The Ontology and Function of Money

Capitalist Thought: Studies in Philosophy, Politics, and Economics

Series Editor: Edward W. Younkins, Wheeling Jesuit University

Mission Statement

This book series is devoted to studying the foundations of capitalism from a number of academic disciplines including, but not limited to, philosophy, political science, economics, law, literature, and history. Recognizing the expansion of the boundaries of economics, this series particularly welcomes proposals for monographs and edited collections that focus on topics from transdisciplinary, interdisciplinary, and multidisciplinary perspectives. Lexington Books will consider a wide range of conceptual, empirical, and methodological submissions, Works in this series will tend to synthesize and integrate knowledge and to build bridges within and between disciplines. They will be of vital concern to academicians, business people, and others in the debate about the proper role of capitalism, business, and business people in economic society.

Advisory Board

Titles in the Series

Economic Morality: Ancient to Modern Readings, by Henry C. Clark and Eric Allison
The Ontology and Function of Money: The Philosophical Fundamentals of Monetary Institutions, by Leonidas Zelmanovitz

The Ontology and Function of Money

The Philosophical Fundamentals of Monetary Institutions

Leonidas Zelmanovitz

LEXINGTON BOOKS
Lanham • Boulder • New York • London

Published by Lexington Books
An imprint of The Rowman & Littlefield Publishing Group, Inc.
4501 Forbes Boulevard, Suite 200, Lanham, Maryland 20706
www.rowman.com

Unit A, Whitacre Mews, 26-34 Stannary Street, London SE11 4AB

First paperback edition

British Library Cataloguing in Publication Information Available

Library of Congress Cataloging-in-Publication Data
The hardback edition of this book was previously cataloged as follows:

Zelmanovitz, Leonidas, 1961- author.
The ontology and function of money : the philosophical fundamentals of monetary institutions / Leonidas Zelmanovitz.
pages cm. -- (Capitalist thought: studies in philosophy, politics, and economics)
Includes bibliographical references and index.
1. Money--Philosophy. 2. Financial institutions. 3. Monetary policy. I. Title.
HG220.3.Z45 2015
332.401--dc23

2015027569

ISBN 978-0-7391-9511-6 (cloth : alk. paper)
ISBN 978-07391-9513-0 (pbk : alk. paper)
ISBN 978-0-7391-9512-3 (electronic)

This book is dedicated to Rosane, Thomas, and Alicia.

Contents

List of Figures and Tables

Acknowledgments

I am grateful to the Liberty Fund in the person of its president, Mr. Chris Talley and to the Department of Applied Economics I of Universidad Rey Juan Carlos in Madrid, Spain, in the persons of its dean, professor Jesús Huerta de Soto, and my dissertation supervisor, professor Gabriel Calzada, for their generous support of my studies, and I admit to a nonjudicious use of my spare time for which I need to apologize to my wife and children because of the time taken from them. There are too many individuals, academics, and practitioners with whom I have exchanged ideas along these years for me to make justice to all of them, but I would like to express my sincere thanks to all who have read previous versions of this work for their support and useful contributions: an anonymous reviewer, Miguel Angel Alonso Neira, Philipp Bagus, Walter Block, Mauro Boianovsky, Gabriel Calzada, Francisco Capella, José Ignacio del Castillo, Roberto Fendt, Jesús Huerta de Soto, Jeff Hummel, Martin Krause, Rolf Luders, Eduardo Mayora Alvarado, Raquel Merino, Leon Montes, James Murphy, Emilio Pacheco (specially), Juan Ramón Rallo, Douglas Rasmussen, Carlos Rodriguez Braun, Douglas Den Uyl, and Leland Yeager for all their generosity with their time and sincere interest in helping me in this research.

The responsibility for any mistake is obviously exclusively mine.

—Leonidas Zelmanovitz, Indianapolis, February 13, 2015.

Preface

The academic debate about monetary policy, sophisticated and innovative as it is today, has seen its philosophical foundations become merely implicit and the shallowness of the debate in the media is discouraging. Worldwide, the political debate about this issue has been even poorer although the ever-changing reality of monetary institutions in the last decades has offered many opportunities to provoke a deeper reflection on the shortcoming of all institutional arrangements as regards money. So, the motivation to study the philosophy of money came, if from nothing else, from the lack of philosophical reflection about the concept of money in my readings on economics, politics, and law. The opportunity to start studying about this and many other issues came in with an invitation to a year-long visiting scholarship; the opportunity to finish my research for the present book came after a master's program in economics, with the incentive I got to present my reasoning as a doctoral dissertation. With this book, I am summarizing some thoughts about money, in order to organize my own ideas and to help others in doing so. This work integrates some concepts about the nature of monetary institutions and what it is possible to know about monetary phenomena in order to present a normative statement about money and thus to have instruments to evaluate monetary policies. Secondly, as a tool for achieving its primary goal, it offers a classification of monetary systems as they exist in history, doctrine, and current observation. Moving from what this book is about, let's examine the sources of the major assumptions and ideas discussed in this work and how I became acquainted with them.

BRAZIL AS A MONETARY LABORATORY

The economist John Exeter once said "The simplest peasant in Brazil understands money better than the American businessman." There is more than a grain of truth in that assertion. From 1964 to 1994, the years in which Brazil lived with widespread indexation, the average annual rate of **inflation** was above 160%. There were major monetary reforms in 1964, 1967, 1979, 1983, 1986, 1987, 1989, 1990, and 1994. Along the way the monetary unit was changed many times (usually but not always cutting three zeros and starting the inflationary process again from a lower denomination); the exchange rate regime changed many times, with pegged parities permeated with episodes of abrupt **devaluation**, price freezes, foreign exchange controls, and more than one attempt of forced de-indexation; many manipulations of the price indexes and even one instance in which all the bank deposits (time and demand deposits alike, including savings accounts and **money market funds**) were seized by the government and partially returned to the investors in installments over the course of two-and-a-half years.

During those years the GSE (government-sponsored enterprise) in charge of providing **liquidity** to the secondary market of residential and commercial mortgages went broke after one of the oddest episodes of de-indexations experienced in the country in 1985 (one in which its assets were depreciated but its liabilities were not). In the process the **banking system** carried uncovered liabilities in the form of "skeletons in their closets" for more than ten years. The federal government finally recognized its obligation and paid an indemnity with a special issuance of twenty-year term Treasury Bonds in an amount equivalent to 5% of the GNP in 1995, which finally restored the health and wealth of the Brazilian financial sector sufficiently to enable it to come out of the land of the living dead. During those years, virtually all demand deposits were transferred electronically to overnight money market instruments (the **commercial banks** were forced to make an overnight compulsory deposit with the Brazilian **central bank** (Bacen) over demand deposits close to 100% anyway). For wages, rents, mortgages, practically any "long-term" contract (more than 30 days), parties had to agree on which of the many indexes in use to execute it. Interest rates were (and still are) the highest in the world in real terms and the deficit in the federal budget alone (not to mention the deficit of the states and municipalities) was bigger than the total domestic savings as a percentage of the GDP.

Still, there were long-term (ten- to fifteen-year) mortgages and private capital formation in the country, and the GNP on average during those years grew slightly faster than the population growth, resulting in small but consistent gains in income per capita.

After 1994 laws of fiscal responsibility prohibited state and local governments from floating bonds and running deficits, they and the federal government got strict limits on what they may spend in current expenditures, the entitlements were partially reformed, the Bacen got formal independence, the federal government started to run a fiscal nominal surplus, and the public net debt was until recently gradually reduced as a percentage of the GDP.

The study of the Brazilian experience invites interest in monetary theory; the research that resulted in this book started as an attempt to try to make sense of the madness of monetary life in Brazil.

GOING BEYOND ECONOMICS AND BECOMING PHILOSOPHICAL

As soon as I started a more systematic research on money, I realized that the answers to most of the questions I had were outside the field of economics, even in its more normative aspects. A breakthrough in my research came with S. Herbert Frankel's *Two Philosophies of Money*, and next I read Nicolas Oresme's *De Moneta*, Ludwig von Mises' *Theory of Money and Credit*, Vera Smith's *The Rationale of Central Banking and the Free Banking Alternative*, Leland Yeager's *The Fluttering Veil*, and Friedrich Hayek's *The Denationalisation of Money*, among many others. The structure of the present book and its main topics reflect the influence of those first readings.

With my initial research, the epistemological problems for the meaningful practice of **inflation targeting** first grabbed my attention. Some readings pointing out the limitations of aggregation in economics and criticizing the use of indexes as a gauge for the effects of inflationary expansion of money and **credit** were pointed out by some scholars as "outdated" in the face of the "success" of inflation targeting policies worldwide. It took me awhile to understand the fallacies of those arguments.

Some studies in moral philosophy were instrumental in allowing me to integrate monetary policy with its philosophical foundations as I attempt to do in this book.

Once engaged in a discussion about whether international economic integration loosens restraints that would otherwise exist at the national level, I have concluded that the internationalization of the structure of production would imply that the effects of inflationary credit expansion, as predicted by the Austrian Business Cycle Theory (ABCT), could only be assessed at the same scale at which that the structure of production was integrated. If financial markets are integrated as well, the price signals as perceived by the floating exchange rates of different fiat currencies would wrongly indicate an increase in the public debt of a given country as an "investment opportunity" for international capital markets. The lesson was clear: monetary phenomena cannot be analyzed out of the context of all other social, political, and economic phenomena. In a world of politically produced money, it is impossible to assess money and banking without considering other policies, fiscal policy chief among them. Another conclusion was the evident necessity to update ABCT to the new realities of financial disintermediation, new monetary arrangements, and consumer credit that did not exist at the time that the theory was formulated.

From my studies on historical and theoretical grounds about the arguments for and against free banking, two important topics called my attention. The first one was David Glasner's "fiscal prevalence hypothesis" in order to explain monetary policy; and the second had to do with the stabilizing effects of the separation of money functions and the propensity for that to happen as argued by Tyler Cowen and Randall Kroszner.

For anyone attentive to the academic debate about the most recent financial crisis, it is not possible to avoid the perception that the current "monetary constitution" is fundamentally flawed, and that the flaws in the monetary arrangements (with too much discretion given to monetary and fiscal authorities), specifically in the United States but more broadly in all the developed world, were ultimately responsible for the 2008 financial crisis; an analysis of what is wrong and how "constitutional" arrangements about money and banking may be reformed is an important part of this project.

Since I read Frankel's *Two Philosophies of Money*, I was familiar with Georg Simmel's contribution to the philosophy of money, among them, his recourse to the concept of intersubjectivity in order to found a justification for money's stability of value under the inflexible gold standard of his time, his thesis about money's evolution towards increasing abstraction, and the key link between the kind of society that money enables to flourish and the very concept of the "good life" in Western societies. These topics helped to shape my ideas presented in this book.

A study of the basic principles of money as proposed by Mises, such as the concepts of "perpetual change" of relative prices and the illusion of price stability, arguments in favor of the nonneutrality of money, and Mises' theory of money value, significantly influenced the ideas exposed in this book about the essential characteristics of money and led to an appreciation of the ideas about monetary equilibrium.

As mentioned above, one of the obvious conclusions about the ABCT is that the mechanism through which Austrian economics describes the business cycle is outdated. That is not necessarily an indictment against the theory itself, but it leaves the door open for arguments that the ABCT does not apply any longer, requiring a new description of the business cycle theory in face of the new economic realities. In regard to the present work, on one hand the entwined relation between money and other institutions regulating economic activity such as the degree of internationalization of the economy, the level of consumer credit, the extent of government support and mandates for investments in housing, and the weaknesses of corporate governance rules among many others would require constant updates to the narrative of ABCT. On the other hand, because of the soundness of its aprioristic assumptions, the essential idea that monetary mismanagement produces and exacerbates business cycles continues to be as valid as it was at the time that the theory was formulated.

A different line of research that most significantly influenced the present book was the study of the monetarist camp; especially the ones that have been utilizing in their models what may be described as the "UCLA micro-foundations." Granted the methodological differences described at length in this work, their acknowledgment of the epistemological limitations of economics, the qualitative analysis required to understand reality, and the relevance of their a priori assumptions about human behavior for their practice of economics reinforced my convictions about the possibility in the future to recreate a consensus about good economics. Some scholars in that tradition do recognize the limitations of inflation targeting as practiced by most central banks and their responsibility for the asset bubbles that happened shortly before the recent crisis. This was at the same time an important contribution to the present book and also a reason for the optimism just mentioned about the possibility of a new synthesis in economics integrating an epistemological skepticism that is not exclusively the domain of Austrian economics.

Concerns about the relation between fiscal and monetary policies have occupied most of my time more recently; and my conclusions about that relation are central to my understanding of the politics of money.

Before we start, one more warning, in what some consider a wrong attribution (Smithin, 2013: 28) Karl Marx once wrote "Gladstone, speaking in a parliamentary debate on Sir Robert Peel's Bank Act of 1844 and 1845, observed that even love has not turned more men into fools than has meditation upon the nature of money" (Marx, 2009: 64). There is no other way to advance our knowledge on the subject of money than accepting that risk; and that is a good reason for us to forgive ourselves and others who are engaged in the same enterprise for eventual lapses.

For obvious reasons in these writings there is great use of philosophical and economical jargon; because of that, the readers are encouraged to utilize the glossary, not only to gain knowledge about new concepts, but, just as importantly, to understand the precise way in which the concepts are used in this paper. Whenever possible, the reader will find in the glossary Mises' terminology, as paraphrased from *Mises Made Easier—A Glossary for Ludwig Von Mises' Human Action* (Greaves: 1974). All terms referred to in the glossary are marked with boldface type the first time that they are used in the paper. In relation to the glossary, a last word of acknowledgement is necessary: the frequent use of Wikipedia helped me to develop definitions that would be comprehensible to laypeople.

Introduction

There is recent crop of books on the nature of money that is part of a healthy search for explanations for our monetary problems, inquiring into their origin and main attributes, and, it is safe to say, they were all motivated by the 2008 financial crisis. Among them are David Graeber's *Debt: The First 5,000 Years*, Felix Martin's *Money: The Unauthorized Biography*, and Nigel Dodd's *The Social Life of Money*. While the first two adhere pretty much to variants of the "State Theory of Money" in order to explain its origin and to derive normative conclusions, in the latter, after describing different orthodox and heterodox theories about the origin of money, the author argues that he sees "no compelling reason" to opt for one. I beg to disagree. This omission implied in just superficially describing the different theories and adding nothing to the existing knowledge on the field leaves the author with no solid foundation for the continuation of his discussion, since, as he acknowledges explicitly (Dodd, 2014: p. 48), he does not settle for any "overarching definition of money"—not a good way to start to discuss anything. But the attempt to explain to a readership of educated laypersons what money is without requiring from them a degree in economics, or offering a different approach—sometimes practical, sometimes from the standpoint of other disciplines—for those who do have a degree in economics, is nothing new. For instance, Hartley Withers states at the very opening page of his 1909 *The Meaning of Money* that "This book is designed to meet the difficulty experienced by the average reader in understanding that part of a newspaper City article which deals with the money market." Although part of the new crop, this book fits in that long tradition. The idea is to approach money as a social institution that may be easily understood from the perspective of philosophy, with a terminology and method common to all sciences. The intention with that is to make comprehensible monetary phenomena at a more sophisticated level for academics from other disciplines than economics in order for them to apply that knowledge in their own researches, for laypersons willing to go beyond the traditional textbook in order to understand an important part of our daily reality and last, for economists, to better assess both descriptions and prescriptions about money going back to what informs the economic way of thinking about the subject. The need for understanding monetary institutions from a broader, or one may say, deeper perspective than the one of pure economics was rightfully identified recently by John Smithin, who in a recent article advocated that a proper understanding of money would require first, a statement of its ontology, next of its epistemology, then its ethics, and finally, its politics (Smithin, 2013: 21). Although this work may have been initiated and the doctoral dissertation on which it is based was defended in 2011, this book may be understood as an attempt to address the four requirements proposed by Smithin.

This inquiry is not exclusively or even primarily historical, and the reason for that is well explained by Joseph Schumpeter, who said that Aristotle has two explanations for the origin of Money, one *Historical*, the other *Logic* (Schumpeter, 1997: 63–64) and the historical is given as an evidence of the latter. For Schumpeter the search for the ancient origin of something to explain its nature is not a valid method because, often, the original version of something is not more simple, but more complex than in its current format, and that seems to me to be a good reason to focus on the function of any object under analysis, instead of risking a genetic fallacy. For these reasons my main effort to try to understand money is a functionalist one.

My intent with this book is neither to do a comprehensive philosophical analysis of money, nor a complete classification of monetary systems, but to call the reader's attention to some of the most important features of this social institution called money and how we can classify the different **institutional arrangements** related to money according to these features. The classification itself came about as a by-product of the larger research.

In these writings, however, are also thoughts about things that economists allegedly ought not to think about: moral knowledge, for one. The reason for such focus is that this work, departing from a position of moral philosophy, aims to evaluate matters of public policy. It considers what exactly a legitimate political order is; or more specifically, what good **monetary policy** is. This approach hints at the fact that a key element in this work is the treatment given to the questions surrounding the "naturalistic fallacy." The basic reasoning here is that in regard to the specific needs of proper human life, or any life for that matter, there are some instruments of teleological value and, therefore, in regard to living beings, it is possible to avoid a naturalistic fallacy, since what they "are" is already impregnated with values about what is proper for them, about what they "ought" to be. In the same way, that exception to the fallacy of deriving an "ought" from an "is" applies to what is instrumental to living beings to realize their potential. In society as we know it, money is one of those things that is instrumental for living a proper human life. And then, it is claimed, it is not merely in ethics that the justification for politics is to be found, but in the metaphysical and epistemological assumptions informing ethics that the ultimate justification for politics lies.

The approach to political economy that emphasizes "how social institutions do or do not facilitate the coordination of human decision making and thus permit or retard societal advance" (Leeson, 2010: 49) is identified with Austrian economics, and institutional economics. It is better to say, perhaps, that it is identified with good political economics, which collects data from other disciplines about the real world and aims to investigate and explain it by the application of praxeology.[1] In this work the other discipline from which raw data is collected is philosophy. The description of metaphysical, epistemological, and ethical concepts are brought to the fore in order to understand the complexity of the social phenomena around money, by deploying, (quoting Peter Leeson again) "what [Friedrich] Hayek called the 'pure logic of choice' or what, using modern parlance, Boettke calls price theory" (2010: 50).

INSTITUTIONS AND PROGRESS

The evolution of a civilization is a matter of historical record.[2] It can be measured by its successes in many different fields. For instance, material progress, increase in population, territorial expansion, artistic and scientific accomplishments are all dimensions of the advancements of a civilization. It is possible to identify a parallel between the evolution of a civilization as recorded by history and its institutions in general and political institutions in particular. That is because political societies are no more than groups of individuals and their institutions are no more than forms of interaction among those individuals, with everyone pursuing his or her own interest in different fields. In other words, it is the sum of the accomplishments of its members in different fields of human interaction and the unintended social results of their individual efforts that is understood as the progress of a civilization. To clarify, perhaps the word "progress" may convey an idea that the evolution of civilizations here mentioned is unidirectional, but that is not the intent. "Progression" is here utilized meaning "whatever lies ahead," not necessarily "good" or "better" circumstances.

For instance, the Greeks, who defeated the Persians twice, were capable of noble and amazing feats that can only be compared in their exceptionality, as time goes by, with the ignoble and mean actions taken by their descendants during the self-destructive Peloponnesian war. The capacity of Greek leaders for two generations to coordinate the actions of a myriad of independent cities against the Persians without compromising their political independence was an amazing achievement; the incapacity of the leaders of the next generation to avoid self-destruction in a fratricidal war is beyond comprehension. This perceived parallel between recorded events and the quality of human interactions as reflected in the many different institutional dimensions of a society is true for an entire civilization and may also be valid for one of its independent political entities. The generation of Athenians that defeated the Persians, built the Parthenon and established supremacy over the Aegean had surely more effective forms of interaction among them and with their neighbors than the generation who faced disaster in Sicily, indulged alternately in democratic excess and tyranny, and was finally defeated in the Peloponnesian war. The argument here is that what history shows, aside from the vagaries of fortune,[3] is the quality, the nature of human interaction in a given social group. It may be understood that the nature of their relationships is embodied in their institutions, in all their dimensions, these institutions being the fruit of the "common will" (those that are product of legislation) mentioned by Carl Menger, or those which "come into being without a common will directed towards establishing them" (Menger, 1963: 146). Understood thus, institutions frame all aspects of social life such as the cultural, social, political, educational, and economical. Obviously, the claims just presented only hold water at a high level of generalization; even during the most unsuccessful responses given by a social group to the challenges facing them at a particular moment, brave and trustworthy characters are to be found, and efficient social arrangements may be in place. The claims presented here may be better interpreted as suggesting the existence of relative differences in time and place between the effectiveness of social institutions.

In order to measure the effectiveness of some institutions, we must agree on their purpose. If bees or ants were the subjects of the present discussion, probably no other criterion other than keeping alive and reproducing their societies would be used to gauge their success. Measuring the success of human societies only by their ability to perpetuate themselves, transmitting to future generations their genetic code, seems a rather bleak perspective of what a human society is; it does not take into consideration the very essence of what a human life is.

Humans by nature have conscience and intelligence and the very purpose of their social arrangements is to enhance their individual opportunities to reach the limits of their potential, to flourish as individuals. Of course, there are many other ethical traditions with different conceptions about the purpose of human life and about political institutions, and this brief introduction is certainly not the place for such inquiries; suffice it to say that the above-mentioned view is the one here espoused.

THE PURPOSE OF GOOD MONEY AND SOME HINDRANCES TO HAVING IT

In relation to the institutional arrangements for the economic activities of a society, the development of the economic capacities of a group of individuals is directly related to the extension of the division of labor among them. Since in human societies the individuals possess specific, local knowledge and subjective as well as technical knowledge about the opportunities for economic activity, the capacity to exercise this "intellectual division of labor," as Jesús Huerta de Soto points out by quoting Mises' *Liberalism* (Huerta de Soto, 2001: 173), is key for overcoming scarcity. History has demonstrated that the best institutions for this purpose are the ones that grant the individuals better opportunities for them to exercise their creativity and their other productive capacities; namely: limited and representative government under the rule of law and individual rights—more specifically, private property rights and freedom of contract, that is, classical liberal institutions.

The availability of adequate money as an instrument for indirect exchanges in society may be understood as encompassed in the institutions mentioned above (classical liberal institutions); but just like independent courts of justice, legal enforcement, and national defense, the supply of a generally accepted **medium of exchange**, of a unit of account, and of an instrument for the store of value, for their importance, deserve a special treatment in any analysis, more than merely being considered as part of the institutions guaranteeing property rights and freedom of contract. Obviously, any monetary institutions that come to be in contradiction with private property rights and freedom of contract (and the other institutions that are instrumental to their effectiveness) will be less than ideal. That is, it is not any monetary arrangement along with private property and freedom of contract that will result in the most effective social interactions aimed to overcome scarcity. And it is gruesome to note that the historical record is full of examples in which governments have intervened in the supply of money, resulting in the production of monies less than adequate for the purpose of enhancing the division of labor by facilitating indirect exchanges.

Returning to the different elements of this work, the historical "sketch" against which I have attached some references was presented rather loosely, as it is not my intention to produce a history of money; however, a more specific historical background is occasionally given in order to support the presentation of some concept. Also, it is not my intention to predict the future by saying what the money of choice will be some years from now; my attempts to deal with this kind of **speculation** serves the purpose of stressing what the trends towards money are based on the most recent developments in this field. In the same way, drafting a utopian model is much more a tool to clarify some of the features that a proper monetary system must have than any romantic dream of influencing public policy.

The thesis here defended is that in order to evaluate monetary policy, it is crucial to have in mind philosophical concepts about money. So, the claim is not a claim about certain conclusions in regard to monetary policy as they could be derived from a philosophical approach to monetary phenomena, although some are reached and defended, but that more precise conclusions about the value of monetary policy can be reached once it is approached from its philosophical fundamentals. Actually, the claim may be formulated as saying that the value of any monetary policy is contingent on its adherence to a coherent set of philosophical assumptions, either explicit or implicitly assumed. Therefore, it is necessary to have a clear idea about the philosophical tenets of money and to "test" any hypothesis about monetary policy in light of those assumptions. An example of the kind of confusion I would like to invite the reader to avoid may be seen in a recent work published by two IMF (International Monetary Fund) economists. Although they seem to value stability of the money supply and in their paper advocate for limiting the capacity of private banks to produce credit instruments with monetary properties as a way to achieve that, they believe in David Graeber's and Stephen Zarlenga's tales about the state origin of money (Benes and Kumhof, 2012:12) and come to the conclusion that not only are governments interested in not inflating credit, but that only governments can do that (page 17). Questionable historical evidence, ideologically motivated theoretical interpretation, even if the intended result is sound, would result in bad prescription about how to achieve it, and not surprisingly, they advocate financial reforms that would give governments the monopoly of money creation. I hope that by the end of this book any reader could be able to perceive the serious mistake involved in their reasoning.

NOTES

1. The possibility of bridging the methodological differences between mainstream economics and Austrian economics has been explored since it became clear that the Austrians did not belong anymore in the mainstream. That is made clear for efforts such as those of Barry Smith who said: "Austrian economics might be conceived not as an alternative to the economics of model-building and prediction but as a preliminary activity of establishing this missing connection to ground-level economic realities" (Barry Smith, 1996: 330). The possibility of such compatibility according to him (see also Barry Smith, 1990) is due to the fact that there is an Aristotelian feature of the Austrian enterprise, and his view of "Austrian Aristotelianism" is one on ontology: "It tells us what the world is like and what its objects, states and processes are like, including those capacities, states and processes we call knowledge and science" (1996: 332). Well, that may be strange at *prima facie* to those accustomed to seeing in Austrian economics only the rule-utilitarianism and possibly the Kantian influences on Mises and Hayek, and fast to see in the mainstream only the positivism stated by Milton Friedman, but the long subjectivist tradition we have been following since Aristotle is the common heritage of both traditions, and the Aristotelian postulates for how to inquire about reality are common heritage to all scientific thinking; so, it should be no surprise that the compatibility of both methodologies seems to be the most fruitful approach to understanding the reality and to guiding us about how to act upon it.

2. Historical here means what really happened in a given time and place, regardless of what we know about any particular civilization.

3. L. M. Lachmann in his book *The Legacy of Max Weber* (Lachmann, 1970: 49) points out that for the actor, formally, there is no difference if the constraints to his actions are produced by nature or by other individuals, although materially, the actions of other individuals are more difficult to predict. Lachmann offers this argument about why institutions tend to be developed in human society (that is, in order to make human behavior more predictable).

I

Metaphysics

ONE

The Origin and Essence of Money

1.1 INTRODUCTION TO THE ORIGIN AND ESSENCE OF MONEY

For more than a century now, the debate about the philosophy of money has been led by two opposing groups. They have disagreements about many philosophical questions, such as what is possible to know about money, and what is right and wrong in terms of monetary policy, but the main divide between them is whether money is an institution that has evolved naturally[1] in society or whether it was created by the state. It is to these two different assumptions about the character of money that each group's position may be traced. But what kind of question does this discussion about the character of money purport to answer? It is undoubtedly a descriptive question. Both groups claim to be describing money's essential features and their efforts to ground their descriptions of money on accounts of the origin of money in society may be understood as just one more aspect of this inquiry into reality. As will be shown later in this book, the conclusions reached through this effort have important normative consequences, but, on the two sides of the divide, the departing point is unmistakably a judgment of reality. On one side of the divide, arguing that money is a creature of the state, we find a group of thinkers, starting with Georg Knapp and including among its leading advocates A. Mitchell Innes, John Maynard Keynes, and F. A. Mann. This group is referred as the **Acatallactics** or **Chartalists** in this work.

For the opposing view, arguing that money is something that is created and develops spontaneously in society, is a group whose main arguments were first proposed by Carl Menger and later were further developed by Georg Simmel,[2] Ludwig von Mises, and Friedrich Hayek.[3] This group here referred as the **catallactic** thinkers.

However, things are a little more complicated than that. Starting with Menger, catallactic theorists have long advocated that the essential character of money is a consequence of its function in society. For them, money is the generally accepted medium of exchange and its uses as unit of account and store of value are conceptually derived from its key function; having said that, despite recognizing that no one can know for sure,[4] they say that historically money was first a medium of exchange and later it became also a unit of account and a store of value.

The Chartalists, in their turn, say that a claim that the essence of something is derived from its origin is some sort of genetic fallacy, and that in arguing that the core characteristic of money is to be a medium of exchange because historically it was so is to use such fallacious reasoning. Furthermore, they argue, there is a better story to tell: money was historically introduced in society by the state to be the unit of account; therefore, the essential character of money results from that. But what do we have here? On one hand, the people saying that money's essence is a consequence of its social function, aside from arguments to justify their argument, have also presented a historical claim, that is, that one can corroborate the explanation about the attributes of money historically. On the other hand, the other group claims that the Catallactics' attempt to explain the essence of money today from its historic development is a sort of fallacy; however, they continue by saying that the history is actually different, and they use the same alleged fallacy themselves. So, here we have apparently two opposing historical accounts; one saying that money started as a medium of exchange and the other saying that money started as a unit of account. These accounts are brought to bear on the discussion respectively by both groups only to corroborate their opposing views about what the essential characteristics of money are as derived from its social use—that is, from its use as the medium of exchange, as argued by one side, or from its use as the unit of account as argued by the other.

This chapter has two purposes. The first purpose is to analyze to what extent it is possible to make the two historical accounts compatible. If the two historical claims are somehow compatible, perhaps the disagreements about which function of money has precedence in order to explain its essence may be better understood on their own merits, and that is the second purpose of this chapter.

A final introductory note is an answer to a question not yet formulated: why is this inquiry on the nature of money important for us today? It is our contention that, as with other social institutions, there are monetary arrangements that are more appropriate than others to the exercise of individual freedom and responsibility in society; these arrangements may be called "good money." But, again, like any other political decision, it is not even possible to recognize, much less to implement, what is "good" if we do not know "good for what?" Since the "right" attributes of money are directly linked with the reasons for its introduction into society, it seems relevant to any person interested in the development of human society to understand the essential character of money.

1.2 MAKING THE HISTORICAL ACCOUNT COMPATIBLE

1.2.1 The Catallactic Historical Claim

The historical account given by the Catallactics is a very straightforward one: they claim that when the conditions for exchange outside the family arose, with an increased division of labor, a medium of exchange was introduced in order to facilitate the exchanges through indirect exchange. With time and the sophistication of society, these initial forms of media of exchange evolved from some merchandise, such as cattle or salt, to metals, and later coined metals until human societies reached the stage of **fiat money** that we have today. Along the way, the generally accepted medium of exchange became the unit of account and also a store of value everywhere. In appendix A, the reader may find a historical "sketch" of such an account.

1.2.2 The Claim of the Chartalists

The Chartalists, on the other hand, have also a very clear account about how we came to the current monetary arrangements. They say that for the last twenty-five centuries, money has been coined money. Not only that, but money has been provided directly or indirectly by state authority. So, according to them, money is the merchandise that was "stamped" by the state to be money. Money, in their account, is the instrument to settle taxes, and its value is a result of the state attribution and whose definition is a unit of account.

In appendix B, some historical references that seem to corroborate the chartalist version are given.

1.2.3 Aren't these Versions Compatible ?

These two versions seem compatible at a first glance: money was created in society spontaneously to primarily perform the function of medium of exchange. Gradually it evolved along with other social developments, which made it ripe for the rulers to authorize a particular form of medium of exchange through a "stamp," which further increased its desirability as an instrument for indirect exchanges. If the Chartalists concede that the first forms of medium of exchange, those that had evolved spontaneously in society, happened before the introduction of coined money; and if the Catallactics accept that money has been provided by the state since the introduction of coined money,[5] the two accounts would suddenly become compatible. The two versions may be interpreted simply as partial accounts, one until the introduction of coined money, and the other afterwards.

Making these two versions compatible seems easy and it actually is; and that is so because the problem remains elsewhere. Both accounts are brought as evidence to support the opposing claims about the nature of money, and these claims in their turn are justifications to normative judgments about money. The problem dividing the scholars is the opposing claims about the nature of money, which we turn to now.

1.3 WHAT IS THE ORTHODOXY?

The idea that money has evolved from barter is generally considered the orthodox view about the origin of money. For instance, in the preface of his book, Mark Peacock argues that the "usual account of the origin of money" is that money originates from barter. Such account, that many attribute to Menger, is nothing but a straw man. The theory of the spontaneous origin of money is not a theory that money "originates from barter," but that it makes sense for individuals to find an instrument more salable than the wares or service they are bringing to the market to procure the goods and services they need; therefore, if a significant number of individuals, in the pursuit of their own interest, start to trade the result of their labor for some easily acceptable merchandise, such merchandise becomes "money," that is, a generally accepted medium of exchange (Menger, 2012: 9). Another thing to consider in assessing how wrong is the claim that "money originates from barter" as an attempt to disparage the thesis of the spontaneous origin of money is that such instrument may well be an instrument representative of a debt owed by the state or even a token created by the state and accepted by the state as an instrument to pay taxes. The relevant aspect of the thesis of the spontaneous origin of money is that it is inherent in society that individuals will better benefit from the division of labor if, after acknowledging that different goods have "different degrees of salableness" (Menger, 2012: 12), they accept the most liquid, the most easily salable, instrument they can get in exchange for the fruit of their labor and go to procure the goods and services they desire with such "money" in their pockets. The thesis that the introduction of money in society resulted just as an unintended consequence of the individuals acting in pursuit of their own interest was made explicit already by Adam Smith in the *Wealth of Nations*, book I, chapter IV, to whom "every prudent man in every period of society, after the establishment of the division of labor, must naturally have endeavoured to manage his affairs in such a manner, as to have at all times by him, besides the peculiar produce of his own industry, a certain quantity of some one commodity or other, such as he imagined few people would be likely to refuse in exchange for the produce of their industry" (Smith,

1981: 38); nonetheless, it is contested. The argument against the spontaneous origin of money is essentially based on the idea that indirect transactions are not necessarily more efficient than barter and to my knowledge the best formulation of such claim is Hillel Steiner's (Steiner, 2013). Yet, his argument is not convincing, it is basically that only third party enforcement (what I suppose, in the case of money would be legal tender laws) would give assurance to the economic agents to accept money in exchange for their goods (2013: 51); and the many cases in which monies have been accepted for millennia outside the jurisdictions in which they are issued is sufficient evidence to prove his thesis wrong. Furthermore, it is totally absent in his model that whatever the economic agents generally decide to use as a medium of exchange, they do so not at a whim, but because such instrument has more liquidity than the alternatives and with that he misses the main reason why it makes sense at an individual level to adopt indirect exchanges (accepting money in payment for his or her goods), and how the selection of what eventually becomes the generally accepted medium of exchange, that is, money, happens. Everything else said and written about the spontaneous origin of money is bogus, misinformed, and misinforming. Authors defending the many versions of the state theory (of the origin) of money like to present themselves as fighting the "orthodoxy;" when in fact, at least since the late 1930s when Keynesianism became the orthodoxy, the state theory of money has been an integral part of such orthodoxy, and one need go no further than to the American Uniform Commercial Code (1958), as quoted by Mann, which "expressly defines money by the test of sanction of government: money is 'a medium of exchange authorized or adopted by government as a part of its currency,'" (Section 1–201 (24)), and who states in the same footnote that "the important fact stated in the text is ignored by far too many scholars who discuss the conception of money" (Mann, 1982: 15). To accept that as an honest error, one needs to think that those authors mistakenly take the general acceptance of a spontaneous origin of indirect exchange by most economists as a rejection of the state theory of money when, in fact, what those economists are accepting, based on the economic way of thinking, is that individuals tend to follow their curves of marginal utility or, in plain English, considering their alternatives, they tend to do, at each circumstance, what, to the limit of their knowledge, they think gives them the most satisfaction; so if, in a given society, what is used as money is a token created by the state because, at a point of a gun, the state forbids anything else from being used as money or simply because, given acceptance by the state of those tokens as payment to any obligation the agents may have with the state, it is more convenient to use, voluntarily, such tokens as money, the individuals will use it spontaneously; that is, having created the institutional setting, no further incentives are necessary; the individuals will use that token created by the state as the instrument in their exchanges. While, in a different institutional setting, they may use silver coins or bitcoins for that matter.

1.4 SETTING THE PREMISES

1.4.1 Money and the Division of Labor

The main difference between a **monetary economy** and a hypothetical barter economy is the limitations of the latter to fully allow the division of labor. A monetary system is a tool to allow and implement the division of labor. The more a system allows the division of labor, the better it is. Besides the absence of money, the division of labor may be constrained by other factors such as the size of market, the cultural background of people, the extent to which property rights are enforceable, et cetera, but it is not part of our goals to inquire about these other constraints. Suffice it to say that ceteris paribus—that is, for societies mainly with same size markets, and also same cultural background, et cetera—it is reasonable to assume a correlation between the intensity in which certain properties are present in the money used by a community and the extension of the division of labor in such community, or, in other words, the complexity of its economic activities. It is a relation that works in both ways: a society that lacks labor specialization does not need monies with all the qualities of good money; it can live with money of lesser quality, and without good money, labor specialization cannot be further developed. It is not just any money that will allow one society to develop industrial activity not to mention complex capital markets. It is worth mentioning that at the time of the Late Roman Republic and Early Roman Empire, they had monies good enough to enable them to run an economy based on trade, agriculture, and slavery for centuries, but even that primitive economy crumbled with the less adequate monies of the late Empire. [6] What makes a coined piece of gold (or any other rare metal for that matter) better money than a bag of salt? Gold coins (from now on, gold will be referred to as a proxy for silver and other metals in this work) were a more convenient medium of exchange than bags of salt, they were easier to carry, cheaper to store, and gold has higher intrinsic value. The introduction of money in general and coined gold in particular was due to the convenience of their use, and the desirability of their properties as we can imagine from something voluntarily adopted by the people. If the "monetary" goods have the properties desired by the money holders, these goods will ease exchanges by diminishing the costs of transacting, and so enhance the division of labor.[7] The complex level of division of labor that we enjoy today would not be possible without an instrument with the two main characteristics of money—that is, its properties as medium of exchange and as unit of account. That is so because the nature of the division of knowledge among individuals determines that only through the price mechanism developed in a free market with private property, liberty of contract, and a fair administration of justice is it possible for them to coordinate actions to the maximum of their potentialities.[8] Without money acting as a unit of account, there would be no market prices; without money performing the role of medium of exchange, there would be no indirect transactions. Therefore the social coordination produced in a moneyless society would always be *suboptimum*. So, money may be understood as a technology for social coordination that has evolved naturally in human society, because it helps human beings, as they are, to develop through the division of labor a complex nexus of social relations that enhances their potential to live a fruitful and happy life. But, for the last twenty-five centuries of our civilization, money has been generally supplied by the state, so how can one say that money is not a creature of the state or that money should not be used to foster government's goals? As Menger says, "The fact that governments treated money as if it actually had been merely the product of the convenience of men in general and of their legislative whims in particular contributed therefore in no small degree to furthering errors about the nature of money" (Huerta de Soto, 2009: 230).

1.4.2 The Problem of Social Coordination at the Dawn of Civilization

The social coordination of individual effort became an extremely relevant issue. As societies evolved, it is reasonable to assume, customary practices alone were no longer enough and other rules were required. Some rules of social behavior were then imposed by religion and power as well. The governors were entitled to sizable amounts of peasants' and artisans' production through the enforcement of those rules and coercive means, like armed guards. The first agro-urban societies were basically societies of command, like an army or a religious order today. An important part of the social interaction was not voluntary.[9] However, another important part of individuals' activities was not coerced, creating new practices that with time became customary and tolerated or even sanctioned by the established powers. How did they come into being, and how were these voluntary activities coordinated? We need to go no further than to one of the most quoted passages of Adam Smith's *Wealth of Nations* to find out. Smith says, "It is not from the benevolence of the butcher, the brewer, or the baker, that we expect our dinner, but from their regard to their own interest" (Adam Smith, 1981: 27).

Or as Adam Smith clarifies a few lines below,

> As it is by treaty, by barter, and by purchase, that we obtain from one another the greater part of those mutual good offices which we stand in need of, so it is this same trucking disposition which originally gives occasion to the division of labor. In a tribe of hunters or shepherds a

> particular person makes bows and arrows, for example, with more readiness and dexterity than any other. He frequently exchanges them for cattle or for venison with his companions; and he finds at last that he can in this manner get more cattle and venison, than if he himself went to the field to catch them. From a regard to this own interest, therefore, the making of bows and arrows grows to be his chief business, and he becomes a sort of armourer.

In sum, they were coordinated spontaneously. There are some emotional responses among human beings that repeatedly generate some patterns of behavior under similar conditions. Human beings are always trying to change from a situation of less pleasure to more pleasure, maximizing their utility, satisfying their hedonism, trying to fulfill their potential the way that suits them best.

1.4.3 Human Action

As Ludwig von Mises wrote quoting Locke and Leibniz: "The incentive that impels a man to act is always some uneasiness" (Mises, 2007: 13). This desire to better their condition, this egoistic motivation is human beings' prime motivation.[10] You can argue whether Mother Teresa in pursuing her altruism was actually doing what she liked most and whether or not it was an egoistic motivation, but even if we recognize (something really easy to do) that human beings have other motivations besides their material betterment, we can count on that prime motivation to build on it a pattern for social interaction—that is, the spontaneous order generated by the market. At the introduction of *Human Action*, while criticizing historicism, Marxism, statism, and irrationalism in general, Ludwig von Mises argued that all scientific inquiry is based on the assumption of: "the uniformity and immutability of the logical structure of human mind as an unquestionable fact" (2007: 2). In the same way, and as a consequence of this uniformity in human nature, we can identify a regularity and uniformity in laws of social cooperation.

The spontaneous order will be a benign one if the institutional arrangements are such that the road for self-betterment is serving others well, or it will be a malign one, like Hobbes' "state of war," if selfish desires can be satisfied in other ways rather than serving others well. But, again, regardless of the moral quality of the interactions, the recurrent responses of human beings have spontaneously generated a pattern of behavior in their social dealings as history has shown us time and again.

1.4.4 Kosmos and Taxis

Along the evolution of a hypothetical timeline of social organization (from the **clan** to the state), of technology (from gathering to metallurgy), which clearly happened over thousands of years with different beginnings in different places and through a process of trial and error, other purely spontaneous social institutions arose: languages as we know them today, for instance. There is no better example of a spontaneously generated social institution than language to draw an analogy with markets. Languages were created many tens of thousands of years before the first states; they appeared to supply a human necessity, and no one commanded their use, it was not necessary. The ability to speak is so intrinsically a human attribute that some perceive it as *the* distinctive human attribute. This link between human nature and a spontaneously generated social institution can be perceived in the markets as well.

Now we are able to differentiate two kinds of social orders, in Hayek's terminology: orders by command (***taxis***), like an army, and spontaneous orders (***kosmos***), like languages. Both orders are human creations, ordering some social interaction. It is important to note that the main distinction between them does not rely on the presence or absence of coercion in each kind of order. For instance, a spontaneous order can be quite coercive (a hierarchy of caste or sex), and freedom can be achieved through an order of command where markets and the rule of law are established by deliberate design and imposition, such as in the United States. Their main distinctions need to be found elsewhere.[11] One may find among the distinguishing properties of spontaneous orders that (a) their degree of complexity is not limited to what a human mind can master, (b) their existence can be based on purely abstract relations, and (c) because they are not consciously created, spontaneous orders cannot be said to have a purpose. Spontaneous orders may serve the purpose of an individual acting according to such orders, but that is obviously a different thing, and that is a key factor to keep in mind when analyzing the role of money in society. When human beings need to coordinate efforts to reach the same goal, command orders are usually preferred, but when the individuals need to coordinate their efforts in order to allow themselves to pursue their own individual goals, spontaneous orders usually are more suitable forms of social coordination. It is this character of spontaneous orders of creating conditions to the normal life of individual agents inside them, that is, to the life according to norms of their own choosing, that may be named its "metanormative" character, a concept we will find again later in this work; for Hayek "Society can thus exist only if by a process of selection rules have evolved which lead individuals to behave in a manner which makes social life possible" (Hayek, 1992: 44).

1.5 UNDERSTANDING WHAT IS MONEY FOR THE CATALLACTICS

1.5.1 Costs of Transaction

For the Austrian economists, money is an institution spontaneously evolved in society that, in order to fulfill its proper role, must have some clearly defined attributes. But to begin with, it is necessary to answer the question, proper for what? We will start here. The proper role of money in human society is to ease bartering among producers, to enhance the division of labor, by lowering **transaction costs** of the exchanges. A medium of exchange was introduced among barterers with the purpose of "clearing" the exchanges, as in a hypothetical **clearance** house for all the barters.[12]

Consistent with Douglass North's observation that the costliness of information is the key to the cost of transacting, part of the transaction cost in any deal is associated with the gathering of information about the best opportunities for trade. How can one acquire knowledge about the relative value of a myriad of different goods without a **unit of exchange**, without a measure of the value of some good against which the value of all the other goods could be measured? So, a unit of exchange was introduced in order to make transactions easier among barterers by lowering their transaction costs in acquiring information about the relative prices among their respective goods and services. This "unit of exchange" is defined in this book as the "unit of account."[13]

Another part of transaction costs that led to the introduction and permanence of money in society is associated with the lack of liquidity in the markets, that is, the lack of information by the economic agents that makes it difficult for them to match supply and demand for a certain product at a certain price. The way to overcome these costs of transaction associated with illiquid markets is by providing a "clearance" service for the community, a service of transferring inventories from where they are abundant to where they are scarce, activity better known as "speculation" or "**arbitrage**." Because in a free society there is no one in command to say what, how much, and where goods and services should be produced, in order to match supply and demand of everything, an immense and complex network of commercial transactions is performed by the economic agents for the purpose of bringing the goods and services that are demanded in the quantity, quality, location, and time that they are demanded. But this activity requires investments in inventories, which in their turn require the existence of "**working capital**." This investment in inventories evidently implies also an investment in everything necessary to produce, store, and transfer such inventories, such as the investment necessary to have the use of capital goods, inputs, labor, et cetera; in essence, all the structure of production of a given society. When the economic agents raise capital, with either equity or debt, a transference of purchasing power happens: the power to dispose of goods and services in society, embodied in the "working" capital, is transferred, in the case we are describing, from the hands of the investor to the hands of the economic agent, and it occurs for a certain period of time. After all, how could obligations with no simultaneous maturities be "cleared" in the hypothetical clearing house of our description? How would one match, for instance, the supply of labor in one place, say, to produce a yearly crop, but which requires weekly remuneration, with the demand for such a crop, all around the world, that is translated into seasonal sales? It would be impossible without the means to dispose of the goods and services necessary to produce, store, and transport those goods, in some cases, literally to the doorsteps of the consumers. So, here we meet another reason for the adoption of money in society: the capacity to readily dispose of goods in society that we described as embodied in the "working capital" must be represented by assets of a very special class. Those assets are such that the owners of the available goods are generally willing to accept them in exchange for their goods without any coercion. The possession of such assets represents "de facto" the capacity to readily dispose of practically everything available in that society. This special class of assets is money.

We have seen so far that there is not a market for everything produced at the time and place that it was produced. From this simple assertion we may develop a number of relevant concepts to understand the nature of money in society. First, as we have discussed above, in order to overcome the needs of identifying which goods are needed, in which amount and quality, when and where, a certain amount of "rights to dispose of everything," that is, "money," must be available to the economic agents. We will discuss later the very important topic of the relation between the amount of these "rights" (stock of money) and the amount of available goods, but, for the moment, suffice it to say that they give access to the stock of existing goods that may be used for productive ends, the "working capital" of society. That is, the stock of money is not "capital;" the stock of money is *representative* of capital. Since everything produced in society may be used either for consumption or production, one does not know for certain which goods and services are "capital," but one may be certain that the stock of capital (that is, the stock of goods that may be used for further production) is part of the stock of available goods or, broadening the definition a little further, part of the stock of goods that may be combined and assembled from the existing goods in society. Second, that assertion may lead us to think that some goods have broader demand than others; certain goods may find a buyer more easily than others and in more places, more frequently, and in less limited quantities. We may say that these goods are more salable than others. That characteristic of greater salability of certain goods is what gives to the economic agents the knowledge that they will be more likely to be successful in finding a buyer for those goods at a predictable price. The uncertainty about the price of those goods tends to be smaller, and with that the chances for arbitrage, bringing the "spread" between the prices to buy and sell those goods to a minimum approaching zero, as is the case with money. And, third, the instrument used by economic agents in a market economy, with private property and freedom of contract, to organize the production of all classes of goods, including the ones with very narrow demand, is to make use of the most liquid merchandise in society, that is, money, to have access to the actual goods and services needed to produce and distribute all other goods. It becomes the preferred medium for indirect exchanges.

It is important to the understanding of our argument (that any generally accepted medium of exchange is money, regardless of the fact that it may be a commodity, a note of credit, or a fiduciary currency) to note that this "working" capital can be raised by either equity or debt. Also, it is important to note that this power of ready disposition of goods available in society is not a common characteristic of any asset. What distinguishes "working" capital from a "fixed asset" conceptually? Which goods embody the proper features required to function as "working" capital that other classes of goods do not have? The answer to these questions will help us understand the proper attributes of money, and the failure of such understanding I would like to describe as "John Law's *second* mistake."[14]

1.6 THE FUNCTIONALITY OF MONEY

1.6.1 The Functions of Money

According to Benjamin M. Anderson, Jr. (Anderson, 1917: 374), the functions of money can be described as:

1. Common measure of values (**standard of value** or unit of account);
2. Medium of Exchange;
3. **Legal tender** for debts;
4. Standard of deferred payments;
5. Reserve for credit instruments, including reserve for government paper money;
6. Store of value;
7. Bearer of options.

As discussed earlier, the crucial function of a unit of account was historically only fulfilled with the introduction of a medium of exchange; the third function seems to be part of the second, the fourth part of the first, and the fifth and seventh part of the sixth. So the classical list of functions of money—that is, standard of value, medium of exchange, and store of value—still holds, in my opinion, although it can be more detailed as described by Anderson.

Other authors noted a fourth function for money: "the strategic financial actions that differentiate among individual natural persons, banks, central banks, and other financial institutions—thereby reflecting money's role in the financial control of the economy" (Quint and Schubik, 2014: 2). The fourth function may be understood as an instrument of political control of the economy, or a fiscal instrument if we accept an understanding of the fisc as a pool of resources extracted from society by political means and not the narrow definition of the government's treasury; ubiquitous as it may be, it is my contention that it is only a derivated function of money. Money may become a fiscal instrument to the extent that it performs its three essential functions.

1.6.2 What is "Good Money"?

A central argument of this work is that "good money" is money that properly fulfills its purpose. If money has all those functions described above, one may wonder if the most suitable characteristics necessary to better fulfill one of its functions may not be the most suitable feature in order to fulfill the other functions. Thinking inside the parameters of the classical list of money functions, I argue that the function of standard of value, of a unit of account, was historically fulfilled by the introduction of a medium of exchange.[15] It is important to note that the function of store of value is better fulfilled by a merchandise with the highest level of liquidity possible, all other things being equal. Therefore, the core function of money is its function of medium of exchange, as proposed by Menger.

It is not my intention with this section to advance a normative discussion about money, something that is the object of part III of this book. My reference here to "good" money has the same meaning as Plato's (*The Republic*: 352e) and Aristotle's (*Nicomachean Ethics*: 1098a) teachings about what makes a "good" knife or a "good" horse; that is, what makes them excel in their function. A knife is made to cut, but depending on the specific use intended for the knife, either to cut meat or to peel a fruit, a different kind of knife will excel, for example; or in reference to a horse, if the function intended is either to ride or use it for traction, a different horse in each case may be more properly deemed "good." Furthermore, an excellent knife for cutting meat does not cease to be a "good" knife if you cut your finger using it, and an excellent horse for riding does not cease to be a "good" horse because it helps a robber to escape. The contention here is that the fact that money was introduced into society in order to ease bartering and that its proper function is to allow and enhance the division of labor are undisputed. History attests to these facts and theory explains them; therefore, to say that "good" money is the money that best performs these functions is not understood here to be a value judgment. For instance, if the division of labor were a bad thing, a "good" enabler of that would be valued as a bad thing also; but in the sense used in this section, it would continue to be considered "good." Later on, I will argue that easing bartering and enhancing the division of labor are desirable things and, therefore, money that excels in allowing those things to happen is "good" money. At that point, it is a value judgment, in the same way that one may say that a "good" knife to cut meat (value neutral) was put to "good" use (value-judgment), say, in cooking a gourmet meal.

I would concede that in dealing with human activity, it is sometimes difficult to distinguish what is and what is not value-laden; some may say that it is impossible to make such a distinction since all human action is purposeful and we may argue in a number of different ways about human motivations, goals, effectiveness, et cetera. If that is so, then in advocating a teleological criterion to what makes good money I am advancing a moral judgment. For someone who does not accept as ontologically possible the distinction that I am trying to make here, then the statement that "good" money is money that performs its function well may indeed be considered an anticipation of the ethical discussion on money, and the reasons given to adopt a teleological criterion to define what is good money given at part III a continuation of the discussion initiated here.

1.6.3 The Naturalistic Fallacy

Regardless of the fact that it may or may not be possible to make a distinct judgment about the adequacy of a tool to a certain purpose from a judgment about the value attributed to the purpose itself, the entire thesis of this book may be understood as an effort to make a value-judgment about a tool (money) for human social interaction from what is accepted as naturally proper for human life (the division of labor). Therefore, it is necessary to address beforehand, even if briefly, any eventual charge that this entire project is just an exercise in the naturalistic fallacy.[16] In this regard we question the assertion that all facts are valueless and consequently it is not possible to derive logically value judgments from facts, the so-called fact-value gap. In discussing the importance of a teleological understanding of human life for their enterprise of basing a nonperfectionist politics on a perfectionist ethics, Douglas Den Uyl and Douglas Rasmussen state:

> If human flourishing is the natural end of human life, and if we understand the human good in terms of that end, then it is simply not the case that all facts are valueless. Indeed, for the class of beings that have natural ends or functions, goodness is ontological in the sense that it is

> a potentiality that is actualized. Hence it is not a fallacy to go from a fact to a value, because some facts are inherently value-laden. (Den Uyl and Rasmussen, 2005: 118)

So, according to the individualistic perfectionism in normative ethics that these authors advocate, there are natural ends to human life, and if their claim that human nature is teleological is accepted without qualification, as it is in this work, such acceptance allows us to avoid a naturalistic fallacy in this project. We can derive normative conclusions about what money should be in order to be a better instrument for human flourishing from our observations about what both human flourishing and money are and from what it is possible to know about money, to the extent that money has come to be defined in terms of its function as an instrument for man's purposes. Such a definition is the object of the next section.[17] But in order to assume it is possible to define a social institution such as money in terms of its functions, we must review the arguments in favor of the validity of such an assumption. Functionalism has a long tradition and it is used in many different disciplines. A good summary of functionalism is the maxim of the modernist philosophy in architecture coined by the American architect Louis Sullivan (1856–1924) that "form must follow function" in order to say that the design and materials of a building should be selected to better support the function for which the building was created. When applied to social institutions, it is impossible to dissociate the characteristics of such institutions from the purposes of individuals to establish society in the first place. The argument presented in this work that money is better understood by a teleological functionalism and that there is nothing logically flawed with that argument is based on the same rejection of the naturalistic fallacy in regard to moral and political philosophy in general.

1.6.4 Carl Menger' s "GAMOE" Definition

A former student at Wabash College (Diamond, 2009) in his blog tells us that his professor of economics, Ben Rogge, in discussing the nature of money, used to say "if a dog eats it, it's dog food" in order to drive home the lesson that if people use something as money, it is money. This aspect of Menger's definition is easy to understand; that is, anything that is generally accepted by the economic agents as an instrument in their indirect transactions becomes, once accepted, money, regardless of whether it is a commodity, a credit, or fiat currency. More difficult is to understand what makes some things better instruments than others to gain general acceptance by economic agents. The answer to this puzzle relies on the "monetary" characteristics of certain things; that is, some things have attributes that are the same attributes usually associated with the monetary merchandise—so much so, that, given the circumstances, they may become money themselves. Foremost among these attributes is "liquidity;" that is, the attribute of some merchandise of being generally accepted at a minimum discount off its face value. In other words, liquidity is essentially a thing's salability, or in Carl Menger's words, "marketability" (absatzfähigkeit).[18] But, because not every good in the market is as salable as the others, the most salable goods become preferably accepted by individuals in exchange for the goods they produce as a medium to acquire other goods they need (defined in this book as medium of exchange).[19] All the other functions of money derive from this primary one, embodied in the very concept of money: the Generally Accepted Medium Of Exchange, or the "GAMOE" definition as first developed by Carl Menger (Menger, 1994: 280) and widely accepted today.[20] Money for us is a "unit of account," a "standard of value," *because* it is the preferred medium of exchange. We could have a unit of exchange that would not be the generally accepted medium of exchange, but in this case the traders would be required to do triangular calculus at each transaction.[21] Money is a "**stock of value**" *because* not all exchanges happen simultaneously and the individuals demand the possession of some easily salable good. What good better fits this purpose? It is the generally accepted medium of exchange, that is, money. Originally money relies on the trust of the individuals accepting a "monetary" good as an instrument to indirectly acquire a certain amount of desirable goods. Any time we are confronted with questions about money, we must remember money's origins in order to understand its desired properties.

The previous paragraph states no more than a lesson learned from Mises who follows, in this regard, strictly the tradition initiated by Menger (Mises, 2007: 401):

> Money is a medium of exchange. It is the most marketable good which people acquire because they want to offer it in later acts of interpersonal exchange. Money is the thing which serves as the generally accepted and commonly used medium of exchange. This is its only function. All the other functions which people ascribe to money are merely particular aspects of its primary and sole function, that of a medium of exchange.

1.6.5 Illusions and Misconceptions about Money

But is money only a medium of exchange generally accepted? Apparently it is not. Once money is introduced and accepted as a medium of exchange, for some people, money becomes much more than simply an instrument to indirectly obtain the goods that they want; it becomes desirable for its own sake, something that neither the "preference for liquidity" rationally suggests, nor any rational use of money as a store of value recommends, but by the sheer illusion that so many people have that equates money with personal power, an enabler to buy everything, even "true love" as Nelson Rodrigues (1912–1980), a Brazilian playwright, once said. The dangers of some people entertaining those irrational ideas about money have been present in philosophy and literature since ancient times.

Because of that, one may argue that our account of money as the instrument for indirect exchanges, an intermediary good, not a final good, may be true as a norm, but not always as a description. This is a point made by some Chartalists that I am prepared to concede with qualifications. My understanding is that precisely because money is always the best instrument for the indirect exchanges, it can fulfill other psychological roles as well, with very dramatic consequences in real life, creating illusions and fostering vices. But that is not an indictment against money, no more than a crime of passion is an indictment against love. Nor is the fact that the possession of the instrument for indirect exchange is sometimes pursued as an end in itself proof against the essential attribute of money having the quality of being the medium of exchange. Other critics of the open society in general and the role that money performs in that society come from Marxist and psychoanalytical interpretations about the role of money in society. The Marxist theory has been proved wrong in so many ways (including in this work, namely, how much Marx's intrinsic metallism informed his view about the origin of money's value) that it does not deserve further comments. The psychoanalytic interpretation of commerce and of the meaning of money deserves at least a brief note. One may say that it was Freud himself who started, with his 1908 "Character and Anal Erotism" to propose, that "Such connections among money, guilt, and loss are most clearly expressed by money's symbolic association with bodily waste." (Dodd, 2014: 151). Freud's main point, if one tries to understand that piece in the context of his work, is that there is a symbolic relation between different "stages" of emotional development and bodily functions and sensations. To understand that the relation is not symbolic but real is, to my judgment, a poor understanding of Freudian theory. To associate the fact that, in order to increase production and productivity of human labor, capital investment is necessary with neurotic propensities to accumulate possessions that may (or may not) be symbolized by retention of feces by the child when she learns how to control her sphincter is, in my opinion, not only bad psychoanalysis but bad sociology. Those claims are so outlandish to a proper understanding of what money actually is that I see no point in further discussing them.

1.7 ARGUMENTS FOR CONCEIVING MONEY AS A CHARTER

1.7.1 Is Money a Creation of the State?

Yet another key characteristic of money could be understood by answering the question: Is money a creation of the state? Georg Friedrich Knapp's 1905 book *State Theory of Money* is the cornerstone of the line of thinking that holds that money is a creation of the state.[22] Knapp starts his book stating: "Money is a creature of Law. A theory of money must therefore deal with legal history" (Knapp, 2003: 1). To Knapp, the essence of a currency resides not in the material that its pieces are made of, "but in the legal ordinances that regulate their use" (2003: 2).

According to the chartalist school initiated by Knapp, money has a much narrower definition than the "GAMOE" definition we are using. Their definition is, money is what the law says that money is; money is what the state determines or authorizes; money is what the state gives a charter to (the reason why this theory is also called *Chartalist*). Knapp goes on to say:

> All money, whether of metal or of paper, is only a special case of the means of payment in general. In legal history the concept of the means of payment is gradually evolved, beginning from simple forms and proceeding to the more complex. There are means of payment which are not yet money; then those which are money; later still those which have ceased to be money. (2003: 2)

There are important consequences of the adoption of this narrower sense for money: first, the value of money becomes "nominal" (the reason why this theory is also called *Nominalist*), that is, the value of money is, even if indirectly, through the control of money supply, determined by the state. Second, since the value of money is determined by the state, the state can change the value of money in order to fulfill its goals and *individuals have no right to complain*—after all, if money is created by the state, it is created to attend to the objectives of the state, and Knapp is quite explicit about that: "Now, when the State alters the means of payment, . . . does anyone lose? Of course; and why not, if the State has paramount reasons for its actions? It can never gain its ends without damage to certain private interests" (2003: 17). One may assume that the state is interested in the division of labor, but the immediate interest of the state is its fiscal considerations and other political goals that it may have. A corollary of this understanding about what money is is that the ideal attributes of money are not the same ones if you accept that the main purpose of money is to allow and enhance the division of labor; these become factors of secondary significance. The primary factors to consider are attributes that one can find in money to make it a more effective tool for achieving government's policies. Among the followers of the theory developed by Knapp, we find John Maynard Keynes, for whom money means essentially the unit of account, the standard of value, (Keynes, 1997: 229) and F. A. Mann who in his 1938 book *The Legal Aspect of Money* wrote:

> Only those chattels are money to which such character has been attributed by law, i.e. by or with the authority of the state. This is the state or chartalist theory of money which in modern times has come to be connected with the name of G. F. Knapp, to whose principal work it has given the title. (Mann, 1982: 13)

Both in the United Kingdom and in the United States of America (and almost everywhere) F. A. Mann's interpretation is incorporated into the *law of the land*.[23] Keynes cannot be more explicit in advocating a chartal theory of money and the state prerogative in monetary matters, almost since the beginning of civilized life:

> The State, therefore, comes in first of all as the authority of law which enforces the payment of the thing which corresponds to the name or description in the contracts. But it comes in doubly when, in addition, it claims the right to determine and declare what thing corresponds to the name, and to vary its declaration from time to time—when, that is to say, it claims the right to re-edit the dictionary. This right is claimed by all modern states and has been so claimed for some four thousand years at least. (Keynes, 1976: 4)

Being the state prerogative in force for so long, obviously, for Keynes, every single case of modern money is a case of chartal money, including all forms of the gold standard. For instance, a 100% backed, freely convertible money would be "commodity money;" at the other extreme is "fiat money," which is not convertible money; and, in between, "managed money"is any arrangement in which the state manages the issuance of money, taking into consideration some relation of its value with something of "objective value" (Keynes, 1976: p. 8).

With Keynes, the understanding of the state prerogative as constrained by the convertibility in **specie**, that is, in something with "objective value," suddenly lost its hold, and the prerogative became understood as the right to "write the dictionary," that is, to manage the value of money as it serves the purposes of the state. To suspend conversion and debase the currency was no longer perceived as something reproachable, to be used only in emergencies, but instead as an acceptable instrument for daily management of the money supply. A follower of Keynes, Abba Lerner, restated the chartalist view about how the state may create a generally accepted medium of exchange as follows:

> Whatever may have been the history of gold, at the present time, in a normally well-working economy, money is a creature of the state. Its general acceptability, which is its all-important attribute, stands or fails by its acceptability by the state. (Lerner, 1943: 313)

The most far-reaching corollary of a state theory of money, however, is the realization by its supporters that once the state imposes taxation on the citizenry, to be paid by the money it creates, it is theoretically consistent to say that the state can "induce" production by simply creating money on one hand and increasing taxation on the other hand. Even more than that, since there is always a demand for cash balances by the economic agents, the state is "forced" to run a deficit or, as stated by Wray in introducing Lerner's concept of "functional finance," "The normal requirement is for a government deficit" (Wray, 2000: 59). Lerner, in explaining what "functional finance" means, states:

> The central idea is that government fiscal policy, its spending and taxing, its borrowing and repayment of loans, its issue of new money, and its withdrawal of money, shall all be undertaken with an eye only to the results of these actions on the economy and not to any established traditional doctrine about what is sound or unsound. (Lerner, 1943: 39)

Further, Lerner explains:

> Functional Finance rejects completely the traditional doctrines of "sound finance" and the principle of trying to balance the budget over a solar year or any other arbitrary period. In their place it prescribes: first, the adjustment of total spending (by everybody in the economy, including the government) in order to eliminate both unemployment and inflation, using government spending when total spending is too low and taxation when total spending is too high; second, the adjustment of public holdings of money and of government bonds, by government borrowing or debt repayment, in order to achieve the rate of interest which results in the most desirable level of investment; and third, the printing, hoarding or destruction of money as needed for carrying out the first two parts of the programme. (Lerner, 1943: 41)

The consequences of this line of reasoning are, therefore, the justification for central planning in monetary matters and as an instrument for central planning in the economy in general, with the elimination of any restraint in transference of wealth from the private sector to the government since, according to the theory, it was actually enhancing production. This ultimate corollary of the state theory of money is stated by Wray as follows:

> Governments issue money to buy what they need; they tax to generate a demand for that money; and then they accept the money in payment of the tax. If a deficit results, that simply indicates that the population wishes to hoard some of the money. The deficit is of no consequence to the government; it merely allows the population to save in the form of government money. If the government wants to, it can let the population trade the money for interest-earning bonds, but the government never needs to borrow its own money from the public. Taxes and bonds, therefore, have nothing to do with financing a government's

spending. They necessarily follow spending rather than precede it. (Wray, 2000: 61)

The chain of reasoning starting with a) the state theory of money's original claims that the state has the monetary prerogative and that the state can create a more useful money for the economic agents by accepting the money created by the state in payment of taxes; followed by b) the argument that the state prerogative comprises the right to define money's value in order to achieve its political goals in war and peace; and resulting in c) the conclusion that the state can create wealth by creating money and increasing the public debt covers the full cycle of the most theoretical aspect of the origin of money to the most practical consequences in the matter of monetary and fiscal policy. All these theoretical developments started from a misconception, in my understanding. The fact that the government enforces the currency is no more proof that the money is a State creature than the definition of a standard grammar by some state-sponsored agency to be adopted by the schools in the country is proof that the language was created by the State, or the enforcement of corporate law is proof that corporations are creatures of the State, or that enforcing civil law in the courts is proof that marriage itself is a creation of the State. Of course it is in the interest of rulers everywhere to say that money is what they say it is because of the corollaries already mentioned, but it does not become true only because a law says so; if traders use other media of exchange rather than the government-sponsored one, they are nevertheless still using money. That people almost always accept fiat money as a medium of exchange whenever legal tender is decreed and enforced is not proof that money is created by the State; if the fiat money is wisely managed as, say, arguably, the American dollar was managed during Greenspan's stewardship, it will be accepted, used, and will keep its value in time and in comparison with other currencies; if the fiat money is badly managed as, for example, the **assignats** were during the French Revolution, it will be rejected. We cannot derive from the fact that nowadays most of the currencies in the world are issued by stated-owned monopolies that money is a creation of the state. Menger already made clear that money in general and coined money in particular are not the same thing and that, generally speaking, money has a spontaneous origin:

> The origin of money (as distinct from coin, which is only one variety of money) is, as we have seen, entirely natural and thus displays legislative influence only in the rarest instances. Money is not an invention of the state. It is not the product of a legislative act. Even the sanction of political authority is not necessary for its existence. (Menger, 1994: 261)

Once laws protecting individuals' property rights against violence and fraud are enforced by the state, a generally accepted medium of exchange—that is, money—will emerge without the necessity of any other state initiative. Saying, however, that money will emerge in society without the necessity of any government's initiative and that adequate money may emerge in society without any government's initiative other than enforcing the protection of private property rights leads one to the question of why the state has been so prominent historically. The reasons for the state prominence in the money supply are, in my opinion, one, because of the rent that can be extracted from society through the establishment of a control of the supply of money, and, two, due to the fact that by having at hand the means of coercion, the rulers can actually impose such controls, admittedly in different degrees, according to the times and circumstances. Yet one may still ask what makes such controls, from the mildest regulations to the most stringent monopoly, legitimate in the eyes of the citizenry? That question admits an empirical answer, and historically the "fiscal" argument in favor of government controls over the money supply has trumped any other arguments against that. When the security of a politically organized community is at risk or seems to be at risk, the government's seizure of the control over the money supply in particular, finances in general, and all sorts of private property rights are more easily accepted than in peacetimes. Again, this opening chapter is not yet the moment to use the analytical tools that are developed in this book to judge either the adequacy of the different possible means of war financing or the legitimacy of the "fiscal" argument for government control of money and banking. For the purposes of this chapter, suffice it to say that the fiscal argument is identified as the main reason for the state prominence in monetary matters.

1.7.2 Max Weber and the Chartal Theory of Money

Even before Keynes, the state theory of money as proposed by Knapp had already achieved academic acceptance, in spite of the critique of Austrian economists. That acceptance seemed to be a result of the evident widespread claim of a state prerogative in monetary matters, limited as that prerogative was understood to be at the beginning of the twentieth century. The money prerogative was an institutional feature of most Western states at the time and as such, regarded as a sociological fact. And it is in that sense that the state theory of money was discussed by Max Weber. Weber accepts that money may be defined as a "legal means of payment;" so, at prima facie, it seems that Weber accepts the chartal theory of money. In his words:

> By passing a suitable law, a state can turn any object into a "legal means of payment" and any chartal object into "money" in the sense of a means of payment. It can establish for them any desired set of "value scales" or, in the case of "market money," "currency relations." (Weber, 1978: 167)

But further analysis reveals that regimenting Weber alongside the Chartalists may not be a correct interpretation. It seems that Weber accepts that the state can create money only in regard to its legal properties. That does not imply that the money created by the state will have any value. So, reductio ad absurdum, the money created by the state may have only formal existence and no real value. This is more like Knapp's nominal theory, for Weber does not offer a complete definition of what money is. Weber does say:

> The definition of money as a legal means of payment and as the creature of the "**Lytric**" administration of political bodies is, from a sociological point of view, not exhaustive. (Weber, 1978: 168)

According to Weber, the real value of the money a government creates may be enhanced when the state gives attributes to its chartal that make it desired by the market, at a certain price, such as: accepting it as a means of payment of the obligations owed to the state, imposing forced tender laws, administering its supply prudently, et cetera. However, in the end, the "substantive" value of money is not in the direct power of the state to define. Weber says:

> The exchange possibility of money against other specific goods, which rests on its valuation in relation to marketable goods, will be called its "substantive" validity, as opposed to its formal, legal validity as a means of payment and the frequently existing legal compulsion for its formal use as a means of exchange. (Weber, 1978: 169)

Weber's acknowledgement that the state has the power to formally define what legal money is can hardly be understood as an endorsement of the chartal theory of money. As an interpretation of that theory, it actually opens the door to the understanding of their claim in a more limited way, one that may be made compatible with a **catallactic** theory of money. That, however, seems not to be the interpretation of the theory's own proponents.

1.7.3 Geoffrey Ingham and the Hybrid Nature of Modern Money: Private Credit Money

It is Geoffrey Ingham who first described how private bank credit money and public issued coinage generated a dual (hybrid) monetary system; and that the landmark development for that to happen was the establishment of the Bank of England in 1694, when "the privately owned Bank of England transformed the sovereign's personal debt into a public debt and, eventually in turn, into a public currency" (Ingham, 2004: 209).[24] Ingham describes how the political compromise established at the time to end absolutism was also extended to the monetary realm, when the merchants organized around the Bank of England gained the privilege to issue (private) notes, backed by debt of the sovereign, while the sovereign gained greater access to credit, thanks to the financial intermediation of the bank and the greater authority to collect taxes and fund the service of the national debt given by parliament. That, of course, is just a development of the seminal work by P. G. M. Dickson (1967), but a novel insight, nonetheless.[25] One may dispute whether that was the moment in which the funding of a national debt by private bankers acting essentially as bond dealers first took place. There is, for instance, abundant evidence that at the time of Charles V and Philip II their bankers were already leveraging their balance sheets to fund the acquisition of their sovereign debt as a stage in the process of placing them with third parties, but the process of monetization of the national debt undoubtedly started with the creation of the Bank of England as pointed out by Ingham and mentioned (without attribution) by Felix Martin in *Money: The Unauthorized Biography*.

The empire of Charles V is on the threshold between a medieval dominion and a modern state. There are many transitional features in the political organization created by Charles V, but our interest is focused on the development of institutions as a response to fiscal needs. Taxation, public finances, and political representation all evolved pressed by his needs to raise current revenues and to mortgage future revenues in order to fund military campaigns.

1.7.4 The "Secret" Weapon of the Sovereign State: Its Monetary Prerogatives

An interesting topic to consider is the extent to which a "modern" sovereign nation-state, the kind of political organization usually considered as having resulted from the Peace of Westphalia of 1648, is a more efficient form of political organization, so much so that practically the entire globe is now subject to one of those states. It seems self-evident that a sovereign nation-state is so much more efficient than other previous forms of political organization such as tribal leagues, loosely connected, dynastic empires, and the like due to the capacity that it has to mobilize fast significant resources in proportion to the total wealth of its citizens to wage war; and the monetary prerogatives are at the core of the mechanism that allow that to happen. However, at the time of Charles V neither his kingdom nor anywhere else were there the kinds of modern states we have today, but all his efforts to centralize power were clearly efforts in that direction, and with that purpose in mind. For some, it is precisely the capacity to mobilize credit, using the coercive collection of taxes as collateral plus the direct manipulation of the money supply, that give such political entities the differential in better providing for defense. Even if not fully understood, it was at least put into practice by Charles V for his dynastic purposes and not necessarily for the defense of life and property of his subjects. For Schumpeter, the centrality of fiscal history to explain the general history could not be overemphasized. Quoting Goldscheid saying that "the budget is the skeleton of the state stripped of all misleading ideologies" (Schumpeter, 1991: 100), it is his opinion that fiscal considerations were the only determinants of Charles V's economic policy (1991: 101). That such power was abused even before it was clearly developed is an indictment against its moral good standing, though. But for now let's remain focused on the implications of the growth of public debt and a monetary base for the European economy in general and the Spanish economy in particular at the time of Charles V. Note, there were some phenomena that can only be explained by qualitative changes, not only by quantitative changes. For instance, at some point during Charles' reign, his bankers started to give him money, no longer against the mortgage and transference of tax collection of ordinary revenues (asientos), but by the acquisition of annuities (juros) under the assumption that they would be sold afterwards. At the time, that assumption seemed reasonable but, susceptible to disruptions by any loss of credit, such as military setbacks, the sequestration of private remittances of gold and silver from the Indies, or a curb on the always-precarious licenses to move bullion out of Spain (partidas), such disruptions resulted from the deterioration of fiscal conditions and induced the leveraging of banking operations at that time.

The deterioration of the balance sheet of Charles' bankers was evident in other ways as well. The Fuggers of Augsburg, Charles' most important bankers, moved from 2 million ducats in assets in 1520, from which only 300,000 were loans to the emperor supported by 1.7 million in capital, to a precarious financial position in 1563 when from 5.7 million ducats in assets, 3.0 million ducats were loaned to Charles V, and their own capital was reduced to 300,000 ducats after losses they faced and capital withdrawals from family members. Neither the extent to which they leveraged their balance sheet and moved from lenders of their own capital to financial intermediaries and, ultimately, dealers of public debt, nor the many parallels that can be traced to banking activities in today's post-2008 financial crisis era can pass unnoticed. The issue, one that I cannot adequately answer, is the extent to which Charles' bankers were practicing fractional reserve banking at his time. In Bernal's book, there is a statement that seventy-five percent of the money in circulation at the end of Charles V's reign was bullion, but that was understood as saying that the other twenty-five percent was token money (velon), composed mainly of copper coins. For me, Bernal was neither referring to inflationary creation of credit by the banks, nor to the monetary attributes that, at one time, were given by the market to the annuities (juros). That latter hypothesis, that is, the monetization of the annuities, may also explain the relaxation in the credit standards required by the bankers funding the public debt. A final aspect of this piling of public debt, inflationary creation of credit by the banks, and acceptance of unsecured debt by the bankers, was the assumption that constant and growing remittances of gold and silver would continue to flow from the Americas. Such a perception that more riches were coming from the Americas which, by the way, ended up materializing during Charles' successor's reign, triggered the expansion of public debt and its consequences to such an unsustainable level that, even when it came to fruition, mainly through the silver mines of Peru and Mexico, it was still not enough to prevent the repeated Philip II bankruptcies.[26]

This historical digression is sufficient to support the claim that, at the time, private bankers were already leveraging their operations by reselling sovereign debt denominated in commodity money, and issuing obligations of their own to be paid in such currency. Granted, the "new era" of hybrid money, in which private credit money began to be used as money in parallel with the commodity money coined by the sovereign may well be established as being initiated with the creation of the Bank of England as claimed by Ingham; although precedents moving financial arrangements in that direction are known to exist for about two centuries before that.

Another important implication of Ingham's work, as it can be deduced from the reasoning mentioned above (Ingham, 2004: 208), as clearly stated by Dodd (2014: 218) is that "The Institutions of strong metallic standards for money provided the financial infrastructure in which credit money could thrive, providing the 'secure socially and politically constructed monetary space,' underpinned by a stable political system and a solid fiscal system, that Ingham regards as the crucial sociological preconditions for full-fledged credit money." Well, that is the clearest statement one can possible make in order to defend the idea that the "Babylonian Madness" of Lord Keynes (more on that later) and all his precursors and followers are wrong in seeing in the clay tallies of ancient Mesopotamia the beginning of money as a unit of account. It only makes sense that the unit of account used—that half a dozen or so goods demanded as taxes, even in a primitive economy with a very low division of labor and under a sociopolitical system in which taxation is collected in kind—had a proportionality of value according to some relation that, even if imposed coercively by the authorities, made some economic sense. Nothing better as an instrument for that than a liquid merchandise that often is used as an instrument for indirect exchanges, as frequent or as infrequent as they may be. So, if the tallies are measured in an amount of silver equivalent to a certain amount of barley that is equivalent to an ox, for example, that is because it makes sense for the priests/kings of old to use silver not only as a unit of account but also as a medium of exchange. We are not talking here about the concrete fact that the unit of account was established by the political authorities, but that it was in the interest of the political authorities to select as the unit of account they will impose on society one that would have the least resistance possible, probably one that had already been in use, and at a certain ratio not much different than the one practiced in the daily transactions of their subjects, in the same way that Ingham describes the great increase in the monetary use of credit instruments once the metallic standard of value became well established and secured by the authority of the state in modern Europe.

There are however other claims, in the most recent presentation of the chartalist thesis that are not easy to accept; for instance, Dodd, on page 96, discussing Graeber, says that the "modern monetary system is rooted in state violence," something with which it is difficult to disagree, but he then says that that started with coinage and not with debt. Let's suppose he is right in his interpretation of Graeber; that requires one to consider that the kings and priests in ancient Mesopotamia did not use violence to collect the debts of their peasants, which is clearly a mistaken assumption.

1.7.5 Contemporary Private Credit Money: The Ideas of Ingham, Minsky, and Strange according to Graeber and Dodd

Having started with the establishment of the Bank of England a hybrid monetary system in which government-issued commodity money and privately created credit money circulated in parallel, it is important to notice that that system only formally ended the moment that the Nixon administration defaulted on the Bretton Woods treaty and all links to gold, however tenuous by then, were completely severed, leaving the world in a still hybrid but by now completely fiat money system.[27] That much is acknowledged by the Chartalists, and we find a quote from Graeber (2011: 362) in Dodd (2014: 98) that Nixon's default on the Bretton Woods treaty instigated a new phase of financial history in which the international monetary system was now based on the (US) national debt. That is an important difference from the system originally described by Ingham, since base money is no longer a scarce commodity, but may be created by fiat. Furthermore, some of the base money, such as bank reserves and bank notes, is not even remunerated; as the Chartalists like to say, they are good only to pay taxes. The fact that the current international division of labor is fundamentally based on a national fiat currency can only be explained for the Chartalists by the hegemonic condition of the United States in the Bretton Woods and post–Bretton Woods era. The international monetary order, therefore, for Graeber, is supported by the military might of the United States (Graeber, 2011: 365), quoted by Dodd (2014: 99). That may well be an important part of the equation, but it is ludicrous to say that it was only that and not take into consideration the economic relevance of the United States and the size of the trade zone developed by the United States; after all, arguably the Russians had or perhaps still have about the same military power and no one is using the ruble.

The concept of private credit money attributed by Dodd (2014: 121) to Minsky is applicable to the securitization of assets and their "monetization," that is, the creation of financial instruments with monetary properties by private financial companies, such as banks through the use of structures such as money market mutual funds (MMMFs). That reveals that the private creation of credits is not necessarily inflationary, although it escapes the control of the state. But what Minsky considers the possible limitless creation of credit (Minsky, 2008: 3), because it is not limited by the banks' own capital, in fact, is limited by the availability in the market of streams of revenue able to be profitably "securitized," so it is not true that that would spiral out of control just because there is no one in charge, a fact that seems to have eluded Minsky. In Dodd, there is still (2014: 121) reference to "Strange Money," that is, the ideas of Susan Strange about the rise of private money, with a distinction between a global financial system, in which private credit money is created outside of the control of governments, and the international monetary system that regulates the relations between sovereign currencies. That, she claims in "The Westfailure System" (Strange, 1999), results from the incapacity of national states as created by the 1648 Westphalia treaty, to deal with problems created, allegedly, by "global capitalism," among them "global financial crises." To the extent that it is possible to identify behind a jungle of unconnected ideas and Marxist jargon any coherence in her arguments, her case is that the creation of credit private monetary instruments gives too much power to private banks at the expense of sovereign governments, or worse still, gives those financial institutions power over sovereign governments. The relevance of her thesis is that she does not consider the fact (perhaps due to the fact that she died in 1998 and therefore missed the counterevidence to her thesis given by the 2008 financial crisis) that the creation of private credit instruments with monetary properties, such as MMMFs, are money until they aren't; the clearest evidence of that were the hundreds of billions of dollars transferred from MMMFs to deposit accounts in the aftermath of Lehman's bankruptcy in a matter of hours that prompted the unprecedented intervention of the central banks into the money market.[28] In the end, the government of the sovereign states created in the framework of the Westphalia treaty with their monopolistic monetary prerogatives proved to be the real power in financial matters. Another minor aspect of her argument is that in discussing international relations (IR), financial matters have been a neglected subject. That cannot be farther from the truth but fits well with a leftist conspiratory worldview. It goes without saying that she is one more proponent of a reform narrowing the role of the banks.

1.7.6 *Graeber on Debt: A Restatement of the State Theory of Money*

I would like to start this review with a compliment to the author's erudition and intellect and a comment with regret for the ideological bias that he imposes upon this work. However, it would be a pity if my comments on Graeber's book were understood as an attack ad hominem due to the fact that the author is a man of the Left. My thesis regarding the origin of the book's flaws comes from Hobbes, for whom it would be difficult to make people agree that the result of two plus two is four if it were in someone's interest to be another answer to this question (Buchanan, 1979: 135). So, I do not criticize the work because its author is of the Left, but because his ideological likeness shows, in some passages, to be stronger than his love for truth.

First, let's describe the book and see how good and original it is. This is a work that uses anthropological evidence on the origin of money to conclude what its nature is in a society. Regarding that, this book fills a large gap in the field as it offers a summary of the existing historic and anthropological knowledge on the development of the instruments that ended up performing the functions that nowadays we associate with money, such as medium of exchange, unit of account, and of store of value. In this book, the author presents and adopts one of the theories on the origin of money and defends it against alternative theories: the theory that money originated as credit, which is one of the versions of the "Chartalist Theory of Money." The Chartalists, beginning with Georg Knapp, defend that money is simply what the state defines it is; money is a "letter," a document. On the other hand, those who sustain the "Credit Theory of Money," of which Mitchell Innes was the pioneer, defend that money is an obligation, a debit. Both theories have in common the idea that the main function of money is to be a unit of exchange and that money has no value besides the one given by the government. In order to support that thesis, the author brings examples from the first societies in Mesopotamia, Old Greece, India, and China, until he gets to our present days and current problems, which he tries to analyze with the tools from this investigation on the origin and essential features of money; by the way, a project that in principle I can only compliment.

Among the provocative original theses the author presents in this book is the idea that the US government public debt in foreign hands was until recently financed almost exclusively by governments and citizens of "American military protectorates" such as Japan, Germany, and Taiwan, and that those investments would only be "tributes" paid for their defense and there would be no US intention, neither an expectation by the lenders, of having those resources paid back eventually (2011: 6). Also, it is possible to notice certain ambivalence by the author towards the state as a violence monopoly; this is almost an anarchist feature of Graeber that comes up, for instance, when he claims that money debts in society are only respected by the use of violence. Such line of thought, like Rousseau, seems to miss a life of primitive simplicity, when people lived in small communities exchanging gifts and where everybody knows "who owes what to whom" (2011: 36) without the need of purchase or sale of goods and services or the use of money unless making reparations for injury caused or ritual and religious obligations like dowry in marriages and offerings in funerals. And here I make a reference in what I judge to be the author's greatest flaw in this work: there is not any recognition of the importance of labor division for the kind of society we have today and the crucial role that money performs in the feasibility of the type of open and complex society we enjoy nowadays. Following a classical tradition, Hugo Grotius affirms that humanity lived, at a certain moment, in a golden era of primitive simplicity and without private property; however "tired of living in caves and covering themselves with the bark of trees," private property and commerce were introduced in society (Grotius, 2005: vol. II, 426). From what we can see, the "golden era" had nothing golden, nonetheless some modern thinkers seem to dream of it as if it had.

I do not want to compare classic myth to the author's anthropological evidence and historic research to explain the origin of money, I only want to call the reader's attention to the fact that one needs more than a gathering of facts to come to a conclusion, even if its veracity is unquestionable.[29] He or she needs not only a theory that has logical coherence, but also a theory that is consistent with the facts that it supposedly supports and other related facts which have not been falsified up to now; and here is where, I argue, Graeber's preferred theory is insufficient. On page 19, he affirms that the idea with this anthropological investigation is to "show" that money and exchange are associated in their origin with violence. Even if that were true, and I am unaware of evidence of that, this thesis used to explain the nature of money suffers from a genetic fallacy. Whatever the origin of money is, it does not necessarily explain what role money performs today in society any better than saying that, alongside the human evolution chain, body hair arose to allow the maintenance of thermal homeostasis explains its practical function for a modern human being.

The credit theory of money, as presented by Graeber, better defines itself in opposition to the theory of the origin of money proposed by Carl Menger, and it is against it that the author presents most of his historic and anthropological evidences. However, some facts appeared to have not been taken into account, such as (i) that, according to Menger, anything that is generally accepted as means of indirect exchange by a certain group is money, and (ii) that the motivation for the adoption of an instrument of indirect exchanges of commodities (C-M-C) is the facilitation of the individual needs' satisfaction by the elimination of the condition of "concomitant desires" which exist in the direct exchanges (C_x-C_y)

when an agent has to find another who not only desires what he has for exchange, but also has some good that the first agent desires. So the idea that indirect exchanges are a more efficient way of promoting job specialization is not to be taken lightly (2011: 34), since doing that would imply rejecting the development of the "transaction costs" concept. Instead, the claim against Menger is based on the lack of anthropological evidence that, at some point, a primitive society had organized its economic activities by direct exchange. For the author this lack of evidence would justify labeling as a "myth" the thesis that money had evolved from direct exchanges by the selection of a good that, through its attributes, would better serve as a tool for exchanges which then became gradually indirect.

After mentioning that the idea that the origin of money as an instrument for exchange began with Aristotle (Graeber, 2011: 25), he attributes it to Adam Smith and says that that "myth" is important because that "desire" for exchange was what led to the division of labor and to civilization, according to Smith. Those advantages of the division of labor seen by Smith do not have the same value for Graeber, who brings up the Nambikwara's example (2011: 29) to claim that one can rarely observe "commercial" exchanges in primitive societies. And here we note an important aspect of Graeber's reasoning: he seems to believe that our ancestors' social arrangements were the same as the arrangement of current primitive peoples. Established as a method of anthropological analysis as it is, it is evidently a mistake because if it were like that, we would still be primitive men today; if our ancestors did the same as today's still primitive peoples, how come our society has evolved and theirs has not? Nevertheless, going back to the lack of recognition for the value of division of labor, this kind of violent inefficient society, not to mention the minimal division of labor and absolute poverty of the Nambikwara, seems to be a poor replacement for the society we have today. The economic inefficiency of the exchanges for "gifts" is patent and it certainly explains why those peoples who practice them are still primitive. According to Graeber (2011: 32), economists resist the idea that the origin of money from exchanges is a myth because without that there would not be the economy discipline; that, however, seems not to be the case—even in those primitive societies he describes, where there are no commercial exchanges but only ritual exchanges of gifts, there is an economic rationality (it is low, but it is there) and with tools of economic analysis, it is possible to better understand and critique them.

However, let's start from the claim (2011: 33) that there has never been a society based on direct exchange. Menger's analysis explains that the exchanges are so inconvenient that it is no surprise that this has never been found. Those rituals, which the author refers to, are inefficient ways of lessening that big inconvenience.[30] In this sense, it is reasonable to say that there is not one minimally complex society with division of labor based on direct exchanges, and those examples of primitive societies with direct exchanges that Graeber mentions are societies with little labor specialization and they themselves are organized in violent and/or mystic ways. Menger's thesis for the origin of money is an application of what later became known as catallactic, as part of praxeology (the science of human behavior). There are different ways of organizing the production and distribution of goods that are necessary, useful, and pleasant for a human life, and for those societies that find themselves in the middle of the forest with the risk of the whole thing becoming a field battle in the hopes of acquiring goods to which other tribes have access and they do not, it is simply an inefficient way of getting those goods. Menger's thesis is nothing more than the axiomatic acknowledgment that the indirect exchanges are more efficient than the direct exchanges and that sooner or later people will adopt them or, in other words, the ones who adopt them thrive and the ones who do not stay in the Stone Age.

Graeber admits (2011: 45) that without money, there would not be the complex division of labor we have today, but that the economists, starting with Adam Smith, lessen the government's role for this to happen and that such division happened thanks to the decision of establishing a coin backed in silver in the England of Smith's time, and that this vision became universally accepted and made others, like Mitchell Innes, who see money as credit, look like cranks. He then affirms (2011: 46) that the credit theory of the origin of money "has to be true," because having gold as money and paper is the same thing, because what deeply matters is the trust in which other people will accept that instrument in their exchanges. Well, there are two different issues here, first is the idea of trust, which is correct in theory, but that does not mean that, in practice, the trust in gold or paper money is the same; second, the idea of liquidity (of the chosen means to intermediate the exchanges) which is missing in the story the author tells. Right after (2011: 48), Graeber refers to Knapp, to the concept of imaginary money proposed by Einaudi, and to the Chartalists' central idea that anything the state defines as money is money. Here, it seems, there is a confusion of ideas because, as Menger said, anything that is generally accepted is money and, as Einaudi explained, if one has an abstract unit of account, one can accept different media of exchange, but that does not eliminate the need for means of exchange. A recourse to theories on the *value* of money would help one to understand that the state cannot define the value that people will give to money they accept. The state may influence, for instance, by accepting the money it produces as an instrument to pay taxes and then creating a "utility" even for pieces of painted paper, but it cannot determine the subjective value which the agents will perceive in this "utility."

Regarding the Chartalists still, Graeber (2011: 50) says that the state theory of money is cursed for economists in the Smith tradition; as if this theory had not become predominantly accepted among economists at least since the Keynesian theories became the dominant mainstream in the economic thought.

Graeber actually mentions Keynes' research on the origin of money in Mesopotamia and affirms that if one does not start from axioms, the only possible conclusion is that the state theory is right. He also says, mentioning Keynes, that it does not matter the origin of money, it has been created by the state in the last 4,000 years. Then, suddenly, Graeber asks himself: If tax is not extortion and governments are not the mob, what justifies the credit theory of the origin of money? And he says that those who adopt this theory do not have such a cynical view of the state. He thinks there are two answers for that question: one is that the government gains legitimacy for providing services such as defense and well-being, and the other is that of "primordial debt theory." This "primordial debt theory" is the idea that the state uses taxes to create demand for the money it produces, that the state is the private debts' "guardian," and that debt is in the origin of the society itself. To my surprise, he candidly affirms that the origin of this theory was the creation of the euro, the effort of ECB and the German government to impose monetary and fiscal discipline in the European Communities (EC) upon the welfare state, and that is why those "theoreticians" came to justify a contrary position to those policies.

Here I am back to reconcile with the anarchist/libertarian Graeber, when he affirms (2011: 69) that the primordial debt theoreticians are not consistent because what they want is to justify an existing social structure. Then, Graeber attributes the pioneering idea that people are born with a debt to a society to Auguste Comte. Here the author presents himself as a critic of the primordial debt theory and the association he establishes between it and positivism is extremely important. On page 71, Graeber says that the primordial debt theory is present in socialism and in nationalism although he affirms that it is a false dichotomy to say that we are born autonomous or as part of the state, because state and market cannot live without each other. Anyway, it is a very interesting acknowledgment that the thesis is collectivist and also interesting is the (implicit) idea that without the organization of a society in a spontaneous way through markets, there would not be states which we could acknowledge as such nowadays. In summary, according to Graeber, the exchange "myth" and the primordial debt "myth" are two sides of the same coin. And based on this theoretical apparatus, he proposes (2011: 214) that the Eurasian history cycles between fiduciary and metallic money would be: (a) 3500 BCE–800 BCE (credit); (b) 800 BCE–600 CE (coins); (c) 600 CE–1450 CE (credit); (d) 1450–1971 (coins); and (e) 1971–today (credit). When explaining the minted coin origin around 800 BC, Graeber claims (2011: 225) that, mentioning David Schaps, minting started with the "de-thesaurizing" caused by wars and the soldiers' will to have light and valuable things to carry as loot; that the first professional armies were organized in that time. I ask myself, why doesn't he think that the society's sophistication led to a larger division of labor and so it began to make sense to the sovereign to pay for the services that they were interested in obtaining with money and not by keeping relations of servitude? Because they might want to get services from manifold people who were not their servants and also they were not organized in a subordinate state, or something like that. Actually, the idea of mercenaries need not be excluded, I believe, but rather is complementary, and is part of the same history of the division of labor which I emphasize.

For Graeber (2011: 335), Adam Smith is wrong in the famous passage on the butcher and baker's self-love from *The Wealth of Nations* (1981: 1.2.2), because the baker used to sell on credit. However, the baker's own interest seems to be at work whether he is selling on credit or not. One may even say that he sells on credit *because* it is in his interest. Graeber's argument appears to be (2011: 334) that Adam Smith made it up that the baker acted in self-interest, just as he made up a story on the origin of money, and that allowed Adam Smith to ignore the importance of benevolence and malevolence in economic (and social) relations; an odd comment about the author of *Theory of Moral Sentiments*. Another historical omission (2011: 337) is the statement that "debasement "became a moral issue" in the time of Adam Smith—when it is already present in Nicolas Oresme or the late Spanish Scholastics, if not before. On the same page, the apparent contradiction that the period of time when the resurgence of gold and silver coin (around 1450) as a substitution for credit happened is also the time when credit grows the most reveals that, for Graeber, the idea of value of money is not only metallism but "intrinsic" metallism.

I end this review as I started it. Despite my doubts about several factual statements and misguided conclusions, I recognize the importance of the book as a gathering of the discussion on the nature of money and the validity of this discussion to help us understand current monetary problems.

1.8 COMPARING THE ARGUMENTS OF THE TWO SCHOOLS

1.8.1 Catallactic and Acatallactic Theories

In Mises' *The Theory of Money and Credit* there is an appendix A on the "Classification of Monetary Theories" (Mises, 1980: 503). In this text, Mises presents a broader distinction between "catallactic" and "acatallactic" monetary doctrines according to which all monetary theories can be classified. He explains that "catallactic" is an adjective meaning something pertaining to exchange, and "catallactics" is a noun meaning the study of commercial exchange. So, the acatallactic[31] theories about the value of money are those not based on market observation but on other factors such as (a) the *valor impositus*, that is, in the command of the state, (b) biological analogies which equate money to blood, (c) "functional" analogies that compare money with speech, and finally (d) legal jargon that considers money as a draft against everybody else.

It is interesting to note that Mises calls our attention to the fact that the theories that identify the value of money with the intrinsic value of the monetary merchandise (that is, its value as derived from every other function besides its function as an instrument for indirect exchanges) are actually acatallactic, since they do not take into account that the value of the medium of exchange results precisely from its function as the instrument for indirect exchanges (although he also notes that this rationale eventually leads to the sources of value of the monetary merchandise and from there to its market value, which inevitably takes into account its monetary potential). Mises even mentions Knapp's definition of metallism that: "The metallist defines the unit of value as a certain quantity of metal" is not what Knapp actually means. According to Mises, for Knapp, any nonnominalistic theory is a metallist one and so comprises catallactic and acatallactic ones. Mises quotes Knapp, saying that Adam Smith and David Ricardo were metallists—an "incomprehensible error" if one considers the writings of these authors on money.

For Mises, a consistently developed theory of money must be merged into a theory of exchange—that is, it must be catallactic—and therefore all acatallactic theories about money are erroneous because they fail to be consistently integrated with the theories about the spontaneous order generated in society by the market interactions of individuals. Mises clearly states this in pointing out the epistemological importance of Carl Menger's theory of money while dealing with "indirect exchange" in *Human Action*. He suggests that the main deficiency of the doctrine sponsored by those authors, who tried to explain the origin of money by the authority of the state or a conscious compact between citizens, is their "assumption that people of an age unfamiliar with indirect exchange and money could design a plan of a new economic order, entirely different from the real conditions of their own age" (Mises, 2007: 405).

This point is particularly important, since for Mises:

> The historical question concerning the origin of indirect exchange and money is after all of no concern to praxeology. The only relevant thing is that indirect exchange and money exist because the conditions for their existence were and are present. (2007: 47)

Consistent with the idea that historical evidence can support a theoretical understanding about human society but can never prove or disprove it due to the complexity of social phenomena, a preliminary conclusion that can be drawn from these passages is that the introduction of state coined money in society happened when the social conditions for the development of that specie of the medium of exchange were already in place; and therefore, even if it is true that the adoption of coined money was primarily motivated by fiscal considerations, money does not lose its catallactic essence because of that.

Back to appendix A of *The Theory of Money and Credit*, discussing the "State Theory of Money" Mises calls our attention to the fact that nominalistic doctrinaires must concede that the state can only establish the validity of money's nominal unit, "but not the validity of these nominal units in commerce" (1980: 507). With that he hopes to demonstrate that there is an implicit recognition of the limitations of the theory to actually explain money's value. But then, he argues, there are always princes interested in the intellectual support of that doctrine for such an important source of revenue as the **debasement** of the currency, which explains its longevity and good health.

Finally, still in opposition to the attempts to find acatallactic definitions of money's value, Mises states in *Human Action*:

> Money is neither an abstract *numéraire* nor a standard of value or prices. It is necessarily an economic good and as such it is valued and appraised on its own merits, i.e., the services which a man expects for holding cash. (2007: 418)

The description by the Catallactics about how some merchandises became perceived by economic agents as useful instruments for their transactions because of their general acceptability, therefore allowing them by indirect transactions to reach their economic goals, is one supported by historical evidence and coherent with the understanding of humans as social beings. In comparison with the catallactic definition of money as the generally accepted medium of exchange, the chartalist definition of money as a chattel that by the authority of the state becomes a means of payment seems tautological: money is what the state says that money is. However, there is more than that in the chartalist definition, which I will try to do justice. One must ask, can the state create value? I think that the answer to that question is undoubtedly yes and all forms of fiat money in circulation today are evidence of that. Yes, the state can conjure a useful instrument to ease the transactions of economic agents and therefore, the government can create value "out of thin air." The proceeds of **seigniorage** accrued by the state are the result of such creation of economic value. For that to happen, it is not even necessary for an imposed monopoly of issuance, a forced tender, or even a legal tender to exist; money created by the state can still be perceived as valuable by economic agents, as was the case at the time that commodity money was freely circulated across borders and governments were still able to charge a premium over the price of **bullion** for their coined money. It is even more evident in our days of forced fiat money, when painted pieces of paper issued by most governments are accepted in payment for goods and services and used by the economic agents even outside their jurisdictions. This creation of value has a number of reasons and I will mention four of them. First, the government may be perceived as trustworthy in assessing purity and weight of bullion; second, the convenience of paying taxes with the money issued by the state may be valuable;[32] third, the forced or legal tender laws also may make it expedient to use the government-issued chattel as money; and, finally, the previous experience that some government-issued monies are generally accepted in daily transactions gives to it, as it would give to any other merchandise in the same circumstance, a value for the economic agents. So, it is based on these evidences that the Chartalists base their claim that by state authority, a chattel may become money. For me, the mistake with this interpretation is that it is the utility perceived by the money users and money holders in accepting the state-issued chattel that gives to it some value, and this value varies according with that perceived utility. So, not everything that the state says is money becomes generally accepted as a medium of exchange, that is, money; and it is not only the chattels issued by the state that are accepted as money. Therefore, the fact that the government can create valuable money does not support the claim of the Chartalists, hence reducing it to a mere tautology.

It is difficult to stress how far "functional finance" as a logical corollary of the state theory of money is from a catallactic theory of money. First, the assumption that it is possible to know what is the "right" interest rate that will result in the "maximum" possible production is to assume that it is possible to have information that will only be generated by the free interaction of economic agents, as will be discussed in the next part of this book; second, it completely disregards the **Cantillon effect** and all the distortions that result from the introduction of state-created money in the economy; third, it leads to the confusion between real wealth and money as representative of such wealth; and fourth, it relies on the supposition that individuals will work and produce just to pay taxes. This last supposition, for instance, may only be conceived from a collectivist approach; the methodological individualism of praxeology would not allow such a naïve assumption to go unchallenged.

1.8.2 Making Compatible what is Possible

Although we have not discussed in detail all the distinctions between the different historical accounts or in what ways one school of thought might misunderstand the views of the other, we can nevertheless accept that many of the reciprocal claims of one school against the other are based on simplistic interpretations and that, therefore, with a more thorough and charitable understanding of the other's position, many of the disagreements might be reduced.

One such instance is the Chartalists' claim that the catallactic theories of money base their views on the nature of money based on its origin.

It is important to note that the critics of catallactic theories are not disputing the account of the origin of money as having evolved from bartering to commodity money per se. The views on money shared by Georg Knapp, A. Mitchell Innes, John Maynard Keynes, and more recently L. Randall Wray differ from the views of the late Spanish Scholastics, Turgot, Galiani, and Say in the Continental tradition; David Hume, Adam Smith, and David Ricardo in the United Kingdom; Carl Menger, Ludwig von Mises, and all modern marginalists; their views differ not mainly or only about history, but most importantly on their conceptions about the essence of what money is. For instance, Stephanie Bell and L. Randall Wray coauthored an introduction to a book on the contribution of Mitchell Innes, in which Wray claims that a "state theory of money" and a "credit theory of money" can be integrated (Ingham, 2014). He further suggests that an early contact with Innes' credit theory of money (1914) was what led Keynes to an interest in Knapp's theory and was instrumental in the development of his own theory as well. Wray and Bell write that the "conventional" view of the evolution of money, as described by Innes, is that "barter is replaced by a commodity money that can be used as a medium of exchange. Only much later is credit discovered, which can substitute [for] money and thereby reduce transaction costs." According to them:

> Innes reverses this evolution, arguing that by its very nature, money is credit—even if it happens to take the physical form of precious metal. This leads to a much different take on markets, on money and on credit relations. (Wray, 2004: 7)[33]

That the origin of a thing does not necessarily explain the essence of that thing is easy to accept.[34] However, it is doubtful that, in any case, when the origin of something is called on to explain its essence, there is confusion. What is understandable is that it may not be accepted, prima facie, that the origin of something necessarily explains its current meaning and context; however, it is perfectly possible that in a particular case the origin of something *does* explain its present form and function.

For Mises (see endnote 4), there are no historically or ethnologically reliable descriptions of the evolution of human societies before the formation of clans; these can only be guessed at.[35] But according to him, praxeology solves that problem (of the lack of historical evidence) by the development of the theoretical apparatus about the benefits of the division of labor, its recognition by individuals, and social results:

> If and as far as labor under the division of labor is more productive than isolated labor, and if and as far as man is able to realize this fact, human action itself tends toward cooperation and association; man becomes a social being not in sacrificing his own concerns for the sake of a mythical Moloch, society, but in aiming at an improvement in his own welfare. (2007: 160)

The reason that higher productivity can be achieved under the division of labor than with just autonomous work, according to Mises, is that "the inborn inequality of men and the inequality in the geographical distribution of the natural factors of production—is real" (2007: 161). It is the recognition of that aspect of reality that enables us "to comprehend the course of social evolution" in general and, I would say with this work, that enables us to understand the evolution of money as well.

Basically, the understanding expressed in this book about the chartalist thesis is that, as a matter of historical record, since money became coined money, almost always, almost everywhere, money production has been monopolized by the state; and, as previously mentioned, that seems to be supported by historical evidence.[36] However, that does not imply that the purpose of money in society is given by the state, or that money should be subordinated to the political goals of the rulers. If we understand their claim in this more limited way, part of the divide between Georg Simmel and the Austrian economists on one side and Knapp and the other Chartalists on the other seems to lose its relevance, since one can accept Simmel's views on the value of money that so significantly influenced Mises' theory of money's value or Menger's views on the purposes of money for society and still recognize that coined money has been provided directly or indirectly by the state since it was introduced twenty-five centuries ago.

A completely different thing is to say that money must be provided by the state or that the state is following the most beneficial course of action for society in keeping its monopoly on money production through legal tender. From a praxeological perspective, it seems that it is more relevant to focus our attention on the essential character of money as a social institution, supported by the fact that men holding political power have monopolized money production in human societies from time immemorial.

Just because it has been so for so long does not imply that it must continue to be so. For example, at the time of the Roman Empire, the state was responsible for the grain supply. In many parts of the world, up until fairly recently, in fact, telephone communications were monopolized by the state. The fact that money has been monopolized by the state does not imply that it is the right thing to do or that it must continue to be that way. When we frame the claim of the Chartalists in this way, the theory loses some of its appeal for economists who had not themselves analyzed the philosophical foundations of monetary institutions; most economists simply see that money has been provided by the state and from that they accept at face value the conclusions of the Chartalists such as Knapp and Keynes that money is primarily an instrument for state policy (which obviously is a non sequitur). Acknowledging the claim that coined money has been produced by the state does not contradict the thesis of the spontaneous origin of money or preclude a principled criticism of monetary policy. As said before, accepting the partial historical account of the Chartalists is not only possible but compatible with the historical account and the thesis of the Catallactics. However, the statement that money is primarily an instrument for state policies not only does not follow from the historical account of the Chartalists, but it also is incompatible with a catallactic theory of money. That money can be used as an instrument for state policy, is obvious; that money may have been produced by the state as an instrument for state policies time and again is also obvious. However, every time that the attributes of the money actually produced are changed from the attributes required by money to best perform its primary function in society, we start to talk about suboptimum money, as this book will make clear.

NOTES

1. There are many possible meanings when it is said that something is "natural." Prescribing that something is in accordance with some "natural law" only compounds the problem. In this book it is assumed that human beings are able to develop complex social relations in order to have an increasingly more specialized division of labor. The statement that money is one of these naturally evolved institutions is meant to say that the creation of money is one of these paths spontaneously followed by different human societies in time and place because humans have been able to realize the benefits of doing so.

2. Although there are authors willing to enlist Simmel on both sides of the debate, I am fully convinced that he should be properly placed among the Catallactics and opposed to the Chartalists. In support of that, it suffices to quote a passage about the origin of money: "Money can have developed only out of previously existing values in such a way that the quality of money, which forms part of every exchangeable object, was realized to a great extent in one particular object; the function of money was at first still exercised, as it were, in intimate association with its previous value significance" (Simmel, 2001: 119).

3. Certainly it has not escaped the attention of the reader that with the exception of Simmel, the scholars identified as Catallactics are all members of the Austrian School of Economics. The mainstream economists, followers of the neoclassical synthesis, even some who are sympathetic to the idea that money is something spontaneously created in society, do not derive normative conclusions from that; and most of them, like Keynes and his followers, simply accept the arguments of the Chartalists. Because of that, in this book the position of neoclassical economists sympathetic to the catallactic position will not be discussed.

4. About the lack of certainty in regard to primitive social groups Mises wrote: "Neither history nor ethnology nor any other branch of knowledge can provide a description of the evolution which has led from the packs and flocks of mankind's nonhuman ancestors to the primitive, yet already highly differentiated, societal groups about which information is provided in excavations, in the most ancient documents of history, and in the reports of explorers and travelers who have met savage tribes" (Mises, 2007: 160).

5. There are innumerable cases in which minting was performed by private individuals; the claim here is that the sovereigns in general have jealously kept for themselves the monetary prerogatives of money supply, even when they grant to some third party the actual production. For instance, the famous Joachimsthaler was first introduced by Stephen, Count of Schilik for the monarchs of Bohemia (Williams, 1997).

6. At least from the second century BCE on (possibly earlier), Roman institutions were adequate to support long-term financial transactions (Andreau, 1999: 152), as M. Rostovtzeff wrote:

> The monetary chaos which reigned in the Greek cities and the Hellenistic monarchies before the period of Roman domination in the East was greatly reduced by the introduction of the paramount currency of the Roman state. (Rostovtzeff, 1926: 171)

Later, however, at the time of the Emperor Alexander Severus (222–235 CE), the situation had deteriorated immensely as described by Rostovtzeff:

> the state resorted to compulsion and to organized robbery. As is well known, one of the most pernicious devices was the abuse of its monopoly of coinage. Looking around for new resources, the state did not shrink from pure forgery by debasing its currency, which the ever-increasing use of alloy made more and more worthless. The result was a tremendous increase in prices and the ruin of sound business. (1926: 380)

7. It comes as a platitude, but the fact that the development of human society towards more specialization in the division of labor has been spontaneously generated does not imply that conscious efforts to shape better (and worse) political institutions have not taken place.

8. Individual potentialities can only be maximized when the individuals have the freedom to act on the best of their knowledge and to benefit or to suffer from the consequences of their actions; that is so because some of the knowledge of special circumstances possessed by the individuals is generated by their own interaction and therefore does not exist outside a free market; any other part of their knowledge, because it is related to their own preferences, cannot reasonably be assumed to be better known by anyone else than the individuals themselves.

9. Most likely no one asked the Egyptians (were they peasants, slaves, or whoever) if they wished to spend their spare time between the harvests building the pyramids.

10. The egoistic motivation referred to here is meant to describe the drive for any human action, as Mises argued, and in this sense it loses most of its power to predict human behavior, since due to the diversity of human beings in their limitations and weaknesses, they may think or feel that they are doing the best for themselves and nevertheless they may be wrong, or the way in which they conceive what is better for them eludes the observer. Also, this concept does not convey any moral judgment; to act in order to eliminate some uneasiness may be a totally altruistic act and, still, under this almost tautological concept, be considered egoistically motivated.

11. Another fact worth mentioning is that it is not the degree of coercion that distinguishes the two kinds of social order referred to in this book either.

12. Note that the proper role for money would continue to be easing the transactions by diminishing their cost, even if at any historical opportunity it was introduced by state coercion and not voluntarily adopted by the barterers.

13. Here it is important to point out the subjective characteristic of money's value. This recognition lies at the very foundation of Austrian economics as seen in Menger's 1871 *Principles of Economics* (edited by Huerta de Soto, 2009: 224). Menger quotes Turgot, saying, "Money, among all possible 'measures of exchange value', is the most suitable and hence also the most common. The only defect of this measure is said to lie in the fact that the value of money is not fixed, but changeable." Then Menger states:

> In my discussion of price theory, however, I have shown that equivalents of goods in the objective sense of the term cannot be observed anywhere in the economy of men, and that the entire theory that presents money as the 'measure of the exchange value' of goods disintegrates into nothingness, since the basis of the theory is a fiction, an error.

Money's use as a unit of account does not require it to have a fixed "objective" value. The relative stability of value of the commodity generally accepted as an instrument for indirect exchanges, that is money, is enough to induce economic agents to use it as a unit of account.

14. At the beginning of the eighteenth century (1716) in France, John Law was the Scotsman who created a system of paper money for the King of France through the *Banque Royale* and its counterpart the *Mississippi Company* that ended in disaster. His *first* mistake was obviously to believe or make others believe that wealth can be created by printing paper money; and what I would like to call his *second* mistake is to pretend that it is possible to "secure" the value of money on fixed assets like land (Rist, 1966: 62).

15. To my knowledge there is no historical evidence of the introduction of a unit of account that is not or was not the medium of exchange generally accepted in society. Incidentally, if one accepts the claim of the Chartalists that most transactions were cleared by compensation of credits in ancient societies, still, the unit of account was the merchandise with best liquidity available, the preferred medium of exchange, even if in practice most of the transactions were cleared by mutual compensation of credits. I also think that this understanding is compatible with the historical account of Menger, Mises, and other catallactic thinkers.

16. According to Den Uyl and Rasmussen, the naturalistic fallacy is "the alleged fallacy of deducing a statement of what ought to be from a statement of what is the case, or a statement about a value from a statement about a fact" (2005: 112).

17. It may be understood that the two central questions of normative ethics are: what is good, and how human beings ought to live their lives. According to the individualistic version of a perfectionist ethics advocated by Den Uyl and Rasmussen, the answer for what is the ultimate good or value for human beings is their flourishing, their self-perfection—that is, eudaemonia (from the Greek, "to be possessed by a good demon" or, as it is usually translated, "happiness"). The answer to the second question is that human beings should try to realize their potential, to be the best human being each individual can be. Therefore, perfectionism for what human beings ought to do is to be what they are, and that has been commonly interpreted as if perfectionism as an ethical theory is logically flawed because of the alleged naturalistic fallacy, the above-mentioned fact-value gap. According to Rasmussen (undated working paper: part one, p. 2), there are five ways to understand that supposed gap: ontologically, logically, semantically, epistemologically, and motivationally. Since the central argument against perfectionism is its logical impossibility, I will reproduce Rasmussen's ethical naturalistic reasoning to answer that:

> a) X is a human being; b) A human being's *ergon* (natural function or *telos*) is human flourishing; c) Human flourishing is what is good for a human being; d) What is good for a human being is what is choice-worthy; e) What is choice-worthy is what ought to be done. Hence X ought to pursue the flourishing life. (undated working paper: part one, p. 5)

With this argument, I hope, the claim that perfectionism as an ethical theory is logically flawed can be safely disregarded.

18. Antal E. Fekete says, "The scientific concept of marketability is due to Carl Menger (Absatzfähigkeit). He based it on the distinction between the bid and asked price. Menger pointed out that it is not possible to buy something in a market, then turn around and sell it at the same price. . . . The difference is the spread. . . . It is the behavior of the spread that determines marketability. According to the Principle of Declining Marginal Utility the bid price is a decreasing function of quantity" (Fekete, 2003: 3).

19. It is important to note, however, that it is possible to have many goods with liquidity close to the most preferred medium of exchange. So, it is possible to conceive that competing media of exchange may exist and that occasionally, with a change in market circumstances, the preferred form of money may be replaced.

20. Incidentally, this idea that the essential attribute of coined money is its suitability to be used as a unit of exchange is already present in Aristotle's *Politics* (Aristotle, I.ix, 1257: 28).

21. In a classic paper entitled "The Theory of Imaginary Money from Charlemagne to the French Revolution," Luigi Einaudi and his English translator argue, quoting Le Banc, that at the time of Charlemagne there were actually silver coins called pennies or denarius, 240 of each cut from a pound weight, and an uncoined silver shilling or solidus was the numerical expression for twelve pennies. Therefore twenty shillings summed a pound, and at that time the pound weight and the pound tale were the same (Einaudi, 1953: 230). With time, centuries of debasement, and political fragmentation (with the correspondent proliferation of different denominations for the media of exchange) that reference of value became just a unit of account adopted in most of Western Europe, although no medium of exchange existed with that denomination anymore. The relevance of this case is, first, that it is an illustration of Mises' regressive theory of money value, since the value of the different media of exchange were "found" in reference to that, then, "imaginary" money. Second, the raison d'être for imaginary money was manifold; first, it was to solve the problem of "duo" metallism, that is, the parallel use of silver and gold without a fixed parity (1953: 241). So, the recourse to an "imaginary" money establishing a known ratio between silver and gold was a useful device, and instead of complicating the transactions, it actually was a way to simplify them, in an environment with perhaps hundreds of different coins of both silver and gold without a fixed parity. (Other reasons mentioned by Einaudi were the existence of a lot of "political money," that is the myriad of denominations of coins with different weights and purity, and the constant debasement and clipping to which the real coins were subject). According to Einaudi, it is important to keep in mind that the idea of a single money denomination per country is a recent one, dating from the French Revolution (1953: 234), which justifies the need for the "imaginary money" and is understood as a useful device to enhance indirect exchanges in those circumstances. This case only reinforces the idea of spontaneously adopted money and the origin of the unit of account in the medium of exchange, although it also gives reason to think about the separation of the functions of medium of exchange and unit of account.

22. According to John Laures (2008: 167) Caroli Molinaei, a French jurist, in *De Mutatione monetarum quaestiones II*, anticipated by three centuries the chartal theory of money in stating that money is solely what the law defines it to be, and that any debt should be considered paid by its nominal amount, regardless of the metal content in it. I am unaware, however, if Georg Knapp had acknowledged Molinaei or any other predecessor in the chartalist theory of money.

23. For Mann, "The State theory of money is the necessary consequence of the sovereign power or the monopoly over currency which over a long period of history the State has succeeded in assuming." For Mann, to permit the circulation of money that is not created or at least authorized by the State would be the denial of the government's monetary prerogative. He brings the definition of money into the Uniform Commercial Code to support that in the United States money is a medium of exchange authorized or adopted by government as part of its currency. For Mann, there is no doubt that in the United States the State monetary prerogative exists and therefore, "the State theory of money rules" (Mann, 1982: 14).

24. Quint and Schubik have expressed the political dimension of the hybrid system of money we have today by saying that: "A society with a large government agent controlling a substantial part of its income has reasonably strong control if the rules of the polity and customs of the society prevent the other agents from introducing partially secured or unsecured credit instruments that serve as money substitutes. Otherwise these serve to provide both leverage and multiple points of partial control" (1949: 313).

25. Dickson (1967) did the groundwork of gathering the relevant information about the financial revolution in England, but it was Douglass North and Barry Weingast with their 1989 article who, based on that evidence, developed the "credible commit-

ment" thesis that institution matters for economic performance. Quoting from Coffman and Neal: "It was Dickson's demonstration that the rise of the capital market for British government debt followed the accession of William and Mary in 1689 that North and Weingast took as 'the single most important piece of evidence' that the necessary condition of securing contracts across time and space, and therefore enabling impersonal exchange, had been fulfilled." (Coffman and Neal, 2013: 2) Although their thesis has been questioned more recently as the departing point for the Industrial Revolution, it seems evident that it has not yet been refuted, and that there is a relation between the limitations on absolute power, through the division of power and political representation as established in England after the Glorious Revolution and the greater security of property rights, including claims against the Crown that gave to the British government debt attributes of greater certainty and liquidity that permitted it eventually to be monetized, enhancing that way the capacity of the British fisc to raise funds when needed.

26. The seminal work on the historical research on the monetary phenomena generated by the New World conquest was Earl James Hamilton's 1934 *American Treasure and the Price Revolution in Spain, 1501–1650*. The statistical data collected by Hamilton established a solid foundation for further research, although his own conclusions were fairly mechanical and unable to explain differing outcomes in other times and places exposed to the same influx of precious metals. Despite acknowledging its importance, the following books: 1) Antonio Miguel Bernal's *España, Proyecto Inacabado: Los Costes/Beneficios del Imperio*; 2) Ramón Carande's *Carlos V y Sus Banqueros*; and 3) Mark Häberlein's *The Fuggers of Augsburg: Pursuing Wealth and Honor in Renaissance Germany* are particularly illuminating about the evolution of banking at the time of Charles V's rule. But not only that, for instance, in *España, Proyecto Inacabado*, Bernal presents his revolutionary insight, "pecunia nervus belli" (money is the sinews of war), as a rationale for mercantilism. He also argues that Spain was "captured" and its future "mortgaged" by the projects of hegemony started by Charles V. The accommodation of the kingdom and its colonies to the demands of empire resulted in a mercantilist structure, which resulted in further problems for the development of Castilla aside from the exactions to fund military campaigns and the debts of previous campaigns.

27. The possible methods of money creation listed by Quint and Schubik (2014: 209) leave no doubts about the hybrid nature of the monetary systems we have today, with money being created either by the government or by private banks.

28. The causes of the 2008 financial crisis are many and will be debated for many years, as the causes of the Great Depression still are; that should not serve as an excuse to evade oneself of expressing his conclusions. If we divide the causes into immediate and mediate causes, the "trigger" of the crisis was to my mind the "run" on the shadow banking system that immediately followed the bankruptcy of Lehman Brothers on September 15, 2008 and the "break of the buck" by the Reserve Primary Fund (RPF) in the aftermath. Suddenly, financial instruments that until the day before were understood as quasi-money had lost their monetary properties, and a "flight to safety" ensued. Too many assets of questionable quality had been "financially engineered" in order to be perceived by economic agents as having investment grade, so much so as to some extent being endowed with monetary properties, and after September 15, 2008 that accepted wisdom had changed, which was the mediate cause of the crisis. Once the quality of the underlying assets came into doubt, a classical run on credit instruments with monetary properties was triggered and a flight to base money began. The result of that is a pressure for deleveraging, as in classical financial crises; the only difference this time is that the run was not on the banking system but on the shadow banking system.

29. On the lack of certainty regarding primitive social groups, see footnote 4.

30. The different meanings and contexts to which gift exchanges eventually mutated in commercial transactions may be understood by their different meanings in the *Odyssey*, as described by von Reden: "This presents itself in the *Odyssey* where evaluation of Odysseus' exchange behaviour depends on the status he adopts. As a hero,

singing of his heroic glory, he receives gifts he will never return; as a human being, telling about his life and his *oikos* at home, he gathers the means of survival in the context of reciprocal guest-friendship, while as a roaming stranger, telling fictitious stories, he strives for profit" (von Reden, 2003:8).

31. Within this work, instead of "acatallactic" these theories are identified as "chartalist," since the main school that argues that money value is not derived from the market is the state theory of money.

32. As already discussed, L. Randall Wray in his account of what modern money is gives such importance to this source of value as to state: "It is the decision of the state to accept at state pay offices, and not legal tender laws, that creates a chartal money" (Wray, 2000: 51). Wray attributes to Adam Smith and Georg Knapp this interpretation of chartalism according to which legislation still does the determination of money, but the nature of money value moves from the direct will (fiat) of the state to the value that the state can generate to the economic agents by its usefulness as an instrument to pay taxes.

33. It is important to note from this quotation that according to Wray, the same reasoning, aiming to explain the essence of money from its origin, is utilized by Innes; in his case, claiming that money is originally, and still remains, essentially a form of credit.

34. This sort of reasoning that confuses the causal origins of a belief with its justification is usually called a "genetic fallacy" and probably was first called as such by Morris Cohen and Ernest Nagel in their *Logic and Scientific Method* (New York: Harcourt, Brace and Co., 1934) according to the *Oxford Companion to Philosophy* (Honderich, 2005: 331).

35. More than that, not only in relation to the origin of society, but also in relation to many aspects of primitive and modern society, the goal of social science, descriptively and normatively, is to identify conceptually the factors that have induced human society to the high level of interdependence that we have today. Mises says, "The task with which science is faced. . . can only consist in the demonstration of those factors which can and must result in association and its progressive intensification" (Mises, 2007: 160).

36. Two recent books discuss in detail instances in which the legal tender faced competition from other issuers. One of them (Selgin: 2008) deals specifically with the case of private "tokens" used in the United Kingdom at the end of the eighteenth century and the beginning of the nineteenth century during a shortage of small denomination coinage until that practice was outlawed in 1821. The other deals with similar cases throughout history since the Middle Ages (Sargent and Velde: 2002). My interpretation of these two books is that they reinforce the understanding that the concept of money is better described by the GAMOE definition; however, there is a tendency for the State to try to impose a monopoly on the money supply. As already stated in this chapter, to accept the reality of the tendency of rulers to try to control the money supply neither contradicts the spontaneous nature of money nor recognizes other ends to proper money than to allow and enhance the division of labor.

TWO

Brief Account of the Intellectual History of Money, Starting with Aristotle

The intention with this chapter is to present a timeline of the development of ideas about money, starting with Aristotle. The first section explores in some detail the contribution of Aristotle to the philosophy of money. The second section brings a short inspection of the different thinkers that carried the debate about the fundamentals of money until the end of the nineteenth century. The third and last section presents a summary of the different contemporary schools on the characteristics of money. The timeline will clarify the evolution of the relevant concepts and the distinctions between the different schools of thought about the main characteristics of money.

2.1 INTRODUCTION TO THE PHILOSOPHY OF MONEY IN ARISTOTLE

In relation to money, like many other concepts, the most long-lasting influence in Western thought can be traced back to Aristotle.[1] And although a treatise on economics is attributed to Aristotle, his treatment of economics in our modern sense of political economy may be found dispersed among his many works, mainly his *Politics* (Aristotle, 1992) and his two treatises on ethics, *The Magna Moralia* (Aristotle, 2006) and *The Nicomachean Ethics* (Aristotle, 1941). *Oeconomica* (Aristotle, 2006), perhaps surprisingly, is essentially a treatment on marriage and the domestic life.

His treatment about money is both descriptive and normative. It can be asserted that, in modern terms, Aristotle recognizes that the bartering of goods (natural wealth) implies transaction costs, and that money was created in order to make the exchanges easier. According to Aristotle, it is from this usefulness and convenience that money draws its *goodness*.

Although in Aristotle it is possible to find statements both in favor of the position that money was spontaneously generated in society and claims that it was created by the state, it is generally understood, consistent with his general philosophy, that he subscribes to the doctrine that money is an institution that evolved naturally *in society*; and that will not be disputed here.

Schumpeter, for instance, also states that Mises would call Aristotle's theory of money "catallactic," because Aristotle acknowledges that the fundamental function of money is to be a medium of exchange. For Schumpeter, Aristotle also thinks that money needs to have a value independent of its monetary use, that is, he is a metallist (1997: 63).

As has been mentioned, for Aristotle, money performs a useful function in social economic life as it is beneficial to the community; however, Aristotle limits his analysis to the assistance that money gives indirectly to the acquisition of desired goods by facilitating exchanges. It is from this narrow understanding about the functions performed by money that Aristotle concludes that money is barren—that is, in his view, money by itself does not help to add to the amount produced, and therefore, charging interest on money lending is unnatural. This conclusion by Aristotle influenced the views of Christian and Islamic religions alike and through them moral views about money that have been instrumental in forming popular opinion and legal norms in most of the world to this day.

The purpose of this section is to suggest that in Aristotle's works it is possible to find elements to support a different conclusion about the description of money given by Aristotle himself and to call attention to what is perceived as a contradiction between Aristotle's own moral views about money and the moral judgment shared by most people supposedly informed by his positions about money.

2.1.1 *Overview of Aristotle on Money and Economics*

From *Politics*, book I, on money (Aristotle, 1992: 1256b26), an early distinction between the "productive" and the "unproductive" sides of the economy can be attributed to Aristotle. This distinction can be based on his concept of "natural wealth," that is, the actual goods traded in society in opposition to purely monetary forms of wealth. This distinction is of crucial importance to understanding Aristotle's description of money because it is from this distinction that comes his conclusion that it is "unnatural" to make money from money dealings. Aristotle describes the natural form of wealth:

> One form then of property-getting is, in accordance with nature, a part of household-management, in that either the goods must be there to start with, or this technique of property-getting must see that they are

> provided; goods, that is, which may be stored up, as being necessary for providing a livelihood, or useful to household or state as associations. And it looks as if wealth in the true sense consists of property such as this. (Aristotle, 1992: 1256b26)

Contrariwise, for Aristotle, (Aristotle, 1992: 1256b40) the other form of wealth, the "unnatural" one, is described as follows:

> But there is another kind of property-getting to which the term "acquisition of goods" is generally and justly applied; and it is due to this that there is thought to be no limit to wealth or property. Because it closely resembles that form of acquisition of goods which we have just been discussing, we may suppose that the two are one and the same. But they are not the same, though admittedly they are not very different; one is natural, the other is not.

For the discussion proposed in this chapter about Aristotle's normative stance on money, it is important to note that Aristotle attributes the introduction of media of exchange, first in the form of bullion and later in the form of coins, to the growth of society; for him, the introduction of coinage was motivated by the need to diminish the costs of assessing the "intrinsic" value of the metal coined, therefore making the exchange of goods easier. Still from *Politics* (Aristotle, 1992: 1257a28) we read:

> as soon as the import of necessities and the export of surplus goods began to facilitate the satisfaction of needs beyond national frontiers, men inevitably resorted to the use of coined money. Not all the things that we naturally need are easily carried; and so for purposes of exchange men entered into an agreement to give to each other and accept from each other some commodity, itself useful for the business of living and also easily handled, such as iron, silver, and the like. The amounts were at first determined by size and weight, but eventually the pieces of metal were stamped. This did away with the necessity of measuring, since the stamp was put on as an indication of the amount.

The next paragraph quoted (Aristotle, 1992: 1257a41) starts with the statement that economic development is a consequence of the introduction of money in society, but then what was an innocent activity (the use of money to make exchange easier) at the beginning developed into what is its excess: *trade*, as we can read below:

> Once a currency was provided, development was rapid and what started as a necessary exchange became *trade* , the other mode of acquiring goods. At first it was probably quite a simple affair, but then it became more systematic as men became more experienced at discovering where and how the greatest profits might be made out of the exchanges. That is why the technique of acquiring goods is held to be concerned primarily with coin, and to have the function of enabling one to see where a great deal of money may be procured.

2.1.2 Why Money is Not a Natural Form of Wealth

The core of Aristotle's argument that holding money is not a natural form of wealth is that the value of money arises in society by convention and ceases to be of value if the economic agents change their minds about it as a consequence of the manipulation of the currency by the government. This argument is based on the assumption that natural wealth, on the other hand, has an absolute value that is independent of the subjective evaluation of the individual engaged in the exchanges, which contradicts part of his own intuition that there is a *valor en uso* (value in use) and a *valor en cambio* (value in exchange) in everything (Huerta de Soto, 2008: 185). The example of this unnatural nature of monetary wealth given by Aristotle is the mythological King Midas, who could not survive from money, as we read below:

> Sometimes on the other hand coinage is regarded as so much convention and artificial trumpery having no root in nature, since, if those who employ a currency system choose to alter it, the coins cease to have their value and can no longer be used to procure the necessities of life. And it will often happen that a man with wealth in the form of coined money will not have enough to eat; and what a ridiculous kind of wealth is that which even in abundance will not save you from dying with hunger! It is like the story told of Midas: because of the inordinate greed of his prayer everything that was set before him was turned to gold. (Aristotle, 1992: 1257b10)

Next, we will see that Aristotle states that striving to make money is not proper, because money is just an instrument, and the purpose of life is to live a good life, not to accumulate the means through which natural wealth can be acquired. Aristotle (Aristotle, 1992: 1257b25, 1257b40) also claims that excess of material goods is not conducive to human flourishing, to the good life, as follows:

> Some people therefore imagine that increase is the function of household-management, and never cease to believe that their store of coined money ought to be either hoarded, or increased without limit. The reason why some people get this notion into their heads may be that they are eager for life but not for the good life; so, desire for life being unlimited, they desire also an unlimited amount of what enables it to go on.

According to Aristotle, the relation of money-making to the art of household management is such that it is all right for the household manager to seek profit in his activities, as long as profit-seeking does not become an end in itself and it is pursued by means of agriculture and not commerce. He writes, "We conclude therefore that the form of acquisition of goods that depends on crop and animal husbandry is for all men in accordance with nature" (Aristotle, 1992: 1258a27).

The consequence of Aristotle's distinction between "natural" and "unnatural" forms of acquiring wealth, as already mentioned, is to condemn usury as the most reproachable form of money-making:

> The acquisition of goods is then, as we have said, of two kinds: one, which is necessary and approved of, is to do with household-management; the other, which is to do with trade and depends on exchange, is justly regarded with disapproval, since it arises not form nature but from men's gaining from each other. Very much disliked also is the practice of charging interest; and the dislike is fully justified, for the gain arises out of currency itself, not as a product of that for which currency was provided. Currency was intended to be a means of exchange, whereas interest represents an increase in the currency itself. Hence its name [usury, τόκος], for each animal produces its like, and interest is currency born of currency. And so of all types of business this is the most contrary to nature. (Aristotle, 1992: 1258a38)

As part of this summary of Aristotle's views on economics in general and money more specifically, it seems worthwhile to question whether monopoly is value-free for Aristotle. It seems from the description below that Aristotle does not distinguish between natural and legal monopolies and, therefore, he does not condemn the latter. There will be consequences for what may be understood as Aristotle's views about what is proper for the state to do in managing the currency. After telling an anecdote about how the philosopher Thales the Milesian cornered the market for olives once, Aristotle states:

> Thales gave proof of his cleverness; but, as we have said, the principle can be applied generally: the way to make money is to get, if you can, a monopoly for yourself. Hence we find states also employing this method when they are short of money: they secure themselves a monopoly. (Aristotle, 1992: 1259a3)

Regarding monopolies and specifically about money, in *Oeconomica* there is a passage about a time when the people of Byzantium were in need of funds and among other things, they established and sold a money-change monopoly. "The right of changing money they sold to a single bank, whose proprietor was given a monopoly of the sale and purchase of coin, protected under penalty of confiscation" (Aristotle, 2006: 1346b25).

2.1.3 Is There a Subjectivist Theory of Value in Aristotle ?

One of the common "mistakes" in economic theorizing attributed to Aristotle is the understanding that exchange happens between things of the same value. This understanding derives from Aristotle's treatment of just exchanges at *Nicomachean Ethics*, book V, chapter V, on money (Aristotle, 1941: 1132b20, 1132b30), and it starts as follows:

> Some think that *reciprocity* is without qualification what is just, as the Pythagoreans said; for they defined justice without qualification as reciprocity. Now *reciprocity* fits neither distributive nor rectificatory justice—yet people *want* even the justice of Rhadamanthus to mean this: "Should a man suffer what he did, right justice would be done." (Aristotle, 1941: 1132b20)

He goes on,

> But in associations for exchange this sort of justice does hold men together—reciprocity in accordance with a proportion and not on the basis of precisely equal return. For it is by proportionate requital that the city holds together. . . . it is by exchange that they hold together. (Aristotle, 1941: 1132b30)

The next Aristotelian position to be presented is his treatment of proportion in trade as derived from the equality of value that for Aristotle is required in order for exchanges to happen. Contrary to Rothbard's position that sees a forerunner of the labor theory of value in the passages quoted below (Rothbard, 2006: vol. I, 16), a more charitable interpretation of the passages below may suggest, as already referred to by Huerta de Soto, that here Aristotle is advancing a subjectivist theory of value,[2] since the equality in proportion is ultimately brought about by a monetary evaluation by each one of the individuals involved in the exchange, and not by some "intrinsic" equality of the traded goods, as may be understood from the following passages:

> Now proportionate return is secured by cross-conjunction. Let A be a builder, B a shoemaker, C a house, D a shoe. The builder, then, must get from the shoemaker the latter's work, and must himself give him in return his own. If, then, first there is proportionate equality of goods, and then reciprocal action takes place, the result we mention will be affected.
>
> If not, the bargain is not equal, and does not hold; for there is nothing to prevent the work of one being better than that of the other; they must therefore be equated to more than the work of the other. Their work, then, must be brought to an equality [or appraised by a common standard of value]. (Aristotle, 1941: 1133a5)
>
> For it is not two doctors that associate for exchange, but a doctor and a farmer, or in general people who are different and unequal; but these must be equated. This is why all things that are exchanged must be somehow comparable. It is for this end that money has been introduced, and it becomes in a sense an intermediate; for it measures all things, and therefore the excess and the defect—how many shoes are equal to a house or to a given amount of food. (Aristotle, 1941: 1133a15)
>
> the shoemaker gets a return for his shoes in proportion to his worth, and the weaver and all other craftsmen do the same. Now here a common measure has been provided in the form of money, and therefore

> everything is referred to this and measured by this. (Aristotle, 1941: 1164a35)

In the second passage above (Aristotle, 1941: 1133a15), it is possible to find support for the *thesis* that the primary purpose of money is to be a unit of account and not a medium of exchange. However, the current discussion about money as primarily a medium of exchange or a unit of value is based on opposing views about the *chronological* precedence of the use of money for one purpose or the other; and it can be understood from Aristotle that money's usefulness as a unit of account derives from its use as medium of exchange. Therefore, it is to be understood that, for Aristotle, the use of money as a medium of exchange took precedence chronologically, siding the philosopher with those who think that money was spontaneously generated in society.

> All goods must therefore be measured by some one thing, as we said before. Now this unit is in truth demand, which holds all things together. . . . but money has become by convention a sort of representative of demand; and this is why it has the name "money" (*nomisma*)—because it exists not by nature but by law (*nomos*) and it is in our power to change it and make it useless. (Aristotle, 1941: 1133a25)

2.1.4 For Aristotle Money has a Utility in Itself

For Aristotle, money provides a means for ready access to the available goods; that is, Aristotle refers to its *liberative* power, which is associated as a characteristic of money with the concept of liquidity. The monetary merchandise is a merchandise that is exchangeable for all other goods at a minimum of cost or trouble. From this we can derive that, for Aristotle, money is not only a tool for easing the bartering of natural goods, but money has a utility in itself. To save money, to save the more salable merchandise, the merchandise that is more easily tradable at a stable value, is a way to reduce uncertainty[3] about our capacity to have desirable goods in the future, as he explains here: "And for the future exchange—that if we do not need a thing now we shall have it if ever we do need it—money is as it were our surety; for it must be possible for us to get what we want by bringing money" (Aristotle, 1941: 1133b10).

One of the essential attributes of money is that it keeps its value relatively constant in terms of the other goods, although its value is not absolute; therefore, it can be inferred that the real value of money is defined in the market, not by the authority. Aristotle says, "Now the same thing happens to money itself as to goods—it is not always worth the same; yet it tends to be steadier" (Aristotle, 1941: 1133b10).

From the next passage quoted from Aristotle, once more we see his line of reasoning linking money as a medium of exchange and as a unit of account with the development of society, revealing clearly that for the philosopher, money is beneficial for man.

> This is why all goods must have a price set on them; for then there will always be exchange, and if so, association of man with man. Money, then, acting as a measure, makes goods commensurate and equates them; for neither would there have been association if there were not exchange, nor exchange if there were not equality, nor equality if there were not commensurability. Now in truth it is impossible that things differing so much should become commensurate, but with reference to demand they may become so sufficiently. There must, then, be a unit, and that fixed by agreement (for which reason it is called money); for it is this that makes all things commensurate, since all things are measured by money. (Aristotle, 1941: 1133b15)

2.1.5 Aristotle 's Constitution of Money

Finally, we will address, from *Politics*, what we can understand about Aristotle's ideas on the "Constitution of Money—in particular, the definition and the limits to the state powers over money. In the passage below Aristotle states his general rule about the relation of the state to property and the very reason for a political association. From this general statement it has been inferred that for Aristotle money does not belong to the state—that is, money is private property, and the politically organized community has no right to alter the value or to take away money from its owners any more than the state has the right to confiscate any other property. That simply would not be in accordance with the very purposes of the state. He states,

> Hence a state needs to own property, but the property is not part of the state. . . . A state is an association of similar persons whose aim is the best life possible. What is best is happiness, and to be happy is an active exercise of virtue and a complete employment of it. (Aristotle, 1992: 1328a33)

2.1.6 Proposition: On Money Aristotle is Not Aristotelian Enough

The proposition here is that, for Aristotle, money is a useful tool for society as an instrument necessary for the production and distribution of wealth. Being necessary and useful for trade, the availability of a medium of exchange is something valuable to individuals in their dealings; therefore, contrary to conventional wisdom and Aristotle's own conclusion[4] from his premises, it is possible to argue that paying for the availability of money (usury) or producing for the market (retail trading) are legitimate activities, and they may be considered "unnatural" only in the sense that they are further developments in human society, like writing or the establishment of governments beyond the tribal forms of subordination.

2.1.7 In Search of a Harmonic Interpretation about the Philosophy of Money in Aristotle

The conventional wisdom about Aristotle's views on money is that money is "barren"—for instance, that it is unnatural to charge interests on money lending, since it would represent an unjust "multiplication" of money. This dogmatic view leaves no room to understand that "usury" is the charging of "excessive" interests. The declaration is absolute: *any* charge is unnatural and therefore unjust. As it has been mentioned, this understanding through Aristotle's influence on Christian and Islamic religious doctrines has been influential to this day, not only among religious people, but also among the population in general, and because of that, it still has informed legislation and the application of law around the world. As we have seen, although supported by explicit claims made by Aristotle, this common understanding may be judged inconsistent with both Aristotle's description about the essential characteristics of money and his clearly stated moral views about money.

2.1.8 Harmonic Interpretation

However, it seems reasonable to make an effort in the interpretation of any text to assume that the author was coherent in his thoughts. Therefore, an important criterion of interpretation is to discard as many contradictory conclusions as possible. It is also reasonable to assume generally that the author was not always successful in his attempt to avoid contradiction. We must be even more vigilant when we are talking about an immense corpus written in Ancient Greek twenty-five centuries ago—and within which we even have doubts about authorship for some of the works; others have many different versions; some came to us only after translation into many different languages, such as Latin and Arabic (both problematic in terms of preciseness); and in any case our most ancient sources were no older than a thousand years, leaving a gap of about fifteen centuries, a period about which we can assert nothing. For all that, it seems acceptable to suggest a corollary for some parts of the Aristotelian corpus that is not consistent with some other parts. In doing that, it is advisable to make an effort to adhere to what is accepted to be Aristotle's core assumptions. Another criterion is to assume that what is suggested is in harmony with the most interconnected parts of Aristotle's body of thought. As Professor Rothbard emphasizes (Rothbard, 2006: 13), Aristotle offers a point-by-point defense of private property against communal property and with all the omissions and equivocations that may be found in Aristotle's economic thought, the defense of private property as a superior institutional arrangement for a human society seems to be at the core of Aristotle's political philosophy.

In the *Nicomachean Ethics,* the philosopher argues[5] that money is useful and necessary for the civil life and for the state; therefore, not only can money not be bad, but it also commands a value on its own, that is, as a medium of exchange, independent of other possible uses for its metal content. Aristotle argues that the excess of money can be bad, but he also claims that the lack of it can be bad. This is because neither a life devoted to the accumulation of wealth seems to Aristotle a way to human flourishing, nor is the good life possible without some material goods and for their acquisition, money is required. Aristotle's advice against engaging in production for the market (retail trading) can only be understood as follows: "if you own a farm and can provide for your subsistence and for the comforts of life, and as long as their enjoyment in moderation is compatible with a good life, do not waste your time in commerce if you can engage in intellectual pursuits, in politics, or the arts."

The claim that usury is unnatural must be understood as "value-free"—that is, money may be understood as unnatural in the sense that money was created by man in society; it does not exist in nature. This interpretation is mentioned by Scott Meikle (2000: 165) and attributed to W. D. Ross, who says, "I don't think he means that it is by an unnatural convention that money breeds money. He appears to regard it as the normal course of things that it should. But it is not the essential nature of money in the truly Aristotelian sense in which nature is equivalent to end" (Cannan, Ross, Bonar and Wicksteed, 1922: 107). Usury, according to this interpretation, can only be regarded unnatural in the sense that, for Aristotle, money was created to ease exchanges and not to be a representation of saved goods that may be put to use in the production of more goods.

The difference in treatment given by Aristotle to economic activity in the household and in retail, summarized by Meikle (2000: 162) as the distinction between producing and selling one commodity in order to get another commodity (C-M-C) and the act of using money to buy a commodity in order to have it sold for more money (M-C-M), may possibly be interpreted as part of Aristotle's propensity to accept what the general practice was in his society as good. According to Meikle, Aristotle was willing to recognize the usefulness of money for its three known functions, but he was unwilling to change his (and the common) dislike for traders and moneylenders; the apparent contradiction in his writing may be a consequence of that prudential desire by the philosopher to not move to an extreme position in either question (Meikle, 2000: 163).

The claim that money is "barren," on the other hand, seems to be a mistake,[6] since from Aristotle's own description about the purpose of using money as medium of exchange, it is a necessary corollary of this assertion that to pay interest in order to have money from someone else seems to be just.

2.1.9 Government and Money

A first question about the state and money may be: Is money a creature of the state? It seems clear that for Aristotle, coined money in Greece at that time was generally minted by state authority if not by the state directly. He even assigns a specific department for that purpose to the royal administration and, by extension, to a free state. He lists it among the four departments identified by him: "namely currency, exports, imports and expenditure" (Aristotle, 1941: 1345b20). As mentioned above, the fact that money is provided by the state does not make money the property of the state or change its character from an instrument to ease commercial transactions in society to an instrument for the achievement of political goals, unless an emergency arises and, in that case, the state may use money as it can use any other private property for attending to the emergency needs of the community. Nicolas Oresme says, "it is clear that a change in money should never be made, unless perhaps under eminent necessity or for the obvious advantage of the whole community" (1956: 13). Other questions that need to be answered are: For Aristotle, what can the state do, and what is the state entitled to do with money? They have decisively different answers. As mentioned before (Aristotle, 1941: 1257b10), for the philosopher, the state can change currency; on the other hand, since the money belongs to individuals and not to the state, debasing the currency, like Hippias of Athens did, is clearly unjust (Aristotle, 1941: 1347a10). As Nicolas Oresme wrote, "Although it is the duty of the prince to put his stamp on the money for the common good, he is not the lord or owner of the money current in his principality" (1956: 10).

From this chapter on Aristotle's philosophy of money, we have a certain historical perspective on the discussion of the essential philosophical attributes of money.

2.2 FROM ARISTOTLE TO THE THEORY OF MARGINAL UTILITY

After Aristotle, the next known discussion about money is from the second and third century Roman jurist Julius Paulus Prudentissimus. Since there is not known to be any case of social coordination with an extended division of labor and monetary economy on a large scale before the late Roman Republic and early Empire, it makes sense that at the time of Paulus, interest in a theoretical discussion about monetary issues would exist. Perhaps not surprisingly for a counselor of emperors and Praetorian prefect, Paulus in his writings advances a nominalist position, arguing that it is not the (metal) content of the coin that gives it is value but its tale (Grice-Hutchinson, 2009: p. 21). With the decline of the Roman Empire and the end of Classical Civilization, cities were deserted, the population decreased, and commerce was greatly reduced in Western Europe and in the Mediterranean basin. The decrease in commercial activity is tantamount to a reduction in indirect exchanges (for which money is required) and the economy returned to small units of production with a low level of division of labor, typical of economies of subsistence. It was only at the end of the Middle Ages that order gradually began to be restored by the institutionalization of the small kingdoms created by the barbarian **tribes** who invaded and destroyed the Roman Empire; the population began to grow again, more extended commercial networks were established, and cities started to be repopulated. Such a turning point may be clearly perceived to have been initiated after the Papal Revolution of the eleventh century, with formal and actual reintroduction of private property rights protection, if by nothing else than the many decrees of "peace of god" extracted from the European rulers by the Catholic church.

It is with St. Thomas Aquinas (1225–1274)—not coincidentally a thinker to whom Aristotle's influence cannot be more significant—in the middle of this resurgence in urban life and monetary economy that an interest in monetary theory arises again. The approach of St. Thomas to money is decisively a teleological one, with an emphasis on its functions and purpose. The next notable contributor to the dialogue on money is the fourteenth century French bishop Nicolas Oresme (1323–1382). Oresme was the translator of Aristotle's *Ethics, Politics and Economics* to French, and his treatise on money, *De Moneta,* is a scholastic interpretation of Aristotle's *Politics* in regard to money. Certainly motivated by the debasement of the currency under Philip IV[7] and John II and the resulting disorganization of social relations, Oresme exposes the Aristotelian ideas that a coin is a defined weight of precious metal whose quantity and purity is attested by the issuer with his stamp, and that the currency in circulation does not belong to the sovereign but to the people that use the money for their own purposes of facilitating exchanges. Therefore, the sovereign has no right to alter the currency in any way without the consent of the people. Oresme also starts an interpretation of debasement under emergency as eventually politically expedient, with the qualification that the value of the currency should be restored as soon as possible (Oresme, 1956: X) that we will see in later thinkers, as Juan de Mariana, for example. Oresme's treatise is credited by Guido Hülsmann as having integrated the thoughts on money of previous thinkers such as Aquinas and John Buridan in what became "the first treatise on money ever" (Hülsmann, 2008: 8).

When the late scholastics of the School of Salamanca in Spain—such as the founder of the school, Francisco de Vitoria; his contemporary, Martin Azpilcueta Navarro; Azpilcueta's pupil, Diego de Covarrubias; Luis de Molina, at the end of the sixteenth century; and Juan de Mariana at the beginning of the seventeenth century—wrote on monetary theory, they were able to draw from John Buridan, Nicolas Oresme, Gabriel Biel, Jean Bodin, Charles Desmoulins, and other members of the French School. Here, too, are many cross-references among the authors and suffice it to say that it is possible to perceive a continuum among the scholastics and late scholastics both in France and Spain in their writing about money, markedly representing Aristotelian influence and Thomist influence funneled through Oresme. According to John Laures, for instance (2008: 163), the 1605 treatise *De Monetae Mutatione* of Juan de Mariana has references to Rene Budelius' *De Monetis* which in its turn lists twenty-nine previous treatises on money, prominently among them, Bodin's *De Republica* and *De Augumento et Deremento Auri et Argenti*, attesting to the knowledge Mariana had of these previous authors and their ideas. According to Grice-Hutchinson:

> The Aristotelian and scholastic ideas about the nature, origin and functions of money were handed on unchanged except for a few elaborations of minor importance. Even today these traditional concepts of money as a medium of exchange and a measure and store of value, together with the customary "historical" account of the inconveniences attendant upon barter economy, are still reflected in our text-books. The School of Salamanca is simply a link in the long chain of writers who have helped to pass on these ideas. (2009: 47)

Perhaps the Spanish late scholastics of Salamanca were in a privileged position to think about money at the beginning of the modern era, brought about by the great navigations. The influx of **precious metals** from America to Spain, the commercial network in Europe centered in Spain and some of its territories, and the chronic fiscal problems of the Spanish empire were all part of the reality surrounding the Spanish scholastics and stimulating their curiosity and analysis, as they were scholars and sometimes counselors to sovereigns and other practical men, such as the merchants of Antwerp who in 1530 counseled Francisco de Vitoria on usury (Grice-Hutchinson, 2009: 42). So, aside from the transmission of traditional concepts, there are many original contributions in monetary theory that may safely be credited to the scholars of Salamanca. Grice-Hutchinson says, "The School's original contribution to monetary theory consists, in my opinion, in its formulation of a psychological theory of value applied to both goods and money, of the quantity theory, and of a theory of foreign exchange that closely resembles the modern purchasing-power theory" (2009: 47).

The marked subjectivism of the Salamanca School was pointed to by other authors as well, and among their other contributions, Huerta de Soto sees in some of these thinkers a "proto-currency school" (1996: 59–81). The School of Salamanca significantly influenced, both directly and indirectly, further thought about money. Direct references to the writings of those in the Salamanca School can be found in Bernardo Davanzati and Ferdinando Galiani in Italy; their subjectivism also can be found in the writings of Étienne Bonnot de Condillac and Anne-Robert-Jacques Turgot and more especially in the utility value theory of Jean-Baptiste Say.

Separating the last of the Salamanca School thinkers from Galiani, the references found in Hugo Grotius about them may be pointed out, quoting again Grice-Hutchinson (2009: 65). And Grotius' ideas about utility as a measure of value and the relevance of relative scarcity to determine money value reached other Protestant thinkers, such as Samuel von Pufendorf (1632–1694) who develops those ideas further still and whose books remained important textbooks on natural law well into the eighteenth century. Ideas of Grotius and Pufendorf about the natural measure of value given by the utility of a given thing to human life and its scarcity were brought to England by Adam Smith's professor, Francis Hutcheson, who also emphasizes the cost of production of the goods in their determination of value, perhaps initiating a line of thought that would result in the labor theory of value of Smith and Ricardo.

In relation to the particular way in which value theory was developed in the United Kingdom, it is worth mentioning that early in the nineteenth century in Germany, having in common a subjective value theory, which was held in opposition to the labor theory of value found in Adam Smith's *Wealth of Nations* (Calzada, 2006: 2), a group of economists became known as members of the use-value school, or *Gebrauchtwertschule*. These economists sought to develop a subjective theory that could be applied to the entire economy; their goal was not to harmonize value and price theory, as certainly was the goal of the Anglo-Saxon thinkers they opposed, but to develop what could well be defined as a moral theory of value. According to Birger P. Priddat, "They did not aim to explain the market allocation on the basis of individual evaluations but rather the relationship between the market and the state economy on the basis of a measure of need" (1998: 1510).

According to Bruno Hildebrand, one of the members of the German use-value school, their particular concept of subjective theory of value may be understood in the following way:

> If the reason for the appreciation lies in the effects of the appreciated thing, i.e. in its suitability for use in satisfying human needs, and not in its causes or in the subjective propensities of the person expressing the appreciation, its value is referred to as use value. If, in turn, the reason for the appreciation is the appreciation of other individuals who would also like to possess the item, it is called exchange value. (Priddat, 1998: 1513)

As it was shown, the subjectivist theory of value of the men of the Salamanca School may well be traced to Ferdinando Galiani (1728–1787) in Italy, to Adam Smith in the United Kingdom, to J. B. Say in France, and to the above-mentioned German school of use-value, among many others. From them it reached the classical economists of the nineteenth century who formulated the concept of marginal utility, such as Jevons, Walras, and Menger, who is explicit in his debt to the *Gebrauchtwertschule* up to the point of being considered by Adolph Wagner, "one of many subjective-value theoreticians" according to Priddat (1998: 1515). The quantitative theory, arguably developed independently by Jean Bodin, was evident in these authors more than a decade earlier, making them, at least intellectually, predecessors of a theory that was only to mature with Irving Fisher at the beginning of the twentieth century.

The commonality between John Locke (1632–1704) and the thinkers of the Salamanca School, specifically Juan de Mariana, may be found, however, in their attempts to define fair government and the limits of political power. Their ideas on money share that general theme, that is, a concern about how to restrain the monetary prerogative and protect economic agents against abuses. In Locke we found a concern about the origins of the public faith required to ensure the broad acceptance of money necessary to produce the good benefits that a trustworthy medium of exchange can bring,[8] and Locke is explicit about that: "Trade, then, is necessary to the producing of riches, and money necessary to the carrying on of trade. . . . Whatsoever, therefore, hinders the lending of money, injures trade" (Locke, 1691/1824: 14).

According to Ludovic Desmedt and Jérôme Blanc in a recent paper (Desmedt and Blanc, 2010: 327), the chronic instability and mistrust in the currency until the end of the sixteenth century is in the background of thinkers like Mariana, Bodin, and Locke that prompted them, in essence, to advocate a "monetary revolution" that eventually led to a more stable monetary system by the beginning of the eighteenth century, a requirement for the availability of the long-term credit instruments that financed the nascent Industrial Revolution. Aside from a clear and open defense of lending with interest and furthermore, freely defined interest, "for the same reason, and upon as good consideration, as the tenant pays rent for your land" (Locke, 1691/1824: 36). Locke's ideas, however, are not exactly revolutionary. His teleological view about the nature of money was drawn from the scholastic tradition; his theory of money value, it is true, in attributing the "intrinsic" value of silver when used as money to the "common consent" of men, perhaps is a step further than the traditional argument based on the scarcity and the psychology of economic agents. Locke's argument for the value of money is not intrinsic, it is not subjective, but is intersubjective (Locke, 1695/1824: 139).[9]

Having arrived in this cursory overview of the history of monetary ideas to the nineteenth-century marginalists, both in the United Kingdom and on the continent, we may initiate a discussion of current ideas on money and exchange.

2.3 CONTEMPORARY SCHOOLS ON THE CHARACTERISTICS OF MONEY

In this section, the intention is to describe succinctly the different schools of thought on the nature of money as they evolved during the twentieth century. In the second section of this chapter, we concluded a brief account of the intellectual history of money with the classical economists of the late nineteenth century, both on the continent and in the United Kingdom, who shared a conception of money value based on the marginal utility theory. An important development in sciences in general and in the philosophy of money in particular is that during the nineteenth century, economics, like many other disciplines, became an independent science, separated from moral and political philosophy, and the discussions about money moved mainly to the new field of economics. That is not to say that money was not the object of inquiry in other fields of knowledge—some old such as law, others new, such as sociology—but the core of the discussions about money, descriptive and normative alike, were centered in the new discipline of economics. But sciences in general, during the same period, were trying to distance themselves from the all-encompassing approach of philosophy. The method of natural sciences, based on observable evidence and testing hypotheses, the search for objectivity, became a powerful reference that was sought by the practitioners in the fields of humanities.

Along with this search for objectivity, positive economics developed. Positive economics became the description of economic events, the development of economic theory, with the pretension that it was a value-free enterprise with no relation whatsoever to metaphysical or ethical considerations about natural ends. Normative economics became the prescription of what to do in order to achieve whatever economic goal happened to be desired.[10] It was not that ethical considerations could not yet influence collective decisions, but they were now perceived as outside the realm of economics, even normative economics. Such was the impact of positivism in the organization of science. In the next part of this book, a brief exposition of the positivist epistemology will be given, to the extent that it is relevant for the purposes of the present work. For now, it is important just to note the importance of the positivist ideology in the transference of the core inquiries about money from philosophy to economics. It was already mentioned that by and large the different conceptions about money may be classified either as part of the catallactic or chartalist schools so, in the present section, some of these different conceptions will just be fleshed out, mainly for the purpose of clarifying why they are classified the way they are. Important discussions about epistemological and political differences among these schools are discussed in other parts of this work.

2.3.1 The State Theory of Money

Since we have already adequately described the state theory of money in chapter 1, here we will mention some of the main characteristics of the neo-chartalist school. The Neo-Chartalists perceive themselves as reclaiming the importance of money in order to explain the real side of economic activity (as opposed to the neoclassical synthesis and its moneyless models). Their conception of money is of something created in society by the state, through its power to raise taxes and formalized by law (Wray, 2000: 51).

Its main feature is the emphasis on the corollary already present in the chartal theory of Knapp and Keynes that the state control over money enables the state to pursue its policies more easily, draining the resources of the community, such as advocated by Abba Lerner's Keynesian "functional finance" (Wray, 2000: 60).

One of the interesting and, at first glance, innovative approaches to the theory of money brought by the Neo-Chartalists, is the idea proposed by Hyman Minsky that the key component for determining the amount of money in circulation is not the demand for money, but the demand for bank credit since, for him, modern money is endogenously created by the banking business. He says, "Money is unique in that it is created in the act of financing by a bank and it is destroyed as the commitments on debt instruments owned by banks are fulfilled. Because money is created and destroyed in the normal course of business, the amount outstanding is responsive to the demand for financing" (Minsky, 1986: 249).

This idea, in a modern setting, means for Minsky that there is a pyramid of obligations with the central bank at the top, the banking system in the middle, and all other economic agents at the bottom. Drawing an analogy with the chartalist thesis that it is the obligation to pay taxes that gives value to money, according to Minsky, it is the fact that debts with the banks can be paid with the cancellation of bank debts that gives value to the money "created" by the banks. Since the state is the biggest debtor, it is again, as in the chartalist account, the obligation to pay taxes that gives value to money, or according to Minsky, "In an economy where government debt is a major asset on the books of the deposit-issuing banks, the fact that taxes need to be paid gives value to the money in the economy . . . [T]he need to pay taxes means that people work and produce in order to get that in which taxes can be paid" (Minsky, 1986: 231).

The Neo-Chartalist insight that the stock of money in circulation is "responsive" to the demand for financing, in a more orthodox terminology, means that in circumstances where a significant portion, if not the majority, of the total liquidity in the economy is represented by money substitutes, mainly public debt and corporate bonds, a deleveraging process results in a reduction in the stock of money. This view is hardly innovative, however. Maybe framing the factors for determining the stock of money in circulation in that way helps one to understand that the total liquidity in the economy results both from changes in the demand and supply of "high-powered" money, and also from changes in the demand and supply of money substitutes, the increases and decreases in the fiscal needs being one of the ways in which the supply of the latter occurs.

In the end, the claims that people produce in order to pay taxes, or that all money is created endogenously by the operations of the banking system, seem exaggerated. The corpus of doctrine that allows for the conclusion that people exist to pay taxes was already discussed in chapter 1; the statement that all money is created by the regular operations of the banking system can only be accepted as true if we consider that it is part of the "normal course of business" to increase the central bank **reserves** by fiat by the addition of figures on its ledgers, or to enter into a transaction in open market operations when the central bank is on one side of the deal and the government is on the other side.

To equate the increase of savings in the banking system, as generated by the unused profits of the economic agents in the process of production (that are, therefore, representative of real wealth), with the accounting gimmicks of the treasury or the central bank through which inflationary credit is generated is to lose the substance of what the balance sheets of the banks represent.

The "creation" of money by the banks in the "normal course of business" can be either representative of a real increase in the wealth saved and therefore available to be invested, or it can be inflationary, that is, the multiplication of simultaneous claims to the existing wealth. This section is not the moment to address this issue in detail, but it is necessary to keep in mind this distinction while evaluating the claims presented here.

2.3.2 The Sociological Theory of Money

The concept that money is a social construct that may be better understood as a social relation between money producers and all other agents in society is at the core of the sociological theory about the origin of money. According to this view, the orthodox economists narrowly conceive of money as a medium of exchange that has spontaneously evolved in society as the result of individuals' propensity for utility maximization (Ingham, 2000: 20). For Geoffrey Ingham, a supporter of the sociological theory, this search for the "microfoundations" of the origin of money is a flawed logical exercise. First, he sees the classical evolutionary conception of money from barter as "a crude teleological functionalism" (Ingham, 2000: 20). Second he sees the Mengerian idea that money was originated as an unintended consequence of the exercise of individuals' rationality as a paradox since he believes that, although it is in the interest of the community to have money, it was not in the immediate interest of individuals to exchange their goods for a medium of exchange which is, in and of itself, useless. And third, he sees the modern explanations based on the rationality of the reduction of costs of transactions as begging the question about the origin of money since, for him, it just says that adoption of money, once it is widely accepted, would be useful for any single agent. Furthermore, he claims that for Menger, the only function of money is as medium of exchange, ignoring money's other functions. According to the sociological conception of the origin of money, it is because money first is a measure of value, a unit of account, that money possesses "the capacity to store abstract value in a universally accepted form that enables it to act as a means of payment" (Ingham, 2000: 21).

As the leading advocate of the sociological theory, Ingham apparently does not consider that for the "orthodox economists" there are objective reasons why at different times and places a given merchandise or token becomes the GAMOE, that these objective reasons can be grasped by individuals, and, therefore, that the "orthodox" explanation that money naturally evolved in society by the uncoordinated, self-motivated action of utility-maximizing individuals and the explanation that money is a social construct may well be saying the same thing. That is not to say that there are not irreconcilable differences, first among them, his stance against the logical consistency of the traditional Aristotelian evolutionary explanation of the origin of money and the fact that it does not depend on historical accuracy for its theoretical validity. Second, Ingham seems to ignore that exactly because money performs a useful function, there is a demand for holding cash balances and therefore there is no paradox in the option taken by individual agents to use indirect exchange in their dealings. Third, he prefers not to recognize the feedback mechanism through which the acceptability of a given merchandise as it becomes generalized increases its desirability as a medium of exchange and therefore results in the dynamic process, by force of which money was created and is constantly selected by individuals. Finally, he accepts the straw man argument that, for Menger, there is only one function for money. However, Ingham brings the authority of N. Dodd to argue that all money is fiduciary in character; the authority of Simmel, Schumpeter, and Hicks to say that all money is fundamentally credit; and so, the three functions of money—as a unit of account, as a medium of exchange, and as a store of abstract value—together explain the origin of money as a social relation (2000: p. 24). If one (a) takes the etymological explanation for the name of money in Greek (*nomos*) as meaning that indirect exchanges and, therefore, the instrument for indirect exchanges, is a social construct; or (b) that the commonly agreed relative value of a monetary merchandise, or a monetary token, for that matter, as arrived at by the sum of the preferences of all economic agents is a social construct; or finally, (c) that money, as representative of all the goods and services available in the economy is a store of abstract value in the sense that it is potentially desired by all economic agents and, as such, is an instrument to access potentially all the concrete goods and services, and that such abstract value is a social construct; then, with that (putting aside, perhaps, questions of precise terminology and the eternal discussion about historical and logical precedence), any "orthodox" economist may agree that, yes, money is a social construct.

Again, it is not the case that the questions of historical and logical precedence are not important or even possible to be reconciled. Ingham concludes his account that money was originated outside the market as chartal money in the command economies of the hydraulic first civilizations in the Middle East: "Monetary practice has its logical origins in the money of account and its historical foundations in the chartal money of early bureaucratic empires. It was not, pace Menger, the spontaneous product of the Market" (2000: 26).

At this time it may be appropriate to return to a quotation of Mises from the first chapter, that "the historical question concerning the origin of indirect exchange and money is after all of no concern to praxeology" (2007: 407). Let us suppose for a moment that although there is no historical evidence, Keynes drew the right conclusion from his "Babylonian Madness,"[11] and the historical account of the introduction of chartal money is correct. Does that mean that money did not have a spontaneous origin? The argument for the spontaneous origin of money, correctly understood, is that every time the social conditions for indirect exchanges present themselves, a medium of exchange gradually gains acceptance because such behavior is ingrained in human nature, because individuals have the rational faculties to time and again perceive the utility that may be derived from the use of such an instrument.[12] There is nothing in the historical account of the origin of chartal money in Babylon or in the claim that a unit of account was first established by the state that contradicts the idea that once conditions arise, individuals will use indirect exchanges to acquire the goods they really want. As already discussed in this work, it is difficult to imagine that the "priests of Babylon" would have selected something as a unit of account by fiat, without regard for what at that time was more or less generally used as medium of exchange, or even something more suitable to be used as a medium of exchange. The very mention made by our author (Ingham, 2000: 26) that the Babylonian shekel first was fixed in a certain amount of barley "and later at a more manageable 8.3 grams of silver" suggests that.

Ingham continues his historical account of the origin of money to say that two thousand years later, coinage was introduced in Greece at a time that political circumstances and technological advances in metallurgy made it possible to integrate all three attributes of money in the same object, and it was with the Roman Empire and its "sound money" that a monetary economy reached a peak, only to be surpassed again in the nineteenth century. With the decline of the Roman Empire in the middle of the fourth century, absent the extensive division of labor and the fiscal flow of the empire, money fell into disuse; minting only reemerged in Europe during the eleventh and twelfth centuries with the consolidation of feudal political institutions. At this time, according to Ingham, two remarkable things happened in regard to money: first, as Einaudi put it in his essay on imaginary money,[13] the delinkage between the unit of account and the media of exchange created the conditions for the second development, capitalist credit money. Or in Ingham's words, "Medieval money was produced in a struggle for control of bullion, coinage and the money of account; it was anarchic and chaotic, but the turmoil provided the conditions for a significant monetary development" (2004: 112).

According to this theory, the emergence of the merchant's bills of exchange became possible by the existence of a stable unit of account, although effective payments were made in the many different coins in circulation at that time. Eventually, credit money became "money proper" again when the states (first, in the Italian city-states during the Renaissance) became the largest receivers and makers of payments in society through the banks. It was the state recognition and enforcement of the legal depersonalization and negotiability of debt that allowed the creation of credit-money. For Ingham: "All subsequent developments have been the extension, elaboration, and refinement of this evolutionary leap in monetary practice" (2000: 28).

The relevance of this development for the sociological theory of money is that the creation of credit money allowed an elasticity of the money supply that made possible, first, the financing of the capitalist enterprise and, second, the modern state. However, once the conditions allowed the creation of credit money, for Ingham (quoting Simmel), all money becomes credit, in the sense that the value of money is based on trust that through money it will be possible to acquire the amount of final goods the money holders want (2000: 29); therefore, given the instability of money value that credit money entails and the pervasive presence of the state in credit money production and regulation, the normative conclusions of the sociological theory of money is that money must be managed by the state. This normative conclusion, on one hand, is a claim for the legitimacy of the state prerogative to do so (given the public interest in having **stable money**); on the other hand, it only becomes possible to be maintained once the state has political legitimacy, that is, if the collective agent of the polity is self-limited in its powers and goals. Ingham says, "The production of trust in money and modern credit money in particular has been inextricably bound up with the rise of the modern constitutional state" (2000: 30).

2.3.3 *The Austrian Economics Theory of Money*

This entire book presents a discussion on the fundamental characteristics of money from an Austrian School of Economics perspective; for that reason, the comments on the school in this section will be limited.

In regard to the origin of money, the epistemological limitations concerning monetary phenomena, and the purposes of good money in society, there is little if any disagreement among Austrian economists. In regard to politics, also, the free banking doctrine is consensual among them. There are obviously differences of methods and emphasis about many aspects of monetary and financial theory among Austrian economists; a case in point is Leland Yeager's emphasis on the disequilibrium between actual and desired holdings of money as an essential component of monetary theory. But the only issue of policy that may be described as critically not consensual inside the school is the issue of bank reserves or fractional banking.[14]

As a general rule, Austrian economists favor: (a) minimum regulations of banking, free banking being just the limit of that trend; (b) the abolition of forced tender and liberal rules for what may be considered legal tender, the privatization of money representing the extreme position on that matter; and (c) minimum exchange controls, a consensus among them, to my knowledge, being the policy of **free exchange**. The abolition of the central bank and severe limitations to the indebtedness of the public sector are just corollaries of the favored policies in regard to money and banking favored by Austrian economists. A general agreement on all these policy prescriptions and, more importantly, on the fundamental theoretical assumptions which lead to them, however, have not settled the dispute about whether or not a one hundred percent reserve requirement should be legally mandated on money issuers and demand deposit banks. In chapter 8, this dispute is discussed in some detail and my own position is offered for consideration; for now, it seems relevant just to point out its existence.

2.3.4 *The Property Theory of Interest and Money*

This theory has been proposed by Gunnar Heinsohn and Otto Steiger, as summarized by John Smithin:

> Heinsohn and Steiger argue that money can only arise in societies based on the institution of private property, and that it is created in a credit contract when property is encumbered and collateralized. (Smithin, 2000: 8)

Their theory has affinity with the sociological theory, to the extent that money for them is a (special) social relation; with the credit theory, since money is created by a credit operation; and with the Neo-Chartalists, to the extent that the state gets access to real wealth by, in their view, "monetizing" its claims on private property that in essence is what its power of taxation means. There are, on the other hand, important differences from these other theories. Contrary to the credit theory, the property theory emphasizes as the key component in money creation not the credit operation, but the property collateralized and encumbered in the credit operation from which results the issuance by the creditor of an anonymous claim against his property that the property theorists call money (Heinsohn and Steiger, 2000: 82). Different from the Neo-Chartalists, they reject the idea that money can be created ex nihilo, by state fiat (Heinsohn and Steiger, 2000: 79), since what the state does when it creates money, according to them, is to use as its claims on property as means of payment.

In their conception, there are only three kinds of economic systems: (a) the *customary* or tribal society, in which production and distribution is assigned to its members by tradition; (b) the *command* society, of which the feudal and the socialist societies are variations, and in which production and distribution is coercively organized by the ruling castes, whether it be an aristocracy or the apparatchiks of the Communist party; and (c) the society based on private *property*, in which free individuals interact voluntarily in order to organize economic activity under a legal system that has abolished most of the traditional rules and commands, and independent courts of law enforce those contractual agreements (Heinsohn and Steiger, 2000: 68).

They argue that under a customary or a command economy, there is no property, just possession, and that "in the possession-based societies the phenomena of money, collateral and interest are notoriously absent" (Heinsohn and Steiger, 2000: 69). Thus, they dispute that a system based on barter is an evolutionary stage preceding a system of indirect exchanges intermediated by money; that is their rationale for having in 1984 proposed the replacement of the evolutionary theory of money origin with the private property paradigm.

For Heinsohn and Steiger, it is not only the traditional evolutionary theory of money that is wrong; for them (and as seen in Harold Demsetz) mainstream economics takes for granted the private property arrangements at the base of capitalist societies without investigating the effects of such arrangements on the behavior of individuals (Heinsohn and Steiger, 2000: 71). Moreover, property ownership dissolves the bonds of tradition and command, creating by "immaterial legal constructs" an entirely new way of social interaction—the market relations we know today.

For them however, even the economists of the institutional school have missed the point that, supposedly, there is a difference between possession and property that does not entail the former to be lumped in as one of the components of private property rights. Consequently, institutional economists can only see the difference between customary or command societies versus property-based societies as centered on the existence of communal property versus private property and not the possession and property dichotomy that they see (Heinsohn and Steiger, 2000: 74).

One of the consequences of neglecting the effect of private property arrangements for Heinsohn and Steiger is present in the neoclassical models of general equilibrium in which the functioning of market economies is analyzed as if it were a moneyless society operated by direct, barter exchanges. In their interpretation of classical economics, it follows that interest is not a monetary phenomenon but the remuneration for thrift and determined by productivity, and they see the lack of treatment to collateralized debt a critical failure of the neoclassical theory. They propose to fill this gap with their claim that interest is a "property premium" paid by the use of collateralized property that by force of a process of credit cum collateralization gains liberative powers, and not for the use of real property.

The mechanism by which money is created according to the theory may be summarized as follows: At the moment that a credit operation is done with a bank, an interest-bearing credit instrument is created: the credit note itself. Simultaneously, the bank creates another note, one that does not bear interest—that is the bank note or the bank deposit that they consider "money proper." In this summarized description of their theory, in the two-layered banking system today in which commercial banks do not issue money proper, they need to offer the central bank, the only one that can create money proper, good collateral in order to have access to money. In this sense the creditworthiness of their nonbank clients, that is, the collateralized property of the interest-bearing notes, supports the production of money. As Bagehot argues, they also see not only the collateralized property of the nonbank clients, but the reserves of the commercial banks and of the central bank itself, as required to the production of "proper money." In regard to the stability of money's value, since there are no physical constraints to the production of money today, the interest rate is what keeps proper money scarce and therefore desirable (Heinsohn and Steiger, 2000: 89).

According to the theory, money proper is not to be confounded with state money; however, since today most of the money produced is produced against public debt and not private debt, Bagehot's "discount window" was replaced by the "open market window" claims that money could be created without collateralized property. Here Heinsohn and Steiger argue that the good credit of the government in issuing its bonds is because "A state which issues debt titles issues property titles. They are underlaid with the entire property of its citizens" (2000: 92). If the capacity of the state to exercise its tax powers to the extent necessary to make good its debts is put in doubt, the market for its bonds will dwindle and the treasury bond will be regarded as the bad securities that Bagehot had in mind; as such, they should not be accepted by a "genuine central bank" (Heinsohn and Steiger, 2000: 92).

Under the property theory framework, a business cycle occurs because the properties given as collateral have no "eternal" value, only market value, and in the middle of the boom stage of the cycle, more and more property owners are willing to take loans, paying interest and giving their properties as collateral in order to get money proper to invest with the expectation of making a profit. That entails an increase in the money production that, in granting a "liquidity" premium to the newly collateralized property, fuels the fear of inflation among creditors. The creditors then demand higher interest rates, the higher interest rates simultaneously decrease the prospects of profits and the present value of the collateralized property, and force the liquidation of debts, which is characteristic of the downside of the business cycle (Heinsohn and Steiger, 2000: 96).

The property theory of money has interesting aspects to be considered. Certainly the emphasis on private property in opposition to mere possession deserves attention. It seems, however, that at the very minimum, it should be refined in order to be considered a theory for the production of "good" money, and questions will still remain about its general validity. After all, it is not just any property that has the attributes necessary to become good collateral in general and even more so, good collateral against which money "proper" will be issued. Real estate property, for instance, is good collateral to the extent that it is generally a good store of value, but its liquidity is low, its liquidation is usually complex and time consuming, so, to issue noninterest bearing titles with the intention of generating liquidity having real estate as collateral may be understood as a case of the *second* of Law's mistakes mentioned at footnote 14 of chapter 1. In the theory apparently there is no effective instrument to limit the production of money in order to produce, to the greatest extent possible, money with the desired attributes of good money, such as (relative) stability in value. It may be questioned, why use a new theoretical paradigm for the analysis of monetary institutions if it does not provide better instruments for the production of good money than the existing ones?

2.3.5 The Credit Theory of Money: The Monetary Circuit Approach

The "Theory of the Monetary Circuit," or TMC, is related to the neoclassical models, to the extent that you can "abstract" money from the circuit of production; and to the neo-chartalist view, to the extent that (a) money value is defined by fiat by the state, (b) it is formally a legally defined title to the communal property, and (c) it is created by the legal mechanisms regulating the operation of the financial institutions. Dodd, for instance (2014: 93) quotes Simmel saying that money creates a relationship of the money holders "with the economic community that accepts the money" (Simmel, 2001: 177) in order to say that all forms of money are forms of debt. In this sense, to state that money is "a claim upon society" (Simmel, 2001: 177) is correct since it represents claims on all available goods whose owners are willing to accept it in payment for their property, but that is quite different from saying that only debts may serve as media of exchange, which is the claim of the "credit theory of money."

In regard to the origin of money, this school follows the concepts of Mitchell Innes, and Heinsohn and Steiger in stating that debt and credit precedes money "because money emerges both causally and historically as a result of prior debt and credit relations" (Parguez and Seccareccia, 2000: 101). However, a crucial difference between TMC and the property theory is that according to TMC, there is no requirement for private property for the existence of credit relations.

According to Parguez and Seccareccia, the two major propositions of the TMC are:

> First, money is, and has always been, a debt created ex nihilo by bank credit advances that are granted either to permit the generation of real wealth or to acquire existing physical assets. Second, there is no alternative between debt financing on the one hand, and the tapping of existing liquid resources (or accumulated savings) to "finance" expenditure, on the other. At the macroeconomic level, spending in a monetary economy is always and everywhere in the nature of debt financing. (2000: 102)

The "Theory of the Monetary Circuit" or TMC holds the conception that, aside from buyers and sellers, money today is one of the many financial instruments created in a modern monetary economy by the operations of third parties, that is, financial institutions. Once debt is created in order to allow private individuals and the state itself to start the production of goods and services, money is generated by the banks in order to be used as a means of payment. Alain Parguez and Mario Seccareccia say, "In this three-way balance sheet relation, every transaction entails the simultaneous creation or destruction of debt, and every seller of goods and services accepts payment of this bank liability on the basis of its general purchasing power or value" (2000: 101).

The emphasis of the theory is that there is a "circuit" in the credit transactions that entails money creation. In the same way that money is created when debt is contracted, money is destroyed when debt is repaid, thus closing the monetary circuit. In their view, the repayment of debts by the sale of the production with a profit is the necessary condition to close the circuit, again generating credits to real goods and services that will be borrowed and made available through the transferences done in the balance sheets of the financial institutions represented, among other things, by money. The purchasing value of the money, for TMC, is a result of the demand for money by the nonbank agents that in their interpretation is needed in order to acquire real resources and generate wealth. As a consequence of that, money for TMC can only be defined as a means of payment (that is, a medium of exchange), and not as a unit of account or store of value (Parguez and Seccareccia, 2000: 105).

For TMC theorists, although credit money is by its nature fiat money and cannot exist outside the state, the state by itself cannot generate stable money, as the experiences of hyperinflation of fiat money may illustrate. According to them, that happens because there should be not quantitative controls guiding money production, but rather what may be understood as "qualitative" controls of the debt underlying money production, as expressed in their definition of money:

> Money is at all times the liabilities issued by banking institutions which have been endorsed by the state primarily for the purpose of financing the formation of future real wealth. This money has a real extrinsic value because every holder of these liabilities has acquired a claim on the future physical wealth that results from the initial bank credit advances. (Parguez and Seccareccia, 2000: 107)

It is impossible for a reader of this definition not come to the conclusion that, as a prescription for money production by the banks, these TMC authors are suggesting the adoption of a criterion comparable with the "Real Bills Doctrine" (RBD). This impression is reinforced by their discussion about the (positive) relation between the value of money and the proportion of the tax liability in the economy as perceived by the Neo-Chartalists.

Along the same line, Smithin argues that credit creation is necessary in order for profits to be generated in an economy with voluntary exchanges and free markets (2013a: 10, 56, and especially 14, where the idea of creation of money and credit as part of a circuit in order for profits to exist is mentioned). Smithin does not take into consideration, however, that nowadays not all money is exogenous or endogenous, but we have a hybrid system of both exogenous money created by the government (the monetary base) and endogenous money (created by the bank with the creation of credit instruments with quasi-monetary properties). The "ideal" creation of money in order to sustain the generation of profits is explained by Smithin (2013a: 16) as "just enough" to allow the greater production without changing the price level, and recognizes that that is easier said than done and that no "updated version of the RBD for the regulation of credit creation could do that. Still, the reference to the RDB is telling. Using the terminology of mainstream economics, the challenge rightly perceived by Smithin is that the demand and supply of money varies, and that an increasing level of economic activity results in an increase in the demand for money, and that requires an increase in the supply of money unless we would like to accept that the price level will fall; that is, that we will have deflation. Deflation, by itself, tends to have a deleterious effect on production, since producers are reluctant to adjust their prices downward, accepting a lower level of sales until they convince themselves that their fares brought to the market are commanding a lower nominal price than previously practiced. That is not to say, however, that production cannot continue to increase in those circumstances; it only says that theoretically, it should be expected to increase less than it otherwise would with a price level kept constant.

The relation between productive investments and the value of money for these theorists, helps distinguish them from state theorists; for instance, for Parguez and Seccareccia, it is not the quantity of taxes that the state can collect that matters. They say, "If the state money is issued merely to finance wasteful expenditures that have no serious positive consequences on the private or collective wealth of the community, the effect in the long run would be to depreciate the value of money, regardless of the power of taxation of the state" (2000:120). It seems therefore, that Parguez and Seccareccia see the description of money production in the theory they champion as supporting their prescription about what sound monetary policy should be. It may be conceded that with their emphasis on the "circuit" of money production and destruction, there is a need, implicit in their reasoning and explicit in their writings, for financial resources to be made available only to profitable investments, which is obviously laudable. However, they seem to ignore all the epistemological problems and the moral hazards that prevent the bureaucracy of the central bank, the commercial bankers, and public in general, for that matter, to know which of the prospective buyers will turn a profit or which of the state expenditures will be of a "productive" character.[15]

2.3.6 Keynesian and Post-Keynesian Theory

Since most relevant aspects of Keynes' monetary theory are discussed in other parts of this book, the account given here is meant just to posit the theory as it relates to Keynes' broader assumptions and some recent developments as proposed by his followers. Keynesian economics promotes a mixed economy where the state is also an economic agent. Keynesian economics seeks to provide solutions to what they perceive as failures of laissez-faire economic liberalism, which advocates that markets and the private sector operate best without state intervention. In Keynes' theory, macroeconomic trends decisively influence the microlevel behavior of individuals, asserting the importance of aggregate demand for goods as the driving factor of the economy. From this Keynes argues that government policies could be used to promote demand at a macro level, to fight unemployment above a structural level. He argues that the solution to depressions is to stimulate the economy ("inducement to invest") through some combination of: increase in the supply of credit money, reduction in interest rates, and government investment in infrastructure. A central conclusion of Keynesian economics is that there is no strong automatic tendency for output and employment to move toward full employment levels. This conclusion conflicts with the tenets of classical economics and with those schools such as supply-side economics or the Austrian school which assume a general tendency towards full employment in a capitalist society summarized in Say's Law. For Keynes, it is not always that the income generated in the process of production is sufficient to acquire the entire production; for him, it is just a special case, and that is why he named his theory of monetary and fiscal management aimed toward full employment as the *General* theory.

In the "Keynesian cross diagram," (figure 2.1) the aggregate demand curve is drawn as a rising line since consumers will have a larger demand with a larger disposable income, which increases with total national out-

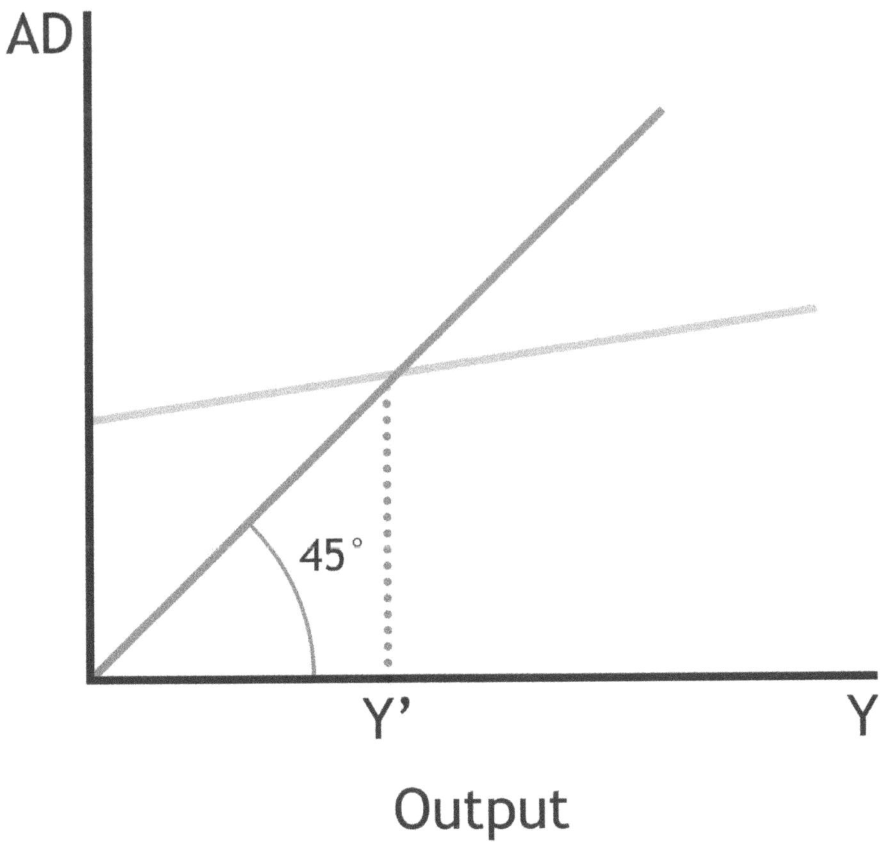

Figure 2.1. Keynesian Cross Diagram

put. This increase is due to the positive relationship between consumption and consumers' disposable income in the consumption function. Aggregate demand may also rise due to increases in investment. Equilibrium in this diagram occurs where total demand, AD, equals the total amount of national output, Y, (which corresponds to total national income or production).[16]

The result of such assumptions is that it is possible to increase the demand for goods if nominal income is increased. Since expansion of consumption and investment by borrowed money would increase the interest rates, effectively "crowding out" other intended investments and expenditures, Keynes advocates as more effective the funding of new investments and expenditures by the creation of more money. Another key element of Keynes' monetary theory is that he claims that it is possible for the state to achieve a multiplied effect of its investments in terms of aggregate demand, that is, the existence of a multiplier, whenever the economy is not at full employment. This is one more reason for Keynes to not worry about the creation of credit money in order to fund these investments.

Keynes was however, developing his theories for a monetary system still somewhat constrained by commodity money; he treats the supply of money "proper" as given. Keynes has many influential writings on monetary policy such as the 1924 *A Tract on Monetary Reform*, but his main works on monetary theory are the 1930 *A Treatise on Money* (*Treatise*) and the 1936 *The General Theory of Employment, Interest and Money* (*General Theory*). It may well be understood that at the time he wrote the *Treatise*, he had realized that the gold-exchange monetary system then in force internationally was unable to impose an external constraint on the money supply by the physical limitations of money proper, that is, gold; this is the reason that he asserts that it is monetary policy that determines the price level. At the time of the General Theory, however, that conclusion would not fit well with his claim that the equilibrium at full employment was only one among the many equilibria possible, and it was omitted. As stated by Colin Rogers and T. K. Rymes, "The key is Keynes's realization that monetary theory had progressed from a world where real and nominal anchors existed, to a world where anchors had been replaced by the banking system, which itself rested on the bedrock of discretionary monetary policy" (Rogers and Rymes, 2000: 257).

In the *Treatise*, Keynes develops a long reasoning about how the commercial banks tend to operate with minimum cash balances even in the face of reserve requirements. From that he adds to his assessment of the monetary system then in force that it was not the **monetary base** that would determine the price level, since its tendency is to zero. These are characteristics of his theoretical model, or in the words of Rogers and Rymes, "Thus, there is a pure Keynesian system with no anchor, no positive base money on which the system rests" (2000: 257).

In such a system, it would be possible to control the liquidity in the economy just by the operation of the bank rate: "The bank rate becomes the price of the services of liquidity which the central bank is providing" (Rogers and Rymes, 2000: 257). Therefore it is through the bank rate that the central bank executes its responsibilities to keep the price level stable. This in essence is the remarkably modern banking theoretical model envisioned in the *Treatise* and gone by the time of the *General Theory* where the rate of interest is determined by the demand and supply of a stock of money that he aims to see increased.

In our days of completely elastic fiat money, increases in the effective demand according to some post-Keynesian scholars are always accompanied by an endogenous increase in the money supply. For them, there are many methods to finance the spending that may prop up the effective demand; therefore, the monetary and financial systems are essential to enable such increases. The relevant aspect to be pointed out here about Keynes' monetary theory as it may be applied today to the circumstances of fiat money is that, according to its proponents, the amount of money in circulation is allegedly determined endogenously. Victoria Chick says,

> The theory of endogenous money states that support of some expenditures and productive process by bank credit creates new money. This new money in turn provides the extra purchasing power needed to raise prices as output expands. In the Post Keynesian vision of endogenous money, not only is the money supply flexible, but the money supply process is connected to the same processes which result in a rise in effective demand. (2000: 124)

A different approach to the importance of Keynes to the debate about the fundamental characteristics of money may be found in the "Irrational Theory of Money." This "Freudo-Keynesian" concept of money argues for the relevance of allegedly irrational attitudes towards money, such as love of money, greed, and propensity for hoarding in order to understand the role of money in modern societies.

That Keynes had substantial knowledge and admiration for Freudian psychoanalysis is well known. As part of the Bloomsbury group, Keynes was acquainted with the introduction of Freudian ideas in the United Kingdom. An interesting sequel of that, for the purposes of this book, is to understand the extent to which there is in Keynes' monetary theory a claim of irrationality that may have a source either in Freud's ideas about money or in similar ideas that Keynes developed independently (Dostaler and Maris, 2000: 242).

Traditional debate about subjective evaluation in economy has been conducted inside the framework of economic agents' rationality. There is a long tradition, traceable back to the Enlightenment, linking the progress of European civilization to the taming of the "passions" by the "interests;" Max Weber in the twentieth century considers capitalism the rational moderation of irrational desires. There are in Keynes, however, claims of unchecked irrationality driving human decisions that should be considered in any assessment of the validity of his ideas.

Gilles Dostaler and Bernard Maris, for instance, argue that in the *General Theory*, at the core of the explanations for economic behavior, there are three psychological motivations identified as (a) the propensity to consume, (b) the marginal efficiency of capital, and (c) liquidity preference. In order to adequately evaluate the merits of Keynes' monetary prescriptions it is necessary to address the validity of his description, and if these motivations are deemed to exist in irrational proportions, then different prescriptions based on an assumption of their reasonability for given circumstances will suffice as an answer.

Arguably, according to Freud's conception, individuals unconsciously reflect their neurosis in their relations with money; Freud saw relations between oral desire and acquisition, between fecal retention and the desire for gold, and between the fear of death and hoarding, for instance.[17] The echo of such ideas may be found in Keynes: "The love of money as a possession—as distinguished from the love of money as a means to the enjoyments and realities of life—will be recognized for what it is, a somewhat disgusting morbidity, one of those semi-criminal, semi-pathological propensities which one hands over with a shudder to the specialists in mental disease" (as quoted from the 1930 *Economic Possibilities for our Grandchildren*).

Specifically about gold, Keynes uses the myth of King Midas as a metaphor for the preference for liquidity. For Keynes, liquidity is associated with uncertainty and the fear of the future, the fear of death that the accumulation of liquid wealth arguably would unconsciously help to appease; the accumulation of wealth, in the *psyche* of the individuals as well as of King Midas, may actually cause their death and with them the economic death of the entire community by the negation of consumption. "Midas, the rentier, the miser, is not only guilty of killing himself, but also of killing the society to which he denies the circulation of his money" (Dostaler and Maris, 2000: p. 245).

It seems evident that with his theory of money, Keynes' intention was to depict the acquisition and accumulation of wealth in general and money in particular as pathological. There is no need to explore other Freudian insights in Keynes to understand his project of bringing irrationality to economics. One interesting question that remains is to understand to what extent the use of those metaphors has only a rhetorical purpose, that is, to convince his audience of the inadequacy of orthodox economic reasoning to solve the economic problems in the 1930s, or if Keynes' project was broader than that.

In regard to the philosophy of money, it seems perfectly fine to explore the emotions known and unknown to individuals that motivate their actions; it also seems reasonable to admit that individuals sometimes have difficulty performing a rational action due to limited knowledge, or because they are blinded by their emotions, traditions, prejudices, et cetera. But nothing in that denies the rational faculty of individuals, and the validity of praxeological assumptions. As already mentioned in section 1.6.5, there are many illusions and misconceptions about money, but that must not be understood as an argument against the possibility of a rational approach to monetary matters, something precluded if one claims that individual action is irrational.

2.3.7 The Monetarist Theory and the Neoclassical Synthesis

The monetary theory of mainstream economics also has been discussed in more details in other parts of this book. Even so, in the general overview of the different schools about the philosophy of money discussed in this chapter, it is important to identify its main characteristics. We left at the end of the second section of this chapter the evolution of the ideas about money with the culmination of the subjective concept of value as was developed by the classical economists with the theory of marginal utility. There I also mentioned the precursors of the quantitative theory of money and the classical and scholastic roots of the ideas of natural prices and equilibrium. Lastly, I referred to the general split of sciences under the influence of Cartesian rationalism, empiricism, and mainly the positivist ideology. At the beginning of the twentieth century, the circumstances were ripe for the development of formal mathematics models for the behavior of economic agents at the micro level along curves of supply and demand, and the aggregation of their behavior at the macro level in models of general equilibrium. The quantitative theory of value was fully developed by Irving Fisher regarding the value of money. A further development with important impact on monetary theory was the statement of economics as a positive science by Milton Friedman. Not only it was advocated that economics as a science was not concerned with metaphysics and morals, but also that, in regards to epistemology, methodology, and the very ontology of the discipline, the validity of the formal models was to be evaluated by the results of the predictions and not by their adequate representation of reality. Incidentally, the theory of value of money of neoclassical economics has as a benchmark the "Arrow-Debreu" model of a closed economy operating in competitive equilibrium with perfect knowledge available to all agents, with an arbitrary unit of account, all the position along the curve of preferences is Pareto efficient, and finally, the value of any good can be defined in terms of any other good. In such a model, money may be dispensed, since the main roles money performs in real life are considered as solved in the model. That is why so often one hears that mainstream economics departs from an unrealistic assumption of a barter economy. In a literal sense, that may be true, still, acknowledging its context, the model can be extremely useful to explain at a conceptual level the subjective nature of relative price change in the economy. Another interesting aspect of the model is that it does not explain the source of value of (fiat) money, as pointed out by Von Hagen and Welker (2014: 31); the explanation for that is exogenous to the model. Meanwhile, for about fifty years, mainstream economics lived with the tension brought about by the Keynesians with their critique of the quantitative theory of money and the new macroeconomics giving intellectual support for policies, on the one hand, and the teachings of classical economics advocated by the economists that became known as the monetarists on the other. In regard to the meaning of monetarism, Michele Fratianni and Jurgen von Hagen said:

> Brunner himself had coined that term (monetarism) in an article published in the *Federal Reserve of St. Louis Review* (Brunner, 1968), describing a school of thought that believes in the self-stabilizing properties of the private economy, that money affects the real economy primarily through changes in the relative asset prices, and that monetary fluctuations are primarily due to the erratic behavior of the **monetary authorities** inspired by the "wrong" model of how money works in the economy. (Fratianni and Hagen, 2001: 644)

Milton Friedman's treatment of the demand for money and the Great Depression is a good example of the different policy conclusions the monetarists elicited from their interpretation of the economic data. As discussed by David Laidler, at the time *Studies in the Quantity Theory of Money* was published (1956), influenced by Keynes, the demand for money was considered to be very elastic in response to changes in the interest rate, and the propensity for consumption was considered rigid. From that came the idea before WWII that "the Great Depression was the result of a collapse in investment, amplified by the multiplier, and monetary policy had been powerless to offset it." That is why the fashionable prescription at the time was to use fiscal policy to promote economic recovery, since the best that could be done by way of the monetary policy was to keep the interest rate low. But that changed with Milton Friedman; his research program gave quantitative theory a new lease on life. According to Laidler:

> Friedman's theory of the Consumption Function (1957) would soon challenge the idea of a stable marginal propensity to consume out of current income, and hence of a stable multiplier, and in 1956 he was suggesting that it was the demand for money function which was the stable relationship in the economy. The implications were soon to be spelled out: the business cycle in general, and the Great Depression in particular were, after all, largely monetary phenomena, (Friedman and Schwartz 1963), and autonomous expenditure variables (including those under the control of the fiscal authorities) had less explanatory

> power over the time path of money income than did fluctuations in the quantity of money (Friedman and Meiselman 1963). (Laidler, 2004: 325)

Eventually, in the last quarter of the twentieth century, a new synthesis, the neoclassical synthesis, was developed, incorporating most, if not all, of Keynes' contributions to macroeconomics in general and monetary theory in particular.

It is safe to say that today the differences among monetarists and Keynesians are by and large not differences of methods or assumptions but of political conclusions as derived from a common descriptive apparatus. In the words of Karl Brunner and Allan Meltzer, two prominent monetarists,

> The term Keynesianism refers to the changing analytic and policy views of a group that have in common their support for activist, discretionary policy. This characteristic distinguishes Keynesians from early and later writers who favored some type of rule. Usually, Keynesians are distinguished from others based on a shared belief that wages adjust more slowly than prices. This view was held by many classical writers—Hume, Thornton, Marshall to name three—and by many, recent non-Keynesian writers who drew different policy conclusions, for example preferring rules to discretion. (Brunner and Meltzer, 1993: 13)

The final development in theory of money of the neoclassical synthesis is inflation targeting policies. There are no more real anchors to the value of money, it is only a policy of control of the liquidity in the economy, mainly by the use of the bank rate, that allows the monetary authorities to fulfill their mandates for price stability. Although the management of monetary policy aiming for relatively low changes on the price level as measured by one or more price indexes is clearly a discretionary exercise, the monetarists among the neoclassical economists usually advocate the use of what became known as the "Taylor Rule" as a guide to achieve that. In his influential 1993 paper, John Taylor argues for a flexible monetary rule that would dictate changes in the bank rate in order to follow rises and declines in the inflation index and GNP, without explicitly determining ex ante the magnitude of such changes, which would avoid the problem brought up by Lucas about the rational expectations of economic agents, and therefore would work well. In Taylor's own words: "monetary policy rules in which the short-term interest rate instrument is raised by the monetary authorities if the price level and real income are above a target and is lowered if the price level and real income are below target, seem to work well" (Taylor, 1993: 200).

In part IV, there is an entire chapter on inflation targeting policies, so there is no need to further discuss them here. The relevant thing to say, at this moment, is that they embodied the fundamental assumptions of the neoclassical synthesis in regard to money. They should not be seen as in any way spurious to mainstream economic assumptions but as its culmination in regard to money.

2.3.8 The Marxist Theory of Commodity Money

The Marxist theory of money is centered on the idea that money is a commodity money (in order to represent "abstract labor," a special commodity must cease to be only a commodity and becomes money); that evidently, is no longer the case with modern money. Marx's idea of money as a special commodity (gold) that fulfills the role of a "universal equivalent" may, therefore, be considered as anachronistic.

But for Karl Marx, to eliminate commodity money would be the same as to "try to retain Catholicism without the Pope" (Marx, 1906: I, II, 6, footnote 48). So how do Marxist theorists come to grips with the reality of a fiat money system without throwing overboard this cornerstone of the Marxist theory in regard to money? It seems worthwhile to understand what Marxists today have to say about money in face of that.

For some Marxists today, such as Steve Fleetwood, one solution is simply to accept that money today is fiat money and therefore money does not need to be a commodity and Marx was wrong; another solution would be to say that the modern economy today does not have a "universal equivalent" anymore—that is, it does not have money, properly speaking (Fleetwood, 2000: 189).

For other thinkers, such as Peter Kennedy, it is possible to develop a Marxist theory of symbolic money. For them it is possible to find in Marx support for the idea that it is not in the intrinsic physical properties of the substance used as money that is to be found the attributes necessary for it to be used as representative of value. Kennedy says, "The idea that money is merely a symbolic of value relations has become acceptable within some quarters of contemporary Marxism" (2000: 197).

Whether Marx was right or wrong about money being a commodity, nonetheless, Marxists seem to accept the need, or rather, the advantages that society may draw from the use of a "universal equivalent" for the function of social coordination in a capitalist setting. Their conclusion is that if there are no more commodity monies in capitalist societies, that is so because the significance of money in those societies, according to the Marxists, has diminished. They claim that in modern Western societies most of the indirect coordination once done by the existence of commodity money is now done directly by the state through other forms of social coordination mechanisms, such as legislation and administrative regulations.

There are many normative conclusions with which one from the Austrian school tradition would not agree. The Marxists' very description of the twentieth century as a time of "managed decline" of capitalism and the idea that we now need a "lesser" money because some of the indirect coordination done in the nineteenth century is now done directly by legislation are highly debatable. However, they seem to understand the relation between the possibility of a worldwide division of labor and the use of gold as a "universal equivalent" that one can only appreciate. Marx's theory of money has another interesting component; that is, he does not accept the state theory of money's origins. He said that "Gold and silver are acceptable by right (law) only because they are acceptable in practice; and they are acceptable in practice because the present organization of production needs a universal medium of exchange" (Marx, 1992: 64). That is because society is already at a level of division of labor that requires a medium of exchange that the state may take advantage of that allows it to collect taxes, not in kind but in money, to pay its ceremonial and military expenses with coined money. That is not uncontroversial, though, Dodd (2000: 53), for instance, states that Marx rejects the spontaneous origin of money. That is clearly wrong. It is true that, in *Capital*, Marx may give some reason for that interpretation by saying that exchange using modern money differs from barter (that is, money's main function is to be a medium of exchange) because, as he points out, C-M-C is different from C-C in the sense that now money may be sought by itself and hoarded (that is, for him, the main feature of money is its possibility of being a store of value). I don't think that Dodd's is a valid conclusion for two reasons: first, because it does not contradict the fact that money in the end is an instrument for real goods and, second, although hoarding by itself fulfills a purpose, that is, to have the "claim on society" open (the nexus rerum or "social pledge," as Marx understands it) in itself does not satisfy any other need (Marx, 1990: 228), so the use of money as a store of value is conditioned on its being generally accepted as a medium of exchange. Furthermore, in *Grundrisse*, Marx clearly states his belief on the spontaneous origin of money: "Money does not arrive by convention, any more than the state does. It arises out of exchange, and arises naturally out of exchange" (1993: 165). The only caveat is that although Marx accepts an spontaneous origin for money, he states that money's original function was as a unit of value and not as a medium of exchange, since it came to be used at a time that most transactions were cleared by barter ("Money appears as measure (in Homer, e.g. oxen) earlier than as a medium of exchange, because in barter each commodity is still its medium of exchange. But it cannot be its own measure or its own standard of comparison" (Marx, 1993: 173).

In *Capital*, volume 3, chapter 15, page 363 (Marx, 1991), Marx blames what he describes sometimes as "excess capital" for cycles of boom and bust; it is not at all clear (as referred to in Dodd, 2014: 56) that here Marx is referring to the same thing that in other passages he describes as fictitious capital (credit money). If that is so, that would be a formulation similar to the theory of the business cycle of the Austrian School of Economics, but I think that that is to read too much into it. For Marx, according to Dodd, only by abolishing money and credit is it that recessions could be avoided, which is obviously false since the problem he is pointing out is one of fractional reserve banking that, even at his time, was already ameliorated by the actions of the Bank of England as a lender of last resort; although I understand that because he is thinking within the framework of the gold standard and fractional reserve banking of his time, and his inclination to understand that only base money is "money" and everything else is credit money how he likely would commit a mistake like that. Marx, in *Capital*, volume 3, page 953 wrote: "Capital is the means of production as transformed into capital, these being no more capital in themselves than gold or silver are money." Dodd (2014: 62) and many Marxists read too much in these passages, when Marx is asserting the obvious that there is a real side in the economy and a "monetary" or "financial" side in which things in the real side are represented. Particularly about "gold and silver," even for someone as intrinsic a metallist as Marx, it is not difficult come to the realization that commodities as they are, gold and silver qua money, that is, as instruments for indirect exchanges (being those exchanges instantaneous or deferred on time) are also a conventional "claim on society" as Marx himself defined. As part of their intrinsic value as a commodity, they performed a socially accepted function of medium of exchange, as a bridge between the products and services one produces and the products and services one desires to consume.

This is not the place to discuss Marx's theory of labor value, but in *Grundrisse,* the chapter on money, pages 134–5 (Marx, 1993), Marx not only states his belief in the intrinsic source of money value ("Convertibility, therefore—legal or not—remains a requirement of every kind of money whose title makes it a value-symbol, i.e. which equates it as a quantity with a third commodity" (page 134)) and equates gold to labor ("gold is labor time accumulated in the past" (page 134), but also clearly accepts that the relation between the value of goods and labor is not a fixed one but changes in time, stating "[w]hat determines value is not the amount of labour time incorporated in products, but rather the amount of labour time necessary at a given moment" (page 135). Such understanding clearly undermines the notion that labor has some sort of objective, stable value; and Marx is clear about that: "if the hour of labour became more productive, then the sheet of paper which represents it would rise in buying power, and vice versa, exactly as a 5 note at present buys more or less depending on whether the relative value of gold in comparison with other commodities rise or falls" (page 135). It is surprising how close to a subjective theory of value he sounds here. Such understanding is shared by some of his interpreters, which label it as an "abstract labor" value theory (Nelson, 2005: 187), although the same interpreters conclude his theory is a variant of the credit theory of money; if that is the case, it is clearly an odd variant because all the other credit theories adhere to a state origin of money, while Marx's clearly does not.

The bottom line that cannot be forgotten is that the entire discussion about money in Marx has a political perspective; it serves as a building block in the justification of his claims about exploitation of laborers by capitalists. Accurate or not as his observations about money may be, it is hard to believe that his entire reasoning was not aimed at a conclusion that he knew beforehand; and more than that, one that was proved wrong long ago, starting with Bohm-Bawerk. There is nothing particular insightful in his ideas about money; they are clearly wrong in many ways—their intrinsic metallism, for instance, his labor theory of value (unless understood as saying the opposite of what most of his interpreters have concluded) is also wrong, his ideas about the business cycle confound problems of real cycles with the ones caused by inflationary credit expansion, and so on and so forth. The reason to study Marx's ideas on money is not that they illuminate our understanding about money, but because they reveal how much monetary theory may be used as an ideological device. As evidence of that, again, in *Capital*, volume 1, page 919, according to Dodd (2014: 64), Marx states that public debt isolates investors from risk, which is a joke, but also that together with taxation, through the state, the forces of society were organized and the transition from feudalism to capitalism was made. That is an interesting thesis, known as the fiscal prevalence hypothesis, according to which the fiscal needs of the state are the main determinants of monetary and banking policies; and furthermore, as said by Dickson and later, Schila, the solutions found for addressing the fiscal needs both in the United Kingdom and the United States helped the creation of the financial infrastructure that helped the development of capitalism. To the extent that Marx really said that, he may be understood as a precursor of that thesis. The idea that colonialism has to do with capitalism, on the other hand is unwarranted; it is exactly because the developed countries in the nineteenth century failed to live up to the promise of free trade, but protectionism was universally condemned, that more and more countries resorted to neocolonialism in order to have through colonial privileges what they could not have by explicit protectionism.

NOTES

1. Whether or not Aristotle is original in all his thoughts or to some extent was compiling the received knowledge at his time is beside the point.

2. Rothbard (2006: 17) also concedes that this is a possible interpretation for some historians.

3. The theme of lesser uncertainty for economic agents in their dealings and the consequent benefits in terms of enhanced production and productivity in society resulting from a monetary policy of hard money is one of the most important indictments of an inflationary policy; such criticism is at the center of perennial discussions

on the reasons for having sound monetary policy, and the assumptions required to reach such a theoretical conclusion are already here.

4. This inconsistency in Aristotle's thought was pointed out by Rothbard (Rothbard, 2006: 14).

5. Aristotle, 1941: 1133a20.

6. Again, Professor Rothbard (2006: 15) has already stated that Aristotle was incorrect in implying that the proceeds of money lending were a "direct" product of money.

7. Dante Alighieri in his *Divina Commedia* suggests that the accidental death of Philip IV (1285–1314) was divine retribution for the debasement of the currency ordered by him (canto 19: Longfellow's translation):

> There shall be seen the woe that on the Seine
> He brings by falsifying of the coin,
> Who by the blow of a wild boar shall die.

It is estimated that debasement at the time Philip IV was the King of France (1285–1314) contributed at times with more than half of the treasury revenue (Kaye, 2000: 22, note 25). Kaye also reports that in the first half of the fourteenth century there were more than 100 changes in the currency (2000: 23); but the lower classes of Paris only rioted when in 1306, he honored a promise to revalue the currency, "which led to the effective tripling of their rents." The end of the riots only came when it was ordained that debts and rents should be paid in the new currency in proportion to the value of the currency at the time the contracts were made (Kaye, 2000: 24, note 40).

8. During his lifetime, in the aftermath of the Glorious Revolution, Locke saw the weight of silver decrease to 45% of its supposed weight, compromising the credibility of the British monetary system. That prompted the debate about fixing the interest rate and depreciating the monetary standard as proposed by William Lowndes, to which Locke responded with his "Considerations of the Consequences of Lowering the Interest and Raising the Value of Money" from 1691 and his "Further Considerations Concerning Raising the Value of Money" in 1695directly refuting Mr. Lowndes' arguments for it.

9. I concede that perhaps I am reading too much into Locke; if that is so, still his argument that the "intrinsic" value of silver is a result of the estimation of the economic agents fits at a minimum with the subjectivist tradition, which thread we have been following since Aristotle.

10. In the field of economics a particular discussion about methodology arose: the ***Methodenstreit der Nationalökonomie***. It was the discussion about epistemology and the method of research in economics, between the Austrian School of Economics and the German Historicists. One may venture to say that, to the extent that the discussion was really about method, at its core there were the opposing conceptions of individualist and collectivist methodology and the role of history in economics. Risking oversimplification, the treatment given in this work to the method proposed by the historicists, in regard to its influence in the philosophy of money, is to equate it to the general claim of the positivists for a "social physics," an understanding endorsed by Mises (Mises, 2003: 12). The only particularity that seems relevant to the historical account presented in this chapter is that even the historicists, with their claims regarding the possibility of deriving positive laws of economic behavior from historical analysis, by the distorted lens of their collectivist method, were ascribing psychological motivations to the economic agents as part of their rejection of materialist determinism; therefore, even the historicists, at their departure point, built on the subjectivist tradition here described.

11. By "Babylonian Madness," Keynes described his studies on numismatics of the first Middle East civilizations in order to understand the historical and logical origins of money (Ingham, 2000: 16).

12. Peter Klein and George Selgin once conducted a very interesting experiment simulating in a laboratory the consistency of Menger's spontaneous account of the

origin of money and they concluded: "Money can emerge spontaneously even where traders have only a very dim perception of the marketability of distinct goods, based on very limited random sampling, and even where all goods are equally marketable at the onset of the evolutionary process" (Klein and Selgin, 2000: 232).

13. See footnote 21 of chapter 1.

14. That is not to say that there are not many disagreements among the Austrian economists in regard to general methodological, epistemological, or political issues, specifically about monetary policy; however, the main point of contention seems to be the issue of fractional banking. In regard to general topics, Peter Boettke listed the following:

> Disagreement within the ranks of Austrian economists still persists over such issues as the role of equilibrium within the theory of the market process, the treatment of expectations from a subjectivist perspective, the incorporation of cultural factors (and social embeddedness) in the analysis of choice and preference formation, and the how and why of knowledge (its conveyance of use). (Boettke, 1996: IV)

15. Proposals of monetary reform propugnating a pure credit system, and in this sense anticipating the idea of a monetary system without base money, in which all money is credit money are more than a century old. Both Wicksell's and Solvay's proposal of "social comptabilism" of the last decade of the nineteenth century were proposals in the opposite direction of some monetary reformers such as Benjamin Anderson and Irving Fisher proposing the elimination of any form of credit money as a way to establish a more stable financial system (Boianovsky and Erreygers, 2005: 122).

16. As with any other individual behavior, ex post facto we can aggregate and build an aggregate curve, such as an aggregate demand curve; however, as noted by Professor Rothbard in the chapter on the fallacies of the Keynesian system in his 1970 book *Man, Economy and the State* (Huerta de Soto, 1987: 12), in the Keynesian system, the consumption function is given *ex ante*. Those curves are useful instruments for analysis of past behavior, and we can draw conclusions and theorize comparing those curves with other data; but even if we accept that we have taken into consideration the most relevant variables that usually explain a given behavior (for example, expected high inflation diminishes the willingness of individuals to hold money balances and they will "chase" the available goods in order to be rid of their money as fast as they can), still we cannot know for sure how individuals will react in the future with any degree of certainty. As stated by Professor Rothbard in the same piece, "The term 'function' is only adequate to the non-motivated and repetitive motions of inorganic material." However, on many occasions, the general trend that may be derived from past events may suffice to our purposes at a given moment, such as, for instance, an expectation that, having inflation, people tend to diminish their money holdings, even if we do not know for certain what the exact relation between a certain level of inflation and the aggregate of money holdings will be.

17. Apparently such pathological and illogical motivations for the "love of money" did not apply to Keynes himself, who earned substantial amounts of money duly rationalized as necessary for him to avoid "salaried drudgery" and to allow him to acquire "beautiful objects" (Dostaler and Maris, 2000: 244).

THREE

Menger, Simmel, and Mises on Money Value

3.1 INTRODUCTION TO SIMMEL AND MISES

Continuing our exploration on the philosophy of money, let's turn now to the ideas of Georg Simmel. Georg Simmel's *Philosophy of Money* is an account of how money evolves. That account can be summarily described as a trend towards more abstract forms of media of exchange. It is extremely important for the argument presented in this chapter to note that Simmel's account of monetary evolution is tightly intertwined with his theory of money value in ways that I expect to make clear in the following pages. Having that in mind, it is relevant to question the importance of monetary thought for Simmel. Simmel's theory of money value as presented in his 1900 *Philosophy of Money* falls between Menger's 1871 *Principles of Economics* and Mises' 1912 *Theory of Money and Credit*. It is the contention of this work that Simmel's ideas about money were influenced by Menger's and in turn influenced Mises'.[1] But Simmel's ideas are also relevant in their own right. One of the topics for which Simmel is most recognized today, perhaps the main theme of his entire intellectual career, is the connection between modern urban societies with individuality. Simmel argues that the idea of individuality that is shared by modern Western societies is only possible in the "Great Society"—the open society with intense and extended division of labor, with commercial relations among strangers, and with the intense urban life that is a common feature now of Western countries. However, that kind of society is only possible with increasingly more sophisticated (abstract, in his terminology) forms of exchanges.

Simmel argues that freedom is always correlated with duty; that is, monetary payment allows individuals more liberty than the obligations of service or payments in kind characteristic of nonmonetary societies. On the other hand, when the use of money is widespread, it induces a rationalization of social activities that tends to be measured in monetary terms, creating a more rational and disciplined society. The paradox for Simmel, however, is only apparent. It is in the growing complexity of life in a monetary society, with its impersonality, rationality, technology, and legality that modern individuality can flourish, unbound to traditional limitations and duties.[2]

Also, for Simmel, it is only in a modern urban setting that it is possible to exercise an individualistic life in its plenitude. The privacy and independence that individuals have in a modern urban environment are only possible in a complex monetary society (Simmel, 1971: 326); and in this way he argues for the relation between individualism and money. Though, it is not just any sort of monetary arrangements that would allow that kind of society to happen, not to mention to prosper. Simmel, therefore, establishes a relation between monetary arrangements, modernity, and individualism and argues that that relation is part of the backbone of the social arrangements most conducive to the exercise of individual freedom and responsibility.

There is no need to emphasize that for Mises also there is a relation between civilized mankind and money (2007: 209). But the similitude between Mises' and Simmel's thoughts on money that I am interested in for this project are the ones related to the subjective source of money value and the evolutionary character of money.

3.1.1 An Identifiable Trend towards Abstraction

It may be claimed that, since a medium of exchange was introduced in society, it has been evolving to more abstract forms. From cattle and other commodities to precious metals in bullion, from bullion to coins, from coins to redeemable banknotes, from redeemable notes to fiat money, from fiat money to checking accounts, and from checking accounts to credit cards; all the evolutions in monetary institutions have been in one direction, from more concrete forms of medium of exchange to more abstract ones. However, this chapter is not the proper place for inquiries about why that is so other than the ones proposed by Simmel; for the purpose of this chapter, it will suffice to understand that this trend exists and the reasons given by Simmel as a possible explanation for that.[3] Briefly, Simmel's argument, in his *The Philosophy of Money*, is that if all goods that can be bought with money constitute one part (of the realm of economics) and money constitutes the other part, then "money (may be) defined as 'abstract' value. As a visible object, money is the substance that embodies abstract economic value" (Simmel, 2001: 120). And as the embodiment of abstract economic value it is only natural for money to become more and more abstract, at the pace that technology and trust in new monetary instruments evolve in society.[4] If the trend regarding money as an institution that spontaneously evolved in human societies is accepted as true by force of the evidence of the repetition of similar paths of monetary evolution, what are the features that can be expected for money in the near future?[5] Can the credit card substitute for banknotes? Are we heading to some innovative monetary system such as the **"BFH" system** discussed by Leland Yeager in his 1997 book *The Fluttering Veil*? Can money become only a unit of exchange, a standard of value, and no longer a medium of exchange? Or will money always be the medium of exchange but perhaps cease to be the unit of exchange and the standard of value? These questions are discussed in the concluding chapter. The reasons for such a discussion are (a) to stress the fact that the trend towards more abstraction in money has not finished its course, and (b) to serve as an introduction for a discussion about the fundamental features of money that may lead to those developments, calling the attention of a contemporary audience to the essential attributes of money which, arguably, were better perceived by Simmel than by anyone else.

3.2 VALUE OF MONEY FOR MENGER

It was mentioned before, Simmel's ideas on money value may be understood as a bridge between Menger's and Mises'. If that is the case, it seems useful to state briefly the theory of money value for Menger.[6] For Menger, the value of monetary merchandise is intrinsically related to its capacity to perform what is perceived to be the purpose of money in society, that is, to facilitate, by indirect exchanges, the division of labor. Therefore, Menger's theory of money value may be deduced from his postulates about that previously discussed in this book.

3.2.1 The Origin of Money for Menger and the Nominalist Dissent

Friedrich Knapp was the first to dissent to Menger's subjectivist and evolutionary explanation for the origin of money value and the introduction of money in society. Knapp starts his argument by accepting the claim that the medium of exchange at a certain moment in history was valued by its weight. However, he argues that it was a long-gone historical event and now, the value of money is given by the state. Knapp states, "In the German language money (geld) always means a formed (morphic) means of payment; but there are morphic means of payment that are pensatory. This however is at a lower stage of development which will be outgrown in the course of history" (2003: 38). For Knapp, money in a "modern sense" has only nominal value, a value that is "declared" by the state:

> For the more exact observer money in the modern sense first comes into being when the morphic means of payment have their validity settled by proclamation and become Chartal. So we get the following answer to the question we have asked. Money always signifies a Chartal means of payment. Every Chartal means of payment we call money. The definition of money is therefore "a Chartal means of payment." (2003: 38)

Menger, however, has an answer for the dissenters' claims: the government can increase the monetary attributes of particular goods, exercising coercion, but it cannot give monetary characteristics to any good.

> But if, in response to the needs of trade, a good receives the sanction of the state as money, the result will be that not only every payment to the state itself but all other payments not explicitly contracted for in other goods can be required or offered, with legally binding effect, in units of that good. . . . Thus, the sanction of the state gives a particular good the attribute of being a universal substitute in exchange, and although the state is not responsible for the existence of the money-character of the good, it is responsible for a significant improvement of its money-character. (1994: 262)

In summary, in Menger we already find a theory of money value in which the value of the monetary merchandise is not defined by law, is not invented by human design, but evolves spontaneously as "each economizing individual" finds engaging in indirect exchange to be in his interest, exchanging his goods for something that he does not need directly, but that he subjectively evaluates as a better instrument to procure the goods that he does need (Menger, 1994: 260). Upon examining the theories of money value of Simmel and Mises, I hope the connection between their contributions and Menger's to the theory of money value will be made clear.

3.3 MISES' THEORY OF MONEY VALUE

For analytical purposes, I think that it is advisable to, unchronologically, describe succinctly Mises' theory of money value before Simmel's. Mises' theory of money value can be described as subjective and catallactic—that is, it is a result of the evaluations made by each individual in the market.

3.3.1 The Subjectivity of Money Value for Mises

First, how does the process by which the individuals determine the value of different goods operate according to Mises? Is this process dependent on money? For Mises, the determination of value happens only in relation to other available goods: it is never a case of absolute value, only of relative value, a process in which the different goods are arranged in order of their significance. Here Mises makes a direct reference to Simmel:

> The process of valuation remains fundamentally the same whether the question is one of transforming labor and flour into bread in the domestic bake house, or of obtaining labor and flour exchange for clothes in the market. . . . For this reason it has been said that every economic act may be regarded as a kind of exchange. * See Simmel, *Philosophie des Geldes*, 2nd Edition, Leipzig, 1907, page 35 (Mises, 1980: 52).

For Mises, the economic activity has no other basis than the value scales utilized by the individuals acting in the market, upon which the exchange ratios of different commodities are established. In stating, "valuation in no way consists in a comparison of two 'quantities of value'," Mises creates the basis to discredit the nominalist/statist conceptions of money value: "If it is impossible to measure subjective use-value, it follows directly that it is impracticable to ascribe 'quantity' to it" (1980: 58).

Although there is no direct quote of Simmel in the following passage, the subjectivism we see in Mises is certainly not derived from Menger: "Modern value theory is based on the fact that it is not the abstract importance of different kinds of needs that determines the scale of values, but the intensity of specific desires" (1980: 59).

To conclude this section about the subjectivity of money value for Mises, the relative, the nonabsolute, character of money value may be stressed, since it is at the center of his criticism of **nominalism**: "What has been said should have made sufficiently plain the unscientific nature of the practice of attributing to money the function of acting as a measure of price or even of value. Subjective value is not measured, it is graded" (1980: 61).

3.3.2 The Sense in which Money has an Objective Value for Mises

It is an idea common to the three authors that are discussed in this chapter that the value of money is a consequence of a subjective act of evaluation; however, they also accept that money has, in a sense, an objective value, as well. This objective value of money is the value that is employed in given transactions. If you pay $12 for a haircut, it can be said that the amount of money involved in that transaction can be objectively determined: "Nowadays exchange is usually carried on by means of money, and since every commodity has therefore a price expressible in money, the exchange value of every commodity can be expressed in terms of money" (Mises, 1980: 61).

For Mises, the role of money as a standard of value, as a tool for economic calculation, is distinct from its value as a medium of exchange: "Because the market enables any commodity to be turned into money and money into any commodity, objective exchange value is expressed in terms of money. Thus money becomes a price index, in Menger's phrase" (1980: 62). And money in this role as an objective "price index" becomes an indispensable intellectual tool: "Money has thus become an aid that the human mind is no longer able to dispense with in making economic calculations" (1980: 62).

As mentioned before, the main attribute of money according to Mises' theory of money value is that the source of money value is subjective. But things are more subtle than that: on the one hand, for Mises (as for Menger and Simmel as well) there is also an objective value, that is, the value that money has in a given transaction:

> If, in accordance with an objective theory of value, the possibility of an objective concept of commodity values is accepted, and exchange is regarded as the reciprocal surrender of equivalent goods, then the conclusion necessarily follows that exchange transactions must be preceded by measurement of the quantity of value contained in each of the objects that are exchanged. And it is then an obvious step to regard money as the measure of value (1980: 51).

But on the other hand, although acknowledging that in each given transaction there is an identifiable money value that is attributed to the merchandise sold or bought, that does not explain at all why that particular agent is willing to surrender that amount of money for the merchandise; therefore, a different starting point is necessary: "But modern value theory has a different starting point. It conceives of value as the significance attributed to individual commodity units by a human being who wishes to consume or otherwise dispose of various commodities to the best advantage" (Mises, 1980: 51).

3.3.3 *Abstract Value of Money in Mises*

Mises starts his discussion about what is abstract in money stating what it has of concreteness, that is, its purchasing power: "The central element in the economic problem of money is the objective exchange value of money, popularly called its purchasing power" (1980: 117).

Next, Mises explains that, contrary to what happens with all other merchandises that have a use-value per se, in the case of money, subjective use-value and subjective exchange value coincide. Mises explains that both are derived from its objective exchange value, for money has no utility other than that arising from the possibility of obtaining other economic goods in exchange for it: "It is impossible to conceive of any function of money, qua money, that can be separated from the fact of its objective exchange value" (1980: 118).

For Mises, before an economic good begins to function as money, it must already possess exchange value based on some reason other than its monetary function. But then Mises explains that money that already functions as such may remain valuable even when the original source of its exchange value has ceased to exist and then he concludes, quoting Simmel, "Its value then is based entirely on its function as common medium of exchange. * See Simmel, *Philosophie des Geldes*, 2nd Edition, Leipzig, 1907, page 115" (Mises, 1980: 132). So, for Mises, whatever the "original source" of the exchange value of money was, money "*qua* money" has its value based "entirely" on its role as the medium of exchange. It is from the subjective evaluation of all economic agents that the value of some merchandise as the instrument for indirect exchanges arises; that merchandise, whose value may have lost all its relation with a previous origin of value, now acquires objectively a value in exchange.

Therefore, for Mises, the value of money is not an absolute value; it has no other source than the subjective evaluations of the economic agents in the market of its utility as a medium for indirect exchanges, and it should be measured in relation to every good and not against all goods and services at the same time, since variations in relative prices in response to changes in the supply of money make the concept of **general price level** meaningless.

As we have seen, for Mises, money: (a) has a value defined by the "intensity of the desires" of each individual in the market and totally severed from its "previous source of value," and (b) has features that had evolved (until 1912) to a level of detachment from commodity money that was difficult to grasp. Now, it is possible to conclude that, for Mises, money had been on the path to increasingly more abstract forms as hypothesized by Simmel.

3.3.4 A Final Note on Mises' Theory of Money's Value in Human Action

Mises wrote his *Theory of Money and Credit* in 1912; in that book Mises built his theory of money, based mainly on Carl Menger's concepts about the evolutionary origin of money in society, its spontaneous nature, and subjective source of value. In that book, a clear statement is found opposing his theory of money to the views that money's purpose in society is to foster state policies and that the value attributed to the medium of exchange by economic agents is determined by the state, or more broadly speaking, that it could be objectively determined at all. So, a relevant question is why Mises judged it necessary to reinstate his theory of money, an effort initiated in 1934 that resulted in the 1940 publication in German of (Nationalökonomie) a predecessor of the English edition of *Human Action* in 1949. And according to Mises, the answer is that:

> My *Nationalőkonomie* finally afforded me the opportunity to present the problems of economic calculation in their full significance. . . . Only in the explanation offered in the third part of my *Nationalőkonomie* did my theory of money achieve completion. Thus I accomplish the project that

> had presented itself to me thirty-five years earlier. I had merged the theory of indirect exchange with that of direct exchange into a coherent system of human action. (Mises, 1978: 112)

Mises' explanation, therefore, is that a discussion about the methodological advancement of integrating a monetary component into the broad framework of economic exchanges (which, until Mises' contributions, was basically a model of barter) was essential to economics as a discipline, but does not alter his statements about money value developed in 1912.

Furthermore, *Human Action* may be understood as a direct continuation of Menger's tradition in general and more specifically of a Mengerian "causal-realistic price theory," in the words of Joseph Salerno (1999: 61). As stated by Menger at the introduction of his *Principles of Economics*:

> I have devoted special attention to the investigation of the causal connections between economic phenomena involving products and the corresponding agents of production, not only for the purpose of establishing a price theory based upon reality and placing all price phenomena (including interest, wages, ground rent, etc.) together under a unified point of view, but also because of the insights we thereby gain into many other economic processes heretofore completely misunderstood (1994: 49).

It is well-established that in Menger's tradition, money is the instrument for indirect exchanges; it is the medium of exchange generally accepted and because of that (historically) it becomes the unit of account and a store of value. The attributes that make something generally preferred by the agents as an instrument for their exchanges are the same as those that will lead them to use the same thing for those other functions. The value of money is derived from its utility for the money holders, as was explained in the initial chapter of this book.

Next, those basic principles are applied in order to explain the business cycles and in order to demystify the idea that changes in the money supply could be neutral. Here the link between money and the theory of prices reveals its relevance. Money as a counterpart in every transaction has an exchange relation with all other present and future goods. As Mises states, "prices are not expressed in money, they are comprised in money." The subjective evaluations of the agents and their individual time preferences are revealed in the market prices for present and future goods, that is, in the price of present goods and in the interest rate(s) that agents are willing to pay or receive in order to anticipate or to postpone the availability of goods and services in any given case.

To conclude, the basic message of Mises in the chapters about money in *Human Action* is that money's purpose in society is to enhance the division of labor by facilitating indirect exchange, and it is from the utility derived from that use that money acquires its purchasing power.

When government manipulates the currency, interfering with its supply, in essence, government is trying to appropriate a share of that value for its own purposes, but in doing so it is decreasing the utility of money for each individual and distorting the signals given to all economic agents by market prices, including the price of goods in time, that is, the interest rate, since money is not neutral as it used to be thought; and that cannot in any way be construed as a negation of Mises' 1912 views presented here.

3.4 SIMMEL'S PHILOSOPHY OF MONEY

3.4.1 The Subjectivity of Any Evaluation

Simmel starts his discussion about the value of money arguing that in nature objects have no value; it is only human beings that classify them by giving them value that is independent of their natural attributes, thereby laying the basis for his claim about the subjectivity of value against any attempt to attribute objective value to the goods (2001: 59).

This evaluation is part of this world, though; it is real, although the criteria utilized are psychological ones, which is why he calls them subjective. He makes clear that value is attributed to the goods as a consequence of their qualities (whether they be real or imaginary). But since there are many different ends for the individuals doing the evaluations, goods with apparently minimal utility for some may be extremely valued by others: "The characteristic feature of value, as it appears in contrast with reality, is usually called its subjectivity. Since one and the same object can have the highest degree of value for one soul and the lowest for another" (Simmel, 2001: 62).

3.4.2 Evaluations are Subjective but Not Capricious

However, it is important to note that, for Simmel, subjective as value may be, it is not devoid of a relation with reality. It is not mere caprice, and the recognition of some good's economic value is nothing more than making "objective" the subjective values of the economic agents (Simmel, 2001: 65). But note the unusual sense in which Simmel utilizes the concept of "objective" value. Objective value is here the actualization of personal preferences in exchange, and not, as a medieval theorist would see it, as something intrinsic to the object: "In the Middle Ages, it was assumed that there was a direct relation between object and money-price, i.e., a relation based upon the independent value of each, which could and should find a 'just' expression" (Simmel, 2001: 126).

Let's concede that Simmel here, in referring to just price, is traveling in murky territory, but still the point that he seems interested in stressing is that value arises from the act of exchange and not that it is intrinsic in the goods exchanged:[7]

> Thus there may be, indeed, a just price for a commodity, but only as the expression of a definite, well-adjusted exchange relationship between this commodity and all others, and not as a consequence of the nature of the commodity itself or the amount of money itself, which stand in no relation to each other and have no reference to the just or the unjust. (Simmel, 2001: 127)

3.4.3 Scarcity and Utility: The Sources of Value

As was previously mentioned, for Simmel, the value of a good is contingent on its scarcity: "The first requirement for an economic object to exist, based upon the disposition of the economic subject, is utility. To this, scarcity must be added as a second determining factor if the object is to acquire a specific value" (Simmel, 2001: 91). "What is really meant is the desire for the object;" however, "real demand" is different from a mere "wish." Therefore, according to Simmel, subjectivity of value does not mean that value is independent of the object. It is true that, for him, evaluation is a sentiment, but value cannot be derived from the evaluator or from the object of evaluation, because it is a relation between the two (Simmel, 2001: 68).

A good example of that is found in his description of why precious metals are proper to be used as money. One component of their value as media of exchange is scarcity, but they cannot be too scarce; it is scarcity above a minimum that makes precious metals appropriate for monetary use because the monetary "attribute" of precious metals depends on them being "generally accepted" as a medium of exchange. If they are too scarce, the quantity necessary for being commonly used will not be available (Simmel, 2001: 72).

3.4.4 Economic Value

There is in Simmel a restatement of Menger's theory of value, although there are no explicit references to it. For Simmel, exchanges are done at objectively equivalent prices, but that does not imply that the subjective evaluations of the traders are the same. Although the agents agree on an objective price to clear their transaction, their marginal preferences are determined subjectively, and there is no way for it to be otherwise: "This emphasis arises from the fact that objects have to be paid for by the patience of waiting, the effort of searching, the exertion of labor, the renunciation of other things in demand. . . . In conceptual terms, price coincides with the economically objective value" (Simmel, 2001: 93).

To say that economic value is objective is tautological for Simmel: "Value is, so to speak, the epigone of price, and the statement that they must be identical is a tautology" (2001: 94). Economic value is, therefore, the monetary representation that embodies the subjective evaluation of the economic agent. Economic value is not an attribute of the object. It is detached from the sentiments of the evaluator and from the causes for his sentiments; it is, in a word, an abstraction, or in Simmel's words, "money is the incarnation and purest expression of the concept of economic value" (2001: 101).

3.4.5 The Intersubjectivity of Money Value

We can say therefore that for Simmel, money value is neither purely objective nor subjective, but it is intersubjective.[8] With this concept, Simmel adds one step to the previous understanding about money. The mere statement that there is subjectivity and objectivity in the value of money would already put Simmel ahead of the neoclassical economists of his time, but the same concept is already present in Menger, as we saw before.[9]

3.4.6 The Stability of Money Value

Simmel needs to develop an explanation for the stability of value of money (as it was perceived in 1900) and he founds that explanation on the intersubjective source of money value. It is not only that money has an objective value, as we can find in any given transaction cleared by money, but also that the value had been (at least for almost a century before 1900) remarkably stable. From the intersubjective source of money value, Simmel derives its perceived stability. For that sort of modern society, urban, cosmopolitan societies of Europe of the fin de siècle , money had been a stable reference for individual exchanges, in the middle of all of the turmoil of war, revolutions, the eruption of nationalisms, et cetera; and yet, money value is not something intrinsic in the **monetary commodity**: "In exchange, value becomes supra-subjective, supra-individual, yet without becoming an objective quality and reality of the things themselves" (Simmel, 2001: 78). But according to Simmel, how does money value become stable? He argues that the money price of every merchandise indicates the degree of exchangeability of that good for all the other goods; to the extent that money expresses the relative value of the different goods, it becomes useful in two ways: first, as an abstract system of measurement (unit of account) and, second, as a medium of exchange. But in order to do that, money must be outside the same realm of every other merchandise: "In order to perform these services, which depend upon its position outside all other goods, money has to be a concrete or specific value itself; and by performing these services it becomes such a value" (Simmel, 2001: 122).

According to Simmel, the stability in money value is acquired by the utility in exchange that is conferred to all economic agents precisely by their preference in using a given monetary merchandise as medium of exchange. Its value is determined fundamentally by the sum of individual preferences, although Simmel recognizes that (at his time of commodity money) the production cost of the monetary merchandise would also be a component of its value: "Its value becomes dependent upon supply and demand; its costs of production exert an influence, however slight, upon its value" (2001: 122).

The monetary merchandise gains an autonomous and stable source of value in exchange, and Simmel points to the fact that economic agents are willing to pay interest to dispose of money as further evidence that it has a value on its own: "The payment of interest is a manifestation of this value which results from the functions of money" (2001: 122). Nowadays, with fiat money, this test gains even more relevance, since economic agents continue to be willing to pay interests in order to dispose of what in essence, aside from its value in exchange, is valueless.

3.4.7 The Essential Quality of Money

For Simmel, money has an essential quality that relates it with everything and at the same time detaches money from everything else:

> Since the basic characteristic of all knowable existence, the interdependence and interaction of everything, also refers to economic value and conveys this principle of life to economic material, the essential quality of money now becomes comprehensible. For the value of things, interpreted as their economic interaction, has its purest expression and embodiment in money. (2001: 119)

3.4.8 Money Evolves

For Simmel, money embodies all intersubjective evaluations of all goods in an amazingly stable fashion. However, money as that abstract, stable, reference of value is not something that came into being in the shape observed at his time. Without committing himself to the controversy about the origin of money, Simmel states the evolutionary characteristic of monetary institutions: "Whatever may be the historical origin of money—and this is far from being clearly established—one fact at least is certain, that money did not suddenly appear in the economy as a finished element corresponding to its purest concept" (2001: 119).

According to Simmel, it is clear that monetary characteristics, that is, the attributes that make some goods seen as media for indirect exchange, evolved from the value of certain goods for other purposes. "Money can have developed only out of previously existing values in such a way that the quality of money, which forms part of every exchangeable object, was realized to a great extent in one particular object; the function of money was at first still exercised, as it were, in intimate association with its previous value significance" (Simmel, 2001: 119).

What remains to be seen is if, for Simmel, the connection between the monetary and the nonmonetary value of money can ever be dissolved. And Simmel answers that question in the affirmative. Money, in its pure essence, has a value that exists apart from any other quality: "It can be seen that money constitutes one party, as it were, and the totality of goods bought by money constitutes the other party; so far as its pure essence is concerned, it must be interpreted simply as money, quite apart from all the secondary qualities that connect it with the contrasting party" (2001: 120).

3.4.9 Money as a Substance with an Abstract Value

For Simmel, as already mentioned, money evolved from the most concrete kinds of goods to increasingly abstract forms. Since the very moment of the introduction of a medium of exchange in society, the use of money has been an evolutionary process. In this process, it is possible to identify, step by step, a tendency towards the dissociation of the direct utility of some goods (the ones that eventually became the monetary merchandise) from their indirect utility: "If money has its origin in barter, it begins to develop only when a single object is exchanged not against another single object but against several others" (Simmel, 2001: 127).

Simmel mentions that one of the main hazards of barter is the problem of divisibility. Patently, that is not the main hazard with bartering—the hazard associated with finding counterparts interested in what you have to offer seems a much more important aggravation (in a post-Coasean time, we can talk about the transaction costs involved in bartering)—still one must not neglect that it is difficult to grasp how many chicken eggs a house is worth if the only medium of exchange you have is an ox. Or in Simmel's words, "The most developed form of divisibility is attained with exchange against money. Money is that divisible object of exchange, the unit of which is commensurable with the value of every indivisible object; thus it facilitates, or even presupposes, the detachment of the abstract value from its particular concrete content" (2001: 128).[10] So money is the instrument to foster indirect exchange, which evolves as required by an increasing complexity of indirect transactions. One of the key steps in its evolution is to become divisible to infinitesimal amounts, which allows the traders to denominate the price of their merchandise in monetary terms with great precision. This role as a unit of account is obviously a step towards abstraction. The concepts of "foot" or "inch" do not refer to an actual foot or inch, and the measurements in the metric system are entirely conventional, that is, arbitrary, and still they are not diminished in their utility for that. Money as an instrument for indirect exchange performs the role that the abstract concepts of meters and centimeters perform in measuring a room, for example. For Simmel, value is an emotion, it is something that can only be felt at a subjective level; still, it is something that the economic agents grade when attributing economic value to the different goods, and in its function either as a unit of account or as a medium of exchange, money is at the same time the gauge and the instrument of the satisfaction of the desire for external goods. The performance of these functions puts money, as an instrument, in a perfectly abstract position, according to Simmel. He says:

> Because money is simply the means to acquire objects, it stands by its very nature at an insurmountable distance from the Ego which craves and enjoys; and in so far as it is the indispensable means between the Ego and the objects, it places the objects, too, at a distance. To be sure, money abolishes the distance again; but by doing so, by transferring the objects to subjective use, it removes them from the objective economic cosmos. (2001: 128)

Finally, Simmel brings to the fore the concept of conventional symbolism. In our social life, there are numerous instances in which certain social relations are given symbols to represent them; and we can infer money is just one more of these cases:

> It is a basic fact of mental life that we symbolize the relations among various elements of our existence by particular objects; these are themselves substantial entities, but their significance for us is only as the visible representatives of a relationship that is more or less closely associated with them. Thus, a wedding ring, but also every letter, every pledge, every official uniform, is a symbol or representative of a moral or intellectual, a legal or political, relationship between men. (Simmel, 2001: 129)

3.4.10 The Greatest Triumph of Money

As has been made clear by now, money epitomizes the pinnacle of abstraction. For Simmel, the capacity of the human mind to create abstractions is perfected with the introduction of a unit of account and a medium of exchange in social relations. As mentioned before, it is not only the fact that money as an abstraction facilitates indirect exchanges, but that it facilitates those exchanges by the reification of many subjective evaluations:

> The projection of mere relations into particular objects is one of the great accomplishments of the mind; when the mind is embodied in objects, these become a vehicle for the mind and endow it with a livelier and more comprehensive activity. The ability to construct such symbolic objects attains its greatest triumph in money. For money repre-

> sents pure interaction in its purest form; it makes comprehensible the most abstract concept; it is an individual thing whose essential significance is to reach beyond individualities. (Simmel, 2001: 129)

3.4.11 *A Judgment of Reality: The Evolution of Money is Towards Abstraction*

At a time when money was still perceived to be a commodity money, when banknotes were rightly or wrongly understood as equivalent to warehouse warrants on deposited precious metals, to say that the value of money, in its pure essence, was totally disconnected from any consideration other than its utility as medium of exchange was really visionary.

Note that Simmel here is not making a value judgment; he is not stating that it is a good thing that the medium of exchange can be purely abstract, he is only stating that in fact it has something of an abstraction: "In this sense money has been defined as abstract value" (2001: 120). For him, the significance of money is that it expresses the relativity of objects of demand through which they become economic values; such significance is not negated by the fact that money also has other qualities that may diminish and obscure its significance, but when that happens, we do not have money in its pure form: "In so far as these qualities are effective, it is not money proper" (Simmel, 2001: 130). The interpretations about Simmel's ideas on money are not uniform, though, Dodd, for instance (on page 330) says that "to all practical intents and purposes, there really is no single, workable solution to the puzzle of perfect money." That is to say that in Simmel's claim that money evolves towards more abstract forms, that "perfect" money would be an instrument of no nonmonetary use (contrariwise to the gold standard in vogue at his time), and that the source of value in money is not objective as claimed by the scholastics nor subjective as claimed by the marginalists, but intersubjective (in the sense that it is formed in society by the interaction of all economic agents, each one with his subjective evaluation), for Dodd, Simmel was searching for something that would be "perfect," "utopic" money. With all due respect, Dodd has no clue about what Simmel is describing in *The Philosophy of Money* ; it has nothing to do with the search for an utopia, it is a down-to-earth, largely successful, and trailblazing effort to understand the social significance of money departing from its function in the kind of modern, cosmopolitan, open, diverse, complex, sophisticated society that the extended division of labor made possible by the extensive use of monetary instruments.

3.4.12 *Was Simmel Talking about Fiat Money?*

Personally, I doubt that Simmel envisaged the replacement of commodity money with fiat money. Certainly, his groundbreaking hypothesis supports the concept that a world monetary order with only fiat money would be perfectly possible, as the world in which we have been living since August 15, 1971 has proved correct. Money can be just the reification of economic value: "As a visible object, money is the substance that embodies abstract economic value" (Simmel, 2001: 120). Money, as representative of abstract value, becomes the autonomous expression of the mutual relations of exchangeability.

3.4.13 Ideal Money

According to Simmel, ideal money is purely **abstract money**, and the argument against abstract money can be summarized by saying that money better performs its monetary role when it does not simply represent "the value of things in pure abstraction" (Simmel, 2001: 165). For instance, those who think that way are those who see in the industrial uses of precious metals something that adds to the monetary value of those metals.

3.4.14 The Displacement of Goals

We have seen so far that for Simmel, money is something that can have no other value on its own than the value that it achieves as an instrument for indirect exchange for the achievement of everything else. In this sense, the desire for money seems to be the desire for the power of having what money can buy, but then, for some, money becomes an object of desire by itself. It becomes the classic example of the displacement of goals. At first, money is valued purely as a means to an end: money is merely of an instrumental value, not an intrinsic value. But over time, some in society begin to value money for its own sake. The universal instrument becomes the universal goal.

3.4.15 Alienation

This theme is not new. Discussions about the manifold forms of alienation engendered by capitalism, including the desire for money, are an infamous feature of Karl Marx's thought. What is new in Simmel is that the alienation induced by money is not inherent in "capitalism" but it is inherent in any modern society with the intense division of labor and indirect exchanges that only sophisticated forms of money can allow:

> The value that objects acquire by their exchangeability, i.e. the metamorphosis through which their value becomes an economic value, emerges more clearly and strongly with the extensive and intensive growth of the economy—a fact that Marx formulates as the elimination of use-value in favor of exchange value in a society based upon commodity production—but this development seems unable to reach its consummation. Only money, in terms of its pure concept, has attained

> this final stage; it is nothing but the pure form of exchangeability. (Simmel, 2001: 130)

For Simmel, valuation is a subjective and individual appraisal, but through social intercourse and exchange, subjective values become objectified into norms and prices. Money is a uniquely objective yet abstract metric whereby all values can be reduced to a common denominator. The abstraction of value inherent in modern money, and not "capitalism," is the reason for this alienation, Simmel argues.

3.5 CONCLUSION OF SIMMEL AND MISES ON MONEY

3.5.1 Money as the Sole Stable Value in Modern Society

At this moment, it seems relevant to question the reason for the development of the concept of *intersubjectivity* in Simmel's theory. It is my hypothesis that he needs an idea of objective value that is more than any value that happens to be agreed upon by the parts in a given transaction; he needs a value that emerges from the sum of all preferences.[11] The reason is that Simmel, who started his inquiry as a subjectivist, sees that without an explanation for the stability of money value, without an account for the extraordinary stability of the objective value of money experienced in Western societies under the gold standard, he would be unable to take even one step further in his reasoning.

This further step is the statement that money is the fixed reference around which we assess the value of all other goods in modern society. Money for Simmel has a stable value in modern society. For him, money is the sole stable reference of value: "Thus it becomes comprehensible that money as abstract value expresses nothing but the relativity of things that constitute value; and, at the same time, that money, as the stable pole, contrasts with the eternal movements, fluctuations and equations of the objects" (Simmel, 2001: 121).

Here, the main characteristics that Simmel finds in money come together: abstraction, intersubjective source of value, and stability. First, the fact that money is abstract, or in other words, that the monetary merchandise at its current value is of no utility other than the one found in exchange, is perceived as essential for its purpose as unit of account and medium of exchange: "If money itself were a specific object, it could never balance every single object or be the bridge between disparate objects" (Simmel, 2001: 125). Next, Simmel argues that one of the most extraordinary and useful characteristics of money is the stability of its value. This stability of value, as it is revealed by the multitude of economic agents in market exchanges, comes from the fact that money is devoid of other actual qualities; again, it comes from the fact that it is an abstraction: "This significance of money shows itself further, in an empirical way, as stability of value, resulting from its interchangeability and lack of specific qualities. This is regarded as one of the outstanding and most useful characteristics of money" (Simmel, 2001: 125).

To conclude this section about the stability of money value, it is perhaps worthwhile to mention what for Simmel is the opposite of that. For Simmel, an increase in the general price level (which in these days of fiat currencies is a direct consequence of the inflation of the medium of exchange in circulation) represents the destruction of the stability of value of the currency: "A general rise in prices would indicate a decrease in the value of money, and when that occurs the stability of money value is destroyed" (2001: 125).

At the time of Simmel, a time of universal (nonnational) commodity money, with episodes of inflation under paper money or debasement far away in history or geography, it is not difficult to imagine why our author does not elaborate on the cases in which that could happen. At his time, money would be the actual gold coins deposited in a bank vault and redeemable at request by cashing a banknote. One may imagine that money would only have its value decreased in the case of a cataclysmic event that would destroy part of money's utility as an instrument for indirect exchanges at a global scale. Today, with national fiat money all around us, that phenomenon is much easier to grasp.

3.5.2 Concluding Summary

This chapter started by positioning Simmel in terms of the history of ideas as a bridge between the theories of money value in Menger and Mises, and also claiming that his contribution for our understanding about money is important in its own right, notably, his idea that money evolves towards more abstract forms as society becomes more complex.

Without discussing why that is so, it was stated that this trend exists and that its course has not yet been completed—in fact, that it is possible that in the future money may lose even its last remaining physical characteristic, that is, the existence of banknotes representative of fiat money. For the sake of clarification, a hypothetical scenario, presented in chapter 11, was drawn with incidental references to the BFH system of payments in which the unit of account is a pure abstraction and divorced from the many media of exchange that were predicted to arise by the authors of that model under such arrangements.

After that, the theories of money value of Menger, Mises, and Simmel were succinctly described, with emphasis on the contributions to Mises' theory of money value that can be traced back to Simmel. In regard to Simmel's theory of money value, first it was argued that Simmel went one step further than Menger in stating that value is not only subjective but also intersubjective, and the causal relation between its intersubjective character and the stability of money value was emphasized. Also, it was argued that that move from a mere subjective to an intersubjective source of money value was a necessary step for Simmel in the development of his argument that there is a trend towards more abstract forms of money as society evolves to become a modern, urban, cosmopolitan society. That is so, because in order for money to be the pure abstract value against which everything else is measured, money needs to be of stable value; and with Simmel already having overcome the medieval conceptions about objective value, it was possible for him to go a step further in search for the source of such a stable value.

The discussion on Simmel's theory of money value continued with a question about whether he ever conceived of a monetary system entirely based on fiat money—one which, at least theoretically, could have a money of stable value. I believe he did not. I think that Simmel never thought outside the framework of a very basic model of the gold standard, a system with Humean characteristics in which the flow of specie would balance prices internationally.

However, that question is beside the point because the fact is that, by following Simmel's reasoning for more abstract forms of monetary arrangements, it is possible to envisage first, an undreamed-of (at his time) system of complete fiat money such as the one that we have had ever since the United States, during the Nixon presidency, defaulted on the Bretton Woods Treaty; and second, that the trend towards even more abstract forms of money has not yet run its course.

The next concluding remark is that Simmel's account of money stability may be understood as valid only under the narrow confines of the gold standard model that he (implicitly) had in mind. It is easy to see why, and it operates more or less according to the following line of reasoning: if the amount of money can be increased in order to alter its perceived scarcity, the utility derived from holding money will change and with that the value given to monetary instruments by economic agents will change as well. In the end, Simmel may be seen as farsighted in perceiving the trend towards abstraction in money, but his assumption about money stability remains valid only under the above-mentioned conditions.

However, those conditions, as mentioned in the brief reference to the BFH system, do not require an orthodox gold standard to be met; it is also possible to meet them under a purely abstract monetary system, one in which the unit of account is no more abstract than the metric system and dissociated from the media of exchange. After all, we may conclude that abstraction and stability in money are not directly related, either positively or negatively.

Having discussed the nature of money and its essential characteristics, it is now time to move to part II of this book and discuss what it is possible to know about monetary phenomena.

NOTES

1. The similitude between Simmel's and Mises' monetary theories in general as well as their theories of knowledge and conceptions about the truth was already pointed out by Oscar Vara Crespo, who in his 2004 paper published by *Procesos de Mercado* also quotes David Laidler and Nicholas Rowe referring to the influence of Menger in Simmel's monetary theory (Crespo, 2004: 224). Nonetheless, in a review of Simmel's book, according to David Frisby (the editor of the English edition), Menger suggests that Simmel's theory of money value does not belong entirely to the marginalist school (Simmel, 2001: 524). With such a suggestion, Menger reserved judgment about Simmel's conclusions, which does not mean that they were not influenced by Menger. Possible reasons for Menger not to endorse wholeheartedly Simmel's ideas are (a) the obvious limitations of Simmel's theoretical knowledge of economics, and, perhaps, (b) that Simmel had among his very few patrons in the exclusive world of German academy at that time none other than Gustav von Schmoller (Simmel, 2001: 513). The claim in this chapter has a more limited scope, though; in this chapter just the conceptions about the theory of money value of Menger, Simmel, and Mises are compared; that is not to say that there were no other important influences in Simmel. For instance, it would be strange for him not be acquainted with the theory of subjective value of the *Gebrauchtwertschule* (although no reference is known). Efforts of the use-value school to find an objective interpretation of use-value are too close to Simmel's use of intersubjectivity to be mere coincidence. Still on the concept of intersubjectivity, the purposes for which Simmel deploys it are clearly related to Eugen Böhm-Bawerk's discussions of the ultimate standard of value—that is, both are in search of a source of value that would not rest solely on the subjective utility perceived by an individual economic agent (but again, there is no indication that Simmel was familiar with Böhm-Bawerk's research).

2. Max Weber too was aware of the changes resulting from an increased monetization of the economy, although he does not attribute to that phenomenon the importance in guiding the development of Western civilization attributed by Simmel. Incidentally, that is just one of the many "neglected affinities" between Weber and Simmel pointed out by James Faught (1985: 167).

3. That is not to say that inquiring about why there is this trend for more abstract forms of money as society becomes more complex is not relevant. For instance, how much of such a trend is a result of state coercion and how much is a consequence of the free interaction of economic agents? These inquiries are crucial to understanding the nature of money and to being able to derive normative conclusions from that. My own thoughts about are presented in the concluding chapter.

4. The monetary institutions of a society do not exist in a vacuum; they change according to the stage of development of the society in which they operate. For instance, it is reasonable to assume that starting during the late Roman Empire and continuing well into the Dark Ages, the quality of money deteriorated just as all other relevant institutions for the maintenance of an urban society with a high level of division of labor in an extended region (almost the totality of the "known world" at the time) did. So it must be acknowledged that the development of monetary institutions follows the development of their respective societies; but that correlation between monetary and other institutions must not be understood as in contradiction to the above-mentioned trend for more abstraction in money. Whenever a society is evolving, its money is evolving in the direction of more abstract forms.

5. An interesting question is whether or not there is an "optimum" abstraction in money; that is, if there is a point beyond which more abstraction may be deleterious for the purposes expected from good money in society. If that is so, what may be seen would be a return to monies with lesser abstraction, not because society is retroceding to a less complex economy, but because the economic agents demanded a more concrete form of money. At first glance, such a hypothesis, advanced here just to illustrate the far-reaching implications of Simmel's thesis, would go against the rationale pro-

posed by Simmel. Such a hypothesis will be discussed in considerable detail in the concluding chapter.

6. Menger's monetary theory is extremely complex and sophisticated. For instance, his insight about the marketability of the **monetary merchandise** (absatzfähigkeit) as its main "monetary" characteristics is sufficient to illustrate that. Specifically this work argues that Simmel and Mises benefited from Menger's concepts on the theory of money value and respectively developed more nuanced theories.

7. Furthermore, we will see an echo of this reasoning later on when Simmel argues for the stability of money value as derived from exchange.

8. The concept of intersubjectivity is used in different disciplines such as philosophy, psychology, and sociology. This concept generally describes a circumstance in which a phenomenon is experienced subjectively by more than one agent, and it is in this sense that it may be applied to Simmel's idea about the origin of money value. The term has been used with other meanings, also; for instance, it is possible to find in Georg Hegel the use of intersubjectivity to define the reciprocal recognition between the self and the other. Between the publication of the 1900/1901 *Logical Investigations* and the 1913 *Ideas Pertaining to a Pure Phenomenology and to a Phenomenological Philosophy* in which the concept of intersubjectivity is fully developed by the German philosopher Edmund Husserl (1859–1938), the father of phenomenology, it is reasonable to suppose that George Simmel came across the concept and decided, with the publication of the 1907 second enlarged edition of his book, to apply it to the problem at hand, that is, how money value can be subjectively defined and at the same time be (relatively) stable. However, as with so many other passages in the book, Simmel does not acknowledge Hegel, Husserl, or anyone else as a source (the book has more than 500 pages and a name index of less than three pages). It is worth mentioning that neither are there references to Husserl in Mises or Hayek, although an author very influenced by the Austrian school of economics, the sociologist Alfred Schutz, applied Husserl's ideas, notably the idea of intersubjectivity, to epistemological problems of economics (Zanotti, 2010: 4).

9. Anderson, in discussing the circularity of the purely subjective theory of money value, argues that Mises in *Theory of Money and Credit* (1981) avoids such circularity by presenting the regressive theorem and bringing in support of that assertion the authority of Wieser and Simmel (Anderson, 1914: 89). That is one of the two passages in Anderson's *The Value of Money* in which Simmel is cited; however, there is no reference in that book to Simmel in regard to the "Theory of Social Value" as an explanation for the value of money. Anderson describes it as follows:

> Finally there is a type of theory, to which the present writer would adhere, which finds a false antithesis in the contrast thus sharply made between society and individual, which holds that the individual is not, in this psychological activity, so much set off from the activities of his fellows, as the contrast would indicate, but rather shares in the give and take of a larger mental life. This larger mental life is completely accounted for when all the individuals are completely accounted for, but it cannot be accounted for by considering the individuals separately. No individual is completely, or primarily, accounted for until his relation to the rest of the group is analyzed. Thinkers who start out with the individuals separately conceived, and then seek to combine them in some arithmetical way, abstract from those organic social relations which constitute the very heart of the phenomenon we are seeking to explain. The parts are in the whole, but the whole is not the sum of the parts. The relationships are not arithmetical, additive, mechanical, but are vital and organic. Men's minds function together, in an organic unity (1914: 18).

Anderson may well have reached his intersubjective explanation for the origin of money's value independently from Simmel; certainly he would be able to do so. Here is not the proper venue to speculate about whether or not that was the case. The important thing to be pointed out here is that there is an equivalence of their theories, with their common features of methodological individualism, negation of an objective explanation for money value, and an acknowledgement of the insufficiency of a simply subjectivist explanation (narrowly understood).

10. Incidentally, here Simmel seems to be talking about coined money and not any GAMOE.

11. The concept of objective value for Simmel means that, in terms of economic evaluations, it is possible to say that there is an objective value when different agents for different reasons come to the same conclusion about the monetary value that some good has for them: "The equation, objectivity = validity for subjects in general, finds its clearest justification in economic value" (Simmel, 2001: 81).

II

Epistemology

FOUR

Comte's Positivist Epistemology and Politics in a Comparative Analysis with the Austrian School of Economics

This chapter's purposes are (a) to show the relation between Auguste Comte's epistemology and its political consequences as described in *Introduction to Positive Philosophy*, referring to other texts when necessary; and (b) to make a comparison between Comte's epistemology and the epistemological assumptions of the Austrian School of Economics. The selection of Auguste Comte's writings to which I will compare the epistemology of the Austrian School of Economics requires an explanation, however. Comte's ideas may be considered *Classical* positivism; his doctrine is the culmination of a process of advocacy for the segregation between moral philosophy and the sciences that resulted from the split of the disciplines from philosophy triggered by Cartesian rationalism. But he is the first, in his epistemology, to expressly state what should be left behind in the path for more advanced knowledge; namely, what he describes as religion and metaphysics. The logical positivism and the radical empiricism of science that followed, starting at the end of the nineteenth century, may be considered the successful result of his advocacy. In this sense, many, if not all, of the intellectual disputes in which Austrian economists have been engaged since the first debate about method that gave birth to the school, it may be argued, have been disputes against doctrines fully inspired by the epistemological assumptions of Classical positivism. Although Bruce Caldwell marks the beginning of the "positivist epoch in economics" as 1938 with the publication of Terence Hutchison's *The Significance and Basic Postulates of Economic Theory* (Caldwell, 1984: 1), as previously mentioned,[1] Mises considers the claims of the historicists as equivalent to Comte's goal to create a "social physics;" if the "positivist epoch in economics" is understood as the moment that Comte's doctrine became influential in economics, it actually started at the time that John Stuart Mill incorporated Comte's core epistemological ideas into his thought. In this sense, Menger's critique of historicism and the birth of the Austrian School of Economics may be considered already a reaction to the positivist influence on economics at that time. But Caldwell is more precise than that in his definition of the "positivist epoch in economics." For him Hutchison's 1938 attempt to define scientific criteria for economics by establishing the threshold that propositions should be "at a minimum, conceivably testable" (Caldwell, 1984: 4) anticipated the trend in economics for empiricism and "mathematization" that would reject all aprioristic theorization as being at most tautological; or as Hutchison quoted Huxley, Haddon, and Carr-Saunders "The essence of science is the appeal to fact" (Hutchison, 1960: 11). It is not that Hutchison rejects totally a priori reasoning or pure theory in economics, such as, for instance, a "geometrical principle," but he just recognizes in them usefulness to organize the empirical evidence, nothing else. Notably, Hutchison was acquainted with the works of Menger, Mises, and Hayek, all of whom are referred to in the book (in a way, he may well be addressing them in claiming that his work aims to help economics to cease to be a "pseudoscience"). It is not that he did not know their arguments; in fact, he rejected them. But according to Caldwell, Hutchison simply anticipated what would come next—he was not the cause of the positivist entrance in economic methodology. In his comments on that, Caldwell proposes a pertinent question: "What forces were responsible for this development?" (Caldwell, 1984: 4). My answer to that question would be that the positivist epistemology of Comte became the implicit assumption of mainstream economics, as will be discussed in this chapter.

4.1 INTRODUCTION

Any political system, regardless of whether it is a theoretical one or an actual one, has some ethical foundation. The relation between some political institutions and their ethical foundations can be more or less precise and explicit or vague and disguised, but it can always be traced.

It may be understood that the ways in which political societies are organized or conceived cannot be analyzed without a previous knowledge of what notions of the good are shared by their political agents or thinkers. That is so, because it is the body of ethical values accepted by political agents and political scientists that would direct the goals to be reached with the political institutions created or envisaged.

The notions of the good (the ethical values), in their turn, can only be established over some concept of what reality is, regarding the inanimate world, living things, human nature, and the history of that society specifically. The different (metaphysical) concepts of human nature are key factors for the development of any account about what is proper for man in general or for the subjects of some political community.

In turn, the idea about how human beings acquire knowledge (epistemology) is an important part of any conception of human nature; it is an important part of any idea about what human beings are.

Comte's ideas about how human beings acquire knowledge generated a conception of what human nature is, that is, a conception of what actually the human condition is and potentially what it could be (in this chapter follows Comte's generalization to humanity as a whole of what he perceived as the historical stage of Western civilization).

Comte's conception of human nature is a key factor in understanding his ideas about the good. Good for Comte, regarding life in society, education of youth, and classification of sciences, is what is necessary to realize the intellectual potential of mankind.[2]

The contrast between Comte's views and views about human individuals and human societies advocated by the Austrian School of Economics cannot be emphasized more than by pointing out the difference between the adoption of the methodology of natural sciences propounded by the positivists for their new science of "social physics" and the one proposed by Hayek for social sciences:

> We can do no better when describing this difference between the approach of the natural and that of the social sciences than to call the former "objective" and the latter "subjective." (Hayek, 1979: 43)

Another important methodological difference between the proponents of a positive social science, Comte's positivist followers among them, and the Austrian School of Economics is that the former tend to adopt a methodological collectivism, treating wholes (like an industry, a social class, or a country) "as definitely given objects about which we can discover laws by observing their behavior as wholes" (Hayek, 1979: 93), while the latter with its specific subjectivist approach adopts what one may call a methodological individualism, searching for knowledge about the individual attitudes of the forming elements in those groups.

The consequences of this fundamental epistemological distinction go far beyond methodological disputes among academics. As stated by Antony Mueller, "Comte's positivism is best described as an ideology of social engineering" (2002: 1). The argument presented here is that the rationale for this ideology may be found in his epistemology. On the other hand, the Austrian School of Economics, departing from a radically different epistemological approach to social science, leads to a completely different normative conclusion.

Therefore, with this chapter, in presenting the logical relation between Comte's positivist epistemology and positivist political institutions and drawing a comparative analysis between the epistemology and politics of Comte's positivism and that of the Austrian School of Economics, I hope to demonstrate the consequences of those methodological (epistemological) assumptions to the economic policy prescribed by the practitioners who adopt them.[3]

4.2 POSITIVISM AS A SCHOOL OF THOUGHT

4.2.1 Positivism and its Origins

Western philosophy was created in ancient Greece. And from more mythical and irrational explanations about life and reality, soon, at the time of pre-Socratic thinkers, Greek philosophy was on the path to a naturalistic and rational interpretation of reality. The philosophy of Plato and Aristotle are to this day the foundation of a rational enquiry about nature, knowledge, ethics, politics, and aesthetics. Their philosophy, with some additions provided by the Stoics, as interpreted by Saint Augustine and Saint Thomas Aquinas and integrated with Christian teachings, became the central tenets of Christian doctrine and Western thought. In all Western Europe, whether countries were influenced by the Reformation or not, Scholastic thought was, in fact, almost the entire corpus of intellectual activity. However, because scholasticism was associated with religious beliefs, with the activities of the religious orders, at the time of the Enlightenment it became tainted by the critics of religious intolerance, abuses of political power in the name of religion, and the imposed limitations to the advancement of scientific knowledge by religious dogma.

It comes as no surprise that as early as Sir Francis Bacon and most notably at the end of the eighteenth century, some intellectuals were willing to distance themselves from Scholastic thought, moving in the direction of more "scientific," "rational" interpretations of reality.

Hayek specifically identifies the source of modern positivism (and modern socialism as well) at the École Polytechnique in Paris. It is in the enthusiasm in France for natural sciences—enthusiasm for its great achievements and its great scientists—he argues, that is the source of the movement to "free (science) from all metaphysical concepts" (Hayek, 1979: p. 187) may be found.

4.3 HENRI DE SAINT-SIMON AND AUGUSTE COMTE

However, it was upon the count Henri de Saint-Simon, a man only informally associated with the École, and, later on, his disciple Auguste Comte that the responsibility "to interpret to the world the significance of scientific progress for the study of society" was bestowed (Hayek, 1979: 242). Through a series of publications, Saint-Simon started to advocate that the organization of society ought to be directed by technological considerations in favor of industrial production. Such dirigisme soon made him depart from liberalism. The "Industrialists" proposed a new political system, with new political bodies such as the *chambre d'invention*, the *chambre d'examination*, and the *chambre d'exécution* (Hayek, 1979: 242). Their stated purpose was to replace the existing political institutions, with their "arbitrariness, incapacity and intrigue" by a system in which "the decisions must be the result of scientific demonstrations totally independent of human will." As quoted by Hayek, Auguste Comte's convictions were that the political reorganization of society could be achieved only after a new intellectual foundation had been laid down through a complete reorganization of all knowledge; and here enters his positivist epistemology (Hayek, 1979: 323).

Before going forward and starting our analysis of positivist epistemology, some explanation seems to be necessary: positivism as a school of thought does not end with Saint-Simon and Comte, far from it. For instance, it has an independently developed Anglo-Saxon branch, where Jeremy Bentham was an exponent, and it left deep marks in all social sciences. However, it can be argued that in economics and jurisprudence it left the most profound marks, since the neoclassical synthesis in economics and legal positivism are still the prevalent schools in those fields even today. Someone, for instance, coming from a continental tradition of law, where legislation is the central piece of the legal system, would think that the Anglo-Saxon countries, with their legal systems supposedly centered on court rulings, would be immune to legal positivism. This person, however, would be surprised. Legal positivism has been part of the jurisprudence in English-speaking countries for as long as it has been on the continent and in the same way, wielding influence over legal thinking. That is why it is so important to understand their philosophical foundations.

4.4 POSITIVE EPISTEMOLOGY

The central tenet of Auguste Comte's philosophy was his idea about the laws governing how human beings acquire knowledge—for the purposes of this paper, what is referred to as his *epistemology*.

In "*Introduction to Positive Philosophy*" (here abbreviated *IPP*), Auguste Comte describes what he identifies as a "great fundamental law" about the development of human intelligence. According to him, the human mind is subject to this law necessarily and invariably, and this law can be demonstrated both theoretically and by historical verification (Comte, 1988: 1).

4.4.1 The Theory of the Three States

The purpose of this section is to offer a brief explanation of Comte's ideas on the development of man's mind. What is the law governing the development of man's mind? In Comte's words:

> This law consists in the fact that each of our principal conceptions, each branch of our knowledge, passes in succession through three different theoretical states: the theological or fictitious state, the metaphysical or abstract state, and the scientific or positive state. In other words, the human mind—by its very nature—makes use successively in each of its researches of three methods of philosophizing whose characters are essentially different and even radically opposed to each other. (Comte, 1988: 1)

For the epistemology of Comte's philosophical system—*Positivism*—there are three kinds of "general systems of conceptions on the aggregate of phenomena . . . which are mutually exclusive of each other" (Comte, 1988: 2).

According to Comte, the human mind "necessarily" starts to understand the world by a theological perspective that evolves into an abstract perspective and finally reaches its "fixed and definitive state," that is, the positive one. Comte describes the three states as follows:

> In the theological state, the human mind directs its researches mainly toward the inner nature of beings, and toward the first and final causes of the phenomena that it observes. . . . It . . . represents these phenomena as being produced by the direct and continuous action of more of less numerous supernatural agents.
>
> In the metaphysical state . . . the supernatural agents are replaced by abstract forces, real entities or personified abstractions, inherent in the different beings of the world. These entities are looked upon as capable of giving rise by themselves to all the phenomena observed.
>
> Finally, in the positive state, the human mind, recognizing the impossibility of obtaining absolute truth, gives up the search after the origin and hidden causes of the universe and knowledge of the final causes of the phenomena. It endeavors now only to discover, by a well-combined use of reasoning and observation, the actual laws of phenomena—that is to say, their invariable relations of succession and likeness. (Comte, 1988: 2).

He describes what he perceives as a general pattern in the way humans acquire and develop knowledge, both as individuals and as societies (*races* in his terminology); and as it has already been mentioned, he thinks that this statement is demonstrable both theoretically and through historical evidence.

To support this statement a passage from *IPP* may be quoted:

> The starting point being necessarily the same in the education of the individual as in that of the race, the various principal phases of the former must reproduce the fundamental epochs of the latter. . . . But in addition to the proofs of the truth of this law furnished by direct observation of the race or the individual, I must, above all, mention in this brief summary the theoretical considerations that show its necessity. (Comte, 1988: 4)

Generally speaking, his law governing the acquisition of knowledge by man describes an evolution in the human perception about the universe, abandoning the supernatural explanations gradually to "abstract forces" and finally "by a well-combined use of reasoning and observation, (to) the actual laws of phenomena" (Comte, 1988: p. 2).

The understanding of what "abstract forces" means, which in Comte's conception are gradually abandoned, is of essential importance to any account of what positivist politics is, as we shall see later. In *Positive Philosophy of Auguste Comte*, book VI, chapter I, "The Metaphysics Policy," he presents the most important principle of metaphysics politics, that is the most important "abstract force": the "Right of Free Inquiry," which brings with it as an immediate consequence the liberty of the press or the freedom to any other mode of expression; and this constitutes, in his words, "an obstacle to reorganization" of society. The second "dogma" is the dogma of "Equality," also blamed as "an obstacle to reorganization" of society (Comte, 1974: 408, 411).

For Comte, liberty and equality, to the extent that they cannot be scientifically defined and observed empirically, they are no more than "dogmas," mere examples of the abstract forces typical of the metaphysical stage of human intellectual development.

4.4.2 What We Could Derive from this Theory in Terms of What is Good for Men and What Ought to be Done in Terms of Political Organization

This section serves the purpose of exposing the argument of what is perceived as a relation between positivist epistemology and despotism, and this relation can only be established by understanding the path through metaphysics and ethics made by the Positivists.

As a premise to this inquiry, some concept definition is advisable for the sake of clarification. "Metaphysics," for the purpose of this paper, is understood as the branch of philosophy that deals with the nature of existence:

> There is a science which investigates being as being and the attributes which belong to this in virtue of its own nature. Now this is not the same as any of the so-called special sciences; for none of these other treats universally of being as being. They cut off a part of being and investigate the attribute of this part; this is what the mathematical sciences for instance do. Now since we are seeking the first principles and

> the highest causes, clearly there must be some thing to which these belong in virtue of its own nature. (Aristotle, 1941a/1992: book IV, chapter 1, 1003a25)

"Metaphysics" for Comte means a different thing, as we can see from the words of John Stuart Mill:

> We use the words Theological, Metaphysical and Positive, because they are chosen by M. Comte . . . In all languages, but especially in English, they excite ideas other than those intended . . . Metaphysical suggests, and suggested even to M. Comte, much that in no way deserves to be included in his denunciation. (Mill, 2002: 10)

Comte himself wrote about the concept of "metaphysics":

> After the Greek division of philosophy into natural and moral, the metaphysical spirit assumed two forms, which, in harmony with the distinction, became gradually antagonistic. The first, of which Plato must be considered the chief organ, most resembled the theological philosophy, which at first tended rather to modify than to destroy. The second, whose type was Aristotle, approached much nearer to the positive philosophy, and tended to disengage the human understanding from all theological guardianship. The one was critical only to the side of polytheism, and superintended the organization of monotheism, under which it was itself absorbed by the theological spirit, and transmuted into religious philosophy: whereas, the other, occupied at first with the study of the external world, could not but be altogether critical, from its anti-theological tendency, in combination with its total lack of power to produce any organization whatever. It was under the direction of this last that the great revolutionary movement went on. Discarded by Platonism, while the best minds were engaged in the organization of the Catholic system, the Aristotelian spirit; which had been perpetually extending its inorganic domain, began to assume the ascendancy in philosophy, by its sway, as soon as the need of a rational philosophy began to prevail. (Comte, 1855/1974: 645)

Here Comte presents the metaphysical stage of development of Western civilization as mingled with the influence of the Scholastics (referred to here by Comte as the best minds engaged in organizing the Catholic system in the Aristotelian spirit) in philosophical thought. Here it is possible to see clearly at what Comte is aiming. The "Aristotelian spirit" is the perfectionist ethics of human flourishing as the ultimate end of the polity, as interpreted by Saint Thomas Aquinas and incorporated into the Christian tradition, both Catholic and Protestant, as natural law.[4]

This is the main issue here: all the limits imposed on the exercise of political will by the idea of natural law/natural rights are consequently put aside by the Positivists.

It may be understood that Comte's description about human nature, his metaphysics in the sense referred to in this chapter, is based on his suppositions about how humans acquire knowledge—for Comte, man is a creature that by his own nature acquires and develops knowledge according to the law envisaged by him—and from this understanding of human nature he or his followers could derive the proper way in which a society of such creatures should be organized.

Also, for Comte, if man is what he is because he is subordinated to the positivist epistemology, then what is proper to man (the highest value in his ethics) is what could lead him to that positive state. Moreover, he presents this in a deterministic fashion: it is inevitable, because "the fundamental character of the positive philosophy is to consider all phenomena as subject to invariable natural laws" (Comte, 1988: 8), including social events, which we can conclude from the following passage from *IPP*: "Now that the human mind has founded celestial physics, terrestrial physics (mechanical and chemical), and organic physics (vegetable and animal), it only remains to complete the system of observational sciences by the foundation of social physics" (1988:13).

Comte's deterministic thought also shows here: "The question being once reduced to these simple terms, the issue cannot remain doubtful, because it is evident for all kinds of reasons, some of the principal of which have been indicated in this chapter, that the positive philosophy is alone destined to prevail in the ordinary course of things" (1988: 29).

It is easy to understand how he reaches his political conclusions once we know of his acceptance of those ideas about what good is and the inevitability of certain events. If someone knows what is right and, furthermore, if it is inevitable, why not force it on others? That is in my understanding the moral justification of positive politics.

4.5 POSITIVE POLITICS

What can we identify in Comte's own account about his political views? First, it is necessary to remember what his goal is, explicated here: "Having by this means acquired the character of universality which as yet it lacks, the positive philosophy, with all its natural superiority, will be able to displace entirely the theological and metaphysical philosophies" (1988: 13).

For Comte, the universality desired for his philosophy is not only an intellectual enterprise, aiming at the discovery of the truth; it is also a project of social engineering, and his intention is to provide the philosophical basis for redesigning human society, that is, a political goal. In his own words:

> There is no need to prove to readers of this work that the world is governed and overturned by ideas, or, in other words, that the whole social mechanism rests finally on opinions. They know, above all, that the great political and moral crisis of existing societies is due at bottom to intellectual anarchy. Our gravest evil consists, indeed, in this pro-

> found divergence that now exists among all minds, with regard to all the fundamental maxims whose fixity is the first condition of a true social order. As long as individual minds are not unanimously agreed upon a certain number of general ideas capable of forming a common social doctrine, we cannot disguise the fact that the nations will necessarily remain in an essentially revolutionary state. (1988: 28)

4.5.1 The Ideal Polity for Comte is an Autocratic Regime

This section presents Comte's ideas on the possibility and desirability of a scientific government. The autocratic goals of Comte's actions could not be made explicit in a better way, and his political goals were nothing less than the "social reorganization that must terminate the crisis in which the most civilized nations have found themselves for so long" (Comte, 1988: 28), based on the positive philosophy, because "if this general agreement upon first principles can once be obtained, the appropriate institutions will necessarily follow" (1988: 29).

The ultimate consequences of his ideas can be better presented through some quotations from the *Positivist Catechism*:

> Is it true my daughter, that the Positivism does not recognize to anybody other right instead the right to perform his duties. . . . The notion of right must disappear from the political domain, as the notion of cause must disappear from the philosophical domain.
>
> The Positivism does not admit nothing else than the duties of everyone with everyone; because its social point of view could not carry a notion of rights, constantly founded on the individuality.
>
> Even though the positivist religion accepts the idea of free human interaction, the positivist religion imposes on everyone the duty of never changing without grave reasons of inferiors and superiors. The very capricious change of customary suppliers is regrettable, because it tends to disturb the operation of the economy which presupposes some fixed demand. (Comte, 1852/1978: 279)

These quotations show some glimpses of Comte's social ideals—his would be a society more rigid than the one envisaged by the Roman Emperor Diocletian; for Comte, the ideal political regime is a kind of industrial feudalism.

In *The Positive Philosophy of Auguste Comte* we see some features of the social order sought out by Comte:

> We have thus to discard altogether the notion of private functions, as belonging to a transitory system, and to consider all as alike social, after having put out of the question whatever functions have to be eliminated; that is, the theological and metaphysical offices which will have expired. The modern economy thus presenting only homogene-

> ous elements, it becomes possible to form a conception of the classification that is to ensue. . . . While on the one hand there will be a universal personal sense of social value, there will be on the other hand an admission of the necessity of systematic discipline; incompatible with a private career. . . . The co-ordinating principle must be the same that I have applied in establishing the hierarchy of the sciences, that of the degree of generality and simplicity of the subject, according to the nature of the phenomena. . . . This was the principle of organization in old societies; and we see vestiges of it yet in the military organization. . . . The office of positive philosophy in this case is to substantiate the common notion of social subordination by connecting it with the principle which forms all hierarchies. The highest rank is held, according to that principle, by the speculative class. (Comte, 1855/1974: 775)

Comte's idea of social coordination is a chain of command; he even argues, "We see vestiges of it yet in the military organization." In his ideal model of political arrangements, there is no room available for free interaction among the members of society.

Another evidence of his disregard for the institutions of an open society is the entirely nominal feature that private property rights have in his ideal model of society. Under Comte's envisaged institutional arrangements, private property rights are not a reality, but exist in name only. Granted, some individuals would hold private properties, but their use would be limited to what could produce "social value" and under "systematic discipline," something that, as it happens, is also "incompatible with private career" (Comte, 1855/1974: 775).

4.5.2 The Right to Obey

The acceptance or not of rights other than the right to obey is a good watershed which can be highlighted in order to show the contrast between natural law and the idea of natural rights on one side and positivism on the other side.

In legal theory there are basically two sources of law: either law is something existing in nature, something inherent to the human condition that should only be discovered and enforced by the coercive apparatus of human societies, or law is something created by convention, brought into existence by the legislative act itself.

If the former idea is accepted, then human beings have rights given to themselves by their nature, justice being one of the abstract forces (a phenomenon not accessible to the human mind) despised by Comte as an example of the metaphysical stage of human intellectual development; and morality and law being impossible to analyze separately.

On the other hand, if the latter idea is accepted, the sole source of right becomes statute, the positive law; law is a convention to be established by society using the positive philosophy, the scientific method.

The total rejection of the natural law concept by positivism can be understood and traced to Comte's thought as noted by Jules Coleman and Brian Leiter in *Legal Positivism* in the *Companion to Philosophy of Law and Legal Theory*:

> All positivists share two central beliefs: first, that what counts as law in any particular society is fundamentally a matter of social fact or convention ("the social thesis"); second, that there is no necessary connection between law and morality ("the separability thesis"). . . . Legal positivists also share with all other philosophers who claim the "positivist" label (in philosophy of science, epistemology, and elsewhere) a commitment to the idea that the phenomena comprising the domain at issue (for example, law, science) must be accessible to the human mind. This admittedly vague commitment does little to convey the richness of positivism as a general philosophical position, but it serves to indicate that the label, though acquiring a very special meaning in legal philosophy, is not utterly discontinuous with its use elsewhere in the philosophical tradition. (Patterson, 2000: 241)

To positivism, any idea about the defense of traditional rights, like property rights, or spontaneous market forces (based on the free interaction of individuals, each of them with his or her own property rights and goals) as instruments to organize society should be considered as examples of metaphysical philosophy, a recourse to "abstract forces," and therefore alien to positive science due to the impossibility of scientific investigation.

Comte's ideas about property rights specifically can be understood from the following passage from *The Positive Philosophy of Auguste Comte*: "The new philosophical action would either obviate or repress all the dangers which attend the institution of property, and correct popular tendencies by a wise analysis of social difficulties, and a salutary conversion of questions of right into questions of duty" (1855/1974: 780).

For Comte, the organization of the society should be done by superior individuals, for the good of the whole, who incidentally do not have any right besides the right to perform their duties, as previously mentioned and as we see here in *The Positive Philosophy of Auguste Comte*:

> When the gradation is once established, it will be preserved from question and confusion, not only by the clearness of its principle, but by the consciousness in each order that its own subordination to the one above is the condition of its superiority to those below it; and the lowest of all is not without its own special privileges . . . and thus the lowest classes really are privileged in that freedom from care, and that thoughtlessness, which would be a serious fault in the higher classes, but are natural to them. (1855/1974: 777)

4.5.3 The Brazilian Case: An Illustration of the Political Consequences of Positivist Philosophy

Positivism has strongly influenced Latin America in general and Brazil in particular. The motto of the Brazilian national flag, "order and progress," comes from Comte's writings. The Brazilian republic was established at the end of the nineteenth century by politicians and military men educated in the positivist doctrine; even Comte's "religion of humanity" took hold in Brazil at the time of the establishment of the republic.[5] The consequences of that education, in a mild form, may be perceived in the myth cherished to this day by Brazilian elites that governmental action may be "scientifically" oriented, which justifies all sorts of interventionist policies, and in a more crude form, by the episodes of dictatorship and chronic disregard in Brazil for individual rights, including private property rights.[6]

Regarding the "mild" political consequences of positivism, it is relevant to quote Antony Mueller:

> Within the positivist system (of thought), scientism and interventionism go hand in hand. The presumed rationality of interventionism rests on the premise of knowing the specific outcome of an economic policy measure in advance. Consequently, when things turn out other than expected—and they always do—more intervention and control is warranted. The result is governments that are overwhelmed by their pretense and humiliated by their failures. (Mueller, 2002: 3)

4.5.4 Positivist Ideology at the Foundation of Dictatorship in Brazil

Regarding the more "crude" consequences, two episodes from Brazilian history are presented in this chapter as historical examples that ideas do have consequences. If you believe that there are no individual rights that should be recognized by the politically organized community (the state), if you believe that any idea of spontaneous order, like markets and traditions, are based on an already superseded stage of human development, then you are prepared to accept brute force as the only source of political power, to accept that the military are the guardians of order, and that the ideal form of government is a "scientific dictatorship."

The Brazilian historian, Décio Freitas, allegedly found original sources about an American journalist called A. Bierce, who was the Buenos Aires correspondent of the *New York Tribune,* and wrote a cable in 1892, narrating our first example:

> Everything indicates that Rio Grande do Sul, the southernmost state of Brazil marches inexorably to the civil war. . . . Although admitting the Republic, Martins and his followers do not accept the Constitution issued in July 14, 1891 by Mr. Castilhos. . . . Being the following the key objections of Mr. Martins and his followers to that constitution: the

> laws are not a prerogative of the legislative . . . and the state governor can be reelected indefinitely. . . . Mr. Castilhos and his followers are feverous sectarian adepts of the French philosopher Auguste Comte's doctrines, who advocate a monocracy and a scientific dictatorship. If his system prevails, Mr. Castilhos shall be described by history as the inventor of an elected dictatorship. (Freitas, 2000: 9)[7]

Another example is that during the last military coup in Brazil in 1964, the army, in order to provide "the restoration of the internal order," changed the constitution, to which they added the following preamble: "The victorious revolution is vested in the Constitutional Power, this power has origin either in popular elections or by revolution. Then, the victorious revolution, as the constitutional power that it is, legitimizes itself" (Institutional Act #1, 1964).

The influence of positivist philosophy in Brazilian political thinking may be understood as a pale example of the influence of positivist ideas in political thinking worldwide. Once one establishes the link between objectivist epistemology, where Comte dismisses "abstract" ideas like liberty, equality, and property and hails the instruments of coercive social coordination on one hand, with the moral obligation of the "superior classes" to provide "order and progress" to society on the other hand, then not only does one establish the path to the "scientific dictatorship," but also a path to legal positivism and the negation of natural rights with all the deleterious consequences to individuals of adopting that doctrine. It is possible to identify in Comte's philosophical position some elitism as well as some determinism; these characteristics helped positivist epistemological ideas to be developed in those above-mentioned political ideas; at the end though, it was the positivist epistemology that supported construction of the positivist authoritarian building.

4.6 THE AUSTRIAN SCHOOL OF ECONOMICS

4.6.1 The Data of Social Sciences has a Subjective Character

The Austrian School of Economics does not reject the idea that there is a natural science related to the physical attributes of men and, in that regard, scientific inquiry is more conducive to applying the methods of natural science. However, social sciences more narrowly defined are moral sciences, and they are concerned with "man's conscious or reflected action" and so in their case, the better method of investigation should follow the character of its object (Hayek, 1952/1979: 42).

In *The Counter-Revolution of Science*, Hayek argues that the behavior that can be expected from individuals is based only on our subjective experience and that no objective test can be performed (Hayek, 1952/

1979: 43). For him, that is the nature of knowledge that it is possible to get from social sciences.

Although economics is more developed than other branches of social sciences, for Hayek, it shares with them its subjective character. He argues that since most economic propositions are statements "about the implications of certain human attitudes toward things and as such necessarily true irrespective of time and place," then what is true about price theory (and economic theory in general) is that "it has nothing to say about the behavior of the price of iron or wool, or things of such and such physical properties, but only about things about which people have certain beliefs and which they want to use in a certain manner" (Hayek, 1952/1979: 56).

Next, Hayek claims that the advance of subjectivism in social science is responsible for a breakthrough in the science of economics that a better understanding about the division of knowledge in society brought about (Hayek, 1952/1979: 57).

4.6.2 The Use of Knowledge in Society

Hayek in his paper "The Use of Knowledge in Society" states that the economic problem is not what the best use of the available means is, but more precisely, to find what the individuals' preferences are and what the available means are. Hayek argues that the information is not available to any individual or group of individuals for them to make a "rational" decision about how to allocate the resources.

According to Hayek:

> The peculiar character of the problem of a rational economic order is determined precisely by the fact that the knowledge of the circumstances of which we must make use never exists in concentrated or integrated form but solely as the dispersed bits of incomplete and frequently contradictory knowledge which all the separate individuals possess (1945: 519).

If only the individuals have the relevant economic information (the one that is subjective, circumstantial, and dispersed in nature and not scientific information that may be found in the hands of experts) not only about their preferences but also about their available means, consequently, the economic problem for Hayek "is rather a problem of how to secure the best use of resources known to any of the members of society, for ends whose relative importance only these individuals know" (1945: 519). So, for Hayek, there is a misconception about what the economic problem of society is and wrong prescriptions about how to solve the problem coming from that misconception. And where does Hayek identify its origin? "This misconception in turn is due to an erroneous transfer to social phenomena of the habits of thought we have developed in dealing with the phenomena of nature" (Hayek, 1945: 520).

The distinction between the epistemological approach of the Austrian School of Economics, which here is represented by Hayek, and the one of the Positivists could not be made clearer. Now, what are the political prescriptions that the Austrian economists derived from their methodological and epistemological assumptions?

4.6.3 The Road to Serfdom

Hayek in his book *The Road to Serfdom,* arguing with those that claim that democracy would not tolerate "capitalism," states, "If 'capitalism' means (here) a competitive system based on free disposal over private property, it is far more important to realize that only within this system democracy is possible" (1944/2007: 73).

Hayek warns, however, that if a society becomes dominated by a "collectivist creed," no democratic regime can survive. But essentially, for Hayek, democracy is only an instrument for the substantial goods provided by a liberal order, that is, the safeguard of internal peace and individual freedom (Hayek, 1944/2007: 73).

4.7 CONCLUSION

If one would like to identify clearly what the fundamental difference between positivism and the Austrian School of Economics is, it is to be found in different views about human nature. For the Positivists, human beings by their own nature, and human societies by a sort of fallacy of composition, have a predetermined path of evolution that leads them to a "scientific" stage of knowledge. And that is a stage in which all "metaphysical" errors, that is, everything that cannot be empirically measured, would be abandoned.

On the other hand, for the Austrian School Economists, human nature has other key features such as the entrepreneurial spirit. Jesús Huerta de Soto says:

> every human being has an innate creative capacity that allows him to appreciate and find the gain opportunities that arise in his environs, and consequently, take action in order to take advantage from them. Entrepreneurship consists, therefore, in the typical human capacity to continually create and find new ends and means. (2004: 48)

And human societies, by the nature of their members, live in constant change, as the only "optimal" stage at which they may aim is one of social creation and coordination. This process of dynamic efficiency, however, "must be framed, i.e., must be submitted to the morals and to the law" (Huerta de Soto, 2004: 57), and the ethical and legal principles most suitable for human beings, considering their nature and the best possible order that they may develop, are the ones consistent with a liberal order. Huerta de Soto states, "The basic problem presented to social conviviality is not, therefore, if society is or is not 'democratically' organized, but, on the contrary, the degree of extension and depth in which systematic coercion is exercised against the liberty for human interaction" (2004: 138).

For the Austrian School of Economics, those who advocate "to master the forces of society in the same manner in which we have learnt to master the forces of nature" are terribly mistaken. Hayek says, "This is not only the path to totalitarianism, but the path to the destruction of our civilization, and a certain way to block future progress" (1944/2007: 73).

That is particularly true in regard to the monetary institutions necessary to enhance the division of labor at the global scale in which we are engaged today. The spontaneous order of a market economy brings coordination to the actions of individual agents by the generation of information that results from their own interaction in response to the incentives given by the market price of goods and services to their actions in pursuit of their interests. The global market that most human beings are part of nowadays is a complex order, far more complex than what can be grasped by any central planning authority or empirically tested by any social scientist. In the world of competing currencies and competing banking jurisdictions where we live today, saying that anyone has access to the relevant information in order to execute a rational monetary policy is simply a bad joke. It is obvious that one can react rationally, with the information one has, to the existing reality; the very existence of the global market we have today is an amazing feat and the biggest testimony ever to the capacity of human beings to coordinate their activities without command if allowed to do so. It is also remarkable that self-interested, short-sighted populists and autocrats, as are the political leaders all around the globe without exception, were able to find it in their interest to keep trade barriers, immigration barriers, capital controls, exchange controls, and tariffs tolerably low; to supply monies that by and large have not often spiraled into inflationary vortexes; to keep maritime lanes more or less open and safe from piracy; and most importantly, to avoid initiating major wars for three generations now. At the conclusion of this chapter on the epistemological differences between Austrian economics and classical positivism, it may be appropriate to offer an interpretation of the Latin phrase *scientia potentia est* (knowledge is power) commonly attributed to Sir Francis Bacon, not as a digression but as an analogy for what to do in regard to money given the limitations of knowledge we have. Although that exact phrase is not found in Bacon's writings, there is the following equivalent expression: "Human knowledge and human power meet in one; for where the cause is not known the effect cannot be produced. Nature to be commanded must be obeyed; and that which in contemplation is as the cause is in operation as the rule" (*Novum Organum*, book 1, aphorism 3). The interpretation I offer is the following: if we want to have the benefits of the natural spontaneous order generated by the free interaction of economic agents, it is necessary to allow liberty for them to interact, so far as we know or at least so far as we may know. Our limitations of knowledge specifically in regard to money are not total—in fact, the accumulated knowledge in monetary matters we have is vast—but it is the realization of these limits that may allow us to act rationally in regard to money, and that is the subject of the next chapter.

NOTES

1. See footnote 11 of chapter 2.

2. However, whether the actualization of that potential is an end in itself or an instrument to other achievements is not even mentioned in this chapter. The fact is that the political system, the educational process, and the classification of the sciences designed by Comte alike are all instrumental to carry mankind to the third stage of human intellectual development, as we shall see in this chapter. This chapter does not discuss the existence of a "feedback" process between the advancement of mankind to the positive stage and the reshaping of society through the implementation of positivist politics.

3. The relation between the method of investigation and what may be deduced from it is true in every field of science, as the options between induction or deduction and methodological individualism or collectivism may illustrate. In the case of economics, as with any other social science, there is a "cry," in the words of Mark Blaug, for not only detached study but evaluation:

> Economics continually touches on questions that are subject to government policy, so that major economic doctrines are not only scientific research programs (SRP) in the sense of Lakatos but also political action programs (PAP). This dual function of economic theories allows for situations in which a particular theory is simultaneously a "degenerating" SRP and a "progressive" PAP, that is, one that offers governments an expanding agenda for policy measures. (1980: 315)

4. Consequently, as Aquinas is considered by many to be the "father" of *Natural Law*, it is no wonder that for the modern legal positivists, "Natural Law" is dismissed as something that is part of Comte's "metaphysical stage."

5. In my hometown of Porto Alegre, capital of the Rio Grande do Sul state, there is one park in the central area that has on three of its corners three buildings built during the first years of the republic in the last decade of the nineteenth century: the law school, the military academy, and the positivist "chapel" respectively. The three of them were, and, in a sense, still are, positivist temples in different ways. Incidentally, the only positivist "church" in the world is in Rio de Janeiro, the former national capital of Brazil.

6. That is not to say that positivism was the only ideological influence in Brazil or that the positivist influence was entirely malign. Brazil is a Catholic country with an important Christian heritage. During the nineteenth century Brazil benefited from classical liberal ideas introduced in the country at the time of the Constitutional Monarchy (which was overthrown by the positivist republicans). Brazil, like any other country on the periphery of Western civilization, has been influenced by all sorts of philosophical and political fashions, not all of them authoritarian. The current constitution from 1988 is remarkable in stating that its bedrock is classical liberal principles

and, with all the real-life problems of a developing country, Brazil has managed to establish fairly decent limitations on government and better protection of individual rights more recently. Still, the history of political movements in Brazil is one in which virtually all political forces both to the left and to the right of the political spectrum are reincarnations of the positivist republican parties of the first republic. Positivist political ideas, perhaps in Brazil more directly than in most other places, are at the foundation for the acceptance of authoritarian and interventionist policies advocated today by Socialists, Social Democrats, and Conservatives, which makes some episodes of Brazilian history good examples of the political implications of positivist philosophy. It is not that Brazil is unique, far from that, it is simply the case that the link is more explicit than, say, in Anglo-Saxon countries where positivist ideas influenced political realities only indirectly.

7. Mr. Freitas, now deceased, has been accused recently of having forged sources for some of his works, and I could not confirm the veracity of this reference; but even if the cable itself is completely false, the facts described in it are not.

FIVE

What is it Possible to Know about Money?

5.1 WHAT IS IT POSSIBLE TO KNOW ABOUT MONEY?

This chapter presents a particular view on the epistemology of money. The main argument here is that the capacity to know about monetary phenomena in society is very limited. This skepticism is reflected in doubts about the ability to know what the quantity of money existing in society is at any given time, doubts about the ability to know the quantity of money desired by money holders or the quantity of goods available to be bought with the existing money, doubts about the grades and rates at which that these quantities may change over time, et cetera.

The view presented in this paper is even skeptical about the capacity to use the concept of "level of prices" in a meaningful way. This skepticism is based on a challenge to the positivist methodology and epistemological assumptions of mainstream economics (the neoclassical synthesis of Keynesian macroeconomics with neoclassical microeconomics) in general and to the general equilibrium theory at its core.

The prevailing monetary arrangements currently in place worldwide are understood as just one more dimension of interventionist and socialist policies. As stated by Huerta de Soto (2001: 36), "The theory of interventionism in general, and of the business cycles in particular are perfectly encompassed in the definition of socialism."

Those policies are underpinned by the descriptions of economic reality and by an understanding about what the economic problem is according to mainstream economics, that is, the same general equilibrium theory. So the same epistemological criticism offered to the neoclassical synthesis by Austrian economics is also valid as a criticism to interventionist and socialist policies resulting, at the end of the continuum, in the theorem of the impossibility of the socialist economic calculus.

Therefore, there are many relations between this skepticism and the theorem of the impossibility of the socialist economic calculus. To the extent that one of the theorem's steps is that, methodologically, the possibility of economic calculus under socialism is based on the equilibrium theory of neoclassic economics, this skepticism shares with the theorem one of its assumptions. To the extent that the theorem itself becomes a tool to assess the validity of epistemological assumptions of economic theory, this skepticism is a result of the theorem's application.

This skepticism is derived fundamentally from Hayek's insights about the limitation of knowledge in society, supported by references to Menger's concept of money as the Generally Accepted Medium Of Exchange—the GAMOE (Menger, 1994: 280) definition, that is adopted throughout this work. In this chapter it is exemplified by mentioning the (greatly unappreciated at the time) complexity of British financial markets in the second half of the nineteenth century, as described by Walter Bagehot.

It must be stressed, however, that this skepticism should not be confounded with nihilism, or as an ode to the uselessness of researching and reasoning about monetary phenomena; quite the opposite! The claim presented here is that in order to properly understand money and what can and cannot be done to and with money, it is imperative to recognize the limitations of knowledge about it.[1] Once these limitations of knowledge are recognized as valid, then the paradigm of the Austrian School of Economics becomes by far the most credible instrument to understand monetary phenomena.

5.2 THE POSITIVIST METHODOLOGY AND EPISTEMOLOGICAL ASSUMPTION OF MAINSTREAM ECONOMICS

In works already quoted in this book, Boettke and Caldwell agree that mainstream economists had chosen by around the late 1930s to adopt a methodology that ended distancing economics from the reality that it supposedly represents. In the words of Boettke:

> Formalistic precision was (and is) followed and the cost was (and is) a loss of relevance of the discipline of economics for the messy world in which we live. Even on the empirical front, fine estimation techniques were developed but the richness of the empirical world remains hidden from scientific view. Theoretically and empirically, I assert, the technology chosen for the task at hand led (ex post) to an intellectual dead-end. (1996: 24)

After the war, in the early 1950s, according to Caldwell, ultra-empiricism had subdued and: "the logical positivist prescription that all scientific statements require independent testing had been replaced by the logical empirical view that theories may contain untestable statements that gain indirect support when the theory as a whole is tested" (1984: 95). That was the state of the discussions on method in economics at the time of Milton Friedman's 1953 "The Methodology of Positive Economics." In that influential paper he summarizes his ideas about what economics is as follows:

> Positive economics is in principle independent of any particular ethical position or normative judgments. As Keynes says, it deals with 'what is,' not with 'what ought to be.' Its task is to provide a system of generalizations that can be used to make correct predictions about the consequences of any change in circumstances. Its performance is to be judged by the precision, scope, and conformity with experience of the predictions it yields. In short, positive economics is, or can be, an 'objective' science, in precisely the same sense as any of the physical sciences. (Friedman, 1953: 4)

For Friedman, any "positive science" is composed by a "language" that is no more than a "set of tautologies," without substance, and a "body of substantive hypothesis" whose evaluation should be done according to its "predictive power" (Friedman, 1953: 8). Friedman is explicit in stating that "assumptions" are never realistic and the relevant question to ask about them is if they are "sufficiently good approximations for the purpose in hand," or, in his widely quoted passage,

> Truly important and significant hypotheses will be found to have "assumptions" that are wildly inaccurate descriptive representations of reality, and, in general, the more significant the theory, the more unrealistic the assumptions. (1953: 14)

The problem for Boettke is that economists, in accepting Friedman's methodology,[2] have forgotten the limitations of mathematic modeling: it does not guarantee realism of assumption, reasoning, or conclusion; it only guarantees the logic of the formulation. Such shift to instrumentalism, he explains, was inspired by a "positivistic image of science" and once the realism of the assumptions was no longer required, economics lost its rudder, or in his words:

> The only way to operationalize positivism in economics was to shift to "as-if"ism and indirect testability. But once permission was granted to abandon all concern with realism of assumptions, theoretical thought experiments could (and did) run wild and scientific exercises can as easily be seen as peculiar forms of escapism as they are viewed as contributions to knowledge. (Boettke, 1996: 24)

The critique offered by Austrian economists to the methodology of the mainstream ones is not only an essentialist one (Menger's rebuke of historicism insisting on the epistemological necessity of theory in social sciences) but also a consequentialist one, that is, formal mathematical models are not good to predict social behavior because they do not capture the complexity of life, and that is why you need theory. Some may argue that those are battles already fought, that modern-day information economics or neo-Keynesian economics recognizes the complexity of the economic phenomena and have introduced *selective realism* into the analysis; Austrian economists, however, argue that that is not enough, because such procedure, in its turn, compromises the universality sought from economics (Boettke, 1996: III).

For instance, Philipp Bagus, in a recent article, calls attention to a number of possible sources of errors in econometric models as listed by Oskar Morgenstern in his book *On the Accuracy of Economic Observation*. For one, econometric models usually do not have error estimates as natural sciences models do. According to Bagus that is a crucial problem, because the data in social sciences tend to be less accurate due to: (a) the lack of designed experiments, (b) the observations which are usually a by-product of some business or government activity and are not produced by the researcher, (c) the lack of incentives for the data producers to be accurate, and sometimes even incentives to outright lie about the data, either underestimating or overestimating in case they are collected in order, respectively, to assess taxes and to pay dividends or ask for subsidies, among other reasons (Bagus, 2010b: 7). To summarize, the available data may not have the precision required to be used in the econometric models in order to make reliable predictions, and, furthermore, economic observations are observations about processes done by different observers, so at different times they may conclude different things about the same event, constituting another important limitation to mathematical modeling in economics.

Friedman's 1953 essay, because of its clarity in stating the positivist position on methodology in economics (and therefore laying bare its limitations), had the beneficial effect of creating a lightning rod, which attracted most of the criticism to the positivist methodology. Starting in 1965 a new stage in the philosophy of economics began, with an increasing number of economists adopting the Thomas Kuhn and Imre Lakatos' "growth of knowledge" approach to economic investigation , aimed at ensuring continuous growth of scientific knowledge by the establishment of less stringent requirements for hypothesis validation such as "falsifiability" and "sufficiency" as opposed to the realism of theories (Caldwell, 1984: p. 260).

Broad as the acceptance of that new paradigm was, it did not solve the methodological disagreements among economists, however, which was made clear by McCloskey, who in 1983 argued that it is worthless to try to separate science from "pseudoscience," as the positivists interpret metaphysical inquiries, so the entire effort of demarcation is pointless.

For McCloskey, the methodology of economics is rhetoric. In the words of Wayne C. Booth quoted by McCloskey:

> Rhetoric is "the art of probing what men believe they ought to believe, rather than proving what is true according to abstract methods"; it is "the art of discovering good reasons, finding what really warrants assent, because any reasonable person ought to be persuaded"; it is "careful weighing of more-or-less good reasons to arrive at more-or-less probable or plausible conclusions—none too secure but better than would be arrived at by chance or unthinking impulse"; it is the "art of discovering warrantable beliefs and improving those beliefs in shared discourse"; its purpose must not be "to talk someone else into a preconceived view; rather, it must be to engage in mutual inquiry." It is what economists, like other dealers in ideas, do anyway: as Booth says elsewhere, "We believe in mutual persuasion as a way of life; we live from conference to conference." Rhetoric is exploring thought by conversation. (McCloskey, 1983: 482, 483)

McCloskey with great acumen sees that hostility to "metaphysics" in modern science is itself metaphysical: "If metaphysics is to be cast into flames, then the methodological declarations of the modernist family from Descartes through Hume and Comte to Russell and Hempel and Popper will be the first to go" (1983: 486). The limitations of the positivist methodology of mainstream economics is a consequence of Comte's conception about how human beings gain knowledge that remained unchallenged although all its weakness was acknowledged by its practitioners.

A further insight critical of the positivist methodology is the one offered by Sarjanovic (2007: 10) that like any other market, the market for money is constantly in disequilibrium and that adds a new dimension of complexity for its understanding, since there is an additional obstacle to any assessment about the establishment and transmission of market prices. As acknowledged by the author, the information generated and provided by this particular market, like any other market, is all the information we can possibly get; therefore, there are not many practical consequences of such realization, other than increasing the awareness for chances for arbitrage even in the most liquid and abstract of markets such as the money market. Another consequence of taking that insight into account is that the practice of monetary policy based on any information revealed by the money market, however better than whimsical policies, is still limited by the limitations of knowledge than even the best-gathered and construed statistical information may reveal about the reality that they purport to represent.

Such limitations about what is possible to know using the mainstream methods of investigation with its unrealistic assumptions, unrealistic models, and disregard for received knowledge dismissed as "mere" tautologies is reflected in the field of monetary investigation as illustrated next in this chapter.

5.3 THE GENERAL EQUILIBRIUM THEORY

The purpose of this section is not to describe the general equilibrium theory but just to emphasize the epistemological assumptions of it. The general equilibrium theory is at the core of mainstream economics today. Its purpose is to describe the behavior of supply, demand, and prices for the entirety of the economy. The first general price model was developed by the French economistLéon Walras(1834–1910). Walras' *Elements of Pure Economics* provides the model of perfect competition based on the assumption of perfect information among others.

Nevertheless, what represents the assumption of perfect information in the model of perfect competition of the general equilibrium theory? Perfect information is assumed in the model ofperfect competition. That is, it is assumed that all agents arerationaland have perfect information, that they will choose the best products, and that the market will reward those who make the best products with higher sales. Perfect information in practice means that all economic agents know all things, about all products, at all times, and therefore they always make the best decision regarding their dealings.

It may be alleged that in competitive markets, perfect competition does not require that agents have complete knowledge about the actions of others, that all relevant information is reflected inprices. Still, complete information about the prices is assumed to be possessed by the economic agents; if that assumption were true, no room for arbitrage would exist, and no entrepreneurial activity would be possible.

The extent to which the general equilibrium theory is explicitly accepted today inside and outside the academic world is difficult to exaggerate. Not only it is taught universally in courses on economics, but it has also been *applied* by governments and governmental institutions such as the World Bank worldwide since the 1970s. Models of Applied General Equilibrium (AGE) have been offered as a method for solving general equilibrium systems for whole economies and even the entire world; that is, assuming to know what is unknown and unknowable, mathematic models have been created and fed with information about prices and quantities of different goods in order to predict which amounts of those variables will result in a balanced economy, as if the reaction of economic agents could be mathematically determined.

The concept of perfect information has often been criticized not only by Austrian economists but also by socialists, although the most important statements about the possibility of economic calculation under socialism are based upon the general equilibrium theory.[3]

For the purposes of this chapter, the acknowledgement by neoclassical and socialist economists of how unrealistic the assumptions about perfect information may be, and any other qualifications about the model of general equilibrium neoclassical economists may have if academic credence continues to be lent to its use are all irrelevant. For instance, as an attempt to avoid the challenge posed by the Lucas Critique, models of general equilibrium based not only on macroeconomic data but taking into account microeconomic principles have been developed and their use advocated. They are the models of "Dynamic Stochastic General Equilibrium" (DSGE). Those models have faced skepticism among mainstream economists both inside and outside the academy for a number of reasons, among them the difficulty they have incorporating some relevant transmission mechanisms and validating empirically some of the data (Tovar, 2008: iii); on the other hand, they may be perceived by Austrian economists as a fundamentally flawed exercise that assumes to know information that it is impossible to know in advance, since the information has not yet been created. Nonetheless, the recognition by the mainstream economists engaged in such efforts that there is a need for adding dynamic and stochastic components to any understanding about the general performance of the economy and that such elements necessarily come from the decision of individual agents taken at a microlevel is a good omen for anyone who hopes one day to see an epistemological consensus reestablished in the field of economics.

5.4 THE USE OF KNOWLEDGE IN SOCIETY AND MONEY

It is our contention that the insights offered by Friedrich Hayek in his paper "The Use of Knowledge in Society" are as applicable to money itself as they are to any other aspect of human economic activity.

In that paper, at first, Hayek argues that the economic problem is not a question of what is the best use of the available resources; rather, the economic problem is about the best way to utilize the dispersed information among the economic agents. In his words, "It is a problem of the utilization of knowledge which is not given to anyone in its totality" (1945: 1). Secondly, he argues that most of the misconceptions in economics are the consequence of methodological problems, "due to an erroneous transfer to social phenomena of the habits of thought we have developed in dealing with the phenomena of nature" (1945: 2). Thirdly, before weighing the options of giving to the central authorities all the dispersed knowledge which ought to be used or conveying to the individuals "additional knowledge as they need in order to enable them to fit their plans with those of others" (1945: 2), we need to recognize first that there are two different kinds of knowledge: one, the knowledge most likely to be at the disposal of particular individuals and, the other, the knowledge expected to be found in the possession of chosen experts. However, the knowledge required by most if not all economic decisions (since technical expertise is only yet another service that can be found available in the market) is of the former type and, furthermore, this kind of knowledge "by its nature cannot enter into the statistics and therefore [be] conveyed to any central authority in statistical form" (1945: 4).

Next, Hayek discredits the "widespread" belief that economic decisions are required only at long intervals; he says that practice is not corroborated empirically by the businessman's experience.

Then, Hayek comes to his fundamental insight that prices convey most of the relevant information needed by individuals to make their own economic decisions; he argues that the **price system** is a mechanism for communicating information in society, a function that it fulfills less perfectly as prices are distorted. The implications of this insight are far-reaching. As mentioned before, the key for diminishing transaction costs relies on the cost of acquiring information; if prices do not convey the precise information about market conditions, the costs of acquiring information about market conditions will rise and the division of labor will not occur to its maximum possible extension, and therefore, productivity will not reach its maximum potential. So, for Hayek, not only is it impossible for the authorities to know about the reality of the market, but also any interference with prices (such as meddling with interest rates and exchange rates directly, and with all other prices indirectly) through manipulations of the money supply, to the extent that they blur the information given by the prices to the economic agents, will result in a less efficient use of resources by all economic agents.

There are many more examples of manipulations of the money supply by national governments with dire consequences for their societies than what can be offered here. The cases in which national governments, under regimes of fiduciary currency and legal tender, have inflated the money supply and therefore provoked a generalized increase of prices across the economy are too many to enumerate. But there are also less obvious ways for a national government to damage the economic performance of a society through interventionist policies on banking and capital markets. For instance, in Brazil, for decades now, in order to float a huge national debt, the national government pays an aggressive interest rate on its bonds, consequently attracting a lot of foreign investors; these foreign investments will first acquire the local currency, resulting in its appreciation. The high interest rate and the appreciated currency will subsequently signal to the economic agents a number of things, inducing them to dispose of their resources not necessarily in the most productive way. Imports will increase not because of comparative advantages of producers in other countries, but because of the appreciation of the local currency "artificially" induced by the massive public debt, and productive investments will be postponed in order to fund the same high yield public debt. Eventually, the national credit will be eroded, and the government will not be able to float the public debt, so a change in course will be required, either an "orthodox" return to fiscal austerity or a "heterodox" default. The change in course in the fiscal policy will induce a correction in the exchange rates and interest rates; these changes, although necessary, are not painless. So, even in a country without controls of capital, with a market-determined exchange rate, free trade, and a management of the national debt by a government that commands a good credit rating such as the United States, there still remains room for intervention on capital markets (such as increasing the public debt up to the point of lowering its credibility, in this example) which may produce terrible results. The lesson here is clear: institutional arrangements that allow such manipulations are decidedly less suitable for any reasonably developed human society.

5.5 SOCIALISM

At this time it is necessary to define what is understood by socialism in this chapter and for that we will refer to the definitions offered by Jesús Huerta de Soto in his book *Socialismo, Cálculo Económico y Función Empresarial*. His first definition encompasses one dimension of the meaning in which the term is used (2001: 25): "Socialism is any system of institutional aggression against the free exercise of human action and entrepreneurial activity."

Next, he brings up the normative dimension of socialism. Socialism is not only applied coercion by institutional means; it is a system that tries to justify politically and scientifically the application of institutional coercion in order to "improve" society, not only in terms of the increased efficiency that it allegedly brings to social interaction but also in terms of an increased fairness that results from it (2001: 86).

As explained by David Hume, every government is based on opinion. And it is worthwhile to mention the socialists' ability to convey a message to significant portions of the public in general and intellectuals in particular that is convincing enough to frame their opinion. It is their success in advocating that institutional coercion may produce a more efficient and fair process of social coordination that has kept the socialist option on the table even after the historical events that contradicted them, notably the demise of "real" socialism in Eastern Europe and China epitomized by the fall of the Berlin Wall in 1989 and the growing integration of China in world trade. That is why discussions about the misguided epistemological premises of socialism are so important; they may help illuminate the debate about the justifications of socialist policies.

Finally, Huerta de Soto adds to his definition the instrument by which all these good things would come into being: "Socialism is any systemic and institutional coercion or aggression that restricts the free exercise of entrepreneurial function in a given area of social activity and that is enforced by a directive organ put in charge of the necessary tasks of social coordination in this area" (2001: 92). This last definition is of crucial importance for the argument presented in this chapter. Virtually everywhere around the globe nowadays the monetary regimes are regimes in which the key features are fiat money, legal tender, and central banking.

These features are obviously interconnected and result in the power monopolized by governments (legal tender) to exercise discretion in relation to their monetary policy (fiat money), and those powers are exercised by a central monetary authority (a central bank).

It is the recognition that the purpose of governments in adopting those regimes is to exercise the role of social coordination by coercion that allows us to discuss the limitations of knowledge for the exercise of monetary policy under the framework of the discussion about the impossibility of the socialist calculus.

5.5.1 Socialism and Central Banks

Central banks have not emerged from the market process; instead, they result from deliberate government intervention in the banking sector. Since they are a widespread phenomenon, one may assume that there are strong incentives for their establishment. These incentives are easy to understand: on the one hand, governments like to take advantage of the banking business, funneling part of the proceeds reaped by the banks due to their privileges into the state; on the other hand, private bankers are quick to realize the benefits they can gain from enlisting the government in orchestrating their rescue during "the recurrent panic and liquidity crisis" that often plagues their business. Because of the convergence of these powerful incentives, "central planning" has been the common feature of the banking and credit markets even in western liberal democracies, resulting in the same problems of lack of social coordination and inefficiency characteristic of socialism for these sectors (Huerta de Soto, 2006: 647).

First and foremost the privilege of fractional banking would compromise social coordination even in a free banking system, but I would like to focus here on the arguments for why the attempt to coordinate society by institutional coercion is an intellectual error. Huerta de Soto states that it is theoretically impossible for the central authority in charge of social coordination to gather the relevant information needed to perform its role by decrees; and it is true for the following reasons (2006: 650):

> First, it is impossible for the agency to constantly assimilate the enormous volume of practical information stored in the minds of different human beings; second, the subjective, practical tacit, and nonverbal nature of most of the necessary information which actors have not yet discovered or created and which simply arises from the free market process, itself a product of entrepreneurship subject to the law, cannot be transmitted; and fourth, coercion keeps entrepreneurs from discovering or creating the information necessary to coordinate society.

This is an elegant summary of the arguments for why the information required to replace the spontaneous coordination of economic activity in society generated by the institutional arrangements of a free market is not possibly known or knowable by the entity charged to exercise such coordination under socialist institutions. These arguments are valid in general for any form of socialist institution; these arguments are not less valid in the case of money and credit.

The current monetary arrangements of private fractional-reserve banking controlled by an official institution (the central bank), like many interventionist (socialist) policies, have been justified primarily with efficiency and fairness arguments.

Mainstream economists argue that the most efficient allocation of savings requires its mobilization through the financial intermediation provided by a fractional-reserve banking system; that is, a banking system leveraged to the limit. The level of leverage required for the "efficient" allocation of savings into productive investment is only possible if the financial system can count on a "**lender of last resort**," since the nonsynchronization of savings and investments would force the banks to be much more prudent in their lending if not for the backing of such lender.

Without the existence of central banks in their capacity of lenders of last resort, so the argument of the neoclassic synthesis goes, the supply of credit would be much more restricted and the efficient mobilization of social "surplus" would be compromised. Since the capacity of central banks to act in such capacity is made effective by fiat money and legal tender institutional arrangements, those arrangements are thus justified.

Furthermore, since exposing investors to the vagaries of market fluctuations would put an unfair burden on small savers, who, after all, fund the massive investments made possible through banking credit, it is also a matter of justice to protect the depositors from banking failures by mechanisms such as the "discount window" of central banks and government-sponsored deposit insurance.

Evidently, these claims are impossible to corroborate or falsify since it is impossible to assess what is counterfactual; it is impossible to know what would have existed if what exists didn't.[4] It is not possible to "prove" either that in the absence of a central bank and deposit insurance the supply of credit would or would not be maximized; that is not to say that we could not deduce aprioristically what one would expect to happen under such circumstances.

In any case, these arguments have been, for all practical purposes, consensual worldwide since the formal establishment of a monopoly of issue was granted to the Bank of England in 1844 creating de facto the first central bank as we know it today.

The fiasco in the management of the money supply during the Great Depression by the major central banks at the time was not enough to destroy that consensus; one may only hope that a positive side effect of the most recent financial crisis may be its accomplishment.

5.6 LOMBARD STREET

We find a very good description of the limits of our knowledge about monetary phenomena and the unintended benefits produced by sound (and spontaneous) monetary arrangements in Bagehot's Lombard Street description of the financial markets in England in the second half of the nineteenth century.

In the very introduction, Bagehot discredits those who saw in the **Peel's Act** of 1844 the foundation of the money market by saying that in his judgment it is only "a subordinate matter" (1999: 3).

Next, Bagehot states the complexity of the money market: "The briefest and truest way of describing Lombard Street is to say that it is by far the greatest combination of economical power and economical delicacy that the world has ever seen" (1999: 4).

Bagehot elucidates the role of the Bank of England in providing liquidity to the British financial markets and, as a consequence, to the world. Incidentally, I do not see his description as praise for the institutional arrangements or for the administration of the Bank of England at that time as wise central banking. If nothing else, it seems to be the opposite—the increased leverage of financial markets resulting from the "de facto" role of the Bank of England as a central bank, in my understanding, is subtly *denounced* by Bagehot. He calls the attention of his readers to the fragility of the entire system (economical delicacy, in his words) based on the enormous confidence commanded at that time by British banks as a consequence of their values, principles, and form of action. He points out the immense benefits that such a preeminence of British banks had reaped for the United Kingdom and the contrast of those benefits with the confessed lack of knowledge about the operation of such a delicate mechanism even among experts and people with their fortunes at stake. Those financial resources and therefore the power to immediately mobilize physical resources made possible through British financial deepening were the motor of the worldwide progress seen in the second half of the nineteenth century. Commanded as they were by British financiers, who funneled the riches of the world through their banks, those resources were available to the French State and to American Railroad tycoons as well: "It is sometimes said that any foreign country can borrow in Lombard Street *at a price*" (1999: 5).

We can even make the case that other nations only managed to have the progress that they experienced at that moment, even without having the same level of monetary stability, *because* they were able to tap into the deep British financial markets.

Living in an era in which most of the money in France and Germany was hoarded because the people in these countries "had confidence in no other securities" (1999: 5), Bagehot was knowledgeable enough to say, "For all other purposes the money hoarded was useless . . . the English money is 'borrowable' money" (1999: 6). Testifying about the availability of financial resources he wrote (1999: 7): "We have entirely lost the idea that any undertaking likely to pay, and seem to be likely to pay, can perish for want of money."

And if in the end the British themselves killed their "golden goose," we cannot find better testimony than that of their lack of understanding about its operations; not that Bagehot does not warn them that it is better to have the government out of the money market, but if the government is to interfere in the market "he must arrange his finances so as not to intensify panics, but to mitigate them" (1999: 11).

5.7 IMPLICATIONS OF THE GAMOE DEFINITION

The GAMOE definition of money utilized in this book, one must recognize, is a rather loose definition; anything that is generally accepted as medium of exchange fits into the definition. It can be a commodity, a coined metal, a certificate that some amount of coined metal has been deposited somewhere, a piece of paper that people accept as medium of exchange just because the government "says so," an IOU or any other title representative of a credit issued by a private company or by the government; it can also be an electronic transaction that performs some accounting entries on the balance sheets of the banks or credit card companies in which the traders have their bank accounts, et cetera. However, it is not everything that has some degree of moneyness (in appendix A: The Introduction of a Medium of Exchange and of a Unit of Account in Society, when discussing the monetary use of salt, the presence and absence of some required attributes was mentioned). Residential properties and artworks can be good instruments to store value, for instance, but because they are not easily divisible, they are not easily transportable, and their value is not easily assessed, the possibility of their use as money may be understood as nonexistent.

If this is the definition of money that we accept, it seems really difficult to differentiate between what money *proper* is and what **quasi-money** is. And our answer is simple, *we cannot.*

Of course, for analytical purposes, we can differentiate assets that we can reasonably assume are more or less ready to be accepted as medium of exchange, and in this sense one can accept an empirical definition of money as advocated by the Chicago School, but we cannot know for certain at any given time the total amount of assets that do have liberative power (the property that something has of being accepted as medium of exchange) in a modern society.

Therefore, definitions of monetary base, **M1**, **M2**, **M3**, or **MZM** may offer good guidance about general trends, they may be helpful to perceive changes in the behavior of either the authorities or money holders, but they are not precise in any meaningful way, being therefore worthless for some of the purposes they are employed in which they are assumed to be precise.

Considering the United States or the European Union today, with tens of billions of United States Dollars and Euro bills circulating abroad, with trillions of private and government bonds held by foreign citizens, what is the amount of money and quasi-money in these societies? If the definitions of money comprise only banknotes circulating inside their borders, these definitions are obviously misrepresenting the total amount of banknotes in circulation because foreigners often use their own banknotes to make transactions in those economies; if the accepted definitions incorporate the total amount of issued banknotes, these definitions will certainly misrepresent the quantity of money available since some banknotes circulate or are even hoarded abroad for many years. Finally, if some ratio is adopted, won't any brisk change in the behavior of the money holders defeat the purpose of the entire enterprise of measuring the available amount of money? I surely think so.

Consideration should be also given to the concept of "velocity of circulation of money." First, it can be understood as tautologically arising from the quantitative theory of money identity. If some aggregate measure of national income and output as representative of quantities and prices is accepted, and given a definition of money that could imply in a measure of its quantity, such as M0 or M1, obviously a multiplier that completes the equation can be found and named "velocity of circulation." One can accept its validity without committing himself to the possibility of actually being able to measure it or any other terms of that identity.[5] A second sense for the concept, the one used by Friedman, states that velocity "is a stable function of a small number of variables—essentially those associated with the opportunity cost of holding money." The neoclassical economists of the Chicago School argue that it is an empirical question and this assumption could be falsified. Also, it can be accepted that, for instance, the higher the opportunity cost of holding money (because of inflation, interest rates, etcetera), the faster money holders will be willing to discharge it, and vice versa, and in any given moment, changes in the behavior of money holders can be empirically identified as related to those factors; therefore the hypothesis of such a relation can be certified or falsified in Popper's terms.[6] But again, acceptance of the existence of the causal relation mentioned before and of the possibility of empirically attesting to it does not imply that the monetary authorities can predict with any reasonable level of certainty the reactions of money holders to changes in the cost of holding money, regardless of whether the unpredictability stems from changes in the money supply imposed by those same authorities such as increases or alleviations of the level of mandatory reserves on bank deposits.

Therefore, is it possible to make "monetary policy" target **monetary aggregates** successfully? I do not think so.

Although it is possible to predict their direction and, more loosely, their intensity, changes in behavior of the economic agents are by no means possible to predict with any certainty, since the quantity of variables to which they react and the different relations among the variables are unknown. Further, as soon as a change in policy is introduced, the behavior of the agents will change in order to adapt to the new reality in ways impossible to predict.[7]

The argument presented here is not an argument against **monetary discipline** under a regime of legal tender or **forced legal tender**; better it should be understood as an argument against the fatal conceit that it is possible to design a model of human behavior that permits control or direction of minutely individual actions through manipulation of the money supply by the government.

The very GAMOE definition of money that we adopt implies this conclusion. If we adopted the definitions of monetary base or any monetary aggregate as our definition of money, then calculation of the effects of changes in the money supply on the behavior of the economic agents would be possible—wrong, but possible. It is worthwhile to emphasize once more that these calculations are surely useful to perceive and identify general trends, but they will not produce results with any level of certainty.

To our knowledge, monetary authorities worldwide have implicitly accepted this understanding for about twenty years now, that is, since they changed their policies from aiming at given monetary aggregate targets to inflation policies.

5.8 MONETARY DISTURBANCES

But then there is another problem: can we talk about a "general price level?" This issue can be better understood by paying attention to the problem of creating a price index as described by Mises in his *The Theory of Money and Credit*. In order to take any measurement, one must assume that the gauge will not change, or as Mises puts it, that the "commodity price of money" (1980: 216) will not change. But if we have more than one commodity, it will be only possible if we (unrealistically) assume that there are no relative price variations among the different commodities. If we add to this problem the fact that the quantity of available goods is not defined because we do not know what the desired goods are, to begin with,[8] we cannot even talk about pondering the quantities of different goods; then, it becomes clear that no price index is reliable to reflect accurately changes in the "general price level" since there is no such thing.[9]

According to Hayek, money is not neutral in the sense that increases in the quantity of money are generally not distributed proportionately to all members of the community in proportion to the quantity of money that they already possess; therefore, in order to identify the changes in prices produced by the introduction of more money in the economy, first an understanding about who is receiving the new money is of key importance. Independently of other factors present in the economy, the introduction of new money will produce disturbances in the relative prices by the increased demand of certain goods and services caused by those with privileged access to the new money (Garrison 1961: 24).

5.9 RATIONAL EXPECTATIONS

In order to summarize the topics discussed in this chapter, perhaps it can be stated that rationality can be generally expected from economic agents, not in the narrow sense of maximizers of monetary returns but in the broader understanding of the motives of human action introduced by Mises.[10]

From these rational expectations of utility maximizing (in the broader sense), nonformal models of actual human behavior may be construed, and they will tell us that outcomes will be systematically what people expect them to be, not always, not for certain, but predictably. As Thomas Sargent in his article about rational expectations of the *Concise Encyclopedia of Economics* (Henderson, 2007: 432) wrote,

> The concept is motivated by the same thinking that led Abraham Lincoln to assert, "You can fool some of the people all of the time, and all of the people some of the time, but you cannot fool all of the people all of the time." From the viewpoint of the rational expectations doctrine, Lincoln's statement gets things right. It does not deny that people often make forecasting errors, but it does suggest that errors will not persistently occur on one side or the other.

The claim made in the first paragraph of this section may be restated as saying that the individual economic agents are able to learn from experience and use the information they get, and it may be understood to be a moderate version of the rational expectation hypothesis. However, according to Brunner and Meltzer, Lucas' models go to an extreme:

> They assume that policy operates according to a relatively precise rule. People are assumed to know the policy rule used by the monetary (and

> fiscal) authorities and to have detailed knowledge about the structure of the economy including the size and timing of responses to shocks of various kinds. These assumptions make the models analytically tractable but, taken literally (as they often are), they distort the economist's view of the policy problem by ignoring uncertainty, incomplete knowledge about the structure of the economy and costs of acquiring information and reducing uncertainty. . . . Costs are assumed (by the rational expectations hypothesis) to be zero or negligible, and they are neglected. In our work, costly information gives rise to institutions such as money as a medium of exchange. Explanations of the role of money, "sticky" prices and other arrangements that are difficult to understand in a new classical analysis become clearer once acquisition of information is recognized as costly. (1993: 38)

Divergences among monetarists and other mainstream economists may be seen here.[11] The "policy ineffectiveness proposition" from rational expectations theoreticians is considered too extreme for them. Again, according to Brunner and Meltzer, "The proposition states that systematic monetary policy does not affect aggregate real demand. The public forms rational expectations about policy action to be taken by the authorities and adjusts nominal values. The only effective action is unanticipated action, that is, policy surprises" (1993: 39).

That is not to say that there isn't more than a grain of truth in there, as the experience of many occasions in which monetary policy changes could be greatly anticipated have shown, as in Brazil at the time of high inflation and widespread indexation, for instance. But this is not a novelty—in Keynes we find the acknowledgement that fully anticipated monetary changes do not produce real effects. The importance of such analysis is to show the necessity of qualitative assessment of the reality under investigation; mere quantitative formulae are not enough.

Therefore, without dismissing the utility of the doctrine of modeling behavior assuming rational expectations, its limitations to forecast actual behavior in any given case must be understood.[12] Incidentally, assuming that agents are irrational will not do the trick either.

The limitations exist regardless of the level of rationality that we may attribute to the agents, because we still face the problems of the limitation of knowledge referred to by Hayek and the impossibility of gathering data that by its nature is dispersed among all the economic agents.[13] Then, the great and ever-increasing complexity of the economic interactions that are possible under sound institutional arrangements must be considered, as referred to by Bagehot. Next, our accepted definition of money imposes limits on what can be known on its own; if money is anything that may be accepted as a medium of exchange, in practice, money can be many different actual things, since many things can perform this role. Finally, even well-accepted concepts such as "general price level" or "price indexes" are shown to be of illusory certainty. So, I end with the conclusion that the limits of what it is possible to know about money falls into the category referred to by Hayek on the occasion of this 1974 Nobel lecture on the "pretence of exact knowledge" that should be resisted by economists.

5.10 SUBJECTIVISM AND THE UNDERSTANDING OF MONEY

The present section is not exactly a concluding section for this chapter, but a post scriptum. The purpose of this final section is to discuss the sense in which the term subjectivism may be understood and applied in economics.

The behavior of economic actors in the market is driven by a desire to remove a felt easiness; each individual agent or subject is the locus for such a motivation, therefore, it may be said that the motivation for human action in the market is subjective.

It is more than mere methodological individualism, because not only must the "unit of analysis" be the individual, and therefore, any tentative attempt to get aggregate information about a collection of individuals will fall short of the reality, but also, one should not expect to fully understand the decisions of a single individual.

This does not imply that individuals are irrational, but simply that knowledge about an individual's motivations is impossible to be rationally apprehended.

It is from the interaction of the individual actors that markets got their praxeologic nature, generating knowledge that will be used by economic agents to coordinate their activities as the result of their own interaction; that is what makes the Walrasian general equilibrium theory with its flawed epistemological assumptions, even in its dynamic variant, unable to explain reality. What is valid for markets in general is valid for monetary theory as well.

As argued by Walter Block (1989: 219), it is necessary to make a "sharp enough distinction" between the general equilibrium propounded by the neoclassic and the tendency towards the equilibrium advocated by the Austrian economists, but that individual actions do tend towards equilibrium must be emphasized.

On the one hand, it is from the subjective nature of individual decisions compounded with the tendency towards equilibrium present in the market economy that "the constant changes on the value of money as a medium of exchange that result unpredictability in its purchasing power" (Huerta de Soto 2001: 193) derives. On the other hand, the tendencies that were aprioristically stated by Menger, Mises, and Hayek make Austrian economics a scientific discipline. If economics is to ever recover from being, in Lincoln's phrase, a "house divided against itself" and the only divisions in economics, using another famous phrase, may be between "good economics and bad economics,"[14] the path for a new synthesis passes, I am convinced, by the establishment of a new epistemological consensus. I don't have much else to say about that other than to emphasize that such an epistemological consensus must incorporate the epistemological assumptions of the Austrian stream of the marginalist revolution and abandon positivist epistemology.

NOTES

1. This chapter title perhaps would be better in the negative since its structure is to show what is not possible to be known about monetary phenomena; still, the realization of such limitations are the key to what reasonably can be known about money, and that is why I chose to keep the title in the affirmative. For instance, among the many aspects of money about which it is possible to gain knowledge are the variations in money with regard to time, to space, to *moneyness*, and to its legal status. Theoretically and empirically it is possible to reason about variations of money in time and space, for example, not only to say that money may evolve in a given society or has evolved differently in different societies, but also to talk about time preference and the different ways in which exchange rates may be understood. It is the existence of such variations and the possibility to know and reason about them that makes possible the classification of monetary systems offered in this work.

2. A profound thinker like Karl Brunner, as late as 1969, in an important paper, sided with Milton Friedman on methodology against the criticism offered by Paul Samuelson (who, incidentally, as pointed out by Caldwell, did not perceive the inconsistency between his stance on that issue and his own methodology) and concluded: "There is no case in which a previously or independently determined 'realism' of 'assumptions' can be used to determine the 'realism' of a theory. Such notions simply result from various strands of logical misconceptions and most particularly a confusion between one's psychology and logical analysis" (Brunner, 1969: 521).

3. Among the several instances of explicit references to "perfect competition" by socialist thinkers in presenting their arguments in favor of the possibility of socialist economic calculation, the case of Oskar Lange, who in his book *On the Economic Theory of Socialism* (Huerta de Soto, 2001: 311), describes the neoclassical price theory and the model of perfect competition as the optimal theoretical foundation for the socialist system, is emblematic.

4. That is not to say that you could not corroborate a given monetary phenomenon with contrafactual arguments, but just to say that if we don't have white, it does not follow necessarily that we will have black, since we may end up with red or blue.

5. This is the understanding of Benjamin Anderson: "To me 'velocity of circulation' seems to be a mere name, denoting, not any simple cause or small set of causes, which can exert a specific influence, but rather a meaningless abstract number, which is the non-essential by-product of a highly heterogeneous lot of activities of men, some of which work one way, and others of which work in another way, in affecting prices" (1917: 180).

6. A good example of this second understanding is the work relating to the demand for money and velocity by Brunner and Meltzer, showing that the demand for cash balances "could be estimated from time series data as a function of an interest rate, some measure of wealth or permanent income and perhaps a small number of other variables." And in such fashion they state:

> By the 1970s we believe the following four propositions were widely accepted about the relation of money to income . . . (1) money growth rises and falls pro-cyclically; (2) accelerations and decelerations of money are frequently followed, after a lag, by cyclical expansions and contractions of

real output; (3) sustained money growth relative to the growth of output is a sufficient condition for inflation; (4) velocity growth is pro-cyclical. A fifth proposition was less widely accepted: (5) discretionary monetary action increases variability by inducing (or augmenting) cyclical expansions and contractions. (Brunner and Meltzer, 1993: 20)

7. For the Chicago School, the quantitative theory of money states precisely the opposite: the demand for money depends on a small number of variables (usually the opportunity cost of holding money and income of money-holders). I do agree that empirically we can test this hypothesis (or the relation between the behavior of economic agents and a limited number of variables) and, therefore, we can use the Quantitative Theory of Money to predict the direction and to some extent the intensity of changes in their behavior, once having data about few variables. But it is impossible to predict, based only on those variables, with certainty, what any specific outcome will be, as shown by the history of quantitative monetary policies.

8. In order to measure changes in the "general price level," should we take into account the stock of real estate properties, or the stock of securities, or the stocks of tradable goods and services existing in other countries? Should we take into account the spare capacity of producing domestically and abroad desirable goods? Mises, (1980: 512), commenting on Schumpeter's attempt to formulate a catallactic claim theory for money, criticizes his claim analogy for money based on the fact that the analogy with any other claim, such as, say, a movie theater ticket is not a valid one. Why? Because (a) we do not know the amount of goods that is on the market to be acquired in exchange for money (the equivalent of the total seats in the movie theater analogy), and (b) we do not know the total amount of money in circulation, because we do not know the amount that individuals want to hold, to hoard, or to constitute their comfortable level of reserves.

9. A mainstream economist may call this position "too strictly Austrian" on "aggregation" in general and on the "general price index" in particular. A neoclassical economist would state that aggregation and the general price index are respectively an old and useful practice and concept. It seems difficult to disagree with that. After all, aggregations in economics serve the logical purpose of generalizations in language, and they are extremely useful for reasoning about categories of entities, but my point is that they suffer the same shortcomings, that is, broad generalizations tend to lose accuracy in describing their components. For example, the category of four-legged animals is less precise than the category of equines, which is less precise than the category of horses, et cetera. Therefore, the broader the generalization is, the more difficult it is to characterize the proper attributes of its components. About general price indexes, the only caveat is that they do not seem to be very precise, but it is not difficult to agree with the point of view that they helped in the past to explain many economic phenomena, and that they will continue to do so in the future. Therefore, with this work I should limit my stance to the skepticism about the possibility of practicing meaningful inflation targeting policies using price indexes as a rudder. I would like to thank Roberto Fendt for the comments that gave origin to this note.

10. Among mainstream economists there are also scholars with a more nuanced understanding of human nature; they reject the theory of knowledge implicit in most social thinking and argue that the REMM model offers an opportunity to unify the approach of social science (Brunner, 1987: 387). Such a claim assumes, however, that methodological individualism is consensual among social scientists, which evidently is not the case. The label REMM—Resourceful, Evaluative, and Maximizing Man—appears in Meckling (1976). Brunner states, "We understand that the individual is not born as an empty slate to be subsequently covered by social experiences, but rather is born with a biological and genetic heritage" (Brunner, 1987: 371). There is a common aspect of that heritage shared by all people, some disposition of behavior that is independent of the society in which the individual was born and influences the way they react to social institutions. So, regardless of moral considerations, there is a physical limitation to how much social engineering can do. That is, nature imposes limits on

nurture. The resourceful individual of the monetarists may be understood as the enterprising individual of the Austrians.

11. Brunner and Meltzer in the work referred to in this section (1993: 50) summarize the divergences in the mainstream about the issues of the validity of the quantitative theory and the effectiveness of active monetary policy dividing the camp in three parts: the Keynesians, the Monetarists, and the Rational Expectations-Real Business Cycle theorists.

12. Quoting Quint and Schubik: "The dichotomy between the individually rational economic actor and behavioral models of the individual is a false dichotomy. The rational economic actor model is merely one among several behavior types. *Homo oeconomicus* provides an upper bound on personalityless abilities, while his companion, the random player, provides a lower bound." (page 311)

13. For example, the compatibility of the ABCT and rational expectations has been contested by some economists on the ground that if economic agents are aware of the cycle, why would they act as if the upside of the cycle will never end? If we understand "rational expectations" as saying that people are aware of changes going on in society and adjust their behavior accordingly it is possible to see why some economists would think like that. However, as pointed out by Simpson (2014a: 104) "being rational does not imply being omniscient;" that is to say, businesspeople may or may not be aware of ABCT and even if they were, they may be wrong on how and when it will exactly play out. So, accepting the limitations of knowledge of agents, and having the ABCT understood as an explanation about how people react to the incentives they are faced with in the marketplace, and taking into account said limitations of the knowledge they have, it makes complete sense to think about it as compatible with assumptions of rational expectations.

14. In the pamphlet "What Is Seen and What is Not Seen" Frédéric Bastiat (1801–1850) wrote: "There is only one difference between a bad economist and a good one: The bad economist confines himself to the visible effect; the good economist takes into account both the effect that can be seen and those effects that must be foreseen."

III

Ethics

SIX

The Ethic of Money

6.1 INTRODUCTION TO THE ETHICS OF MONEY

6.1.1 What Does the Nature of Money Have to Do with Monetary Policy?

It seems necessary that in order to evaluate monetary policy, aside from the obvious knowledge about monetary history and command of economic theory, one should have, at a more fundamental level, first, a clear idea about what the nature of money is and, second, an idea about what it is possible to know about money. It is from the foundations provided by a conceptual assumption of the nature of monetary institutions and by taking into consideration the available knowledge about their operations that one may develop an understanding about what is right and wrong as regards money. That is to say that without a metaphysical and epistemological foundation, there is no possibility of developing a meaningful ethics for money, and without it one cannot offer a normative position about monetary policy.

For instance, Dodd mentions the claim that Islamic finance is ethically superior to western finance (Maurer, 2005: 149). If we consider that the prohibition of charging interest has limited the range in which consenting adults may engage in what they think are mutually beneficial relations, and that those relations could have been productive relations, Islamic financial regulations have been the cause of lives and societies living below their potential to individual flourishing for generations. It is difficult to consider, even by a collectivist point of view, how that could be considered "morally superior" to the greater freedom of contract so far enjoyed in the West.

6.1.2 *Two Schools about the Nature of Money*

Therefore, an acceptable departing point for these inquiries seems to be the discussions on the nature of money, which we did at the first part of this book. Broadly speaking, it is possible to classify the different conceptions about the nature of money into two opposing schools: (a) the "State Theory of Money," whose followers believe that money is a creature of the state, conjured as an instrument for political purposes such as to facilitate tax collection; and (b) the "Catallactic Theory of Money," whose members believe that money has evolved spontaneously in society in order to allow and enhance the division of labor. If one endorses the views of the state school of money, accepting that money was created by the government, and more than that, that money was created by the government as an instrument to foster the achievement of political goals, how can this person say that there is something wrong in manipulating the money supply in order to, say, enhance government's revenue? In accepting that money is a creature of the state and its corollary, that money's purpose is to help government in achieving its policies, the division of labor ceases to be understood as the sole value or even as the main goal to be achieved through the introduction of money to society.

On the other hand, if one sees money as a naturally evolved institution in society and its purpose is to enhance the division of labor, any action by one or more private citizens that may compromise its function, like, say, counterfeiting, will be deemed morally "wrong" and deserving of punishment. By the same token, any action taken by the political body, that is, a "policy," that works against the purpose of money may be judged as morally "wrong" as well and deserves condemnation.

6.1.3 *What is Possible to Know about Money?*

The very understanding of what money really is and what it is possible to know about money may influence critically the design of monetary policy. In part II of this book a somewhat detailed epistemological analysis of money was proposed; however, at the beginning of this chapter it is adequate to point out the existence of greater limitations to what is known and what is knowable in terms of the monetary institutions of a free society than what is assumed by neoclassical economists. Suffice it to say that Mises' insights about the fact that money is not neutral and Hayek's insights about the use of knowledge in society put in serious doubt the validity of any attempt to understand the impact of changes in the money supply by the application of any of the many different formulations of the "Quantitative Theory of Money" on society. As mentioned in part II of this book, there are limitations on our possibility to know objectively what the value of money is at any given time. Since the purchasing power of money (PPM) results from the interaction of all the economic agents in the market, their desire to keep cash balances, and the subjective evaluation of the value of the goods and services they have to offer, given the institutional framework in which they are, it is impossible to say at any given moment what the "price of money" or the "price level" is with precision, since relative prices are constantly changing and adjusting to the supply and demand for money in different ways. In the words of Leland Yeager:

> The point relevant to what concerns us here is that imbalance between the actual quantity of money and the total of desired cash balances cannot readily be forestalled or corrected through adjustment of the price of money on the market of money because money, in contrast with all other things, does not have a single price and a single market of its own. (1983: 307)

That is not to say that one cannot talk about these abstractions and reason using these concepts, but the awareness of the imprecision involved should limit what we could expect from its use. A good example of that is the almost universal adoption of inflation targeting policies pioneered by the Reserve Bank of New Zealand in 1990. Nowadays, it is considered "state of the art" in terms of monetary policy, and it has been applied either implicitly or explicitly. Its perceived effectiveness is a consequence of an assumption that closely scrutinizing general price indexes or consumer price indexes and regulating the money supply through manipulation of the interest rate and other mechanisms in order to prevent those indexes either from going down (deflation) or from climbing faster than the "acceptable" level of inflation suffices for a sound monetary policy.

However, the amount of the American trade deficit nowadays and the bubbles experienced first in technology stocks, next in residential properties, and later in all types of investment assets, which led us to the financial crisis started in 2008, tell us another story. Pretending that money is what money is not and pretending to know what is not known or even knowable are not sound foundations for monetary policy.

Therefore, one may say that the best possible normative monetary theories are the ones with the best descriptive apparatus possible to apprehend through reason from the observation of human experience how monetary institutions operate.

What this chapter argues is that there is a given ethical perspective that adequately establishes a relation between the conclusions about the evolutionary nature of money and the moderately realist, antipositivist epistemological approach with some prescriptions for monetary policy; that is done arguing that a flawed monetary policy limits the opportunities of the individuals in society to achieve their potential. It seems difficult to think about a better criterion to define what is right and wrong with social arrangements than measuring them in light of their capacity to allow and to promote human flourishing. Next this criterion will be compared with other options.

6.2 A POSSIBLE CLASSIFICATION OF THE SCHOOLS OF THOUGHT ABOUT MONEY ACCORDING TO THEIR CONCEPTIONS ABOUT THE SOURCE OF MONEY'S VALUE

At the beginning of this inquiry in the quest for an adequate normative stance on money, it seems worthwhile to reflect on the different lines of thought according to their conceptions about the sources of the value of money.

Using a terminology proposed by Ayn Rand, the different lines of thought on the value of money may be classified into three different categories: the intrinsic, the subjectivist, and the objectivist. The first are theorists who see the value of money as an attribute inherent to the monetary merchandise; the second are those who see the value of money as attributed to it by someone; and the third are those who see the value of money in the role that a given monetary merchandise performs in a given social context.[1]

Incidentally, Younkins' project of a paradigm of an "Aristotelian Classical Liberalism," demonstrates that the alleged incompatibility between the claims of Austrian economists that values are subjective and claims by Objectivists that values are objective actually does not exist. As shown by Younkins, these claims are not about the same things because they exist in a different sphere of analysis (Younkins, 2011: 137); and that is why it seems worthwhile to reflect on the different conceptions about the sources of value.

6.2.1 Metallism

The intrinsic theorists are the sensu stricto metallist ones, those who only recognize the market value of the monetary merchandise as practiced for all other uses *besides* the monetary use. The main limitation of sensu stricto metallism as a theory to explain the value of money is that once a commodity acquires liberative power by reason of becoming generally accepted as a medium of exchange, along with its new utility it acquires a new source of value and, therefore, its value can no longer be construed as being only its value for its nonmonetary uses. Nor does metallism explain what the source of money value is when money is not redeemable money.[2]

6.2.2 Statism

The subjectivist theorists are the nominalistic ones, those who see the value of money as named by some authority. Among the subjectivists, we can point out those who see in the command of the state (the Statists or Chartalists) the attribution of value to the currency.[3] These theorists are the ones that see the command given by the state (and formalized in a chattel) as the only source of value for money. This theory is unable to answer, however, what gives value for money when economic agents are unwilling to use a currency at the value "given" by the state. It can be seen, for instance, when there is an "official" and a "parallel" market for foreign exchange; it can also be seen when a currency loses its value in the middle of an inflationary process. Therefore, these theories also fall short of reality.[4]

6.2.3 Catallactic

Finally, the objectivist theorists are the theorists that advocate that the value of money derives from its utility for the money holders; it derives from the benefits they get from using it and it is defined every moment by the sum of their individual evaluations (that is, *intersubjectively*) in their daily transactions. Money value is something that is created in the market as a result of the spontaneous actions of economic agents. In Ayn Rand's terminology, the objectivist theorists are *catallactic* theorists. It may be understood that this theory is the only one in line with the empirical evidence, and the argument that it is not a theory but a tautology can be disputed; the theory is not about what the value of money is (the value of the monetary merchandise is the value given in the market), it is rather a theory about the nature of money's value, about the source of value seen by the agents in the market. In this sense, it is obviously not a tautology. The value of money derives from the benefits accrued by the agents in using it as a medium of exchange for their transactions, by the services it renders. If a given currency is only accepted in the jurisdiction of a small country, if that currency loses value daily and is only accepted at all by some because of the coercive power of the government issuing it, its value for the agents will be significantly less than another currency generally voluntarily accepted in a broader region and relatively more stable in value. Different currencies with different attributes command different values in the market and these attributes are the real source of value, reflected in the market price of the currency. Perhaps, in this sense (and only in this sense) one can say that the value of the currency is discovered in the market and not given by the market.[5]

From this classification one may conclude that the catallactic theory of money is the one that more adequately answers the requisite of better capturing the reality of human experience with money posed at the end of the previous section. Therefore, it is in a moral theory amicable to a catallactic view of economic activity that should be found the next tool for evaluating monetary policies.

6.3 MORAL THEORIES

Reluctant as one may be to open a discussion that is part of the continued philosophical issues and therefore cannot be briefly addressed in the narrow confines of this work, one must locate the preferred ethical tradition underlying this writing within the broad framework of current moral theories on economic activity. There are many ways to categorize the different ideas on the foundation of moral value, but it is impossible even to mention all of them here.

6.3.1 Is the Right the Will of the Strongest Party?

Plato's Socrates in book I of *The Republic* discusses whether "telling the truth and returning what we have borrowed" is enough for one to be considered a good man, and whether the right is what is just or the will of the strongest party (Plato, 1974). Here one can find not only questions about Cephalus' views on what it means to be good in private life, but also opposing views about what the concept of good in social life is. Although the conventional view of justice is clearly shown as an insufficient answer to what being a good man implies, no other view is offered. On the other hand, two opposing views are offered during the discussion about what is right (what is good in a social context): Thrasymachus argues that justice or right is simply the will of the strongest party, while Socrates argues that being just is a more intelligent choice; it results in more effective action and therefore is conducive to happiness. This aligns Socrates with a consequentialist justification for justice.

6.3.2 Human Flourishing and the Virtue of Prudence

Later, Aristotle develops his perfectionist ethics in which eudaemonia, or human flourishing (sometimes translated as happiness), is understood as the ultimate goal of human life, the realization of the potential that each human being possesses and something to be achieved, mainly, by the application of practical wisdom or *phronesis*, (or *prudentia* in its Latinized form). It is relevant to note that the cardinal virtue of "prudence" for the ancients did not have the narrow meaning of utility maximization associated to the *homo oeconomicus* that it has today. Quite the opposite, it was understood as an instrument in each human individual's search for perfecting him or herself (Den Uyl, 1991: 1).

Until modern times (and that can be traced back no further than the sixteenth or seventeenth centuries), notions of just conduct both in individual and social contexts in Christendom were based either on a perfectionist ethics of Aristotelian origin or in a Platonist more collectivist, consequentialist foundation as transmitted respectively by Saint Thomas Aquinas and Saint Augustine.

6.3.3 Kant's Deontological Ethics

In regard to the philosophy of money, the intellectual contributions of Immanuel Kant were mainly indirectly perceived on the history of ideas. The abandonment of instrumentalism, that is, teleological justifications for social institutions and a search for "mechanical" justifications became possible in part thanks to Kant. The abandonment of metaphysical considerations in politics also can be traced to Kantian ideas. Even projects of global (or at very least, pan-European) monetary management and abdication of sovereignty have a distinctly Kantian pedigree. Collectivist methodology in social sciences is another idea whose origin may be found in Kant's idea about the limitations of free will in the face of a distinctly historically deterministic concept of "natural necessity"; it is impossible not to see these ideas at the root of German historicism. Finally, his deontological ethics is *the* moral justification (or excuse, if you will) behind every single proposal for government intervention and, for example, were very influential on Keynes. Obviously, it is not possible to trace clear-cut lines of Kantian influence on later thinkers: Kantian ideas were used by intellectuals in support of the Prussian regime, for example, and many neo-Kantian ideas were enlisted against positivism. However, the importance of his ideas for the intellectual developments listed above is undeniable.

In the spirit of the Enlightenment, like Hume, Kant delved into the fact/value split that had constrained natural sciences since ancient times. In that regard, his claims that values are not part of a space/temporal reality (and therefore can be neither proved nor disproved by the same criteria by which the meaning and truth of facts are assessed) became the fulcrum of the lever of the future development of positivist epistemology. In his writing about teleology, Kant argued that explaining a given organism by its purposes merely confirms that you can use a means-end concept to do so, but that is not "an assertion about what 'really' produces a given state of affairs" (Jones, 1980: 97); that is, you can talk about the purpose of a given object, but that is not an explanation for its existence. To talk about purposiveness in organisms is to talk as if they were created by an intelligent maker, but that is a question of faith and therefore, outside the realm of science. In his political writings, Kant immensely displeased the Prussian government in arguing that states were known in the state of nature as individuals were before—that the "antisocial" actions of states were only exponentially multiplied by the existence of standing armies (Durant, 1991: 219), and that the solution for such a state of affairs was the creation of a universal government with the abrogation of all sovereignties. More than that, Kant, who died in 1804, saw in the French Revolution and the Napoleonic military expansions the seed of such a new "Universal Republic," ideas which certainly did not endear him to the King. In regard to human nature, Kantian thought is very tortuous in trying to avoid a contradiction between his belief that every event is predetermined by previous historical events and the necessity of freedom to the very existence of a moral life.

> Kant admitted that to attribute freedom and natural necessity to the very same self is to become involved in contradictions. But he held that there are two selves, the noumenal self and the empirical self. It is the noumenal self that freely chooses and hence is morally responsible, and it is the empirical self whose behavior is completely determined by antecedent events in time. Thus, according to Kant, the contradiction is removed. (Jones, 1980: 85)

In other words, the sense in which a man may be free is not in relation to what he actually does, since that is determined by the historical conditions of his own upbringing, his community, et cetera, but in relation to what he "transcendentally" chooses as an "autonomous legislator" of what "ought" to be his moral rules. In regard to our topic, that leaves, in practice, no room for individual methodology in social sciences. Following Kant's reasoning, the protagonist in history is not the individual, but some collective, such as the class, the corporation, or the nation.

But it is on the development of an ethics based on duties and not on a conception of good that his influence is most perceived in the philosophy of money; that is, it is not because his influence is directly related to monetary questions, but because it was wholeheartedly adopted by later thinkers willing to justify their preferred policies not on grounds of their consequences for actual individuals, not even by crude utilitarian considerations, but for some sense of a higher good that only they, due to their virtuous character could grasp, and here, specifically, but obviously not only, to John Maynard Keynes. Kant, in trying to escape from what he perceived as the weaknesses of consequentialism in morals, that is, its subjectivism, argued that the only unqualified good is a *Good Will*, and the only virtuous action is to have a good intention, or as Kant himself says, "Nothing can possibly be conceived in the world, or even out of it, which can be called good, without qualification, except a Good Will" (1927: 9).

That means that virtue exists in actions regardless of their results. Kant says, "A good will is good not because of what it performs or effects, not by its aptness for the attainment of some proposed end, but simply by virtue of the volition, that is, it is good in itself" (1927: 10).

Therefore, for Kant, the solution for the moral problem is that whenever we have a moral choice to make we ought to choose—more than that, we have the duty to choose—a good will. Duty being so central to Kant's moral, what is duty for him? For Kant:

> Duty is the necessity of acting from respect for the law. . . . Now an action done from duty must wholly exclude the influence of inclination, and with it every object of the will, so that nothing remains which can determine the will except objectively the law. . . . The preeminent good which we call moral can therefore consist in nothing else than the conception of law in itself. (1927: 16)

There is no need to go much further to understand the problems posed by this account of what is moral. The comparison presented by Kant between two philanthropists, one that takes pleasure in what he does and the other who acts solely out of duty and his statement that only the latter is virtuous makes that crystal clear. For him, in the words of Philippa Foot, "If a man who is willing to do an act of injustice to help a friend, or for the common good, is supposed to act out of charity, and he so acts where a just man will not, it should be said that the unjust man has more charity than the just man" (Foot, 2002: 15).

The consequences of such inversion can be seen around us in multiple ways.

6.3.4 The Greater Happiness for the Greater Number

During the eighteenth and nineteenth centuries, the new utilitarian school was developed in the United Kingdom. From the seminal works of Bernard Mandeville, Jeremy Bentham, and John Stuart Mill a sophisticated criterion for human action based on Bentham's maxim of "The Greater Happiness for the Greater Number" was developed (Hospers, 1996: 138). This school of thought clearly bases moral judgment on the collective "utility" or consequence of any action. Positivist philosophy and legal positivism may be understood as developments parallel to utilitarianism, with which they share a common history and common values.

It is by consequentialist (utilitarian) justifications that all interventionists and socialist policies are justified; it is by consequentialist (again, utilitarian) justifications that most classical liberals justify liberalism as a political doctrine. We find, for instance, already in Jeremy Bentham a moral defense of usury, albeit, his moral criterion of utility made it dependent on "The perceived benefits of the practice to the collective or the Nation" (Brook, 2007:25). The problem is that once an institution such as usury is (morally) justified by its social benefits, government intervention becomes almost inevitable, although it is not a logical outcome of that justification.

6.3.5 *A Perfectionist Ethics for a Nonperfectionist Politics*

However, a tradition started by Aristotle, developed by Saint Thomas Aquinas, and well-developed in the doctrines of Natural Law and Natural Rights, found the justification for policy in human nature, which decrees what is proper for man in what nature requires from him in order to have a human life. It can be found in Baruch Spinoza, it can be found in Lord Acton, but since then, until the second half of the twentieth century with the appearance of neo-Aristotelian philosophers, that tradition seemed to be relegated to the backstage. In their most recent book *Norms of Liberty*, two of these neo-Aristotelian philosophers, Douglas Den Uyl and Douglas Rasmussen, argue "that there is at least a version of neo-Aristotelian ethics and a version of liberalism that are compatible." Their central tenet is that there is a problem of political philosophy that liberalism answers by its metanormative character. They argue that the need (and justification) for metanorms is better understood by a neo-Aristotelian ethics that puts human flourishing (virtuous activity) at its center and demands from the political body something that ordinary normative ethics cannot justify. The liberalism problem may be summarized in the following question: "What are the principles by which to establish a political and legal order whose structure will allow for the possibility that different individuals might be able to flourish and realize virtue in very different ways?" (Den Uyl and Rasmussen, 2005: XV).

They argue that only a negative, natural right to liberty with its corollary rights to life and property (if properly understood as metanormative principles because they protect the self-direction in a social context instead of prescribing what is the good) is the proper justification for classical liberalism, thus reviving the Aristotelian tradition in political philosophy.

6.4 THE MORAL JUSTIFICATION OF THE "FISCAL PROVISO"

Even if one disagrees with consequentialist justifications for what ought to be considered right, it is necessary to keep in mind that notwithstanding strong protection of private property rights, the lesson from the history of money and banking generally has been one of relativization of those rights, especially through interventions in the monetary and financial arrangements every time that the necessities of war financing so required.

In the historical record are countless episodes in which, for fiscal reasons resulting from a state of war, a government intervened in the monetary institutions sometimes with disastrous effects for the economic performance of society, and that is a reality that must be dealt with.[6]

Let's assume, like Larry White and George Selgin do (Selgin and White, 1999), that "fiscal necessities" are the ultimate justification for government's control over money and banking, or in any case, that they are a better explanation than "market failures."[7] After all, the evidence from history shows many occasions in which a sovereign, rightly or wrongly, seeing no other means to wage war but by trumping private property rights, to the extent that he was able to do it, seized private property for that purpose. That is, sovereign powers have acted throughout history as if, under some circumstances, specifically in cases of armed struggle, the protection of private property was not absolute.[8]

Is an armed struggle an argument strong enough to overcome most, if not all, limitations on political power as well? Is this an argument of "realpolitik" (the government has the guns, they can take your horse, there is nothing you can do about that) or is there also a "moral" argument to be made?

This is perhaps the opportunity to discuss whether there are persuasive justifications to limit the state to a minimum other than the moral tradition that evolved into individual rights, as argued by Robert Nozick, for instance. Or, in other words, for the thinkers not satisfied with Nozick's claim that there is "an area in moral space around an individual" (Nozick, 1974: 54) that no one, even the polity, can trespass, are there other arguments to offer in favor of a state with limited powers?

The argument in favor of an unlimited state is traditionally associated with the social contract described by Thomas Hobbes, in which the individuals surrender their liberty to the sovereign in exchange for protection against others. Since the entity then created by the covenant among those individuals, Hobbes' Leviathan, has the right to prevent the use of violence and fraud among the contractors and to marshal them for the purpose of common defense. Since according to Hobbes, "whosoever has the right to the End, has right to the Means," it follows that the sovereign has the "right" to use whatever means he deems expedient, including the private property of his subjects, to provide for the peace and security of the community. As the Hobbesian argument goes, the sovereign has legitimate authority to take any liberty his subjects have retained; and that seems to justify morally the fiscal proviso.

But the problem with such line of reasoning is that it serves to justify anything else the sovereign might do. According to Michael Levin, it is here that a distinction between Hobbes' supposedly unlimited state and Nozick's state, which is constrained by inalienable rights possessed by the individuals, may be drawn: "Nozick believes there are 'side constrains' on the state's action even in pursuit of its legitimate goal, and thus disagrees with the end-means maxim. For him, the right to keep peace entails the right to means to keep peace which do not violate the side constraints" (Levin, 1982: 342); or in the words of Jan Narveson, for Nozick "rights are rigid, incapable of being legitimately violated even for the sake of preventing wholesale further violation by others" (Narveson, 2001: 324).

However, as Levin argues, there are reasons for the contractors to give up their "swords" but not their "plows." Essentially, it may be expected that once everyone abdicates the use of violence, even if the sovereign is not good at enforcing peace, the level of violence tends to diminish; at the extreme, if everyone adheres to the pact, the sovereign does not need to do anything to establish security.

As in relation to everything else, figuratively represented in Levin's paper by the "plows," the sovereign, prima facie, cannot provide for the individuals by monopolizing the means to do so better than the individuals can do for themselves.

This may be considered his central argument in favor of "A Hobbesian Minimal State": there is no reason for the individuals in the state of nature to establish a social contract with a broader scope than surrendering to the sovereign their "swords" in exchange for the expectancy of peace and security. Anything else the Leviathan decides to do is only justified in light of the original contract to the extent that it is necessary to achieve that goal; nothing else.[9]

Granted, the one who decides what is necessary is the sovereign, and that does not solve the problem that the fiscal proviso represents for the claim that individual rights in general and private property rights in particular are absolute, since the needs for defense still may justify expropriation of private property in the Hobbesian Minimal State. Furthermore, an argument against the fitness of absolutist states, with weak protection of individual rights to better provide peace and security than, say, a constitutionally limited government may be made on historical grounds. So, the "Hobbesian" covenant here may be understood as limiting the degree to which private property may be conditioned to the circumstances, at a minimum, justifying a protection of these rights, for all practical purposes,[10] similar to the one advocated under the natural law–individual rights tradition.

That is, at least, the exception Buchanan takes with Thomas Hobbes, who "failed to see that resolution of the problem raised by the presumed anarchistic chaos does not require the all-powerful sovereign, and that such resolution requires, instead, only the limited sovereign which enforces property and contract" (Buchanan, 2005: 66).

To the extent that the fiscal proviso on the absoluteness of private property rights with allowance for government intervention in money and banking is an argument of political realism, it will be discussed in the next part of this book, but it does not carry moral weight; the sovereign may take what is necessary for the survival of his regime simply because he can without regard to what he or others know to be right. Quoting Von Hagen and Welker: "governments hold the monopoly of money production because they are the only institution in society with the power to usurp and defend that monopoly" (2014: 28). The recognition that that is a fact of life, that persons in positions of power may abuse of their positions for personal benefit knowing that is not fair, is an important part of the description of the reality discussed in this book and therefore it needs to be taken into account, but it is not part of the normative discussion conducted in this chapter.[11]

To the extent that the fiscal proviso is an ethical argument, it may be considered in two ways; first, it may be considered in a very narrow form, and in this case only differing from a conception of absolute private property in the sense that it would allow, in emergencies, the use of property to be compensated for later on; and in the second form, it may simply be equated with the bleak and cynical moral position argued by Thrasymachus in the dialogue depicted in the first book of Plato's *The Republic*. The argument for the morality of the very narrow limits in which the fiscal necessities of the state may justify a temporary and further compensated mitigation of private property rights may be found in the authority of Juan de Mariana when he wrote, "In case of urgent need the king might also debase the coinage without the explicit consent of the people but would be under obligation to restore the old coinage as soon as normal conditions returned and to make good any loss sustained by those concerned" (Laures, 2008: 126). As is well known, Juan de Mariana argued that debasing the currency is equivalent to a tax and, therefore, subject to the consent of the subjects, and punishable with excommunication, as prescribed by the papal bull *In Coena Domini* at least since 1478 when such an article was introduced by Pope Martino V, and was amended several times until the 1587 version of Pope Sixtus V in force at the time of *De Monetae Mutatione* (Lopez, 1768/2011: 17).[12] Still, the exception of emergency, if duly compensated, is considered morally acceptable by Mariana.

6.5 HOW TO FIT A CATALLACTIC MONETARY THEORY INTO THE DIVIDE IN MORAL PHILOSOPHY

Edward Younkins suggests a solid justification for a capitalist society integrating moral and political philosophy, and economics in support of public policy. Younkins arguments in favor of the compatibility of Austrian economics with neo-Aristotelian philosophy as the best justification for a free society. That synthesis is understood by many as unsustainable, but with his research he challenges that common assumption.

Younkins, after surveying different justifications for an open, market economy society from the perspective of leading economists, philosophers, and other social thinkers, set himself to offer a synthesis of some of those justifications. According to Younkins, in a nutshell, the best justification for the existence of a legal monopoly of violence is the enforcement of rules of just conduct by an agent entrusted by the community with such responsibility; rules that are required to accommodate the many different ways in which individuals may reach the maximum of their potential or, to say it differently, may flourish. This centrality of individualized human flourishing for the definition of what is moral is based on an Aristotelian perfectionism in ethics as pointed out by Younkins. For Younkins, a libertarian minimal state is one that does not try to impose a special way for all the citizens to flourish; that is, a society organized around *no-perfectionist* policies. Younkins attributes the idea of justifying such political arrangements on the *perfectionist* Aristotelian ethics mentioned above to the works of contemporary neo-Aristotelian philosophers, among them Douglas Rasmussen, Douglas Den Uyl, and Eric Mack. Younkins could have included Ayn Rand among those neo-Aristotelian moral thinkers, but perhaps because of important differences[13] between her and the others on metaphysical conceptions, he chooses to explore the epistemological contributions of Ayn Rand to the debate about the limitations and uses of knowledge in society and in this way to approximate Rand's objectivism to Austrian economics.

It is my understanding that the most fundamental moral basis for political action may be found on either side of the divide between methodological collectivism, consequentialism, and positivism on one side and methodological individualism, ethical perfectionism, and natural law on the other.[14] And with the Austrian School of Economics being so significantly influenced by late scholasticism as argued by Rothbard and others, one may understand that the catallactic concepts of spontaneous order, limitation of knowledge, entrepreneurship, limited government under the rule of law, respect for property rights, and many others that are bedrocks of Austrian economics and jurisprudence seem to fit better in the neo-Aristotelian tradition described above.[15]

It is our contention that the "Theory of Dynamic Efficiency" as presented by Huerta de Soto establishes a possible link between the Aristotelian tradition in moral philosophy and economic policy in general and monetary policy in particular under the catallactic framework proposed by Mises and Hayek and later developed by other members of the Austrian School of Economics such as Israel Kirzner, Murray Rothbard, Roger Garrison, and others.

6.6 THE DYNAMIC EFFICIENCY THEORY

In the field of economics the actualization of individuals' potentialities may be understood by their ability in a given social context to achieve their material goals to the extent of their capacity. In economic jargon it has been termed "efficiency."

6.6.1 Paretian Concept of Efficiency

Neoclassical economics adopts a basic model with a static concept of efficiency as the maximization of the relation between given desired ends and also given means (technology and resources). So, in the concept of efficiency attributed to Vilfredo Pareto, given the resources available, once no more "Pareto improvements" can be made, that is, it is no longer possible to make one economic agent better off without making anyone else worse off, it is considered that a "Pareto Optimal" level of economic efficiency has been achieved. So, in neoclassical analysis it is possible to envisage infinite equilibriums, all of them consistent with the Paretian concept of efficiency in this static sense, along "production possibilities curves" (PPC) of "maximum production." Since there is no qualitative dimension in this concept of efficiency, given the resources available and the goods to be produced, any combination that maximizes production would be considered efficient in this sense. In the formal microeconomic models of mainstream economics these multiple possible Pareto efficient equilibria are frequently termed as "production possibilities frontiers" (PPF). These curves illustrate the production possibilities of an economy, that is, the alternative combinations of two goods that an economy can produce with given resources and technology.

6.6.2 The Dynamic Dimension of Efficiency

According to Huerta de Soto, an entire dimension of efficiency is neglected by this concept, a dimension with a long tradition that he traces back to Xenophon in ancient Greece, through Saint Bernardino of Siena, all the way to Austrian economists today: the dimension of dynamic efficiency (Huerta de Soto, 2004: 14).

Dynamic efficiency may be understood as "the increase in the supply of goods by entrepreneurial creativity, i.e., by commerce and speculation, more than by avoiding the waste of known resources" (Huerta de Soto, 2004: 15).

The study of dynamic efficiency is the study of the factors that may lead to changes in what is considered as given in the static dimension of efficiency (technology and resources) by virtue of the creative, coordinating potential of entrepreneurial activity. And paramount among those factors are the ethical values informing the legal and social institutions and the prevailing morals in society.

But then we are again in need of justifying social arrangements by their informing normative conceptions and grounding those normative conceptions on reality (metaphysics) and our capacity to understand it (epistemology).

6.6.3 Creating Value in an Unpredictable Environment

Huerta de Soto claims that the application of the dynamic concept of efficiency is imperative, and it is based on the following assumption:

> that in real life neither the resources nor the technology is given, but may vary and actually vary continuously as a result of entrepreneurial creativity. And if they vary, it is obvious that there is an entire dimension of the concept of efficiency (the dynamic one) . . . which [to] disregard comes with a heavy cost for the economic analysis of reality. (Huerta de Soto, 2004: 19)

A possible interpretation of his argument is that the unpredictable and ever-changing character of reality is better described by a theory that does not consider it as stable, and that it is only by the actions of entrepreneurs, capable of reacting to market signals, that the dispersed knowledge in a modern open society can be harnessed into economic goods, either by improving the modes of production of the ones already known or by creating new ones. And with that, I venture to say, Huerta de Soto captures the metaphysical and epistemological grounds for the set of institutions (as informed by the individualistic and perfectionist moral values described above), that in his argument are more conducive to the economic development of society. In his words, "the truly relevant, more than moving the system to the frontier of maximum production, . . . consists in applying systematically the criterion of dynamic efficiency, the one focused on the system's capacity to "move" continuously to the "right" of the curve of production possibilities" (Huerta de Soto, 2004: 26)

The truth is that perhaps the neoclassical definition of the realm of economics is too narrow, but the problem that economics as a science purports to answer is still an economic problem—that is, the creation of economic value—and the importance of the dynamic concept of efficiency must be understood to the extent that it helps the achievement of that goal.

6.6.4 Human Nature and Natural Rights

Entrepreneurship is just one venue for the essentially human capacity to continuously create and find new ends and means. And therefore in the field of social ethics, one must conclude that this concept of man as able to create and coordinate with other human beings in their creative endeavors implies the right of the creative individuals to benefit from the results of their activities, or quoting Huerta de Soto once more:

> [That is,] the private appropriation of the fruits created and discovered by the entrepreneurs is a principle of natural right, because, if the agent could not appropriate what he has created or discovered, as a consequence, his capacity to detect opportunities would be blocked and the incentive for him to persevere in his actions would be gone. (2004: 48)

6.7 THE THEORY OF DYNAMIC EFFICIENCY AND MONEY

6.7.1 A Generally Accepted Medium of Exchange Embodies the Character of Dynamic Efficiency

Before the existence of public mints, before even the existence of national states or even city-states, before the first coined money was struck out of Croesus' mint, a unit of account and a medium of exchange had already been a social reality for thousands of years.

Without a unit of account and a medium of exchange, the division of labor at a minimum level would have been impossible, and so Carl Menger developed his hypothesis about the customary and evolutionary introduction of money into society.

Therefore, money in its GAMOE definition embodies the character of dynamic efficiency. It is by the spontaneous activity of some economic agents that the advantages of no longer making direct exchanges but trading in goods that could more easily be traded for other goods that the "monetary" characteristics of certain commodities was perceived and its use became widespread.

6.7.2 Under Static Equilibrium No Cash Balances would be Necessary

Huerta de Soto also notes that under the assumptions of a model of static equilibrium, no demand for cash balances would be necessary, but since "real life is plagued with uncertainty about the future," it at the same time is cause and consequence of entrepreneurial activity. But the entrepreneurial activity constantly generates new information and modifies market circumstances; therefore, it is unavoidable to keep cash balances. In this way, yet another link between money and the dynamic character of market economy in the face of entrepreneurial creativity is established (Huerta de Soto, 2004: 63).

6.7.3 Good Money and the Goal of the Dynamic Efficiency Theory

We have seen that money was created by entrepreneurial creativity and enhances productivity by making possible a more developed division of labor as a result of opening new options for the exercise of entrepreneurial creativity and coordination.

That is precisely why it is important that monetary institutions do not make the processes of entrepreneurial coordination more difficult. Societies that manage to provide good institutions to solve economic problems—that is, institutions that foster and enhance the division of labor (and among them private property, personal security, and good money are paramount)—are the societies that offer the individuals better chances to actualize their potentialities, which in economic terms means the goal of dynamic efficiency.

6.8 SELECTED ATTRIBUTES OF A PROPER MONETARY SYSTEM

The previous chapters of this book presented authoritative views about what money is and about what it is possible to know about money; and there I advocated for reasons to opt for a market base valuation of money. Next, I presented brief descriptions of some moral theories, as well as the "Theory of Dynamic Efficiency" and how it applies specifically to an analysis of monetary institutions. Now, in light of the insights offered by the "Theory of Dynamic Efficiency," it is time to explore what may be considered right and wrong about money and the criteria to make this judgment. Here I will present a claim that in order to fulfill its purpose—that is, to foster the division of labor by allowing and enhancing the exercise of entrepreneurial activity, for any potential instrument of indirect exchange to become generally accepted as a medium of exchange, it must have liquidity, which was already referred to as the essence of *moneyness*. In order to have liquidity, money must be trusted to be relatively stable in value, nonexpensive—or to say it differently, cost effective—and available in the proper amounts required by the market.[16]

6.8.1 Stability of Value

One of the desired attributes of a currency seems to be the relative stability of the Purchasing Power of Money (PPM). As an instrument for commerce and speculation, money's stability of value seems to be its most desirable attribute. It may be argued, as James Buchanan does (Buchanan, 1962), like Irving Fisher before him, that "predictability" would be a better criterion than "stability" to evaluate monetary policy for having good money. Fisher says, "It will also simplify our problem if we remember that our ideal is not primarily constancy of the dollar but rather dependability. Fluctuations which can be foreseen and allowed for are not evils" (2007: 223).

Obviously, predictability in changes of money's value is better than unpredictable changes, but in order to remove the necessity of factoring risks and costs associated with changes in money value for economic agents, the more stable the value of money is, the better it fulfills its purpose.[17] Fisher says, "But while there is much to be hoped for from a greater foreknowledge of price changes, a lessening of the price changes themselves would be still more desirable" (2007: 323).

Other authors, however, may give the impression that stability of the PPM is not an attribute *absolutely* necessary for good money; I am prepared to concede that. Philipp Bagus , for instance, while criticizing

Mises ' approach to deflation , and bringing the authority of Hülsmann and Salerno in his support, states: "Falling prices per se are not an economic problem for the economy as a whole" (Bagus, 2008: 138). I do not think, however, that some tolerance for a steady deflation under a monetary regime in which the monetary base is considerably inflexible may be construed as an argument against the desirability for relatively stable money. It may be argued that redemption in specie, under a gold standard with a 100% reserve requirement and hard constraints to the monetization of time deposits, would force prices steadily down, assuming increases in real output above the yield of gold mining, and therefore it would not be a recipe for stability but for deflation. Redemption is listed here as one external constraint on the supply of money. Under a requirement that would limit increases of the monetary base to increases of the stock of gold and considering also growth in production superior to that, deflation is to be expected; but the argument here is that redemption has been used historically as an instrument to achieve relatively more stable PPM and not that its result is absolute stability, if that could even be possible.

Incidentally, that prices in the economy are not strictly rigid and therefore there is some room for debt monetization (for replacing interest-paying bonds with interest-free banknotes and reserves) without stocking increases in general prices, is something that the evidence of the years since 2007 has shown, if more proof is needed. But if that is the case, a legitimate question would be—why bother then? Let the music continue! An adequate answer to that question is that prices in general are not completely elastic either, that there are physical barriers in the real world for how much individual producers may be induced by monetary illusion to expand production before starting to raise prices. Cynically or unwittingly creating an atmosphere of uncertainty in order to increase the demand for cash balances may help governments to crowd out individuals in favor of the beneficiaries of their largesse, but that is not something that can go on forever. The reality is that new claims to existing goods are being created and given to economic agents in exchange of their goods and services and although most of them are not using those claims to bid for goods in the real economy, the imbalance between what is going on in the financial side and the real side of the economy is not getting smaller. In 2011 the Fed purchased more than 60% of all Treasury issuance according to Lawrence Goodman ("Demand for U.S. Debt Is Not Limitless," in the *Wall Street Journal*, March 27, 2012); although that percentage has been reduced in recent years, a substantial part of the federal deficit of the United States has been funded with increases in the monetary base.

Another proposal for a better attribute than stability of value is the productivity norm; that is, arguably, the targeting of some nominal income parameter by the monetary authorities instead of a zero inflation target would be an arrangement that would reduce costs of transactions for economic agents, allowing swifter changes in relative prices than the alternative (Selgin, 1997). The basic difference between Selgin's proposal and the idea of constant prices as a monetary goal is that in his proposal, while changes in the velocity of money would trigger countermeasures in order to prevent changes in the price level, on the other hand, events that would reduce the general level of productivity in the economy—"adverse 'supply shocks' like wars and harvest failures"—would be allowed to have their effects reflected on the price of produced goods, in the same way that gains in productivity "would be allowed to reduce prices permanently" (Selgin, 1997: 10). His proposal may be understood as a "refinement" of professor Leland Yeager's theories about the deleterious effects of monetary disequilibrium, that is, "a discrepancy between actual and desired holdings of money at the prevailing price level" (Yeager, 1986: 370), to the extent that it intends to overcome some of the shortcomings perceived by Selgin in Yeager's theory, such as the difficulty to instantly equilibrate the price level (Selgin, 1997: 16). But the most relevant aspect of Selgin's thesis is his proposed solution: to allow, by making banking freer, an even more endogenous production of money substitutes by private competitive banks in order to match supply and demand for money in the economy without the (dis)allocative effects of exogenously supplied money. To the extent that Selgin's thesis about a "productive norm" is proposed to be achieved by the spontaneous and uncoordinated action of competitive money providers, it is similar to the goal of (as) stable (as possible) prices as an attribute of good money; and indeed, it may be considered a refinement in the concept of what "price stability" means ideally. However, if that may be achieved under the system of hybrid provision of base money by the government and money substitutes by private banks, I tend to disagree, but that is a discussion for other part of this book (see section 11.3: Banking Architecture).

But what are the instruments to achieve stability in value? There are three possible instruments for reaching stability: a clause of redemption in specie; a self-imposed constraint, like a constitutional limit on issuing new money; and a competitive constraint, a market constraint that could lead to a competition among different issuers, as further discussed in this book.

6.8.2 The Example of the American Dollar

If we take as an example the American dollar, which has been the reserve currency of the world for more than half a century now, it is easy to see that it has not been a model of stability. Since it is not redeemable in specie, it is issued by a monopolistic agency of a government subject to political pressure; it comes as no surprise that its record as a store of value is a poor one.

According to the Consumer Price Index (CPI) calculator provided by the Bureau of Labor Statistics of the United States Department of Labor on their website, 100 USD in 1913 had the same buying power as $2,391.27 in 2014; or to say it differently, the US dollar lost 95.82% of its purchasing power in that period.

6.8.3 Stability Achieved by Redemption in Specie

If the reasons just mentioned above compromise its stability, which arrangements would best produce stable money? In order to answer this question, we must go back to the properties of money: to the extent that a currency maintains constant its capacity of being exchangeable for desirable goods, it may be deemed trustworthy by economic agents and suitable for use in their commercial and speculative activities. One way that an issuer of a currency can guarantee its capacity of being exchangeable is by a contractual assurance lawfully enforced by the state that the currency is retrievable in specie. For a banknote to be redeemable in specie, it may be no more than the "warehouse warrants" mentioned in the specialized literature, or, under fractional reserve arrangements, a claim against the issuing bank that it can be redeemed in specie.

6.8.4 Stability Achieved by a Constitutional Rule

A second theoretical source of stability in value would be the rule of a constitutionally mandated growth of the money supply, originally proposed by Friedman. However, that proposal was never put into practice, remaining purely a theoretical model. But somewhat derived from that model is the monetary regime currently in use in most Western countries under fiat money, central banking, and floating exchange in which only an "inflation target" anchors the value of the currency. Arrangements under an "inflation target" framework may not be described purely as a "rule" monetary regime, but they are not regimes of pure "discretion" either; they would be the closest to Friedman's proposal ever put in force. The results are not exactly satisfactory, though.

6.8.5 Inflation Targeting and the Business Cycle

Current monetary arrangements of inflation targeting were directly responsible for the inflationary expansion of the money supply seen during the last decade, which ended in the 2008 crisis. It was the imbalance between the level of investments financed by credit expansion and the actual growth of voluntary savings in most Western countries, mainly in the United States, that has produced a "grave lack of coordination and intertemporal imbalance between investors and consumers" that has now been purged (Huerta de Soto, 2004: 64). These grave imbalances have produced the most damaging consequences for entrepreneurial activity around the globe in more than sixty years.

The current monetary regimes, guided solely by the impact of increases in the money supply on consumer price indexes or, at most, general price indexes, have utterly failed to limit the discretion of central bankers in inflating the supply of money. The tragedy of our current circumstances described by the "Austrian Business Cycle Theory" can only be compared to a desolation caused by a disease for which a vaccine was already invented but not made available due to prejudice.

6.8.6 Stability of the Value of Money under Competitive Currencies

A third circumstance in which an issuer of a currency is forced to offer a guarantee that he will maintain constant the value of the issued currency happens when he is forced to do so by issuing competitors. This regime may be properly described as "Free Banking ," and one theoretical possibility of a competitive monetary regime is the one described by Hayek in his essay on the "Denationalization of Money" originally published in October 1976.[18]

In the specialized literature, there is a discussion about the possibility of effectively constraining the supply of money if a free banking arrangement is designed based on fiat money, as Hayek suggests. Selgin and White, for instance, argue that: "Hayek's proposal for private fiat-type money unfortunately fails to secure the quantity and value of money" (Selgin and White, 1996: 86).

The argument presented here is that stability of value may be sought by the establishment of a regime of competitive issuance that would force the issuers to be more restrained than otherwise. That is to say that it is one more instrument to achieve stability and not to say that in the particular case of a competitive regime and fiat money that competition would suffice to assure absolute stability of value, as in Hayek's proposal. Nor do I think that Selgin and White meant that. My understanding of their argument is that, under competitive currency and fiat money, circumstances may arise in which all issuers may have room to increase the supply of money without constraints, if the only existing constraint is competition.

A competitive constraint is considered here an automatic constraint on the issuers, imposed by the spontaneous acceptability of their notes, which may vary, and therefore it allows them to expand the money supply under certain circumstances. To illustrate my reasoning, it is possible to draw a parallel with a regime of commodity money and no minimum reserve requirement. If there is no minimum reserve requirement, an increase in the confidence of the money holders about the ability of the money issuers to redeem their claims may well allow them to multiply the stock of money in circulation to many times the stock of base money;

that is, if competition does not force the money issuers to limit money production, redeemability in the absence of strong reserve requirements will not do either.[19] To distinguish the claims here, White says, "The creation and maintenance of that confidence was the product of a scarce good" (1995: 91); that is, by itself competition would not suffice to restrain the money issuers, redeemability for a scarce merchandize is also necessary. For Hayek, on the other hand, the key factor that would allow a claim to circulate as a medium of exchange is the public trust in the issuer's commitment to keep its value more or less stable, and such commitment is reinforced by competition up to a point in which redeemability may be dispensed.

6.8.7 Another Attribute is its Availability at the Desired Level

Money, under the GAMOE definition, is a merchandise with a very definite purpose in society, that is, to allow and to enhance the division of labor by the exercise of entrepreneurial creativity of all economic agents. As such, money has its own supply and demand. Our current monetary arrangements are characterized by a monopoly of issuance in almost every country; these arrangements have inherited this monopolistic feature from the monetary regimes in place in Western countries at least since the first quarter of the nineteenth century. It is difficult, under such arrangements, to visualize how the supply of money could be regulated by the market; or for that matter, why it should be regulated by the market. Nonetheless, a truly praxeological currency is one that not only will not hinder entrepreneurial activity, but one that would even offer a venue for the entrepreneurial spirit. Such currency in itself is a currency that, by the action of competing suppliers, could have its supply matching a varying demand for cash balances by economic agents.

This attribute can be achieved neither by the redemption in specie that follows the actual production constraints for the monetary commodity nor by a self-imposed constraint by the issuer because he is unable to know what the quantity desired by his consumers, the "money holders," is. It can only be achieved by competition among issuers, producing the amount of money that the market demands, neither more nor less. It can be argued that since an "inflation target" type of monetary policy has a loose approach to the monetary aggregates, it may well perform the job of supplying the "optimum" amount of money demanded by the agents. I am not prepared to totally disregard this claim; however, I would like to point out that, as the recent history of money supply in the United States has shown, say, since the beginning of Mr. Greenspan's administration of the **Fed** until the present day, it is very difficult to know what the inflation is in order to have it targeted. Are the securities' prices included in the inflation index? And are the prices of residences and other real estate assets included in the price index? I have my reservations about the possibility of a monetary authority having enough information about what the changes in the general prices level are, or to put it another way, if even the concept of changes in the general level of prices is a meaningful one.

6.8.8 Difficulties in Achieving Stability in the Purchasing Power of Money through Redeemability

Achieving trustworthiness through reserves in order to guarantee the redeemability of a fiduciary media has an important cost consideration. We could take a model of a fiduciary currency backed for 100% reserves in gold as an extreme example. In accordance with historical experience, we may note that many consider this model as very difficult to implement and to maintain. There are many considerations supporting such an opinion. In particular, the cost of this model, one of the most common objections raised against a 100% reserve requirement, will be discussed in the next section. But there are other considerations, such as the arguably insurmountable difficulty of enforcing it.[20] Among other doubts, there is the fact that the supply of gold is subject to unknown factors outside human control. The lack of human control, which is usually considered one of the blessings of such a system by forcing the depoliticization of the money supply, may well be considered a curse in some extreme thought experiments, such as the theoretical possibility that, after a system like the one described has been adopted and used for some time all over the world, something like the "El Dorado" or something as mystical as that could be discovered and the price of gold would suffer a stupendous drop.

An argument downplaying the catastrophic effects predicted as a consequence of that hypothesis is that something like this already happened at least three times in the past. First, in the fourteenth century, the decimation of the European population by the Plague produced an effect of a relative increase in the amount of precious metals in circulation. Second, soon after the discovery of America and the influx of specie to Europe, again the amount of gold in circulation increased stupendously in a relatively short period of time. And finally, after the Gold Rush in California, which was followed by the discoveries in Alaska and South Africa, the available quantity of gold increased so rapidly that, as a result of it, 90% of the existing gold today was mined after 1840.[21] Yet, at the time of the big gold discoveries in the middle of the nineteenth century, the gold standard was in force almost everywhere, and no monetary crisis was reported because of it.

The increase in the money supply considered in isolation theoretically would produce an increase in the general level of prices; however, from 1865 (end of the Civil War) until 1876 deflation was very high in the United States, although redemption suspended during the Civil War only resumed in 1879 due to the tightening in liquidity by the federal government. From 1876 to 1896, deflation subsided in the United States, but it was still 1.5 % per year; after that, inflation resumed and was 2% per year until 1914 (Friedman, 1994: 76). Obviously, flexibility in adapting to the existing money supply was only possible under flexible labor markets and, in comparison with today, the general economic openness that resulted in the huge gains of productivity that happened during the second half of the nineteenth century, not to mention the economic impact of the Civil War.

But if no inflationary crisis can be associated with the increase in gold supply during the second half of the nineteenth century, we may well attribute it to external circumstances and not necessarily to some inner feature of the gold standard model of monetary arrangements. That is why we cannot infer based on those events that the market behavior in response to a hypothetical discovery of an "El Dorado" would be the same another time around as it was in that period.

6.8.9 Taking Cost into Consideration as a Desirable Attribute of Good Money

In a now classic essay, Roger Garrison argued that a comparison among different monetary systems based on their costs would "not be meaningful unless the corresponding benefits are brought into view" (Garrison, 1985: 61).[22] The cost of a gold standard should not be considered in isolation from its benefits. Furthermore, talking specifically about the *resource* cost of gold, Garrison points out that we cannot assume that they will be zero under fiat money arrangements:

> The effectiveness of the resource-cost argument against the gold standard rests on the popular perception that the activities of mining gold, refining it, casting it into bars or minting it into coins, storing it, and guarding it are collectively wasteful activities and the implicit assumption that if the gold standard were supplanted by a paper standard, these activities would cease. (Garrison, 1985: 70)

Evidently, gold has not lost its luster because it has lost its attribute of legal tender. However, Garrison's argument still leaves open the possibility that gold continues to be mined because of its industrial uses. But White argues that whether or not it pays to incur the resource cost of a gold standard versus the resource cost under a fiat money regime is a question that may be answered empirically and that in measuring it we may find an argument to support the thesis that the resource cost of the current fiat money arrangements worldwide are *higher* than the resource cost of the gold standard in its different forms in the fifty years or so before it was abolished. He argues that if we assume that the demand for gold for other uses has remained constant since the 1920s, any difference in the "real" price of gold (as measured by the CPI) is due to changes in its "monetary" demand; and "the question of whether world resource costs are lower under fiat regimes reduces to the question of whether the monetary stock demand for gold has fallen" (White, 1999: 43). His answer is yes, even at the record low prices of the late 1990s: "$300 per ounce in 1998 is equivalent to more than $60 at 1967 prices, whereas gold was $35 per ounce in 1967. It is equivalent to more than $31 at 1929 prices, whereas gold was $20.67 per ounce in 1929" (1999: 43).

Garrison's argument for an opportunity cost approach and White's evidence suggest that a gold standard with 100% reserves and no legal (or forced) tender system is not necessarily the one that has the highest "social" cost. Still, it would be worthwhile to examine if for each individual agent it would be the case. Or, in other words, how were the economic agents concretely nudged out of the gold standard gradually during the nineteenth and twentieth centuries? Basically, they were induced to accept apparently comparably trustworthy forms of money and thereby avoid the expenses of keeping the stock of gold safe, to print paper money, to organize archives, et cetera.

As an example, if an issuing bank started to issue USD 1 billion per year and charged the bullion owners a fee of 2%, this bank could not bear more than USD 20 million of administrative costs during the period in which the issue remained outstanding.

Could we assume what the average period of money issued remaining outstanding would be?

Would the public be willing to pay a 2% fee to hold this trustworthy money? A well-known and often-cited estimate for the United States (Friedman and Schwartz, 1993: 5) places the annual resource cost of a "pure commodity standard" at 2.5 per cent of net national product (White, 1995: 148).

With the known limitations that such an estimation has (such as not distinguishing the "initial" cost of acquiring the bullion necessary to start the system from the "flow" cost of maintaining it), it is necessary to emphasize that the estimate is for a gold standard with a 100% reserve requirement not only for the issuance of banknotes and demand deposits but most time-deposits as well, since it was based on the cost to acquire gold enough to cover any increase in M2.

White has argued that a monetary system of free banking and no reserve requirement mirrored in the nineteenth-century Scottish system would not require holding more than 2% of its demand liabilities in reserve, which would imply basically a cost of about one-fiftieth of Milton Friedman's estimate, that is 0.05% of GNP.

Can we have a trustworthy monetary system without the cost that a 100% reserve requirement implies? The answer to this question is particularly relevant to the question of the desirability of a precious metallic standard, because the most common objections to specie standard have been the expense of exclusively metallic money and the supposed inherent instability of a banking system that economizes on specie by introducing **fractional reserves**.

An opportunity cost approach when talking about the cost of the gold standard system under fractional reserves shows its irrelevance because the problem with that system is its trustworthiness, due to its inherent weakness to confront a crisis, and not its cost, as White's numbers just mentioned demonstrate. Perhaps, it can be argued that a gold standard system with fractional reserves has a good relation of costs and benefits and therefore discussing the cost of this system may be justified after all. But it seems to me that if the purpose of incurring any cost is to have some asset in reserve in order to redeem the currency, we need to ask first what the intended purpose of that is. A gold standard system with fractional reserves can have a central bank like in England in the second half of the nineteenth century or concurrent issuing banks like in Scotland at about the same time. In the former case, the effective guarantor of the system is the perceived capacity of the lender of last resort (in the case of the Bank of England, its implicit banking by the British government) and in the latter case, the discipline imposed by competition. Well, if so, then the trustworthiness of a gold standard system with fractional reserves does not rely *directly* on the reserves and so, again, there is no purpose in arguing about an optimum amount of reserves and the cost of achieving it. Under a hypothetical free banking system, the reason for incurring any cost at all to establish reserves is only justifiable if proved that the discipline imposed by competition would not be sufficient to provide adequate limitation on the money supply and therefore that some cost should be incurred in order to add an extra institutional feature to assure such control; then, the amount of reserves will be determined by the demonstrated preference of the economic agents in their dealings with the banks and not by legislated fiat.

Here is not the proper place to enter into a full discussion on a gold standard with fractional reserves; this topic was brought up just to emphasize the need to evaluate the cost of any monetary arrangement according to the attributes of good money.

The cost of any monetary system has two dimensions that may be taken into account. The first one is the cost of different possible monetary arrangements to the community in general. In defining the legal institutions that will regulate the medium, or media, of exchange, it would be desirable for the political agents to take cost into consideration, preferably using the already-mentioned opportunity cost approach suggested by Ronald Coase. To the extent that the decision about some attributes of the medium of exchange is left to the citizenry not as voters but as economic agents that may influence the end result by the sum of their individual decisions, it is naturally expected that they will evaluate the costs and benefits of their individual decisions within the boundaries allowed by the institutional framework for them to demonstrate their preferences.

The widespread monetary system of forced tender, central bank, fiduciary currency, and exchange controls is considered by the criteria of direct resource cost the cheapest of the monetary systems. Theoretically, not only there is no cost to build reserves either at the commercial banks or at the central bank, but there are also no limits to the seigniorage, and therefore, under normal circumstances, the system is actually a profit center for the government. We have seen, however, that it is exactly the potential for monetary disequilibrium under such a system that leads some economic agents, public and private alike, to use gold as a store of value in proportions even bigger than under the diluted forms of the gold exchange systems in place in the interwar period and later the one established by the Bretton Woods Treaty.[23] Still, theoretically, if we could count on angelical central bankers and therefore abstract the other reasons against such arrangements, that system would be the least expensive way to provide a medium of exchange.

6.8.10 Ideal Money and the Requirements for Dynamic Efficiency

In between, the system of substitution with legal tender, no central bank, substitution, and free exchange like in Panama is costlier than the system of forced tender, central bank, currency board, and fractional reserves like it used to be in Argentina under their "convertibility law" (from 1994–2001).[24]

In Panama with "**dollarization**," not only is there no seigniorage for the local government (only for the US government), but also there is the cost to the country of acquiring 100% of the **hard currency** that is actually used as money. Who actually bears this cost is subject to controversy, though. In Panama, the private banks (mainly foreigners) usually provide the domestic market with the necessary banknotes, the amount regulated by the spread between the interests in the domestic market vis-à-vis the interests in the international capital markets pondered by the country's risk. The money holders in their turn have a power to access goods not only in the domestic market but also worldwide, so it cannot be simply considered a "net" cost of this arrangement since there are gains associated with the use of the US dollar for the money holders inside the country.

In Argentina, the local government used to have, to some extent, a seigniorage income and did not have the acquisition cost of 100% reserves (because they did not have it), and at same time the Central Bank could collect interest on the reserves that it effectively held.

Juan Luis Moreno-Villalaz in "Cost of Using the Dollar as Currency" uses the comprehensive opportunity cost approach mentioned earlier and concludes:

> Previous studies about the financial cost of a unified currency system concluded that it entails a substantial seigniorage cost. These studies, however, did not compare the cost and total foreign exchange used in a unified currency system with the cost and international reserves of an autonomous monetary system. Furthermore, these studies overestimated the currency to GDP ratios in the dollar system. A new estimate, taking into account the opportunity cost of a monetary system, shows that a) the dollar system used less international currency, four to six percentage points of GDP less than the autonomous system; b) the opportunity costs of either monetary system are more or less equal. Thus, a unified currency system, or Dollarization, does not impose a cost to the economy. However, it has the benefit of stability, low interest, no banking crisis, automatic adjustment mechanism, and the savings of not having central banks. (Moreno-Villalaz, 1998: 18)

Along this continuum from the least expensive to the most expensive monetary system, if the resource cost is considered in isolation, how could it be made comparable?[25] White proposes a methodology to do so (1999: 48). It was mentioned that the estimates for a commodity money with a 100% reserve requirement and virtually no room for the production of fiduciary media may be estimated around 2.5% of the GNP, and that the resource cost of a commodity money system with no reserve requirement may be estimated between the range of 2.5% and 0.05% of the GNP subject to the expressed preference of the money holders for more or less reserves. Quoting 1994 research done by A. J. Rolnick and W. E. Weber from the Minneapolis Federal Reserve Bank, White assumes that the annual inflation under commodity money was *minus* 0.5%. On the other hand, the average annual inflation in the fifteen countries selected in their research, eliminating from the calculation episodes of hyperinflation, was 6.5%; this 7% annual spread is the "benefit" brought by commodity money in a comparison with fiat money. Using a standard approach to measure the welfare cost of inflation, White concludes that a fiat standard may cost about 0.5% of GNP if it results on average in an inflation of 6.5% per annum (1999: 49). According to that estimation, a monetary system with fiat money may be well worth it if it results in an average inflation rate lower than that, even if compared with the cost of a monetary system with commodity money, if the percentage of total liabilities in reserves held by the banks does not exceed 20%.

However, the above calculation, it is important to point out, is presented here simply to illustrate the necessity to take cost into consideration as an attribute of any monetary system and does not imply an endorsement of its results. For one, the effects of inflation on the coordination function of the price mechanism may be higher than considered in the above calculation. For instance, I think that episodes of hyperinflation must be taken into consideration (which increases the average inflation to the level of 18% annually and increases dramatically the welfare cost of fiat money); after all, it is through hyperinflation that some of the monetary claims against the governments are cancelled out, and therefore they are not extemporaneous episodes but inherent to the (mis)management that fiat money regimes allow.

6.9 CONCLUSION

In the same way that the dynamic dimension of economic efficiency does not contradict the static dimension, it may be understood that the broad sense in which prudence as a virtue was described in this work also does not contradict the narrow sense of utility maximization commonly adopted today.

In the realm of economics, it can be argued that the "Theory of Dynamic Efficiency" better describes the reality of economic process and the central role that entrepreneurship has in answering the economic problems faced by society; it offers a valuable instrument for evaluating economic policy in general and monetary policy in particular.

In this book I argue that the three attributes of money, (i) stability of value, (ii) availability in the amounts needed for trade, and (iii) cost maximization, can be deduced or derived from Dynamic Efficiency theory.[26]

The relation between the stability of value in money and the desire that social institutions do not hinder the exercise of entrepreneurial activity is a straightforward relation. The importance of keeping the value of money relatively stable is a necessary corollary once one accepts the concept of dynamic efficiency as the criterion for analysis of monetary policy. The relations between the theory of dynamic efficiency and the desirability for an adaptable supply of money to the demand for cash balances and the costs considerations of money deserve more reflection, more than what can possibly be addressed here.

It seems that, under specific circumstances, a case can be made for the desirability of a variable supply of medium of exchange for the enhancement of entrepreneurial activity, therefore making it easier to move the curve of maximum production "to the right;" and hence, with qualifications, the advocacy of some flexibility in the money supply can also be directly derived from the application of the concept of dynamic efficiency. It may be restated as follows: the equilibrium between supply and demand for cash balances is achieved not only by changes in the demand for money that must be adjusted to a fixed supply, but also by changes in the supply of money, so long as these changes are not arbitrary but as a consequence of the sum of the decisions by the individual money suppliers acting in competition. However, the criterion of cost maximization in the supply of money may be understood as only indirectly related to the concept of dynamic efficiency, and only under the (reasonable) assumption that it is not in contradiction with the concept of static efficiency. A decision to use the least expensive money, as it results from balancing the costs and benefits of the adoption of a given medium of exchange, addresses a concern of static efficiency more properly, and such behavior is based on the very human tendency of utility maximization.

NOTES

1. Ayn Rand, in the chapter "What Is Capitalism?" of her book *Capitalism: The Unknown Ideal*, uses these three categories to classify the different schools of thought about the nature of the good (1965:21).

2. Still, in order to understand how serious thinkers in the past, such as Sir Issac Newton adopted such theory, it is important to remind ourselves that he made an extensive report of the coins circulating in London in the decade preceding the report's publication in 1719, at the time he was the Master of the British Mint, and the empirical evidence he found "reaffirms the principle that coins were truly looked upon as bullion in the eighteenth century. His data lends support to other ample evidence that Latin American coins were the dominant moneys, not only of our American colonies, but also of the entire world." (Lasser et all, 1997: 5) So, it was not him the intrinsic metallist, everybody were. The commentator may disagree with the sum of individuals' evaluations as revealed by their behavior, but intellectual honesty requires that to be acknowledged as a fact. And the historical context explain that, it is hardly surprising at a time that there were literally thousands of different coins in circulation, with varied weights and grades of purity, that mostly, if not all coins were assessed by their weight and purity, unless there were a taker of them as a higher value than their intrinsic value.

3. I personally think that it is regrettable that the theory of money value of the Austrian School of economists came to be known as a subjectivist theory, when they stressed that their theory is a Catallactic one, one in which value is created by the spontaneous interaction of the agents in the free market. Obviously, I understand the long history of the subjectivist theory of value and the fact that Menger's marginalist theory is the culmination of such a long process (as described in chapter I.2, "Brief Account of the Intellectual History of Money, Starting with Aristotle"). Furthermore, the theory of Austrian economics is directly opposed to the Statist or Nominalistic ones and that is why it became known as a Subjectivist one; but I continue to think that naming their Catallactic theory as a subjectivist one is really unfortunate.

4. For the sake of precision, a qualification may be made. As already described, (see footnote 35), some *Chartalists* argue that the state does not give value to its money by fiat, but by making it really useful to the money holders as an instrument to pay taxes. Also I mentioned other ways in which the state may create valuable money or enhance the value of money by legislating uses for its money. That does not contradict what is stated in this paragraph; to the extent that their claim ceases to be one that the state creates value for its money regardless of the utility that economic agents may derive from its use, they can no longer be considered *Nominalists*. In essence, this is a claim that it is not by state fiat that money value is created, but that indirectly, by the utility that may be derived from money, that the state may create value. However, this claim can not be used as an argument for giving free rein to the government to do whatever it wants to money, since, on multiple grounds, the government then may be called to justify why it is varying the usefulness of its money for the money holders.

5. One may be reluctant to use, however, this terminology, since it could imply that someone may know better than the market what the "objective" value of money is and therefore de-characterize the *Catallatic* theories as objective ones. I dispute that. At any given time, the value of money is what it is, i.e., the market value. Perhaps someone knows or thinks that he knows about future political events, or natural events, or whatever, that will impact the *future* value of the currency. He may be right,

or he may be wrong. If he is right, eventually this knowledge will come to the market and the impact of the events will be reflected in the market price for that currency. If he is wrong, it will be only another wrong bet.

The value of the money is, in my understanding, at the same time objective and Catallactic, in the sense that if the attributes of given money are not recognized by the market, they do not produce the good results that may be expected from them; and, therefore, these attributes reside in the realm of intentions and not in the reality. Is the money trusted to be stable and generally accepted? Is the money non-expensive? If it is, it is so because it is perceived by the economic agents in the market to be so.

The finance minister may be Bishop Nicolas Oresme himself, the State may be as solid as Gibraltar Rock, the money may be redeemable and gold reserves may exist to redeem all outstanding money; even so, if these facts (true or false as they may be), for whatever reason, are not acknowledged by the economic agents, the money will not be a reliable, stable, and non-expensive medium of exchange; therefore it will not be possible to say, objectively, that it has a corresponding value. And just to stress the argument, when these facts come to be proven true, and they become accepted in the market, then it will command a different value in the market, because it will produce benefits that otherwise it would not.

6. On that, Mariana's remark, as quoted by Laurel (2008:142), that "It is said that statesmen very often act according to the principle that necessity knows no law" should be taken at face value.

7. Arguments for fiscal needs as the ultimate justification for government's intervention in monetary matters may be also found in David Glasner (2005: 36) and James Buchanan (2000) among others. Incidentally, Buchanan's description of the government as a "revenue-maximizing ogre" is a very illustrative one.

8. That, legally, private property rights are not absolute is a matter of positive law everywhere, to my knowledge; the issue discussed in this section is if ethically, in terms of reasoning about what is moral, one may find arguments against a conception of absolute rights.

9. Admittedly, this "Hobbesian Minimal State" is a departure from the Hobbes mature ideas that all property rights are conventional and therefore the Sovereign is not limited by previously acquired property over "plows" since there were none previous to civil society; indeed in Part I of *Behemoth, or the epitome of the Civil Wars of England,* Hobbes explicitly rejects the idea: "the people in general were so ignorant of their duty, as that not one perhaps of ten thousand knew what right any man had to command him, or what necessity there was of King or Commonwealth, for which he was to part with his money against his will; but thought himself to be so much master of whatsoever he possessed, that it could not be taken from him upon any pretence of common safety without his own consent" (Hobbes, 1839).

Still the concept of a "Hobbesian Minimal State" is conforming to Hobbes ideas about the origin and purposes of civil society and in this sense it is applied here. That is the sense in which Levin uses the concept of "Hobbesian Minimal State" and also, in my understanding, equivalent to the identification James Buchanan has with a "Hobbesian" world view, one in which individuals are utility maximizers, everyone prefers order to anarchy, only the sovereign can establish order, but there are no controls over the sovereign's passions.

For Buchanan, that view is compatible with Public Choice theory, although it was empirically disproved; after all, history tells us that almost always the sovereigns have been constrained (Buchanan, 1979: 274). So, here the "Hobbesian" view, as for the "Virginia school," should be blended with contractualism (Buchanan, 2000: 7) and should not be understood as literally and narrowly derived from Hobbes thought.

In the same line, according to May (2013) it is possible to categorize the limitations to the sovereign power in the following categories: moral, prudential, legal and structural, international, and self-imposed limitations. For him, Hobbes accepts all those limitations on the powers of the sovereign, having those, more or less "teeth" as they may have, being some only in foro interno.

Still, the relevant question for our inquiry is to recognize Hobbes as a natural law jurist, and therefore, his concept of sovereignty, considering the salus populi (safety of the people) ultimate source of its legitimacy, is bound by that law and other prudential considerations. One does not need to think about a Hobbesian sovereign as bound by the Rule of Law or Constitutional order as we think today to see that it is in the long term interest of the sovereign to establish positive laws defining and protecting private property rights and to enforce those laws; particularly in money and banking.

10. For all practical purposes, because it must be assumed that under the Hobbesian covenant, the sovereign will utilize every means at his disposal to restore or compensate any property taken in an emergency to the defense of the polity.

11. Still, evidently, there is a qualitative distinction, both legal and moral, between taxation and expropriation and that will soon be explored.

12. As common an opinion of the sixteenth-century theologians as the censure of excommunication in the case of a king imposing new taxes without the consent of the people would be (Laures, 2008: 125), that was not necessarily the opinion of the kings in Europe and Spain in particular, more inclined to see the Bull as an intromission into secular affairs, as the publication of Don Juan Luis Lopez' "Historia Legal de la Bula llamada "In Coena Domini" and the legal opinion of Josef de Ledesma show.

13. For instance, as mentioned by Younkins (2011: 14), for Rand life is an ultimate end and a goal in itself. The neo-Aristotelian philosophers mentioned by Younkins, specifically the ones named here, would have said that it is not any life, but a life proper to a human being, a life that is the actualization of the individual's potentialities that is the ultimate end. Here is not the place to develop the corollaries of that distinction, suffice it to say that the difference exists and it is metaphysical in its character.

14. As an explanation why I have excluded deontology from consideration here, I would propose that deontology in morals, as in Kant, although it is intended to depart from utilitarian considerations, in the end results in a collectivist approach to political action and a disregard for the consequences of political decisions for individuals, allowing us, for these reasons, to seat Kantian justifications on the same side of the divide as the positivists and utilitarians. I understand that this is a huge and controversial claim that requires defense, but this is not the place to attempt that.

15. There are some problems here, problems that I do not hope to solve but that at least should be acknowledged. The problems I am mentioning are all of them related to the centrality of Ludwig von Mises contributions to what we understand today as Austrian Economics; and these problems are (a) Mises' ethical utilitarianism, (b) his neo-Kantian epistemology, and (c) his assertion that economics as a science is value-free. If one accepts these statements about Mises' view on ethics, epistemology and philosophy of science as truly representative of Mises philosophical views without qualification and out of context, one may deem them to contradict Younkins' conclusion that may be summarized as stating that a synthesis among neo-Aristotelism in ethics, Objectivism in epistemology and Austrian Economics in politics is not only possible but indeed, once they are put together, they become the best justification for a Classical Liberal Order.

In regard to Mises' utilitarianism in ethics, my conclusion from the 2000 contribution of Leland Yeager and the discussion between Walter Block and J. Patrick Gunning in 2002 in the American Journal of Economics and Sociology is that it is true that Mises adhered to a form of rule-utilitarianism—that is, the moral guide for political action is the establishment of rules that may lead to good consequences. But these rules may well be the ones protecting natural rights, and the good consequences may well be perfectionist at an individual level; that is, the rules most suitable for fostering the division of labor are the ones that better allow individuals to flourish. That is the conclusion of Edward W. Younkins (Younkins, 2005) and it seems a reasonable one to me. In support of that understanding, Pacheco, in his doctoral dissertation (1986:1), states that "several writers presented moral theories in which utilitarian considerations support strong theories of rights." His thesis is that such compatibility with natural rights of a consequentialist moral theory such as utilitarism, may be understood by a simple silogism:

- PM—Private property generates wealth;
- PM—Natural Rights protect private property;
- Conclusion—Therefore, Natural Rights enhances the generation of wealth.

That is better understood, argues Pacheco (page 4) if the utilitarian in consideration is a "rule-utilitarian," that is, one which accepts an "indirect utilitarianism" in the sense proposed by John Gray in which "utility serves as a principle of evaluation of whole systems of rules and not of any given action." (page 5) Well, I argue, that is exactly the case of Mises. In regard to Mises' neo-Kantian epistemology, I will rely again on Younkins, this time his account of to what amounts to Mises' neo-Kantianism in epistemology:

> Rothbard could not accept Mises' Kantian extreme aprioristic position in epistemology. Mises held that the axiom of human action was true a priori to human experience and was, in fact, a synthetic a priori category. Mises considered the action axiom to be a law of thought and thus a categorical truth prior to all human experience. Murray Rothbard agreed that the action axiom is universally true and self-evident but argued that a person becomes aware of that axiom and its subsidiary axioms through experience in the world. (Younkins, 2004)

If the discussion about the neo-Kantian influence in Mises' epistemology may be limited to whether or not Mises apriorism is a law of thought or deduced from previous experiences, that does not seem to compromise our Rothbardian stance presented in this paragraph (incidentally, I also agree with Rothbard on the nature of any aprioristic thinking).

Finally, in regard to Mises' idea of economics as a "value-free" science, it seems clear to me that in that regard Mises was narrowing the scope of all inquiry in economics to what is purely descriptive; and to the extent that that is possible, again, it does not seem to be a problem to the claim that Catallatics better fit a neo-Aristotelian perfectionist individualistic tradition in ethics. That seems to be the case, for instance, if you agree that the (ethical) value of the division of labor for human beings is a given to be accepted aprioristically as a fact. I personally dispute that that is possible, the advantages of the division of labor are vast, a constant in human society, and they may be understood as derived from deeply ingrain attributes of human beings; but all that must be hypothesized, evidence must be collected, a due consideration to whom the starting hypothesis is a different one and to possible contrary evidence must be given (not to mention recognition that there are those who attribute moral value to things that are in contradiction with the advancement of the division of labor). All of that is just to say that even some of the most obvious and basic of our assumptions may require justification because they are deduced and therefore, not intrinsically aprioristic regardless of the source of aprioristic knowledge as said before; and furthermore, even if we agree as an aprioristic assumption on the economic benefits of the division of labor, still it is possible that someone would not attribute a higher moral value to them than others which possibly may be in contradiction with the division of labor.

Back to Mises, if you think about economic theory in the "extreme aprioristic position in epistemology" criticized by Rothbard and mentioned by Younkins above, then you may conclude that the entire realm of descriptive economics is "value-free." So, Mises' claim that economics should deal purely with facts may be understood as a consequence of his ideas about the nature of aprioristic theories and as applicable (only) to the descriptive aspect of economics, which again does seem to me sufficient to prevent the claim discussed in the paragraph which gave occasion to this footnote.

16. As money is the generally accepted medium of exchange, and as the instrument that economic agents tend to select to perform their indirect transactions would be one with the highest liquidity, which is the one easiest to sell at a minimum, or possibly,

zero discount, as has been previously argued, the following discussion is about the attributes that make something the preferred instrument for indirect transactions (footnote 21). That is, what makes something the most salable; what causes a certain instrument to be preferred and selected?

17. Gerald O'Driscoll, in discussing stable money, argued that stability of purchasing power to the extent that it could be measured by a price index is not an unqualified good; under fiat money, if the monetary authorities were able to "perfectly" balance the supply and demand for money in order to keep its purchasing power stable by recurring to deep swings in its supply, the cost of such policy would be sharp changes in the economy, or in his words, "Unless a monetary policy of stabilizing PPM is neutral even in the short run, it can itself become a source of instability of real economic activity" (O'Driscoll, 1983: 329). O'Driscoll's hypothesis leads us to think that stability of value is not an "ultimate goal." Stability of value is, perhaps, the most important attribute that appeals to the economic agents in their search for an instrument for their indirect exchanges, but nonetheless, it is just one of the many attributes sought, and not an end in itself. So, as a criterion to select among possible instruments for indirect exchanges, if everything else is equal, it seems to me that the one that offers more stability would be preferred by the majority of the economic agents. That is not to say that a rigorous policy to keep the inflation target at zero, no matter what, under a government with monopolistic fiat money, would be a good thing. This leads us to another thought: there is a difference between some instruments for indirect exchange that have an inherently more stable exchange ratio in relation to other goods (that is, their supply is less elastic to positive changes in prices) than others—say, precious metals versus base metals—and that would make them preferable to be used as money if the decision was spontaneously made by the free interaction of the economic agents. That is hardly a novel thought, but it helps to convey the confined sense in which stability of value is a desirable attribute of money.

18. There are no recent cases of monetary systems organized under free banking arrangements. With the exception of Hong Kong between 1973 and 1983, issuing currency has been a monopoly almost everywhere since the beginning of the twentieth century. Nowadays, despite being allowed private issued currency, the Hong Kong case is more precisely a system of "currency board," since the issuing banks operate with foreign exchange reserves backing their note issuance business. Although there are no free banking monetary systems nowadays, some competitive constraint has been in force, however attenuated in its effects, by the freedom of trade in foreign currencies that exists in the capitalist countries.

19. According to White: "In sophisticated gold-based banking systems without legal restrictions on reserve ratios, like Scotland's in the nineteenth century, the stock of bank reserves equaled about 2 percent of demand liabilities" (White, 1999: 47).

20. Quoting Yeager: "Efforts to enforce 100 percent banking in the face of contrary incentives and private ingenuity would require unacceptably extreme government interference" (Yeager, 1983: 318).

21. Gold.org. Accessed March 20, 2015.

22. As Garrison points out the argument for a comprehensive opportunity cost analysis while comparing different monetary systems is a particular case of Ronald Coase's claim for a comparative analysis of alternative social arragnements (Garrison, 1985: 77).

23. The total reserves of Gold hold as a store of value by governments and individuals were estimated by Mike Hewitt in his blog (http://dollardaze.org) to be 34% of the total of 161.000 tons of above ground gold inventory in existence, based on data released in September 2008 by the World Gold Council, which represents at current prices for gold at the time about 3.1 trillion US Dollars. At the same time Hewitt estimated using available M1 data that the major currencies in the world converted to USD would amount to 18.4 trillion USD. The relation therefore between the amount of money kept by governments and individuals and the amount of fiat money and demand deposits is one of about 18.15%.

24. In Argentina both the US Dollar and the Peso used to be legal tender. Nowadays, the Peso is forced tender.

25. If one considers that this continuum has at one extreme, as the most expensive monetary system, the one with commodity money and 100% reserve requirement and on the other extreme a fiat money system, with systems with fractional reserve in between, one may ask, where does free banking fit into this continuum? My answer to that question is that hypothetically all systems along the continuum could have free banking arrangements, or none. That is, the discussion about the feature of free banking does not belong to the discussion about the cost of alternative monetary systems; it is another dimension of the general discussion about how to classify monetary systems.

26. Section 6.6—The Dynamic Efficiency Theory

IV

Politics

SEVEN

Are There Unsurmountable Arguments for Monetary Prerogatives?

The inquiry so far conducted in this book has been a purely abstract intellectual exercise. Now it is time to apply some of the concepts presented in regard to the metaphysics, epistemology, and ethics of money to politics. In order to do that, a number of different cases will be discussed.

The practical goal with this first inquiry is to evaluate if there is an argument that cannot be put aside in favor of "central banking;" and by central banking I mean the government's prerogative to regulate money and credit. I start by identifying three different categories of arguments in favor of central banking and I have confidence that I have found sufficient grounds to dismiss the first two. In order to deal with the third argument, we will discuss philosophically whether the institutions of private property and freedom of contract in general and good money in particular are of a higher value than national defense; also we will analyze if there are other ways to provide funds for national defense instead of manipulation of money and credit.

There are many arguments in favor of the government's monetary prerogatives. Such prerogatives generally include the power to define what can be used as money, who will be authorized to produce it, what the rules are, if any, for its production. It also includes the power to authorize banks to operate and regulate them, and perhaps, most importantly, how those powers will be used as an instrument for government's policies; that is, the ways in which monetary and fiscal policy will be deployed to mutually support each other and the ultimate goals of the state. The government may use its prerogative benignly or malignly. A benign use of monetary prerogatives by the government would be the definition of a monetary regime with no forced tender, allowing competitive supply of money, for instance. A malign use of the monetary prerogatives happens when the government manipulates money and credit and by *that* I mean the enforcement of rules for money and credit that would infringe on property rights and freedom of contract.[1]

Since it is the existence of the monetary prerogatives which gives occasion for monetary manipulation, an important question to ask is on which grounds such prerogative is advocated. In its modern incarnation, most interventionism in money and banking has been delegated to a government agency generally called the Central Bank. Although that was not so in the past, a modern discussion about monetary prerogatives is, in essence, a discussion about justifications for central banking.

Central banks' primary purpose in regard to the economic life of a country is to provide a medium of exchange where a single medium of exchange is permitted or to regulate its supply where there are competing suppliers. Since banking everywhere is fractional reserve banking to a greater or lesser extent, there is always a risk of crisis of liquidity at short notice in the banking industry, and therefore, a second important responsibility of the central bank is to be the "lender of last resort" for the financial system. And most, if not all, responsibilities of a central bank towards the private sector are encompassed in these two categories. But central banks have another purpose, actually their original purpose, that is, they are agents of the government's treasury; they are responsible for facilitating public funding either by helping the government to borrow or by directly crediting the government's newly produced money.

That is why we cannot discuss the rationale for central banking without taking into account fiscal policy; or as stated by Vera Smith "it must be admitted that it is almost certain that by far [the] most powerful reason leading to the maintenance of Government intervention in the banking sphere, at a time when it was on the decline in other industries, was that power over the issue of paper money, whether such power is direct or indirect, is an exceedingly welcome weapon in the armory of State finance" (1990: 9). Said differently, central banks perform their roles as money providers, lenders of last resort, and all other instrumental functions in order to better perform their original function, that is, to become a better agent to the state in general and particularly to the fisc.[2]

A discussion about the rationale for central banking should, therefore, be divided between justifications in regard to the central bank's role for the private sector and in regard to its role as a direct arm of the treasury and indirectly of state policy in general.

That money does not need to be monopolistically produced or to have its supply regulated by the state can be attested by the fact that money monopolistically produced in one jurisdiction may be use voluntarily by economic agents in other jurisdictions as has been the case for millennia.

Since historical evidence demonstrates that the government's monopoly on money production is not a necessary condition to having a medium of exchange available to economic agents to facilitate their indirect transactions, that should be discarded as the reason for such monopoly.[3]

But how about the group efficiency effect, where gains to all agents may be accrued from the fact they are using the same currency? This argument of efficiency in itself cannot be denied, although the transaction costs minimized by the use of a common currency may be overstated in these days of electronic and instantaneous transactions.[4] The main issue here is that to the extent that the use of a single currency offers economic benefits to individual agents, it is for them to discover and establish that by the sum of their individual decisions; it may be the case that apparent or real benefits do not pay off in comparison with the costs associated with the use of multiple currencies. In any case, the economic argument for the benefits of using a single currency, everything else being equal, is not an argument for the imposition of a monopoly, something that with the excuse of giving something of value to economic agents is taking from them the capacity to judge the supposed benefit for themselves as to what is morally wrong, evidently. Another argument for giving the state the power to regulate money is found in Hamilton's 1791 report "On the Establishment of a Mint" which states that the money produced by other sovereigns may not be reliable, as was evidenced by the debasement of the Spanish silver coin named "dollar" at the end of the eighteenth century when it was the most important medium of exchange and unit of account in the new republic of the United States of America.[5] Sound as that argument may be, it does not follow, that giving monopolistic powers to the US government or to any government for that matter to regulate money would result in better money than allowing the use of money supplied competitively. To limit for now the argument about what constitutes good money to the criterion of stability of value, the history of a state monopoly on money has been one that demonstrates that governments do not necessarily produce good and reliable money [6] even when constrained by self-imposed constraints such as a clause of convertibility; after all, those clauses can always be rescinded. So, the goal to assure "good" money is also a rationale for central banking that can be falsified; that is, central banking is neither a necessary condition nor a sufficient condition to have good money. You can have good money without central banking and central banking does not guarantee good money.[7]

That leaves us with the conclusion that the reason why governments establish such a monopoly is neither because it is necessary in order to have money available to the economic agents, nor because that allows them to produce better money than otherwise.

Returning to our assumption that modern usage of monetary prerogatives through a central bank fulfills the three purposes of (i) providing money to the daily economic activity of the citizenry, (ii) acting as a lender of last resort, and (iii) helping the government in its political goals, having disposed of the first of the three possible rationales we are left then with the other two hypotheses for governments to assume a monopoly of money production. The first is to be a better lender of last resort and the second is because that allows the central bank to better fulfill its role as enabler of the fisc.

In absolute terms, the existence of a lender of last resort is not a necessary condition for a monetary economy as is attested by the fact that for millennia, there was none; but perhaps one may say that it was unfortunate that it took so long to create a lender of last resort. Then, the argument for central banking based on the need for a lender of last resort must shift towards the question about whether central banking allows a swifter adjustment of the economy to economic fluctuations. [8]

One may argue that an inflexible supply of money may not leave enough wiggle room for adjustments to sudden or even secular changes in the demand for money without sudden or continuous changes in the value of money that would be detrimental to economic development and, therefore, the existence of a government's agency with the authority and the instruments to make changes in the money supply is necessary in order to avoid economic shocks. However, in order for the central bank to have the instruments to make changes in the supply of money by fiat, either the government establishes a legal monopoly of money production that allows it to create base money by fiat, or the government allows inflationary credit creation directly or indirectly, that is, the creation of credits without the preexisting savings, something which is done through fractional reserve arrangements in a broad sense. Furthermore, a banking system organized under fractional reserve arrangements—that is, a system in which financial intermediaries are not only leveraged but there are time mismatches in the financial operations as well—is a system that, on one hand, can mobilize existing savings more rapidly and to a greater extent by funneling them to particular uses, among them supplying the treasury with funds; on the other hand, it is more unstable. If the banking system can create multiple claims over the same amount of financial resources (for instance, by lending money at longer maturities than the maturities required from the depositors to retrieve their deposits) that allow the banking system to allocate resources as it sees fit, it may be based on a criterion of economic efficiency, or it may be based on a political mandate. The fact is that, under fractional reserve arrangements, the bankers and the politicians with power to regulate the banks can mobilize resources on a scale and with a speed that otherwise they would not be able to. And note that that can be done in any arrangement that allows the creation of multiple simultaneous claims over the same resources, not only in the case of fractional reserves on demand deposits.

The problem with leverage (borrowing in order to lend) and time mismatches (borrowing with shorter maturities than the maturities of the lending activities) is that sometimes in periods in which there are crises of confidence in the banking system or periods of increased demand for liquidity not necessarily associated with a confidence crisis in the banking system, the banks are forced to "deleverage," that is, to call back the loans they made in order to repay the investors/depositors. Since the very essence of the system is the creation of multiple financial claims over the same amount of base money, or said differently, of multiple claims on the monetary side of the economy not represented on the real side of the economy for actual goods, that liquidation becomes problematic.

It is under such arrangements of multiple claims over same assets and time mismatches that a lender of last resort becomes an important component of the system, an essential component of the system. But if not for the significantly improved conditions for the banking system to fund the government under such arrangements, it is doubtful that that would be the "architecture" of choice for a financial system and therefore for the need of a central bank; or to say it differently: what compels the government to come to the rescue of the banks in times of crisis of liquidity if not for the need governments have to tap into the inflationary creation of credits conjured by the banks through fractional reserve banking?

Not long ago (before 1844), the ratio of reserves to bank liabilities in England was about 30%; when the role of the Bank of England (BoE) as the lender of last resort became known and trusted, that ratio started to decline. Aside from the general interest in having a healthy financial system as an instrument for economic growth that most politicians have, the state has a vested interest in the solvency of the banking system to the extent that the banks are agents of the treasury in its effort to raise liquidity to fund public expenses. However, that role is limited when money production is limited by external factors, such as the refusal by economic agents, both domestically and abroad, to accept things other than precious metals as money and to accept those only at their intrinsic value and not at their face value. But today, base money is everywhere fiat money so, at least for mainstream theorists, central banks around the world can increase the money supply and drive down interest rates on treasury bonds almost indefinitely and that allows them to be more effective lenders of last resort than before. But one should not accept that a fiat money regime allows for easier increases of the money supply and see in that a good thing when the government is supporting the banks; after all, if not forced to divert saving to fund the public debt in one way or other, and not being caught in the moral hazard problem that a lender of last resort creates, the banks would not have needed a lender of last resort in first place.[9] So, on what does the answer to the question of whether a central bank with the power to manipulate the money supply, either by the inflationary creation of money or by credit, is a stabilizer factor in the economy and therefore an acceptable rationale for a central bank depend? It depends on the idea that banking arrangements are not only of the fractional reserve kind but that there is the implicit or explicit guarantee given by the government that they will come to the rescue of the financial system if needed. And the bankers may be sure of such a thing because the government, if nothing else, needs the financial system to float the public debt. If not for the need to place public debt in the market, the government would be freer to make clear to economic agents in general that a rescue of the banks with public funds, real or inflationary, is not to be expected, and therefore, the banks would be required to operate much more prudently than otherwise.

To conclude, the argument that central banks are necessary to act as lenders of last resort in order to give stability to the financial system starts from the premise that central banks add more stability than the instability they bring. That presumption obviously is a *praesumptio* iuris tantum , that is, a rebuttable presumption; therefore, this assumption only offers a rationale for central banking if it is proved that the net result of central banking is superior to the result in the absence of central banking. If not for the guarantee that the government will intervene to provide liquidity for the banks, a guarantee that becomes credible only when the government depends on the banks for its fiscal needs, the banks would be more prudent and the lender of last resort would not be necessary.

Of course if the government needs the banks to pool individuals' savings in order to fund the public debt, the banking system will be less stable than otherwise and therefore, the presence of a lender of last resort becomes a stabilizing factor; but absent that need, mere existence of a lender of last resort induces nonprudent behavior.

So, as exemplified by the historical evidence, we can also reject on logic grounds that a lender of last resort is a stabilizing factor in the economy and therefore it is an acceptable rationale for central banking, since that is only the case when the government fiscal needs impose on the banks a pressure to act irresponsibly.

Having attributed the very need of a lender of last resort to the instabilities introduced in the banking system by the privileges granted to them by the government (incidentally, access to a lender of last resort being one of them), that leaves us with one hypothesis to analyze, that is, with the rationale for central banking based on its function as an instrument for state policy, in particular, state financing.

Regardless of what event we choose as our departing point for the history of central banking, either the establishment of the Bank of England (BoE) or the Peel's Act which gave monopoly of issuance to the BoE, we will see that governments saw it was to their benefit to authorize an agent to produce and regulate the money supply as an instrument to create a market for public debt.

And the most pressing necessity that governments may face that forces them to raise money quickly is that of national defense. We could expand this concept to encompass all threats to the survival of a given political regime, not only external but also internal, not only conventional war, but also rebellion.

However, that expansion of the concept of national defense for the purposes of this work would only complicate things unnecessarily; so for the purposes of the argument presented here, national defense will be considered as an external military threat not only to the political regime, but to the lives and properties of all citizenry as well.

7.1 THE PROBLEM WAR FINANCE POSES FOR THE INTEGRITY OF PRIVATE PROPERTY RIGHTS

Among all the possible justifications for the relativization of private property rights in general and by the manipulation of money and banking rules in particular, the needs of war financing seem to carry more weight than anything else. Individuals prepared to resist attacks on private property rights based on any other reason face moral doubts once confronted with the needs to fund defense. What is the rationale behind the apparent difference in value judgment in the case of war finance?

In dealing with moral justifications for taxation, Eric Mack sees private property rights as: "a moral *presumption* against forced takings, a presumption that might, at least in principle, be overcome in special cases—specifically, cases that do not fit the paradigm of unjustified forced *redistribution*" (1986: 489). Mack goes on saying that he finds no sufficient basis to actually overthrow that presumption "unless, of course, one retreats to utilitarianism" (1986: 509). Most people would accept social utility as a perfectly acceptable moral criterion to evaluate the morality of taxation, but let's try first without that. The "special case" referred to by Professor Mack is the case of an "authentic" public good, and national defense is the quintessential one; so, the recourse to voluntary financing of national defense would imply accepting a distribution of benefits not proportional to the contributions in favor of the "free-riders," which is morally acceptable from a right's perspective, so long as all the contributors are better off. Nonetheless, Mack argues that national defense financed by coercion, that is, taxation, still needs to pass the test of proving that it is provided in an efficient manner and that "even if social utility were thereby greatly enhanced" (1986: 509), that no group of individuals will be worse off. But since in the real world we live in, knowledge is extremely imperfect, Mack proposes a litmus test to find out if it is morally acceptable in a given circumstance of tax-financed national defense; and the test consists of a comparison with a "genuinely defensive system, one truly protective of our lives, liberties, and property" (1986: 511). If the cost of that system were in the "ballpark" of current levels of expenditure, the tax-financed national defense would be acceptable in principle. Yet, Mack believes that it would be possible to finance national defense voluntarily; the economic gains of an effective defense system would bring the cost to what is acceptable to a "rational purchaser" regardless of the fact that there are free-riders.

I disagree with his conclusion, but I think that his proposed test offers a practical instrument to evaluate the morality of coercive financing of national defense without descending into a utilitarian calculation that Mack clearly rejects.

There are two elements that I would add to be factored in to his proposed method of assessment; and the first one is that the size of the army you need to field is not an ideal number, but it is a consequence of the strength of the forces you face, as stated by Hobbes.[10] Even though it would be impossible to know what the personal preference for security of each individual is and to give a price tag to it, still, we can know for certain that the cost of national defense is not related to the aggregate of those figures. The cost of national defense is determined by the military threats the nation faces and not by any internal circumstance. Therefore, if protection of life and property is of personal value for all individuals, in different circumstances, different efforts may be necessary, regardless of their individual preferences.[11]

The other element, also from Hobbes, is that the arrangements for defense need to be permanent: "Nor is it enough for security, which men desire should last all the time of their life, that they be governed and directed by one judgment for a limited time, as in one battle or one war" (1994: 107). And that makes sense. The apparatus of defense should be built to protect not only against existing threats, but also potential threats and there are gains of specialization in this field of endeavor as in any other; therefore, the effective defense of the lives and property of every individual citizen requires a permanent organization, reasonably, prudently supplied with the means to dissuade and if necessary to confront military threats.

The requirements of defense of individual rights to life and property cannot be evaluated in a metaphysical and epistemological vacuum. Mankind and human political societies being what they are, it is not reasonable to expect that national defense could be effectively conducted by any means other than by a permanent apparatus of military defense funded not voluntarily according to the personal preferences of each individual, but compulsorily. Negating that is tantamount to negating reality. And the morality of such a system should not be condemned by the mere fact that it is funded by taxation, but by an evaluation of the entire context in regard to its efficacy and reasonableness, by considering, for instance: (a) whether tax-funded defense has been consented to by the individual members of a given polity by legitimate instruments of collective decision, (b) whether the means of legitimate coercion are used only to achieve that purpose or if some redistribution is also pursued, (c) whether individual rights are observed, including property rights (albeit mitigated by the provision for defense), (d) if the total cost estimated for national defense meets Mack's criterion of being measurable with the cost of the same service provided by a private rational agency, et cetera.[12]

7.2 THE NATURE OF MONEY AND THE FRAMEWORK FOR THE DEBATE ON WAR FINANCE

For more than a century now, the main divide about the nature of money has been among those who see money as a spontaneously evolved institution in society whose purpose is one of allowing and enhancing the division of labor, and those who see money as an institution created by the state as an instrument for its policies. The debate about war finance, in all its dimensions, from the description of its instruments to the evaluation of their efficacy and the justifications for their use in each given circumstance, may be better understood in the context provided by the discussion on the nature of money. If money is just one more instrument for the implementation of state policies, then there are no limits in that regard to what the government can do to money. On the other hand, if money is understood as the instrument for indirect exchanges, then there are ethical limits to what can be done to money. A precise understanding about what money is may inform the best ways to provide for war finance when necessary.

However, this work is neither to discuss philosophically whether the institutions of private property and freedom of contract in general or good money in particular are always of a higher value than national defense, nor to analyze contrafactually if ways to provide the funds for national defense without interventionism in the money supply would have been better, say, for the American society. The sole purpose of this chapter is to offer a presentation and an interpretation of a historical[13] view on the relation between the fiscal necessities brought about by war and interventionism in money and banking in the United States up to World War I, with the purpose of illustrating the theoretical questions in regard to monetary policy and war finance; therefore, it is a reflection on the ideas behind the historical events more than anything else.[14] And as stated above, it is axiomatic that money was introduced in society and its main function still is to facilitate indirect exchanges; and in that regard, the introduction of specific forms of money, including credit or state money, only becomes possible, and ultimately successful, because they perform that basic function. So, the fact that some monies, including our monies today, may have been introduced by the state does not contradict the thesis that instruments of facilitating indirect exchanges are introduced in society not by command but because they perform a useful function for individuals.

So, not even (what I would recognize as a genetic fallacy) stating that money was created by the state and therefore its main purpose is to be an instrument for the state gives legitimacy to the claim that because our monies were created by the state, the rulers can do whatever they wish with money as if there were no moral constraints. Money becomes and remains a morally accepted instrument for the state to the extent that it remains adequate for its basic function; and its basic function is to enhance the division of labor in society, not to serve state's policies.

So far we have talked about justifications for central banking without trying to distinguish what kind of justifications they are. Basically, we are in search of justifications on grounds of economics and ethics. Our understanding is that justifications on those grounds would appeal to all constituencies interested in this topic. And the matrix of our inquiry, so far, is the following:

7.3 INSTRUMENTS FOR WAR FINANCE AND THE SINEWS OF POWER

If a theoretical study of the economic consequences of the different methods of war financing is the object here, it seems advisable to start describing those methods. Following Mises in *Nation, State, and Economy*, Gabriel Calzada Alvares separates the methods into four categories: conscription-confiscation, taxation, inflation, and war bonds (Calzada, 2005: 149).[15]

In the context of Mises' distinction between a "Soldier's War," a somewhat limited form of war that may be compatible with a market economy and civilization itself, and "Total War," conscription, or the "Blood Tax" as Mises used to call it, is the very beginning of unlimited warfare. The rationale that may be inferred here is that once the populace consents to the government enslaving part of the citizenry and potentially sending them to death, any other limitation on the power of government, such as private property, free speech, whatever, loses its legitimacy. After all, how can someone have the right to refuse to give up his property if others are forced to give their lives?[16]

Regarding confiscation, according to Calzada, the taking of already-produced goods and means of production would eliminate the incentives for entrepreneurs to make the necessary adjustments to transform the structure of production in order to deliver war supplies; therefore it is a self-defeating method.

Considering taxation, inflation, and public debt as instruments to raise the resources to wage war, it is important to take into consideration Mises' lesson that "War can be waged only with present goods" (Mises, 2006: 139). Accepting Mises' assumption, from an economic standpoint, that is, deciding on the use of the scarce resources available, a generation that wages war must bear its material cost. However, it must be under-

Table 7.1. Matrix of Rationales for Central Banking

Justifications for Central Banking	Economic Grounds	Ethical Grounds
A Central Bank is necessary in order to have (good) money provided for society.	Central banking is neither necessary nor sufficient to have good money; no solid economic case for central banking based on the monopoly of money production exists. The group efficiency effect argument for the selection of a single currency does not imply that such currency should be provided without competition.	Central banking is neither necessary nor sufficient to have good money; no solid moral case for central banking based on the monopoly of money production exists. Stealing from the individuals the right to use a currency of their choice is morally wrong.
A Central Bank is necessary in order to have a stable financial system by its actions as a (effective) lender of last resort	Central banking allows effective lending of last resort under fiat money and fractional reserve arrangements, which are unstable by nature, defeating the purpose of greater stability through central banking.	There are no necessary social good achievable through central banking whose deficiency is not a consequence of the introduction of central banking.
A Central Bank is a (Relevant) instrument of the fisc in cases of emergencies.	The mitigation of private property by the manipulation of money may be the best way to have fast access to real existing savings under emergencies, short-term extreme circumstances, but a strong real economic sector, "deep" financial markets, and sound management of public finances are the most efficient policy for peacetime and all but extreme cases, as a way for the state to have access to existing goods necessary to wage war.	In case of war, is the survival of the political body a "higher value" than private property rights? Is the "fiscal proviso" morally justifiable? My answer is yes, it is. But since it is not possible to evaluate morally central banking regardless of its economic efficiency, this answer admits important qualifications.

stood that sometimes the share of the existing wealth that is required for the war effort is bigger than what can possibly be taken from the taxpayers without forcing them to fire-sell nonliquid assets, producing strong redistributive impacts; or, simply, the state might not have the tax-collection mechanisms to raise the amount required in a timely and orderly manner. These are considerations that may lead to the use of one form of taxation over others or may induce the government to have recourse to debt or inflation in order to respectively spread the burden of the material cost of the war among owners of liquid and illiquid assets and to collect more resources than would otherwise be possible to collect via taxation. Calzada's argument in regard to the efficiency of the different methods of war finance as read from Mises and Rothbard is that taxation is to be preferred to inflation and, to a lesser degree, war bonds, due to the distortions that they introduce into all sectors of the economy.

Calzada concludes that among different forms of taxation, a general sales tax combines "the best possible mobilizing effects" with "the least violent attack on private property" (2005: 168).

In concrete terms, the access to a broader pool of resources that debt allows in comparison with taxation (since taxation is always aimed at profits and revenue but not at the principal; it is aimed at the capital gains, but not at the capital) is what makes the capacity to fill the public coffers by raising liquid resources through financial instruments so essential in cases of war.

There are some goods that by their nature cannot be used for the war effort; still their owners may be called to pay for the acquisition of other goods that can have military use. Still, the mobilization of resources to wage war is limited to the capacity of the economy to produce military supplies, but that capacity is different from the capacity to pay for those supplies.

Let's assume, for instance, that in a given society there are 80 billion dollars in fixed assets and 20 billion in liquid assets and at the same time the annual income is 12 billion and from that income, 8 billion is current expenditures and 4 billion are investments. If it is for the government to wage war taxing only income or consumption, it is doubtful that more than say, 6 billion could be raised, and even that at an "economy of war" kind of economic system. However, if the war is financed with debt, some of the existing liquid assets and even some of the fixed assets can be mobilized for war production, to the extent that owners of liquid assets may buy war bonds and fixed assets may be diverted to war production if the state has the resources to pay for their use. Theoretically, war procurement could be, for some time, totally financed by debt without even denting civil consumption. Obviously, that is not sustainable in the long run and here is not the place to discuss why that is so. But it is sufficient for our purposes to demonstrate that debt allows the government to draw resources from the existing wealth, while taxes only allow (without forcing fire-sale liquidations) the government to draw from the existing income; even if the goods diverted to war, in the end, are limited by the capacity of the economy to convert capital and other resources from their civil uses to military ones.

7.3.1 The Financial Revolution in England

The classical account of the relation between money and war is P. G. M. Dickson's *The Financial Revolution in England: A Study in the Development of Public Credit, 1688–1756*. The central thesis of the book is that it was thanks to the capacity of the British Crown to raise money beyond its taxing capacity, through borrowing, that England was able to field the military forces necessary to succeed in war against France and its allies. So much so that a contemporary source (Isaac de Pinto) states that the astonishing capture of Havana in 1762 "would not have been possible if one-third fewer ships and troops had been assigned to the task" (Dickson, 1967: 9).

Dickson then describes the features of the new system of public finance developed in that period, the development of the market for short-term and long-term public debt, and the relations between the treasury and the financial markets in general.

However, his argument about the relation between the fiscal necessities of the crown and the development of British financial markets can be understood as operating in two directions; that is, the creation of a stable and efficient government was a precondition for the development of successful public borrowing in the same way that such borrowing ended shaping, out of necessity, a more efficient and stable government in the United Kingdom.

Dickson's argument was further developed in both directions by other authors. One direction is to say, like Niall Ferguson does,[17] that the existence of a central bank (formally introduced in the United Kingdom with the privilege of monopoly of issuance to the Bank of England by the Peel Act of 1844) is crucial for governments to deal with emergencies like wars by the flexibility in the money supply that they allow (Ferguson, 2008: 100). For instance, talking about the reaction to the crisis of 1914 he writes, "Then, as now, the authorities reacted to a liquidity crisis by printing money" (2008: 301).

The other direction is to stress the importance of the fiscal needs of the state forming and shaping financial markets. This direction is the one presented by Richard Sylla with his essay "Shaping the US Financial System, 1690–1913" in *The State, the Financial System, and Economic Modernization*. According to him, the financial requirements and policies of the state "determine the ways in which private financial institutions and markets emerge and develop" (Sylla et al., 2007: 250). For the author, the financial program of Alexander Hamilton, which was aimed at providing one more weapon to the republic's arsenal, resulted in launching a banking system and a securities market in the United States; for him, the lesson of history is that "virtually" every major financial innovation is just a reaction to fiscal needs and policies.

*7.3.2 The "*Fiscal Proviso*" in Practice*

The fiscal proviso undoubtedly implies the dilution of private property rights, especially through interventions in the monetary and financial arrangements, every time that the contingencies of war financing so require.

In the historical record, there are countless episodes in which, for fiscal reasons resulting from a state of war, a government intervened in the monetary institutions sometimes with disastrous effects for the economic performance of society and that is a reality that must be dealt with. For radical opponents to the governments' monetary prerogatives, Riegel proposes the adoption of "nonpolitical" money as a way to limit government's power. "Money can be issued only in the act of buying, and can be backed only in the act of selling." (1944: 9). For the author, "The issue between private enterprise and collectivism is not a matter of choice as long as the political money system prevails. If the government holds the money issuing power, it will either buy out the people and control them or ruin their enterprise system thorough inflation." (1944: 11) The author, oddly in the middle of the war against totalitarianism, a war that was not initiated by the United States, although recognizing the relation between finance and war ("The money power is the war power"—page 30) seems to think that monetary prerogatives are used only in wars or aggression, not in defensive wars; when the American experience, starting with the Revolutionary War demonstrates that ill-managed as the monetary prerogative may be, it has been used, critically, as an instrument for defense.

7.4 WAR FINANCE IN THE MONETARY HISTORY OF THE UNITED STATES

This work has already mentioned the importance of understanding how much the "quality" of social interactions (as crystallized in the institutions) is necessary in order to explain the general performance of a society. That reasoning also applies to the monetary arrangements of any society, and these arrangements, in their turn, are decisively influenced by the fiscal needs of the state, especially in cases of armed conflict. In those circumstances, history shows the fundamental importance of having efficient arrangements to procure the resources necessary to wage war. The multiple perspectives from which the issue of war finance may be approached include not only considerations of efficiency, but also moral considerations, and they are key to understanding the legitimacy of war procurement in all its forms. These topics are essential to have in mind when discussing war financing and monetary history in the United States.

7.5 THE MONETARY SYSTEM IN PLACE IN COLONIAL TIMES

Rothbard starts his book, *History of Money and Banking in the United States* (*HMBUS*), describing the monetary system in place in colonial America. He notes that the colonies adopted the monetary system of the colonial power, and despite being legally in a silver standard, England was in fact in a bimetallic standard with a fixed parity. Precious metals being internationally traded in the absence of a legal prohibition (which happened in the United States only by act of Congress in 1857), foreign coins used to circulate freely. In fact, gold and silver foreign coins comprised the bulk of the circulating medium in the colonies at the end of the seventeenth century. The leading specie currency in the colonies was by far the Spanish silver dollar, which happened to be the world's most important coin since the early sixteenth century and also the most stable coin in the Western world for three centuries (2005: 49). As early as colonial times the government attempted to manipulate currency, both when England forbade the minting and the export of English coins to the colonies and when the colonial governments, in their attempts to make their exports more competitive, debased the shilling in favor of the Spanish dollar, which was outlawed by England as early as 1707.

Aside from those attempts to manipulate the currency, the monetary system in place in the colonies at the end of the seventeenth century was basically a classic bimetallic system with no fixed parity between gold and silver, with a free flow of coins in and out of the colonies, and with no forced tender of a national currency.

7.5.1 Massachusetts' First Issue of Government Fiat Paper Money

It is generally accepted that it was medieval China that pioneered government paper money, starting as early as the ninth century with government paper money redeemable in specie that three centuries later "evolved" into irredeemable fiat paper money. The next experience with government fiat paper money happened in colonial America. The colonial government of Massachusetts was the first government, apart from China, ever to issue fiat paper money, which they did in 1690 (Rothbard, 2005: 51). It is important to understand the circumstance in which that policy was adopted. Lightheartedly,[18] Rothbard says the Massachusetts colonial government was "accustomed to launch plundering expeditions against the prosperous French colony in Quebec," noting that they were usually "successful." But one day, they were beaten and the expedition came back to Boston without booty to sell and pay the "soldiers." With no money to pay the soldiers and afraid of a mutiny, the colonial government tried to borrow money from Boston merchants but "its credit rating was not the best" and they failed in this attempt to raise the necessary money. Finally, in December 1690, in order to pay the soldiers, the colonial government decided to print £7,000 in paper notes, but "suspecting that the public would not accept irredeemable paper" the government of Massachusetts framed that political decision pledging that it would redeem the notes in specie "in a few years" (it actually took forty years to do so) and that no more paper money would be issued; however, as soon as February 1691, the government issued £40,000 more to repay "all of its outstanding debt" (Rothbard, 2005: 52). However, the skepticism of the colonists with that first experience soon was perceived by the notes' depreciation of about 40% against specie. That led the government to make the notes compulsory legal tender for all payments contracted in specie.

The next relevant event happened in 1711, when Massachusetts issued £500,000 "to pay for another failed expedition against Quebec." That massive issuance forced a devaluation of the notes, legal tender notwithstanding. Attempts by the British Crown to force Massachusetts back into a specie currency failed because the colony was unable to retire the notes au pair. Then, again in 1744, Rothbard tells us that "another losing expedition against the French led Massachusetts to issue an enormous amount of paper money over the next several years." By 1748, Massachusetts alone had issued £2,500,000 and the depreciated shilling was valued 1/10 of its value in silver in 1690.

7.5.2 Government Paper Money in the Other Colonies

By 1740 all the colonies but Virginia had adopted fiat paper money. In the late 1750s even the colony of Virginia "in trying to finance part of the French and Indian War against the French" (1754–1763) followed suit (Rothbard, 2005: 54).

After the end of the Seven Years War (1756–1763), in 1764 parliament extended the 1751 prohibition of new issues of government paper money in New England to all colonies and required the gradual retirement of outstanding notes, forcing the colonies back into a specie **monetary standard**, and ending the government paper money experiment in colonial America.

It is possible to see from this narrative the direct link between the necessities of war financing and drastic manipulation of the money supply by the government; in this case, the introduction of government fiat paper money. The door is open for questions on the merits of the measure. Objectively, is war a sufficient justification for the government to defraud the money supply by adopting fiat paper money? Rothbard's (2005: 55) comments first on the British Crown forcing the retirement of paper money in the middle of the Seven Years War, and second on the "remarkable" stability of the specie standard during the conflict may induce a reader to think that, as a matter of policy, war finance does not necessarily imply inflation, and, "remarkable" as it may be, it is not impossible to keep a "stable" specie standard in middle of a major armed struggle.

7.6 REVOLUTIONARY WAR FINANCE

The financing of the Revolutionary War resulted in an expansion of the money supply from $12 million in 1775 at the beginning of hostilities to $225 million in five years due to the issue of nonredeemable fiat paper money by the Continental Congress. Such monetary expansion made the "Continental" paper money depreciate from a parity of $1 to $1.25 in specie at the end of 1776 to $1 to $168 by the spring of 1781, when it became "virtually worthless" (Rothbard, 2005: 60).

The issuance of government fiat paper money by the states only came on top of that calamity, adding $210 million by the end of the war to the nation's currency, followed by various attempts by the states to slow the depreciation of fiat money by price controls and forced tender laws. Other measures against private property rights also happened, such as the seizure of supplies by the Continental Army, forcing the farmers and merchants to accept devaluated currency or "certificates" issued by the army's quartermasters. From these certificates, the federal government issued $200 million.

By 1779, having turned the government issued fiat paper money into something worthless, the Continental Congress started to issue "loan certificates," which technically were part of the public debt but in essence were one more form of circulating currency (Rothbard, 2005: 61). Those loan certificates had devaluated in less than a year to a 24-to-1 ratio with the specie, and by the end of the war $600 million of them were issued.

The chapter about the financing of the American Revolutionary War ends with "maneuvers" by congressman Robert Morris to pay au pair in specie the depreciated loan certificates. According to Rothbard (2005: 62), Morris' two reasons were, first, to subsidize the speculators, and second, to make the case for granting the Continental Congress with taxing powers, which they lacked under the Articles of Confederation, showing once more the relation between the needs of war finance and the trend towards an aggrandizement of the state. A more benevolent interpretation, however, would be that, conscious of the affront to private property that only nominal redemption of the federal debt would represent, Morris made a good faith effort to prevent the creditors from being defrauded. Furthermore, it is worthwhile to mention that as a congressman, Morris was instrumental in advocating the issuance of debt as an attempt to stop the devaluation of the currency; he was personally involved in the push to attract investors to the federal debt (Rappleye, 2010: 110).

Besides Morris' personal involvement with the loans, it is also important to have in mind how much the Revolutionary War was funded not by taxation but by debt, and the untold times in which the confederacy was on the verge of disintegrating due to the lack of funds during five years of relentless war against the most powerful nation at the time. In the middle of the war, in 1779 at a time in which the confederation was unable to pay interests on the existing debt, Morris, for instance, wrote a "Report on Public Credit" outlined by Rappleye as follows: "America must do justice to its creditors, and afford itself access to future loans, by raising revenue to pay the interest and eventually the principal on its debt" (2010: 303), hardly the words of an unscrupulous and self-interested politician.

One need not be naïve about the speculative character of the investments in the public debt of the confederation to understand that many expedients used to fund the Revolution trumped private property rights such as the issuance of devalued continentals and loan certificates, cases dictated by the dire fiscal considerations of the new nation. To regard the initiatives to create the conditions to honor those debts in full at the very first moment that the circumstances would allow and yet to understand the "fiscal proviso" as a mere act of force, deprived of any moral justification, even utilitarian ones, seems very unrealistic in light of the future events in the monetary history of the United States.

7.6.1 The Bank of North America 1782–1783

The establishment of a fractional reserve commercial bank with a monopoly of banking and issuance—in effect, the first central bank in the United States—was the Bank of North America, which started its operations in 1782. The Treasury controlled the bank (with 5/8 of its capital) and congressman Robert Morris was its first president. In exchange for its privileges, the bank "lent most of its newly created money to the federal government to purchase public debt" (generated during the war). The new **bank notes**, although nominally redeemable in specie, soon were discredited, and in 1783, after the end of the war, the bank was sold to private investors and recharted in Philadelphia as a private bank, concluding the history of the first central bank in the United States.

Also of note was the deflationary and recessionary "scarcity of money" provoked by the contraction of paper money when the federal and state governments started repaying the wartime public debt. Some states tried to reinflate currency in order to honor these payments without needing to increase taxation. These attempts ultimately failed because the states were forbidden to issue unredeemable paper money, and the effect of Gresham's law only made specie scarcer.

In *HMBUS* there is a value judgment about the propriety of the inflationary expansion of the money supply in order to finance the Revolutionary War and about the granting of banking privileges; in labeling as "catastrophic" the inflation produced by the fiat paper money, certificates, and loan certificates issuance, Rothbard is clearly not only describing the consequences of such policies but expressing his opinion about them as well.

Can it be inferred from the acts of the Founding Fathers that the foundation of the United States was an end that justified the means? The very first "financial" committee of the Continental Congress in 1776, composed by Benjamin Franklin, Robert Morris, William Duer, and Reverend Witherspoon, among others, under the constraints imposed by the lack of taxing power, had little choice other than to raise the debt in order to face the "financial demands, pressing and immediate" of the revolutionary government (Rappleye, 2010: 110).

As already said, the moral justification for abridgments of individual rights by the polity such as inflating the currency can only be understood as an emergency measure in the case that the very survival of the polity is at risk and with the full commitment of the community to restore the rights of those infringed upon at the first opportunity. One cannot be sure of his or her own motivations, much less so those of others, and it is harder still with historical figures during events that occurred more than two centuries ago, but the inflationary sources of funding for the Revolutionary War and the measures taken after the war to retire the debt give some credibility to the belief that the revolutionary government was fully aware of the violence it was perpetrating and was committed to repaying those who supported the War of Independence. The best evidence that the Continental government was perceived in such a fashion by a significant portion of its contemporaries is the ability it retained during the entire war to continue to get financial support.

7.7 THE MONETARY CONSTITUTION OF THE UNITED STATES

The American constitution in 1787 established a bimetallic monetary system, with legal but not forced tender, allowing therefore the circulation of foreign currency and forbidding the states to issue money. The provisions of the constitution regarding money were regulated in 1792 by the Coinage Act that established a fixed parity of 15 to 1 between silver and gold. Thus, the American dollar became defined as either a weight of 371.25 grains of pure silver or 24.75 grains of pure gold.

The constitutional provisions were respectively a reflection: a) of the circumstances at that time (Rothbard mentions an estimation that by 1800 about 80% of the coins in circulation were foreign); b) of the recent experience (with inflationary creation of paper money both by the states and by the confederation); and c) of the prevailing ideas at the time (bimetallism with fixed parity was then the monetary regime in England).

7.7.1 The First Bank of the United States 1791–1811

Even before regulating the currency, a central bank, The First Bank of the United States, was established as a cornerstone for the monetary arrangements of the new republic in a fashion similar to that in the United Kingdom in which the Bank of England was de facto a central bank. Hamilton's "Report on a National Bank" delivered to the House of Representatives in 1790 states the reasons for the establishment of a national bank, and the second one is particularly relevant for our present project, that is, the "greater facility to the Government in obtaining pecuniary aids, especially in sudden emergencies" (Hamilton, 1790). After some questioning (the constitutionality of a national bank was questioned even by the treasury secretary and the attorney general), the ank was established in 1791 as a fractional reserve bank.

At a time that taxes were paid in specie, the privilege of paying taxes with bank notes, giving them a quasi legal-tender status, plus the monopoly of a national charter, the deposits of all taxes, and the federal stake in the institution contributed to the success of the bank in its inflationary credit expansion; most of it funneled into financing the floating of the "newly assumed federal debt," in Rothbard's words.

However, on the eve of the 1812–1815 War, a proposal to renew the charter of the bank was defeated in congress and the bank was liquidated in 1811.

7.7.2 The War of 1812 and its Aftermath

The financial system put in place at the beginning of the republic aimed to fund the federal and state public debt acquired during the War of Independence with federal taxation; the restrictions on state paper money and any fiat money in general may be understood as reactions against the abuses of the Revolutionary War. In this sense, the liquidation of the First Bank of the United States, with its inflationary credit expansion, may be accepted as "solving" an internal conflict in the first monetary policy of the United States that soon would be tested again by the needs of financing a military struggle.

7.7.3 Rothbard's Comments on War Finance

The chapter of *HMBUS* on the 1812 War starts: "War has generally had grave and fateful consequences for the American monetary and financial system. We have seen that the Revolutionary War occasioned a mass of depreciated fiat paper, worthless Continentals, a huge public debt, and the beginning of central banking in the Bank of North America" (2005: 72).

The 1812 War was financed predominantly by the acquisition of public debt by an inflationary bank credit expansion, and according to Rothbard, government encouraged the formation of more banks. There were 117 banks in 1811, and 212 incorporated plus 35 unincorporated banks in 1815. Rothbard estimates an increase of 87.2% of banknotes and deposits from 1811 to 1815 while the specie in reserves declined by 9.4%, forcing the reserve ratio from 0.27 in 1811 to 0.17 in 1815 (2005: 73).

Due to the increased demand for redemption in specie in proportion to the increase of outstanding banknotes, most banks in the country soon were facing insolvency and, with that, risking the war-financing scheme in place. Therefore, in August 1814, the federal government permitted the banks to suspend redemption in specie. Specie payments were not resumed until February 1817, two years after the war was over.

Rothbard comments about this suspension: "in one of the most flagrant violations of property rights in American history, the banks were permitted to waive their contractual obligations to pay in specie while they themselves could expand their loans and operations and force their own debtors to repay their loans as usual" (2005: 74).

Another form of war financing was the issuance of treasury notes, and that also contributed to the wartime inflation of 35% on average, since those notes were used not only by the public in their transactions but also by the banks as "high-powered money" in the form of reserves upon which they would pyramid their credit expansion.

For Rothbard, the precedent of the suspension of payments in specie was more important than inflation and "at least as important as the wreckage of the monetary system" (2005: 76). His reasoning is that in case of any general crisis the banks would be allowed to suspend payments in specie again, creating a moral hazard that in fact made null the natural restraint imposed on the banks by the risk of facing a run in case of general crisis. The monetary system in the United States before the Civil War may be described as one of "Decentralization without Freedom," and it is implicit that individual banks may have been restrained by the risk of facing a run in case of lost of confidence, but the entire banking system was encouraged to discount the risk of a general run and therefore "economize" in reserves.

7.7.4 The Second Bank of the United States, 1816–1833

For the present discussion, the establishment of the Second Bank of the United States is important only to illustrate the path of monetary policy after the War of 1812–1815. The banks, checked only by the public perception of their competing strengths, continued the inflationary credit expansion of wartime. To put a stop to that, according to Rothbard, there were two possible paths: the first was the path of hard money, and the other was the path of a new central bank, which was chosen this time.

The Second Bank of the United States, like the first, was a private corporation with 20% of the shares owned by the federal government; it enjoyed a monopoly over creating a national paper currency to purchase the public debt and to monopolize the deposit of funds of the US treasury. The bank was able to support the local banks in resuming redemption in specie, essentially because with its support, the perception of the strength of local banks was enhanced and claims for redemption dwindled, allowing the banking system to continue with its inflationary expansion. Eventually, as early as 1818, the bank started to suffer a drain of specie, forcing it to adopt "heroic" contractions, that led to the panic of 1819, starting the first cycle of boom and bust in America and creating the background for the first articulate reaction to the status quo in money and banking, the movement led by Andrew Jackson.

7.7.5 The Jacksonian Movement

In trying to understand the impact of war finance in the monetary history of the United States, it is important to describe the changes introduced in the monetary constitution of the United States by Andrew Jackson and his associates, since the new institutional arrangements promoted during Jackson's administration were basically the ones in place at the beginning of the Civil War. The Jacksonians, in *HMBUS*, are described by Rothbard as libertarians who pioneered the concepts of the Currency School in their policies. They succeeded in: (a) their fight against fractional banking in general and the central bank status of the Second Bank of the United States in particular; (b) severing all links between the federal government and the banking system, operating exclusively with paper 100% backed by specie; (c) allowing the free circulation of foreign currency in the country; and (d) retiring the federal debt in its entirety. According to Leonard Liggio: "Ideally, if Jackson had his own way, he preferred a financial system in which the government placed its funds in a government treasury, dealt solely in gold and silver and demanded specie for the payment of taxes" (Liggio, 2011: 3).[19] In 1857, however, an important part of Jackson's monetary reform was repealed when Congress stripped the legal tender power of foreign coins.

It is worthwhile to note an important feature of the banking system of the United States previous to the Civil War, that is, the "free banking" arrangements under which the banking business, although open to competition with very small hurdles, was regulated by the states. That feature induced the state-chartered banks to pyramid the issuing of their banknotes on state public debt (as a quid pro quo by their charters) and at same time offered a protection against a systemic crisis by allowing the banking system as a whole periodic general suspensions of specie payments whenever necessary (the latest episode before the Civil War was in 1857).

With all its real life problems, many features of the monetary arrangements of the United States before the Civil War are praiseworthy, such as the clearance mechanism spontaneously developed into the system and administered by the Suffolk Bank. That clearance mechanism was interrupted in 1858 by political pressure, and any hope of the reestablishment of an equivalent mechanism was lost with the beginning of the confrontation.

7.8 THE CIVIL WAR

From any perspective, a description of the impact of the Civil War on American finances is a sobering one. It was the cause for the United States to suspend redemption in December 1861, for the first time since the 1814–1817 episode caused by the 1812 War; and this time it lasted two decades. Once in an inconvertible fiat standard, the federal government soon started to inflate the money supply, which was done through the Legal Tender Act of February 1862.

Federal expenditures increased exponentially during the war, rising from $66 million in 1861 to $1.3 billion in 1865. Those expenditures were mostly financed by public debt and not by issuance of fiat money. The deficit accumulated during the war reached the amount of $2.614 billion, of which $432 million were financed by printing fiat money, and all the rest was borrowed. In order to fund this borrowing, all the savings in the country had to be drained, and the banking system was the instrument to achieve that goal.

Chief among the structural changes was the new architecture of the banking system that resulted from the effort of war financing; with a "quasi-centralized fractional reserve national banking system" (Rothbard, 2005: 122). The new structure ended the separation between federal government and the banks introduced by the Jacksonians and, "(w)hereas the effects of the greenbacks were finally eliminated by the resumption of specie payments in 1879, the effects of the national banking system are still with us" (Rothbard, 2005: 137).

The new banking system was effectively built as an inverted pyramid, with the banks, in issuing their notes and multiplying their reserves, now composed basically of federal debt. On top of that, the country banks, which were not required to have specie reserves anymore, could have their reserves deposited with city banks, and these, in their turn, could have their reserves deposited with banks in New York City, which held their reserves both in fiat money and specie; it worked to an extent that the money supply rose from $454 million to $1.773 billion during the war.

The process of replacing gold as bank reserve and the continuous attempts to curb the gold market by treasury secretary Salmon Chase while in office were necessary to force the country to adopt public debt and fiat money as a medium of exchange and "**high powered money**" at the pace required by the funding of the war effort. With the creation of this new banking system "the federal government had an assured, built-in market for its debt" (Rothbard, 2005: 142).

The well-documented chasing (no pun intended) of "gold speculators" and other forms of violence against private property and freedom of contract as part of government policy did not passed unchallenged, though. Not only did states such as California and Oregon effectively repudiate the fiat money by not accepting it in payment for state taxes and legislating "specific currencies contracts," but judicial institutions also helped to protect individuals from the depreciation of the "greenbacks." Wholesale prices rose at a rate of 22.2% per year during the war.

7.8.1 The Monetary and Fiscal Consequences of the War

In short, the monetary and fiscal consequences of the war were that the United States, at the end of it, had a "depreciated inconvertible greenback currency, and a heavy burden of public debt" (Rothbard, 2005: 147). Then, yet another deleterious consequence of the war came into play: the perverse incentives for political forces to mobilize for the continuation of the inflationary credit expansion, summarized in Carey's gospel (after the economist Henry C. Carey) of "high tariffs and soft money" (Rothbard, 2005: 148). One may identify even *avant la lettre* Keynesian schemes of public spending among the inflationists. They advocated public spending, even if it was not necessary or conducive to better productivity in general, such as "pyramid building or digging holes in the ground;" he also describes the importance of the railroad lobby among the inflationists (Rothbard, 2005: 149). The actions of the inflationists prevented serious talk about resuming redemption until 1879, almost two decades after it was suspended.

The final enduring change in the American monetary constitution as a consequence of the Civil War came about when the greenback question reached the US Supreme Court in the case of *Hepburn v. Griswold,* which was decided in February 1870, and the acts of the Treasury Secretary were declared as "unnecessary and Unconstitutional" by a majority of 5–3. But a new court, with two new judges, by a new majority of 5–4 in the case of *Knox v. Lee* declared paper money as constitutional in May 1871.

A last note about the struggle to resume normalcy in monetary matters after the war, with the resumption of redemption in specie, is about the compromise on bimetallism and silver purchases that in 1879 came into being along with the return to a redeemable currency. Usually the decision to return to bimetallism is understood as an inflationary concession to the populists, agrarian interests, or whomever. A more benign interpretation would be that the return to bimetallism was simply that, a return to the traditional monetary system in place before independence. Specifically silver purchases may be understood as part of the centuries-old tradition of a bimetallic system with fixed parity. For instance, Juan de Mariana, in the 1609 "*De Monetae Mutatione*" according to Father Laures (2008: 142) advocates a regulated parity around "their natural relationship," although recognizing that, like all commodities, the supply and demand for gold and silver may vary. The traditional bimetallism with fixed parity[20] was one in which the parity was "fixed" at a certain ratio, until it wasn't; that is, when long-term market conditions changed, the regulated parity was expected to accommodate the new "natural relationship." The program of silver acquisitions may be seen as simply part of those short-term maladjustments resulting from the ever-changing "natural relationship" between the supply and demand of the two metals and not, necessarily, an inflationary conspiracy.

For Rothbard, the Civil War was a turning moment in American monetary history, and the consequences of the war in terms of money and banking were all negative. So, with the chapters on the Civil War, Rothbard, as quoted above in different passages, makes clear his discomfort with the consequences resulting from the effort of war financing and its enduring marks on the monetary institutional arrangements of the United States.

7.9 THE FIRST WORLD WAR

7.9.1 The Golden Years

The years between 1879 and 1913 were the years of the gold standard in the United States. It was the time of the "free banking" system in which there were: a) nonnote issuing banks regulated by the states, and b) national banks, issuing banknotes.[21] The banknotes were redeemable in specie, and they used to operate with fractional reserves; these reserves were cumulatively deposited in major cities around the country and ultimately in banks in New York City.

An analysis of those arrangements is not the object of the present chapter; however, understanding the problems of having banks investing their reserves in state and federal bonds does not require much thought.

Another problem brewing was the commitment to high tariffs (and what was perceived by some as a soft money policy) of the Republican party, expressed in the Sherman Silver Purchase Act (which doubled the purchases of silver by the Treasury and made the US dollar redeemable in either gold or silver at the Treasury's discretion) and the McKinley Tariff Act, both from 1890.

In those years, many attempts to institutionalize bimetallism happened, shaking the confidence in the US dollar and the American commitment to a pure gold standard. Not even the repealing of the Sherman Silver Purchase Act by the end of 1893 restored confidence, since other anti-gold political movements were active.

Nevertheless, it was a time of mild deflation, low interest rates, increased productivity, and economic growth with the resulting growth in income per capita; but a transformation in the political landscape in America was in place at the end of the nineteenth century. The elections in 1896 represented the end of the Democratic party as "America's great laissez-faire, hard-money libertarian party," and its political space was occupied by the new "corporate, statist ideology of progressivism." The policies under which that long period of economic development happened yielded no more majority support and were replaced for a different set of values that would shape policymaking in the years to come. Rothbard states, "The Progressive Era of 1900–1918 fastened a welfare-warfare state on America which has set the mold for the rest of the twentieth century" (2005: 178).

7.9.2 The Federal Reserve System

The Federal Reserve System must be understood as part of the reshaping of American political institutions inspired by progressivism. Although the different initiatives of the Progressive Era were perceived by the public as motivated by "moral" concerns and guided by a "scientific" approach to the problems, specifically in the case of the central bank, those motivations matched nicely with the concerns of banks in general and the big banks in particular with the lack of "elasticity" of the money supply under the existing bank arrangements at the time.[22] It was their inability to expand money and credit "as much as they wished" that led the banks to advocate for the establishment of a central bank with the responsibility of a lender of last resort. It was done through third parties identified justly or unjustly as "grassroots," such as the ones gathered at the Indianapolis Monetary Convention in 1897 (Rothbard, 2005: 190).

The formal establishment of the Federal Reserve System as a central bank was not a complete novelty, however, since the Treasury to an extent had been functioning as a de facto central bank (Rothbard, 2005: 207).

The political movement for the creation of a central bank finally succeeded in December 1913 when the Federal Reserve Act was passed creating the Federal Reserve System (the Fed).

7.9.3 The Gold-Exchange Standard

The monetary standard in place around the world in the decades that preceded the Great War, more than a fractional reserve gold standard, was a fractional reserve gold-exchange standard, under which reserves were not kept in gold but in a convertible currency, mainly in pounds sterling or US dollars in a minor scale.

This system, which in effect pyramided the inflation on money supply in different countries around the world on top of already inflated pounds or dollars, actually loosened the constraints on note issuance by American and English banks, at the same time that it lent the prestige of gold to the currency of peripheral countries as long as they integrated their financial systems globally. As stated by Rothbard, "In that way, if U.S. banks inflated their credit, there would be no danger of losing gold abroad, as would happen under a genuine gold standard" (2005: 219).

Bringing more and more countries to this system, justified as it was by some economic theories about the existence of "surplus" capital in the relatively more developed countries and clearly in the interest of their banking systems, became part of the foreign policy of both the United Kingdom and the United States prior to the Great War and soon afterwards—a foreign policy that became indistinctly imperialist.

7.9.4 Money and Banking in the United States During the Great War

The monetary policy in the United States during World War I is directly linked to the operations of the Fed from 1914 to 1928, the years that Benjamin Strong was the governor of the New York Fed. References in the historiography of those years about the links between the Fed's policy, the interests of the House of Morgan, and British interests are common. It has been argued that one of the main reasons for the Fed to have adopted an inflationary policy during the war, which lasted with short interruptions until 1928, was to help Britain to finance its war effort and later to help the United Kingdom in its catastrophic decision to return to the gold-exchange standard at the rate of 1914. In Rothbard's words, "The United States inflated its money and credit in order to prevent Britain from losing gold to the United States, a loss which would endanger the new, jerry-built 'gold standard' structure" (2005: 271).

Actually, there is evidence of the inflationary expansion of money and credit in the United States as part of American war financing. Aside from that, we see the aggrandizement of government during the Great War—for example, the methods of "intimidation of business" employed by Hoover when he was "food czar in World War I" to the activities of Eugene Meyer as managing director of the War Finance Corporation (WFC) in propping up the market for federal bonds and subsidizing American industries. Rothbard even traces many of the initiatives to fight the Great Depression, such as the Reconstruction Finance Corporation (RFC), back to the collectivism engendered during World War I (2005: 280).

However, it is necessary to go to other sources in order to find precise data about money and credit expansion in the war years, and Friedman and Schwartz's *A Monetary History of the United States* shows that the wholesale price index in the United States from 1914 to 1918 rose from 65 to 130, on a scale where the wholesale price level of 1926 equals 100; the money stock rose roughly from $15 billion in 1914 to $30 billion in 1918 (Friedman and Schwartz, 1993: 197).

The federal debt increased immensely during the war; from $32 billion of total expenditures by the federal government from April 1917 to June 1919, no less than $23 billion were funded by borrowing and money creation (Friedman and Schwartz, 1993: 216).

The Fed could not possibly come into being at a more suitable moment, since the raison d'être of a central bank was precisely, as Alexander Hamilton wrote in his "Report on a National Bank," to be of "greater facility to the Government in obtaining pecuniary aids, especially in sudden emergencies," as mentioned before. That was precisely what the Fed did in the face of the necessities of war financing. In the words of Friedman and Schwartz, "The Federal Reserve became to all intents and purposes the bond-selling window of the Treasury, using its monetary powers almost exclusively to that end. Although no 'greenbacks' were printed, the same result was achieved by more indirect methods using Federal Reserve notes and Federal Reserve deposits" (1993: 216).

Summarizing the monetary impacts of the war finance, Friedman and Schwartz state that from the $34 billion in expenses ($32 billion in federal deficit plus $2 billion in additional Treasury cash balances), 25% was financed by taxes, 70% was borrowed, and 5% was money creation. They also note that due to the fractional reserve system, the money supply increased $6.4 billion, or $4.8 billion more than the fiduciary currency issued by the government.

During World War I, the Fed proved its utility, but the cost came in the form of post-war inflation, and it was big: it was roughly of the same magnitude of the variation in the money supply accumulated since the beginning of belligerence. From 1914 to 1920, the per-year change in wholesale prices in the United States was 15%, the annual change in the money supply was 13%, and the per-year change in "high-powered money" was 12% (Friedman and Schwartz, 1993: 206).

There are many lessons to learn from the monetary history of World War I; if nothing else, the account given by Friedman and Schwartz serves to reinforce the general theme of Rothbard's book on the role of central banking in war finance.

7.10 CONCLUDING NOTES

The subject of war finance is a broad one. War financing in the monetary history of the United States is still too broad a topic. Some conclusions, however, may be ventured. As a matter of fact, it seems clear that one cannot expect from American government respect for private property rights and freedom of contract in general, and sound money and free banking in particular, in the presence of armed conflict. This attitude of disregard for individual property rights is the "natural" response of different governments in different historical moments. It is a "fact of life." The acceptance of this attitude as the "natural" response from government in the face of military struggle does not imply in any way that the survival of the polity justifies the relativization of private property in general and sound money and free banking in particular unconditionally.

A discussion on alternative ways to finance war other than debasing the currency and regimenting the banking system to drain the savings of the country in the shortest period of time possible, if one has sufficient detachment, is a valid intellectual exercise on contrafactual arguments, but in this chapter we are dealing with those arguments of *força maior* that in the face of the circumstances were the basis for actual decisions.

It is reasonable to acknowledge the fact that it is in the "depth" of financial markets (as the concept, more recently, has been utilized), that is, in the complexity and extension of capital markets, that a country may find the instruments appropriate for financing emergencies, and the "deepness" of a financial market is a direct function of the extension of the protection of private property rights and freedom of contract in that society. On the other hand, desperate times require desperate measures, and it is not always the case that political leaders are at leisure to think in any time frame other than the shortest possible.

To distinguish between moments—say, at the beginning of the American Revolutionary War (in which the situation could not seem more desperate) and the circumstances of American federal finances during World War I (in which no "greenbacks" were issued because it was not deemed to be necessary)—would be an exercise in casuistry and the result of such an exercise would likely be that sometimes the interest of the community may be understood as a morally superior value to individual rights by the majority of the population, or by the political leaders, or the intellectual elite, or whomever. To engage in this utilitarian reasoning as an acceptable guide for moral evaluation is exactly the point about the pervasiveness of a "fiscal proviso" as a matter of realpolitik.

The different episodes in American history in which the federal government has intervened with money and banking in order to provide for war finance allow one, from the comfort of one's armchair, to identify two different arguments against governments trumping private property rights in cases of emergencies: the first one is that it is not an efficient way to gather the resources necessary to face the emergencies, and the second is that it is not in the best interest of the community to do that in the long run.

The first argument can be easily granted; that is, it is not so difficult to show how, through the protection of private property, the government may create the trust necessary to raise more resources than through rapacious means. That is an argument that, without denying the moral case for trumping private property rights, gives practical reasons for limiting it to the circumstances of the most extreme and desperate emergencies.

The second argument is more difficult to defend; that is, what if there is really no time to gather the resources necessary to face the emergency by any means other than confiscation? Does any individual have the right to refuse his property when the very survival of the community as an independent political body is at risk, and with that his own life and the remainder of his property? The answer to this question is far from consensual in America and, in any event, historically, the government in the United States has not refrained from trumping private property rights in case of emergencies out of respect for individual rights.

The way I see it, the recognition that even American political institutions will allow the relativization of individual rights in the case of emergencies is the main lesson left by the history of war financing in the United States. A major challenge that remains unmet is to show all involved parties that it is possible to create a principled way to deal with such cases.[23]

If a central bank is understood as a modern proxy to the monetary prerogatives of government in general, only to be used in cases of extreme emergencies, then a moral defense for its existence may be found in this work. However, if the central bank is understood as just one more instrument to manage fiat money for any other purpose than the defense of the life and property of individuals, I advocate that it is morally wrong, tantamount to forgery, economically unnecessary, and also damaging to the purposes of individual human flourishing that are the ultimate rationale for political institutions.

NOTES

1. The exercise of monetary prerogatives may be equated to the power to establish a "monetary constitution." The "constitutional" rules about money and credit do not necessarily infringe private property rights and freedom of contract. For instance, the definition of a unit of account that economic agents may use in their calculations or the supply of a medium of exchange stable in value would be an exercise of such prerogatives without infringement of private property and freedom of contract.

2. One may argue that there were no fiscal considerations in play at the creation of the Federal Reserve System (FRS) as the *fourth* central bank in the United States; true or false as that may be, it does not diminish the fact that the previous three central banks (The Bank of North America, The First Bank of the United States, and the Second Bank of the United States) were created primarily with that purpose in mind, and that the bank created in 1913 was completely mobilized as an agent of the Treasury by 1917 and has performed that role ever since. In regard to the Bank of England, however, there is no doubt that not only was it established in 1694 in order to provide funds to the British Crown but also that privileges such as the management of the national debt, the acceptance of its notes in payment of taxes, and, later, the granting

of legal tender status to them, among others, were extended in order to facilitate the bank's purpose as an instrument of war finance.

3. Even after the establishment of a mint, in the United States, foreign coins had legal tender status as late as 1854 (the Spanish silver dollar retained that status until 1857), demonstrating that a monopoly of the money supply is not a necessary requirement to having money supplied. The relative merits of providing the supply of money either monopolistically or competitively is a different discussion.

4. For instance, credit card companies incorporate the cost of foreign exchange transactions in their regular fees for some of the credit card contracts they offer in order to have more business, which allows some of their customers to do transactions in multiple currencies for no additional cost other than what they implicitly pay for transactions in their domestic currencies.

5. "The dollar, originally contemplated in the money transactions of this country, by successive diminutions of its weight and fineness, has sustained a depreciation of five per cent, and yet the new dollar has a currency in all payments in place of the old, with scarcely any attention to the difference between them. The operation of this in depreciating the value of property, depending upon past contracts, and (as far as inattention to the alteration in the coin may be supposed to leave prices stationary) of all other property, is apparent. Nor can it require argument to prove that a nation ought not to suffer the value of the property of its citizens to fluctuate with the fluctuations of a foreign mint, and to change with the changes in the regulations of a foreign sovereign" (Hamilton, 1790/1904).

6. Cases of debasement of the national currency, at the time of commodity money, and cases of inflation of the money supply by the sovereign, in cases in which convertibility was suspended temporarily or definitively, are well known and too many to be enumerated.

7. All the historical examples of debasement, suspension of convertibility, and inflation demonstrate beyond doubt that central banking does not guarantee good money, but good money being supplied without central banking requires some explanation. The argument here is that in the absence of forced tender, economic agents will choose the money that best suits their necessities, it may be the US dollar in Panama or Ecuador, or the Spanish silver dollar during colonial times and later in the antebellum United States. It is not an argument that there will always be a better money available than the one provided by the central bank but that the monopoly of the money supply as embodied by the central banks worldwide, because of the attribute of being a monopoly, precludes the possibility of economic agents using a better money that may be available.

8. The lender of last resort argument for central banking and the flexibility of the money supply as an instrument to smooth economic fluctuations are folded together because the former only becomes necessary once the government intervenes with money and banking in order to achieve the latter, as will be explained in the next paragraphs.

9. Since we are dealing with counterfactuals, I can only support this claim with the logical argument that a lender of last resort only becomes necessary when the banks operate not only with fractional reserves, but also with time mismatches, being that a bank operation under fractional reserves but no time mismatches the kind of operation recommended by the "Real Bills" doctrine, for instance. Fractional reserve banking and time mismatches may occur without the moral hazard created by a lender of last resort or the implicit (or explicit) guarantee by the government that convertibility will be suspended or deposits on demand will be frozen if needed but they tend to be isolated events, given that the consequence of reckless behavior is bankruptcy; they become systemic events when the bankers know that the government will not allow them to go broke and that happens when they know that the government needs them to pool short-term savings to float long-term public debts, that is, the government needs them to do exactly what will make their banks insolvent in the event that confidence is lost.

10. "The multitude sufficient to confide in for our security is not determined by any certain number, but by comparison with the enemy we fear; and is then sufficient when the odds of the enemy is not of so visible and conspicuous moment to determine the event of war, as to move him to attempt" (Hobbes, 1994:107).

11. One may say that not everybody values his life or the life of his family so highly as to fight for them and therefore it would be an infringement of their rights to ask them for their blood or treasury for the common defense. However, I think that a distinction can be made between the "blood tax" of conscription and taxation no matter how onerous a given taxation may be. The most desperate circumstances do not give the sovereign a right to enslave his subjects and to force them to fight, nor do I think that a suicidal defense or a confiscation and commitment of the destruction of everything that is valuable in order to try to prevent their loss is morally justifiable. In deciding what to commit to national defense, the sovereign needs to apply practical reasoning, prudence, as with everything else in life, and a sensible form of government is one that makes rulers accountable to the people for that. Furthermore, the right not to be forced into the army and the right to sell one's goods and emigrate is part of the individual rights which all human beings are entitled to. But once a situation of emergency has started, if your property is needed for common defense, the right you have is to expect compensation, once the emergency has ceased and conditioned on the sovereign not having been defeated.

12. As previously stated, the sum of individual preferences is not the only determinant of the amount to be raised for national defense, since external circumstances such as the size of the military threat faced by a given society and the need to keep a standing army are not determined by the sum of those preferences. However, the *ex ante* conclusion of a cost and benefit analysis between the expenditures of national defense and the value of the life and property that each individual has in that given society is a determinant factor in each one's assessment that he is a net gainer or a net loser for each level of expenditure and may determine whether he judges that the best option is to leave that society or to surrender that society whose defense, according to his or her criterion of evaluation, it does not pay to defend. Under assumptions of perfect knowledge, it would be possible to talk about an objective assessment of all the values involved in such decision, and the closer each subjective decision maker comes to that objective evaluation, the better, but ultimately, each individual will decide based on the knowledge about his internal and external circumstances he possesses and, of course, he may be wrong in objective terms.

13. It is historical in the sense of an enquiry into certain events as discussed by Oakeshott in his essay "On History" (1999: 1).

14. In his introduction to the 2005 edition of *HMBUS*, Joseph T. Salerno quotes Mises' statement that since history is the record of human effort to better their condition and this evaluation is an intellectual endeavor, "Thus, ideas are the main theme of the study of History," particularly the ones based on the values directing human action. For the historian, action and judgments of value, according to Mises, "Are the starting points of a specific mode of reflection, of the specific understanding of the historical sciences of human action" (Rothbard, 2005: 12).

15. See Mises, "Covering the State's War Costs," in *Nation, State, and the Economy* (2006).

16. The same point is made by Robert Higgs in *Crisis and Leviathan* quoting the economist Wesley C. Mitchell, who wrote in 1943 that "When lives themselves are treated as means (to the end of military victory) so is property" (Higgs, 1987: 202).

17. See Niall Ferguson's "Of Human Bondage" in *The Ascent of Money* (2008).

18. Without a personal statement, and I am unaware of any, it seems impossible to know for certain what the mood of Rothbard was while writing that passage. One can only guess that he was in a humorous mood in describing the pathetic events which led to the first experience with government fiat paper money in modern times.

19. Rothbard, while writing his dissertation thesis on The Panic of 1919, worked with the historian Joseph Dorfman. Dorfman, who wrote the five volumes of *The*

Economic Mind in American Civilization, is famous for having discredited the claims, most conspicuously advanced by Arthur Schlesinger, Jr. in *The Age of Jackson*, that the Jacksonian movement was a sort of *avant la lettre* New Deal. According to Leonard Liggio (Liggio, 1995: 2) Dorfman showed that the Jacksonian movement was actually a radical laissez-faire movement, contrary to the understanding about the Jacksonians so forcefully advanced after World War II by some research programs interested in finding a pedigree in American history for interventionist policies.

20. The difference between "duometallism" and "bimetallism" according to Einaudi (Einaudi, 1953: 238), is that under the former there is no fixed parity and, therefore, the prices are quoted both in silver and gold, with the use of an "imaginary" coin as unit of account linked to the actual weight in silver in each coin being instrumental to economic agents to facilitate the exchanges. On imaginary money see footnote 21 of chapter 1.

21. According to Vera Smith, in 1913, there were about 20,000 banks in the United States, 7,000 of them note-issuing national banks, regulated by the National Bank Act, and the others organized in accordance with the laws of the respective states in which they were established (Smith, 1990: 146).

22. The perception that a monetary system in which there is only the issuance of banknotes with the deposit of bullion, such as the currency boards attempted by Brazil and Argentina at the end of the nineteenth century, by the beginning of the twentieth century was already considered lacking a required *elasticity* which was supported by one of the main theorists of fiat money at the time of the traditional gold standard, the Chilean economist Guillermo Subercaseaux (Subercaseaux, 1912/2014: 380).

23. Other episodes of relativization of private property rights in the face of a perceived emergency are the Gold Clause Cases in the 1930s. When Franklin D. Roosevelt in 1933 devalued the US dollar from about 22 dollars per ounce to 35 dollars per ounce, a Joint Resolution of Congress invalidated all contracts establishing payments at the pre-devaluation parity. That was challenged in court, and in *Perry v. United States*, 294 U.S. 330 (1935) as in *Marbury v. Madison*, 5 U.S. 137 (1803) before that, the decision denied a remedy to the claimants in order to avoid a confrontation with the President. Franklin Roosevelt made clear to the Justices that out of necessity, he would not obey a decision upholding the Gold Clauses, forcing them to risk a constitutional crisis. But, as stated by Gerard N. Magliocca in an undated working paper (Magliocca, 2012: 32), "The most plausible source of that necessary duty is the Commander in Chief Clause, but even the most eager apologist for executive power could not stretch that provision to cover monetary action in peacetime." That basically draws the line between what was an emergency, in which case qualified action would be morally acceptable, and what, in essence, was a pure exercise of power.

EIGHT

The Demand for Money, the Business Cycle, and the Current Monetary Regime

8.1 INTRODUCTION TO THE DEMAND FOR MONEY

In any society with a monetary regime that allows expansion of monetary instruments beyond the availability of goods and services in the real economy, business cycles are to be expected, reflecting periods of overconsumption and overinvestment followed by contractions necessary to adjust supply and demand in the real sector as mediated by the competing claims represented by money and quasi-money over a limited amount of real resources. In the real economy, the distortions introduced during an expansionist period are reversed by the "**Ricardo effect**," but in the financial sector, that mismatch between the competing claims and the available resources is reflected in a time mismatch between financial assets and liabilities.

Obviously, different monetary regimes are more or less conducive to the expansion of money and credit according to their different features. A gold standard with banknote issue and bank deposits fully backed in bullion is less prone to inflation of the money supply than a gold standard with fractional reserves, and both systems are potentially less inflationary than a regime of forced tender fiat money, fractional banking, and a central bank, which are currently in force almost everywhere.

Under fractional banking, therefore, busyness cycles are expected potentially to happen more often and with sharper swings than under regimes of fully backed money supply. That is not to say, however, that under a 100% reserve system for the issuing of banknotes and deposits on demand, mismatches as the above-mentioned cannot occur.[1]

The fluctuations in the supply of money and credit, as briefly stated above, may produce upturns and downturns in economic activity, and the fluctuations under fractional banking, everything else being equal, are expected to be sharper than under arrangements with 100% reserves. But it is important to note that fractional banking is not only good in increasing the money supply, but also in decreasing the money supply (as described in 9.2.1 On Money Creation by the Banks). So, under the monetary regimes today, with their features of fractional reserves, fiat money, legal tender, and in most cases, forced tender, there are not only moments when the money supply can increase with few constraints in the short run, but also moments in which it can decrease very dramatically.[2]

A parallel phenomenon is the one of variations in the demand for money. Obviously supply and demand for money are related in a number of different ways; the most obvious of them is that when the supply of money increases to the point of affecting its purchasing power, it is reasonable to expect that the demand for holding money tends to decrease. But there are many other ways in which they are interconnected. In this chapter we will deal with the one where an increase in the demand for money leads to a decrease in the money supply at the turning point from an upturn into a downturn in the business cycle, and that happens when some monetary instruments cease to be money, that is, they lose their **monetary properties** in the middle of a "flight to liquidity." So, under the monetary arrangements of fractional banking, fiat money, and central bank, at the tipping point of the business cycle, the central bank can allow the money supply to increase, to decrease, or it can attempt to keep the money supply constant. Although these options will not be discussed in this chapter, it is part of the argument presented here that the variations in the demand for money must be taken into consideration on the central bank's decision about which course of action to follow. But more than that, what this chapter purports to demonstrate is that none of the possible courses of action open to the central bank lead to an optimum result for society. It is true that this chapter prescribes a course of action the central bank should adopt in the face of an increased demand for money at the beginning of a downturn, but the entire exercise is much more than an instrument to conclude which monetary policy to follow under those circumstances. The entire exercise must be understood as an argument against the current monetary regime and not as a way to mend it.

8.1.1 The Demand for Money

There is a difference between the amount of money that each individual uses on any given day to perform his transactions and the amount of money that he aims to keep at the end of the day. The latter may be referred as "cash balance," and it is the aggregate preference of all economic agents for holding cash balances that represent the *demand for money* in society.

8.1.2 The Supply of Money

The *supply of money*, on the other hand, may be supplied competitively or by a monopoly.[3] Money is supplied competitively when there is no legal forced tender, that is, when there is no legal provision mandating the use of a given currency by the economic agents; and there is a monopoly of the money supply when such a legal provision is in force.

8.1.3 Money is Like Any Other Economic Good

All economic goods may be classified into three categories: i) capital goods, ii) consumer goods, and iii) media of exchange. Capital goods are those that have their utility derived from their capacity to produce other goods; consumer goods are those that have their utility derived from the satisfaction of human wants that they provide; and the media of exchange derive their utility from being instrumental in the acquisition of other goods, which may also be understood as a consequence of its liquidity. Since the utility of media of exchange is a consequence of their instrumentality for the acquisition of other goods, some authors classify them as capital goods. Incidentally, the idea that money is the most liquid instrument is summarized in the dictum "Money buys goods and goods buy money, but goods do not buy goods." (Von Hagen and Welker, 2014: 26). Whether or not the media of exchange is a capital good is not a relevant issue for the topic discussed in this paper.[4] What is relevant is the fact that money is an economic good like capital and consumer goods and, therefore, money is subject to the same laws that command the behavior of individuals in relation to those other goods.

8.1.4 Money is a Generally Accepted Medium of Exchange

As previously stated, the definition of money that is adopted in this book is the GAMOE definition of money, that money is the Generally Accepted Medium Of Exchange.[5]

So, this chapter presents the contention that the generally accepted medium of exchange in society is subject to the laws of supply and demand in a similar fashion to any other economic good.

Due to the fact that money is generally not only the medium of exchange but also the unit of account in society, the variation of its price in relation to all other goods must be understood as a change in its purchasing power.[6]

So, like any other economic good, money is subject to the laws of supply and demand; money is an economic good that derives its utility from its use as a medium of exchange; the aggregated amount of money that each one of the economic agents chooses to keep as cash balance is the demand of money; and the supply of money may be institutionally framed to be provided competitively by the market or monopolistically by the state.

8.1.5 Why Keep a Cash Balance?

Going forward, an intriguing question that may be asked is, why do economic agents choose to keep cash balances?

Since the utility provided by money is a consequence of its attribute of being generally accepted in exchange for other goods, it is in this "stored potential" to have ready access to the available economic goods in the market that one must search for the answer.

It has been said that if individuals had perfect knowledge about the future, no money would be necessary: "the main function of money for most people is to bridge the gap between present and future, which is necessitated by the uncertainty of the latter. If the future were known with certainty, there would be no need for money" (Barnett II and Block, 2005: 189).

Obviously, the above statement is just an exaggeration made by its authors in order to stress a point. After all: a) money is needed in order to ease the daily transactions of economic agents; b) even if they knew the future "with certainty," each family and business would still experience uneven inflows and outflows of cash; and c) one must not forget that there are higher transaction costs in buying and selling any other form of wealth.

Exaggeration though it is, the link between uncertainty about the future and the decision of keeping cash balances is crucial to understanding the demand for money. In the words of Mises:

> The uncertainty of the future makes it seem advisable to hold a larger or smaller part of one's possessions in a form that will facilitate a change from one way of using wealth to another, or transition from the ownership of one good to that of another, in order to preserve the opportunity of being able without difficulty to satisfy urgent demands that may possibly arise in the future for goods that will have to be obtained by way of exchange. (Mises, 1981: 170)

As can be easily understood, aside from the uncertainty regarding the future, there are many factors influencing the amount of cash balances that economic agents may choose to keep at any given time; furthermore, as stated by Rothbard (2009: 776), there is nothing "antisocial" in keeping cash balances, contrary to Keynes' normative arguments. In the same chapter, Rothbard is clear in stating that any quantitative limits to cash balances are arbitrary and unjustified.

One of the factors influencing the desire to keep cash balances is the amount of transactions that the economic agents usually do in the short run, and this amount is strongly correlated to their income, so it can be said that the size of cash balances is a function of income level.

Another factor is the extent to which cash flows match the aggregate of the economic agents. For instance, a society with a great percentage of formal employment tends to have a lower demand for money than a society in which the majority of the population is self-employed, say, in different seasonal economic activities.

The level of sophistication of financial instruments also plays a role in determining the demand for money; if the transaction costs to invest in income-generating financial assets are relatively low, money can be transferred into financial investments and back into cash more often, in shorter periods of time than otherwise, diminishing the necessity of holding cash in order to pay for the expected transactions in those periods.[7]

The short-term interest rate is obviously one more key element that affects the determination by each economic agent of the cash balances he would like to keep.[8]

8.1.6 Problems Originated by Variations in the Supply and Demand for Money

Related to the problem of fluctuations in the demand for money is the problem of variations in the supply of money and the changes in the purchasing power of the medium of exchange. Actually, most of the literature about the supply and demand for money deals with changes in the supply of money and emphasizes that the relevant changes for determining the demand for money are the real changes and not the merely nominal changes provoked by an inflationary expansion of the medium of exchange.

My hypothesis here is that, in a monetary framework, the supply of money is provided competitively, that is, provided by different suppliers; the problems that may arise to accommodate the supply and demand for money are of a lesser magnitude than when the supply of money is monopolistically provided by the state, since under competitive money supply, the adjustments of supply and demand for money are operated endogenously by the interaction of the preferences of economic agents, each one with his or her own marginal utility, and not by the guessing of a central banker. It is when the supply of money is provided by a state monopoly that serious problems may be expected to happen. The most commonly identified problems are the ones that arise when a society with a given demand for money experiences an inflationary increase in the money supply. In this case of inflation of the money supply, a predictable consequence is a decrease of the purchasing power of the medium of exchange; others result from all sorts of misallocations that the nonneutral characteristic of these variations in the money supply may cause.

As confirmed by the empirical evidence time and again, the economic crisis, the recessions, and the depressions are, in most cases, nothing more than the more or less prolonged and severe period (according to the circumstances of each business cycle) of time required to correct all the misallocations provoked by the inflationary expansions of the money supply.

But periods of economic crisis are moments of increased uncertainty and, as mentioned above, uncertainty about the future is one of the key elements that may drive an increase in the demand for money.

8.1.7 What is the Proper Response to an Economic Crisis?

If the government monopolistically controls the supply of money, what should be the government's "proper" response in the case of a perceived increase in the demand for money in the middle of an economic crisis?

Is it proper for the government to increase (again) the money supply in order to match the increased demand? Or is the proper response *f iat justitia ruat caelum*?[9]

If the government keeps the supply of money constant in face of an increased demand for money, or worse, allow its contraction, it will force asset liquidations beyond the misallocations that need to be corrected, producing even bigger economic devastation, human suffering, and social unrest.

If the government supplies extra money in proportion to its estimate for its demand, a plethora of bad things may happen: a) it will generate an excess supply of money as soon as confidence is restored unless the government later "mops" up the excess supplied (something to be skeptical about); b) given the nonneutral characteristic of money, it will result in other misallocations; and c) it may generate all sorts of privileges, moral hazards, and an increase in the size of the state sector, to name a few.

Having said all that, it is the contention presented in this chapter that under the institutional framework of fiat money, legal forced tender, and central banking, the proper action for the government to take is to attend to the increased demand for money with an increase in the money supply; this course of action being justified, by prudential reasons given below, as the lesser evil.

A traditional approach among Austrian economists[10] to this dilemma is to frame this discussion as a choice between the alternatives of a lengthier or deeper recession. Paul Cwik says, "It seems that economists and policy setters face a trade-off between the length of the recession and its depth" (2009: 8).

The three courses of action open to the central bank are to expand the supply of money, to keep it constant, or to allow it to contract. The expansion of the money supply is associated with the option of lengthening the recession in order to avoid a depression, and the options of maintaining constant the money supply or allowing its contraction are usually associated with accepting a deeper recession, which will bring a faster correction of the existing misallocations and therefore a faster recovery.

This chapter does not dispute that traditional approach; it just suggests a new element for analysis: that is, changes in the demand for money. Let's suppose that the preference for holding cash balances has not changed significantly at the beginning of the recession. In that case, keeping the supply of money constant would match the existing demand for money. But what if most of the economic agents have panicked, and the desire to hold cash balances has increased dramatically in a true "flight to liquidity?" In those circumstances, some forms of monetary instruments, quasi-money, that were part of the money supply because of their liberative power (liquidity), may have lost their liquidity once the agents start a flight to "hard" money. That is the case when investments in credit instruments, such as "securitized" credits, corporate bonds, mortgages, and treasury bills, held in money market mutual funds and regarded as de facto money, start to be traded or risk being traded at a discount when money holders start to move their liquidity from **MMMFs** to bank deposits or cash.[11] In such cases, in light of the GAMOE definition of money, should an increase in the monetary base that prevents a decrease in M2 by compensating the reduction in credit by an increase in bank credits with the central bank be considered an increase in the money supply or simply a policy to keep the money supply constant? The "flight to liquidity" seen during the crisis suggests that part of the increase in the monetary base just compensated for the decrease in the perception that some credit instruments were part of the money supply.[12]

8.1.8 Final Introductory Remarks

The course of action of expanding the monetary base by "quantitative easing," even if just to keep the money supply constant in the broad sense of GAMOE used here, as mentioned above, has terrible consequences. Therefore, if, under the current monetary arrangements in place almost everywhere in the world, the best thing that can be done is a terrible thing, a case may be made that the entire institutional edifice of a state-controlled monopoly of the money supply is a flawed one, and a new monetary constitution must be thought out.[13]

8.2 THE NEOCLASSICAL MODELS FOR THE DEMAND FOR MONEY

8.2.1 The Demand for Money Function

Neoclassical economists consider money, like any other good, as subject to market forces, and therefore, models to illustrate the supply and demand for money have been created since the moment that mathematical formulation has been used in economics. As written by David Laidler in *The Demand for Money*, "We study the demand for any item mainly so that we may make predictions about the consequences of changes in its supply. This statement is as true of money as of anything else" (1993: 3).

The supply and demand for money, therefore, may be expressed in the classical form of curves of supply and demand as with any other good.[14]

According to Laidler, an analysis of supply and demand shows first that "in face of a shift in the supply function, . . . at least one . . . of the variables on which demand depends must change;" second, it shows that the extent of the changes (in those variables) depends on a relation between such variable(s) and the quantities demanded; and third, that the

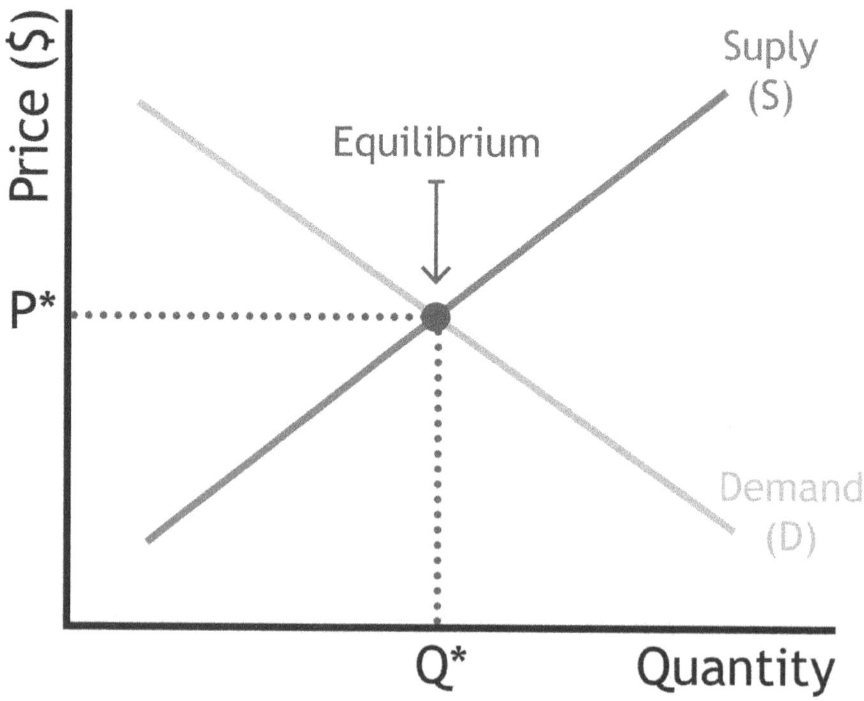

Figure 8.1. Supply and Demand

outcome of any shift in the supply, though "heavily conditioned" by the nature of the demand curve, is not determined exclusively by that.

These simple principles are particularly important in the case of money. As pointed out by Laidler, because the demand for money is strongly influenced by some variables such as interest rates, the level of national income, and the price level, the government can influence systematically the demand for money through manipulating the quantity of the money supplied; and as Laidler also stresses, in "virtually all contemporary economies" it is something under government's control (1993: 6).

A most interesting aspect of Laidler's exposition is a recognition that "We must consider the possibility that all of the factors on which the demand for money depends will respond simultaneously to a change in its supply" (1993: 7) and, therefore, we must accept the necessity of a dynamic analysis in order to understand the consequences of a change in the supply of money.

There are many subjective factors implicit in the neoclassical analysis though, and Laidler explicitly states that "Theories of the demand for money . . . are not logically incompatible with the notion that the demand for money in fact arises from its usefulness in making transactions or with the proposition that it is an excellent hedge against the risks inherent in holding assets," and he concludes his overview on the demand for money stating that "all theories of the demand for money rest on considerations having to do with uncertainty and the passage of time" (1993: 45).

Having said that, the demand for money in the neoclassical paradigm is presented as a simple alternative between holding cash or bonds and, therefore, as a function of the rate of interest at any given income level.

8.2.2 The IS-LM Model

For any level of income (Y) and any rate of interest (i) it is possible to describe a preference for liquidity, that is, a curve for the demand for money (LM) that will be in *equilibrium* with the level of savings and investments (IS) curve. According to the neoclassical economists, the IS-LM model can be understood as the special case of the supply and demand for money in which the demand for money is determined by the national income and the rate of interest. Since the rate of interest is assumed to possibly be manipulated by the government by means of changes in the money supply, the theoretical apparatus for the sort of interventions advocated by both monetarists and Keynesians on the two sides of the *neoclassical consensus* is the one provided for the neoclassical model of equilibrium as applied to the supply and demand for money.

8.2.3 The Quantitative Theory of Money

The quantitative theory of money must be understood simply as an application of the general theory of supply and demand for the case of money; after all, the existence of a ratio between money and all available goods, as the essence of the quantitative theory of money, is the same as with any other exchange. Its main flaw, of course, is to assume that money is neutral and not to state that there is a causal relation between prices and the quantity of money as stated by Mises in his book *Human Action* (1949/2007: 405).

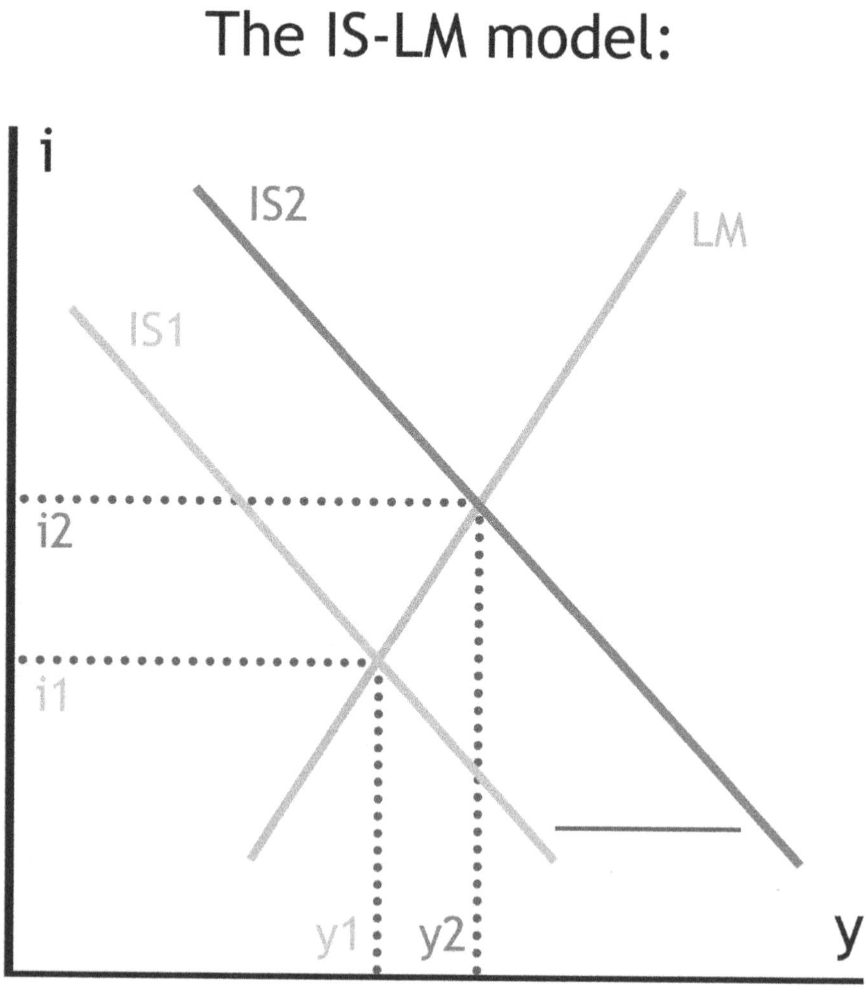

Figure 8.2. The IS-LM Model

This work is not the right place to discuss the many methodological and conceptual differences between the neoclassical consensus and Austrian economics but the opposite; the purpose of this section is to stress that from a shared understanding of the essential role of money in society (medium of exchange), of its main feature (liquidity), and of its ***endogenous* determination of value**, neoclassical and Austrian economists alike can accept that subjective evaluations about uncertainty and risk are key factors in determining the demand for money. Or can't they?

8.3 IS ANY AMOUNT OF MONEY AS GOOD AS ANY OTHER?

8.3.1 What Does Austrian Economics Have to Say about the Optimum Amount of Money?

Mises, arguing that any amount of money is as good as any other and therefore that it would be a waste of social resources to add to any existing quantity, wrote, "the services which money renders can be neither improved nor repaired by changing the supply of money" (1949/2007: 421).

If any further evidence is required about what is supposed to be the view of Austrian economics on the optimum amount of money, Barnett and Block state: "It is pretty well established within Austrian Economics that the optimum quantity of money is whatever level is established at any given time" (2004: 39).

It must be emphasized that this statement admits a qualification; in the same article from which the quotation above was drawn, Barnett and Block assume that (it) "is obvious from Mises' (and Rothbard's) statements, both are referring to a commodity money" (2004: 43).

However, it seems to be implicit in a praxeological analysis about the demand for money, understood as the aggregation of the individual preferences for cash balances, that the "optimum" amount of money is a consequence of the aggregate of individual preferences. In the framework of competitively provided commodity money, these preferences may be accommodated by an increase or decrease respectively (i) in the supply of money, (ii) in the preference for cash balances, or (iii) by a change in the purchasing power of the commodity money. "The optimum quantity of money is not, then, whatever quantity happens to exist, but rather whatever amount of gold as coins the free-market process creates" (Barnett and Block, 2004: 48).

If this interpretation is correct, then it may be accepted from an Austrian economics standpoint that it is not any existing quantity of money in use by society at a given time that performs the services desired by economic agents, but fluctuations in the supply and demand for money should accommodate the sum of personal preferences like the functions of demand and supply for any other good. And as with any other good, these preferences may vary, resulting in a short-term disequilibrium.

8.3.2 What Would be a Function of the Demand for Money from an Austrian Economics Perspective under the Current Monetary Arrangements with Fiat Money?

Since under a gold standard the supply of money constantly changes according to the actions of the economic agents in depositing and retrieving bullion from the issuing banks as stated above, in principle, it does not seem that the postulate of "any amount of money is as good as any other" holds water in the specific case of commodity money. If the postulate that any amount of money that happens to be in use in society is the optimum amount of money is not even valid for commodity money, what would be a general "demand function for money" from an Austrian economics perspective? As stated above, the aggregate of individual preferences will intersubjectively determine how the supply and demand for money will be accommodated regardless of the specific monetary regime enforced. For instance, if the supply of money obeys a *Friedmanesque* constant rule and the demand for money either increases or diminishes differently from the established rule, the conclusion that the accommodation will happen by changes in the prices and quantities of marketed goods and services seems to be consistent with a praxeological approach. Violent changes in the preferences for cash balances will generate violent changes in prices and quantities traded plus or minus the variation in the money supply according to the established rule. But if that is so, from an Austrian economics perspective, what can be said about the demand for money under monetary arrangements of fiat money in which the cost of creating money is marginally insignificant and there is no constant rule for the money supply such as the one mentioned in the example above?

In the imperfect markets of mixed-economy societies today, all sorts of rigidities and limitations are imposed on the free exchange of goods and services and the labor market is one of the most regulated markets, by far. Under the just-mentioned circumstances, a case may be made that when society is in a downturn as part of a business cycle, the cost of making any adjustment of supply and demand of goods and services by deflation is relatively more expensive than allowing the adjustment to happen by keeping the purchase power of the money constant. The hypothesis that keeping prices stable during a downturn is a relatively less expensive solution results from the fact that adding fiat money to the money supply is relatively cheap. It is undisputed that in the face of an increase in the demand for money, a nonflexible money supply will force the prices down. Why that is so painful is a legitimate source of controversy, though. That this phenomenon has a psychological origin may well be assumed; after all, it is a common behavior already observed in different times and places. It may be ventured that economic agents have a sense of entitlement to the relative value of their goods and skills and, generally speaking, are reluctant to be the first to accept a loss in what they perceive as the "current" price of their property, individually. Yeager says, "Elements of price and wage stickiness, though utterly rational from the individual points of view of the decision-makers involved, do keep downward price and wage adjustments from absorbing the full impact of the reduced willingness to spend associated with efforts to build or maintain cash balances" (1983: 306).

The fact is that the trend towards a lower price level in order to match an increased preference for money to a constant money supply is expected to produce a decrease in production since prices are not, due to the circumstances above, as elastic to the downside as they are to the upside. And, price stability in times of crisis can be achieved by increasing the supply of money in order to accommodate an increased demand for cash balances in the economy.[15]

All the analysis presented so far seems to fit fairly as a description of the reality from the perspective, first, of the neoclassical economists and, next, of the Austrian economists. Now, it is time to deal with the normative side of this problem, since any increase in the demand for cash balances in a regime of state monopoly of money must be supplied to the money holders by the central bank through the banking system.

I have argued elsewhere[16] that prudence should be the guide for how to respond to financial crises.

8.4 THE REASONS FOR ADVOCATING A PRUDENTIAL RESPONSE

8.4.1 A Matter of Principles

Could the 2008 (or any) economic crisis be considered an emergency case, such as an armed conflict?[17] Do the principles on which civil society are based not apply because civility is replaced by a state of war?[18] Apparently not; therefore, the solution for an economic crisis must be consistent with the principles best suited to organize a society of human beings.[19]

Has the 2008 economic crisis changed the paradigm of a pluralistic society, based on private property rights, with a representative government limited by individual rights as the best society for human flourishing? The answer is also no; no new argument in favor of replacing a spontaneous order for an order of command was offered.

Nonetheless, the response to the crisis worldwide was more protectionism (so far mild), industrial subsidies, financial regulation, fiscal and monetary stimuli. Are they not against the principles of an open society and free markets? It seems to be beyond any doubt that commercial protectionism, subsidies, and protection for noncompetitive industries or political favorites and increased governmental expenditures are against the principles of limited government best suited for a society of free and responsible individuals, and no aspect of the reality seems to justify departing from those principles.

But are the bailouts of banks and insurance companies by governmental loans financed by massive increases in the public debt or straightforward increase of the money supply in a narrow sense ("quantitative easing") also not regrettable? Yes, they are regrettable, but here, the answer may be nuanced.[20] For good or evil, the law of the land in the United States, for instance, has been one of a state monopoly of the money supply, legal forced tender, fractional reserve banking, and central banking since 1913 when the Federal Reserve System (Fed) was created.[21]

Any decision by the central bank to close the discount window and to prevent financial institutions from gaining access to hard money, giving in guarantee well-performing assets they may have, would in practice represent a contraction of the liquidity in the economy forcing a deflationary adjustment beyond the adjustments necessary in the structure of production in order to correct the malinvestments done on the upturn of the business cycle. In a now famous article, Hayek, by 1937 talking about the Great Depression, argued that, "a movement towards more liquid types of money causes an actual decrease in the total supply of money," and under those circumstances, the proper thing for the central bank to do is to "offset . . . as far as possible the effect of changes in the demand for liquid assets on the total quantity of the circulating medium" (Miller, 2009: 32).[22]

It seems that a case may be made that there is a difference in not supporting the malinvestments done during the boom stage of the cycle with easy money and not allowing the supply of money to decrease, which under fractional reserve and central bank arrangements may imply increasing the amount of hard money in order to compensate for the increased preference for liquidity. That is so because, contrary to what would happen under a regime of a competitive supply of money, that is, an increased demand for money would be matched by an increased production of coins,[23] under a governmental monopoly of the money supply, only the government can at least try to act as the private suppliers would have done. That the government cannot mimic the spontaneous actions of economic agents in a free marketplace goes without saying, but that is part of the argument against the entire regime of a fractional reserve bank and central banking and not an argument against trying to alleviate the bad consequences of the existing regime while it is still in force.

One last comment is this: if given the lack of knowledge that the central bankers possess and the nonneutral character of money it is impossible to know if an increase in the money supply is upholding investments that should be liquidated or avoiding unnecessary deflation, it seems again an argument against the regime that leaves such an action as the least disastrous course of action to follow and not an argument against taking such a course, if the circumstances are the ones described.

8.4.2 What to Do in the Case of a "Secondary Depression"?

The discussion above resembles the one about *"secondary depression"* championed by Wilhelm Röpke and explained by Huerta de Soto as this: "Under certain conditions, government and union intervention, along with the institutional rigidity of the markets, may prevent the necessary readjustments which precede any recovery of economic activity. . . . Under these circumstances a cumulative process of contraction may be triggered" (Huerta de Soto, 2006: 453).

The position of Austrian economists is clear on this regard: the measures to avoid a "secondary depression" are the ones required to eliminate the rigidities and inefficiencies in the economy, and not to produce further credit expansion. But as pointed out by Huerta de Soto, the intriguing and relevant question for our analysis is what to do if "it appears politically 'impossible' to take the measures necessary . . . ?" (2006: 454).

In the same section Huerta de Soto reminds us, "Hayek himself admitted that, under certain circumstances, a situation might become so desperate that politically the only remaining option would be to intervene again," which brings up the issue of which "type of monetary expansion would be the least disturbing from an economic standpoint?" (2006: 455). So, it is not alien to Austrian economists to accept that cases of "special circumstances" that may require nuanced responses can happen; and it is the intention with the final part of this paper to propose to frame these nuanced responses, when they are required, in a principled way. The way to identify what could be principled responses to special circumstances of emergencies is by appealing to the virtue of *Prudence*.

8.4.3 The Virtue of Prudence

Prudence nowadays is understood as equivalent to utility maximization, but in premodern times, it was not only one of the four cardinal virtues (along with justice, courage, and temperance), but it was also considered the supreme virtue. The sense in which prudence is utilized in this paper is its premodern one, or more precisely, according to the teachings of Aristotle, as an *intellectual* virtue. In Aristotle's words, "Prudence is that virtue of the understanding which enables men to come to wise decisions about the relation to happiness of the goods and evils that have been previously mentioned" (Aristotle, 1366b19–22).

In a modern, "Neo-Aristotelian" definition, "Prudence is the intelligent management of the components needed for living a good human life. As we have argued, some of the components are given by nature, others by our environment, and still others are fashioned by the logic of our own choices" (Den Uyl, 1991: 267).

It is in the sense in which self-perfection is the way to achieve a good life, that prudence, with the meaning of *practical wisdom* adopted in this paper, may be understood as the most important of the cardinal virtues. And it is in this sense that an appeal for an "intelligent management" of the circumstances in order to restore, to maintain, and to develop the best conditions possible for a good life may be understood as a principle for action in the context of our discussion.

8.4.4 The Lender of Last Resort

In a regime of state monopoly fiat money, central banking, and fractional banking, the central bank has the obligation to act as lender of last resort for the financial system. This obligation is a legal obligation, but more than that, it is a logically necessary consequence of the existing structure of the financial system. As stated by Huerta de Soto, "The very existence of a fractional-reserve banking system invariably leads to the emergence of a central bank as a lender of last resort" (Huerta de Soto, 2006: 638).

It has been accepted by the majority of the economic profession that the current financial arrangements of a fractional reserve banking system with a central bank with the legal mandate to act as a lender of last resort are the most efficient arrangements for money and banking possible.

Actually, as argued in Bagehot's *Lombard Street*, that has been the predominant view in the profession since Peel's Act of 1844 granted a monopoly of the money supply for the Bank of England in exchange for its role as lender of last resort; it became the underpinning of the financial systems of the entire world, allowing the mobilization of financial resources on an unprecedented scale, fueling the progress of mankind.[24]

However neither a recourse to authority nor the number of supporters of one idea proves its validity, and the dissonant voices of Austrian economists have incessantly pointed out the shortcomings of the current monetary arrangements adopted with variations globally. But what needs to be made clear in relation to the monetary expansion post–September 2008 promoted by the central banks in the United States, Europe, Asia, et cetera, is that it is an integral part of the financial systems as they are structured.

The different forms by which a central bank may provide liquidity for the financial system is not part of what has been discussed in this paper, and if most of lending is now done outside regular commercial banks, it is only to be expected that the central banks will provide liquidity for financial transactions outside the regular banking system as well. In the same way, it is not part of the inquiry conducted here to analyze the correctness of the different actions taken by all central banks in general or the Fed in particular; however, the perception that privileges and moral hazards are a necessary consequence of the process must be weighed in any evaluation of the current system.

8.5 CONCLUSIONS

A first conclusion that can be reached for this chapter is that in providing liquidity for the financial systems, the central banks are honoring their legal and logical obligation of acting as lenders of last resort for the financial system as it is currently organized.

Having money supply increased by the central bank in order to provide liquidity for financial institutions is no more an evil per se than any other essential feature of the current monetary constitution. It must be understood that it is not an optional feature of the system, but a defining component of it, and therefore, it cannot be evaluated apart from the rest of the monetary arrangements in place.

A second conclusion is that even if the increase in the money supply in order to provide liquidity for the financial system comes to be understood as something wrong per se, a vision shared by many sensible people, still it must be evaluated in the context of the entire financial edifice of which it is an essential feature.

Our final conclusion for this chapter is that if the process of increasing the money supply in order to provide liquidity for the financial system is perceived as a source of further misallocations, as a source of inefficiencies, privileges, and moral hazards—in sum, if it comes to be understood as an unpardonable flaw—it means a condemnation of the entire edifice. If it comes to be accepted that fractional banking cannot subsist without a lender of last resort and that this lender of last resort may not have another instrument to fund its operations other than the printing machine, it must be understood as a condemnation of fractional reserve banking and not of last resort lending. "The only way to tend this vicious circle is to recognize that the origin of the entire problem lies in fractional-reserve banking" (Huerta de Soto, 2006: 638).

8.6 POST SCRIPTUM

The current monetary constitutions are not the ideal monetary arrangements for a free society. Nonetheless, they command enormous legitimacy. Therefore, while the current monetary constitution remains in place, any decision by the central bank of not providing more liquidity for the banks, and consequently forcing all economic agents, in their increased demand for cash balances, to compete for a fixed supply of money, would represent an additional effort of adaptation from society on top of the effort required to liquidate all the existing misallocations. Depending on the severity of the crisis, it is difficult to exaggerate the dire consequences for the well-being of the economic agents of forcing down the prices in the market.[25] The progress of socialist and totalitarian experiments represented by the New Deal, Fascism, and Nazism, plus World War II, the Holocaust, and the subjugation of Eastern Europe by Soviet Imperialism come to mind as some of the dire consequences that happened the last time that the central banks failed to live up to their promises and left the financial systems worldwide to be almost completely destroyed, resulting in the bankruptcies of thousands of financial institutions in the United States alone. Any decision by the central bank to renounce its obligations would conspire against the economic foundations of the different nations around the globe. At this time, it seems bloodily clear that the best course of action possible under the current arrangements is the lesser of two evils and not a clear-cut position. This must be understood as a definitive flaw in the current arrangement and a most powerful indictment against it, a most powerful claim for its revamping. The abolition of legal tender seems to be the right place to start. All of this may be accepted as sufficient argument for a prudential evaluation about the best way to replace the current unsatisfactory arrangements regarding money and banking.

NOTES

1. See footnote 13 of chapter 9.
2. Obviously, it is not any quantity of base money that will be absorbed by the money holders; it is not any quantity of credit money that could be generated by the banking system leveraging the available amount of base money without significant and considerably fast impact on the purchasing power of money. But, to the extent that the initial circumstances permit, substantial amounts of financial claims over and above the increase in real savings can be created under the current monetary arrangements almost everywhere until it starts to compromise the purchasing power of money and the credibility of the banking system.
3. For the purposes of this work, when a monopoly of the money supply is referred to, I mean a monopoly created by law and not a natural monopoly in the supply of money that may spontaneously arise under a competitive framework.
4. For a discussion on money as a capital good, see William Barnett II and Walter Block, "Money: Capital Good, Consumer's Good or (Media of) Exchange Good?" in *The Review of Austrian Economics* 18, no. 2 (2005): 179–194.
5. As discussed in chapter 1, the GAMOE definition of money was first developed by Carl Menger, and assumes that money is a spontaneous social institution that is developed in society in order to facilitate economic transactions and therefore allow and enhance the division of labor by diminishing the transaction costs of bartering. Key features of the GAMOE conception of money are that the monetary institutions are subject to the same evolutionary pattern of other spontaneous institutions and that the central attribute of monetary merchandise is its suitability to perform the function of medium of exchange. Importantly, the other two main functions of money, that is,

its capacity to be used as a unit of account and as a store of value, are derived from its central attribute. Opposed to the GAMOE definition of money is the *nominalist* concept that the value of money is nominal, that is, given by law. This concept was first developed by Georg Knapp. According to this conception, money is a creature of the state, created as an instrument for state policy and the value of money is the one attributed to it by the state.

6. If the GAMOE definition of money is accepted, money becomes anything that comes to be generally accepted as a medium of exchange. So, not only commodity money, but also fiat money, bank deposits available on demand, and credit instruments with extremely high liberative power may be considered money under this definition. In fact, the distinction between money and quasi-money becomes somewhat blurred because, given some circumstances, some financial instruments may lose or acquire liquidity to a degree of becoming "money," while a fiat currency may totally lose the confidence of the money holders and cease to be considered money. As written by Leland Yeager in his book *The Fluttering Veil*, "At some point, apparently, the shading or drift from the properties of close near moneys toward those of money become a jump from a difference in degree to a difference in kind" (Yeager, 1997: 109). Since the definition of money adopted in this work is the GAMOE definition, the use here of the concept of "money supply" must be understood not only as variations in the monetary base, but variations in the monetary aggregates as well. For instance, prior to the 2008 financial crisis, certain credit instruments such as mortgage-backed securities issued by government-sponsored enterprises (GSEs, quasi-governmental federal agencies with the implicit support of the US Treasury), such as the mortgage securitization giants Fannie Mae and Freddie Mac, were deemed by the agents in international capital market as so liquid as to be required to be held as the invested assets of money market mutual funds. As money market funds are a form of investment with availability at D+1, with virtually no transaction costs, assets parked in these funds have indirectly acquired practically the same liquidity as resources deposited in checking accounts. At the peak of the financial crisis, however, these instruments lost their former level of credibility, risking being traded at a discount. If that was allowed to happen, with the loss of their liquidity, they would cease to be perceived as possessing quasi-monetary attributes and one may say that the trillions of US dollars invested in those assets in a matter of days at the end of 2008 would have ceased, for all practical purposes, to be considered by the economic agents as quasi-money as before. That is the rationale behind the movement of trillions of US dollars in a matter of hours away of money market mutual funds (MMMFs) in the direction of checking accounts, and it explains some of the desperate measures undertaken by the American monetary authorities at that time, such as the takeover of those entities by the American Treasury, making explicit what before was just an implicit warranty. An example of the relevance of the "monetization" of mortgage-backed securities by the GSEs is the statement of a typical American money market fund one year later. At the end of the 2009 fiscal year the MMF TIAA-CREF (ticker: TIRXX) had 39.6% of its assets in securities issued by them. Recent data released by the Fed and quoted in the December 1, 2010 *Wall Street Journal* article, "Absent Help, More Funds Might Have Broken Buck" by Ben Levisohn and Daisy Maxey, shows that nine out of the ten largest money market fund companies in the United States at the time of the crisis managed two-thirds of the total assets invested in MMFs at that moment, and used a first-aid program from the Fed called the "Asset-Backed Commercial Paper Money-Market Mutual Fund Liquidity Facility." Under that program, the funds sold securities to commercial banks in order to solve their liquidity problems and the banks used funds from the Fed to make such purchases. That is more evidence of the amount of "de-monetization" that happened in financial markets at the end of 2008 following the panic provoked by the collapse of Lehman Brothers.

7. As will be shown in this chapter, all the classical models for the demand of money compare the opportunity costs of the expected gains with interest-bearing

financial instruments, considered the net of the transaction costs to move money to and from financial instruments.

8. Incidentally, aware of the existence of many factors influencing the decisions about the cash balances that individuals may choose to keep, illustrated by the examples mentioned above, one would hardly be surprised that sometimes the demand for money may vary substantially in a short period of time. Even if most of the time the different factors may annul each other—say, increases in income and financial sophistication may run in opposite directions, turning the demand for money into a fairly stable function—sometimes they may act in unison resulting in fast variations.

9. *Fiat justitia ruat caelum* is a legal phrase in Latin that may be translated as "Do justice and let the sky fall." The maxim signifies the belief that justice must be realized regardless of consequences. It can have a positive or a negative connotation. In the case of judging the proper course of action for the monetary authorities to adopt in case of a higher demand for money due to an increase in uncertainty in the middle of an economic crisis, first it must be understood whether it is a case that admits only a principled response or a case that admits a prudential response. Perhaps in this case, as in any other case in which what is required is a moral choice, a definitive response may be an elusive goal. The best that can be hoped is for someone to state as clearly as possible the reasons for adopting one position or another. The reasons for advocating a prudential response to this case are outlined at the concluding section of this chapter.

10. Rothbard, in *Man, Economy, and State*, describes the "liquidationist" point of view against the prudential response suggested above: "It may well be true that the deflationary process will overshoot the free-market equilibrium point and raise price differentials and the interest rate above it. But if so, no harm will be done, since a credit contraction can create no malinvestments and therefore does not generate another boom-bust cycle" (Rothbard, 2009: 1006). As it is argued in this chapter, there are other harms to be considered aside from the generation of another cycle.

11. The discussion about forcing the MMMFs to float their NAV (net asset value) would be a decision, in essence to "de-monetize" those funds, that is, to make them lose their monetary properties. The MMMFs in America have shrunk their assets from 3.8 trillion USD at the end of 2008 to 2.9 trillion USD at the end of 2012 ("Money-Market Funds: Running from the Shadows," in *The Economist*, November 24, 2012, page 79), to 2.6 trillion USD ("SEC Approves New Rules for Money Funds," *Wall Street Journal*, July 24, 2014); still, without monetary properties it is doubtful that they would be able to carry so many assets and therefore a decision to de-monetize them would have fiscal considerations aside from considerations about the shrinking of the money stock. Perhaps it is for that reason that the SEC in its regulation of July 2014 determined that only "prime" funds catering to institutional investors, that is, money market funds investing in corporate bonds and municipal bonds but not in US Treasury bonds and catering only to professional investors, not retail investors, are subject to the new rules, for what comprises approximately 30% of the market ("Regulators Ready Money-Fund Rules," *Wall Street Journal*, July 10, 2014). A further comment is that the decline from 3.8 to 2.6 trillion USD in assets of US-based MMMFs since 2008 is already a consequence of a perceived loss of monetary properties by those funds.

12. Note in the case under discussion that if assets held in MMMFs are sold in order to repay investments in those funds that have their shares or units redeemed by the investors, that does not alter the immediate availability or maturity of credit. The structure of credit remains the same, although the loss of monetary properties of those classes of assets may force the banks to apply to rediscount with the central bank. In the absence of that option, if the discount window is closed, it may result in a forced liquidation of those assets. Those will be the alternatives every time that there is an explicit or implicit warranty of the financial institutions that the investors in MMMFs have a "debt" claim against the banks and not an equity position. This work is not the place to discuss the policies followed by the Fed during the 2008 financial crisis, but it must be kept in mind in evaluating the course of action followed that if the investors in MMMFs had had the perception that the principal of their investments would be at

risk, the "flight to liquidity" would have been much greater than it actually was (with catastrophic and unpredictable consequences for the entire financial system).

13. Considering that in virtually every inhabited corner of this planet there is a national government claiming jurisdiction over the territory, and that legal forced tender monetary regimes are equally universally adopted, any change in the monetary constitution anywhere will require a piece of legislation. Even if only to abolish the legal tender, or to define a new monetary standard, or to eliminate banking regulations, or to close the central bank, legislation will be required. May any change in the current monetary arrangements be construed as being constructivist? Yes, obviously, it may be understood as constructivist, but such a claim seems to be unwarranted. A constructivist solution for the current malaise does not result from proposing legislation but from proposing legislation with certain features such as proposing to "fine-tune" the system, introducing more banking controls, expanding the role of the central bank from lender of last resort to reinsurer of last resort, and et cetera.

14. It must be emphasized that the purpose of this chapter is not to present the classical theory of equilibrium, but only to comment on some of the features of the demand for money function for neoclassical economics.

15. George Selgin, in the introduction to Leland Yeager's *Fluttering Veil*, argues that it is not only in a mixed economy that a downward rigidity in prices is to be found. He argues that it is a consequence of a "*network externality*." He says, "each seller has an incentive to wait for others to go first in making desirable adjustments" (Yeager, 1997: xvi).

16. In the article "In Face of Changes in the Demand for Money, What is the Proper Response by the Central Bank?" in *Criterio Libre*, Volume 8, number 13, pages 69–94, edition Julio-Diciembre 2010.

17. In order to evaluate to what extent a financial crisis may or may not justify extraordinary measures, it seems relevant here to keep in mind Ayn Rand's definition of emergency:

> An emergency is an unchosen, unexpected event, limited in time, that creates condition under which human survival is impossible. . . . In an emergency situation, men's primary goal is to combat the disaster, escape the danger and restore normal conditions. . . . By "normal" conditions I mean metaphysically normal, normal in the nature of things, and appropriate to human existence. . . . By its nature, an emergency situation is temporary . . . the principle that one should help men in an emergency cannot be extended to regard all human suffering as an emergency and to turn the misfortune of some into a first mortgage on the lives of others." (Rand, 1963: 55)

18. Robert Higgs describes in chapter 8, "The Great Depression: 'An Emergency More Serious than War'," the ways in which an artificial crisis was created by president Franklin Delano Roosevelt soon after his inauguration on March 1933 (claiming dubious powers given by the Trading with the Enemy Act of 1917) by proclaiming a banking holiday (Higgs, 1987: 170). Abuses such as that and others carried on by Roosevelt under the "New Deal" such as the seizure of gold and the devaluation of the gold content of the US dollar were largely avoided during the 2008 financial crisis.

19. According to Den Uyl and Rasmussen, there are three views on principles: the empiricist, the constructivist, and the naturalist. For an empiricist like Hume, principles are abstractions apprehended from reality by empirical observation, less complex than reality itself, and therefore subject to qualifications. A constructivist is someone like Kant that understands reality as too chaotic to be understood, and so it is the mind that provides principles and laws necessary to make sense of reality. For a constructivist, there is nothing in practice that may justify abandoning a principle. And finally, for the naturalist, like Aristotle, principles are not distortions of reality, but generalizations of nature and, therefore, if the principles are rightfully apprehended, they are

useful to guide our action when appearances seem to deceive us. In this work a naturalistic understanding of principles is adopted.

20. The Federal Reserve program called the Overnight Reverse Repurchase Facility, commonly referred as ON RRP, allows the Fed to sell part of its portfolio signing an agreement to "repurchase" it the next day. By the end of the first quarter of 2014 a total of 242 billion USD have been regularly repurchased, mainly by MMMFs and other institutional investors according to the former chairman of the Federal Deposit Insurance Corporation ("The Federal Reserve's Risky Reverse Repurchase Scheme," in *Wall Street Journal*, July 5, 2014). This facility allows MMMFs to carry as part of their assets Treasuries and other securities of any maturity, since the "repos" by the Fed is what counts against their regulatory limitations; in practice, the Fed is, through this facility, helping the MMMFs to monetize the federal debt. That, in a sense, may have come as a "response" to the very squeeze of the shadow banking system by the Fed with Quantitative Easing (QE) related by Andy Kessler ("The Fed Squeezes the Shadow-Banking System," in *Wall Street Journal*, May 23, 2013). The purchases of Treasury bonds by the Fed has the unintended consequence of limiting the "rehypothecation" of securities in the "repo" market, estimated by Kessler to be about three times its "base" assets. So, when QE takes, say, 100 USD in highly liquid bonds from the market it, in effect, is diminishing the stock of quasi-money by three times the amount collected with the bond sale (one of the possible explanations why it has been so ineffective in producing increases in the price level), and these "reverse repos" may be the Fed's answer to that.

21. Obviously the monetary constitution of the United States is not the same today as it was at the time of the founding. During the Civil War redemption in gold was suspended. The period between the late 1870s until the end of World War I was the time when the United States had a gold standard with fractional reserve banking charted both by the federal and state governments. In 1913 with the establishment of the Fed, however, a major change, one may say a constitutional change, if not formally at least de facto, was introduced. At the end of World War I, under the new monetary regime, a first important change was introduced when the gold standard was replaced by a gold-exchange standard. A second relevant change to the monetary institutions of the United States post-1913 was the adoption of a fixed parity in 1944 with the Bretton Woods treaty. A third fundamental change was the denunciation of that treaty in 1971 and the adoption of a free-floating currency. Important as these changes were, they did not substantially change the current monetary constitution of the country introduced in 1913, which has been in place for almost a century. If nothing else, these three changes consubstantiate the trend towards fiat money completed in 1971.

22. Specifically about the desirability of deflation, Hayek was quoted in a recent article by Larry White (White, 2008: 27) as saying, "I would no longer maintain, as I did in the early 1930s . . . a short period of deflation may be desirable. Today I believe that deflation has no recognizable function whatever, and that there is no justification for supporting or permitting a process of deflation" (Hayek, 1975: 5).

23. See Barnett and Block, 2004: 48.

24. It is disputable if Bagehot in his book was making an apology for central banking or, on the contrary, if he was actually calling attention to the real underpinning of British financial markets (trust) and the inherent fragility of the fractional reserve system in place.

25. Mises says, "Deflation and credit contraction no less than inflation and credit expansion are elements disarranging the smooth course of economic activities" (Mises, 2007: 567).

NINE

Incentives to Supply an *Optimum* Amount of Credit Under a 100% Reserve Requirement

One of the main criticisms against the proposals for restructuring the monetary system under a 100% reserve requirement is that it would not allow for the most efficient allocation of financial resources; money would stay "hoarded" by the banks, hindering the supply of credit from reaching its potential. This chapter explores whether or not that claim may be true.

9.1 THE BACKGROUND FRAMED FOR ANALYSIS

9.1.1 Human Action

In *Human Action*, Mises states that the motivation behind any action taken by a human being is a desire by each individual to better his condition. The individual in question may be wrong about the means to achieve that end, the end itself may be odd as a consequence of the many imperfections that human beings are subject to, but one fact remains: to the limit of his or her intellectual capacity, the agent *thinks* that he will be better off taking that action than abstaining from taking it.

Suicide, the use of addicting drugs, donation of all one's worldly possessions to a new church recently established by someone who served time in jail for felony, and indulging in a diet of fried fatty foods are examples of conscious actions taken by some individuals based on the belief that they would gain more satisfaction (or suffer less despair) than if they had not followed those courses of action. For most people, in most of the circumstances that they may find themselves, those acts would not bring any satisfaction; but the individuals who engage in them do think they will.

Because preferences are subjective and conditioned by the circumstances of time and place in which each individual finds himself, the understanding that any action is motivated by a desire for the betterment of the agent is not a moral compass, it is not a tool to predict human behavior in any particular case, it is just a description of the psychological mechanism behind any human action.

Imprecise as it is to assert how any specific individual will act in a given circumstance, the knowledge about how the human *psyche* operates is the central tenet of *praxeology*, the science of human action.

If you have some knowledge about what, in a specific set of circumstances, most individuals regard as their good, you can fairly presume that having the opportunity to act, they will act in order to achieve, if not in its entirety, at least partially, those things that they regard as beneficial to them.

In this sense of a description of human psychology, this postulate that human action is always motivated by a desire for betterment is a universal one—it applies to all individuals in all times in all places—and the question is to what extent it can be assumed that, given the right set of incentives, the egoistic motivations of the bankers will result in an amount of bank lending that approaches the limits of real savings under a banking system of 100% reserve.

9.1.2 Ludwig von Mises' Classification

Before starting to discuss the possible responses of some economic agents to incentives under a 100% reserve banking system, it would be advisable to put into context the system that will be analyzed. A good way to start is by presenting Mises' classification of actual "gold standard" regimes as presented in his book *The Theory of Money and Credit*, chapter 22 (Mises, 1981: 471) in order to emphasize that none of them had a 100% reserve requirement. Mises' classification may be summarized as follows:

- The Inflexible Gold Standard:

  The mark of all the varieties of the gold standard and the gold-exchange standard as they existed on the eve of World War I was the gold parity of the country's monetary unit, precisely determined by a duly promulgated law. (Mises, 1981: 471)
- The Flexible Standard:

  The flexible standard, a development of the period between World War I and World War II, originated from the gold-exchange standard. Its characteristic features are: 1) the domestic standard's parity as against gold and foreign exchange is not fixed by a law but simply by the government agency entrusted with the conduct of monetary affairs; 2) this parity is subject to sudden changes without previous notice to the public; 3) The only method available for preventing a currency's exchange value from dropping below the parity chosen is unconditional redemption of any amount offered. (Mises, 1981: 472)

- The Freely Vacillating Currency:

  The characteristic mark of this freely vacillating currency is that the owner of any amount of it has no claim whatever, against the Treasury, a bank, or any other agency. There is no redemption either de jure or de facto. The pieces are not money substitutes but money *proper* in themselves. (Mises, 1981: 473)

  The outstanding instance of a freely vacillating currency today [at the time of the 1952 edition] is the United States Dollar, the New Deal Dollar. The administration is committed to an inflationary policy, increasing more and more the amount of notes in circulation and of bank deposits subject to check. (Mises, 1981: 474)
- The Illusive Standard:

  It is based on a falsehood. The government decrees that there exists parity between the domestic currency and gold or foreign exchange. . . . It knows that nothing is done to make the illusory parity an effective parity. It is known that there is no convertibility. But it clings to its pretence and forbids transactions at a ratio deviating from its fictitious exchange rate. . . . It expropriates all the foreign currency owned by its subjects and indemnifies the expropriated by paying them the amount of domestic currency which according to the official decree is the equivalent of the confiscated foreign-exchange holdings. These confiscations convey to the government the national monopoly of dealing with foreign exchange. In compliance with its own decree it should sell foreign exchange at the official rate. (Mises, 1981: 474)

When describing the Illusive Standard, Mises makes an analogy between this system and the process that the **Purchasing Power Parity** (PPP for short) theory of foreign exchange describes. He argues that the process described by PPP theorists is one in which the market is not handicapped by government interference and there prevails a tendency to establish and maintain an exchange ratio between the domestic and foreign currencies such that it does not matter if one sells or buys merchandise using either currency. According to Mises, this policy "pretentiously called foreign-exchange control tries to counteract the operation of the PPP principle" (Mises, 1981: 475), but it always fails.

9.1.3 A Gold Reserve System

Monetary institutional arrangements that could be defined as a reserve system have the issuance of banknotes redeemable in specie by the note-issuing banks as a central feature. As seen above, there are many variants of this monetary system. It is possible to think about arrangements in which there is or is not an issuing monopoly, in which there is or is not a legal definition of what the metals are in which the banknotes are redeemable.[1] Having adopted a bimetallist standard, a possible variation is whether or not the rate between gold and silver is fixed. The most important of all is whether or not the rules allow the banks to issue bills backed by fractional reserves, and all these variants are entirely compatible with the central feature of a reserve system.

As an illustration of how the actual "gold standard" systems moved away from a 100% reserve requirement, a last development in the evolution of trading instruments that deserves to be pointed out before mentioning that the origin of banknotes is the development of the **bill of exchange** in London. During the nineteenth century, some houses specialized in accepting bills of exchange on behalf of traders. A note accepted by one of these houses came to command worldwide credibility, credibility comparable to gold, therefore fulfilling the role of an international medium of exchange.

After the Great War, their use as an international currency was impaired by many factors (among which currency controls were not a minor one) that we do not intend to discuss here, but there is an almost poetic passage in George Winder's book about them that it is worth quoting: "Like all other sound forms of modern money, the Bill on London was the product of honor, integrity, and freedom" (Winder, 1959: 33). Another quotation from the same book (1959: 35) leads us to our next topic: "The origin of the modern bank note can be found in the receipt given by the goldsmith of the Middle Ages to those depositing with him gold or silver money for safe keeping."

At the end of the Middle Ages, aside from the circulation of bills of exchange issued by merchants as a consequence of their trade and receipts of deposits of coins and gold in bullion issued by banks of deposit, redeemable in person in Western Europe, a new instrument appeared: the receipt of deposit of money redeemable by any person at its presentation. As mentioned in the quotation above, it is in these receipts and not in the bills of exchange that we find the origin of the modern banknote. The availability of trusted persons with whom merchants could deposit their coins and bullion and get a transferable written instrument with which they could acquire goods and services in the market enhanced immensely the opportunities for trade. Important as the availability of respected coins was, having banknotes was a blessing; after all, carrying bags of coins through the streets and roads of the unsafe medieval times in Europe was a risky proposition, to say the least. The perceived advantages for traders carrying receipts of deposits of money to trade with, instead of carrying actual coins or bullion, was the motor behind the development of the first issuing banks at the dawn of the Renaissance in Italy. By the time of the Renaissance, with the development of paper production and the introduction of printing technology in Europe, the means for developing full-fledged reserve monetary systems, and later fiat money, became available.[2]

Originally, a fee was charged for having some money deposited. Soon, however, "the miracle of banking deposits and loans" (Weatherford, 1997: 76) under fractional reserve arrangements imposed itself as a consequence of the perverse incentives resulting from the privileges given to the bankers by the state. It may be accepted that the development of banking activities happened because of the obvious returns resulting from the fast reintroduction of the money in circulation, specifically in the hands of individuals able to put it to productive purposes, money that otherwise would have stayed hoarded. Hoarded money would remain outside banking institutions.

What remains to be seen is whether or not the incentive to put hoarded money into circulation would be severely constrained in the case of a 100% reserve requirement system.

It is known that the Bank of Amsterdam, established in 1609, operated "for all intents and purposes" (Huerta de Soto, 2006: 99) for more than 150 years under a 100% reserve system. Based on the experience of that bank, can it be concluded that the 100% reserve requirement is not an impediment to the full utilization of the existing savings in a given society?

The case for a 100% reserve requirement is a compelling one because the argument that fractional reserve banking generates bank lending in "excess" of the existing savings which results in the known sequence of booms and busts has been perceived as a truthful description of the facts under such a system.

On the other hand, aside from the vested interests of bankers and governments in having the power to create new lending capabilities out of thin air, there is the legitimate concern of serious economists that the 100% reserve requirement may be a hindrance to the full employment of the existing savings, resulting in a suboptimum rate of investments.

The intention with this chapter is to address the latter concern; but first let's try to address the question of the validity of the claim in favor of a 100% reserve requirement for both banknotes and bank deposits, and in order to do that, a description about the main characteristics of the monetary system that will be analyzed in this chapter is necessary.

9.1.4 The Imaginary Construct under Analysis

The discussions in this chapter about the proper incentives for bankers to lend money are circumscribed to what could possibly happen in a certain institutional framework that is an imaginary construct: that is, it is not an existing monetary system, but a hypothetical one, because there are no actual systems with the features to be analyzed.

This imaginary framework that will be discussed in this chapter is the one described by Huerta de Soto (2006: 736) and consists in a monetary and banking system (a) with no legal or forced tender, that is, not only does the government not issue money, but economic agents are also free to make their transactions in any currency they wish, (b) there is no central bank or any other lender of last resort, (c) in this system the government is mandated to operate without deficits in times of peace, (d) entitlements and taxation are limited to a relatively low proportion of GDP in order not to be an impediment to an acceptable rate of economic growth, and (e) international capital flows are also relatively free. Other key features of this system are (f) that the banking business is open to competition, (g) there is no mandated deposit insurance, (h) the banking deposits operate under the traditional rule that deposits on demand must be subject to a 100% reserve requirement, (i) with the 100% reserve requirement, any formal barrier for banking and insurance activities to be conducted by the same firms ceases to exist, and finally (j) after a transitional period in which all the private competing issuers of money would be required to have their issuances backed by gold, they will be free to back their issuances in any other assets.[3]

Which system would result from the application of these rules? A first observation is that we are not talking about any of the gold standard arrangements described by Mises, not even the inflexible standard prior to the Great War. Notable distinctions showing how far the gold standard, even in its most inflexible actual form, had already moved away from free banking principles are absent in Mises' inflexible standard of a 100% reserve requirement, the existence in Britain of a central bank, and at the eve of the war, monometallism. But, it is not the purpose here to develop a full account of a free banking system, which has already been done by Huerta de Soto as referred to above, so the description that follows is a very schematic one. Basically, it is possible to assume that the banks will operate five distinct core activities: the issuance of banknotes, deposits on demand, time deposits, brokerage, and fiduciary activities. Lending activities will necessarily be funded directly by their time deposits and indirectly by their fiduciary activities through the placement of commercial papers and bonds in the capital markets. Brokerage activities in equity, commodities, and fixed income markets are also expected to be core activities for financial companies. On the other hand, insurance services do not seem prima facie to be a core banking activity; however, it is to be expected that in an unregulated market some integration between insurance and other financial services tends to occur.[4]

A key feature of this system is that there is no legally defined monetary standard and therefore, theoretically, many different specie currencies may coexist. Following Huerta de Soto's assumption that given the regressive theorem of money (2006: 739), a transitory period in which gold will be the single monetary standard, that could very well be gold in the metric system (one gram, ten grams, one kilo, et cetera); and also, following again Huerta de Soto and Kirzner (Huerta de Soto, 2006: 736 and 743), it is impossible to theorize a priori about the future evolution or to know for certain what the future institutions will be, so the analysis developed in this chapter will assume that banknotes are 100% backed by gold, being no more than warehouse "warrants" for gold.

9.2 THE ASSUMPTIONS

9.2.1 *On Money Creation by the Banks*

Before discussing the behavior of bankers under a system with a 100% reserve requirement, such as the *onde* described by Huerta de Soto, let's discuss "money creation" by the banks under fractional reserves. When a commercial bank accepts the deposit of funds subject to withdrawal on demand and subsequently gives credit by opening credit accounts, it does not "create" money proper, it expands credit. The credit will be used by the debtor to acquire something, by issuing a check or authorizing an electronic transfer, for example, and the seller will be entitled to withdraw the money from the account; as long as the demand on the bank remains outstanding, someone is giving credit to someone, not creating money proper. It becomes clear if we think about what happens as soon as the bank pays the check, as is shown in the example below.

At the beginning (first moment), the bank has an asset that is the money, and a debt that is the obligation to retrieve the deposit:

Secondly, there is a credit operation that increases its assets and liabilities as long as it remains outstanding:

Thirdly, after the check is withdrawn, the bank becomes short of cash to match the demands of its clients who had funds deposited on demand at the bank:

Table 9.1. Bank Balance Sheet, Three Steps Mutations: 1st

	Assets	Liabilities	
Cash	10	10	**Deposit on demand**
Total	10	10	**Total**

Table 9.1. Bank Balance Sheet, Three Steps Mutations: 2nd

	Assets	Liabilities	
Cash	10	10	**Deposit on demand**
Credit contract	5	5	**Credit account**
Total	15	15	**Total**

The case of a society without money may be illustrative; all the transactions were cleared by the exchange of real goods. In any monetary society (and not only in the imaginary construct under analysis), the result, in essence, is the same: to acquire some good by paying for it with money, either the buyer surrenders a right to acquire other available goods instantaneously to the seller, or this seller or someone else is giving credit to the buyer. The seller is giving to the buyer his actual goods in exchange for a "promise to pay" in the future with the production of some other actual good or service.

Going back to the assumption that banks "create" money, just because someone has credit against the bank of a given amount of money previously deposited with a bank and someone else who got a loan from the same bank is on a spending spree, it does not mean that both have the money at the same time (as explained above), although there may be competing claims if there is a time mismatch between the maturity terms of the bank's assets and liabilities. In any event, the bank was only the intermediary instrument, the middleman (regardless of its own responsibility to repay the lender/depositor) by which the owner of the bank deposit loaned the money to the borrower. As soon as the owner of the deposit decides to withdraw it, he ceases to be a creditor of the bank and gets his money back, while the bank will find another source to fund the outstanding loans it has. Therefore, no money is created or multiplied by banks, since the money is not utilized *at the same time* by more than one economic agent. What happens under a fractional reserve system is not creation of money, but credit expansion of two concurrent claims against the same amount of money.

Moving our analysis for a minute to the "real" side of the economy, we may note that financial instruments representative of debts in the economy with their multiplicity of maturities and levels of liquidity are representative of available goods "saved" for future or uncertain uses in the economy; such representation is never perfect, automatic, or directly correlated, if you wish, it is just an approximation and the uncertainty of that relation is what allows "wiggle room" for monetary authorities to play with the demand for money in the benefit of the fisc. However, there is a quote from Simpson (2014b: 136) which makes clear the limits of doing that: "Changing the mix of assets one holds as one's savings does not increase savings in real terms because it does not increase the supply

Table 9.1. Bank Balance Sheet, Three Steps Mutations: 3rd

	Assets	Liabilities	
Cash	5	10	**Deposit on demand**
Credit contract	5	0	**Credit account**
Total	10	10	**Total**

of physical assets in the economy that are productively employed or the amount of physical assets that last many time periods and that can be used in future periods (such as homes)." There is a limit of how much bonds of long maturity can be held as short-time investments with sufficient liquidity to acquire monetary properties; and such changes in the composition of one's portfolio, as stated by Simpson, if they are not a reflex of a real change in the composition of saved goods in the economy, or to say it differently, if the change in the composition of the stock of financial assets is not endogenous, it will eventually go out of synch with what is going on in the real economy, resulting in simultaneous claims on existing goods that would be impossible to satisfy at the same time, generating a crisis that will need to be solved by some legal or political expedient.

A banking system of fractional reserve may be understood as one in which there is no 100% reserve requirement for specie currency, or if it is a system of fiat money, one in which any fraction of the demand deposits is not compulsorily transferred to the central bank. Under such a system, since bank deposits are by definition part of the money supply (M1) and a fractional reserve system multiplies temporarily, as explained above, any initial deposit, once a fractional reserve bank system is established, at any given time for statistical purposes, the money supply (M1) will be larger than the monetary base (M0). So, it must be understood that the so-called creation of money by the banks is in fact an expansion of credit above the existing savings and the fact remains that all those claims that the depositors have against the banks cannot be retrieved simultaneously without bringing the nominal amount of the money supply (M1) to the actual size of the monetary base (M0).[5]

Consider the following: under a fractional reserve banking system, the bank operations will make M1 larger than M0, and that will maximize the monetary use of M0, to the extent that the tendency is to have any part of M0 deposited with a bank, instead of hoarded in the bank vaults, being loaned to someone else. But that tendency will be limited to the actual size of M0, that is, nominally, M1 may increase substantially with the "multiplication" of money proper produced by the bank loans funded with the deposits on demand, but that increase will only last as long as the money is *not* used and remains deposited. As soon as the money is actually used, it will produce a ratio between M1 and M0 that reflects the average amount of M0 constantly left deposited with the banks that they put aside, not lend out.

In monetary terms, it is the existence of the concurrent claims described above that creates the forced liquidation of assets and the "liquidity crisis" during the halving and final step of a business cycle, also referred to as "credit contraction" (Huerta de Soto, 2006: 254).

But until now we have been talking about the monetary limits that the banks have to lend and the bad consequences that result when they exceed these limits by the practice of fractional reserve banking; let's deal next with what the constraints for credit in the real side of the economy are.

9.2.2 Schumpeter and the Creation of Credit by the Banks

The creation of credit by banks is an idea well described by Schumpeter (1997: page 1114); for him, an acknowledgement of the fact that banks create money by giving loans is counterintuitive and, for many, morally tainted; that is why it took so long to be accepted. Although he explains the possibility of banks creating credit that may be used to promote further production or consumption than what would exist without them by referring to Wicksell's distinction "between money and real rates of interest" (page 1118), perhaps one more step back could be helpful to understand the phenomenon. One useful way to understand the economy is to think about it without money; it is to think about all the economic agents producing their goods and services, exchanging them for other goods and services, saving real goods for future consumption, investing real goods in order to increase future production, keeping inventories of goods for sale, all of that as if money were not necessary to liquidate all the present and deferred payments resulting from all the exchanges. In that fictional economy, the "real" rate of interest would be a result of the temporal preference of the agents for real goods (how much more they are willing to pay to have the goods now instead of later when they are borrowing, and how much they would like to charge someone to receive back some good later instead of now, when they are lending), to the extent that a single time preference could be aggregated, but that is a different issue. Of course, even in that hypothetical moneyless economy there would be many different rates of interest depending on creditworthiness, the nature of the goods borrowed, et cetera. Still, all those rates would be premiums to be paid by the use of real goods, and for analytical purposes, if we could aggregate them, that would be the "real" rate of interest. Think now about the same economy with monetary instruments. Payments now are done by the transference of those instruments; and savings, investments, and inventories are now all represented by financial instruments. That is why, sometimes, economists refer to the economy as having a real and a monetary side, the monetary side being a "representation" of the real side, with monetary and financial transactions "mimicking" what happens in the real economy. However, money performs this very useful and necessary function of clearing the many exchanges in the economy. As already mentioned many times, the division of labor we now enjoy would not be possible if instruments representative of real wealth were not widely accepted by the other agents with whom one interacts in his daily economic activities. Because of that, in principle, we can think about the rate of interest on money as just one more "real" interest rate, that is, the aggregate time preference for a liquid instrument that gives to its holder power to buy the most ample range of goods available in the real economy. Yet, in order to understand the difference between the interest rates on money and the time preference in that particular society one needs to add one more component to the equation: that is the quantity of "money." In our now monetized economy the nominal price level is given by the relation between all the available goods in the economy (everything money can buy) and the stock of all forms of money. If we think that only gold coins are accepted as money—not even banknotes representative of gold coins stored in the bank—and we know that there are in circulation only one million gold coins, each one with a nominal value of, say, 10 dollars, then, the price of everything measured in gold coins would result in a relation between the quantity of that good and the existing demand for that good measured in the only money that exists, a fixed amount of 10 million gold dollars. Well, let's think next that the gold coins may be deposited in banks and the banks may issue notes representative of those coins deposited; that, by itself would not represent an increase in the money supply, and therefore, has no impact on the price level. But if we add the component that the banks may be allowed to issue more banknotes than the ones they have in their safes, or if we allow the bank to open lines of credit to people giving them credit cards, or crediting their deposit accounts and allowing them to make payments by issuing checks against those deposit accounts or using their debit cards against those borrowed funds deposited in their accounts, then we have an increase in the "money" supply, by credit expansion. Back to Wicksell's explanation, now that the size of the money supply may change independently of the changes in the amount of available goods, it does make sense to talk about an interest rate on money different from the "natural" interest rate on real goods as revealed by the aggregation of the temporal preferences of all economic agents. But what are the impacts of that and how does that "prove" that inflationary creation of credit by the banks (that is, credit created not by intermediation of savings deposited with them, but by conceding credit lines "out of thin air") may in fact lead to increases in real production and consumption? Again, we should think that once money is introduced in the economy, economic agents get used to making their transactions using money and there is nothing in an "inflationary" banknote or credit line that would distinguish them from the previously existing ones; therefore, there is no reason for economic agents not to sell their goods and services in exchange of those forms of money. Continuing in this line of reasoning, if we further realize that except for the circumstance in which all the productive capacity that that given society is able to mobilize is already employed, in which case, any addition to the money supply would be transmitted directly to the prices, raising the price level without affecting production, it is reasonable to expect that some elasticity of prices would exist, along with some idleness of real resources; therefore, it is also reasonable to expect that inflationary credit creation by the banks would result in a stimulating effect on employment, regardless of any detrimental effect it may also have of dislocating factors of production to the sectors of the economy with better access to bank credit, beginning with the bankers themselves. There are many particular circumstances that may allow banks to create more or less credit, such as the level of concentration of the banking system, the level of "reserves" (real deposits) they may keep in order to pay for withdraws, the existence of a lender of last resort that may help them in case they become illiquid, et cetera, but the theoretical case for some positive effect on employment due to the multiplication of credit by the banks cannot be denied. However, in this, as in much else, the devil is in the details, and the qualifications done in the previous sentence and many others allow us to see with great skepticism the possibility of positive results for the leveraging of banks due to inflationary credit creation. There are many ways in which financial institutions may engage in fractional reserve banking, that is, in keeping only a fraction of the resources deposited with them in their vaults to pay for withdrawals on demand. Let's just say that in an institutional setting in which there are no barriers of entry to financial services and in which the government does not monopolize the supply of high-powered money (no legal tender laws), does not offer guaranties as lender of last resort to the financial system, and does not mandate the financial system to hold public debt, the capacity of the banks to create credit is extremely limited. It may well indeed marginally help to increase the full employment of resources, to the extent that some real financial instruments may remain idle in the banks because their owners prefer to have access to liquidity on demand, at the expense of remuneration for their employment, even in the short run. The banks, on the other hand, are well positioned to benefit from this increased (although marginal) efficiency in the use of actual resources and therefore, under those circumstances, and with those qualifications which, incidentally, almost never happen in the real world, the inflationary creation of credit may have positive effects and what the banks accrue for that creation may be considered a fair remuneration for allowing that added economic efficiency to be created in the real side of the economy. What we see, most of the time, however, is that the banks are forced to use the inflationary creation of credit to fund public expenses, expenses which generally are not the most productive employment of those resources one may find, or not productive at all. In those circumstances, the inflationary creation of credit, even if it does not result in a direct raise in the price level, creates dislocation of resources in the economy, favoring some uses at the expense of others.

9.2.3 Limits to the Capacity of Giving Credit

In any society, the capacity to concede "credit" is limited, constrained by some actual factors and, in the long run, not influenced by the nominal quantity of money in circulation. Thinking again about a hypothetical moneyless society may help explain this topic: the capacity of a society to allow some individuals to consume goods "on credit" is limited by its capacity to make those goods available. It can be done in a number of different ways. First, it can be done by restricting consumption by some of its members; second, it can be done by increasing production, to the extent that the inputs are available or can also be bought by credit; and finally, it can be achieved by borrowing those goods from other societies. Putting money back in the picture, we can see that giving "credit," that is, lending money to some individuals, may allow them to dispose of the available goods, but it cannot make more goods available in the long run. But why have this qualification about the "long run?" Since in open, capitalist, monetary societies, the price system serves the function of signaling the demand for some goods but the price system cannot differentiate existing money from "new" money, for some time, until economic agents start to perceive the inflation of the medium of exchange and start acting accordingly, an increase of the supply of the medium of exchange will produce a dislocation of goods into the hands of the individuals who got the new money first from the hands of the issuer and this dislocation may well result in increased production either domestically or abroad. But again, as soon as the economic agents take notice of what is going on, they will take the increased supply of fiat money into consideration and start acting accordingly, that is, they will assume a certain constant rate of devaluation of the real, constant value expected for the currency. As soon as the inflationary expectations are taken into account, the supply of goods will not increase because of increases in the money supply at the expected rate.

Can the statement about the short-term effects of monetary expansion of the previous paragraph be construed as an endorsement of "Keynesianism?"[6] It is hoped not! It should not be considered an endorsement first because it is not conceded that one could predict the exact behavior of economic agents along curves of aggregate demand;[7] and second, it is worth mentioning that other factors such as labor laws, exchange rate regimes, the political environment, and the existing structure of production may lead to very different results for different societies at different times. Furthermore, there is no way to assess what "short term" is, what the "proper" amount of money is to increase in order to have this or that increase in production as a result, and much more relevant than this, it is impossible to know the unintended consequences of messing with the money supply, examples throughout history attest.[8] If the money holders in a particular society have all the money that they want to hold, the introduction of more of the "monetary merchandise" to the money stock will only depreciate the value of such merchandise. It is impossible to generate, enhance, or facilitate the production of more goods by adding money to the existing stock unless there is a demand for it.[9] Once the demand for liquidity is satisfied; the excess of money added to the stock of money will only produce "devaluation" of the real value of the currency in the face of prices of the available goods, that is, what is generally called "inflation." At the time that the generally accepted medium of exchange used to be redeemable for a real merchandise, like a piece of specie, the introduction of money in circulation in excess of the demand for money would (a) domestically result in the concentration of bullion in the more conservative banks as consequence of the operation of the "reflux mechanism",[10] and (b) internationally it would lead to the exportation of bullion, self-correcting the liquidity level to that desired by the money holders without increasing the amount of credit available in the long run.

Incidentally, it was already noted that in nineteenth-century England the operation of this external drain of specie would only work in order to keep the monetary system "neutral", that is, neither promoting nor reducing the business cycle under a hypothetical purely metallic currency as described by Hume in his essay "Of the Balance of Trade" (Hume, 1987: 308). Under the gold reserve system with a central bank of that time, its effects were not immediately perceived, taking some time to happen, as mentioned by White (1995: 115). Now, in our times of fiat money, increases in the money supply tend to lead straight, although not immediately and not in any direct correlation, to "debasement" of money value as a medium of exchange.

Contrariwise, limiting the supply of money only to the financing necessities of trade as intended by the followers of the "Real Bills Doctrine" is to neglect that money performs a much broader role in society than fostering the commercial operations in the narrow sense meant by its proponents.[11]

9.2.4 Fractional Reserve Banking and Moral Hazards

From the digression of the previous paragraphs, it is possible to conclude that the monetary flows of money to and from a banking system of fractional reserve do not increase the capacity of the economic agents in a given society to concede more credit than the actual availability of goods not necessary for consumption would allow; that is, "money creation" by credit expansion, driven exclusively by price signals would be endogenous. However, attempts to artificially expand credit would end reflecting in the monetary side of the economy the creation of concurrent claims over the available goods, producing changes in the general prices and changes in the relative prices of the different goods and services. But if that is the case, where do the incentives for bankers to (over) expand credit under fractional reserve arrangements come from? They come from the commitment of the lender of last resort to rescue the banks anytime the bankers misjudge how much of the deposits on demand they must keep available, therefore, creating a moral hazard that only encourages more reckless behavior, exacerbating an economic crisis (Huerta de Soto, 2006: 636).

It may be concluded that the institution of fractional reserve banking is, in essence, a privilege granted to bankers that allows them to have access to present goods and services that are saved by some economic agents in society for future and not immediate consumption. That leads eventually to the cycles of boom and bust in the economy with all the deleterious consequences associated with them, but these institutions represent in fact a source of wealth for the individuals involved and as long as holding only fractional reserves coupled with guarantees of financial backing by the authorities continues to be allowed to banks, there is no reason to suppose that this reality will change.

Clearly, there are incentives that can easily be perceived rationally by bankers that induce them to try to expand credit to the limits allowed by the regulations or even to try to go beyond those limits.[12] That does not increase the amount of investment in society to more than its actual savings, but in the process it makes available to the banks resources that otherwise would not be accessible to them, making them invested in the maintenance of the status quo.

9.3 THE ANALYSIS

9.3.1 The Link between Deposits on Demand and Actual Savings

The operation of a fractional reserve system is well understood. The banks help to mobilize some portion of the available savings in productive investments through their activities as financial intermediaries but not through their activities accepting deposits on demand. The deposits on demand represent a certain portion of the actual savings that the economic agents would like to keep readily available for all of the conceivable reasons that one may have to keep liquidity.[13]

9.3.2 *Hypothesis about the Behavior of the Depositors on Demand*

The first step in our analysis shows us that the holders of deposits on demand must be sensible to changes in the interest rate and to the different maturities in which cash balances could be invested, and that is the basis on which further reasoning about the behavior of the bankers will be developed in this chapter. The next step is the recognition that from the total amount of savings existing in society at any given time, the proportion that the saver would like to keep available on demand is but a fraction of the total. So, being sensitive to the availability of higher interest rates and to relatively short-term investments, it is possible to speculate that noninterest bearing deposits on demand (most likely subject to maintenance fees) would be kept to the minimum required by the economic agents to execute their normal transactions.

9.3.3 *Hypothesis about the Behavior of Bankers*

One should recognize that bankers have similar gain potentials in their different core activities that financial institutions may have in a 100% reserve requirement free-banking system. If the "rules of the game" do not grant the banks authorization to lend deposits held on demand, bankers will have a strong interest in keeping deposits on demand as low as possible.[14] Having identified different time horizons for different depositors, the "efficiency" in the allocation of savings claimed to exist under fractional reserve banking is expected to operate, but in a different fashion: bankers will compete to "match" the different time preferences for liquidity of their depositors with investments of different maturities.[15]

Based on current banking operations, it is reasonable to expect that a fiduciary activity that may gain importance over time in the banking system under analysis is the management of "mutual funds."

Mutual funds are a kind of fiduciary property—that is, a multiplicity of investors are the "beneficiaries" of a pool of securities held in co-ownership in the "mutual fund." Mutual funds may invest in equities or in fixed income, in assets of different levels of liquidity, and the "shares" in the mutual funds themselves may be traded in capital markets according to the "open-ended" or "close-ended" character of a mutual fund in particular. So, in the same fashion that today investors are able to invest in "money market funds" that invest in fixed income assets of extreme liquidity, up to the point of being part of the more liquid monetary aggregates such as M2 (like treasury bonds and AAA-rated corporate bonds), and having liquidity at D+1 (the next day), it is to be expected that similar instruments will be offered to prospective depositors and investors to keep their cash balances and investments with different maturities, even ones of very short maturity.

9.4 COMPARING FRACTIONAL RESERVE BANKING AND 100% RESERVE BANKING FROM THE PERSPECTIVE OF BANKERS' INCENTIVES

In this chapter, a fractional reserve banking system has been compared with a hypothetical 100% reserve free-banking system in order to analyze whether the argument that the former offers an efficient allocation of existing savings and the latter does not holds water.

The conclusion of this inquiry is that the same profit motivation experienced by the bankers under fractional reserve requirements, to keep them vested in the status quo and lending to the greatest limit possible the resources trusted to them on demand, operates under a 100% reserve requirement. Their profit motivation makes them interested in maximizing the returns of their depositors by keeping deposits on demand to a minimum, diverting funds to more appealing investments such as mutual funds and other short-term interest-bearing investments.

Neither under a fractional reserve or a 100% reserve baking system can investments sustainably be carried out above the level of existing savings minus the cash balances. If we accept that one finds in the 100% reserve free-banking system profit motivations that will lead bankers to supply prospective depositors and savers with financial products in order to maximize their returns, keeping deposits on demand at a minimum, then a case for equivalent efficiency among the two systems can be made and the claim in favor of the fractional reserve system as more efficient can be dismissed.[16]

9.5 NARROW BANKING: THE ARGUMENT OF ALLOCATIVE EFFICIENCY OF FRACTIONAL RESERVE BANKING (FRB)

The most common argument in favor of fractional reserve banking (FRB) is that such a scheme to multiply the monetary base is necessary in order to increase the efficient use of available resources on the real side of the economy. In order to evaluate such a claim, it is important first to understand that whatever the impact that FRB has on the efficient allocation of resources, we are talking about efficiency "under the curve" (of production possibility) and not about expanding it as shown in figure 9.1.That is, the capacity to invest in the economy is limited to the availability of real resources suitable to being invested in productive endeavors; we may discuss whether FRB helps the society to achieve the most efficient allocation possible of the available resources by eliminating any idleness, but one thing is certain, FRB does not expand the frontier of production beyond the availability of real resources.

To accept that FRB by creating inflationary credit may distort the scale of relative prices and would increase the availability of capital goods is to

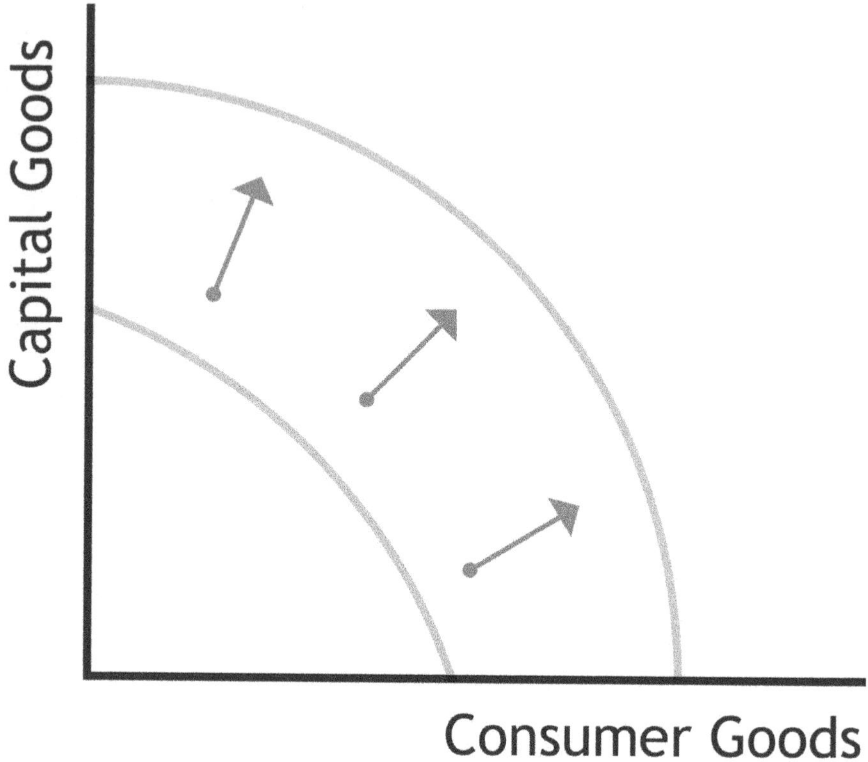

Figure 9.1. Moving Beyond the Possibility Curve

consider, first, that the very production of capital goods has some price elasticity, that is, that any increase in the demand for them would imply an increase in production and not solely an increase in their prices; and second, that the allocation of credit does not follow the "natural" rate of the propensity for investment and consumption (otherwise the result would be neutral between consumption and investment, and there would not be a movement to a different point along the curve). Those assumptions lead to other speculations about how much changes in short-time relative prices due to inflationary credit creation are sustainable in the long run and whether the consequences of allocation of credit by political fiat against the "natural" propensity for investments may produce anything other than a boom in malinvestments that eventually will go bust. Aside from heroic assumptions well discussed and rebuked in the literature about the "Austrian Business Cycle Theory" (ABCT), there is not much else to be said against such a possibility; so let's stick with the argument that FRB increases the efficiency "under the curve" of possibilities, but neither results in changes "along" the curve nor does it "move" the curve to the right.

Constrained by those reasonable assumptions, FRB should then be compared with other possible ways to maximize the use of saved real resources instead of leaving them idle. Considering that FRB does leave banks exposed to runs as we have seen, if we could find a way to achieve at least the same results without exposing the economy to sharp declines in credit and liquidity in case of a crisis of confidence in the banking system, that would be a strong reason to pursue it and abandon FRB. Just before we analyze that, there is one more thing to consider, that is, the impact of deposit guarantees. Under FRB, it has been argued that sharp reductions in credit may be avoided by introducing deposit insurance; and, generally speaking, it is true that once bank deposits are guaranteed by a third reliable party, runs on the banks are no longer in the interest of depositors. But on the other hand, neither is a prudent selection of the bank in which one will deposit his money nor prudent management of liquid reserves by the bankers. So, the guarantees of liquidity offered or mandated by the government through last resort lending facilities or deposit insurance mechanisms are sources of a different problem, the problem of moral hazard, which induces imprudent behavior on the part of depositors and bankers. If we accept that such problems possibly are, or may be even more compromising of economic growth as a suboptimum use of saved resources, then we can make the case that they are not an adequate solution for the problem at hand.

Let's suppose then that we have shifted from FRB to a system of narrow banking (NB), one in which all liquid instruments redeemable on demand are base money (bank deposits have 100% reserve in high-powered money, money produced by the state, either banknotes or bank reserves with the central bank) and all credit is given by the financial intermediaries on behalf of mutual funds with 100% of equity (or possibly time-matched liabilities). There are many different forms to make a transition to a system with those characteristics, some of them already mentioned in this work such as the 1930s' Chicago Plan of Irving Fisher and Henry Simon, Friedman's version of the Chicago Plan, Huerta de Soto's proposal of 100% reserve banking, et cetera. But what all of these have in common is that the profit motivations for banks (financial intermediaries) to raise capital in capital markets to make loans would continue to exist; true, there would be no more inflationary credit expansion, just noninflationary credit expansion, but the profit motive would still be there. Other thing to consider is that the monetary base, under most known proposals of NB, would continue to be money supplied by the government at its discretion. So, no lack of money in the economy is to be expected, including money to be invested in the mutual funds that will lend money for prospective borrowers. A final note about these proposed arrangements is that they leave some problems unanswered, such as the convenience of leaving the production of money as a monopoly in the hands of government and limits to government's indebtedness; those will be addressed soon.

NOTES

1. The introduction of a "gold standard" by legal definition can be traced to Lord Liverpool's Coinage Act of 1816, which declared that in the future gold coins would be the sole measure of value and would be legal tender for any amount (Winder, 1959: 24). Until then, money in Britain (and all around the world) consisted of myriad forms of payment to be settled in many different ways; by the middle of the nineteenth century that had changed, with people getting used to thinking about "their bills and coins as means of exchange in an homogeneous system held together by a universal principle: the gold standard" (Dick, 2013: 2). It is not that people did not use "ideal" conceptions of monetary value before that in order to assess the media of exchange at hand—it is hard to imagine how they could not have done so; but the economic hegemony of Great Britain was now lending its support to the concept of a universal and homogeneous money.

2. References to contemporary experiments with paper money in China were reported by Marco Polo and Ibn-Battuta, respectively in the thirteenth and fourteenth centuries, but three important features distinguishing both experiments must be pointed out: first, the technology to make paper was reported to be known in China at least since the second century CE, but it remained confined to that country for at least one millennium; second, once paper money was introduced in Europe, first as fiduciary money under a reserve system such the ones discussed in this section, and later as fiat money, it was never abandoned, something that happened in China as soon as the fourteenth century; and finally, the introduction of paper money in Europe was voluntary, spontaneous, not centralized, and it had the purpose of facilitating trade, while in China it was introduced during the Mongol Empire in order to impose a monopoly on gold and silver and to enhance taxation (Weatherford, 1997: 126).

3. Simpson (2014b), on page 256 (correctly) describes Huerta de Soto's proposal of monetary reform as one in which the banks are transformed in mutual-fund managers, effectively "narrowing" the scope of banking activity. I agree with the description of Huerta de Soto's plan; I lament the lack of mention of the fact that his proposal is of the "narrow banking" variety.

4. That is not to say, however, that banking services and insurance services have the same nature, as Huerta de Soto writes: "the contract of life insurance bears no relation to the monetary irregular-deposit contract" (2006: 161). Insurance policies are aleatory contracts, in which present defined goods are given in exchange for uncertain goods in the future; they are made possible by actuarial calculation and not by the creation of competing claims to present goods.

5. According to the GAMOE definition of money, anything that comes to be generally accepted as money is money; so if sometimes credit is accepted as money and banks give credit, then banks would, in a broad sense, be creating money; however, for the analysis conducted in this chapter, banking lending activities will continue to be referred to as credit expansion.

6. See an introduction to Keynes' monetary theory in 2.3.6 Keynesian and Post-Keynesian Theory.

7. The limitations of using the "Keynesian cross diagram" as an instrument to predict the behavior of economic agents is discussed in footnote 17 of chapter 2.

8. Just to mention one case, one may refer to the decline of about one-third of the money supply in the United States from 1929 to 1933, as reported by Milton Friedman and Anna Schwartz (Friedman and Schwartz, 1993: 302). Had the Fed kept the supply

of money stable after the 1929 crack in the stock market, the recession that followed would have been much less tragic.

9. Every society has at any given moment a structure of production composed by the sum of buildings, equipments, inventories, and individuals engaged in productive activities. They operate in a given cycle of production, shorter for industrialized goods of consumption, longer for agricultural goods, perhaps even longer for capital goods. Every structure of production requires a certain liquidity expressed by a quantity of medium of exchange available in order to operate the economic transactions. This quantity of medium of exchange can be available because the economic agents themselves have enough capital to do their transactions or it can be made available through credit. But the fact is that, at any given moment, the economic agents require neither more nor less money than that which is necessary to do their transactions. This can be considered the "optimum" amount of money, and this optimum varies all the time with the variation in circumstances. A necessity of increasing inventories or expanding productive capacity through the introduction of new technology or fixed assets may demand increases in the optimum amount of money; alternatively, better management techniques and lean production processes may liberate resources and imply a reduction of the money demanded by that society at that moment. This understanding is a generalization of the "Needs of Trade Doctrine" advocated by the members of the "Banking School" in the debates on monetary policy in the middle of the nineteenth century in Britain. Although their arguments were in favor of allowing the local banks to have some elasticity on the issuance of banknotes in different regions of Great Britain at different times during the year in order to accommodate the "needs of trade" (White, 1995: 123), their arguments may be accepted as a general principle about money given the "stiffness" of price and contracts, since in those circumstances the adjustment cannot be made as easily by price changes.

10. The reflux mechanism operates under a gold reserve system in which banknotes are cleared among different and competing issuing banks, as it was in Scotland during the second half of the nineteenth century. A more aggressive bank would have systematically negative balances at the daily clearing and would be forced to give reserves to the more conservative ones, inducing the aggressive bank to scale back and start to operate at the same level of exposure as the other banks. However, this mechanism is not a guarantee against a general expansion of the bank's leverage as pointed out by J. R. McCulloch and quoted by Lawrence White (1995: 103).

11. For the members of the Banking School, under the "Real Bills Doctrine"—RBD, for short—banks should be allowed to issue banknotes in any quantity demanded by merchants presenting bills of exchange against other merchants. The main fallacies of this doctrine in regard to its sufficiency to control the supply of credit money and therefore the price level, such as the "nominalist" fallacy and the "inelastic-supply-of-bills" fallacy, were well exposed by White (1995: 122). The key issue in regard to the "Real Bills Doctrine" seems to me to be that it may be understood as an effective guide to prudent commercial bank management, but nothing more than that may be expected from it. It is not a guide for central bank policy, if there is a central bank in the system under consideration, and it is not sufficient to guarantee the stability of the supply of money and the price level. The doctrine was elaborated *before* the 1844 Peel's Act, at a time that the gold standard in operation in England was one *without* an institutionalized and monopolistic central bank. The control of the supply of money was not a result of the operation of the RBD, but of the operations of a gold standard without a central bank in which the external component of the economy was by and large kept automatically under control by the *Humean* mechanism. If you have a gold standard in operation with no central bank to discount bills as a lender of last resort that you could rely on, it seems reasonable to manage prudently a private bank giving credit only on short term and against self-liquidating good collateral and not engaging with short-term funding in long-term or risky financing such as industrial or agricultural lending. But the application of such a doctrine as a policy guide to the central bank even under a gold standard or, worse, under a fiat money institutional arrange-

ment, is a compound mistake. It is to assume that a mechanism is built into the doctrine to control the supply of money, which it is not, and it is to assume that the doctrine was meant to guide public policy, which is also not true. To try to apply the doctrine outside the context in which it was developed, for a purpose different from its original purpose is a compound mistake. I would like to thank Rolf Luders for clarifying this point to me. Posting in his blog, Koning presents a 2x2 matrix to help classify the many versions of the Real Bills Doctrine among those which are or are not what they say they are and are or are not true to themselves. Koning (2013) ends listing some of the variants of the RBD, such as Lloyd Mint's version to whom he attributes the coining of the phrase "real bills doctrine" in 1945, Adam Smith's version, the version of the Bank (of England) directors, and others. The relevant point here is to understand that there is more than one version about what the doctrine is.

12. A substantial part of the innovations in finance are driven by the profits that increased leverage may generate; furthermore, that leverage is conveniently hidden behind formal adherence to the regulatory limits on leverage. The attempt by regulators to limit leverage and by financial institutions to bypass those limits is, under the current regulatory regime in most Western countries, a neverending "cat and mouse" story.

13. In the discussion that follows, no consideration is given to the impact of international flows of goods— neither to the real flows nor to the financial flows—because it is not necessary to develop a more complex model in order to present the argument intended. That is not to say that time mismatches between the availability of real goods in the economy and competing financial claims on them may not be accentuated by international flows; any attempt to apply this theoretical apparatus to understand reality should take that aspect of reality (international flows) into consideration.

14. See footnote 22 of chapter 6.

15. The assumption here is not that "human ingenuity will be capable of finding ever more sophisticated means of fraudulently evading universal legal principles and that therefore in practice they will never be obeyed and defended" (Huerta de Soto, 2006: 160). I agree with Huerta de Soto that with more or less well-designed regulation and stringent enforcement, it is possible to prevent a good amount of, if not most, fraud. The argument here is that it is not necessary to commit fraud to maximize returns by matching the time preferences of savers and investors. It is based on the assumption that in normal circumstances the amount of savings that economic agents would like to keep readily accessible on demand is a fraction of total savings. Therefore, it would be expected that law-abiding financial institutions will have the incentive to induce economic agents to keep deposits on demand in as relatively low a proportion of total savings as possible, maximizing the efficient use of resources. If today, with the opposite incentives, deposits on demand are a fairly low proportion of the total amount of financial assets with monetary and quasi-monetary properties, it is to be expected that under a different institutional setting in which there are no profits to be made by the multiplication of deposits on demand, their proportion of total monetary aggregates will be even lower.

16. As shown in this chapter, the profit motivation of bankers is expected to operate in ways in which the deposits on demand will be kept to a minimum and other financial instruments will be made available to prospective investors. That is to say, some investors may be nudged into investments of longer maturities than they originally desired, and this nudging may be done by not only offering attractive interest rates, but also repurchase agreements and other instruments to liquidate investments before their maturity that may end up causing a maturity mismatch for the financial institutions. As argued by Philipp Bagus (2010a: 1–18), mismatches in the maturity of investments and financial liabilities may cause misallocations and business cycles even under a 100% reserve requirement. Although it is not the objective of this chapter, the analysis just developed can be seen as a corroboration of Bagus' insight.

TEN

"Inflation Targeting": Neither New nor Effective

Since 1990, the "state of the art" in monetary policy has been "inflation targeting."[1] Inflation targeting policies have been regarded as capable of keeping inflation low under fiat money and fluctuating-exchange-rate arrangements while allowing the "flexibility" to manage monetary policy required to support politically the "independence" of central banks, namely easing credit as an attempt to promote stable growth with the least possible unemployment.

This chapter contends that inflation targeting policies, understood as a strategy for monetary management conducted more or less in a discretionary form aiming primarily at the achievement of a target for the variation of consumers' prices, are neither something "new"[2] nor have these policies been effective in preventing the boom and bust cycles produced by loose (flexible, if you will) monetary management, as they themselves are directly responsible for the current financial crisis by allowing gross speculation in investment assets not "perceived" by the general price indexes utilized to gauge those policies. That, incidentally, is one of the many epistemological arguments that may be raised against the use of inflation targeting policies.

In order to discuss these ideas, in the second section of this chapter we will deal with the concept of inflation targeting policies, presenting a brief historical overview, their key elements, and how to classify them in accordance with the traditional modes of rules and discretion. The third section offers a review of the performance of monetary policies in selected developed countries as empirical evidence for some of the arguments presented with this paper. In the fourth section, some elements of the monetary policy in the United States and the authority of Allan Meltzer, Murray Rothbard, and Richard Timberlake are brought up in support of this paper's main contention mentioned above and presented in the concluding fifth section.

10.1 THE FORMULATION OF "INFLATION TARGETING" POLICIES

On August 15, 1971, the United States under the watch of President Nixon defaulted on the Bretton Woods agreement and severed the tenuous link still existing between the US dollar and gold by closing the "gold window" under which US dollars were redeemable by central banks of signatory countries at the fixed rate of US$ 35.00 per ounce. A new short-lived parity was established, but in 1973 the fixed-exchange-rate monetary regime in force since the end of World War II came to an end. Central banks around the world scrambled for a new "anchor."

In a world left only with fluctuating fiat money, the only possible "anchor" to the value of a currency was a "nominal" one to be implemented at a national level.

10.1.1 Precursors to Inflation Targeting

The Deutsche Bundesbank and the Swiss Central Bank as early as December 1974 and the American Federal Reserve System (Fed) and the Bank of Canada during 1975 started to "state" a "growth" target that they were aiming at. At the beginning, the effort of central banks was to make known to society the evolution (growth) in the monetary aggregates and with them, the "expected" changes in the general price levels as mechanically derived from the application of the "Quantitative Theory of Money." However, these arrangements still constrained the central banks, forcing them to adopt certain marks in terms of changes in the money supply, the resultant price level being just a consequence of their intended commitment.

Pressures to make changes to the goals in terms of expansion of the money supply were soon felt. Real factors and political factors contributed from time to time to force central banks out of their stated goals for monetary expansion, thereby compromising their credibility. At times, with relatively low inflation but a small rate of growth, some further monetary expansion seemed to be possible and pressure to promote that was felt; at other times, a more stringent monetary policy was perceived by the monetary authorities as necessary to keep inflation low, frustrating the expectation (if from no one else, from the Treasury) that the stated monetary expansion would happen. In sum, the claim for "discretion" was a constant.

It was only in 1990 when the Reserve Bank of New Zealand (its central bank) adopted an explicit inflation target with no more reference to limits on monetary expansion but to an aimed-at price level measured by a given price index that the adoption of an "inflation targeting" policy in a narrow sense officially began, according to Bernanke et al. (2001: 86).

10.1.2 What is Inflation Targeting?

But, what is inflation targeting? In their book *Inflation Targeting—Lessons from the International Experience,* Dr. Bernanke and his coauthors offer the following definition: "Inflation targeting is a framework for monetary policy characterized by the public announcement of official quantitative targets (or target ranges) for the inflation rate over one or more time horizons, and by explicit acknowledgement that low, stable inflation is monetary policy's primary long-run goal" (2001: 14).

Since the 1930s most of the debate about monetary policies tries to classify them as strategies based on either "rules" or "discretion," the gold standard, for instance, being a "rule." A discretionary approach happens when a central bank makes no public commitment about its actions. Dr. Bernanke describes inflation targeting as a "framework" in order not to pinpoint it as either a "rule" or as a "discretionary" kind of policy.

In other words, under the "framework" of an inflation target, the central bank is free to take any measure it sees fit, so far and so long as the price level at the end of a certain period of time comes close to the previously stated price level "goal" as measured by the chosen price index. Under the inflation target framework, the central bank claims to be able to pursue other political goals without falling into the discredited monetary "activism" of the bad old days before the "Great Moderation," as the period of discreet monetary management by the main central banks between the start of Paul Volcker's chairmanship at the Fed and the beginning of the recent financial crises became known.

10.1.3 Key Elements of Inflation Targeting Policies

One may summarize an inflation targeting policy as composed of two key elements: first, a high level of discretion about the use of the tools available to the central bank, and second, a "formal" commitment to keep inflation low. Central bankers perceive the first component as required to show the "strength" of their institutions and, therefore, along with the second element, to convey the idea that the monetary authorities are committed to a low level of inflation and have the power to make it come about.

The second element may be understood in at least two different ways. First, strictly speaking about an inflation target in the narrow sense of the strategies first introduced by the Reserve Bank of New Zealand in 1990, the formal commitment to keep inflation low may be stated in a piece of legislation or in an operational agreement between the government and the independent monetary authorities, or it may be made public through the release of some official document by the monetary authorities or simply through the press. The other possible meaning for this second element may be the one in which the monetary authorities, without any legal mandate, agreement with the government, or even by making their goal public, still operationally act driven towards the achievement of an inflation goal, though only a few top officials may know it.

The advocates of inflation target policies claim it is possible to create a "nominal anchor" to the price level by the communication to the public of a target which would result in certain "psychological" market conditions favorable to the achievement of the very same inflation goal (Bernanke et al., 2001: 19). They believe that, if the market knows that the central bank has the power to do one or all of the following, this knowledge will help them achieve the goal of keeping inflation low: (a) to expand or contract the money supply, (b) to raise or to lower interest rates, (c) to impose exchange controls, (d) to alter the level of compulsory reserves, (e) to alter the classes of assets and the conditions under which they will grant access to discount facilities, and in most cases, the power (f) to impose new bank regulations. Along with their stated goal of keeping the inflation low, the knowledge that the central bank has such power would create, so believe the advocates of such policies, the "psychological" conditions necessary to actually achieve the inflation goal. Bernanke could not be clearer about the psychological benefits expected from using everything available in the central bank "tool kit": "Evidence suggests that the only way for central banks to earn credibility is the hard way: by demonstrating that they have the means and the will to reduce inflation and to keep it low for a period of time" (Bernanke et al., 2001: 308). Furthermore, the element of discretion offers the central bank the capacity to pursue "other" political objectives deemed necessary by the circumstances without compromising the achievement of the stated goal so long as the "psychological" conditions remain under control.

10.1.4 Rules vs. Discretion

Proponents of inflation targeting policies argue that history shows that "rules" are no protection against changes in monetary policy. Since changing circumstances "require" flexibility, even the gold standard offers no protection against political decisions to suspend payments in gold in case of war, for instance.

Therefore, so the argument goes, all monetary policies are "discretionary" to a certain degree, and the best you can get is a "framework" such as the one provided by the adoption of a "nominal" anchor.

If we consider that there are no more commodity monies, there are no more fixed-exchange-rate mechanisms, as the Friedmanesque proposal for a legally (constitutionally) defined rate of expansion for the money supply never gained acceptance anywhere because it was considered "too rigid," as the experience of stating monetary expansion goals since 1974 has proved, we are left only with discretionary regimes. Among them, the inflation target framework is the only one in sight carrying some limitations to monetary expansion.

10.1.5 Epistemological Problems for Inflation Targeting Policies

It may be said that those policies are not necessarily dependent on any knowledge about the actual quantity of money in circulation in the economy, since there are variations in the supply and demand of money that are observed and acted upon and that the most frequent objection to the idea of inflation targeting is in relation to the time lags between the occurrence of the imbalances and the corrective actions.[3] That interpretation seems to me to be too benevolent.[4] Price indexes, even if they could perceive changes in the "general price level," cannot perceive them with the precision necessary for the meaningful practice of inflation targeting policies based on them.[5] It is not only that the corrective actions can only be taken when the effects of the disturbances have already occurred,[6] but also, that it is not possible to know how the transmission of monetary changes has happened and, therefore, how it could be "corrected." That is to say, there is a qualitative dimension that cannot be perceived by quantitative measurements, regardless of how precise they are meant to be. A final epistemological question in regard to the practice of inflation targeting policies is that they may be regarded as having been developed precisely to address the limitations of knowledge afflicting policies targeting quantitative measurements of the money supply in vogue before the 1990s, and therefore are a step in the right direction. Evidently inflation targeting policies assume it is necessary to know much less than policies applying the quantitative theory of money to monetary aggregates; but, as argued in this chapter, they still assume more than what is reasonable to assume is known or even knowable.[7]

10.2 Monetary Policy Since 1990

Since the precursory adoption of an inflation targeting policy in New Zealand with the passage of the Reserve Bank of New Zealand Act of December 15, 1989, and the adoption of a similar policy by Canada one year later, it has gradually become the policy of choice worldwide due to its seeming success.

With different grades of formality and public commitment, the establishment of price level goals by the monetary authorities without any other commitment about how those goals would be achieved has become the common practice around the globe.

10.2.1 Track Record of Inflation Targeting Policies

The historically low levels of inflation achieved under the inflation targeting framework, wherever it has been adopted, according to its proponents, seem to prove that it is the solution for price stability under fiat money and fluctuating exchange rates. And the statistical record gives credit to that assessment, at least until the beginning of the current financial crisis.

In order to analyze the validity of the claims made by the proponents of inflation targeting policies, I present the table 10.1 with the Consumer Price Indexes of nine selected developed countries, with data from 1970 to 2007. The countries shown on the table are representative of modern Western societies as a result of the size of their economies and their leadership in institutional developments.

10.2.2 The Final Years under the Bretton Woods Treaty

Until February 1973 the international monetary arrangements were the ones established in 1944 by the Treaty of Bretton Woods with fixed exchange rates pegging all currencies of the signing countries to the US dollar until 1971, convertible (only by their correspondent central banks) in gold at a fixed parity of US$ 35.00 per ounce. However, the charter above shows that the average inflation level in the nine selected developed countries for the period 1970–1972 was well above 5% per year. Those arrangements were clearly unsustainable in the long run, being incompatible with a regime of fixed exchange rates. The weakened link to the gold standard provided by the Bretton Woods Treaty until August 1971 proved to be insufficient to check inflationary expansions of the money supply among the Western developed countries, and the abandonment of those arrangements became inevitable.

10.2.3 In Search of a New "Anchor" for the Value of Monies

The American *default* on its obligations to redeem the US dollar in gold under the Bretton Woods Treaty came as shock for financial markets worldwide. The impacts were huge and long-lasting. From 1973 until 1983, we saw an increase in prices in the selected countries at the time that they were striving to find a new "anchor" for the value of their currencies. That was the period of failed attempts to control inflation establishing targets for the growth of monetary aggregates. The price of gold in US dollars for the period 1964 to 1984 is illustrative of that loss of confidence. Until 1968 world markets perceived that the promise by the American government to redeem US dollars at the agreed parity of US$ 35.00 per ounce was credible. From 1968 to 1971, when the pledge was finally broken, increases in gold prices showed that the confidence in that

Table 10.1. Consumer Price Indexes, Selected Developed Countries 1970–2007(Percentage changes based on national price indexes published by each country)

Year	US	CA	JP	FR	DE	IT	SE	CH	UK
1970	5.9	3.3	7.6	5.9	3.4	5.0	7.0	3.6	6.4
1971	4.2	2.9	6.4	5.5	5.2	4.9	7.4	6.6	9.5
1972	3.3	4.9	4.8	6.2	5.5	5.7	6.0	6.7	7.1
1973	6.3	7.6	11.7	7.3	7.0	10.8	6.7	8.8	9.2
1974	11.0	10.9	23.2	13.7	7.0	19.1	9.9	9.8	16.0
1975	9.1	10.7	11.7	11.8	5.9	17.1	9.8	6.7	24.3
1976	5.8	7.6	9.4	9.6	4.3	16.7	10.3	1.7	16.7
1977	6.5	8.0	8.2	9.4	3.7	18.5	11.4	1.3	15.8
1978	7.6	9.0	4.2	9.0	2.7	12.0	10.0	1.1	8.6
1979	11.3	9.1	3.7	10.8	4.1	14.8	7.2	3.7	12.6
1980	13.5	10.2	7.8	13.0	5.5	21.3	13.7	4.0	16.9
1981	10.4	12.4	4.9	13.3	6.3	19.5	12.1	6.5	12.2
1982	4.0	10.7	2.8	12.0	5.3	16.5	8.6	5.7	8.5
1983	5.3	5.9	1.9	9.5	3.3	14.6	8.9	3.0	5.2
1984	4.4	4.4	2.3	7.7	2.4	10.9	8.0	2.9	4.5
1985	3.5	4.0	2.0	5.8	2.1	9.1	7.4	3.5	5.2
1986	1.9	4.2	0.6	2.5	-0.1	5.8	4.2	0.8	3.6
1987	3.7	4.4	0.1	3.3	0.2	4.8	4.2	1.4	4.1
1988	4.1	4.0	0.7	2.7	1.3	5.1	5.8	1.9	4.6
1989	4.8	5.0	2.3	3.5	2.8	6.3	6.4	3.1	5.9
1990	5.4	4.8	3.1	3.4	2.7	6.5	10.5	5.4	8.2
1991	4.2	5.6	3.3	3.2	3.5	6.3	9.3	5.9	6.8
1992	3.0	1.5	1.7	2.4	5.1	5.3	2.3	4.0	4,7
1993	3.0	1.8	1.2	2.1	4.5	4.6	4.7	3.3	3.0
1994	2.6	0.2	0.7	1.7	2.7	4.1	2.2	0.9	2.4
1995	2.8	2.2	-0.1	1.8	1.8	5.3	2.5	1.8	3.5
1996	3.0	1.5	0.1	2.0	1.4	4.0	0.5	0.8	2.4
1997	2.3	1.7	1.9	1.2	1.9	2.0	0.7	0.5	3.1
1998	1.6	1.0	0.6	0.7	1.0	2.0	-0.3	0.0	3.4
1999	2.2	1.8	-0.3	0.5	0.6	1.7	0.5	0.9	1.5
2000	3.3	2.7	-0.8	1.7	1.4	2.5	0.9	1.5	3.0
2001	2.8	2.5	-0.7	1.7	1.9	2.7	2.4	1.0	1.8

2002	1.6	2.2	-0.9	1.9	1.5	2.5	2.2	0.6	1.7
2003	2.3	2.8	-0.3	2.1	1.0	2.7	1.9	0.6	2.9
2004	2.7	1.8	0.0	2.1	1.7	2.2	0.4	0.8	3.0
2005	3.4	2.2	-0.3	1.8	1.5	2.0	0.5	1.1	2.8
2006	3.2	2.0	0.3	1.6	1.6	2.1	1.4	1.1	3.2
2007	2.8	2.2	0.0	1.5	2.3	1.8	2.2	0.7	4.3

CA = Canada; JP = Japan; FR = France; DE = Germany; IT = Italy; SE = Sweden; CH = Switzerland.

promise had somewhat diminished. Under the Smithsonian Agreement of December 1971, an attempt to fix exchange rates at a devalued US dollar without a link to actual gold faced skepticism, and gold in 1971 closed at the record price of US$ 44.20 per ounce. In February 1973, the Bretton Woods exchange market formally closed, reopening in March 1973 in a floating regime. From that year onwards, the increase of gold prices in US dollars reflects more correctly the *devaluation* of the US dollar in gold terms than an increase in the price of gold as a single commodity as evidenced by data collected by the National Mining Association. [8]

10.2.4 The Years of Recovering Credibility

Nineteen eighty-four is the first of a number of years in which the data shows the results of more conservative policies adopted by monetary authorities in developed countries. The galloping inflation during the Carter presidency led Paul Volcker to the head of the Fed. Mr. Volcker implemented a monetary policy of quantitative control of monetary aggregates that eventually curbed the increases in consumer prices. Similar policies were adopted in Europe since 1979 with the creation of the European Monetary System. But in order to impose an effective control on the growth of monetary aggregates, these policies resulted, as a byproduct, in a short but significant recession during the year 1980 with a double dip at the end of 1981, beginning of 1982. Although those policies proved successful, eventually new inflationary pressures came into the scenario. And regardless of how brief a recession is, it is intolerable in many political circles and the reason why cries for more "discretionary" policies continue to be listened to even today coming from political representatives from almost every persuasion aside from classical liberals, every time the economy in a country with a central bank enters into a downturn.

10.2.5 New Inflationary Pressures and the Adoption of Inflation Targeting Policies

More conservative monetary policies became fashionable after 1982's recession ended. However, three events of historical proportions may explain the increase in the general price levels until 1991. The first of them was the Black Monday in October 1987 when the stock market in the United States plunged and the recently appointed Fed chairman, Alan Greenspan, took charge of the problem, flooding the market with dollars. The second one was the fall of the Berlin Wall in 1988 with the required effort made by developed countries to integrate the Eastern European countries into the new world order. And the third one was the invasion of Kuwait and the first war in the Persian Gulf with the correspondent shock in the world oil supply.

No doubt the massive inflationary expansion determined by those events resulted in increases in the consumer price indexes in the selected countries. But they were counterweighted by the concomitant increases in productivity generated by the enlargement of the division of labor with: (a) the integration of China and the countries behind the Iron Curtain into the world markets, (b) liberalization of trade worldwide with the creation of the World Trade Organization (WTO), (c) the benefits in terms of lower barriers for the trade of goods, labor, services, and finances in an expanded Euro-zone with the final adoption of the euro ten years ago, and last but not least, (d) the advances in information technology.

A twenty-year period of prosperity had begun. Foreign trade was the motor in the real economy behind the miracle, and economic expansion and increasing tax revenues lessened the political cost of adopting relatively more conservative fiscal policies in developed countries.

With a regained credibility in their management of fiscal and monetary policy, governments and monetary authorities started to adopt, explicit or tacitly, the inflation target framework.

The United States is one of these countries where, to this day, inflation targets are not formally adopted; nevertheless American monetary policy is guided primarily by a focus on the inflation rate. Mr. Alan Greenspan commented about monetary policy in his *memoirs* in 1994, and defended keeping the Fed Funds rate unchanged, arguing that it was the first time since the 1960s in which the inflation rate had been under 3% per year for three consecutive years. About the monetary policy in 1996, in the seventh year of the most consistent bull market in record, he argues that the Fed "has no explicit mandate under the law to try to contain a stock market bubble" and that it was established that "price stability is [the] central [Fed's concern] to [promote] long-term economic growth." In December of that year, the famous concept of "irrational exuberance" was offered during a speech at the American Enterprise Institute's annual dinner, yet no change to the inflationary easy credit policy was made since the consumer price indexes did not show any impact from that policy (Greenspan 2007: 178).

The adoption of the inflation-target framework perfectly coincides with the beginning of the twenty-year expansion mentioned above. Up to a point in which the inflation-target framework has been credited with the prosperity experienced until 2007, claims have been made that it is the "perfect" balance between rules and discretion in monetary policy.

What remains to be assessed is to what extent the current crisis proved that inflation targeting policy is the best strategy possible for monetary policy, since it gives room for the monetary authorities to react to the crisis with every instrument at their disposal; or whether it proved to be no more than a new dress for the recurrent mistake of credit expansion that in the end caused the crisis.

In order to assess that, it is worthwhile to revisit the monetary policies of the early 1920s.

10.3 THE MONETARY POLICY OF THE 1920S

It is commonly believed that the years between the Great War and the Depression were years in which the monetary excesses provoked by war financing were interrupted in Europe and in the United States, that resuming redemption in gold was a signal of a regained monetary stability under the venerable gold standard, and that the wild speculation with equities during the 1920s was mainly due to the lack of regulation in the stock markets.[9]

The available data, however, tells us a different story: From June 30, 1921 to June 30, 1929 the total money supply of the United States in billions of dollars rose from 45.30 to 73.26. That means there was an increase of 28 billion dollars during those eight years, or 61.8% (Rothbard 2008: 92).

For those who are skeptical about Rothbard's statistics, a more traditional measurement for the money supply, that is, M2, shows a story not so different. Measured by the M2 criterion, the increase in the money supply in the United States for the same period was 13.75 billion dollars, or 41.86% as shown in the table 10.2.

There was an unequivocal increase in the money supply during the 1920s, *an increase not perceived by the CPI*, an increase that happened almost exclusively on credit money and not at the monetary base or in money proper as the much referred to charts of M1 from that period show. Incidentally, that distinction—that is, when measured by the monetary base, the Fed policy was deflationary in the 1920s, but when measured by M2 it was inflationary—did not pass unnoticed by Allan Meltzer, who attributes such difference to innovations by the banks in face of

Table 10.2. Consumer Price Index and M2 Money Supply: 1921–1929 (M2 in billions of dollars)

Yea r	CPI 1967 = 100	Percent Change	M2 Money Supply	M2 Percent Change
1921	53.6	-10.67	32.85	-5.60
1922	50.2	-6.34	33.72	2.65
1923	51.1	1.79	36.60	8.54
1924	51.2	0.20	38.58	5.41
1925	52.5	2.54	42.05	8.99
1926	53.0	0.95	43.68	3.88
1927	52.0	-1.89	44.73	2.40
1928	51.3	-1.35	46.42	3.78
1929	51.3	0.00	46.60	0.39

restrictions to obtain powered money from the Fed, such as nudging their clients to move from demand deposits to time deposits (Meltzer, 2003: 257).

Many other mechanisms were used to expand the money supply given the limitations of the still-prevailing gold standard (more properly a gold-exchange standard) and the constraints imposed by Fed policies; the currency in circulation, for instance, stayed fairly constant at around $3.7 billion during the period. The truth of the matter is that the entire monetary expansion happened on money-substitutes,[10] that is, through credit expansion.

But does the gold standard not have an inbuilt mechanism to self-correct imbalances preventing inflationary expansions? It seems that not all monetary regimes based on a gold standard are created equal. It was already noted in nineteenth-century England that the operation of an external drain of specie would only work in order to keep the monetary system "neutral," that is, neither promoting nor reducing the business cycle under a hypothetical purely metallic currency as described by Hume (1987: 308) in his essay "Of the Balance of Trade." Under the gold-exchange system with a central bank, the anti-inflationary effects of a specie drain mechanism were not immediately perceived, if ever (White, 1995:115).

10.3.1 Rothbard on the Monetary Policy of the 1920s in the USA

In *America's Great Depression*, Rothbard demonstrates that in the 1920s the system utilized the concept of "Total Dollar Claims" to represent the total money supply on top of gold reserves. The data retrieved by Rothbard from the Banking and Monetary Statistics published by the Fed in

1943 (Rothbard, 2008: 94) actually shows that the regime of gold-exchange standard of the 1920s, in which governments no longer redeemed their currency in gold domestically, and redemption by foreigners, although formally available, was politically constrained, posed no real limits to monetary expansion. Furthermore, as argued by Timberlake, the main factor behind the monetary management executed by the Fed through its open-market operations in that decade was not an imperfect understanding of the operations of a gold standard, not even an adherence to the real bills doctrine enshrined in its legal mandate, but an ad hoc political decision resulting from the flood of gold arriving at the Fed from abroad: "To prevent current gold monetization and inflation, and a subsequent deflation on the gold's anticipated return to European banking systems, Fed policy sterilized the gold and instituted a stable price level policy" (Timberlake, 2005: 210).[11]

Whatever were the rationales for the actions of the Fed, the fact remains that the monetary policy in the 1920s was de facto a policy aiming at price stability, and we will next discuss its intellectual origins.

10.3.2 Intellectual Roots of Inflation Targeting may be Found in the 1920s

Rothbard considers Yale professor Irving Fisher as the major theoretician of the inflationists in the years of the Great Depression, someone "who mechanistically had believed that since the price level was not rising in the 1920s, there was no inflation to worry about and no coming crash" (2005: 303). After the crash happened, Fisher urged President Roosevelt to abandon the gold standard and rejoiced when the President finally did that. But the important lesson is what history tells us about the monetary policy before the Great Depression, and what we now know is that the only actual limits to monetary expansion at that time were already the self-limitations adopted by different central banks with eyes only on the price levels, anticipating by sixty years the strategy of conducting monetary policy primarily by aiming at a certain inflation level, and using discretion in the management of the money supply in order to achieve that goal, a policy now known as inflation targeting. And in the face of the supposed success of Fed Governor Strong in stabilizing wholesale prices during the late 1920s, Fisher was again the leader in the economic profession in welcoming the arrival of an era of continued prosperity assured by the "new" policy of managed money in America and in the world, ignorant of the fact of mounting malinvestments induced by the inflationary policies in practice during the 1920s.[12] About this in particular, Rothbard (2005: 449) states, "Fisher was particularly critical of the minority of skeptical economists who warned of overexpansion in the stock and real estate markets due to cheap money."

As stated by Rothbard in *America's Great Depression* (2008: 169), "One of the reasons that most economists in of the 1920s did not recognize the existence of an inflationary problem was the widespread adoption of a stable price level as the goal and criterion for monetary policy."

In that book, Rothbard is explicit in stating that the Federal Reserve was guided not only by the desire to help the United Kingdom in its inflationist monetary policy or to help farmers, but "by the fashionable economic theory of a stable price level as the goal of monetary manipulation" (2008: 181).

Timberlake draws similar conclusions from his research on the money market operations and other activities of the Fed between 1923 and 1928. According to Timberlake, the Fed was not acting solely in order to make the supply of money elastic or acting as a lender of last resort as was prescribed in its legal mandate. The Fed was actively engaged in managing gold flows and executing its open-market operations with price stability as its goal. For Timberlake:

> Strong was particularly inclined towards price level stabilization and, as a policymaker, was willing to promote it. Besides his practical experience as a banker who had witnessed clearinghouse operations in the Panic of 1907, he had the counsel of Professor Irving Fisher and some other economists who proposed such a policy through control over the quantity of money. (Timberlake, 2005: p 211)

Meltzer also mentions the maintenance of price stability as one of the goals of the Fed's policies in the 1920s. For him, the Fed was also aiming at the reestablishment of the gold standard as an international exchange system and curbs on speculation without a return of the high interest rates of the early 1920s (Meltzer, 2003: 139). Meltzer ultimately attributes the failures of the monetary policy in the 1920s to a conflict between the long-term goals of their activist interventions, such as the restoration of the gold standard at the international level, with their short-term policy of price stability (Meltzer, 2003: 210). Be that as it may, one fact remains: the guide of the monetary policy in the 1920s was the achievement of price stability through activist management of money (abhorrent as it was to Governor Strong) through manipulation of interest rates, access to rediscount facilities, sterilization of the monetary base, et cetera.

10.4 CONCLUSION

The monetary policy known as "Inflation Targeting" is neither new nor effective. Seen by most economists today as the "state of the art" in monetary policy, the inflation-target framework can be understood as a relabeled version of the monetary management that central banks had gradually begun to exercise worldwide once the gold standard was diluted into the gold-exchange standard.

It is not the objective of this chapter to discuss the historical evolution of the gold standard, but suffice it to say that the golden era of the international gold standard with a fractional reserves banking system structured as a pyramid with the Bank of England on the top that took form after Peel's Act of 1844[13] was already a regime with room for monetary management by the central bank, and the gradual transformation of that system to a system of gold-exchange, then limited gold-exchange, then fixed exchange rates, and finally fiat money with floating exchange rates just gave more and more room for the exercise of discretionary monetary policy.

Taking the fractional reserves system under the umbrella of the Bank of England as our departing point, inflationary credit expansion was possible, first by diminishing the prudent ratio of reserves to assets by the implicit support of the banking system by the British Crown. Later, after the Great War, under a regime formally with a central bank, as described by Rothbard, the direct trade on money-substitutes by the Fed, the Bank of England, and other leading central banks was a source of inflationary credit expansion worldwide. And finally, since 1973, under fiat currency and floating exchange rates, inflationary expansion of the money supply is possible by the total discretion that central banks have today.

All along the way, the "nominal" anchor, that is, an implicit or explicit commitment of the monetary authorities to avoiding increases in the price level as gauged commonly by a consumer price index, gradually became the only limitation to inflationary expansion and also the only guide to the exercise of monetary policy.

The surprising thing about policies that in essence allow discretionary expansion of the money supply so long as the Consumer Price Index does not increase more than some "accepted" rate is that the shortcomings of the theoretical apparatus behind those policies have been known in academic circles for about eighty years now. The intertemporal implications of inflationary changes in the money supply, and the limitations imposed by the structure of production for monetary "management" presented by the Austrian Business Cycle Theory are concepts that have been well-known since the early 1930s; yet, during the Great Depression and again about eighty years later during the recent financial crisis, many economists were surprised by the effects of inflationary expansion of credit in distorting economic activity and leading to malinvestments that eventually need to be purged by a recession. Again quoting Rothbard (2008: 169): "The fact that general prices were more or less stable during the 1920s told most economists that there was no inflationary threat, and therefore the events of the Great Depression caught them completely unaware."

Inflation targeting strategies do not prevent inflationary credit expansions and therefore do not prevent the cycles of boom and bust irremediably associated with them. Moreover, distortions in relative prices produced by inflationary credit expansion as described by the Austrian Business Cycle Theory are not easily perceived by price indexes, since usually they do not include assets in their composition. Massive increases in the money supply can produce sizable appreciation in certain classes of assets but barely affect consumer prices or more generally the price level as measured by general price indexes.

Nowadays, it can be affirmed that the existing flexibility to engage for long periods of time in inflationary credit expansion under an inflation-target framework can be exercised without compromising the achievement of an inflation goal as measured by most price indexes. It was true during the 1920s; it had been true since the 1990s. However, the fact remains that an inflationary credit expansion distorts relative prices and provokes economic booms that eventually will end in a downturn.

Therefore, we may conclude that policies guided solely by targeting a certain price level as measured by an index while allowing discretion to the monetary authorities to pursue "growth" is an insufficient institutional arrangement for a society that purports to offer a good money as a fair instrument to individuals for enhancing the division of labor, productivity, and prosperity in the long run.

NOTES

1. Perhaps the most influential academic paper proposing an inflation target as the central criterion for monetary policy is John B. Taylor's "Discretion Versus Policy Rules in Practice" (Taylor, 1993). Its main credit, however, is that it endorsed what at that time became common practice among central banks. Bernanke et al. (2001), first published in 1999, is also widely quoted in academic discussions about inflation targeting for the collection of data supporting the claim for the effectiveness of inflation targets.

2. Proposals "for targeting monetary policy on a broad price index" were already deemed "old" by Yeager in a 1983 paper (Yeager, 1983: 308); and rightly so, since, as will be argued in this chapter, their root may be found in the monetary policy of the 1920s. Specifically, the similitude between the 1920s and the 1990s was already noticed by Barry Eichengreen, who wrote that observers "see parallels, in other words, between the 'new economy' of the 1990s and the 'new age' of the 1920s" (2002: 9).

3. See Yeager, 1983: 309.

4. Here the discussion of aggregation in 5.8 Monetary Disturbances must be revisited, especially footnote 9 of chapter 5. Bagus in his already-mentioned paper on Morgenstern's contributions brings the example of Gardiner Mean's doctrine of administered prices as a case in which inaccurate aggregation of data led to a "problematic" thesis; once the data was reevaluated it showed weak or no support for the thesis supposedly based on them (Bagus, 2010b: 13).

5. In the same article mentioned in the footnote above, Bagus lists a number of problems of limitation of knowledge that may influence the quality of the aggregated data produced as a price index. For instance, he mentions that some goods have more than one publicly quoted price, and that many goods and services have nonmonetary components to their prices. He argues that "These non-monetary components of prices are, of course, relevant for an econometrician who wants to test the hypothesis that changes in the money supply have an influence on prices" (Bagus, 2010b: 14).

6. Incidentally, the time lag may be considered as yet another epistemological objection to inflation targeting, since it is only after the monetary disturbances are

perceived by the price index that monetary authorities will have the information that some corrective action is necessary.

7. This last point about the fact that the exact knowledge assumed to exist in order to practice inflation-targeting policies is actually nonexistent is made clear by Bagus when he states that error estimates are not provided in econometrics because "there is not a precise way of calculating them" (Bagus, 2010b: 28).

8. "Historical Gold Prices–1833 to Present" accessed March 20, 2015. www.nma.org/pdf/gold/his_gold_prices.pdf.

9. Timberlake quotes the *Annual Report* of the Board of Governors of the Federal Reserve System for the year 1920 in which the blame for the post-war inflation was attributed not to the accommodation of the Fed to the requirements of the Treasury and the resulting credit expansion but to: "an unprecedented orgy of extravagance . . . overextended business, and general demoralization of the agencies of production and distribution" (Timberlake, 2005).

10. The distinguishing characteristic of money-substitutes is that they are believed to be converted, au pair and on demand, to money. Under this definition, demand deposits, money market funds, mutual funds, and corporate and public debt instruments, among others, may be considered money-substitutes. The most important implication of the existence of money-substitutes is that the amount of money in the market becomes something of an unknown, unknowable magnitude. Under Menger's GAMOE definition, any commodity or title that due to its characteristics comes to be generally accepted as medium of exchange becomes money. In this broad sense, money-substitutes are money as long as they continue to command au pair liquidity. However, the legal definition of money in the United States prescribes that "money is a medium of exchange authorized or adopted by government as part of its currency" as mentioned in footnote 23 of chapter 1. From this definition comes the necessity to talk about money-substitutes.

11. Incidentally, such policy may explain in part why most of the monetary increase happened on credit money.

12. When Irving Fisher in 1920 wrote *Stabilizing the Dollar*, he described his ideas about monetary management assuming "automatic" controls of gold and credit supply. At the time he wrote *The Money Illusion* in 1928, the practice of discretionary credit management by the monetary authorities had become the rule and he wrote: "This, when duly perfected and duly safeguarded, will greatly simplify and improve the technique of stabilization and will make gold control secondary to credit control" (Fisher, 1928/2009: 193). In describing the evolution of the understanding about monetary policy by the Fed in the 1920s Thomas Humphrey states that the attempts starting in 1923 to reconcile the RBD with the new mechanism of open market operations express a more bleak view than Fisher: "Such operations, constituting as they did, activist, discretionary policy intervention, conflicted with the doctrine's notion of policy as a passively accommodating and automatically self-correcting affair. The resulting reconciliation saw member bank borrowing and market interest rates emerge in the mid- to late 1920s as the doctrine's key policy indicators" (Humphrey, 2001: 296). Here perhaps, it could be added that the volume of re-discount and the interbank interest rate were the key indicators for the policy response in its activist pursuit of price stability.

13. The Peel's Act of 1844 gave to the Bank of England (BoE) the monopoly of issuance of paper money, solidifying its role as de facto central bank. In such a role the BoE used to concentrate most of the British gold reserves while the other banks used to have BoE notes instead of gold in their vaults, creating a two-layered system, or reserves which "economized" in gold and allowed an already highly leveraged ratio of gold to banknotes.

ELEVEN

The Future of Money

11.1 JUSTIFICATION FOR THE ACTUAL STATE OF AFFAIRS

What are the justifications for the adoption of a state-issued fiat money monetary system prevailing today? If the benefits of good money are so evident and the flaws of the fiat money arrangements are so blatantly clear, why does everybody have fiat money and nobody have competitive or specie-backed money? There are many answers but not a definitive one.

In considering the advantages of having state-issued money in terms of standardization,[1] we must consider the history of money in Western societies. After much abuse, a commodity standard crystallized with free circulation of a myriad of gold, silver, and copper coin denominations in the first half of the nineteenth century, which gradually evolved to an institutional design that attributed more and more discretionary power to the governments. The force behind that trend may be found in the fiscal benefits in terms of seigniorage; such benefits are so enormous that no politician or public official trying to maximize his own interest as a "**political entrepreneur**" would agree to surrender this power back to society unless a real shift in the balance of political power happened. These changes in mature countries like the United States and Canada are uncommon due to the stability of political forces, and in developing countries, the very absence of constitutional limitations on the abuse of money is an invitation to whoever comes to power to be tempted to abuse it for his own benefit and the benefit of his faction.

The perception of the advantages of a different institutional arrangement is something only acquired through a massive investment in information gathering, and is by no means easy to grasp even when the information is presented. The citizenry cannot opt for what they do not know even in a democratic regime. Needless to say, societies with better education and more democratic institutions usually have the relatively better currencies, increasing the opportunity cost of the investment in political changes due to the fact that, for most people, the money provided is a money good enough for their needs.[2]

11.1.1 When does a Quantitative Difference become a Qualitative One?

That quantitative differences may become qualitative ones is why still today the US dollar is a better currency than the Venezuelan bolívar, the nonconvertible Cuban peso, or the Iranian rial, even though all of them are fiat currencies. The differences among them are not in their specific monetary arrangements, but in the general political arrangements of those different societies. If the money supply is a matter of state policy, no wonder those institutional arrangements in a broader sense make the difference in its output.

In fact, I think that the euro and its predecessors, the deutschmark, the US dollar, the yen, the pound sterling, and the Swiss franc, to name some, have been relatively good currencies for more than half a century, first under the Bretton Woods Treaty and later during the "Great Moderation," the 1970s being the exception. It is only reasonable to expect no big fuss about something that people in general are happy with and not aware of the fact that something better could exist. After all, it must be recognized that a certain level of ignorance is rational by the citizenry.

The people of countries in the periphery can recur to currency boards in an institutional fashion; they can invest in better currencies as private investors, or in real assets, as most people in Latin America do. We must remember that even perceiving the failure of their national money, they usually do not have much knowledge of the alternatives, not to mention the channels to express their desires and transform those into institutional changes due to the autocratic characteristic of their political regimes.

A former Brazilian politician, diplomat, and scholar, now deceased, José Guilherme Merquior once wrote: "The nature of the process (of civilization) is the progress of liberty" (1982: 198). There is an optimistic assumption implicit in this statement, a belief that we are living a process towards more civilized mores, a belief, incidentally, which I share. But this process is, at the most, not a linear one, as the occurrence of the Dark Ages after the classical period in Western history has shown us. We can expect that with time the competition among different societies with different institutional arrangements will teach humanity what the best institutions are. At least some human beings have understood the value of private property, monogamy, separation of church and state, and limited government in this trial and error way. These values are the values of the most successful societies of our times; other human beings can adopt those institutions and benefit from the results in accepting those values in their constitutions or they can insist on their less efficient arrangements. The results can be perceived in the long run, as we can already see when comparing countries that, fifty years ago, used to have about the same income per capita, like Taiwan and South Korea on the one hand, and North Korea and Myanmar on the other.

Another extremely relevant aspect to be considered is the interconnection between monetary arrangements and the banking system. This interconnection is a powerful force for the maintenance of the status quo. Without obviously saying that it is a good thing, it is only possible to have a full-fledged lender of last resort such as the ones in place today all around the world if the money is fiat money. The constant abrogation of the payments in specie and constant bank holidays in England, in the United States, and anywhere else during the nineteenth century made that clear.

Arguably, the actual level of credit in the economy, or at least, the level of public debt in particular, is made possible with the incentives provided by a banking system organized under the umbrella of a central bank acting as a lender of last resort.[3] This is true for central countries and the ones in the periphery, as a rule, respecting only quantitative differences according to the specific level of sophistication of their economies.

Could another arrangement lead to about the same "efficiency" in the allocation of savings to investments? Maybe so, maybe not. The same features of our monetary systems today, which have generated confidence in the banking system and confidence in the relatively stable value of currencies, are those that could destroy the existing confidence and, with that confidence, the "efficiency" of the allocation of resources could be destroyed as well. What are those features? They are the political origin of our money today and the politically driven regulations of the banking system.

Anyway, even if it is generally accepted that other arrangements could lead to better times, the transition would not be costless, and we must consider that the transition would be a transition not only to a different monetary system but to a different banking system as well.

By accepting the lessons about the limitations of knowledge and natural motivation of public agents, are we condemned to have fiat money or at best purely abstract money with a regulated banking system? Maybe.

If so, in order to understand the differences among the existing currencies, their performances, and future trends in regard to money, it would be useful to keep in mind an examination of the main characteristics by which different monetary systems may be classified.

11.2 AN ATTEMPT TO CLASSIFY THE POSSIBLE MODERN MONETARY SYSTEMS

In order to do such an analysis, this section starts with a classification of monetary systems cross-grouping characteristics to name the systems. This is not the approach used in the past and it is not the approach utilized in a recent attempt to classify modern monetary systems.[4] Although Schuler's classification refers to many features of the different monetary systems, it tends to focus on the legal status of the currency. Instead, the proposed classification below focuses on the different features, legal status being just one of them.

11.2.1 Legal Status

In relation to the attribute of its legal status, it is possible to envisage first the possibility of having the *No Legal Tender* system in which the economic agents in a given territory are either explicitly or implicitly free to adopt the monies of their preference without any legal mandate to use a given currency as medium of exchange for their transactions. Second, if there is a legal mandate, then it is possible to separate this mandate into two categories: First, the attribute imposed by law that the currency defined as *Legal Tender* must be accepted as payment for any debt in a certain territory; and second, the currency defined as legal tender must be the ONLY currency accepted as payment in that territory, in which case we can refer to it as *Forced Tender*.

11.2.2 In Relation to the Existence of a Monetary Authority

In relation to the existence of a monetary authority in charge of manipulating and regulating the money supply, we can classify a given monetary system either as one of a *Central Bank* or one of *Free Banking*; there is no middle ground. Admittedly, there are different intervention levels that a central bank may exercise; and so, in regard to this characteristic, we can further differentiate monetary systems as follows:

a. systems with a central bank as solely an issuer of money;
b. systems with a central bank that regulates the issuance of money by other issuing banks, whether the central bank is an issuer itself or not;
c. systems with a central bank that, aside from regulating and/or engaging in money issuing, is also a regulator of the financial system;
d. systems with a central bank that, aside from regulating and/or engaging in money issuing and regulating the financial system, is also a treasury agent, lending money to the government; or
e. Free banking systems with no monetary authority.

Those jurisdictions with a central bank can also be differentiated from those with an *Independent Central Bank* and a *subordinated* one. Independence of the monetary authority usually means independence from the executive branch of power to the extent that the central bank is accountable to the legislative branch of power, or its board of directors is appointed by the chief of the executive branch of power for fixed terms that usually do not coincide with its own, such as is the case with the American Fed or the Colombian *Banco de La Repú blica*. The independence of the central bank allegedly correlates with sounder monetary policies, since it supposedly does not need to be bound by political considerations as directly as a central bank whose directors risk being dismissed *ad nutum*. The independence of the central bank can be enhanced in different ways, from fixed terms for its officials to legal mandates forbidding the central bank to lend money to the government such as established in the charter of the Chilean central bank, for instance.

A Free Banking System is a monetary system with no central bank and with free entrance of new firms into the banking trade. In a Free Banking Monetary System, the issuers of money are private although they could be regulated by some governmental agency, such as the Treasury Secretary. To the extent that the treasury in a given jurisdiction regulates minutely the private issuance of money, that may be considered a jurisdiction with de facto central banking.

11.2.3 The Source of Value of the Monetary Unit

The source of value of the monetary unit may rely on its being redeemable by some specie or other currency (fiduciary currency), or it can be purely based on the confidence that the issuer will provide for the stability of its value (fiat money). As different ways to give value for the monetary unit it is possible to identify:

1. Fiduciary Currency: Basically, a currency is defined as *Fiduciary* when it is retrievable in money proper, either in some commodity money or in other (hard) currency as may be the case in a gold standard.

    a. Gold Standard. A currency has a *Gold Standard* when the paper money is redeemable in specie, usually gold, at some fixed quantity. This characteristic is compatible with (a) bimetallism in which the bank notes are redeemable both in gold and silver at a given parity, (b) having metal coins in addition to redeemable bank notes, (c) a monopoly or a multiplicity of issuing banks, (d) legal tender or not, (e) a legal definition of the unit or not, (f) the existence of a central bank or not, (g) the currency being redeemable for any money holder or only for central banks, and finally (h) fractional reserves or a 100% reserve requirement. To my knowledge, currently there is not a single example of a monetary system with a gold standard.

b. Currency Board: A currency has the characteristic of a *Currency Board* when the paper money is freely redeemable in a hard currency at a fixed rate; then it is a currency board in sensu stricto. Variants are (a) the possibility for money issuers to hold fractional reserves or not and (b) to have only the reserve currency supporting the value of the locally issued currency or, if securities nominated in that currency are also admitted, then it must be determined which securities qualify.[5]

2. Substitution: A monetary regime may be characterized as one of *Substitution* when some currency issued by a political entity other than the national government of the country in question has the status of legal tender and is the currency used by the public. The cases of "dollarization" in Panama and Ecuador are cases of substitution as was the adoption of the euro by most countries in the European Community. These examples are sufficient to clarify that even substitution admits a number of variables, such as (a) the existence or not of a central bank, (b) the imposition of foreign currency only as legal tender or forced tender, (c) whether or not some locally issued currency also competes with the foreign currency, for example, whether or not this local currency is redeemable in the foreign currency, et cetera.
3. Fiat Currency: Basically, a currency is defined *as Fiat* when it is irretrievable in some good as gold or in other (hard) currency and the public confidence in its value is based only on the confidence that the issuer will maintain its amount approximately constant. In the case of fiat money, the value of the currency results from the political decisions of the issuer in managing its supply and utility for the money holders.[6]

11.2.4 Instruments for Sustaining the Value of the Monetary Unit

Regardless of which institutional arrangements are in place to give value to a currency, it is necessary for the issuers to have the capacity to sustain that value. The most important instrument is the availability of reserves to the issuers whenever the source of value for a currency relies on its being redeemable or when a given exchange rate is being supported by the monetary authorities. Another instrument usually used by some *desesperado* as a resource of last resort is the adoption of an indexed unit of exchange while the value of the actual medium of exchange continues to deteriorate. As mentioned below, it is also possible to envisage a monetary arrangement in which there is a unit of exchange but no physical currency.

1. *Reserves*: To back the capacity to redeem paper money for gold or for a hard currency, the issuing banks hold a certain percentage of gold or hard currency and investment-graded securities nominated in the hard currency as *Reserves*. There are basically two different possibilities related to this attribute, either a system with 100% of reserves or a fractional system with only a fraction in reserves of the total amount issued.[7] Reserves are also kept and utilized as instruments by the monetary authorities to manipulate exchange rates in any regime that is not of free exchange.
2. *Exchange*: One important mechanism to sustain the value of a currency is through competition. In the case of national currencies as we have today, that means through *Foreign Exchange*, that is, the different regimes in which a currency can be exchanged for other currencies. If the regime of foreign exchange is one of *Free Exchange*, with no administrative and no fiscal barriers and no manipulation by the authorities of the exchange rate, the value of the currency is given by the market, and it fluctuates according to changes in the supply and demand for that currency as a consequence of the financial and commercial transactions nominated in that currency. Other regimes of foreign exchange such as the "Peg" (at a fixed exchange rate), the "**Dirty Flow**," the "**Crawling Peg**," and the "Fluctuation inside Bands" regimes are types of *Controlled Exchange*; they are attempts by the monetary authorities to sustain more or less strictly a "price" for the currency defined according to political considerations.[8] These attempts can be sustained with interventions in the foreign exchange markets backed by reserves or they can be imposed through legal and administrative rules such as a monopoly of foreign exchange, and limiting the action of the economic agents, to some extent and for some time, depending on the willingness of the authorities in sustaining their writ.[9]
3. *Dissociation*: We can envisage a system in which the medium of exchange is one thing and the unit of exchange is another; that is, in which there is *Dissociation* between the medium of exchange and the unit of exchange. In this case there is a lack of identity between the GAMOE and the unit of exchange, the standard of value. It happened in the Middle Ages with the "ideal money" referred to by Einaudi, it happened in Brazil for more than ten years in the late 1980s and early 1990s at the time of high inflation and almost complete indexation, and it could happen again in a future moment in which a state-issued currency ceases to exist and only a unit of exchange, a standard of value, is taken as a reference by the eco-

nomic agents in their transactions that will be cleared with the use of different media of exchange.[10]

As mentioned before, nowadays there is no country where the gold standard is enforced, so all the existing monetary systems are either fiduciary currency with currency boards or purely fiat money systems. In most countries the currency is not only fiduciary but also forced tender. There are some countries with legal tender but not forced tender. Currently, there are no countries without legal tender.

Most of the countries adopt a central bank system but there are some small countries that still may be described as free banking systems.

These are the different attributes through which it is proposed to differentiate all existing monetary systems. Next, we will turn to future trends in regard to money, taking into consideration what has been discussed so far.

11.3 BANKING ARCHITECTURE

11.3.1 What is Narrow Banking?

There are many different ways to define "narrow banking," or perhaps, to say it differently, there are many different models according to which banking may be "narrowed" and I intend to discuss some in this chapter. But a good place to start is by giving the rationale for changing the institutional design of money and banking from the perspective of supporters of narrow banking, and the best of those for me is Buchanan's argument for narrow banking: fiat money makes fractional reserve anachronistic (Buchanan, 2010: 251–258). An edifice designed to economize base money makes (economic) sense when base money is expensive, even if it adds instability to the economy; the moment base money is no longer expensive, the trade-off does not pay anymore and a less stable financial system should be conceived of or allowed to evolve. Ideas about narrowing bank activities, with different degrees, shapes, and forms, may be traced as far back as David Hume who "reluctantly" advocated for a government monopoly of deposit banking with a 100% reserve requirement and no loaning banks allowed (Paganelli, 2014: 979); such policy was based on his intrinsic metallist understanding of money, and his concern that any "paper credit" would result in inflation and therefore, in misguided price signs to the economy. The attention on ways of reforming banking arrangements naturally increases with financial crisis; for instance, one of the first contemporary proposals for narrowing the banks was the Chicago Plan, later elaborated by Irving Fisher with his 1935 proposal for a "100% Money" (Fisher, 2011: 47–58). Fisher's proposal goes to the core of the matter, the elimination of fractional reserve banking. Other proposals, such as John Kay's, advocate for narrow banking with a different meaning; he advocates for a change of financial architecture, replacing the existing one for one of "narrow banking"; however for Kay narrow banking means not so much the elimination of time mismatches caused by different forms of fractional reserve banking, but the separation of current financial conglomerates into many different financial firms, each one with its activity narrowly limited. His proposal comes close to the meaning used here in advocating that only deposit banks could use the name "bank" and their assets should be only UK treasuries; in that sense it resembles John Cochrane's proposal and for the same reasons I judge that insufficient. Among economists from the Austrian School, recently, in *Procesos de Mercado*, Alok Basu published an article entitled "How to create a banking and monetary system for the 21st century: the Huerta de Soto and Chicago plans reworked" (Basu, 2014: 13–66); and in the same edition, Philipp Bagus published the article "Austrian economics and new currency theory on 100% banking: a response to Huber" (Bagus, 2014: 105–136). Both articles discuss ideas about narrow banking, showing the interest for new institutional designs. along the lines of limiting the capacity of the banks to create inflationary credit, among economists from different traditions. Another example of that is Benes' and Kumhof's "The Chicago Plan Revisited" working paper for the IMF (Benes and Kumhof, 2012). Because the most comprehensive and consequential defense of the idea presently is the one of John Cochrane, the commentaries on the topic are based on his work.

11.3.2 John Cochrane and his Narrow Banking

In "Toward a run-free financial system" (2014), Cochrane, presents the case for narrow banking. I am limiting my comments to things that I have a different opinion about or some thought that may be of value for the readers; all the praise I have for his work and how much I agree with his basic premise that it is a fallacy to say that "banks must try to 'transform' maturity" in order to match society's demand for money-like assets go without saying.

My comments are the following:

Comment 1: Cochrane starts saying that "money-market funds, or overnight debt must be baked entirely by short-term Treasuries," (2014: 2) later, (2014: 45) Cochrane qualifies that by saying that "Narrow banking backed by Treasuries is only perfectly safe so long as Treasuries themselves are perfectly safe." He also mentions (2014: 25) the current "fiscal profligacy" in the United States. I cannot agree more with the last remark and, because of that, I think that to tie the success of narrow banking to the continuous creditworthiness of the American federal government would be a strategic mistake (to the cause of helping the establishment of a "run-free" financial system); although it may make tactical sense. Better, I would argue, would be to limit financial instruments with quasi-monetary properties such as money market mutual funds to very short-term corporate notes issued against their receivables, in a modern version of the Real Bills Doctrine as it was originally conceived (see footnote 8 of chapter 9).

Comment 2: That brings me to what perhaps is my main concern: I tend to think that the main reason why governments in general support the financial system is because they need financial intermediaries to float their consolidated debt; or to put it differently, the more a government runs a deficit, the more that government cannot afford to allow its channels to place their bonds with savers to dry out. Because of that, I think it is unrealistic to think that governments will ever relinquish their monetary prerogatives; on the other hand, I also think that a default on the public debt is inevitable, so, as much as I like his idea (2014: 45) of granting the government the power to lower or eliminate the payment of interest in their long-term debt, I don't think it is wise to allow the government to have short-term debt at all, much less to allow investors to hold them as quasi-money (it would be bad enough for someone to buy a 90-day Treasury Note and put it in a drawer until it matures; it is quite another thing for people to hold shares in Money Market Funds with D+1 liquidity invested in those notes). So, I don't think it is a good idea to encourage economic agents, or worse, to force individuals and corporations to carry their liquidity in instruments backed by short-term public debt if that government will be unable to honor them some time in the future (which may happen in the long run or tomorrow, in case of a "perfect storm"). Cochrane may argue that the government may default on their long-term bonds and still honor their short-term liabilities, and that much is true, but if the Brazilian experience in the 1980s serves as a guide, the moment there is a default, although with different levels of severity, the government likely will default on everybody. That reminds me that at the time of Charles the V in Spain, the Crown-preferred form of consolidated debt was that of perpetuities, which did not prevent Philip II from defaulting on them and on short-term borrowing, granted, with different levels of "haircuts" to different creditors (according to their political clout).

Comment 3: I like very much his discussion about the fact that people no longer need to have their "liquidity" represented by run-prone securities (2014: 3). Still, considering the properties people look for when choosing their money, I like to think that financial instruments representing "liquidity" should be as close as possible to being of a "fixed-value" nature and payable-on-demand. Furthermore, I like to think that the "ideal" inventory of "liquid" instruments should represent the availability of saved resources in the real side of the economy which are able to be mobilized for the different uses that the uncertainty in the structure of production may dictate. So, if the reason people want to have "liquidity" is because they are uncertain about when and what goods and services they may need in order to satisfy their needs, those "liquid" resources should be a representation in the financial/monetary/abstract side of the economy of the available resources for immediate disposal in the real side of the economy. If we lose that from our perspective I think we may engage in wrong diagnosis and wrong prescriptions. In that sense, it makes sense to me that if we are using credit instruments as the medium of exchange, those instruments should be as closely related as possible with the production of goods and services going on in the economy. And short-term public debt, creditworthy as it may be (given the ability of the government to extract income through taxes from the private sector), is not a good gauge for the availability of resources in the real sector; and a bubble of public debt may provoke an increase in the claims against real goods that may be solved only at a different (and higher) price level); that is, with inflation.

Comment 4: That leads me to a topic dismissed by Cochrane (2014: 45) that is dear to me: the pursuit of a fundamentally different monetary standard. I am sympathetic to ideas of segregation of monetary functions. Again, perhaps that is a consequence of living in Brazil through thirty years with average annual inflation around 160% between 1964 and 1994, but I really think that what saved the day during those years was indexation. If not for the existence of fairly stable (in real terms) units of account and freedom to contract on them, the daily melting of the real value of the medium of exchange would not have allowed capital formation, and a modicum of rational economic life as we had at that time in the middle of fiscal, financial, monetary, political, moral chaos in the country . . . Separation of monetary functions seems to me the best solution to have stable value in the units of account combined with a supply of the media of exchange flexible enough to accommodate changes in the demand for money, even abrupt and unexpected ones. Because of that, ideas of narrow banking coupled with segregation of monetary functions such as those advocated by Yeager with his BFH proposal seem to me as close to an "ideal" monetary/financial system as we can possibly get.

Comment 5: In regard to Cochrane's perspective on the 2008 financial crisis, I agree completely that it may adequately be described as "a run in the 'shadow banking system.'" I would emphasize, though, the fact that some money market mutual funds that until the day that Lehman Brothers went belly-up were perceived as "quasi-money," given their monetary properties, suddenly had the perception about them changed, when worries that they could "break the buck" became widespread. In a matter of hours, hundreds of billions of dollars left them, being moved to checking accounts and other perfect substitutes of money in a "flight to quality" as Cochrane mentions (2014: 12). That raises the issue, however, that even narrow banking arrangements would not prevent a run if there is an implicit warranty of the banks managing the MMMFs that they will not allow their investors to suffer losses and that

that warranty is fully supported by the monetary authorities. For me, the real question then is why the government did not want the MMMFs to lose their monetary properties? The only compelling answer that comes to my mind, strong enough to justify all the actions of the US federal government at the beginning of the financial crisis, is that it could not afford to allow the MMMFs to lose their monetary properties because without them, they could not float the entirety of the federal debt at interest rates sufficiently low as they would like. Since there are not enough takers for its bonds and notes to maturity, even the shortest of maturities, the government could only keep those bonds and notes floating if economic agents in search of liquidity would take them as instruments to keep almost instantaneous liquidity (D+1) like the MMMFs permit. How much of the assets of MMMFs in general at the eve of the crisis were treasuries and GSE debt? More than 30% (see footnote 3 of chapter 8). So, if I am right in my reasoning, unless the assets held by MMMFs might *exclude* government debt, we will not escape the temptation for the government (pressing need, one may say) to intervene again. It is clear that Cochrane thinks that if a rule revealing that ETF (exchange-traded fund) MMMFs are equity investments open to losses of principal is introduced, the problem is solved. I would like to invite the reader to think about why that rule has not yet been adopted, and I think, the answer is that monetary authorities are afraid that that would force a reallocation of resources back into high-powered money or, at the very least, into more perfect money substitutes which would significantly limit their capacity to monetize the federal debt (see footnote 8 of chapter 8). If we accept the idea that many instruments may be used as media of exchange, including debt instruments, that will only happen if those debt instruments have "monetary properties" and one of them, obviously, is liquidity as represented by a zero spread between the buy-sell asked price. The moment there is a risk of loss, that spread will no longer be zero and therefore, the debt instruments held (by economic agents in search of keeping a portion of their savings in liquid assets) as if they were money will no longer appeal to that class of investors. So, short-, medium-, or long-term maturity bonds, even if the solvency of the government is not in dispute, have a more limited market among investors willing to hold them to maturity; they may be able to sell them in other, secondary markets if they can get them placed in MMMFs in which the shares have the implicit or even explicit assurance that they may be redeemed anytime in D+1 at its nominal price plus some interests, minimal as they may be today.

Comment 6: Proposals for "bail-in" schemes (2014: 17, 30) seem to be the fairest solution for bankrupted banks, and again, there are precedents in the recent Brazilian banking history. In 1985, at the end of the military regime, some banks propped up by the former regime went bust because the new regime refused to continue to support them. By the same token, the new federal administration refused to bail out their investors, forcing a "bail-in" scheme in which investors with credits above the (small) deposit insurance for both checking accounts and saving accounts then in place, investors in credit instruments issued by the banks such as CDs (certificates of deposit), and investors holding shares of fixed income mutual funds holding as a portion of their portfolios those same credit instruments (something that at that time was legal) got shares of those banks which emerged from bankruptcy no longer with charts to operate as financial intermediaries but only as holding companies, which diminished even further the net present value of those enterprises. An unintended consequence of such action was that, suddenly, investors became much more cautious in their investments and immediately after that what happened was a "flight to security," weakening the Brazilian financial system even further as well as the ability of the government at all levels (local, state, and federal) to float its consolidated debts, since fixed income mutual funds were a major investor in those funds already at that time. Diminished capacity to float public debt, a weakened financial system with resources moving to foreign-owned institutions and local conglomerates, a flight to real assets—all of these contributed to the closing of many avenues to float the public debt, forcing the government to accelerate inflation as a way to fund the deficit and, as a response to that, to implement the first of many "packages" of monetary/banking/fiscal reforms that plagued Brazil starting in 1986 with "haircuts" in financial investments, banking holidays, tax hikes, devaluations, price controls, wage controls, and all sorts of "heterodox" economic measures, until finally a minimum of financial sanity was restored in 1994. In retrospect, the "bail-in" imposed on the investors of those banks, if it was surely not the sole cause, arguably triggered the tailspin into which Brazil fell, resulting in a "lost decade" for the country. So, bail-in schemes may destroy confidence in bank deposits and therefore, while they may be the best solution once you have created a "narrow" banking model, they are not a solution for the run-prone system we have today.

Comment 7: Cochrane suggests government should not subsidize banks in holding/buying "short-term debt" in or for their MMMFs and that the implicit (deposit insurance) and explicit (bailout) guarantees are the major subsidies to debt and that is what creates the incentives for banks to have run-prone assets. I dispute however that it is realistic to think that governments could be limited to the point of being able to "credibly pre-commit against bailouts" (Cochrane, 2014, 18).

Comment 8: I agree that not even floating NAV (net asset value) would solve the problem of having MMMFs draining cash from the banks managing them, as happened with the "Reserve Fund" which "broke the buck" in 2008 because it had a significant position in Lehman Brothers' debt. However, the interpretation that money market mutual funds "are 'banks' with no equity" (Cochrane, 2014: 21) I think is wrong. I agree with Cochrane's prescription that those funds should have a 100% cushion or be allowed to float their values in order to be considered equity investments instead of fixed income investments. However, that is what they (legally/formally) already are: the investors are owners of the shares and the funds should have 100% in assets as a proportion of the capital invested. However, due to the regulation of those funds there is the assumption that they had a "fixed" nominal value. Supported implicitly by the banks managing them, they acquired "monetary properties;" that is, investors chose to invest in those funds as part of their liquid investments, with the expectation that the spread between the ask/sell price of those shares would be zero and therefore, the banks were able to "monetize" the assets held in those funds. In other words, the managers were able to find buyers for those assets who in other circumstances would not be interested in holding them to their maturity at the interest rate they were paying. I would reiterate my comment about Cochrane's suggestions: I don't think limiting MMMFs to the acquisition of short-term treasuries would solve the problem; I actually think that would aggravate the problem. Short-term treasuries are the most perfect candidates to being monetized because they are the closest credit instruments to have monetary properties, but still, they are not "high-powered" money and in a case where the government loses its creditworthiness, again, we will see a run on those funds. So, the only solution would be to have the investors facing the risk of fluctuations in the NAV and *forbid* the money market funds from holding treasuries; with that, they will lose their "monetary properties" and investors will understand that they are short-term investments, but not "perfect" money substitutes. Other than that, we will follow a long path and still end in a place in which funds will hold run-prone assets; and I quote Cochrane in support of that: "Of course, risk and maturity 'transformation' are fallacies. Maturity and credit risk can be sliced and diced, pooled and tranched, but they cannot be removed" (2014: 23).

Comment 9: Cochrane also proposes the transition to run-free banking with the nationalization of all demand deposits (1.5 trillion dollars) and money market mutual funds (2 trillion dollars) by forcing the banks to buy 100% of those resources in treasures like the bank reserves they have today with the Fed.[11] I don't think that a mandate to use all liquidity in the economy to fund the floating of the public debt is a good idea; that would create a number of inefficiencies in the economy and increase uncertainty, as much as the goal of having a 100% deposits in the bank system is a worthwhile one. Anyway, the key issue for Cochrane is that, and I quote: "We have used private intermediation to create a multiplier, to create a larger volume of interest-paying claims that promise payment of a limited amount of government short-term debt. The vast volume of government debt, together with the much lower fundamental economic demand for run-prone assets, means we no longer need this multiplier"

(2014: 25). Or to say it differently, once the production of base money becomes as cheap as it is since base money became purely fiat money, there is no more economic reason to have a banking system designed to "economize" base money at the expense of becoming "run-prone" for creating time mismatches between banking assets and liabilities, or to put it yet another way, for adopting "fractional reserves." The really fundamental question is how to establish a banking system that will create financial instruments that may more adequately represent in the monetary side of the economy the different classes of assets and different classes of claims over those assets in the real sector of the economy.

Comment 10: Cochrane reminds us that "before the lender-of-last-resort function, banks had developed a clearinghouse system to deal with runs and that all posterior interventions such as "deposit insurance, explicit and implicit guarantees, ex-post creditor bailouts, a lender of last resort, asset price manipulation, and other firefighting measures" (2014: 40) had the unintended consequence of making financial markets less stable, which is a good reminder of how much the banking architecture we have today is likely not the one that would have evolved absent government's intervention.

Comment 11: The last topic and perhaps the most polemic (and relevant) in Cochrane's article is the possibility of creating a financial system immune both to private and public default, not by making any substantial change in the financial architecture, but by innovations in public debt, one in which the government would issue long-term debt, possibly in perpetuity, with a clause of reduction or suspension of interest payments "without triggering a legal or formal default," then the risk of government's debt would be transferred to investors and all would be fine. Unfortunately, history shows that perpetuity subject to suspension of interest payments is not a good idea (vide what happened with them at the time of Philip II in Spain) nor is resuming payments at par after some crisis such as a war (in which a significant inflation took effect and the fiscal situation deteriorated instead of improved; vide what happened to the British with their return to the Gold Standard after World War I). Investors will demand a deep discount to buy such a paper and such a paper will never be able to be a "perfect money substitute," therefore, people will be unable to use it as if it were money; but if that is the case, if the government is willing to limit itself to selling bonds that will not be monetized in any shape or form, that will not be used as bank reserves or assets of money market funds in the modern iteration of those schemes, then you don't need to pursue that path which would only increase the cost of the public debt. Perhaps, as a second thought, forbidding the government to issue papers under those conditions would be a good idea (in order to limit public indebtness in peacetime). However, one should not be naïve enough to think that in an emergency the government will not get rid of those limitations. Therefore, and again, the only solution is limiting the indebtness that the government may incur in peacetime to the minimum possible, which is still the best measure to prevent or minimize financial problems in case of emergencies.

11.3.3 Narrow Banking: The View from the Left

The American Monetary Institute, founded in 1996 has been one of the leftist organizations engaged in the public advocacy of narrow banking as inspired by the Chicago Plan from the 1930s and explained in the "Comprehensive Explanation of Monetary Reform" written by its president, Stephen Zarlenga (2011). They propose, by the elimination of fractional reserve banking, a separation between "banking" and "money creation" and with that the restoration of the government's "monopoly" of the latter. One does not need to agree with all the supposed benefits their advocates see in the measure (presented in December 17, 2010 by the former congressman Dennis Kucinich, Democrat-OH, to Congress as the HR 6550 proposed piece of legislation named NEED "National Employment Emergency Act") to agree with the idea of narrow banking, though. But the objective of eliminating entirely the capacity of the banking system to endogenously accommodate changes in the demand for money is one that may be challenged on grounds of monetary theory alone (as will be discussed in the next section), leaving aside all other considerations about the problems of granting such absolute control to the government.

11.3.4 Narrow Banking, Macroprudential Regulations, and Other Ideas to Make Banking More Stable

The idea of narrow banking is usually associated with stringent regulations of the banking industry, a cause of financial repression. It is not necessary for it to be so, but often it is. As a conclusion of his research on the stability of British banks from 1800 to the present age, John Turner sees only two possible paths of reform in order to enhance bank stability: "banks may face stringent economic regulations as they did during the era of financial repression, or bank shareholders must be held to account by making them liable for capital calls in the event of a bank failure. Because the stringent regulations associated with financial repression are highly inefficient due to capital misallocation, holding shareholders to account appears to be only viable policy choice" (Turner, 2014: 11). I would consider such a policy prescription in the category of those skeptical of macroprudential regulations. Still, contrary to Turner (2014: 208) I would argue that narrowing the banks (according to the premise proposed by Buchanan that it does not make sense in a time of fiat money to have banking arrangements leveraging a base money that costs close to nothing to be produced) would be more effective for the purposes of achieving greater stability. A reform eliminating limited liability for bankers and bank shareholders would impose on them a welcomed discipline, as the experience in Brazil since 1964, for instance, has shown. But if banks continue to be seen by governments as instruments to monetize their debts or, at the very least, as dealers of the public debt on which they rely to find investors willing to carry their bonds, and furthermore, if special privileges are granted to the same banks in order to facilitate the fulfillment of their responsibilities as agents of the fisc, it seems doubtful that any reform of bankers' liabilities would have any real consequence, however correct in theoretical terms it may be.

Ideas of narrowing the banks—be that by imposing higher reserve requirements such as the Basel rules; limiting the kind of proprietary trading the banks can do, such as the Volcker rule; reestablishing a separation of commercial and investment banking, like the ideas to resuscitate the Glass-Steagall Act; or radically changing the nature of banking by imposing a strict version of narrow banking by limiting financial institutions' capacity to lend any money against their own balance sheets, transforming them into just fund managers—all have in common a realization that banks are inherently unstable today. Macroprudential regulations, such as increased regulatory oversight and enhanced capital requirements, therefore, may be understood as part of the many forms in which banking activity may be "narrowed" in order to become more stable. In a recent paper Marcelo Prates (Madureira Prates, 2013) pointed out the most cogent reason why macroprudential regulations are expected to fail to prevent future crises: because they assume it is possible for the bureaucrats imposing those regulations to know better the circumstances of capital markets than do the agents themselves and, as a consequence of that, Prates proposes as an alternative to those regulations the definition of rules for banking that would make it in the interest of bankers to act more prudently. If we add to that the arguments already presented in favor of narrow banking, a shape of what a more stable banking system might look like may be envisaged.

11.3.5 The "Fiscal Proviso," Narrow Banking, and Finacial Stability

Calomiris and Haber present their version of the "Fiscal Proviso" asking rhetorically "why are banks so essential to statehood that they are more ubiquitous than armies and taxes? (2014:60). And they answer that referring to the institutional innovations starting in the sixteenth century in which monarchs, merchants and financiers accommodated their interests with the establishment of a chartered bank. That is obviously, not a novel theory; incidentally, they pay tribute to Charles Tilly quoting his phrase "War made the state and the state made war" (2014: 83) but the essential role of chartered banking, new sovereign debt contracts, and fiat money, for the emergence of the nation-state is clearly emphasized by them: "the ability to use banks to mobilize funds on a large scale to serve newly empowered domestic political interests was central to the statecraft of the new era" (2014: 76).

Having explored Calomiris and Haber's thesis and having largely agreed with it, one finishes their book with the impression that they have almost crossed a large river, but have not arrived yet at the other side. That is to say, that the unstable nature of financial arrangements and the political uses of credit allocation, especially given the example of Brazil they use in the book, lead to a natural conclusion that the way to design a more stable financial system is to eliminate the multiple claims over a limited monetary base, and to allow competitive, noncentralized, allocation of credit. In their book, they never reach this other side, but we may do so.

11.3.6 Narrow Banking: A Final Word of Caution

The idea of changing radically the banking architecture by narrowing the banks, by "destroying banking as we know it," is opposed by many serious thinkers. Their argument is that, bad as it is, the current hybrid system we have in which the government creates base money and (mostly private) banks create credit instruments with monetary properties allows for some level of endogenous money creation; that is, the creation of credit by the banks (both funded in previous savings and inflation) is what allows the supply and demand of credit to match without having anyone in control of it (assuming that central banks only pretend to be in control of the demand of credit, since actually, what they do is react to changes in the economy that, by definition, precede their actions). That is not an argument to dismiss lightly, but it is not an argument that cannot be contradicted either. From the comments offered in this section, I think it was made clear that a system of "narrow banking"—as open and competitive as possible in which banks are able to create (fully funded by previous savings) short-term credit instruments with sufficient monetary properties to be used as money, while the government is forbidden both to issue base money and to create public debt in peacetime (although governments may create the unit(s) of account and fiscalize financial markets)—would fit the requirements of a "run-free" system without throwing the baby (of endogenous money creation) out with the water (of fractional reserve banking) and ending with a system more politically managed then the one in place in which precisely that characteristic (of being politically run) is the cause of its most important defects.

11.4 THE FUTURE OF MONEY

One of the main themes of this book is the evolution of money from coined metals into paper notes representative of coined money, and the evolution from those into fiat money and bank accounts representative of fiat money.

Since 1971, money all around the world is only fiat money; and due to technological innovations, even banknotes and checks, considered as instruments to move bank credits, have been replaced by electronic transactions.[12]

This stage of further abstraction has been the reality for many years now and inquiries into "the changing nature of money and banking in the information age" have been done for more than a decade. The works collected by James A. Dorn in his 1997 book on *The Future of Money in the Information Age* are one good example.

By and large, there is no disagreement between the many conclusions presented in Dorn's book and what is discussed in this chapter. The goal with the present exposition is perhaps to go further or, to put it another way, to put conceivable further developments in money in the perspective of the trend towards abstraction already mentioned and not to inquire about what possibly, through the lens of acute spectators gathered by Dorn in 1987, the future of money in the information era will be. In chapter 2, Larry White notes that e-money is not money of a different nature from the fiat money into which it is convertible (Dorn, 1997: 3); but what if banknotes disappear entirely? What if US dollars now, hypothetically, are only "credits"[13] in the bank accounts and become the only units of account, segregated from the actual media of exchange?

White shows that even if all analog currency disappears from circulation, still there will be a monetary "base" composed of bank deposits with the Fed (Dorn, 1997: 18). This would be yet another step towards more abstract forms of money but, this description is still a description about a possible future in which there would be a monetary "base," depicts a future in which all quasi-money assets would ultimately be claims on a very narrow monetary stock that would represent simultaneously the unit of account and the medium of exchange.

What remains to be seen is if it is possible to have a monetary system in the future in which the monetary "base" has shrunk to zero, the money becoming split into a unit of account with no material existence and one medium or many media of exchange. In sum, could the credit card substitute for banknotes? Is this the path to a system of separation between the medium of exchange and the unit of account such as Yeager's and Greenfield's BFH monetary system? Could money become only a unit of account, a standard of value, and no longer a medium of exchange? Or will money always be the medium of exchange but perhaps no longer the unit of account, the standard of value?[14]

In the United States today, a middle-class citizen probably makes more than 95% of the value of his or her economic transactions without using dollar bills. The amount of money in this sense of actual banknotes in proportion to all transactions cleared by "money" is, therefore, minimal.

According with data provided by the Fed,[15] the ratio between currency held by the public and M2 is approximately 1/10. But, although in April 2008 M1 was approximately $1.4 trillion, more than half of which consisted of currency, according to the New York Fed, as much as two-thirds of US currency in circulation is estimated to be held outside the United States (and all currency held by the public is included in the money supply). Therefore, using the ratio between currency held inside the United States and M2 as a proxy for the relation of transactions cleared by banknotes and the ones cleared by other forms of money and quasi-money, the ratio is 3.5%.

In the near future, can money cease to exist physically, cease to be a medium of exchange and become only a unit of exchange, a standard of value? I think that we are pretty close to it. Suppose that next Friday, the Fed determined that all money holders should go to the banks and deposit all bills and coins in their possession, because in the following week, all banknotes and coins would cease being legal tender. From then on, all economic agents, the public in general, would be able to do economic transactions using only credit cards, debit cards, and checks. All the accounting would continue to be made in US dollars.

As pointed out by Menger (Menger, 1994: 261) and Mises (Mises, 1981: 44), all merchandises have a certain level of liquidity and only the merchandise with the most liquidity prevails as a monetary merchandise. On the other hand, at any given time, a certain amount of a monetary merchandise is necessary as medium for the transactions in society in order to allow individuals the benefits of the labor division. This amount is determined by real conditions in the economy, factoring in psychological conditions, and it is expressed in the value attributed to the monetary merchandise.

Suppose that all economic agents in the United States, for example, to generate a GNP of, say, $15 trillion in 2010, required $1.5 trillion in money (M1) in order to clear all of their economic transactions. Now, if a change in the real economy happens and the demand for "liquidity" (as measured by M1) increases to $1.55 trillion or decreases to $1.45 trillion, regardless of the reason for this change (it may be a change in technology, in habits, et cetera), the fact is that the demand to hold money has changed.

Consider what would happen today: the Fed, as the monopolistic provider of money and having the authority to adjust the required amount of money, would correct the imbalance between the stock and the demand for holding money, but if the Fed lacked the ability or, more likely, the information and the time to act upon the available information, the adjustment would happen only imperfectly.

But in our future "without money," would the demand for liquidity disappear? I don't think so. In a world in which the unit of account becomes completely abstract, in which it is totally separated from the media of exchange, a demand for a medium of exchange (and I cannot think of a better definition of liquidity) will still exist.

The generally accepted medium of exchange is representative of a "right" to ready access to the entire stock of available goods in a monetary society. It is representative of a right to dispose immediately of the existing goods. Since the stock of existing goods is limited at any given time, and also at any given moment, there is a rate at which the availability of goods changes over time, the amount of medium of exchange is limited, although it may increase slowly and steadily in a thriving society.

But in a society in which the money became purely abstract and totally dissociated from the unit of account, how would changes in the medium of exchange happen?[16]

Suppose that the medium of exchange became only electronic transactions nominated in a unit of account, a purely abstract standard of value that, for the sake of simplification, we continue to call "dollar," but not a single dollar banknote would exist anymore. How, in the course of the economic transactions of daily life, could one increase his or her "credits" in the bank? How could the total stock of "credits" be increased?

The stock of securities in which the liquid capital of the community is invested would become "a" *monetary merchandise,* but not the unit of account. Without bills the next most liquid assets after banknotes would perform the function of sole monetary merchandise, which today would be the preferred assets for agents that are satisfied with "Day + 1" liquidity such as money market mutual funds.

There is, however, a relevant issue in regard to the definition of money that must be explicitly addressed at this time. As explained in the previous paragraph, in this hypothetical scenario "without money," in which the monetary base has shrunk to zero, liquid claims and equities such as bank accounts and money market funds would become the media of exchange. In that scenario, I argue that money market funds, although they represent an equity investment and not a cash claim, must be considered as part of the money supply. Actually, although recognizing that I am in a minority position, and against the best judgment of Salerno (Salerno, 1987: 1–6) and Shostak (Shostak, 2000: 69–76) who do not consider them as part of the TMS (**True Money Supply**), I think that even under our current monetary arrangements, MMMFs should be considered part of the money supply as argued by Haymond (Haymond, 2000: 53–68). For me his position is coherent with the GAMOE definition; and, therefore, money parked in MMMFs should be considered part of the money supply in theory as it is in practice.[17] If we consider that today the total liquid assets of the community (United States) to the point they start losing monetary properties is, say, M3 (we must be arbitrary), then the "actual money" (M0) among all monetary assets is no more than 10%. What does that mean? It means that, today, 90% of the "money" holders prefer other monetary assets to money proper. The time for a monetary system in which the unit of account will be entirely abstract and all monetary merchandise will be securities is very close. I think that the evolution to that even more abstract form of money is unstoppable.

One reason for this is because of the proper nature of money as described by Simmel and discussed in this work. But how does that operate? Maybe the decision by economic agents to have most of their liquidity not in money, but in money equivalents such as bonds, is seen as a way to hold better money, one that cannot be inflated as easily as fiat money today (bonds pay interest, so keeping liquidity in money market funds is better than keeping it in checking accounts).

11.4.1What Determines the Value of a Purely Abstract Dollar? Or, Be Careful What You Wish For

In fact, thinking again about the hypothetical society "without money," it would be harder (but not impossible) to inflate the stock of the medium of exchange without the possibility of printing bills.[18] But what would be the value of the US dollar on Monday, the first working day after our hypothetical day in which all banknotes (and checks, for that matter) were abolished? Unlike the moment that the US dollar ceased to be redeemable in gold and a huge inflation in the monetary stock happened, I think that the value of the US dollar would remain more or less the same as it was on the previous Friday, but only under certain conditions.

In a society where the unit of account is purely abstract and it is only a "credit" in a bank account, the stock of liquid capital in society is represented by the sum of all liquid credits (that is, ones tradable in an equivalent of a money market) at any given time. In this sort of monetary arrangement, the commercial banks really become money "creators," not because they are allowed to "issue" money, but because of their role as financial intermediaries.

For example, today, whenever one transfers money from a money market account to a checking account in order to make some commercial transaction that will imply "withdrawing" money from his account and "depositing" it in someone else's account, first the bank needs to "sell" the securities backing the money market investment, that is, to find someone willing to keep the money in the bank available to be loaned to a third person through the intermediation of the bank. Every time someone creates some wealth through the production and sale of goods or services, the entire chain of commercial operations generates new "credits" through the financial intermediation of those operations.

For instance, suppose that the Producer "P" will sell services to retailer "R" worth $1,000 to be paid in a month, but he needs to use a share of the proceeds of that sale to pay his suppliers, all of them bought from wholesaler "W." What does he do? He goes to the bank and discounts the $1,000 bill of exchange against "R" receiving, say, $800 in order to pay "W." In order to simplify our example, suppose that "W" deposits the proceeds with the bank, buying a thirty-day Certificate of Deposit. At the end of the month, "R" pays the bill, "P" pays the bank and keeps his net margin of, say, $100 invested with the bank for his retirement.

After the clearing of these transactions, the net worth of "P" and of the community as a whole has increased by $100, duly deposited with the bank, which at the beginning of the cycle had $800 to loan and at the end has $900 to loan. The increase in the wealth of the community was able to generate a "credit" that may be deposited and used by the banks, through regular commercial loans.

However, this mechanism only holds if there is in force a prohibition on the issuing of new debt by the government in order to finance current expenses (otherwise, we would be talking about a scenario similar to White's).

Investments may go sour, consumers may go bankrupt, and these unfortunate events will diminish the available wealth of society and eventually some of the "credits" on the bank balance sheets will need to be written off.[19] But when the government finances current expenses adding more debt to the existing stock, it is increasing the quantity of quasi-money in the economy without a corresponding increase of available goods.

11.4.2 Is Completely Abstract Money a Cure for Inflation?

Does this mean inflation will no longer be a threat? Not necessarily; the threat of inflation will disappear only under the conditions mentioned before.[20] Because the government has such economic power, it can flood the market with its debts, it can force its employees and contractors to accept its promises to pay nominated in the unit of exchange and with these actions generate the devaluation of the standard of value. To summarize, if base money comes to zero and the stock of money becomes only what is today quasi-money, then inflating the stock of quasi-money will have the same effects as it has today.

Because money is so interwoven with the social fabric, because money can only perform the maximum potential of its proper function when society abandons the pursuit of political goals through money, the only moment in which we could have proper money is in the future when: central banks are abolished; currency is privately issued; banks are deregulated; public debt is paid and new public debt is forbidden; and the government is constitutionally and effectively limited to some safe percentage of the GNP like 15% (at all levels), for example.[21]

Aside from that institutional arrangement in which society would expect from money only what is proper in it, money will always be subjected to being used as a political tool to achieve governmental ends and not purely the best medium of exchange possible, which is the best money possible in order to enhance productivity, the best currency possible in order to allow individuals an efficient tool for more easily achieving their goals.

11.4.3 The BFH System

In which aspects does the monetary system described above diverge from the BFH system? The BFH system implies the elimination of fiat money as the unit of account and medium of exchange. The role of unit of account would be performed by a "price index," the value of some bundle of commodities, and the medium of exchange, actually media of exchange, would be liquid, tradable assets, such as bonds and shares in mutual funds. The system is not a system of "monetary bigamy" in which there are two units of account, one constant in nominal terms that happens also to be the medium of exchange, and the other constant in real terms (the price index); as in the experiences of some developing countries during the last decades of the twentieth century with indexation, notably Brazil and Israel (Yeager, 1997: 369). According to the proposed system, the new unit of account, tentatively named "U," representing the price of the bundle of commodities, would be the only unit of account (Yeager, 1997: 413).

Although this work is not the proper place to discuss the BFH system in detail, nonetheless, we are aware of some of the criticisms raised against Yeager's proposal. For instance, Steven Horwitz quotes Larry White's (1989) critique of the BFH system with the argument that the cleavage between the unit of account and the medium of exchange tends to fail in practice (Horwitz, 2010: 20).The reason they offered is that these functions tend to evolve together, they need government intervention, and they would not prosper in a competitive environment. Against that we can point to the actual cases of dissociation in Brazil and Israel. In these particular cases, dissociation works in producing more stability of value for the unit of account than the available instruments for indirect exchanges with those functions integrated. No one was forced to use the separated unit of account in his or her dealings; they just had an interest in doing so. Therefore, the fact that these functions have so far coevolved together does not preclude the possibility that they may evolve separately in the future if the right circumstances arise to make that a better option for economic agents.

Let's suppose that the unit of account of choice in a competitive environment becomes the weight of gold by the metric system (1 gram, 10 grams, and so on) and in a free banking environment, issuers are allowed to produce media of exchange that, although backed by other assets, are nominated in gold. Would that arrangement not be competitive?[22] In *Explorations in the New Monetary Economics*, Tyler Cowen and Randall Kroszner mention three price incentives for the reemergence of monetary separation (Cowen and Kroszner, 1994: 30): first, the desire to capture monetary returns on interest-bearing media of exchange; second, the cost of gathering information about the quality of different media of exchange; and third they argue that differences in the bid-ask spreads does not disappear when the unit of account and the medium of exchange are unified; they simply are charged as fees paid to the financial intermediaries. They explain this last incentive as follows:

> Explicit bid-ask spreads have not prevented the use of return-bearing securities for transactions even in today's world. Money market funds and Cash Management Accounts, for instance, are used by many individuals for ordinary checking purposes. The superior returns on money market funds (compared with demand deposits) more than compensate for the loss on bid-ask spread incurred when assets are bought and sold. That is, the explicit bid-ask spread is often less costly than the implicit fee that must be paid for its removal. (Cowen and Kroszner, 1994: 33)

Anyway, for our purposes suffice it to say that the BFH system resembles the monetary system with a purely abstract dollar described above in regard to the elimination of fiat money and the adoption of money market funds as media of exchange. It differs in the sense that it anchors the value of the unit of account to the daily prices of a bundle of commodities.

Both the BFH system and the system of a purely abstract dollar are proposals for a more abstract monetary arrangement, one in which the link to a physical paper money is severed. It is not to say, however, that only separation of (monetary) functions is able to keep the price level stable. As pointed out by Boianovsky, the stabilization of the price level by the manipulation of the interest rate by the central bank, even in a "pure credit economy," was already described by Wicksell in *Interest and Prices* (Boianovsky, 1998: 582). The difference between what Wicksell describes and what is proposed by "New Monetary Economics" (NME), aside from the fact that in the latter there is a separation of monetary functions, is that in the former, in order to keep the price level constant, interest rates must be raised in order to quench the market of "excess" liquidity, resulting in "exogenous" changes in the money supply that will have consequences in the level of economic activity. Under a system of separation of functions as proposed by NME, in which the government does not issue a medium of exchange, attempts by government and private companies to float more bonds than what the market is willing to absorb may likewise have consequences for the interest rates practiced in the market, but that is not necessary to keep prices stable since the unit of account is not the medium of exchange but a more or less abstract unit, such as a price index of a certain bundle of goods and services. In the kind of fiat money economy we have today that precisely corresponds to Wicksell's "pure credit economy," except for the fact that implicit in his reasoning was the gold standard of his time (Boianovsky, 1998: 582), the only way for the central bank to try to keep the price level stable is by manipulations of the interest rate, which may result in deleterious effects for the level of economic activity, while under separation of functions, that would not be the case.

11.4.4 Bitcoin and the Future of Money

The introduction of cryptocurrencies such as bitcoin has been an interesting recent phenomenon. Appropriately described by George Selgin as "Synthetic commodity money" (Selgin, 2013) bitcoin has being favored by libertarians as a "nonstate" alternative for the money supply. Because bitcoins are "free of the power of the state" (Velde, 2013: 3), they have found a "niche" in the demand for money as an instrument to circumvent government controls, being those capital controls in Cyprus or mainland China, or to clear illegal transactions, and that has been the main drive of its wild fluctuations. Thinking about the attributes of good money discussed in this work, the lack of an "ultimate" utility, such as to pay taxes, the natural unwillingness of governments to facilitate its use as money, its fiduciary character, and its relative small stock has made bitcoin value utterly dependent on the demand for people trying to avoid one government control or another and making the currency a speculative asset of high risk.

The unwillingness of governments to foster the monetary properties of currencies they have not issued themselves becomes evident in other cases such as the case of the Liberty Dollars according to Seth Lipsky ("A Monetary Gadfly in an Age of Fiat Money," in *Wall Street Journal*, December 2, 2014).

Speculation aside, the relative success of bitcoin as a medium of exchange has raised some interesting theoretical questions, such as the validity of Mises' regression theorem. If the theorem is understood as saying that the objective value of money (its purchasing power) can always be traced to the intrinsic value of a commodity in which previously a given currency was redeemable, it may be said that bitcoin came to disprove that; however, that would be a mistake. The proper interpretation of the theorem is that the purchasing power of any medium of exchange is subjectively determined (or rather, intersubjectively determined), that is, by the subjective evaluation of all agents willing to use that money. So, if there is a utility for bitcoin, such as evading government controls, it will get some "objective" value in the marketplace, that is, it will have some purchasing power.

The other side of the coin, so to speak, of bitcoins are the proposals for abolishing notes and coins altogether (already discussed in section IV.11.4). One of the benefits for the proposal of phasing out banknotes and coins is exactly that, to prevent the kind of use that has given to bitcoin its purchasing power, to clear illegal transactions, as a recent article by Kenneth Rogoff has proposed (Rogoff, 2014).

11.4.5 The Development of a Monetary System under Laissez-Faire

The exposition we have presented so far has been partially an exposition of historical events, and partly an exploration of theoretical proposals. We have conducted these discussions without always differentiating those that would require overcoming the key aspect of reality—that the sovereign has interest in regulating money and banking—from other scenarios in which that change was not considered. This paragraph will describe a path for monetary evolution under laissez-faire as proposed by Kevin Dowd in his paper "The Invisible Hand and the Evolution of the Monetary System" (2000: 139–156). In it there are references to Huerta de Soto's laissez-faire proposal for monetary reform (2006: 736–744) and also Dowd's theoretical laissez-faire model. The interesting aspect of Dowd's proposal is that his conclusion about the evolutionary developments of the monetary institutions in a regime of natural liberty would end with roughly the same arrangements envisaged in this concluding chapter for money and banking, taking into consideration government intervention guided by the fiscal proviso, properly understood (that is, the arrangements that would best enhance the ready availability of financial resources by the government in case of emergencies). The stages of Dowd's monetary evolution may be summarized as presented in table 11.1 (Dowd, 2000: 153):

Another perspective about how a monetary system would look without coercion is given by Simpson (2014b: 114) who argues that government, and not banks, is responsible for the creation of money through fractional reserve banking, for allowing that to happen and supporting banks is the consequence of such behavior. The very imposition of fiat money is entirely attributed to governments. As a logical conclusion of his reasoning, he argues that a free market monetary system would move in the direction of 100% reserves (2014b: 125). I would agree that absent coercion, more stable monetary systems would emerge; however, the historical experience when banking was least regulated or intervened with (say, in England before Peel's Act) was one of higher reserves comparatively with later moments, but a far cry from 100%. So, the general as-

Table 11.1. The Stages of Development of the Monetary System under Laissez-Faire

Stages of Development	Key Features	Comments
Coinage	Gold as MOE Gold as MOA/UA	Use of gold coins as full-bodied money
Directly—convertible Gold Standard	Bank currency as MOE Gold as MOA/UA/anchor Gold as MOR	Textbook gold standard Bank currency displaces coins as MOE
Indirectly—convertible Gold Standard	Bank currency as MOE Gold as MOA/UA/anchor Financial assets as MOR	Financial assets replace gold as MOR
Indirectly—convertible Commodity—Basket Standard	Bank currency as MOE Commodity basket as MOA/UA/anchor Financial assets as MOR	Commodity basket replaces gold as MOA/UA/anchor Gold has no monetary role

sumption seems correct, the tendency under less coercion is towards more inherently stable money, even if it never reaches the limit of the equation.

11.5 THE GOLD STANDARD IS NOT AN ADEQUATE ALTERNATIVE TO THE CURRENT MONETARY PROBLEMS

11.5.1 Introduction

With this section I intend to argue that neither our current monetary systems of national legal tender fiat money nor any variation of the gold standard are the answer for an ideal monetary system. The problem with those systems is that the medium of exchange and the unit of account are the same. Because of that duplicity of functions, a system which may have features adequate to fulfill one of those functions may not have the features adequate to perform the other function, and that is what happens with fiat money and gold standard systems alike. While the flexibility of the money supply under fiat money arrangements is damaging for price stability, but may be good to supply a changing demand for money the (relatively lower) flexibility of the money supply under gold standard arrangements is good for price stability, but it makes the system exposed to violent ruptures when there are sudden increases in the demand for money. Therefore, the argument in this chapter is that if it is properly understood that the deficiencies of those systems rely on a key element of their institutional design (that is, the simultaneous functions of medium of exchange and unit of account that modern monies perform), the search for an ideal monetary system should lead to a different institutional arrangement and we will discuss which one it is.

11.5.2 The Dimension of Flexibility in the Money Supply

One of the dimensions along which monetary systems may vary is how flexible the money supply is under each arrangement. But before going forward, note that when we discuss flexibility of the money supply, we may use the concept with two different meanings.

The first meaning is the literal sense of flexibility. In this sense, at one extreme of the continuum there would be a system with a "numerus clausus" amount of "money" as referred to by Alexander Del Mar. There will be, say, an issuance of one million bills of one "dollar" and that number cannot be changed, and nothing else will be accepted as money. At the opposite extreme, there will be a monetary system with no restrictions whatsoever on the production of money, no monopoly of the money supply, no legal tender laws, and no banking rules in regard to the expansion of the money multiplier. However, it is not in this sense that we usually talk about flexibility in the money supply; commonly, we use the concept of flexibility to classify how much the changes in the money supply are determined by conscious and centralized human decision; that is, by fiat. In this second sense, the two monetary systems that represent the extremes in regard to how much flexibility to have in the money supply are, at one extreme, an inflexible gold standard and, at the other extreme, a national fiat money with forced tender and central banking.

These two extremes are ideal types and we may define them as follows:

A totally inflexible commodity standard is the system that perhaps existed in Greece and Rome during Classical Antiquity in which the media of exchange were gold and silver coins and there were no banknotes or other forms of credit money. The money supply was limited to the existence of bullion and the mining production of precious metals. Even under that system, one may note, there was the possibility of increasing the money supply by imports of bullion and coin and by the mining production, and nonmonetized forms of credit were available although monetized forms of credit did not exist; and therefore, even under that most inflexible of the conceivable systems, it is true that money could not be created by fiat, but still the supply of a medium for indirect exchanges[23] was not totally inflexible in the first sense.

We may also note that a monetary system with 100% reserve requirement over bank deposits, incidentally, a system that has never existed in practice, would be more flexible in the supply of money than the pure metallic of gold just described, to the extent that, for instance, at the very least, time-deposits may be monetized through instruments such as money market mutual funds (MMMFs).

The monetary system with the most flexible money supply conceivable in this second sense is one in which the money is supplied monopolistically by the government, that money is not only legal tender but forced tender as well (that is, not only it is good to clear all payments but also it is the only way to clear payments in the given jurisdiction), the currency is not convertible into other currencies, there are capital controls, and banking regulations give discretion to the monetary and fiscal authorities to mobilize as much of the existing savings as they wish, which allows them to some extent to monetize public debt. It is important to note that even in this most flexible of the systems, the money supply still faces constraints; as much as the demand for money can be manipulated, it cannot be controlled, and therefore, there is a limit to how much money can be produced without collapsing the monetary system. In regard to actual monetary systems, all of them have features that allow us to classify them along that dimension either closer to one extreme or to the other, and those in existence today are very close to the extreme of a flexible supply in both senses of unlimited variations and total discretion. Flexibility of the money supply in the second sense, that is, the extent to which the monetary authorities have discretion to make changes in the money supply is not necessarily a bad thing; and its contrary is not necessarily a good thing. That is, a supply of money that varies as little as possible (first sense) and its variations, which do occur, occur most often as a consequence of the unconscious sum of individual decisions and not by human design (second sense).

The first argument against flexibility in the money supply is that it will be abused and more money will be produced than the money holders have interest to hold, therefore the value of money will be diluted. There are other arguments against a flexible money supply, but the one just mentioned suffices to impinge on it. Let's mention now an argument against an inflexible money supply. Let's assume that the demand for money may vary under some circumstances rather dramatically. It may be a war or other catastrophe that results in great anxiety about the future, and with that comes an increased demand for money. A relatively constant amount of money chased by a sudden increased demand will force fire sales and economic disruption. Even under relatively calm circumstances, a relatively inflexible monetary supply is not necessarily one that would adjust automatically to changes in the demand for money without somewhat important changes in money value. Because we are using the concept of (in)flexibility of the money supply in the sense of not being subject to human design, that does not mean that the other meaning never plays out. A system that would attend perfectly the "demands of trade,"[24] that is, that would match perfectly and automatically the supply and demand for money is not necessarily one in which the supply of money is determined by the vagaries of gold mining, for instance. A commodity constraint is, it is true, a limitation on the supply of money, but that will not result in an automatically "perfect" supply of money.

So, by now we can conclude that the monetary system that provides the "ideal" supply of money is not necessarily one that has no flexibility (in the literal sense), nor one in which there is total discretion in money production, but one in which the supply of money is the closest possible to the actual demand for money at any given time at a stable value.

NOTES

1. In his 1791 *Report on the Subject of a Mint,* presented to Congress, the first American Treasury secretary Alexander Hamilton advocates the establishment of a mint basically for the government to establish a standard coin not subject to having its metal content altered by a foreign mint and to avoid the cost of transactions resulting from duometallism, that is, the parallel use of gold and silver without a fixed parity (Viera, 1997: 98). That was the justification for the 1792 Coinage Act with which the provisions of the constitution regarding money were regulated and a fixed parity of 15 to 1 between silver and gold was established.

2. The ways in which an issuer promotes and maintains the value of fiat money and therefore the desire of the economic agents to hold cash balances was discussed in many passages throughout this dissertation; basically, it is through the utility that economic agents derive from the use of a given fiat currency that its value may be established. Such utility results mainly from laws establishing given currencies as legal or forced tender in given jurisdictions, not only for transactions among private individuals but also as a means of payment of taxes, which may make them valuable inclusively outside such jurisdictions. A relatively prudent management on the one hand of its supply, and on other hand of the possibilities for its use may result in the maintenance of a relatively stable or at least predictably changing value for long periods of time. One may be surprised by the demand to hold cash balances in US dollars, yens, or euros, but the fact is that there is such demand and the value of those currencies, although subject to discretionary actions of political agents, has not melted down like many Latin American currencies.

3. It is impossible for any government to conjure real savings from the printing machine. It is impossible for any government to mobilize more savings than the amount in existence by management of the money supply. What remains to be seen is if there is a case for the full mobilization of existing savings through government backing of the bank system; such investigation, however, goes well beyond the scope of this work. However, as was argued in chapter 9 about the likely result in terms of the allocation of savings for productive investments under an institutional setting requiring a 100% reserve, given the proper incentives of profit maximization, bankers and depositors will tend to narrow time mismatches in the absence of a lender of last resort or government-sponsored warranties for inflationary credit creation by the banks.

4. I refer to the classification offered by Dr. Kurt Schuler in his 1996 work *Should Developing Countries Have Central Banks?* (1996) in which he describes a monetary system with a central bank and describes the alternatives. Schuler describes eight alternatives to the central bank system, as follows: 1) The Currency Board (frequent in British colonies); 2) the Monetary Institute (a monetary authority in-between a currency board and a central bank, common in French colonies); 3) The Private Commercial Bank with Monopoly Note Issue (examples given by Schuler are the French *Banque de l'Indochine* and the Portuguese *Banco Nacional Ultramarino*); 4) Free Banking ("a system of competitive issue of notes and deposits, with low legal barriers to entry into the banking business and few legal constraints on bank operations;" according to Schuler,

this system, common during the eighteenth and nineteenth centuries, became extinct in 1962 when Namibia adopted the currency issued in South Africa. True to this implicit criterion, the system in Panama is not one of free banking, since it adopts the currency issued by a central bank elsewhere; 5) Foreign Currency ("Dollarization"), and the example given by Schuler is Panama; 6) Occupation Currency, as utilized shortly after World War II when the currency of the occupying country was in use; 7) The "Free-Issue" System as adopted in Hong Kong from 1973–1983 when a floating exchange rate and no monetary authority was in place until an exchange-rate crisis provoked a return to a currency board system in order to reestablish confidence; and 8) Direct Government Currency Issue, a system similar to the one in which the central bank has no independence. Finally, the Central Bank System is described as one in which there is a monetary authority with some level of independence in the management of the monetary policy (1996: 15). Schuler's work is the remarkable result of extensive research and deals with the key characteristics of the different monetary systems. Since, to my understanding, the classification that he offers in his work has the sole purpose of differentiating the Central Bank System from the existing and possible alternatives, it cannot be blamed for being unsystematic because, for the purpose of his book, the classification that he proposes fulfills its function.

5. In April 2001, the Argentinean government changed the charter of the Central Bank of Argentina. In essence they changed the rules of their currency board, admitting from that moment on a higher proportion than the previously existing one of one-third of Argentinean government-issued bonds nominated in US dollars as part of their reserves supporting the value of the redeemable Argentinean pesos at the parity of one peso to one dollar. With that change they continued to be under a "Currency Board System;" however, obviously, the system was no longer the same and the credibility that it initially commanded started to be eroded.

6. A fiat currency may be considered "hard currency" based on the confidence that the public has that the issuer will keep its value relatively stable and not based on its being redeemable or not. Among different fiat currencies there is a difference in the degree of confidence enjoyed by some of those currencies that are not a difference in their essence; for example, the US dollar is a fiat currency and not a fiduciary currency and to this day it is still considered a "hard" currency. Depending on the foreign exchange regime in practice, a fiat currency can enjoy great confidence on the part of money holders.

7. The arguments in favor of a banking system with a 100% reserve requirement are compelling. As will be argued later in this chapter, the tendency towards a purely abstract unit of account implies the adoption of a monetary system in which the banks would only operate under such requirement. Therefore, it may be advocated that the soundness of those arguments will be vindicated as a consequence of the natural evolution of monetary institutions when the movement towards abstract money runs its course. Imposing this requirement, however, may be understood as in contradiction with the principles of maximum liberty, although the case for such a requirement in the case of fiduciary commodity and fiat money may be made. As pointed out by Huerta de Soto (2006: 769), since British Parliament with Peel's Act of 1844 neglected to impose a 100% reserve requirement, the prevailing monetary systems in the world have been ones with central banking (at least a de facto one) and fractional reserves. So, it is difficult to know if, in the absence of a central bank and by stripping the national governments of their capacity to manipulate money markets through their treasuries (by imposing limits to their indebtedness and spending), the "insurance" costs for fractional banking would not be so great as to make a 100% reserve requirement cost effective.

8. Miguel Ángel Alonso Neira has in his book *Teoría Económica de las Crisis Monetarias y Financieras y de los Controles de Capital* a table with the advantages and drawbacks of different foreign exchange policies (Alonso Neira, 2004: 224) as an illustration of the relation between foreign exchange policy and monetary policy as a whole.

9. Perhaps, in order to clarify the distinctions among the different regimes of foreign exchange, we can call attention to the difference between the Canadian model of "free exchange" in which the Canadian central bank is constrained to intervene in the foreign exchange rate only indirectly through changes in the interest rates, and the Chilean model in which its central bank is mandated to not intervene in the foreign exchange unless in "exceptional" circumstances; in our classification of different systems in the next section, both systems are considered among the few with "free exchange."

10. The proposal of a unit of account physically defined in terms of a basket of commodities and not by the regulation of the quantity of the medium of exchange or its redeemability, as in the "BFH" system proposed by Yeager and Greenfield, is clearly a serious contender to be the standard of value of choice under a regime of dissociation (Yeager 1997: 367).

11. Such proposals resemble Huerta de Soto's proposed transition to a 100% banking system (2006: 736–744).

12. The obvious interest of governments around the world to exercise control over the possession of money must be considered an important factor inducing money holders to keep their liquidity in forms of money like bank deposits and to do their transactions in ways traceable by the governments such as electronic transactions. The instruments for such inducements have been laws against money-laundering and anti-terror laws, but the main consequence of governments' ability to trace every single transaction and to know to the last cent the amount of money that any individual possesses is the availability of a very powerful tool of social control in the hands of governments. The extent to which the movement away from physical money and physical transactions has been induced by governments may be difficult to be quantified but cannot be denied.

13. Credit here is being used to mean a claim against the bank, an entry on its ledger as a liability, and not a credit operation.

14. The hypothesis of a banking system without reserves, albeit conceived of at a time that reserves were kept in bullion, was already contemplated by Wicksell and the discussion of what would happen under those circumstances was part of his "conversation" with Fisher. Not that any would recommend that as sound monetary policy, since, as described by Boianovsky, Fisher agreed with Wicksell that "under a pure credit economy money becomes endogenous and the traditional quantity theory of money does not hold" (Boianovsky, 2013: 20). That may be understood in two ways, the first is that without a gold standard there is no limit to what the central bank can do; the second, is that the price level becomes dependent on the interest rate level. For us living today in a "pure credit economy" (that is, with fiat money only), that is not much of a revelation, but, in theoretical terms, it gives us an idea about what monetary policy would look like in a system where the only media of exchange were credit instruments and M0 would be zero. Like today, the price level would be determined not by the quantity of money (in sensu stricto) but by the interest rate.

15. "The Money Supply," Federal Reserve Bank of New York, accessed March 20, 2015. http://www.newyorkfed.org/aboutthefed/fedpoint/fed49.html.

16. The case of "ideal money" in the Middle Ages and the cases of almost complete indexation in Brazil (and Israel) offer a response to that question. An abstract unit of account with constant value may exist while the supply of the medium or media of exchange may continue even in an inflationary way. For the purposes of the reasoning we are trying to develop here, the important aspect to keep in mind is that if money proper ceases to exist and the unit of account becomes purely abstract, the instruments for indirect exchanges will become what before were forms of quasi-money or other forms of quasi-money that will be created by the agents or by the government.

17. It is noteworthy however, to mention that money market mutual funds (MMMFs) command trust until they don't, something already mentioned at footnote 2 of chapter 8. The current financial crisis reached its peak at the end of 2008, when in a matter of hours about two trillion dollars were moved from MMMFs to checking

accounts, since many investors realized that the assets in which some MMMFs were invested were MBS (mortgage-backed securities) guaranteed by Fannie Mae and Freddy Mac, two GSEs (government-sponsored enterprises) which at that time had an "implicit" guarantee from the US Treasury. Doubts about the willingness of the US government to back such entities made their corporate debt, if briefly, lose its status as quasi-T-bills. That would imply having those titles traded at a discount, and therefore, the MMMFs held by investors in such securities would no longer be redeemed au pair, resulting in the above-mentioned massive withdrawals. It was only with the influx of capital by the US government in those entities transforming them into GOE (government-owned enterprises) and a number of other initiatives to support the banks in their efforts to sustain the au pair value of their MMMFs that the crisis of confidence was overcome. Many lessons can be drawn from that episode, but in regard to the topic of the present discussion, the fact is that investors perceived MMMFs as money, and the banks, regulators, and financial authorities did not dare to allow the market to think otherwise. Before the crisis, investors perceived some of the assets usually held by the MMMFs as having "monetary properties" of certainty and liquidity, but with the crisis, the assets lost the confidence of the investors, and with that, the same thing happened with the MMMFs holding them or thought to be holding them.

18. The scenario discussed by White in Dorn's book is one in which there is a monetary base, a monetary base no longer represented by paper money in the hands of the public plus deposits with the Fed, but only the latter. Under that scenario, the Fed would be able to increase the monetary base simply by crediting third parties, the US government, for instance, in their accounts. White's scenario is somewhat different from what I am trying to describe in this paragraph. The "purely abstract" US dollar would be purely a unit of account and the amount of media of exchange could not be increased in quantity by government's fiat by other means than by increasing the public debt. If the monetary base ceases to exist, the Fed will no longer be able to "credit" the Treasury with deposits on its balance sheet.

19. That is what Steven Horwitz calls a "productivity norm." Horwitz argues that the "productivity norm" is more important than predictability (by keeping the price level constant); that is, if the productivity goes down, say, because of war, it is more important for prices to reflect that than to try to keep prices stable (Horwitz, 2010: 22). Therefore, for Horwitz, the monetary arrangements ideally should have some automatic mechanism to accommodate reductions in the stock of money in case of reductions in productivity (on that see also the already-mentioned Selgin, 1997).

20. Abstract money is not equivalent to constant money. In this work it is argued that money at the time of the inflexible standard was relatively more stable in value than other commodities and that equivalent relative stability may be generated again by the reintroduction of the gold standard or by the adoption of price indexes as units of account. But relative stability does not mean absolute stability, does not mean constancy. In that the position argued in this dissertation differs from the lesson of Ferdinando Galiani who is quoted by Einaudi as arguing that although "in this world one cannot hope for . . . perpetual stability" and that "a constant and unchangeable measure need not be desired or sought," he still admits the possibility of a constant unit of account: "If imaginary money were a term for a definite number expressing an idea of price, and if this idea were fixed in our minds and so detached from everything that it would not be affected by any disturbances, then it would certainly be invariable and constant" (Einaudi, 1936: 232).

21. Against the assertion that central banks should be abolished, again, the claim that "inflation target" policies are working may be raised. However, as argued in chapter 10 "'Inflation Targeting': Neither New nor Effective," there is an epistemological problem with these policies; since, it seems to me, it is impossible to know what the rate of inflation actually is in order to measure it. But aside from this epistemological consideration, a public choice argument against central banks can be made. Are not central banks public bureaucracies? Are not central bankers susceptible to putting their personal interest and the interest of their corporations, family, and friends first? I

do not think that anyone could argue against these facts. Therefore, a central bank cannot be trusted more than any other public bureaucracy. And even if we put angels in charge of the central bank, if things really went sour, what would happen? During a military coup in Brazil, someone asked the Supreme Court for a habeas corpus and the Chief Justice replied: "If I gave you a *habeas corpus,* who would give a *habeas corpus* to the Supreme Court judges?" Similarly, who would defend the central bank against the executive and legislative branches if they decided to strip it of its "constitutional" guarantees? Would it be the Supreme Court? And then, who would provide a habeas corpus to the Justices themselves? This statement should not be construed as an argument against the independence of central banks, or as a proof of despair about the efficacy of attempts to impose transparency and accountability on central bankers. On the other hand, if we take into account the performance of the Fed, both in terms of its perceived "dependence" on the political agenda and the mismanagement of the monetary supply, and, on top of that, the ticking time bomb of the deficit of the Federal budget, the landscape is not inspiring and public choice arguments must be weighed.

22. Ricardo Lagos in a recent paper in which he argues for the possibility of the co-existence of money with financial assets yielding a real return wrote: "Nothing in the environment prevents agents from using equity along with money, or instead of money, as a means of payment" (Lagos, 2010: 309). It seems to me that there are no a priori reasons to disregard that possibility.

23. Although narrower definitions such as "Monetary Base" or "Monetary Aggregates" would add precision, it is my contention that their use represents a less adequate representation of reality and therefore the preference for the GAMOE definition.

24. We have already discussed the "Real Bills Doctrine." I will only reiterate that there is a demand for money, that such demand varies, and that an ideal monetary system would be one in which the supply and demand for money match at any single time without drastic variations in the real value of money.

TWELVE

Concluding Chapter

At this point, it is important to recapitulate some of the key concepts that we have been discussing throughout this book and the chain of interconnected conclusions reached along the way.[1]

Money is defined as the generally accepted medium of exchange, the instrument for indirect exchanges, and a first conclusion reached at the beginning of this work is that the nature of money is not a result of history or determined by legal definition but it is given by the proper function of the monetary institutions in society, that is, to allow and enhance the division of labor by facilitating through indirect exchanges the acquisition of desired goods and services. Money is undoubtedly a social institution, but a social institution of a special kind, not one rationally construed but one that has evolved spontaneously in society. Money is in the same category of social institutions as language. A second conclusion reached at the beginning of this research is that the aspects of the reality that have given cause to the introduction of money in society are the gains of a more developed division of labor that the introduction of money generates. Such gains are resulting, in a very broad sense, from the elimination of transaction costs, which have induced, spontaneously, time and again, human societies everywhere to adopt as an instrument for their indirect exchanges a generally accepted medium of exchange.

A third conclusion, still in regard to the nature of money, is that once a commodity becomes perceived by economic agents as having more salability than others, that is, the arbitrage in its price comes closer to the limit of the trend towards its elimination, it is the very embodiment of the monetary attribute of liquidity: it becomes money.

The most liquid commodities, the ones that are more easily tradable at a minimum discount, become the most generally acceptable media of exchange. A forth metaphysical conclusion reached in this investigation is that it is not any commodity that becomes money; there are objective reasons why at a given place and time it is a certain commodity that becomes money and not others. At an early stage of civilization, rare and not-so-rare metals, such as gold, silver, and copper, for their intrinsic properties of relative scarcity, high intrinsic value, divisibility, and durability, became the preferred media of exchange; they have been referred to in this book simply as gold. Along with its use as a GAMOE, gold was naturally used also for the other two essential social functions: a unit of account and a store of value. As we have discussed, Mises has demonstrated that aside from special circumstances such as the ones during the Middle Ages in Western Europe (in which a duometallic system was in use with a myriad of unreliable denominations in parallel circulation making the use of a medium of exchange as the unit of account very troublesome and ineffective), the unit of account tends to be the generally accepted medium of exchange in order to avoid triangular calculations. The raison d'être for the use of an "ideal" money as an abstract unit of account in the Middle Ages is precisely because doing a single and known triangular calculation is better than trying to tabulate the many media of exchange times the products available. Therefore, a fifth conclusion reached in this work is that it is only when the media of exchange lack some essential features such as stability or, at a minimum, predictability in value, or when it is not standardized enough that an "abstract" unit of account evolves. But again, that evolution is spontaneously driven by economic concerns even if adopted and enforced by the government; that is, it is a result of the same forces that in other circumstances would lead to the adoption of the GAMOE as the unit of account.

That is why, incidentally, that as a sixth conclusion, this work insists on the spontaneous origin of money in society even recognizing that the historical evidence has shown that at least since the introduction of coinage, most, if not all, monies either have been produced directly by the state or authorized by the state.

It is understood also that the logical necessity for a unit of account is a separate necessity from the medium of exchange. It may even be accepted, for the sake of the argument, that in some cultures, the necessity for a unit of account may have arisen *before* the existence of a GAMOE. For instance, it may be accepted that in Babylon, the priests defined coercively a unit of account to collect levies in specie before the existence of any generally accepted medium of exchange. As such, as the seventh conclusion, it is insisted that this hypothesis, if ever proved to be historically accurate, does not contradict the thesis of the spontaneous origin of money. The thesis of the spontaneous origin of money results from economic agents grasping the benefits that they may gain from the use of an instrument to do indirect transactions in their striving to acquire desired goods and services. If, in a given society, at a given moment, there happens to exist a unit of account, a measured weight of some widely available good, such as barley, for instance, by the application of *praxeological* principles, the conclusion that economic agents would start to use such instrument to facilitate their indirect exchanges is the logical one. Let's stress this conclusion once more, far from denying it, one may derive from Keynes's "Babylon madness" a lesson that reinforces the logical consistency of the thesis of the spontaneous origin of money.

That is not to say, however, that the essential function of money actually changes or should change because of that. The fiscal considerations have no higher moral standing than money's role as an instrument for indirect exchanges. If nothing else, it is the attribute of liquidity, of being generally accepted, that made coined gold become such a good instrument for the purposes of the sovereign once the division of labor in society evolved beyond the stratified system of the hydraulic mideastern societies of the Bronze age. Therefore, an eighth and key conclusion of this research is that in evaluating what good money is, the attributes most adequate for money to perform its function of allowing and enhancing the division of labor take precedence over the attributes that may make money a better instrument for political purposes.[2] And derived from that, the ninth conclusion is that the fact that coined money has been produced by the sovereign does not morally justify considering money an instrument for state policy above or independently of its natural function for human societies in their spontaneous quest for an ever more complex and expanded division of labor. Incidentally, the tenth conclusion argued here is that it is the realization that good money allows and enhances society to achieve this summum bonum that makes Mises' *rule-utilitarianism* compatible with a neo-Aristotelian *perfectionist* ethics that sees in individual human flourishing the ultimate end of political society; and, as an eleventh conclusion, it is the understanding that the *catallactic* interactions of human beings are more adequately described by a concept of dynamic efficiency that allows us to make Kirzner's and Huerta de Soto's concept of dynamic efficiency a possible bridge between those ethical conceptions and actual political economy in general and monetary policy in particular.

The de facto precedence that fiscal considerations have taken over monetary matters since men in power first grasped the potential to use money manipulation as an instrument to readily dispose of the existing goods and services in society must be understood as what it is, that is, an exercise of brute force, an act of extortion on the part of those who have the necessary means of coercion.

The only qualification to such indictment is the old one, present already in Oresme and Juan de Mariana, that if the very security of the individuals is at risk, it is excusable for the government to use the liquid wealth of the same individuals for their defense to the same extent that it uses any other form of wealth, and once the emergency ceases, the private property taken from some or all of the citizens should be restored or adequate compensation must be paid. Again, as the twelfth conclusion of this investigation, it is stated that there are aspects of reality, economic considerations, that make inevitable the mobilization of liquid assets by men in power in the case of war. It is through the use of liquid assets that they may have access to dispose of the available goods in amounts well above the current yield of all capital goods in society without forcing their liquidation, which, incidentally, would be very damaging to production, as Mises points out. That is inclusively, what makes the organization of political societies in the form of national states the prevalent form of political organization in our days. The thirteenth conclusion of this work, derived from the previous one, is that national states are in a better condition to readily dispose not only of current production, but also of accumulated wealth in society by manipulation of money and banking rules. In sum, the political organization of human societies in national states with the power to manipulate money and banking has proved to be a more efficient arrangement to readily provide for the sinews of war than other forms of political organization.

It is on this consideration of realpolitik that I see with immense skepticism any idea of getting away from the national state or its presence in monetary matters.

But as Ayn Rand wrote, you do not define what is morally right in normal conditions in society from the perspective of survivors from a sunken ship clinging to a raft (Rand, 1963:56).[3]

The fourteenth conclusion in this research is the recognition that the most adequate monetary institutions are those most suitable for its essential function; if it is understood that the survival of the political community is a good in itself [4] that may, in case of an emergency, justify the use of accumulated resources of the individuals in such community for defense, then a fiscal proviso may be made in the regulations of money and banking in order to allow to the sovereign to draw on the depth of the financial markets for the resources necessary to wage war. But even that should be done, to the greatest extent possible, without eliminating the attributes of money that make it appropriate for its main function; otherwise, there will be no deep financial markets to draw from.

Along the evolution of human societies towards a more developed division of labor, more abstract forms of money have evolved. Monetary institutions are part of the bundle of social institutions regulating social life. A life of self-sustaining agriculture in small plots of land and occasional plunder does not require very sophisticated forms of media of exchange. As society evolves, most, if not all, social institutions evolve, admittedly, at different paces. As was shown by the example of the introduction of a sophisticated monetary economy by the late Roman Republic in the Mediterranean basin replacing the unreliable monies of the Hellenistic kingdoms that preceded them, and its later demise by self-inflicted mismanagement at the time of the late Roman Empire, when society regresses to more primitive arrangements, money regresses as well. That is the trend towards abstraction pointed out by Simmel, and as the fifteenth conclusion of this investigation, I see no reason to disagree with his observation. Although he stopped his analysis at the fiduciary money of his time, a money redeemable in gold, it is only a natural sequence of his reasoning to reach the forms of purely fiat money we have today, or to envisage a "zero" base monetary system or a dissociation of functions in order to have a purely abstract unit of account as we have described above in the example of the BFH system.

The issue then is whether or not there is an optimum level of abstraction in money for it to perform its functions. An answer for such a question may be attempted by adhering to the idea that money evolves alongside society; that is, as the sixteenth conclusion of this work it is argued that for each stage of institutional development in society, there should be an optimum level of abstraction in money, and absent coercive constraints, society should spontaneously converge to that level.

A key element to have in mind in order to understand whether or not there is an optimum level of abstraction in money is another concept utilized by Simmel, that is, the related concept of *intersubjectivity*. For Simmel, the trend towards abstraction in money has to do with the advantages in terms of stability of value that more abstract forms of money allegedly possess as a consequence of being more detached from other uses apart from its natural uses as medium of exchange and unit of account. In Simmel's account, the stable money of his time, the inflexible gold standard, in Mises' terminology, with banknotes redeemable in gold at a fixed parity, was a consequence of the sum of all individual subjective evaluations of the relative value of gold; that is, it is a result of an intersubjective evaluation. It may be pointed out that, because of the value Simmel gives to the relative (not absolute) stability of money value in regard to other goods, he leaves the door open to the possibility that other arrangements, which may produce the same result more efficiently, may be adopted in the future.

Here, a pause is advisable. As already emphasized, the evolution of the monetary systems in Western societies for the last two hundred years has been decisively influenced by fiscal considerations; therefore, the seventeenth conclusion in this investigation is that the evolution we saw is what happened under such influence—we do not know what the evolution would have been absent such coercive influence. For instance, we saw an evolution for the last two hundred years towards monetary and banking arrangements tweaked in favor of economizing in specie, until its elimination (at least from the governments' perspective). While that was what actually happened, our eighteenth conclusion is that one would have thought that the "natural" evolution, absent coercion, would be an evolution of financial instruments that: (a) would produce and reflect the benefits of minimizing the time mismatch between real savings and investment, while (b) keeping a supply of money relatively stable in value, that is, preventing it from inflating, and (c) with a supply flexible enough to accommodate increases in the demand for cash balances without forcing a deflation against which there is a natural resistance among economic agents (something that existed even under the Adam Smith regime of "natural liberty").

The evolution of the monetary regimes in Western societies during the last two hundred years started with the transformation of the regimes of commodity money at the beginning of the nineteenth century where individual banks used to keep their reserves prudently around 30% of demand deposits, first, into regimes of gold standard with two-layered fractional reserves and central banks with aggregate reserves of about 5% of demand deposits; later into regimes of gold-exchange standards with reserves of less than 2% of demand deposits; and, finally, since 1971, into regimes of fiat money with no required gold reserves whatsoever. Analyzing such evolution from the perspective of increased discretion given to the governments to manipulate money, to produce seigniorage gains, and to readily dispose of financial resources in cases of emergencies, it all makes sense, although it is not the kind of evolution that, absent coercion, one would expect.[5]

12.1 THE EVOLUTION OF MONEY: THE PRESENT

Along the way money became less predictable, at times its supply became too flexible, at others too inflexible. Overall, as we have seen, the cost of keeping gold reserves has not diminished (since individuals and governments are using gold reserves as a store of value in higher amounts than during the last spell of a so-called gold standard, the gold-exchange standard of the interwar period), and money supply became so entwined with fiscal considerations that today those considerations have taken total precedence over any other in the design of monetary and banking arrangements.

The spontaneous order, however, continues to operate, at times by the uncoordinated action of economic agents, at other times, by the revenue-enhancing interests of men in power acting out of wisdom or pressured by "**bond *vigilantes***" and the like.

The introduction of coined money in ancient Greece happened at a time in which the circumstances would suggest the use of an instrument like that to collect revenue and pay for the expenses of the sovereign. That is, if the society was not already structured in a more complex way than the hydraulic societies of the near East, the tallies of old would have continued to be used. The fact that money first arose in small city-states and not in big empires was pointed out by Von Hagen and Welker (2014: 115) as evidence that they were the social conditions of a more complex and decentralized society that created the conditions for the introduction of money, as we have argued. That does not mean, however, that once the "social technology" of organizing social cooperation through monetization was begun, which was not quickly adopted in Persia, as the Persepolis treasure tables attest, that by 469 BCE the economy of that city was completely monetized (Von Hagen and Welker, 2014: 142).

In the same way, it is our twentieth conclusion, that the sovereign has a vested interest in producing good money or allowing the production of good money under normal circumstances, precisely to be able to use it as an instrument in case of emergencies.

At the same time, financial instruments created by market agents to economize in the high-powered money of today have in fact expanded the amount of quasi-money 100%-backed to a percentage of total liquidity *superior* to the levels of reserves of the commodity regimes prior to 1844.

If we consider the balance sheets of financial institutions today, most of their assets and liabilities are held in *fiducia,* and not as part of their own equity. That is, most of the liquid assets in financial markets today are held in money market mutual funds in which the financial institutions have assets in the proportion of 100% of their liabilities.

That is the reason why, as our twenty-first conclusion, it is contended here that the issue of 100% reserve, per se, has lost relevance. That is not to say that enforcing a 100% reserve requirement for demand deposits should not be done; of course it must be done. But today, demand deposits represent in advanced countries just a fraction—less than 10% and most of the time half of that—of the money supply as measured by M2.[6]

The demise of the gold standard and the search for other sources of stability has led the banking system to move to the deleveraging of their balance sheets in the last forty years. Our current financial problems are elsewhere. The responsibility for the current financial problems worldwide, the main culprit for the 2008 financial crisis, relies on the amount of liquidity today represented directly and indirectly by public debt. Let's be clear on that: at the same time that private commercial banks were deleveraging their balance sheets from commercial loans since the 1980s, the same banks and other financial institutions (in the "shadow banking system) became dealers in public bonds, taking them in mutual funds nominally without leveraging their balance sheets; the net result, however, is a record level of what is assumed to be sound assets backing financial liabilities.

It is not the intention here to dissect current financial problems, but with our twenty-second conclusion, this book makes clear that transactions in the financial sector of the economy should reflect the match in time and quantity of the availability of real resources saved vis-à-vis the commitments to invest them. When the debt of the sovereign comes into play, being nothing more than claims on future tax revenues, it distorts financial markets and leads to the crisis like the most recent one, even if the ratio of reserves to liquid financial instruments is at a record high. The lesson is that 100% reserve requirements to issue banknotes and demand deposits, even a 100% reserve requirement to issue shares in MMMFs, which are the most widespread instrument to hold liquidity today, are not a sufficient arrangement to prevent time mismatches if among the accepted assets backing those obligations there is public debt or some other mandate that may distort monetary equilibrium, such as implicit government backing of financial institutions, government-sponsored deposit "insurance" schemes, and so on.

We discussed the epistemological limitations to implementing policies of inflation targeting, learning from the experience of the last time that monetary policy was conducted primarily with eyes on price indexes in the interwar period. But it may be accepted that the discussion was mainly limited to quantitative aspects, since, and that is our twenty-third conclusion, the epistemological limitations on practicing inflation targeting policies are the same that prevent us from pointing out where they are mistaken. Still, the amount of public debt that represents claims over existing goods but has future tax revenues as its only backing may well be singled out as the main factor blurring the perception of economic agents and misguiding them in their idea that the relative stability of consumer price indexes means that there is no inflationary credit expansion going on. One may not know precisely how the existence of a stock of 18 trillion US dollars in national public debt[7] distorts the signals to the economic agents in an economy of 17 trillion US dollars of GDP[8] like the economy of the United States today, but one does not need to know in order to realize that it must result in huge qualitative (allocative) distortions, not only to the American economy but to the entire world as well, given the communications between the American economy and global markets.

It is my firm belief that the fights for the return of a gold standard or for a 100% reserve requirement are today proxies for the fight to curb government issuance of public debt as a means to appropriate resources that in the minds of the savers were to be invested in order to be available in the future. The time of reckoning is coming, and when financial markets realize that the so-called savings do not exist anymore, that they were wasted in public spending and that the sovereign cannot honor all of his obligations, the next financial crisis will ensue.

12.2 THE EVOLUTION OF MONEY: THE FUTURE

Let's return to the trend toward more abstract forms of money.

We have seen so far that it is unrealistic to eliminate the government from the picture. On the other hand, the ingenuity of economic agents continues to operate. Given the right incentives, they may lead to more sophisticated forms of money. On the other hand, if the burden of government debt continues to increase, that will inevitably result in a flight to real assets, to a decrease in the level of abstraction in money, among other things.

The scenario that we propose to explore is the one in which the division of labor at a global level intensifies, where the rule of law becomes more widespread around the world, and some moderation in public spending is imposed in order to produce a gradual reduction in the stock of public debt as a percentage of global production, and therefore the catastrophe of a debt crisis by loss of confidence in financial assets representative of public debt is avoided. The description of such a scenario has in itself a key element of the things to come, that is, some limitations on the use of financial instruments by the government in normal circumstances. That may take the form of constitutionally mandated limits on public spending, such as balanced budget mandates, or the sovereign may relinquish some of its monetary prerogatives.

In any case, in talking about the future of money we are not talking about what would be the development of money in the absence of government coercion, but one that will be accompanied and to a great extent guided by that.

Our twenty-fourth conclusion is that it is only in this scenario and having this factor in mind that a movement towards a "zero" base arrangement with a purely abstract dollar as the unit of account and the use of liquid financial instruments as media of exchange may be conceived.

That arrangement, however, is one that does not offer much in terms of stability for the standard of value, since the creation of inflationary credit would still be possible and with that the devaluation of the abstract standard.

It is given to that consideration that an evolution towards a purely abstract unit of account however linked to some bundle of commodities, that is, something like the monetary bigamy of Brazil and Israel in the 1980s with widespread indexation, Fisher's tabular system, or Yeager's BFH system, comes into play.

The twenty-fifth conclusion of this work, another of its key conclusions, is that the ideal attributes for a monetary system include as its main features the production of money stable in value, with a supply flexible enough to accommodate changes in the demand for cash balances, which is inexpensive for economic agents, and which would prevent the production of inflationary credit expansion, that is, it would be able to prevent the counterpart in the financial sector from a mismatch in time and quantity between savings and investments in the real sector.

With that blueprint, one might say that a regime of a free-banking gold standard with the enforcement of a 100% reserve requirement on banknote issuance and deposits on demand would fit the bill. I disagree with that. In my judgment, there are a number of reasons why such a system, first, hardly will get political support to be implemented, and second, even if implemented, it will not succeed in delivering the results expected from it. As I once heard Allan Meltzer say, he is not against the gold standard because he does not know how it operates, but because he does.[9]

The aspects of free banking and 100% reserve requirements on deposits and banknote issuance are not questioned. There are abundant and convincing arguments in favor of them in the Austrian economics literature in general, and in Huerta de Soto's writings in particular. Proposals in that direction come also from other perspectives on economics as already mentioned in this book with reference to the Chicago Plan, the 100% Dollar plans of Irving Fisher and Milton Friedman, and more recently, proposals to "narrow" banking activities ranging from leftist monetary cranks to the serious and well-thought-out proposal of John Cochrane (it is important to keep in mind that although all those proposals grant monopolistically to the government the prerogative to produce money, that is not an inherent feature of narrow banking). Ultimately, the argument in favor of a 100% reserve requirement that convinced me is Buchanan's argument that once base money is no longer expensive to produce, there is no more reason to have a banking system designed to economize on it.

That under normal circumstances, the supply of gold may have the level of flexibility sufficient to accommodate increases in the demand for cash balances and at the same time be inflexible enough to not produce inflation is disputable, however. The literature of inflation under the gold standard, even conceding that the most reliable of it reflects changes in prices under fractional reserve arrangements, shows that some disequilibrium is to be expected. The problem seems to be that in case of sudden changes in the demand for cash balances, motivated by a sudden increase in uncertainty, for whatever reason (such as political unrest, natural catastrophes, et cetera), or in the case of sustained growth at a faster pace than the physical conditions to increase gold production, the inflexible aspect of the gold standard may result in monetary disequilibrium with undesirable effects on production. But that, however, is not the most important argument against the system of free-banking gold standard and 100% reserve requirement in regard to the flexibility of the supply of money. After all, it is to be doubted that any other conceivable system would produce, under normal circumstances, better results in terms of price stability.

In that regard, our twenty-sixth conclusion is that the argument that the supply of money should not be left to the vagaries of mining is an argument with considerably more weight. It is not an absolute argument though. If proven that there is no better way to have an "automatic," that is, nondiscretionarily commanded supply of money than by leaving it to the *fortuna* of gold miners, that would be a compelling argument in favor of a gold standard. However, I argue that the 100% reserve requirement of *any* liquid asset for the production of money would be enough, at the same time, to eliminate the discretion in money production without leaving it subject to the performance of gold mining. It is possible to offer arguments for that while discussing the last two features of an "ideal" system, that is, to be cost effective and to prevent inflationary credit expansion, and they may be addressed at the same time.

A twenty-seventh conclusion in this research is that the gold standard, specifically in its version with a 100% reserve requirement on banknotes and demand deposits, is a kind of monetary arrangement that imposes on economic agents an elevated opportunity cost to hold banknotes and demand deposits. That is why it is believed that under such arrangements there will be strong incentives to money holders and financial managers to economize in gold reserves by reducing, to the extent of what is legally permissible, the use of banknotes and demand deposits, as already mentioned.[10] Furthermore, such a system would not preclude the possibility of time mismatch between the assets and liabilities of financial institutions in their time deposits, and consequently, that would defeat the purpose of the entire enterprise. Even if successful in implementing such a system, the risk of business cycles would not be eliminated. However, if the unit of account and the medium of exchange were dissociated and liquid credit instruments could be used as media of exchange, it would be possible for liquidity, even at a very short term, to be held in interest-bearing instruments, and at the same time, to extend the 100% reserve requirement to time deposits, if those instruments could be used as collateral for those deposits, as the assets of MMMFs are today. The twenty-eighth conclusion is not difficult to understand that with the financial intermediaries required to match in a timely manner 100% of their liabilities with corresponding assets of good quality and no government-sponsored warranty or other mandated distortions, it would be expected that the monetary arrangements would be as close to the ideal as possible, that is, they would be the "optimum" in abstraction: a purely abstract unit of account and many media of exchange issued according to the demand of money holders against the deposit of good and liquid collateral in the proportion of 100%. Dissociation of functions and the adoption of multiple liquid assets to back the issuance of financial instruments with liberative power (including not only, but not exclusively, gold) seem to be a better answer to the search for "ideal" monetary arrangements.

As Huerta de Soto said, "It is not possible to theorize a priori about the future evolution of money" (Huerta de Soto, 2006: 737). That is why we can mention some specific characteristics of money, and psychological and social realities that may influence the evolution of money in the future, but it is not possible to be certain about a phenomenon contingent on so many future events.

The final conclusion of the reasoning developed in this book is that among the many proposals for monetary reform, the proposal suggested by Huerta de Soto, of free-banking, privatized money, 100% reserve requirement, and "permitting the spontaneous and gradual entrance of other monetary standards besides gold" (Huerta de Soto, 2006: 739) is compatible with the idea of an abstract unit of account separated into many media of exchange as proposed by Yeager with his BFH system that, according to our analysis, better accommodates the supply and demand for media of exchange than relying on the production of a single commodity. It is our contention also, that although it is not possible to eliminate the fiscal proviso that de facto entitles the sovereign to intervene in money and banking arrangements, it is possible to limit the moral support to these interventions to the needs of war financing, and no state monopoly of money, central bank, laws of legal tender, or authorization for peacetime public financing are necessary for that. Actually, to the extent that they introduce into the monetary arrangements attributes that are inimical to the ones best suited to money's natural function by the introduction of instability of the money supply, they compromise the possibilities of floating war bonds in case of need.

NOTES

1. For the sake of clarity the conclusions will be enumerated. As for the conclusions themselves, some are original and others are not. This is so because, as stated at the introduction of this work, the central thesis of this work is that, in order to evaluate monetary policy, it is necessary to have an understanding about what is moral in regard to money as informed by the nature of money and the limitations of the knowledge about money. Therefore, some of the conclusions mentioned at this summary are only intermediary steps in the reasoning developed and the reasoning itself is only an application of the central thesis. It is hoped that the quotations and references offered throughout this work make clear what is not original in the reasoning here presented.

2. Quint and Schubik acknowledge that "an economy that includes government as a strategic agent is a political economy . . . But the control mechanisms are operationally different, depending upon the nature of the money to be used." (2014: 317) It is inescapable that there will be political control over the economy, but the nature of the money used makes that control different; or to put it another way, there is a correlation between the money used in a given society and the political relations in that society and that is on a continuum. Quoting Quint and Schubik (2014: 308) again, "the concept of (government) control is on a continuum, with the lower bound being 'no-control' (anarchy) and the upper bound being 'total control' (a centralized government that removes all economic choice from the individual small agents)."

3. According to her, "It is important to differentiate between the rules of conduct in an emergency situation and the rules of conduct in the normal conditions of human existence. This does not mean a double standard of morality: the standard and the basic principles remain the same, but their application to either case requires precise definitions" (1963: 54).

4. Since each individual may choose to vote with his feet and leave a given polity with his family and his property if he judges that the cost in terms of blood and treasure to defend it as an independent political entity is not worthwhile, it is perfectly possible for a polity to realize that a commitment for its defense would likely be a suicidal pact and surrender its independence instead. Furthermore, such individual right to leave, in my understanding, can be exercised at any time, well into the conflagration.

5. Quint and Schubik, quoting from Ricardo and Mises, state that the greatest virtue of the traditional gold standard was "emancipating the system from the changing influences of party politics and government interference" (Mises, 1935: 20), that there is no alternative than either "trusting gold and trusting politicians" (Quint and Schubik: 318). Quoting Ricardo (1821/1965: 322): "Experience . . . shows that neither state nor a bank ever have had the unrestricted power of issuing paper without abusing that power; in all states, therefore, the issue of paper money ought to be under some check and control; and none seems so proper for that purpose as that of subjecting the issuers of paper money to the obligation of paying their notes either in gold coin or bullion" (Ricardo, 1821/1965: 24), they emphasize the need for trust, and that only with "check and control" over the issuers will the power to issue paper money not be abused. Well, gold undoubtedly serves that purpose, but with all the known shortcomings it has. To leave money to be endogenously created by the market continues to be the ideal to pursue and finding a way to do that without creating a system prone to systemic risks seems to be the challenge at hand.

6. At this juncture, perhaps it is the moment to address one of the multiple issues that may arise in a transition from the money and banking system that we have today to a new system of free banking which, it is hoped, will produce better results. Although not always acknowledged by authors advancing transitional proposals for free banking arrangements, the pure and simple elimination of the central bank would likely induce an immediate bank run. Such an event is predictable in the circumstance of government retrieval of its support for the banking system, since the time mismatches and the dubious quality of bank assets today accumulated after decades of privileges and easy money policies are too big to be swept under the carpet. That is why a 100% reserve requirement is a key principle of the model for banking reform proposed by Huerta de Soto (2006: 715).

7. U.S. National Debt Clock: The Outstanding Public Debt as of 05 Dec 2012 at 02:50:29 PM GMT is: $ 16,344,688,650,537.39. ("U.S. National Debt Clock," brillig.com. http://www.brillig.com/debt_clock/.)

8. Current-dollar GDP—the market value of the nation's output of goods and services—in the third quarter of 2012 reached the level of $15,797.4 billion. ("National Income and Product Accounts: Gross Domestic Product: Fourth Quarter and Annual 2014 (Second Estimate)," Bureau of Economic Analysis, accessed March 20, 2015. http://www.bea.gov/newsreleases/national/gdp/gdpnewsrelease.htm.)

9. Another caveat, in regard to the possibility of restating an international monetary system based on a gold standard, is that there are two major working hypotheses about the establishment and maintenance of the gold standard for about a century between the Napoleonic wars and the Great War, the spontaneous explanation and the hegemonic stability theory (Kindleberger, 1986). The latter basically states that British hegemony was necessary in order to keep a liberal world order. Both hypotheses have been only partially confirmed by historical evidence according to Reti (1998: 2). Also, according to Reti, it is Barry Eichengreen (1990: 293) who suggested an alternative interpretation of the actual events during the classical gold standard, one that is consistent with coordination based on shared interests and beliefs, and he states that "Great Britain provided 'a focal point for policy harmonization' in the context of 'an international consensus on the objectives and formulations of monetary policy'" (Reti, 1998:2). So, even if there were a hegemonic political power in favor of such regime, it is not at all certain that that would be sufficient to align interests among the international community in that direction.

10. The structure of the Bank of England in the second half of the nineteenth century, that is, post-1844, as described by Bagehot, illustrates nicely the legal argument in favor of a 100% reserve requirement for some banking liabilities. It is not that the arrangements of the BoE were ideal, far from it, but they offer a good illustration of the different kinds of banking liabilities in regard to the legal aspects of the 100% reserve requirement. The BoE at that time was divided basically in two, for legal purposes: the issuing department and the banking department. If a client entered the bank at that time to deposit some gold and get banknotes, the bank was legally required to keep 100% reserve of gold bullion in its coffers backing those new banknotes issued. But if the same client entered the bank to deposit his good as a demand deposit or as a time deposit, no reserve requirement was legally required. The difference that such operational division illustrates is the difference between what was considered by the British banking laws to be a service of safeguarding the gold for the client (as performed by the issuing department) and what was considered to be a credit claim against the bank (as performed by the banking department). The problem is that deposits on demand, by their nature, like the issuance of banknotes redeemable in specie on demand, also are agreements with the legal nature of custody, of safekeeping, as noted by Huerta de Soto (2006: 18). Therefore, only time deposits are (legally) typical monetary loans, and therefore it is only in regard to their liabilities resulting from time deposits that bankers are at leisure to decide how much in reserves they will keep based on prudential considerations; in regard to their note-issuing and demand deposit activities they (should be) legally obliged to keep 100% reserves. It is only the privileges given to banks, contrary to the Western legal tradition, that allow them to lump together all of their obligations as if the ownership of the assets was completely transferred to them by their clients when it is obvious that in regard to the issuance of banknotes and the acceptance of demand deposits, they were not. Quoting George Reisman's *Capitalism* on page 957, Simpson argues that fractional reserve is not legally wrong, or should not be made illegal as argued by Huerta de Soto, but is philosophically wrong, for infringing the law of the excluded middle (Simpson, 2014b: 130) which says that something is either A or non-A and that money cannot be at the same time available to two claimants. However, this "philosophical" error is the same error pointed out by Huerta de Soto, who uses Roman law with its evolutionary tradition as a proxy for logical reasoning. The problem with both alleged infringements of logic is that a credit may be so liquid as to have monetary properties; in this sense, does the claim of someone to some money deposited in a bank and a credit against the same bank to which someone else is entitled have the same liberative power even if, at the end of the day, the bank can only honor one of them? Furthermore, during the restriction of convertibility in the middle of the Napoleonic wars, the argument of the unconstitutionality in England of the mandate to the director of the Bank of England "of regulating, in a certain degree, the standard of the currency of the kingdom, and of varying this standard at their pleasure" (King, 1803/2014: 84) was already made. That was somewhat different from the legal argument against fractional reserve banking, since it was even more general in its scope and linked the reprobation of the arrangement (in that case, the suspension of convertibility) to its economic consequences, to its practical consequences, not to formal legal reasoning under the paradigm of Roman law.

V

Appendixes

The Introduction of a Medium of Exchange and of a Unit of Account in Society

A.1 SOME HINTS FROM PALEOANTHROPOLOGY

As currently accepted by paleoanthropologists, our species, the *Homo sapiens*, originated in Africa about 160,000 years ago and started to migrate about sixty thousand years ago, eventually colonizing all continents except for Antarctica, and in the process displacing other *Homo* species (*Science Daily*, May 2007). About ten thousand years BCE, the end of the last glacial era coincided with the end of the Paleolithic era and found human beings living in **bands** scantily sprawled all over the world. Those bands, probably organized in clans (no more than the extended family), practiced hunting and gathering in order to survive. Some males, females, and their offspring composed those clans, but it was already an evolution in comparison with the apelike bands that were the prevailing *Homo* genus group for millions of years, centered on an alpha male, and which expelled from the group or killed any young grown-up male.[1]

At the beginning, the individuals inside the bands performed the same activities, with no function specialization among them. As time went by, the labor specialization benefits were perceived and individuals began to organize their groups in order to implement more and more labor specialization. As stated by Ludwig von Mises: "The factor that brought about primitive society and daily works toward its progressive intensification is human action that is animated by the insight into the higher productivity of labor achieved under the division of labor" (2007: 160).

Some became hunters (the males), others became gatherers (the women and children), and others became the repository of the accumulated knowledge of the group (the very few surviving seniors at a time when life expectancy, on average, was less than thirty years). Indications of a certain division of labor at the time of the Upper Paleolithic (from 30,000 to 10,000 BCE) were found among the Cro-Magnon to attest to this (Burns, 1975: 12).

Coerced as it may have been, the division of labor increased in social importance with the growing gains of productivity derived from agriculture and the labor specialization itself, since it is a self-generating and self-improving phenomenon.

From the bands of hunters we can skip forward a few thousand years and go to the beginning of the Neolithic, the introduction of agriculture, and the first pre-urban societies about 5000 BCE in Europe,[2] 7000 BCE in Egypt, and probably earlier than that in the Middle East (Burns, 1975: 15). The people were then living in small villages, surviving mainly on domesticated animals and plants. At that time, they were probably organized in tribes. Those tribes were composed of an amalgamation of the previously existing clans, each tribe numbered maybe hundreds of individuals, and the labor specialization was a fact dictated by custom and, it is reasonable to assume, enforced by brute force in most places.

The individuals in those societies were entitled to the product of others basically by customary rules and a **barter system** organized more or less according to what we would consider today as "commercial transactions," or quoting Hingston Quiggin: "Somewhere in between the insignificant giving of presents and recognized money transactions there are two customs of worldwide, though sporadic distribution, 'silent trade' and 'gift-exchange'." (Quiggin, 1949: 11). The "witch doctors" probably received their maintenance from the group because the other members of the group were customarily obliged to pay them. The artisans, who specialized in the production of weaponry, probably resorted to barter to acquire food, and the women most likely performed the provision of shelter and clothes also in customary form, regardless of the level of coercion involved.[3]

A.2 THE INTRODUCTION OF A UNIT OF ACCOUNT

Even at the most primitive stages of society, human exchanges require some sort of commensuration. Even for bartering, criteria of proportionality must be generated, since barter is already a complex form of human interaction under the division of labor. As stated by Mises, "Monetary calculation is the guiding star of action under the social system of division of labor. It is the compass of the man embarking upon production" (2007: 209).

What makes, at a given place and time, two oranges for an apple and, at other times, two apples for an orange a fair (voluntarily accepted) deal? Many other human interactions require a commonly accepted standard of value. You need to compare incommensurables in order to pay a corvée, tithes, taxes, gift exchanges, et cetera. The logical necessity for a unit of account derives precisely from this.

However, it seems reasonable to presume that that necessity was fulfilled by the introduction of some medium of exchange and not by the creation of some abstract unit of account. As explained by Mises:

> The system of economic calculation in monetary terms is conditioned by certain social institutions. It can operate only in an institutional setting of the division of labor and private ownership of the means of production in which goods and services of all orders are bought and sold against a generally used medium of exchange, i.e., money. (2007: 229)

It seems acceptable to suppose that, for millennia, all those proportionalities among different goods, services, and obligations in the primitive societies were established quite arbitrarily, with only vague proportionality. That was so because in the absence of a unit of account, rational calculation was not possible, and there are no known references in history to abstract units of account before recent times. So, for our purposes, although it is conceded that the necessity for a unit of account is different from the necessity for a medium of exchange, since that necessity was only satisfied by the introduction of some medium of exchange (being it tallies, bills of exchange, or any other merchandise with monetary characteristics) in dealing with the introduction of the latter in society, this work also deals with the introduction of the former.[4]

A.3 THE INTRODUCTION OF MEDIA OF EXCHANGE

At this point in our schematic timeline, the conditions for the introduction of money in human society had arisen, but it took several thousand years more of experimentation and evolution to a medium of exchange to take the form of coined rare metals.

In those pre-urban tribes, each individual or group of individuals started to specialize in the production of some desirable good in order to barter with others. Those tribesmen must have had great difficulty finding counterparts for their barters. For example, a wheat producer willing to exchange his production for cattle had to find a cattle grower wanting wheat; they needed to match their reciprocal necessities, otherwise no barter would occur.

Aside from the daily exchanges inside the tribes, we can imagine the occasional meetings with people of other tribes; we can imagine that if no evident martial advantage had been present in favor of one group, they would prefer to practice commerce to war or, at least one can assume, only the descendants of those who more consistently adopted that behavior prospered. To engage in commerce with foreigners (tribe "B"), who presumably were not interested in the goods produced by local people (tribe "A"), a third merchandise could be used as means of exchange.

For example, suppose that both tribes "A" (farmers) and "B" (farmers and ranchers) needed salt, but only tribe "A" would have access to tribe "C," salt producers dwelling on the sea shore. So, tribe "A" in contact with tribe "C" on the beach could exchange some of their farm products for salt. And in their turn they would be able to acquire ranch goods from tribe "B" using not their own products but salt in their barter.

That salt performed the function of "medium of exchange." In our example, salt becomes a suitable commodity to perform that role due to the following attributes: It is divisible in small amounts; it is easily tested or tasted if you wish; and it maintains its properties for a long time. The main drawbacks to the use of salt as a medium of exchange are its small intrinsic value (you need to carry a load of salt to have a reasonable value) and the fact that it is perishable.

With time and the introduction of metallurgy, precious metals, or any metal for that matter, were identified by the people as ideal media of exchange. Metals were then used as proxy to the barters, fulfilling the role of salt in our example as medium of exchange, not in the coined form of later but by their weight. All the costs of scaling and assessing the metals' quantity and purity involved in a transaction were tradeoffs assumed by the participants in that transaction.

We were then at the beginning of civilization—the Neolithic faded out, the Bronze age started about 3300 BCE and the Iron age started about 1200 BCE, according to the "three age system" proposed by Danish archaeologist Christian Jürgensen Thomsen. The establishment of cities was contemporary with the invention of writing, of metallurgy, and the use of metals in bullion as medium of exchange. Living in cities, the tribes became dissolved in the proto-states of those times. By then human societies numbered thousands of individuals and the labor specialization was already assumed as a given feature of society at that time. New classes of individuals such as warriors, scribes, priests, artisans, and peasants arose at those times, and human societies became increasingly complex.

NOTES

1. . This description is based on the insights of Sigmund Freud in his 1913 book *Totem und Tabu* since, as stated by Mises, we do not have actual knowledge about primeval social groups (see footnote 4 of chapter 1).

2. . Although there are still today clans of hunters, tribes of illiterate farmers and so on, evidencing different chronologies of social development, in order to understand the role of money for us today, in this work we follow a schematic time line representative of modern western civilization history as the history of our predecessors.

3. . It seems relevant to call the reader's attention to the fact that the case for liberty does not rest on trying to show that our ancestors were rational and free. We can assume a fair amount of coercion in the primitive societies and still argue that by a process of trial and error, humanity learned the benefits of the division of labor and then the natural necessity for liberty arose.

4. . It seems also relevant to address the difference between the logical necessity for a unit of account and for a medium of exchange, without accepting, however, that in primitive societies the former could be supplied by any means other than by the introduction of the latter. For instance, at the beginning of the Late Bronze age (about 1,600 BC), Quiggin quotes Charles Seltman (1933: 4) as saying: "While the northerners and highlanders reckoned in cattle the Egyptians and the peoples of Mesopotamia

were using gold, silver, electrum (a natural amalgam of silver and gold) and bronze which they had learnt to weigh in the balance for the purpose of estimating its value." And he concludes: "These diverse standards were adjusted to a common unit, that of the ox, and the ox had its equivalent in gold or in copper talents; the gold talent (weighting some 8.5 grammes) was in the form of bars, which could be cut up into sections like Chinese silver; in rings of various shapes, and in dumps, the fore-runners of stamped coins; the copper talent, beaten out into a flattish plate, weighed some 25.5 kilo or about 60 pounds" (Quiggin, 1949: 272). The different peoples of the Late Bronze age eastern Mediterranean, using different primitive moneys, found a minimum denominator for their currencies, the ox, and known quantities of gold, silver, and copper were representatives of a value similar to an ox.

The Introduction of Coined Money in Greece

The life of a peasant or an artisan at the dawn of human history was not easy with all those warriors and priests giving orders and seizing the output. The first states were political societies in which, generally speaking, the subjects were not allowed to have individual goals, and the entire group was coerced into pursuing the social goals revealed by the deities as traditionally proclaimed by the priests and enforced by the kings.

But the archeological evidence of many small shops and small farms from the "Hydraulic Societies" in Mesopotamia, ancient Egypt, and India attests that even at those dark times when the light of civilization was rare in a world almost entirely dominated by brute force, individuality thrived. The autocrats of that time, and of all times for that matter, fundamentally lacking capacity, regardless of their will or even interest in organizing the entire social life in command format, left some space for individual initiative. Granting differences in time and place, there is evidence that portions of the economic activities inside the cities were not commanded; also, it may be inferred from the historical records that most of the intercity trade was also not state-owned, although it may have been monopolized, and for sure it was regulated and taxed. It was the beginning of the markets. There were markets for farm products inside the cities, markets for foreign goods, et cetera. Most of those markets were organized on certain days in some venues where buyers and sellers met to trade. At that time, markets were not an abstract concept but an actual place in which buyers and sellers could meet.

At that stage of human evolution (anytime between about five thousand and two thousand five hundred years ago), the use of a metallic medium of exchange was widespread. Rare metals such as gold and silver were perceived as the ideal medium of exchange among traders. An Egyptian trader could acquire timber in Tyro paying in gold, afterwards he could travel to Crete to sell the timber in exchange for copper, he could then acquire olive oil in Israel paying with the copper, and travel back to Luxor to sell the oil and receive gold bullion (mined in Ethiopia) once more.[1] People, regions, and countries could then specialize in the production of certain goods and services and trade them using metals, both bare and rare, as media of exchange; but a further step was still necessary for the Fertile Crescent and Mediterranean ancient civilizations to have something recognizable today as money; that is, coinage.

B.1 COINED MONEY

According to George Winder (Winder, 1959: 20), the Chinese were the first to manufacture gold coins (in the shape of knives and spades). Winder, quoting Sir George Macdonald, attributes the invention of coins in Europe to Greek merchants who did so in order to facilitate the circulation of their stocks of metals. He also says that the first European rulers to strike coins were the Kings of Lydia, a fact that is well established.[2]

About 600 BCE, in the Lydian kingdom, located in where part of Turkey is today, under King Croesus, the first known gold and silver coins (the Lydian Lion as it is known is made of a gold and silver alloy called electrum and known as white gold in ancient times) were minted. According to Herodotus in his *Histories*, "[The Lydians] were the first of all people we know of to use coinage struck from gold and silver, and the first to become retailers of goods they did not themselves produce" (1.94.1, 2007: 55). They managed to do just that, and by spreading the concept to neighboring countries, they helped establish the first monetary societies, the first societies in which indirect exchanges were cleared with coined money.

Coinage was a certification of the weight and purity of that specific piece of metal with a seal stamped on it for this purpose given by someone credible to the community. From then on, metallic money became available; prices in the markets could no longer be referred to by their equivalent in some weight of metal, but rather in pieces of metal, in coins. The premises for all further monetary developments were settled.

B.2 WHAT IF MONEY WERE INTRODUCED IN SOCIETY AS A UNIT OF ACCOUNT?

Let's suppose that, as a matter of historical account, the Chartalists are right in stating that *coined* money in the western civilization started with the fiscal needs of the state.

Quoting Thomas Martin, "The current consensus among ancient historians and numismatists seems to be that the state's need for a convenient medium of exchange to pay for official expenditures motivated the initial adoption of coinage in the Greek *polis*" (1996: 258).

Does it prove that a unit of account was first introduced in human society by force of authority and not because it is convenient to think in terms of comparable goods? It seems difficult to be absolute in either way.

Does it prove that the purpose of money in society is to foster state policy and not to allow and enhance the division of labor? Again, even if it is accepted that money was created by the state, from that assumption it does not follow that money was introduced in society in order to foster state policy.

Incidentally, it is precisely because traditional forms of compulsory service were in disuse as they had been replaced by a market-oriented division of labor that the authorities needed money, as explained by Martin: "Lacking a central authority to compel contributions or labor through the threat of force, the urbanizing Greek city-state had to find other ways to pay for and to maintain the common structures and services of its ever more complex physical and festal infrastructure" (1996: 270).

As clearly stated by Martin, it does not matter much if the original intent in minting coins can be singled out and found to be a fiscal one. At the beginning of our civilization coinage was mingled with the evolution of our civilization, from a more primitive, traditionally ruled society, to a more sophisticated, market-oriented one, and the introduction of coinage helped to foster a further development of commercial activities and the division of labor regardless of the motivation behind its creation:

> It seems reasonable to hold as a premise of the investigation that this connection had its roots in the earliest history of coinage in the *polis*, which of course does not mean that the original reasons for the adoption of coinage by city-states necessarily remained the only reasons that they continued to mint coins over the succeeding centuries. Coinage, like other technological innovations, surely had unintended consequences over the long run. In any case, speculation (and that is all our evidence allows) about the perhaps diverse reasons why Greeks living in city-states originally adopted the use of coinage seems an appropriate way to begin thinking about the multi-faceted issue of the significance of archaic and classical Greek coinage in and for the *polis* as a political community. (Martin, 1996: 258)

To summarize, the known evidence does not allow us to establish with certainty what were the motivations of the first rulers who minted coins in ancient Greece; evidence about the introduction of coined money in other civilizations is scant as well, allowing us to generalize that there is no concrete historical evidence about the cause for the introduction of coinage. However, that does not imply that the introduction of coinage did not happen at a time and under circumstances that demanded low transaction cost tools for the coordination of economic activity among individuals, which was, in turn, cause and consequence of the expansion of the division of labor. It was in this environment of multiple relatively small city-states in the Hellenistic world trading and fighting among each other that the circumstances for the introduction of coined money arose. The fact that the fiscal needs of the city-state could be better addressed by the collection of coined money through taxation than by the imposition of

Egyptian-like forced labor may be understood as an argument to reinforce the catallactic theory of the origin of money and not to contradict it.

NOTES

1. The discovery of the Uluburun shipwreck in 1982 and her ill-fated journey by way of the east Mediterranean around the fourteenth century BCE as it was deduced from the goods salvaged from the wreck gives evidence for the existence of a sea route for the transport of copper, tin, and other raw materials (Pulak, 1998: 191). The main cargo was about 10 tons of copper from Cyprus, in the form of 354 ingots; and at this time it does not matter much whether the ship was on an official mission or not, if there were private merchants on board (there are evidences given by the multiple sets of weights found in the shipwreck that at least three different merchants were on board) or only government officials, whether the copper and other raw materials in the cargo were intended as "gifts" among different sovereigns or more recognizable "trade" by modern observers. The fact is that those ingots in differing weights (and therefore subject to weighing at each commercial transaction) were decidedly acquired in Cyprus, most likely by an Egyptian agent, in order to be exchanged in the eastern Mediterranean for other goods; that is, precisely the point I want to make (Pulak, 2005: 34).

2. In his aforementioned 1959 *A Short History of Money*, George Winder also says that Croesus, in order to face the problem posed by the variance in the amalgam of the two metals composing the electrum, abandoned it for a double system of gold and silver coins, a statement that I am unable to confirm.

"Dollarization" and Euro-Like Currencies

Many countries have recently adopted a monetary system based on the US dollar. Although the US dollar is a fiat money currency like most currencies in Latin America, it is perceived by the public as "hard currency," if for no other reason than its relative greater stability in comparison with the other American currencies, with the possible exception of the Canadian dollar.

C.1 DIFFERENT FORMS OF DOLLARIZATION

Nevertheless, the dollarization process has many forms in its appearances, and we can single out different processes generally understood as "dollarization." There are several ways of adopting a monetary system based on the US dollar. We will try to classify them not only by using the attributes listed above, but also considering the fact that the adoption of the US dollar as base money for a monetary system may be implemented with or without any agreement with the US government.

Dollarization can be classified as either a bilateral or unilateral process. An agreement related to the use of the US dollar deals essentially with two issues: First, has the Fed agreed to be a "lender of last resort" to the country's "banking system?" And second, has the Fed agreed to share the profits of "seigniorage?" As far as I know, the US government does not have any agreement of that sort with any country. So up until now, all "dollarization processes" have been unilateral measures.

Until now (January 2010) the American government policy related to the adoption of the US dollar as currency by other countries has been a nonsupportive one.

C.2 THE DOLLARIZATION PROCESS IN LATIN AMERICA

The dollarization process in Latin America has been conducted along the lines described below:

C.2.1 Dollarization through Substitution, Dollarization Sensu Stricto: The Panama Case

In Panama, there is no central bank, which means that there is no political control of the amount of money in circulation in the country. On the one hand, this feature of the dollarization process in Panama implies a low level of restrictions to banking activity; on the other hand, it implies that there is no lender of last resort for the banking system. This system has been in force in Panama for more than a century now and it has been argued that the system has managed to survive without a central bank because of the steady flow of US dollars brought into the country by the Panama Canal, or because of the small size of Panama's economy or even because the American banks in Panama can recur to the Fed as a lender of last resort. First, the flow of US dollars into Panama is no greater than the flow into any other country with a strong exporting sector. Second, the size of the dollarized economy is only relevant in relation to the extension of its links with financial markets; in the case of Panama, since there are few bank restrictions, the country is well-connected to the financial markets worldwide. In this sense, even the economy of the United Kingdom or France or Italy may be considered small. Third, since the US dollar is not redeemable in specie, and since most of the commercial banks with branches in Panama have headquarters in the United States, it is true that the Fed is effectively a lender of last resort for these banks, but there are not only American banks in Panama, and what gives depth to the financial resources that Panamanian banks can tap into are the connections that they have with capital markets abroad, not only the United States. The fact that there is no currency risk for money lenders in Panama is also a factor diminishing the risk of lending in that country, after all, the US dollar is in use directly by the people, and the amount of money available in the economy is given by the aggregate activity of the commercial banks; the banks bring US dollars to Panama when there are profitable opportunities to do so and invest domestic savings abroad when there is a demand for that.

C.2.2 Dollarization through Substitution with a Central Bank: The Cases of Ecuador and El Salvador

In Ecuador and in El Salvador, the US dollar has substituted respectively the sucre and the colon, and now it is used directly by the people. The main difference from the Panama case is the fact that the banking reserves cannot fluctuate so freely to match demand for liquidity inside the country due to the central bank regulations. The central banks in Ecuador and in El Salvador have abandoned the responsibility of lenders of last resort to the banking system, or at least they have had this capacity lowered, and considering that the Fed had not previously agreed to assume this responsibility, as in Panama, the headquarters of the international banks in these countries have become the lenders of last resort to the system. That is, you can have management of bank reserves a) by a central bank, or b) by the spontaneous actions of the different banks in pursuit of their own business,[1] or c) you can have both in the case of substitution with a central bank. The central bank has no revenue from seigniorage since it is not the issuer of the money in circulation.

C.2.3 Dollarization through a Currency Board 100% Backed: The Cases of Belize and Hong Kong

Both in Hong Kong and in Belize, the local currency is backed in 100% reserves of hard currency, mainly the US dollar. In this case, the government can always stop the redemption of the local currency, but then society will incur the costs associated with the issuing of nonbacked money, mainly related to the lesser degree of confidence that the fiat money may command. In a small city-state like Hong Kong was before its devolution to China, the menace of a military invasion or economic blockade was present during the entire Cold War. Under those circumstances, the availability of the reserves (invested and deposited abroad) was a strong support for the currency value; likewise, the decision by the Chinese authorities to keep the Hong Kong dollar redeemable in US dollars has been an important factor in favor of the financial stability of the Hong Kong economy. In this system, the issuer does make a profit with some of the seigniorage revenue, that is, the issuer can lend on interest the money deposited with him in exchange for the locally issued money, deposits over which he pays no interest and which constitute its reserves. To my knowledge, the weakness of the economy in Belize and the political instability of the region recommend some sort of arrangement in order to support the value of the currency, and a currency board has been a traditional option for former British colonies.

C.2.4 Dollarization through a Currency Board Fractionally Backed: The Failed Argentinean Case

In Argentina, since the introduction of their currency board, the central bank used to hold insufficient reserves to redeem all the monetary assets of the country in hard currency since they were allowed to have as part of their reserves a significant percentage of Argentinean treasury bonds. Later, soon before the collapse of their system, the rules were changed in order to allow an even bigger percentage of government debt nominated in US dollars as part of the reserves, effectively destroying any remaining credibility that the "convertibility" may have had at that time. During the years in which the regime of "convertibility" was in force, the country still had a central bank, theoretically with the responsibility of a lender of last resort; then the international banks were supposed to only provide liquidity for their own branches or subsidiaries, not for the entire system. This implicit "shared" responsibility or "double" guarantee of deposits in US dollars at the branches of foreign banks in Argentina proved to be misleading since the government, the effective debtor of most bonds nominated in US dollars, when it finally decided to walk out of the redeemable currency, was able to decree a bank holiday and simply changed the laws in force to that effect. The result was that foreign banks returned to the investors the proceeds of their holdings, now in Argentinean pesos, at a devalued exchange rate.

C.2.5 Dollarization through the Abolishment of Forced Tender: The Cases of Uruguay and Most Other Countries in Which, to a Lesser Degree, the Local Currency has Lost its Forced Tender Feature and has Become Only Legal Tender

In Uruguay, the US dollar has legal tender status and the local currencies are no longer forced tender, although US dollars are legal tender, local currencies have also remained legal tender. This system accepts that, for most deals (like mortgages, commercial loans, rents), the US dollar takes the function of unit of exchange. But conditioned to the size of the government in the economy and its ability to conduct monetary policy, the local currency can maintain a relevant role in the economy. Since the risk of currency exchange persists, most of the benefits of a dollarization are not achieved in this format. The extent of the financial controls can also effectively limit the financial integration of a country in international financial markets simply by the abolition of the forced tender feature of its currency. The extent to which the economic agents actually have the liberty to use other currencies aside from the local one will determine the extension of the economic benefits reaped by the country with this model.

C.3 WHY IS DOLLARIZATION (STILL) AN OPTION TO CONSIDER?

The American government, through its monetary authority, the Fed, has not been supportive of the adoption of the US dollar as legal tender in other countries. I think that they worry about the possibility of being called in the capacity of lender of last resort to foreign governments. In my understanding, that is why they have been reluctant to accept dollarization through substitution, even without any formal obligation on the part of the United States. The risk of political pressure to inflate the currency in order to bail out a foreign government or foreign branches of American banks is real, and it is a major difficulty in the adoption of the dollar as common currency for the Americas. Therefore, there are no indications of changes in this policy, so, any discussion about dollarization must happen inside the framework of a unilateral move by the interested country.

Today, the American government issues bonds, and capitalizes the "IMF," a multilateral institution that bails out the countries with irrational policies. No direct effect is produced on the quantity of money proper, although the increase in "T-Bills" has effects on the allocation of resources in the world economy and, to the extent that they are used as assets backing MMMFs, they do generate inflationary credit expansion and increases in global liquidity with severe allocative effects. If all the countries in the Americas came to adopt the US dollar as their currency, the pressure to inflate the medium of exchange stock and the consequent increase in the general price level would be irresistible to the American government. However, these fears seem unjustified to me, since a new pool of goods and services would be available to holders of US dollars and, therefore, the substitution of local currencies in the Americas would not necessarily imply (additional) inflationary trends.

Not only would the substitution of local currencies by the US dollar not necessarily imply inflation, but also, duly followed with the liberalization of trade in goods, in services, and ideally, of labor, it would increase the productivity of all the economies in the hemisphere.

Since the US dollar is no safe harbor against political mismanagement and its consequences for the quality of money, as the record of the last years has shown, the "dollarization" of other countries in the Americas must be seen as a step towards more liberal policies.

Perhaps this process may not or should not even be called "dollarization," but the process throughout different countries may abolish the forced feature of their currency, liberate foreign exchange controls, and limit access of their governments to financing by the monetary authorities, and it seems to be well on its way. Its results in terms of more stable currencies can be experimented with all around the continent. If the fate of the US dollar as reserve currency comes to be saved from the imbalances of the American federal government and all of their deleterious consequences for the American economy, the liberalization of the monetary arrangements in the Americas may well be a process of "dollarization;" if not, it will be a process of "euronization," "yuanization," or whatever.

C.4 CONSIDERING A EURO-LIKE CURRENCY AS AN ALTERNATIVE

C.4.1 The Euro as a Model for a Monetary System

The supranational single currency adopted in 1999 by the European Economic and Monetary Union (EMU), the euro rivals the US dollar today for the title of reserve currency of the world. It is a greater success than could have possibly been imagined only ten years ago at its launching, not only by the skeptics but also by its supporters. Hayek starts his book on *The Denationalisation of Money —The Argument Refined* arguing that monetary competition would be a "proposal more practicable than utopian European currency" (1990: 23.) For him, the different European governments would not be willing to abandon their national currencies; and in that he was proved wrong. However, his judgment was not only about the practicality of a common currency being adopted but also about the practicality of its operation and its merits.

The jury is still out on the practicality of its operation—only ten years of "fair weather" have elapsed since its adoption; one must see how the ECB (European Central Bank), the European Union and the different member states will react during the aftermath of the recent financial crisis in order to make an assessment about the "extreme unlikelihood," in Hayek's terms, of some countries getting a better currency than the one they used to have. Hayek is adamant about the faults and dangers of a common currency; for him a common European currency (1990: 23) "would ultimately only have the effect of more deeply entrenching the source and root of all monetary evil, the government monopoly of the issue and control of money."

As regards whether or not the adoption of a common currency may be a good tactical move toward achieving competitive currencies, only time will tell:[2] however, what is beyond questioning is the fact that the common currency gave a new lease on life to the idea of government (even if supranational) monopoly over money.[3]

Due to all these doubts associated with the euro as an actual case, perhaps a theoretical model of a supranational currency may help to evaluate it as an option for a possible monetary arrangement.

C.4.2 Main Characteristics of a Euro-Like System

Could, for instance, the different countries in the Americas, the United States among them, accept as a currency one issued by a supranational entity? Could the Organization of American States (OAS) or any other like entity be entitled to issue the american, or the colombian, or whichever name a common currency for the Americas would have? I think that it could demand higher doses of restraint on active monetary policy than the American government would be willing to accept. For the other countries, it could be an alternative with fewer political problems than straight dollarization. It needs to be understood, however, that this change, per se, means nothing if the political mandate and the independence to pursue its mandate of a hypothetical American Central Bank (ACB) are not the same as the European Central Bank (ECB) currently enjoys. Euro is a fiat currency, the European Central Bank is an institution subordinated to the Brussels (although supranational) government, the constitutional restraint on money-issuing, the alleged independence of their central bank, and the noninflationary tradition of the German central bank still do not represent a bullet-proof guarantee of sound money, not to mention a guarantee that they could provide the money Europeans really want for the time being.

Is it better to have a supranational issuer? If this condition is achieved through a governmental grant, one may be excused for being doubtful. For all practical purposes, the dollarization through a currency board in Argentina during the 1990s would not have been different if instead of the dollar the peg had been made with the euro.

A straight substitution for a supranational currency instead of a substitution for a foreign national currency could result in a better distribution of the seigniorage revenue and in less impact of the monetary policy of the national issuer on the supply of money, but it could result in little else.

To be fair, it may be accepted that governmentally issued supranational money could be understood as a step in the right direction: the direction of a money supply independent of national governmental intervention, a supply of money closer in its attributes to the money desired by money holders. Still, it is only one more step in a surely long journey, not the end of the journey.

In *Should Developing Countries Have Central Banks?* Kurt Schuler (1996: 52) states that economic growth is not a measure of monetary quality, but rather that inflation is the most used measure. He is straightforward about the money that would be desired by the money holders: "monetary performance is the extent to which a currency fulfills the textbook functions of money as a medium of exchange, unit of account, and store of value." In discussing disagreements among specialists about how to supply a quality currency to developing countries, Dr. Schuler concludes by quoting Larry White: "Their disagreements point to the flaw in the theory: it assumes economists know better than market participants which currencies people should use."

C.5 POSSIBLE MONETARY SYSTEMS TO BE CONSIDERED

In the realm of theoretical speculation it is possible to conceive of the following alternative scenarios for the monetary arrangements that we have today in the Americas:

a. Different national fiat currencies;
b. A single national fiat currency adopted in the entire continent;
c. A single supranational fiat currency for the entire continent;
d. Different national purely abstract currencies;
e. A single national purely abstract currency;
f. A single supranational purely abstract currency;
g. A deregulated currency supplied by the market;
h. A single national "indexed currency" adopted in the entire continent;
i. A single supranational indexed currency adopted in the entire continent;
j. Different national indexed currencies;
k. Different national "backed currencies";
l. A single national backed currency adopted in the entire continent; and
m. A single supranational backed currency adopted in the entire continent.

In real life, though, fiscal problems of the United States, political idiosyncrasies of the different American countries, the implications of the North American Free Trade Agreement, and the trend toward purely abstract money must be considered. While in an optimistic mood, one would bet on the euro-like scenario F as the one with better probabilities for the Americas in the near future. With pessimism about the evolution of political institutions in the region, a bet on scenario A may be more rewarding, because the trend to purely abstract currency depends on a higher level of confidence than that pessimist assumption can provide. But all those predictions are about what is realistic to expect, which is still far from what is ideal.

NOTES

1. The entire debate in England about the special role of the Bank of England in opposition to the "Free Banking" system in place in Scotland at the time that Peel's Act was introduced in the middle of the nineteenth century was about these alternatives.

2. Rothbard in *What Has Government Done to our Money?* (1990: 110), considering that the establishment of a common currency and a central bank for the European Union would enhance coordination among the major central banks, even asks, "could a World Central Bank be far behind?" This clearly shows skepticism that the adoption of a supranational currency could be a step toward more monetary freedom.

3. In his recent book on *The Tragedy of the Euro*, Philipp Bagus argues that the euro may be seen as an instrument for the socialist view of Europe associated with the idea of political union or the "Roman Empire" vision of Europe; while competition among currencies is associated with the classical liberal view of simple economic union in Europe, without political union, or the "Christian Europe" in the words of Charles Gave (Bagus, 2010c: 8). However, if one takes into account the Hobbesian view adopted by Alexander Hamilton at the time of the Constitutional Convention that there is no ideal size for an army, that the number of troops you need to field is correspondent to the strength of the enemy you may face (the reason why he advocated a federation instead of the existing confederation, since to wage war against the British Empire, the isolated states would likely succumb one after the other), one may conclude that political and monetary union are not necessarily socialist plots. It may be argued that given proper consideration to the subsidiary principle, political union may be the instrument to promote democracy while providing for common defense like on the other side of the Atlantic. Western Europe, since the end of World War II, has abdicated from the responsibility to provide for its own defense and has instead relied on the presence of American troops, the American nuclear shield, and the protection of NATO article 5 to fend off the Soviets, keep open supply lines, and even to prevent genocide in the Balkans among other things. In this sense, political union has not been necessary since all Western European countries are friends and allies of the "Roman Empire." I would suggest that the euro cannot be evaluated outside the context in which it was created; and it is not possible to know what would be necessary to keep peace and open borders in Europe in the absence of the military forces that support the "Pax Americana." Europe has been so far very fortunate that the American demands in exchange for the military protection it has given to Europe have been reasonable and for mutual benefit; but like the French political elite, other Europeans may be willing to take their destiny into their own hands, and for that, political union would be essential. A confederation of despotic states would not be more democratic than a federation ruled by the principle of subsidiarity. Although I consider competition among private issuers of currency a better arrangement than state monopoly provision of money, monetary and banking arrangements cannot be considered outside the contexts of the societies using them. In the case of Europe today, one may theorize about better arrangements than the euro, but an answer for the kind of political arrangements that would support these new monetary institutions must be fleshed out first. That, incidentally, is exactly what Bagus did in discussing in his book the two visions of Europe mentioned above. My only observation is that perhaps those two visions do not capture the complexity of the situation.

Monetary Arrangements, Resource Curse, and the "Dutch Disease"

In this appendix I argue that the "Dutch disease" is an effect of the changes in relative prices both domestically and internationally, a situation that can only be explained a) under the current monetary arrangements, when the monetary authorities allow the real foreign exchange rate to appreciate, and b) when the institutional arrangements in regard to a booming economic sector permit rents to be extracted and distributed through the political process.

D.1 INTRODUCTION

The approach of this inquiry about what I consider essentially a monetary phenomenon is to apply basic concepts about the nature of money as a social institution to the set of specific circumstances of the case in order to better describe them and possibly to be able to prescribe, drawing lessons from that inquiry, what to do in order to get a money better suited to its social function.

For some time now, it has been discussed why the exploitation of mineral resources in general, and oil more specifically, seems to be associated with bad economic and political problems, generating the so-called "resource curse." That discussion has motivated me to develop these thoughts, with the hope of analyzing that aspect of the "resource curse"—also called "Dutch disease"—as a phenomenon, considering how monetary and political arrangements affect the "real" sector of the economy and foreign trade.

Before continuing some clarifications are in order. First, according to Fernando Postali, "the 'Dutch disease' is a chronic competitiveness loss faced by resource-dependent economies resulting from the overvalued exchange rate. The term 'Dutch disease' firstly appeared to describe the impact of natural gas discoveries on the Dutch economy by the 1960s, when the subsequent export boom contributed to overvalue the exchange rate. As a consequence, the competitiveness of manufactured exports was negatively impacted and the economic growth was impaired. Although there are several variants, the 'Dutch disease' started to represent the general description of similar phenomena regarding the adverse effect of overvalued currencies on the economic dynamism" (Postali, 2009: 207).

Second, the extent of the impact of the dependency on mineral "**rents**" varies in intensity according to the shortcomings in the public governance. Therefore, although the paper deals with the "Dutch disease" as a monetary phenomenon, it also reflects on the nature of a ***rentier* state.**[1]

Built on these concepts, my thesis is that "Dutch disease" is a story of the changes in relative prices both domestically and internationally, something that can only be explained under the current monetary arrangements if the monetary authorities allow the real foreign exchange rate to appreciate, but it is also a story that requires substantial rents to happen.

D.2 THE "DUTCH DISEASE": ESSENTIAL ELEMENTS

A widely accepted definition of the "Dutch disease" is "the coexistence within the traded goods sector of progressing and declining, or booming and lagging, sub-sectors" (Corden and Neary, 1982: 825). Since the booming sector is usually of an extractive kind and the lagging sector is a manufacturing sector, the emphasis of the discussion is about the phenomenon of deindustrialization. Some of the most respected analyses on the "Dutch disease" ignore monetary considerations entirely and focus on real variables. As already stated, my understanding is that the phenomenon can only happen under the current arrangements of national fiat money legal tender regimes, and therefore it cannot be understood separately from the monetary regime. For instance, W. Max Corden and J. Peter Neary describe two transmission mechanisms through which the effects of a boom in mineral exploitation is felt by the entire economy: the first, the *resource effect,* is one in which some mobile resource (labor) is attracted to the booming sector, mainly through variations in the real exchange rate; the second, the *spending effect,* occurs when the extra income in the booming sector is spent in services and produces real variation in prices, that is, an appreciation of the real exchange rate (1982: 827). These authors explain the real exchange rate appreciation with the boom in a tradable sector by a diminution in the supply of nontradable goods/services (the resource effect) and an increase in the demand for services/nontradable goods (the spending effect) (1982: 831). They conclude that deindustrialization may be caused directly by the boom in a tradable good and indirectly by the exchange rate appreciation, and the way to ameliorate that is to allow more flexibility in the use of resources (1982: 841).

As already mentioned, for these authors, variations in the exchange rate may be explained solely by variations in relative prices in the domestic market between tradable and nontradable goods. That understanding of real exchange rate is in line with the neoclassical literature that assumes money as neutral in the long run. However, under the assumptions of Austrian economics, in which money is not neutral, the deficiencies of such a definition become clear. Furthermore, it does not allow the analyst to perceive that the changes in the exchange rate—if those changes are understood as changes in the nominal and real parity between different currencies—are crucial to understanding the mechanism through which the "Dutch disease" is transmitted.[2]

In contrast, Michael Ross' definition of the "Dutch disease"—composed of (a) the appreciation of the real exchange rate and (b) the attraction of labor and capital by the booming sector from other sectors in the economy—seems to be more appropriate (1999: 306). In Ross' scheme, the issue of the changes in the real exchange rate is brought into the analysis, and it leads to the crucial question of how the attraction of labor and capital happens, inviting an exploration of the transmission mechanism.

D.3 THE "DUTCH DISEASE" AND MONETARY SYSTEMS

The main argument in this appendix is that the "Dutch disease" is a phenomenon that can only happen under the international monetary system we have today based in national, fiat money currencies and floating exchange rates. The thesis is not a denial that there are dislocations of resources in the real sector driven by the profitability of one industry of tradable goods such as minerals. First such reallocations can hardly be called a disease, and second, the argument is that on top of those movements of resources from other sectors to the booming sector, the "Dutch disease" manifests itself by further dislocations, mostly driven by incentives generated and transmitted by the current monetary system of national, floating fiat monies. Once the first (monetary) condition is present, the thesis is also that the "Dutch disease" manifests itself more strongly when the institutional arrangements in regard to the booming sector permit rents to be extracted and distributed through the political process.

The premises of my thesis are three. First, considering the characteristics of fiat money regimes in place around the world, one cannot expect foreign trade imbalances to be "automatically" corrected, since there are no more "automatic" correction mechanisms such as (with a varied degree of effectiveness, and thanks to the gold standard) existed as late as the early 1970s, when the Nixon administration defaulted on its obligations under the Bretton Woods Treaty. That means that governments are less constrained than they have ever been to pursue active monetary policy without (too much) regard for the impact of those policies on the balance of trade, since they perceive themselves as able also to "manage" that variable.

Second, in order to achieve the different political goals that the respective governments may explicitly or implicitly pursue by using monetary policy as a tool (such as full employment, international competitiveness, and so on), not a single national currency today is free from government's manipulation. Therefore, if money is not neutral, it may be expected that an active monetary policy will create a different allocation of resources in the economy from the one that would happen under a neutral monetary policy (that is, in the absence of any monetary intervention). In turn, those government-guided misallocations would result in arbitrage opportunities for a reallocation of factors in international markets.

Third, mineral wealth is a unique kind of economic good. In traditional economic analysis, increases in production tend to happen at the margin. That is, more efficient producers, under a given state of technological knowledge, marginally and gradually advance production with their profits always tending to approach zero. In regard to mineral wealth, the quality and accessibility of the mineral deposits are such an important component of the costs of production that the success of prospection, even without significant technological changes, may bring to the market a new producer, far from the margin of zero profitability. That is, the law of diminishing returns does not apply to the aggregate of mineral exploitation in the long run (Simon, 1983: 53). Incidentally, it is exactly this characteristic that creates such opportunity for "rents" in that industry.

D.4 THE STORY OF DUTCHLAND

Now, imagine that not so long ago there was a country with a fairly diversified, although small, economy, and a tolerable government, with some degree of political representation, respect for individual rights, and economic links with the international community—so much so that there were no controls of capital flows and the government allowed some fluctuations of the exchange rate of the local currency in relation to their major commercial partners. Let's call that country *Dutchland.* That society also had a monetary regime of legal tender fiat money. The national currency of *Dutchland* was not a "reserve" currency, more because of the size of their economy than because of any terrible mistake in its management, and, therefore, all of its foreign transactions were done in one of the world's reserve currencies. We may mention, in passing, that *Dutchland's* government had some political goals of its own, goals that would be easier to pursue under a lax monetary policy, say, running a loose fiscal policy.

Suddenly, some new mineral findings in *Dutchland* [3] gave rise to the creation of a very lucrative and internationally competitive new industry of mineral exports. The government, in nationalistic fervor and anticipating increases in public revenues, took the lead to extract an important "rent" from the new activity. That did not go well with the owners of the lands where the mineral deposits were found, since they expected to get the rent for themselves, but in the end the government settled with some of them for a tiny fraction of the royalties, proportional to their political clout, and they learned to live with that; the others are still waiting for their day in court and probably will fare no better than the first group, if they get anything at all.

Dutchland soon found itself in a situation in which there were significant inflows of foreign currency derived from the mineral sales. Given the legal tender character of the monetary system, the influx of reserve currency was deposited in the central bank, and the latter credited the government in the local currency (let's call it the "guilder").[4] Since the government had appropriated most of the "rent" for itself, the new revenue was immediately spent in current public expenses, which sharply increased. The government suppliers of goods and services started to use their new income to buy goods in the domestic market.

Under legal tender fiat money arrangements, the monetary authorities are able to control either the general price level or the exchange rate by their manipulation of interest rates and supply of base money. They can even, to some extent, strike a balance between the two, but they could not control both at the same time.

Let's say that the monetary authorities in *Dutchland* were more concerned with keeping the inflation and unemployment low than with the appreciation of the exchange rate, and therefore, in order to prevent the general price level from rising or being forced to raise the interest rate to levels that could damage the economic activity, they allowed the guilder to appreciate in relation to the reserve currencies by "sterilizing" the increases in the money supply generated by the exchange of foreign currency for local currency. The increased demand for exchanging local for foreign currency and a constant supply of local currency forced the exchange rate up, as measured in the guilder.

The moment that the monetary authorities decided to allow the currency to appreciate, the international competitiveness of all tradable goods in the economy started to diminish to some degree. Different goods suffered in different degrees according to the extent that their costs were more or less rigidly linked to prices in the domestic market. For instance, if there had been many "***maquiladoras***" in *Dutchland*, an appreciation of the guilder would not have been that bad for them. On the other hand, if there had been other industries with complex supply chains and substantial costs in local currency not easily replaceable by foreign suppliers, those industries would have suffered immediately from the appreciation of the local currency.

The supply chain of minerals is pretty much straightforward: a mine, means of transportation in bulk, and a harbor. The industry is very intensive in capital, and generally with very low intensity in labor costs. If we assume that the mines are not at the margin of mining worldwide, and that transportation and harbors are not terribly inefficient, the government may give up some of the "rents" to gain market share in international markets and keep exports for a long time, even if that would produce an appreciation of the local currency and diminish the competitiveness of other tradable goods.

The story told in this section illustrates that the impact of the "Dutch disease" in a given country is a necessary consequence of the legal tender fiat money with floating exchange rate regime to the extent that under such regime the proceeds of mineral exports allow for the appreciation of the exchange rate if the monetary authorities so decide.

One also sees that the "Dutch disease" is dependent on: (1) how marginally efficient the mineral production is; (2) the extent to which the state may extract rents from the mineral sector; (3) and the rigidities faced by the other sectors of the economy.

Before moving to the analysis of the "Dutch disease" in the next sections, one important aspect should be considered: Why bother with what is happening to the industrial sector?[5] If manufacturing is losing competitiveness because there are now better uses for capital and labor in mining, society will be better off with less industry. However, it is my understanding that we are not talking here about a matter of better allocation of resources to their most productive uses. I would be the last person in the world to advocate any restriction to the freedom of entrepreneurs to allocate resources the way they see fit. And I do not think that a country necessarily needs to have a big industrial sector to be wealthy and productive.

I think that it is possible to distinguish justifications for industrial protection from the analysis of the "Dutch disease," and I propose to compare what would have been the impact of inflows of revenue generated by mineral exports under a monetary system of commodity international money with the impact under the monetary regimes of national fiat money currencies we have today in order to make such distinction. If the lagging sectors of the economy are losing competitiveness, not because of a natural reallocation of resources to their most productive uses, but because the nature of the monetary system is such that the inflow of revenue of the booming sector is changing the purchasing power parity of the domestic currency and making the lagging sector less competitive (whether or not the resources they use may be transferred to other uses or simply liquidated), I think that one can make the case against such a monetary regime on purely economic grounds and without being understood as a supporter of industrial protectionism or noneconomic motivations.

D.5 A CLASSIFICATION OF MONETARY SYSTEMS ACCORDING TO THEIR MAIN CHARACTERISTICS

There are many dimensions along which a monetary system may be evaluated. Among them the legal status of the currency produced (whether there is legal or forced tender), the scope of action of the monetary authorities (the extent of their formal independence), the sources of value for the money produced (such as currency board), supporting mechanisms of money's relative value (such as international reserves) utilized by the monetary authorities, et cetera. Once one has in mind many of those dimension one may successfully classify different monetary systems according to their main features.

If we would classify them, nowadays the majority of monetary systems around the world share the common characteristics of: (1) having a national fiat money currency to which it is attributed legal tender; (2) the currency is issued by a state-owned central bank; (3) the monetary authorities (usually a central bank) have authority to regulate what other financial institutions can do and to buy and sell public debt in order to influence the interest rate, through management of the supply and demand of money and credit; and (4) the monetary authorities also engage in and regulate foreign transactions in order to influence exchange rates.

There are important differences among monetary systems, and those differences are what explain the different performances of, say, the Chilean and the Argentinean pesos. But those differences are quantitative differences not qualitative ones; that is, for instance, there are degrees of independence of the central bank but nowadays there is not a single system around the world without the government's regulation of money. If no graduation were accepted, no differentiation among most modern monetary regimes would be perceivable and they would be pigeonholed together, which would not to be very useful to explain their comparative merits.

Incidentally, in order to explain the performance of different currencies, it is necessary also to keep in mind that monetary institutions do not exist in a vacuum; and the quality of the institutional arrangements in general, what may broadly be defined as the adherence to the "Rule of Law," is an important component to explain the way in which a given currency is valued relatively to other goods and currencies. Aside from the degree of adherence to the principles of "Rule of Law," the quality of many "instrumental" institutions is also essential to have in mind when comparing different monetary arrangements; after all, if the powers of criminal prosecution in the name of the state may be abused, for instance, because public attorneys are not sufficiently accountable, one cannot talk about "a fair distribution of justice" and the uncertainty about what you can do with your money increases to the point of affecting its value, even if we cannot measure that effect.

That is an important concept to remember: the value of fiat money currencies is always a relative value; since, by definition, it has no intrinsic value. And that is what makes it possible for monetary authorities to use the manipulation of foreign exchange transactions as an instrument to support the value of their currency.

Among the different foreign exchange regimes that monetary authorities may decide to follow, there are variations ranging from relatively more to relatively less elbow-room allowed for the exchange rate to fluctuate, a regime of fixed parity being the regime with the least room for fluctuation. That shows, incidentally, that the foreign-exchange regime has nothing to do with the general "openness" of an economy; since, for instance, you can have a currency "pegged" to another and have free flow of goods and services on one hand (for example, China) and a free-floating exchange rate with very cumbersome commercial and financial regulations on the other hand (for example, the Euro-zone).

A last remark about the essential features of money seems required. If money is assumed to be a generally accepted medium of exchange, money could be anything used as media of exchange by the economic agents, and that which has satisfactory liquidity (the bid-ask price gap is as close to zero as possible) may be used as such. It is granted that such definition is not as precise as legal definitions of money and its aggregates, but it is better at describing the real uses of money, which has important implications for our thesis.

D.6 EXCHANGE RATES AND CONTROL CASES

In an ideal world in which there were no barriers of any kind to the free flow of goods, services, labor, and capital across borders, it would be expected for nominal exchange rates to reflect the purchasing power parity of the different national currencies to acquire all goods and services in their respective countries, tradable and nontradable goods alike, in the same way that under a classical gold standard, like the one in force until 1914, the exchange rate of British sovereigns and 20-franc French angels tended to reflect their different gold content.

Since we do not live in an ideal world, a number of national idiosyncrasies result so that there is a difference between the nominal exchange rate of any currency in relation to other currencies and the differences of their relative purchasing power.[6] It is relevant for our purposes to recognize that there are differences in purchasing power among different currencies, and that those differences are not automatically corrected with changes in nominal exchange rates.

But now consider that you are living, say, in a mineral-rich country around the 1900s. The balance of trade has a substantial surplus, but the local currency, at the time was in the gold standard, so the inflow of foreign exchange, likely British pounds, brought by the sales of, say, copper are re-exported in order to keep equilibrium between the price of gold in the domestic market and abroad. In that country at the beginning of the twentieth century, the supply of base money changes with the increase in the deposits of gold with the banks of issuance. At that time, sterling pounds were as good as gold, and therefore the inflow of foreign exchange would, without the interference of government, produce an increase in the money supply. But the demand for money is a variable independent of the money supply. Let's say that at first, the banks would use the new reserves to try to expand credit; eventually the interest rate will go down below its opportunity cost. The next action is to re-export the excess deposits of gold equivalents. Therefore, if there were more deposits of gold equivalents than the demand for money, the banks would automatically, without the interference of the government, keep not only the money supply but also the exchange rate "in equilibrium."[7]

Let's consider another case, the case of Panama for its entire history as an independent country, but particularly today when the sovereignty over the Panama Canal and the proceeds from the use of the canal unquestionably belong to the Panamanian Government. Panama gives legal tender status to the United States dollar, and Panama does not have a central bank; therefore, the constant inflow of fees paid to the authorities in charge of the Panama Canal operation and spread throughout the Panamanian economy in the form of wages, remuneration of goods and services, etc., are all US dollars. Why do we not talk about a "Dutch disease" in Panama? Why are other sectors of the Panamanian economy not put out of competitiveness because of the inflow of foreign currency and the positive balance of trade Panama has enjoyed for more than a century now? The answer is that, like in the cases of the gold standard, monetary unions, and currency boards, there are no fluctuations of the exchange rate, and the supply of money is not politically determined but it is independently variable.

The decision to highlight these cases was not to advocate a return to the gold standard, a substitution of national currencies by the US dollar, or the introduction of a currency board. These actions should be analyzed by their own merits and challenges, and it is not the place here to do that. The reason to bring up these cases is just to show that the inflow of foreign currency brought by the mineral exports or the exploration of other natural resources—although attracting factors of production from other sectors of the economy and generating income that will be spent in the domestic market, pricing up nontradable goods—does not produce an appreciation of the local currency, because either the exchange rate is independently defined (in the case of the gold standard) or there simply is no exchange rate because the country is in a sort of monetary union with its main commercial partners, by force of the substitution of the local currency or by force of a currency board.

D.7 THE MODEL AND ITS ELEMENTS: FOREIGN EXCHANGE IMPACT IN FIVE SCENARIOS

In order to present my main argument, it is useful to analyze the impact of the increased inflow of foreign exchange and its impact on the economy in five scenarios: first, an economy without money; second, one under a constrained gold standard; third, one under a fiat money regime with fixed exchange rate; and two scenarios under a fiat money regime with floating exchange rate: one in which the monetary policy accepts inflation but not an exchange rate appreciation, and one in which the monetary policy allows the appreciation of the currency.

It is enough to consider this economy with three sectors: the booming tradable sector, which we will call "oil," the lagging tradable sector, which we will call "shoes," and the sector of nontradable goods and services which we will call "hospitality."

We assume that there are two factors of production, "labor" and "imports," and all the production of tradable goods is "exports."

There are two time periods: time one before the boom, and time two after the boom has started.

We will call the foreign currency the "dollar," and the local currency the "peso." The foreign exchange rate at time one is one dollar to ten pesos.

At time one let's say that the revenue of "oil" is zero, the production of "shoes" is about 200 pesos, and the remuneration of hospitality is 200 pesos. The export of shoes generates revenue of 200 pesos, 200 pesos are imported, and the balance of trade is in equilibrium.

At time two there is a production of 200 pesos in oil, consuming 150 pesos in factors of production, 100 pesos in labor acquired in the domestic market (the remaining 50 pesos we may call "rents"), the production of shoes has declined to 100 pesos, and the remuneration of hospitality has remained 200 pesos, but is now consuming 150 in factors of production, which results in a "profit" of 50 pesos. Now the exports of oil and shoes generate revenue of 300 pesos, the imports are now 200 pesos, and there is a foreign trade surplus of 100 pesos.

The existing factors in the domestic market in time one generated an income of 400 pesos and in time two received a remuneration of 500 pesos.

Regardless of any reallocation of factors of production that may be caused and transmitted by the monetary system, this model offers an obvious case in which some resources previously utilized in the production of shoes and hospitality were now invested in the oil business, and the increased demand for nontradable goods and services in the economy increased its remuneration in the domestic market.

This model without money leaves the question of what to do with the trade surplus unanswered, but for the purposes of our comparison, it is not necessary to elaborate further.

Now let's introduce money into the model. First, we will use the gold standard scenario. The only change in the model is that now the balance of trade will be cleared by the Humean "specie" mechanism.[8]

With this scenario we intend to prove that aside from the reallocation of factors of production motivated by the opportunity of more productive uses in the economy, there is no need for an appreciation of the currency to occur, as long as the monetary system is such that there is an automatic "correction" mechanism to keep purchasing power parity between prices in the domestic and foreign markets.

Again, for the purposes of our comparison, we do not need to elaborate what will be done with the gold acquired by the clearance of the balance of trade.

Now let's consider a scenario with fiat money but with foreign exchange with a fixed parity. The central bank, in order to keep the fixed parity, will borrow money in the domestic market with "money market operations" in order to "mop up" the excess liquidity. That will force interest rates up, and impose a burden to the Treasury, since the government will be forced to pay to keep those resources "sterilized" in the central bank. We do not need to elaborate further; suffice it to say that for awhile the policy of "fixed exchange rate," by definition, will prevent the exchange rate from appreciating and therefore will prevent further dislocations in the economy, but these arrangements are unsustainable in the long run.

Chart D.1. Foreign Exchange Impact in a Scenario Without Money

	Time 1 Revenue	Time 1 Expenses	Time 2 Revenue	Time 2 Expenses
Oil	0	0	200	50 imports 100 labor 50 rents
Shoes	200	100 imports 100 labor		50 imports 50 labor
Hospitality	200	100 labor	200	100 imports 50 labor 50 profits
GDP	400	400	500	500
Exports/ Imports	200		300	200
Balance of Trade	0	200	100	

Chart D.2. Foreign Exchange Impact in a Scenario with Gold Standard

	Time 1 Revenue	Time 1 Expenses	Time 2 Revenue	Time 2 Expenses
Oil	0	0	200	50 imports 100 labor 50 rents
Shoes	200	100 imports 100 labor	100	50 imports 50 labor
Hospitality	200	100 imports 100 labor	200	100 imports 50 labor 50 profits
GDP	400	400	500	500
Exports		200	300	500
Imports	200			200 production factors
Balance of Trade	0	200 production factors	0	100 gold imports

Now, let's consider the same variables under two scenarios of floating exchange rates. The first one to consider is the one in which the monetary authorities prefer inflation to the appreciation of the foreign exchange rate.

They will acquire foreign currency with the creation of new domestic money and with that inflate the money supply. Although in nominal terms the exchange rate will go up, the exchange rate measured in constant values, that is, the real exchange rate, may remain stable.

There are all sorts of consequences and repercussions of such a decision by the monetary authorities, but, for the purposes of our comparison, to highlight the fact that no appreciation of the exchange rate necessarily happens is enough.

Let's now discuss the fifth and last scenario, the one with floating exchange rate and noninflationary monetary policy. Under such conditions, the entire surplus in the balance of trade will force an appreciation of the local currency if brought into the country. This is the scenario that describes how the existence of rents in the "booming tradable sector" translates into a change in the purchasing power parity of all domestic prices in relation to the international market, compromising the competitiveness of the "lagging tradable sector" further than the simple reallocation of production factors to the most efficient uses. Again, in order to keep the model simple, we will not try to describe here the impact of the appreciation of the currency or any other corollary of this scenario. We believe that it is a sufficient tool to conclude that only under certain

Chart D.3. Foreign Exchange Impact in a Scenario with a Fixed Exchange Rate

	Time 1 Revenue	Time 1 Expenses	Time 2 Revenue	Time 2 Expenses
Oil	0	0	200	50 imports 100 labor 50 rents
Shoes	200	100 imports 100 labor	100	50 imports 50 labor
Hospitality	200	100 imports 100 labor	200	100 imports 50 labor 50 profits
GDP	400	400	500	500
Exports/Imports	200		300	200
Balance of Trade	0	200	100	
Money Market Operations	0		100	
Exchange Rate	1/10		1/10	

monetary arrangements will the appreciation of the foreign exchange rate associated with the "Dutch disease" happen.

D.8 AN "AUSTRIAN" CONCERN

The "Austrian Business Cycle Theory" (ABCT, for short) is a theory about how the effects of inflationary expansion of credit are transmitted to the real sector of the economy producing a cycle of boom and bust in the economic activity. ABCT is based on the assumption that the transmission mechanism of monetary phenomena does not affect the entire economy equally: the inflationary increase of credit money affects different sectors of the economy at different times and produces different effects. So, this recognition that changes in the money supply affect not only the general price level but relative prices as well, and that changes in relative prices transmit information from the monetary side to the real side of the economy with impact on the structure of production is a central claim of the ABCT.

A useful analogy to establish, for the purposes of this thesis is that given, among other things, the fact that supply and demand factors of production are not perfectly elastic, and neither are they perfectly interchangeable, an increase in the international demand for some goods results in changes in relative prices in the domestic market in the same way that a Cantillon effect is observable during an Austrian Business Cycle. Those changes in relative prices would have happened even in the mon-

Chart D.4. Foreign Exchange Impact in a Scenario with a Floating Exchange Rate and an Inflationary Monetary Policy

	Time 1 Revenue	Time 1 Expenses	Time 2 Revenue	Time 2 Expenses
Oil	0	0	200	50 imports 100 labor 50 rents
Shoes	200	100 imports 100 labor	100	50 imports 50 labor
Hospitality	200	100 imports 100 labor	200	100 imports 50 labor 50 profits
GDP	400	400	500	500
Exports/Imports	200		300	200
Balance of Trade	0	200	100	
Money is created by the Central Bank and exchanged by the surplus of foreign currency, inflating the money	0		100	
Exchange rate kept constant (in real terms)	1/10		1/10	

eyless society of the textbooks; therefore, we insist, there are real movements of factors when the products of one sector of the economy are in higher demand, but that will only have an impact on the exchange rate under a certain kind of monetary arrangement.

Also, it is important to consider that the openness of a national economy to the free flow of goods, services, labor, and capital and the elasticity of domestic prices (that is, the lack of laws and regulations imposing price rigidities) certainly influence the extent to which international demand may distort relative prices in the domestic market. In other words, the amount of time for distortions in relative prices in the domestic market to be "corrected" (that is, for relative prices in the domestic market to get closer to relative prices in international markets) is greatly influenced by coercive domestic measures in force, in the same way that coercive measures may increase the time necessary for the Ricardo effect to operate in the downturn of an Austrian Business Cycle.

D.9 RENT-SEEKING AND THE RESOURCE CURSE

A sensible way to describe the resource curse is to think about it as composed of two elements. The first element is the trigger of rent-seeking activity targeting the "rents" generated by the exploitation of mineral

Chart D.5. Foreign Exchange Impact in a Scenario with a Floating Exchange Rate and Noninflationary Monetary Policy

	Time 1 Revenue	Time 1 Expenses	Time 2 Revenue	Time 2 Expenses
Oil	0	0	200	50 imports 100 labor 50 rents
Shoes	200	100 imports 100 labor	100	50 imports 50 labor
Hospitality	200	100 imports 100 labor	200	100 imports 50 labor 50 profits
GDP	400	400	500	500
Exports/Imports	200		300	200
Balance of Trade	0		100	
Exporters bring into the country the surplus of foreign currency, buying pesos in the market, thus appreciating the domestic currency	0	200	100	
Exchange rate appreciates 20%	1/10		1/8	

wealth that manifests itself by the introduction of perverse incentives in the political sphere. The second element is the bundle of economic problems generated by the appreciation of exchange rates, specifically, the loss of competitiveness of other tradable goods as a consequence of the exports of minerals, the so-called "Dutch disease" (*The Economist*, 2012).

Christa Brunnschweiler and Erwin Bulte distinguish between abundance and dependence on oil revenue: oil revenues approaching 50% of export revenues cease to be abundance and become dependence. While abundance leads to faster growth, dependence may be detrimental if coupled with poor political institutions (Brunnschweiler and Bulte, 2008). So, according to these authors, a key element in determining the outcome of oil revenue is the quality of the political institutions and not so much the aspects of the economic structure in place at the time the oil revenue begins.

Some supporting evidence for their thesis may be found in F. Postali, who makes a comparative analysis of the economic performance of municipalities in Brazil with the highest royalty revenues in relation to a representative group of other towns. He concludes that:

> Results suggest the existence of a phenomenon that resembles the so-called resource curse, to the extent that high resource-dependence

> seems to impact negatively on local economic growth. Higher royalty revenues tend to reduce the economic growth of municipalities entitled to receive them compared to the control group (Postali, 2009: 211).

Since all municipalities in Brazil use the same currency and there is unimpeded labor and capital mobility in the country, we cannot say that exchange rates or crowding out of resources are responsible for those consequences. Therefore, Postali argues that the "Dutch disease" is not a valid explanation for the poor performance of those local governments; further, he thinks that "blaming local institutions and opportunistic behavior for inefficiencies in the use of those revenues" may be tempting, but it is premature (2009: 212). I have only anecdotal evidence to support my disagreement that such a conclusion is premature, but for now, the relevant conclusion is that poor political arrangements may be understood as an independent variable from the "Dutch disease" to explain the "resource curse."[9] Aside from the "Dutch disease," Postali offers other explanations for the resource curse, such as the crowding out of capital for investments, the peculiar production path of mineral exploration, the influence of mineral exploration in the institutional design, the decline in the terms of trade, the inherent instability of the market price for natural resources and, last but not least, the misuse of rents (2009: 207). Regardless of the fact that all these explanations cannot be true at the same time and some of them are not true at all, it is important to stress the independence of the two variables we are discussing here: one may witness bad economic results from the misuse of rents even if other parts of the same economic area are thriving; and it is also possible to have a significant percentage of total export revenue proceeding from mineral exploitation without that causing a manifestation of "Dutch disease," much less "resource curse."

It is worth exploring what at prima facie seems to be contrary evidence to the thesis that the resource curse is a consequence of political decision-making in regard to mineral wealth generating rent-seeking. That is the case of Norway. Ola Listhaug argues that, in the Norwegian case, bringing oil wealth under political control was a good thing (Listhaug, 2005: 835). The argument raises the question of whether it is possible to explain, using "Public Choice Theory," the Norwegian government's perceived position of trying to save oil revenue and not spend it. To answer that one needs to study particularities such as the composition of parliament and the division of power between elected politicians and bureaucrats who have different time preferences for public spending. Anyway, the author's emphasis is on trust in the government; he seems to think that some skepticism is salutary but cynicism is not. For the author, the purpose of the oil fund is to "handle" fluctuations of revenue flows into the domestic economy and to provide for pensions, a goal that in his view the government-managed fund has performed satisfactorily so far (2005: 838). The author recognizes, however, that putting the oil revenue in an oil fund postponed but did not eliminate the rent-seeking problem; the oil fund became the target of rent-seeking (2005: 839). True, the data presented in that paper does not support the hypothesis that oil wealth has undermined confidence in democratic institutions in Norway; perhaps it never will, but what seems to be the most clear conclusion from the analysis of the Norwegian case is that better instrumental institutions, such as a well-designed perpetual fund with a policy of sharing annual dividends throughout the population and a culture of limited and representative government, create checks to the perverse incentives that are at the core of the resource curse.

A final argument in favor of the idea that the resource curse is essentially a political and not an economic problem[10] is the argument claiming there are antidemocratic properties in mineral wealth appropriated by the state, which Michael Ross defines as the rentier effect. For him, the rentier effect operates through taxation, expenditure, and group formation (2001: 335). The taxation effect implies that states that fund themselves more with personal and corporate taxes are more democratic. The expenditure effect implies that states with higher government consumption as a percentage of GDP are less democratic. Looking for a group formation effect, higher government share of the GDP would imply less democracy (2000: 347). According to this interpretation, a resource curse is one more example of the tragedy of the commons (Shaxson, 2007:1128), and the two elements of lack of accountability of the political class and the perverse incentives generated by rent-seeking would be eliminated if there were a direct distribution of oil revenue, preferably through private property and funding the needs of the state through tax collection (2007: 1135).

D.10 CONCLUSIONS

The "Dutch disease," as I define it here, is a specific effect of the appreciation of the real exchange rate of a national legal tender fiat currency. That appreciation is caused by the conversion of increasing amounts of foreign currency earned by nationals in their exports of minerals, when a substantial part of those earnings is constituted by "artificial rents" and not factors of production. If there were no government intervention in the mineral industry, that is, if all factors of production were open to be privately appropriated, there would not be, by definition, "artificial rents." So the way in which the revenue of mineral exports will be used is a function of the extent to which government's intervention in the mineral sector generates "artificial rents," and changes in relative prices both domestically and internationally can be derived from that intervention.

In an effort to prevent the excess liquidity produced by capital inflows from generating inflation, the government may either allow the local currency to appreciate or may build up reserves, which puts pressure on the public budget. In any case, in a context with no "automatic" mechanisms to balance the supply and demand of liquidity under national monetary arrangements, and in the presence of rigidities in the economy, there may be no "good" solution to cope with the above-mentioned problem. In that context, any policy directed towards fighting the excess liquidity will tend to generate fiscal imbalances or will induce a lack of competitiveness in other sectors of the economy.[11]

A final note is that the different models I have presented here may suggest an indictment against floating exchange rates. Given the fact that prices generally tend to be rigid downwards, it is "less painful" to adjust the purchasing power domestically by inflation than by deflation. But one may not assume that the foreign trading partners would not react to such policy, for example by implementing protectionist measures. Understanding this is one more reason to conclude that, as long as we have national fiat monies, there will not be monetary policies without undesired unintended consequences.

NOTES

1. For Michael Ross, the rentier-state explanation for the resource curse is based on the assumption that the state is not a revenue maximizer (Ross, 1999: 313). I disagree. Statesmen may act rationally in limiting taxation and accountability; a certain amount of taxation without too much accountability might be the greatest possible result in terms of revenue maximization for the politician.

2. J. Peter Neary, in his treatment of the real and monetary aspects of the "Dutch disease," introduces a third effect which he labels *liquidity effect*. Such an effect, unequivocally monetary, is the transmission mechanism through which, under a fixed-exchange-rate regime, there is a build-up of foreign exchange reserves delaying the real effects of the boom (Neary, 1982: 18), and under a floating regime, it makes the exchange rate "bear all the brunt of ensuring that the money market clears at the new higher level of real income" (1982: 21). My conclusions are similar to the conclusions of his monetary model, although Neary, accepting the treatment of real exchange rates as a story of changes in relative prices in the domestic market, does not take into consideration changes in the purchasing power parity, which, I argue, is essential to understanding the "Dutch disease."

3. For an actual description of the events related to the findings of the Slochteren gas fields in the Groningen province in the Netherlands in the late 1950s and their economic consequences, see Rudd (1996).

4. It does not matter much whether the government intervenes directly in the foreign exchange market by centralizing all foreign exchange transactions, or if it allows private clearing of foreign exchange transactions and intervenes only indirectly by providing liquidity to financial institutions, through the manipulation of the demand for money via the interest rates, et cetera. In the former case, the influx of foreign currency will be acquired in exchange for newly printed domestic currency and kept in reserves with the central bank, and the latter will need to sell bonds (previously bought from the treasury) to "mop up" the excess liquidity in the economy and avoid too much inflationary pressure. In the latter case, the central bank will

need first to sell public debt in order to raise funds to provide the government with local currency in exchange for the foreign currency earned with the mineral exports, and next it will need to provide liquidity to the financial system to prevent the interest rate from going up. Either way, the monetary authorities, by issuing a mixture of base money and public debt, will provide the necessary liquidity in the domestic currency for the clearance of foreign transactions and will try to control the impact of the increased liquidity in the general price level by inducing some of that money to be "sterilized" in public debt.

5. Neary, in a paper written solo, in the same year of his seminal paper on the "Dutch disease" with Corden, concluded that: "de-industrialization following a resource boom is a 'disease' requiring treatment only if a large manufacturing sector is desired for the sake of some non-economic objective, or if distortions (such as wage stickiness) impede the smooth reallocation of resources" (Neary, 1982: 26).

6. Because that fact is well recognized, models of "Purchasing Power Parity" are usually displayed in order to better compare "real" exchange rates. Purchasing power parity theory was popularized by the Big Mac Index created and regularly published by *The Economist* under the assumption that the famous sandwich is a sufficiently representative and uniform bundle of goods and services; so much so, that the discrepancy between its price in different countries and the nominal exchange rate may be used as gauge of how much "real" and "nominal" exchange rates are at variance.

7. There is an interesting case reported by Carnies (1873) about the increase in wages in Australia in the middle of the nineteenth century due to the massive discoveries of gold that is well explained by Mauro Boianovsky, the author of "A Brief History of Economic Thought on Dutch Disease," (Sinnott et al., 2010: 15, box 3.2). Due to the particular circumstances that wages were paid in gold and that the abundant and efficiently produced mineral wealth was precisely gold, although the country was part of the international gold standard at that time, the phenomenon was one of real appreciation of the exchange rate, more than one of changes in relative domestic prices; after all, not all farmers moved to work in the gold mines. That is precisely the phenomenon that I argue operates nowadays as rents of the mineral exports are transmitted to the rest of the economy through floating exchange rates.

8. Here, for the sake of the model, we are using a very basic model of a gold standard, a system with Humean characteristics in which the flow of specie would balance prices internationally. Incidentally, it was already noted that in nineteenth-century England the operation of this external drain of specie would only work in order to keep the monetary system "neutral," that is, neither promoting nor reducing the business cycle under a hypothetical purely metallic currency as described by Hume in his essay "Of the Balance of Trade" (1987: 308). Under the gold reserve system with a central bank of that time, its effects were not immediately perceived, but took some time to happen, as L. White mentions (1995: 115).

9. For other authors the resource curse is entirely a political and not an economic problem, and the increased levels of external intervention and the lower levels of checks on political power precisely because of a lesser dependence on tax revenues may explain it. For one of these authors, the solution is to implement via a "fiscal social contract" political reforms to diminish rent-seeking activities through transparence and accountability (Karl, 2007: 256).

10. For an Exxon Mobil spokesperson, there is not an "oil" curse but a "governance" curse (Shaxson, 2007: 1125).

11. In the specific case of Brazil, the increase in investments in the oil and gas industry in the last decade may have already caused "Dutch disease," not yet as a consequence of the oil exports, but from the influx of foreign currency that produces the same effect as exports in exerting pressure on the exchange rate.

Financial Repression

A Study Based on the History of Viscount of Maua

This appendix explores the role of financial repression in nineteenth-century Brazil and its consequences for development and freedom in the country and is brought as evidence of accepting the normative implications of the state theory of money's origins.

The general topic of financial repression, obviously, is of much larger application than just for the Brazilian case. Based on their observation that the distribution of banking crises follows a nonrandom pattern, Calomiris and Haber noted that in the United States fourteen banking crises were reported in the last 180 years, while in Canada they had two (Calomiris and Haber, 2014: 5). Bank crises are correlated with low income countries, that is, with other institutional shortcomings, but why is the United States on that list? (Calomiris and Haber, 2014: 7). Calomiris and Haber's answer to this question is that "the fragility of banks and the scarcity of bank credit reflect the structure of a country fundamental political institutions" (Calomiris and Haber, 2014: 12). This understanding is based on the assumption that the government policies reflect the "real constitution" of the country; that is, the political settlement among the most powerful political groups in society, as first proposed by Ferdinand Lassalle (1862), is not necessarily the written code that usually embodies it. The logical conclusion of their thesis is that banking arrangements are mainly guided by a political logic, not by criteria of market efficiency (Calomiris and Haber, 2014: 13) and the evolution of banking institutions is not the consequence of a "free market" but have been driven by the same political considerations (2014: 38), that is, by coercion. In their effort to demonstrate that the key factors shaping banking arrangements are political, Calomiris and Haber draw heavily on Brazilian banking history (2014: 22), as McKinnon did before (1973) when he first proposed the concept of "financial repression."

Banking regulations, argue Calomiris and Haber, are prone to inconsistencies in addressing the property rights issues making banking arrangements unstable, not only because in the government many conflicting interests are represented, but mainly, because banks are inescapably instruments of public finance (2014: 34).

The taxonomy proposed by Calomiris and Haber of regimes and banking systems in figure 2.1 (2014: 42) leaves clear the link between the political regime and banking arrangements. Evidently, it is a generalization, and the range between competitive banking and politically centralized credit allocation is a continuum that tends to be correlated with more or less limited and representative government and with a smaller or bigger role of government in the economy in general. Nevertheless, it is an excellent visual presentation of varied forms of banking regulations and their relation with the political settlements in different societies.

Back to the Brazilian case, in *Maua , Empresario do Imperio* (*the Entrepreneur of the* [Brazilian] *Empire*), Jorge Caldeira argues that, from the nineteenth century on, financial repression in Brazil and the political restrictions on the concession of credit were used as instruments to control society. Irineu Evangelista de Sousa, the Viscount of Maua (1813–1889), was a Brazilian entrepreneur, industrialist, banker, and politician. A pioneer in several areas of the economy of Brazil, one of his greatest achievements was to start the construction of the Maua Railroad, the first railroad in Brazil. At his peak, Maua controlled eight of the country's ten largest companies (the remaining two were state-owned) and his banking interests stretched over to Britain, France, the United States, and Argentina. However, his fortunes turned around with the decay of the empire after the Paraguayan War. By the time he died, Maua had lost most of his wealth. At a time in which Brazil was dominated by government-protected landowners who prioritized exports in a slave-based economy, Maua defended free enterprise, liberalism, industrialization, and the abolition of slavery.

Financial repression consists of any of the measures that governments employ to channel themselves funds which would go elsewhere in a deregulated market; and the creation of such institutional arrangements in the second half of nineteenth century in Brazil is exactly what Jorge Caldeira tries to describe with his book. In chapter 28, Caldeira describes the solution found by Maua to fund his enterprises: accessing international financial markets. In chapter 29, Caldeira discusses not only how Maua tried to create a culture of "prudent risk taking" inside his conglomerate, but also the difference between productive investment and wasteful spending. And finally, in chapter 30, Caldeira gives an account of how politics in the court and economic policy were intertwined during the nineteenth century in Brazil and the dire consequences of that for Maua. Mr. Caldeira's book therefore is an excellent source to discuss the phenomenon of "financial repression" at the time that it was being established in Brazil; it not only allows the reader to understand the phenomenon in its simplest form, but also it offers sufficient detachment for the discussion to be focused on the topic without the distractions that proximity with persons and ideas sometimes brings to the discussion of current events. And in this sense it offers, in my judgment, the ideal departing point for a discussion on the Ronald McKinnon thesis, first proposed in his 1973 *Money & Capital in Economic Development*. In chapter 7, McKinnon describes, with express reference to the Brazilian case in the late 1960s, the consequences of regulations imposing constraints on bank lending in general for the development of credit markets and economic development. Although his interest at the time was to argue for the possibility to fight inflation without compromising economic growth (it would just be sufficient to reduce the fiscal imbalances of the public sector and eliminate mandates forcing savings to inefficient sectors at subsidized rates of interest, he argued), the description of the phenomenon of political allocation of credit, so prevalent in Brazil, became an important element of economic analysis and an important tool to explain how and why intervention with money and credit is so important for politicians, so damaging for the economy, and so difficult to eliminate.

In this appendix we are discussing first the implications of political control of finances and monetary policy in the development of private enterprise in nineteenth-century Brazil, with Maua as an example. The final sections are dedicated to exploring the theory of and practical evidence for "financial repression" and the consequences for economic development of the political control of money and credit.

I hope readers will consider the Brazilian experience, both in the nineteenth and twenty-first centuries, as relevant for every country today, and it may serve as a cautionary tale about how NOT to try to stimulate economic growth.

E.1 MAUA, THE MAN AND HIS ACHIEVEMENTS

More than Maua's achievements, it is good to start discussing what caused the demise of Maua's business empire. Maua was too close to the government for comfort, the same government which could give him privileges could and did take his businesses from him; although Maua had no alternative but to be close to the government, considering the patrimonialism of Brazilian society at that time as that Weberian term has been applied to explain the kind of institutional arrangement that emerged in Brazil with the arrival of the Portuguese and the kind of society they built there. We should remind ourselves that Brazil was a mercantilist society, but not only Brazil; foreign investment around the world during the nineteenth century was not capitalism as one finds in textbooks: railroads and other major infrastructure and industrial projects demanded and often got from local governments warranties of minimal return for their investors, monopolies, protective tariffs, and subsidies, usually in land, and direct subsidies in cash were not unheard-of as well. Maua was obviously an accomplished entrepreneur, able to perceive opportunities to exercise his entrepreneurial skills, but the limitations of Brazilian capital markets—in which there was almost no capital available and in which most savings were invested in slaves or land, and in which he was competing with the government to have access to the little there was—posed a real barrier for his growth. We may consider though that there was more to it than that; even if one does not consider the "suicidal" decision to lend money to the Uruguayan government, having a substantial part of his fortune at risk of being seized in the country, even if one does not consider Maua's ill-advised decisions to run a "parallel" foreign policy or his opposition to the domestic policies of many conservative cabinets, still, it would have been possible for him to raise capital in London or to develop capital markets in Brazil, if not for the desire of political control over financial matters of the Brazilian imperial government. Think about the figure of Maua in Brazilian historiography; after being considered one of the three leading figures of the nineteenth century, a mere "lackey of British interests," and being relegated to oblivion, the renewed discussion about the role of the government in the economy after the redemocratization of Brazil in the 1980s gave cause to a renewed interest in Maua as emblematic of private enterprise in fields in which Brazilians were used to seeing a monopoly of state action. Unfortunately, like in the nineteenth century, given the regulatory institutional framework, twenty-first century private business in Brazil (operating in the same infrastructure and financial sectors as Maua), are as subject to government's fiat as he was; and willingly or not, as much part of the political process as Maua found himself. And of course, they are exposed to the same risks.

E.2 MAUA, THE MAN AND HIS CIRCUMSTANCES

In Maua's saga, it is possible to discern the Iberian origin of Brazilian centralized government, inhibitor of progress, perfectly captured in the framework described by the patrimonial typology of Max Weber. Such typology was applied to explain Brazilian reality by many authors as summarized by Ricardo Velez Rodriguez in the piece *Patrimonialismo e a Realidade Latino-americana* (Velez Rodriguez, 2006); each one with different emphasis, but common in their understanding that Brazilian social structure had not evolved from feudal Europe but from patrimonialistic Europe. Such assertion is not accepted by all, however; for some, Weber's distinction is more a question of degree than one of different quality. It was said that in the Iberian Peninsula in medieval times, "the law makes the king," while later, in modern times under absolutism, "the king makes the law." In this sense, Brazilian centralism was attributed to the "modernizing" reforms of Marques de Pombal, the all-powerful prime minister of the Portuguese King Joseph I from 1750 to 1777 and epitome of the absolutism in the Portuguese empire. The distinction between a feudal and a patrimonialistic heritage being one of degree as it may be, for most commentators, the character of private appropriation of political power, of conduction of public business as an extension of the family, the existence of a society not as mobile as a class society nor as rigid as a caste society, but one in which there is a (bureaucratic) "stratum" is evident in the formation of the Brazilian society. What all seem to agree on is that restatement of feudal prerogatives, or newly invented limitations on absolutism, and the overcoming of abuses of power happened by the establishment of a constitutionally limited government. But before engaging in a discussion about how far Brazil has evolved in the direction of a constitutional government, perhaps we should delve into a discussion about the origin of the state and the material conditions for totalitarianism. The concept of "hydraulic societies" of Karl August Wittfogel (one in which the need for massive collective projects, much bigger than what can be done by individual families may explain centralization of power) may or may not be a valid explanation for authoritarianism in ancient Egypt or Mesopotamia, but it was certainly not a valid explanation for Soviet Russia as was Wittfogel's intention. Perhaps the need of a strong national government to keep slavery was an important component in the explanation of why Portuguese America remained unified as a country, but this is not the place to explore that further. In any case, the "stationary bandit" theory about the origin of the state shared by many scholars, including the Brazilian Darcy Pereira de Azambuja (1903–1970), as a consequence of which it is silly to think that public officials are remotely concerned with the common good, is a realistic explanation for the origin and nature of political power, and the understanding of the government as a "stratum" of society which has evolved from an "occupation force" better explains the relation between government and subjects than any romantic theory about the nature of political power; it better explains the need and the limitations of what is possible to achieve under constitutional government. Although it is difficult to say that Brazil lives nowadays under a constitutionally representative and limited government under which there is to some extent the "Rule of Law," the country is better off in that sense as it has ever been, although the current leftist government is doing its best to move the country backwards.

E.3 MAUA, THE MAN AND HIS DEBACLE

To understand Maua's change in fortune it is necessary to understand what went wrong with Maua's investments in Uruguay. The definition of the southern border between the Portuguese and the Spanish empires in South America was one of fierce disputes due to the ambition of the Portuguese to share control of the Rio de la Plata occupying its oriental band, that is, Uruguay, and also the fierce determination of the Spaniards to deny that. When Maua started to exercise influence on Uruguay, even more so when he decided on the unorthodox move of lending to the Uruguayan government in its attempts to become independent from both Argentina and Brazil, Maua lost the support of the Brazilian government; and that was a terrible mistake at the time since the last resort to collect sovereign debt were the gunboats. Even granting this misstep in meddling with a contentious issue of foreign policy, one may ask why the Brazilian government denied Maua the right to incorporate a bank, the main reason, other than the Uruguayan debacle, why Maua's business failed. Possible reasons, ranging from personal differences to the "logic of financial repression," that is, the conscious effort to control financial resources by the state, tend to converge on two possible sets of explanations: first, in the "real" set of explanations, there is the hypothesis that Maua's enterprises and the government were in competition for available savings in the domestic market, and also that banks were banks of issuance about that time, and therefore, the Brazilian government then was not willing to share with Maua, an outspoken member of the Liberal opposition, such an important part of the government's prerogatives; on the side of "theoretical" explanations, first, it may be said that the demand for credit necessary to keep Maua's many enterprises afloat would require the abandonment of the "Real Bills Doctrine" since what he needed was long-term funding for his infrastructure projects, such as railroads and the like; and, second, there was another genuine "theoretical" issue at stake, that is, whether it was convenient to have multiple banks of issuance or if it was more satisfactory to have a monopoly of issuance. Those theoretical and practical issues may be seen as two sides of the same issue, the limitation of available "real" savings in the domestic market and the unwillingness of politicians to lose the power of regulating the inflow of foreign capital into the country. A parallel discussion about the circumstances in which Maua found himself at odds with the Brazilian government was whether or not the Brazilian government was "weak" to the point of being afraid of Maua's economic prowess or if it was making too strong a point in capriciously curbing progress that was not happening at its command. It is difficult to end this discussion with a clear opinion about that; on one hand, the Brazilian government seemed too weak to accomplish things, entangled in a net of conflicting interests, lack of reliable information, lack of disposable income, et cetera; on the other hand, there were 250,000 free men at the service of the Brazilian emperor, the biggest power structure in the Western hemisphere at that time.

E.4 COMPARING THE EFFICIENCY OF DIFFERENT STRUCTURES OF FINANCIAL MARKETS

It was in the seminal piece by Ronald McKinnon on "Financial Repression and Inflation" (McKinnon, 1973) where the concept of financial repression was first proposed. An important element that immediately calls the attention of the reader in that work is the need of having the relation between "real" savings and "real" investments in mind and the fact that the financial flows should be properly understood as representations of that relation. In England, for instance, wealth had been accumulated for centuries before the second half of the nineteenth century (the time the events discussed in this chapter took place), furthermore, there were institutional conditions in terms of protection of private property, freedom of contract, and (relatively) mature financial markets for such accumulation to take place, the availability of "real" savings, that is, of real goods that could be mobilized for investment was huge. In Brazil, on the other hand, the availability of real goods necessary to make any investment was minimal; the actual rails, the equipment, the engines, almost everything to build a railroad, for example, needed to be procured abroad, and that limitation in actual goods and the ways in which access to financial instruments might shift access to them from those making the savings and those managing the saved funds offers the economic rationale for the concept of financial repression. Another important component of the complex phenomena we are trying to understand is the fact that at that time, although Brazil had a nonconvertible currency, it was nominally in the gold standard (Franco, 2005: 9–33). What happened is that the Brazilian paper currency, because redemption was suspended most of the time, was exchanged at a discount for British pounds (which were redeemable in gold at a fixed parity). In order to prevent a deterioration of the exchange rate between Brazilian currency and British pounds, the Brazilian government was forced to impose some control on how many banknotes the banks would issue; and that caused a constant complaint voiced by the farmers and merchants that there was a "scarcity" of money. The limitations of actual savings for all the demands for investments (be they productive or not) have been a common feature of the Brazilian reality since the nineteenth century. Governments are quite willing to issue money or to monetize debt in order to give their favorites access to existing goods or to a limited extent, to imported goods, but in doing so, they create claims to those goods above and beyond their availability, which creates the conflict that is reflected from time to time in the mismatch between time deposits and bank assets, or in the devaluation of the exchange rate. The instruments of financial repression were not clearly understood by the government, nor even applied with a conspiratorial intent; it is possible that some public servants were simply reacting to consequences in the financial sector of political decisions with consequences in the real economy that they could not understand within the theoretical apparatus and under the limitations of the institutional arrangements of that time; for instance, nowadays we do not see the reasons for the debate between the "bullionists" and the defenders of fiat money because the constant devaluations of weaker paper money currencies "solve" that problem, while at the time of Maua, breaking the parity between two currencies theoretically linked to the gold standard was unthinkable. Again, many obligations of the Brazilian central government were in either gold or British pounds, and therefore, they were only reacting to the circumstances—when limiting the expansion of paper money by the banks, they were only trying to keep the purchasing power of their tax revenues.

E.5 THE AFTERMATH: CURRENT PUBLIC DEBT POLICY

This is the first section in this appendix focused entirely on current events; and the phenomenon of "crowding out" of private, productive investments by public spending takes center stage. There are many ways in which the resources necessary to satisfy the public sector financial needs (PSFN) may be obtained. The government may establish regulations inducing or mandating that some classes of investors are required to buy public bonds, the government may raise the interests it is willing to pay and "price out" other potential takers of resources, the government may mandate the banks to do certain investments which favor privileged sectors, the government may establish some compulsory mechanisms to funnel savings to be managed by the government directly or indirectly, reducing the amount of savings to be allocated by the market, and et cetera.

All of these forms are present in many different instances in Brazil today. That is why the interest rates in Brazil are still the highest in the world, and no legitimate long-term investment can be made in the country either without bringing resources raised abroad or obtained at a subsidized rate in the domestic market by political decision (Franco, 2011). The economic power that gives to the government over the private sector is tremendous and often not realized by many foreign observers. The BNDES (the Brazilian national development bank) with its multibillion dollar budget, with funds obtained from a compulsory saving scheme linked to the payroll of all employees in the formal labor market in the country, with an often negative return, is not a "mistake" of the economic policy of the country, it is an intentional feature of the status quo, a machine through which political patronage is exchanged for subsidized credit. Another important aspect of Brazilian capital markets is the very low trust investors have in the public debt; although it is no longer true that all public debt is essentially rolled overnight, most of the public debt is still financed at very short periods, measured in a few days or weeks, and even that at the highest interest rates in the world. Brazilian capital markets barely have the semblance of normality and will remain like that while the PSFN de facto represent so significant a part of the gross domestic product (GDP). A final topic of discussion is what the PSFN actually are since the "captive" markets for treasury bonds, on top of dubious methodological assumptions such as the understanding that the principal of the public debt is rolled in perpetuity when the government cannot find takers for more than few months, raise a smokescreen over the market, making it difficult for any analyst to calculate the amount of those needs.

E.6 THE AFTERMATH: CURRENT FOREIGN EXCHANGE REGIME

At this closing section we should focus on the issue of the foreign exchange regime. It may be illustrated as a dispute between some economists in the central bank and in the treasury; on one hand, papers such as *Globalizacao e inconversibilidade monetaria* (Carneiro, 2007) were commissioned to support the opposition to more competition in currencies in Brazil. However, even the proposal of a fully convertible Brazilian currency defended in papers such as "Conversibilidade do real e inserção internacional da economia brasileira" (Tavares de Araujo, 2009) are not bold enough, since regulation forbidding the adoption of foreign currency as a means of payment in domestic contracts would not be abolished. In the end, although a weakening of the forced tender status of the Brazilian real would be welcomed as a baby step in the right direction, a most significant constraint on the power of the authorities to manipulate the money supply would only be established by the total abolition of forced tender laws (under the assumption that the abolishment of legal tender laws is impossible to contemplate at this time). Next, it may be argued that the relatively small size of foreign trade as a percentage of GDP in Brazil is an impediment for the adoption of Brazilian currency even by its closest trade partners. On the other hand, that was never the intention of the proposal of allowing free convertibility of the Brazilian real; the goal has always been to impose a constraint on the ability of the government to expand the money supply. If questioned about what the ideal exchange rate regime would be, it may be said that the adoption by Greece in 2001 of a single currency with other countries in Europe with fewer rigidities in their economic arrangements was not a shot in the foot, it was a shot to the head, and one may be afraid that the same would happen with Brazil under full convertibility. In reply to that, I would say that full convertibility does not imply convertibility at a fixed parity and that allowing the exchange rate to reflect the actual relative scarcity of the

Brazilian real in comparison with other currency would make capital markets more, not less efficient, since a market price would be revealed and available to be used as a guide for individuals' decisions. We may conclude this discussion mentioning the Brazilian "law of fiscal responsibility" (LFR) as the actual bedrock of economic and political stability in the country, since it is thanks to the LFR that the federal government can at least curb the state and local governments in their profligacy and has to wear a fiscal straitjacket itself. It is not that the LFR is perfect or that it has improved the fiscal situation of the country, but at least it has effectively prevented it from deteriorating even more. Whether other limitations of the ability of the government to monetize debt, such as the full convertibility of the Brazilian real or a straight abolishment of forced tender laws, would be (politically) possible to implement, I remain skeptical, but that they would help to improve market conditions in Brazil, I have no doubts.

Glossary

- Abstract Money—a monetary unit without physical representation, a pure unit of account, such as a price index under current fiat money arrangements. It is my contention that there is a trend toward purely abstract monetary arrangements in the developed countries.
- Acatallactic—the opposite of Catallactic (see below), not resulting from free market interactions.
- Arbitrage—**Arbitrage** is the practice of taking advantage of the knowledge about a price differential between two or more markets.
- Assignats—paper money issued during the French Revolution soon discredited (1794) because of its inflation.
- Backed Currency—A currency issued under a gold reserve system or a currency board system in which the banknotes are redeemable in the assets backing the value of the currency in question.
- Band—The most ancient and simplest form of human society is a **band**. Consisting of a small kin group, a band usually is no larger than the extended family or clan.
- Banking System—The body of financial institutions specializing in deposits, issuing, lending, capital markets, insurance markets, mortgage markets, exchange trade, et cetera.
- Banknotes—Paper bills.
- Barter System—A **barter system** is a system of direct exchanges that presumes a coincidence of wants among traders. In a barter system, for an exchange to happen, traders must want what the other has to offer, when and where it is offered.
- BFH System—Leland Yeager developed with Robert Greenfield the layout for a new monetary system from the contributions of Fischer Black, Eugene Fama, and Robert Hall, which they named the "**BFH system**." Yeager and Greenfield describe the system as a payment system, in which a medium of exchange ceases to exist and people use only the clearance of bonds and mutual fund shares to pay for their debts. Under this system, the unit of account ceases to be defined physically by a basket of commodities, and is no longer regulated by its quantity or redeemability. According to Yeager and Greenfield, the BFH system requires minimal governmental intervention. In their proposal, "Apart from defining the unit and enforcing contracts, the government would practice laissez-faire to-

ward the medium of exchange and the banking and financial system" (Yeager, 1997: 364).

- Bill of Exchange—The earliest written document dealing with money of which we have record, a **bill of exchange** is defined by the British Bills of Exchange Act of 1882, part II, article 3(1) to be "An unconditional order in writing, addressed by one person to another, signed by the person giving it, requiring the person to whom it is addressed to pay on demand or at a fixed or determinable future time a sum certain in money to or to the order of a specified person, or to bearer."
- Bond Vigilantes—This phrase refers to the global investors who, in demanding higher Treasury bond yields from the late 1970s through the 1990s whenever irresponsible fiscal policies resulted in the expectation of higher inflation, in the end forced some discipline to policy makers in the United States.
- Bullion—Precious metals in bulk form are known as **bullion** and are traded on commodity markets. Bullion metals may be cast into ingots, or minted into coins. The defining attribute of bullion is that it is valued by its mass and purity rather than by a face value as money.
- *Cantillon* Effect—Richard Cantillon (1680–1734), a successful speculator during the "Mississippi Bubble" in early eighteenth-century France, wrote an essay in economics where, among many original contributions to economic theory, he developed the idea that money is not neutral and that the introduction of new money into the economy benefits most those who first receive it, since it is only gradually that the consciousness of the monetary inflation will be transmitted to different prices in the economy (the ***Cantillon* effect**).
- Catallactic—resulting from free exchange. **Catallactic** is a word that Friedrich Hayek coined from the Greek verb "katallattein," which means not only "to exchange" but also "to admit in the community" and "to change from enemy into friend" (F. A. Hayek, *Law, Legislation and Liberty*, vol. 2, 1976: 108–109).
- Central Bank—The institution that by legal definition essentially has the authority of defining criteria for money value, including authority over money issuing, and bank regulation. It can exercise the authority over money directly or through other institutions, and it can be part of the government or private (such as the Bank of England used to be). Usually, in order to impose bank regulation and since it has control over money issuing, the **Central Bank** becomes a lender of last resort, being responsible for providing liquidity to the banking system. It may or may not have other powers such as the power to trade on government debt, the power of

imposing foreign exchange controls, or the power to control capital, insurance, or mortgage markets .

- Chartalist—That which has a charta, a parchment, a document (given) by the government.
- Clan—A **clan** is a group of people united by kinship and descent, which is defined by perceived descent from a common ancestor. In political terms it is a part of a bigger group such as a tribe.
- Clearance—**Clearance** is utilized in this work with the meaning of matching supply and demand in the market.
- Commercial Bank—A financial institution that accepts money deposits, opens accounts from which resources can be claimed on demand and transferred by checks, and gives (usually short-term) loans, typically, for commercial activities.
- Crawling Peg—A system of exchange rate adjustment in which a currency with a government-mandated fixed exchange rate is allowed to fluctuate within a band of rates.
- Credit—**Credit** is an exchange deferred in time. One party provides resources (such as granting a loan) to another party, and that second party does not immediately pay the first party for the resources. A deferred exchange generates a debt, and arrangements are made for the debtor to either pay the equivalent value or to return those resources at a later date.
- Currency Exchange—The international market for currencies, usually expressed as exchange rates in which different currencies are nominated in dollar terms and the dollar is rated in sterling pounds.
- Debasement—**Debasement** is the practice of lowering the comparative value of commodity money such as gold or silver coins. A coin is debased if its content of gold or silver is reduced either by replacing the amount of the most expensive metal in the alloy for less expensive ones or by reducing the weight of the coin and keeping its nominal value.
- Devaluation—**Devaluation** can be used either to represent the diminishing in real value of a currency as a consequence of the increase of its quantity or the diminishing in its exchange rate for other currencies.
- Dirty Flow—The currency exchange regime in which a central bank allows some room for the fluctuation of its currency, although amid constant intervention.
- Dollarization—A common denomination to the different ways in which the US dollar can be used as currency for another country; this use being as medium of exchange, standard of value, or as reserves for its own currency.
- Endogenous determination of money value—The determination of money value is considered endogenous to economic activity when

it is derived from the utility perceived by economic agents in holding money, which is a consequence of its attributes.

- Fed—Federal Reserve—American Central Bank, established in 1913 by act of the US Congress.
- Fiat Money—A currency that is not redeemable in any other asset.
- Fixed Assets—**Fixed Assets** is an accounting term that describes tangible property used in the operation of a business such as buildings, furniture, and equipment.
- Fractional Reserves—System in which the issuers of a redeemable currency are allowed to maintain commodities in reserve amounting to only a fraction of the issue to back the demand for redemption. Fractional reserve banking in general is a banking system under which banks may accept deposits without the obligation of keeping them untouched in a safe; although they are obliged to redeem the deposits on demand, they may keep reserves of only a fraction of their deposits for that purpose. In an even broader definition, any banking arrangement in which there is a time mismatch in which banking liabilities are of a shorter maturity than banking assets implies fractional reserve banking.
- Free Exchange—The currency exchange regime in which the exchange rate fluctuates only due to the market forces of supply and demand.
- Forced Legal Tender, Forced Tender, Forced Currency—This is one currency that economic agents are forced to accept and to adopt in their dealings by force of law.
- General Price Level—It is the aggregate level of prices in an economy, usually represented by a price index. Although not excluding the possibility of relative changes in prices, the utilization of a general price level in economic calculation tends to lead to the understanding that all prices move in accordance with the index of prices.
- Hard Currency—A currency that is perceived in the market as having good monetary attributes, whether or not redeemable in other assets.
- High-Powered Money—The stock of paper money in circulation plus the deposits held by the commercial banks with the central bank form the monetary base. It is also called **high-powered** because an increase in the monetary base (M0) in the absence of reserve requirements (as is usually the case under fractional-reserve banking arrangements), may magnify the supply of bank money (bank deposits), an effect often referred to as the money multiplier.
- Indexed Currency—See abstract money.
- Institutional Arrangement—a body of legal regulations.
- IMF—International Monetary Fund.
- Inflation—*Inflation* is defined as the increase in the general level of prices of goods and services in a given economy over a period of

time (although the increases are not the same for all goods and services). As said by Milton Friedman, inflation is always a monetary phenomenon, that is, it is always caused by high rates of growth of the money supply in comparison with the growth of available goods.

- Inflation Target—**Inflation targeting** is an economic policy in which a central bank estimates and makes public a projected, or "target," inflation rate and then attempts to steer actual inflation towards the target through the use of interest rate changes and other monetary tools.
- IOU—**IOU** is anacronym that means a note and acknowledgment of personal debt (from the phrase "I owe you"). A promise to pay.
- Kosmos—Classical Greek word for the spontaneous order of society, meaning originally "a right order in a state or a community" according to Friedrich A. Hayek in *Law, Legislation and Liberty*, University of Chicago Press, 1983, volume 1, "Cosmos and Taxis," page 37.
- Legal Tender—A currency that by law is accepted as medium of exchange in a given territory although the law does not force it as the sole currency to be accepted or adopted by economic agents.
- Lender of Last Resort—The role performed by the central bank in providing liquidity to the banking system under institutional arrangements in which banks are forbidden to refuse withdrawals on demand or to decree bank holidays.
- Liquidity—Market **liquidity** is a term that refers to an asset's quality of being easily exchanged without causing a significant movement in the price and with minimum loss of value. The liquidity of a given asset is considered to increase as the spread between its ask and bid prices tends to zero. The essential characteristic of a liquid market is that there are ready and willing buyers and sellers at all times.
- Lytric—It is part of the terminology developed by George Knapp, according to Claus Wittich (Weber, 1978: 210). It derives from the Greek *lytron* that means "means of payment." **Lytric** is used by Knapp to designate the institutions that regulate payment instruments.
- Maquiladoras—***Maquiladoras*** are assembly industries in which the immense majority of the inputs were imported and the component of local costs was relatively small.
- Medium of Exchange—A **medium of exchange** is an instrument for indirect exchanges (C-M-C), used in trade to avoid the inconveniences of a barter system with direct exchanges (C-C).
- Methodenstreit—Literally, ***Methodenstreit*** means a discussion about method. Specifically the *Methodenstreit der Nationalökonomie* is the discussion on method in economics, which raged at the end of

nineteenth century between the Austrian School of Economics led by Carl Menger and the German Historicists led by Gustav von Schmoller over the approach to history and apriorism in economics.

- MMDA—**Money Market Deposit Accounts** constitute cash claims against the banks, that are redeemable au pair, on demand, and in the United States they are insured as other bank deposits (Salerno, 1987: 3).
- MMMF—**Money Market Mutual Funds** are equity funds that invest in highly liquid assets such as Treasury Bills and Commercial Papers. The assets bought by MMMFs are usually of short-term maturity and high quality, which in the general perception of the investors allows the shares of the MMMFs to be redeemed au pair, on demand, even if the fund needs first to divest some assets before redeeming an investor (Haymond, 2000: 55).
- Monetary Aggregates—In macroeconomics, monetary aggregates or **money supply** is the quantity of currency, money in bank accounts, and other financial instruments with monetary properties in the hands of the public available within an economy to purchase goods and services.
- Monetary Authorities—According to the North American Industry Classification System of the Bureau of Labor Statistics, "The **Monetary Authorities**—central bank subsector group establishments that engage in performing central banking functions, such as issuing currency, managing the nation's money supply and international reserves, holding deposits that represent the reserves of other banks and other central banks, and acting as a fiscal agent for the central government." (www.bls.gov/iag/tgs/iag521.htm accessed March 20, 2015)
- Monetary Base—Actual Money—(M0)—The **monetary base** is a term related to the volume of money in the economy, or money supply. The monetary base comprises only currency (banknotes and coins) and commercial banks' reserves with the central bank. As such, it is a narrow definition of money supply, consisting of only the most liquid forms of money. Wider definitions of the money supply include the public's bank deposits and are therefore larger in volume and encompass money of a lower liquidity.
- Monetary Commodity—see monetary goods.
- Monetary Discipline—**Monetary discipline** means a prudent management of the money supply by the monetary authorities aimed at price stability; it is an attempt to avoid producing inflation or deflation as a consequence of this management.
- Monetary Economy—A society in which economic transactions are made using coined money as a medium of exchange instead of barter.

- Monetary Goods—Some merchandise that, due to their properties, can be used as media of exchange.
- Monetary Merchandise—See monetary goods.
- Monetary Policy—Monetary policy is the process by which the government through the monetary authorities, nowadays, the central bank, manages the supply of money and credit.
- Monetary Properties—Monetary Properties are the attributes possessed by the medium of exchange that allow it to perform that function. Being generally accepted as medium of exchange is a consequence of a perception by economic agents that it will be accepted, and that it will be useful for them to perform their exchanges. It is the degree to which economic agents trust that the monetary merchandise, be it a commodity, a credit, or just fiduciary media, will be liquid at a stable value that makes such merchandise able to perform, in different degrees, its role as money.
- Monetary Standard—See standard of value.
- Money Market—Expression used by Walter Bagehot in his book *Lombard Street* to describe English monetary arrangements in the second part of the nineteenth century, its institutions, legal and customary, and its business practices.
- MZM—**Money of Zero Maturity** is a measurement of money that comprises all monetary instruments which are redeemable au pair, on demand; such as currency, deposits on demand, traveler's checks, saving accounts, and money market mutual funds (MMMFs).
- M1—Monetary aggregate that comprises the stock of money consisting of checkable deposits and currency held by the nonbank public.
- M2—**M2** by definition of the Fed comprises M1 plus other assets such as savings, time deposits, overnight repurchase agreements, foreign currency deposits, and balances of money market mutual funds maintained by the private sector with local banks.
- M3—The category of the money supply that includes M2 as well as all large time deposits, institutional money market funds, short-term repurchase agreements, along with other larger liquid assets. This is the broadest measure of money usually utilized by economists to estimate the entire supply of money within an economy.
- Nominalism—Theory about the value of money that understands the value of money as the value attributed to it by the state.
- Notes of Credit—See Bill of Exchange.
- Peel's Act—**Peel's Act** of 1844 centralized the issue of banknotes in the hands of the Bank of England, establishing issuing limits that the bank directors were quite willing to conform to in exchange for the "legalization" of their de facto monopoly on note issuance. Bagehot is right in asserting that it is beside the point whether the

implicit backing by the British government of the financial system is done through one bank or many banks, and whether the limits on the ratio of reserves and issuing is established by law or enforced by the monopolist (discretionarily refusing to back expansionist banks). The fact is that in England of that time a system of fractional reserves got a two-layered feature, with the Bank of England acting as a lender of last resort with the implicit backing of the British government and a limit on the minimum ratio of fractional reserves being actually enforced by the Bank of England.

- Political Entrepreneur—Someone that thinks it to be in his interest (however broadly defined his own interest may be) to take the initiative to propose some change in policy.
- Price System—The sum of monetary prices practiced in a free market for all goods and services conveying the relevant information about its supply and demand that act as a signal for the action of economic agents.
- Precious Metals—A **metal** is deemed to be **precious** according to its rarity. The discovery of new sources of ore or improvements in mining or refining processes may cause the cost of production of a precious metal to diminish and with that its availability, as in the example of aluminum before the Hall-Héroult process made it possible to extract aluminum on a large scale. Like everything else, the demand for a "precious" metal is determined by its utility; before new printing methods made possible banknotes not easily falsifiable, silver was used for the coinage of coins for daily transactions, after that, silver gradually lost some of its monetary properties and although it remains a rare metal it does not command the same price relative to gold that it once had.
- PPP—Purchasing Power Parity—It is the estimation of imbalances in the exchange rate between different currencies assuming that the market price of similar goods in different countries tends to converge. In other words, the exchange rate adjusts so that an identical good in two different countries has the same price when expressed in the same currency. The most famous application of this theory is the "Big Mac Index" produced by *The Economist* that compares the price of the famous sandwich in different countries to estimate how much one currency is over-valued or devalued in comparison with the US dollar.
- Quasi-money—**Quasi-money**, near money, and money substitutes are terms used to describe highly liquid assets that, given their properties, may easily be converted into cash and therefore may perform the functions of money. The most common money substitutes in use nowadays are money market funds. In economics, quasi-money is usually understood by the monetary aggregate known as M2.

- Rents—The classic concept of **rents** is that rents are considered the returns "in excess" of the ones obtainable by the resource owners "in perfect competition." There are more elaborate definitions of "rents," but it may be useful to keep in mind that for Adam Smith they are simply the "activities of people who reap what they do not sow" (Karl, 2007: 259). It is also important to distinguish "artificial rents," such as the ones generated and appropriated by the political process, from "natural rents," such as the ones, for instance, commanded by the owners of the most productive lands referred to by Ricardo. That is, by the terminology used here, those "excess" returns obtained by force of private property rights arrangements are considered "natural rents," while the same income, once captured by the government, becomes "artificial rents."
- Rentier State—A **rentier state** is one in which a substantial portion of government's revenues come from the rents obtained with the exports of some natural endowment of the country.
- Reserves—**Bank reserves** are the amounts held by the banks in accounts with the central bank plus the currency they hold in their ownvaults. In most countries the monetary authorities set minimum reserve requirements for the banks.
- Ricardo Effect—The **Ricardo Effect** is the mechanism through which misdirected resources are drawn back from capital-intensive modes of production to less intensive ones, reversing the economy back to a sustainable structure of production.
- SEC—Securities Exchange Commission.
- Seigniorage—The gains made by the issuer of a currency.
- Specie—Any monetary merchandise, usually a rare metal such as gold.
- Speculation—see Arbitrage.
- Stable Money—Stable currency, any currency redeemable or otherwise that has the attribute of being able to keep its value for long periods of time.
- Standard of Value—A value used as reference for price definition, a unit of measurement used as reference of value for economic exchanges.
- Stock of Value—Or store of value. This is one of the functions that money can perform because of "the fact that money is the most appropriate medium for accumulating that portion of a person's wealth by means of which he intends to acquire other goods" (Menger, 1871/1994: 278).
- Taxis—Classical Greek word for a made order such as an order of battle, according to Friedrich A. Hayek in *Law, Legislation and Liberty* (Hayek, 1976: 37).
- TMS—The **True Money Supply** is a monetary aggregate formulated by Rothbard and is proposed to represent the amount of money

readily available in the economy. The TMS consists of the currency component of M1, checking deposits, savings deposits, US government deposits on demand, and demand deposits due to foreign banks and governments (mises.org).

- Transaction Costs—Transaction costs consist of the costs of measuring the valuable attributes of what is being exchanged and the costs of protecting rights and enforcing agreements, according to Douglass C. North in *Institutions, Institutional Change and Economic Performance,* Cambridge University Press, 2005, chapter 4, "A transaction cost theory of exchange," page 27.
- Tribes—**Tribes** are distinguished from bands and clans in that tribes are generally larger social groups, consisting of many families. Tribes have more social institutions than smaller and more primitive forms of societies, such as a chief, big man, or elders. Many tribes are divided into clans.
- Unit of Exchange—See standard of value.
- Working Capital—**Working capital** represents the amount of day-by-day operating liquidity available to a business. It is representative in monetary terms of the resources needed to pay for daily expenses, to keep inventories, and to give credit to customers.

Bibliography

Aligheiri, Dante. *The Divine Comedy*. Translated by Henry Wadsworth Longfellow. 1997. Project Gutenberg Etext. Accessed October 2015. Available at http://www.gutenberg.org/cache/epub/1004/pg1004.html.

Alonso Neira, Miguel Ángel. *Teoría Económica de las Crisis Monetarias y Financieras y de los Controles de Capital*. Colección Estudios. Madrid: Instituto de Estudios Económicos, 2004.

Anderson Jr., Benjamin M. *The Value of Money*. New York: Macmillan Company edition, 1917. Reprint, Grove City, PA: Libertarian Press, Inc., 2009.

Andreau, Jean. *Banking and Business in the Roman World*. Cambridge, UK: Cambridge University Press, 1999.

Aristotle. *Metaphysics*. In *The Basic Works of Aristotle*. Edited by Richard McKeon. Thirty-fifth printing. New York: Random House, (1941a) 1992.

———. *The Nicomachean Ethics*. In *The Basic Works of Aristotle*. Edited by Richard McKeon. Thirty-fifth printing. New York: Random House, 1941b.

———. *Rhetoric*. In *The Basic Works of Aristotle*. Edited by Richard McKeon. Thirty-fifth printing. New York: Random House, 1941c.

———. *Magna Moralia*. In *Loeb Classical Library*, Aristotle XVIII, LCL 287. Cambridge: Harvard University Press, 2006.

———. *Oeconomica*. In *Loeb Classical Library*, Aristotle XVIII, LCL 287. Cambridge: Harvard University Press, 2006.

———. *The Politics*. Trevor J. Saunders, ed. London: Penguin Classics, Penguin Books, 1992.

Bacon, Francis. *Novum Organum*, Book 1, Aphorism 3. Forgotten Books, 2012.

Bagehot, W. *Lombard Street: A Description of the Money Market* . London: Wiley & Sons, Inc., 1999.

Bagus, Philipp. "Austrian Business Cycle Theory: Are 100 Percent Reserves Sufficient to Prevent a Business Cycle?" *Libertarian Papers* 2, 2 (2010a): 1–18. Available online at: www.libertarianpapers.org.

———. "Austrian Economics and New Currency Theory on 100% Banking: A Response to Huber." *Procesos de Mercado: Revista Europea de Economía Política* XI, no. I (Primavera, 2014): 105–136.

———. "Monetary Reform and Deflation—A Critique of Mises, Rothbard, Huerta de Soto and Sennholz." *New Perspectives on Political Economy* 4, no. 2 (2008): 131–157.

———. "Morgenstern's Forgotten Contribution: A Stab to the Heart of Modern Economics." 2010b. To be published in the *American Journal for Sociology and Economics*.

———. *The Tragedy of the Euro*. Auburn, Alabama: The Ludwig von Mises Institute, 2010c.

Barnett II, William, and Walter Block. "Money: Capital Good, Consumer's Good or (Media of) Exchange Good?" *The Review of Austrian Economics* 18, no. 2 (2005): 179–194.

———. "On the Optimum Quantity of Money." *The Quarterly Journal of Austrian Economics* 7, no. 1 (Spring 2004): 39–52.

Basu, Alok. "How to Create a Banking & Monetary System for the 21st Century: The Huerta de Soto and Chicago Plans Reworked." in *Procesos de Mercado: Revista Europea de Economia Politica* XI, no. I, (Primavera, 2014): 13–66.

Belluzzo, Luiz Gonzaga, and Ricardo Carneiro. "O Mito da Conversibilidade." *Revista de Economia Politica* 24, no. 2, 994 (April–June, 2004): 218–222.

Benes, Jaromir, and Kumhof, Michael. "The Chicago Plan Revisited." IMF working paper, wp/12/202 (2012). Accessed March 20, 2015. https://www.imf.org/external/pubs/ft/wp/2012/wp12202.pdf.

Bernal, Antonio Miguel. *España, P r oyecto Inacabado — Costes/Beneficios del Imperio.* Madrid: Fundación Carolina, 2005.

Bernanke, Ben S., Thomas Laubach, Frederic S. Mishkin, and Adam S. Posen. *Inflation Targeting, Lessons from the International Experience.* Princeton: Princeton University Press, 2001.

Blaug, Mark. *The Methodology of Economics.* Cambridge: Cambridge University Press, 1980.

Block, Walter. "A Look at Subjectivism, Intelligibility and Economic Understanding." *The Review of Austrian Economics* 3 (1989): 215–236.

———. "Value Freedom, Laissez Faire, Mises, and Rothbard: A Comment on Professor Gunning." *American Journal of Economics and Society* vol. 64, no. 3 (July 2005): 939–960.

Boettke, Peter J. "What is Wrong with Neoclassical Economics." In *Beyond Neoclassical Economics—Heterodox Approaches to Economic Theory.* Edited by Fred Foldvary. Cheltenham, UK: Edward Elgar Publishing, 1996.

Boianovsky, Mauro. "A Brief History of Economic Thought on Dutch Disease." (box 3.1). In *Natural Resources in Latin America and the Caribbean—Beyond Booms and Busts?* Emily Sinnott, John Nash, and Augusto de la Torre. Washington, DC: World Bank, 2010. Accessed at openknowledge.worldbank.org/bitstream/handle/10986/2482/555500PUB0Natu1EPI1991501801PUBLIC1.pdf?sequence=1.

———. "Fisher and Wicksell on Money: A Reconstructed Conversation." *The European Journal of the History of Economic Thought* (2013). Accessed at dx.doi.org/10.1080/09672567.2012.758757.

———. "Real Balances, the Price Level and the Unit of Account: From Wicksell to Patinkin and Beyond." *American Journal of Economics and Sociology* 57, no. 4 (October, 1998).

Boianovsky, Mauro, and Guido Erreygers. "Social Comptabilism and Pure Credit Systems—Solvay and Wicksell on Monetary Reform." In *The Experiment in the History of Economics.* Edited by Philippe Fontaine and Robert Leonard. Abingdon, UK: Routledge, 2005.

Brook, Yaron. "The Morality of Moneylending: A Short History." Originally published in *The Objective Standard* 2, no. 3 (Fall, 2007).

Brunner, Karl. "Assumptions and the Cognitive Quality of Theories." *Synthese* 20 (1969): 501–525.

———. "The Perception of Man and the Conception of Society." *Economic Inquiry* XXV, no. 3 (July 1987): 367–388.

Brunner, Karl, and Allan H. Meltzer. *Money and the Economy: Issues in Monetary Analysis.* Cambridge: Cambridge University Press, 1993.

Brunnschweiler, Christa N., and Erwin H. Bulte. "The Resource Curse Revisited and Revised: A Tale of Paradoxes and Red Herrings." *Journal of Environmental Economics and Management* 55, no. 3 (2008): 248–264.

Buchanan, James M. "The Constitutionalization of Money." *The Cato Journal* 30, no. 2 (Spring/Summer 2010): 251–258.

———. "Predictability: The Criterion of Monetary Constitutions." In *In Search of a Monetary Constitution.* Edited by Leland B. Yeager. Cambridge: Harvard University Press, 1962.

———. *The Power to Tax—The Collected Works of James M. Buchanan* , vol. IX. Indianapolis: Liberty Fund, Inc., 2000.

———. *What Should Economists Do?* Indianapolis: Liberty Fund, Inc., 1979.

———. *Why I, Too, Am Not a Conservative—The Normative Vision of Classical Liberalism.* Cheltenham, UK: Edward Elgar Publishing Limited, 2005.

Bureau of Labor Statistics. "Top Picks: Consumer Price Index-All Urban Consumers." Accessed March 25, 2015. data.bls.gov/cgi-bin/surveymost?cu.

Burns, Edward McNall. *História da Civilizaç ã o Ocidental*. Porto Alegre, Editora Globo, 1975.
Caldeira, Jorge. *Maua : Empresário do Império*. Rio de Janeiro: Companhia das Letras, 1995.
Caldwell, Bruce, ed. *Appraisal and Criticism in Economics— A Book of Readings*. Winchester, MA: Allen & Unwin, Inc., 1984.
Calomiris, Charles W., and Stephen H. Haber. *Fragile By Design: The Political Origins of Banking Crises & Scarce Credit*. Princeton, NJ: Princeton University Press, 2014.
Calzada Álvares, Gabriel. "La fuente de los Principios." Instituto Juan de Mariana, last modified April 13, 2006. www.juandemariana.org/comentario/607/fuente/principios/.
———. "Mises and Rothbard on War Finance." *Procesos de Mercado: Revista Europea de Economía Política* II, no. 1 (Primavera, 2005): 147–170.
Cannan, E., W. D. Ross, J. Bonar, and P. H. Wicksteed. "Who said 'Barren Metal'? A Symposium." *Economica* 5 (June 1922): 105–111.
Carande, Ramón. *Carlos V y Sus Banque r os*. Barcelona: Editorial Critica, SL, 2004.
Carneiro, Ricardo. "Globalizacao e inconversibilidade monetaria." IE/UNICAMP, Brazil (August, 2007): 1–23.
Chick, Victoria. "Money and Effective Demand." Chapter 6 in *What is Money?* Edited by John Smithin. Abingdon, England: Routledge, 2000.
Cochrane, John H. "Toward a Run-Free Financial System." University of Chicago Booth School of Business, April 16, 2014, available on John Cochrane's blog.
Coffman, D'Maris, and Larry Neal. "Introduction." In *Questioning Credible Commitment—Perspectives on the Rise of Financial Capitalism*. Edited by D'Maris Coffman, Adrian Leonard, and Larry Neal. Cambridge, UK: Cambridge University Press, 2013.
Comte, Auguste. "Eleventh Conference, on The Public Regime." In *Positivist Catechism*, 1852. Reprint, *Augusto Comte, Selected Works*. São Paulo: Editora Abril Cultural, 1978.
———. *Introduction to Positive Philosophy*. Indianapolis: Hackett Publishing Company, Inc., 1988.
———. *Positive Philosophy of Auguste Comte*. Translated by Harriet Martineau. 1855. Reprint, New York: AMS Press, Inc., 1974.
Concord Coalition. "U.S. Budget and Economic Data." Accessed March 25, 2015. pw1.netcom.com/~rdavis2/budget.html.
Corden, W. Max, and J. Peter Neary. "Booming Sector and De-Industrialisation in a Small Open Economy." *The Economic Journal* 92, no. 368 (December, 1982): 825–848.
Cowen, Tyler, and Randall Kroszner. *Explorations in the New Monetary Economics*. Cambridge, MA: Blackwell Publishers, 1994.
Crespo, Oscar V. "La Fundamental Homogeneidad de las Teorías Monetarias de Georg Simmel y Ludwig von Mises." *Procesos de Mercado* I, no. 1 (Primavera, 2004): 223–250.
Cwik, Paul F. "Recession Economics and Non Neutral Money." Working paper presented at the Austrian Scholars Conference, 2009. Available at mises.org/journals/scholar/cwik4.pdf .
Debreu, Gerard. *Theory of Value: An Axiomatic Analysis of Economic Equilibrium*. Cowles Foundation Monographs Series. New Haven, CT: Yale University Press, 1972.
Den Uyl, Douglas. "The Virtue of Prudence." In *Studies in Moral Philosophy*, vol. 5. New York: Peter Lang Publishing, Inc., 1991.
Den Uyl, D., and Rasmussen, D. *Norms of Liberty, A Perfectionist Basis for Non-Perfectionist Politics*. University Park, PA: The Pennsylvania State University Press, 2005.
Desmedt, Ludovic, and Jérôme Blanc. "Counteracting Counterfeiting? Bodin, Mariana, and Locke on False Money as a Multidimensional Issue." *History of Political Economy* 42, no. 2 (2010): 323–360.
Diamond, Art. *Mackerel Money: "If a Dog Eats It, It's Dog Food."* (blog). 2009. Available at Art Diamond blog, artdiamondblog.com.

Dick, Alexander. *Romanticism and the Gold Standard—Money, Literature, and Economic Debate in Britain 1790–1830*. Hampshire, UK: Palgrave Macmillan, 2013.

Dickson, P. G. M. *The Financial Revolution in England: A Study in the Development of Public Credit, 1688–1756*. London: Macmillan, 1967.

Dodd, Nigel. *The Social Life of Money*. Princeton, NJ: Princeton University Press, 2014.

Dorfman, Joseph. *The Economic Mind in American Civilization*. New York: August M. Kelley, 1959.

Dorn, James A. *The Future of Money in the Information Age*. Washington, DC: Cato Institute, 1997.

Dostaler, Gilles, and Bernard Maris. "Dr. Freud and Mr. Keynes on Money and Capitalism." Chapter 12 in *What is Money?* Edited by John Smithin. Abingdon, England: Routledge, 2000.

Dowd, Kevin. "The Invisible Hand and the Evolution of the Monetary System." Chapter 7 in *What is Money?* Edited by John Smithin. Abingdon, England: Routledge, 2000.

Durant, William. *A História da Filosofia*. Rio de Janeiro, Brazil: Editora Record S.A., 1991.

The Economist. "The Oil Barons Have a Ball." February 18, 2012.

Eichengreen, Barry. "Hegemonic Stability Theories of the International System." In *Elusive Stability: Essays in the History of International Finance 1919–1939*, 271–311. Cambridge, UK: Cambridge University Press, 1990.

———. "Still Fettered After All These Years." In *NBER Working Papers Series*, paper 9276, 2002.

Einaudi, Luigi. "The Theory of Imaginary Money from Charlemagne to the French Revolution." Chapter 14 in section II, "Money and Prices." *Enterprise and Secular Change—Readings in Economic History*. Edited by Frederic C. Lane and Jelle C. Riemersma. Homewood, IL: Richard D. Irwin, Inc., 1953. Originally published in *Rivista di Storia Economica*, 1936.

Faught, James. "Neglected Affinities: Max Weber and Georg Simmel." *The British Journal of Sociology* 36, no. 2 (June 1985): 155–174.

Fekete, Antal E. "The Gold-Demonetization Hoax—Gary North is Wrong on Gold." 2003. Available online at www.professorfekete.com/articles.asp.

Ferguson, Niall. *The Ascent of Money: A Financial History of the World*. New York: Penguin Press, 2008.

Ferrari Filho, Fernando, Frederico G. Jayme Jr., Gilberto Tadeu Lima, José Luiz Oureiro and Luiz Fernando de Paula. "Uma Avaliação Crítica da Proposta de Conversibilidade Plena do Real," in *Revista de Economia Politica* 25, no. 1 (January–March, 2005): 133–151.

Fisher, Irving. *The Money Illusion*. 1928. Reprint, Mansfield Centre, CT: Martino Publishing, 2009.

———. *Stabilizing the Dollar: A Plan to Stabilize the General Price Level without Fixing Individual Prices*. Nabu Press, 2010.

———. *100% Money: Designed to Keep Checking Banks 100% Liquid; to Prevent Inflation and Deflation; Largely to Cure or Prevent Depression; and to Wipe out Much of the National Debt*. New York, NY: Adelphi Company, 2011, originally published 1935.

———. *The Purchasing Power of Money: Its Determination and Relation to Credit Interest and Crisis*. 1912. Reprint, New York: Cosimo Books, 2007.

Fleetwood, Steve. "A Marxist Theory of *Commodity* Money Revisited." Chapter 9 in *What is Money?* Edited by John Smithin. Abingdon, England: Routledge, 2000.

Foot, Philippa. *Virtues and Vices and Other Essays in Moral Philosophy*. Oxford: Clarendon Press, 2002.

Franco, Gustavo H. B. *O papel e a baixa do câ mbio*. Rio de Janeiro: Reler Editora Ltda., 2005. "Preface," 9–33.

———. "Por que juros tão altos, e o caminho para a normalidade." CLP—Centro de Liderança Publica and Casa do Saber, Brazil (June 13, 2011): 1–21.

Frankel, S. Herbert. *Two Philosophies of Money*. New York: St. Martin's Press, 1978.

Fratianni, Michele, and Jürgen von Hagen. "The Konstanz Seminar on Monetary Theory and Policy at 30." *European Journal of Political Economy* 17 (2001): 641–664.
Freitas, Décio. *The Man Who Invented the Dictatorship in Brazil*. Porto Alegre, Brazil: Editora Sulina, 2000.
Friedman, Milton. "The Methodology of Positive Economics." In *Essays in Positive Economics*. Chicago: University of Chicago Press, 1953.
———. *Money Mischief—Episodes in Monetary History*. New York: Harcourt Brace & Company, 1994.
Friedman, Milton, and Anna Jacobson Schwartz. *A Monetary History of the United States, 1867–1960*. Princeton: Princeton University Press, 1993.
Garrison, Roger W. *Austrian Macroeconomics: A Diagrammatical Exposition*. Menlo Park, California: Institute for Humane Studies, 1961.
———. "The Costs of a Gold Standard." Chapter 4 in *The Gold Standard—An Austrian Perspective*. Edited by Llewellyn H. Rockwell, Jr. Lexington, MA: D. C. Heath and Co., 1985.
Glasner, David. *Free Banking and Monetary Reform*. Cambridge: Cambridge University Press, 2005.
Goethe, Johann Wolfgang von. "Faust." In *Goethe's Works Illustrated by the Best German Artists*. 5 volumes (volume 2). Philadelphia: G. Barrie, 1885.
Goldsborough, Reid. *World's First Coin: The Lydian Lion, 2003*. First Coins—First coin—Lydian Trites.htm.
Goodman, Lawrence. "Demand for U.S. Debt Is Not Limitless," in the *Wall Street Journal*, March 27, 2012.
Graeber, David. *Debt: The First 5,000 Years*. Brooklyn, NY: Melville House Publishing, 2011. ISBN: 978-1-933633-86-2.
Greaves, Percy L. *Mises Made Easier—A Glossary for Ludwig Von Mises' Human Action*. Irvington, NY: Free Market Books, 1974.
Greenspan, A. *The Age of Turbulence*. New York: The Penguin Press, 2007.
Grice-Hutchinson, Marjorie. *The School of Salamanca—Readings in Spanish Monetary Theory, 1544–1605*. Auburn, AL: The Ludwig von Mises Institute, 2009.
Grotius, Hugo. *The Rights of War and Peace*. Indianapolis: Liberty Fund, Inc., 2005.
Gunning, J. P. "Did Mises Err? Was He a Utilitarian?" *American Journal of Economics and Society* vol. 64, no. 3 (July 2005): 939–960.
Häberlein, Mark. *The Fuggers of Augsburg: Pursuing Wealth and Honor in Renaissance Germany*. Charlottesville: University of Virginia Press, 2012.
Hagen, Jürgen von, and Michael Welker. *Money as God? The Monetization of the Market and its Impact on Religion, Politics, Law, and Ethics*. Cambridge: Cambridge University Press, 2014.
Hamilton, Alexander. "On the Establishment of a Mint." In *The Works of Alexander Hamilton*. 12 volumes, volume 4. Edited by Henry Cabot Lodge. Federal Edition, 1790. New York: G. P. Putnam's Sons, 1904. Available online:oll.libertyfund.org/?option=com_staticxt&staticfile=show.php%3Ftitle=1381&chapter=64330&layout=html&Itemid=27.
———. "Report on a National Bank." 1790. Published by *The Executive Intelligence Review* accessed atwww.larouchepub.com/.
Hamilton, Earl James. *American Terasure and the Price Revolution in Spain, 1501–1650*. Harvard Economic Studies, Book 43. Harvard University Press, 1934. Cambridge, MA: Harvard University Press, 1934.
Hartwick, John M. "Intergenerational Equity and the Investing of Rents from Exhaustible Resources." *The American Economic Review* 67, no. 5 (December, 1977): 972–974.
Hayek, Friedrich A. *A Discussion with Friedrich Von Hayek.*, Domestic Affairs Studies, no. 39. Held at the American Enterprise Institute, April 9, 1975. Washington, DC: American Enterprise Institute for Public Policy Research.
———. *The Counter-Revolution of Science*. 1952. Reprint, Indianapolis: Liberty Press, 1979.

———. *The Denationalisation of Money —The Argument Refined.* Hobart Papers, no. 70. London: IEA, 1990.

———. *Law, Legislation and Liberty*. Chicago: University of Chicago Press, 1976. Reprint 1992.

———. *The Road to Serfdom*. 1944. Reprint, Abington, UK: Routledge Classics, 2007.

———. "The Use of Knowledge in Society." *American Economic Review* XXXV, no. 4 (September 1945): 519–30. Available at www.econlib.org.

Haymond, Jeff. "Are MMMFs Money?" *The Quarterly Journal of Austrian Economics* 3, No. 4 (Winter 2000): 53–68.

Heinsohn, Gunnar, and Otto Steiger. "The Property Theory of Interest and Money." Chapter 4 in *What is Money?* Edited by John Smithin. Abingdon, England: Routledge, 2000.

Henderson, D. R. *The Concise Encyclopedia of Economics*. Indianapolis: Liberty Fund, Inc., 2008.

Herodotus. "The Histories." In *The Landmark Herodotus*. Edited by Robert B. Strassler. New York: Pantheon Books, a division of Random House, Inc., 2007.

Higgs, Robert. *Crisis and Leviathan:, Critical Episodes in the Growth of American Government*. Oxford: Oxford University Press, 1987.

Hobbes, Thomas. The English Works of Thomas Hobbes of Malmesbury; Now First Collected and Edited by Sir William Molesworth, Bart. (London: Bohn, 1839–1845). 11 volumes.

———. *Leviathan : With Selected Variants from the Latin Edition of 1668*. New York: Hackett Pub. Co., 1994.

Honderich, Ted. *The Oxford Companion to Philosophy*. New Edition. Oxford: Oxford University Press, 2005.

Horwitz, Steven. "Do We Need a Distinct Monetary Constitution?" Prepared for the Fund for the Spontaneous Order's Lifetime Achievement Award Conference in honor of James M. Buchanan, Fairfax, VA, 2010.

Hospers, J. *Human Conduct, Problems of Ethics*. Belmont, CA: Thomson Learning, Inc., 1996.

Hotelling, Harold. "The Economics of Exhaustible Resources." *The Journal of Political Economy* 39, no. 2 (April, 1931): 137–175.

Huerta de Soto, Jesús, ed. *Lecturas de Economía Política*. Volume I. Madrid: Unión Editorial, 2009.

———, ed. *Lecturas de Economía Política*. Volume II. Madrid: Unión Editorial, 1987.

———. *Money, Bank Credit , and Economic Cycles*. Auburn, AL: Ludwig von Mises Institute, 2006.

———. "New Light on the Prehistory of the Theory Banking and the School of Salamanca." *Review of Austrian Economics* 9, no. 2 (1996): 59–81.

———. "El Pensamiento Económico en la Antigua Grecia." *Procesos de Mercado: Revista Europea de Economía Política* V, no. 1 (Primavera, 2008): 177–188.

———. *Socialismo, Cálculo Económico y Función Empresarial*. Secunda edición. Madrid: Unión Editorial, 2001.

———. "La Teoría de La Eficiencia Dinámica." *Procesos de Mercado: Revista Europea de Economía Política* I, no. 1 (Primavera, 2004): 11–72.

Hume, D. *Essays Moral, Political and Literary*. Indianapolis: Liberty Fund, Inc., 1987.

Humphrey, Thomas. "The Choice of a Monetary Policy Framework: Lessons from the 1920s." *Cato Journal* 21, no. 2 (2001): 285–313.

Hülsmann, Jörg Guido. *The Ethics of Money Production*. Auburn, AL: Ludwig von Mises Institute, 2008.

Hutchison, Terence. *The Significance and Basic Postulates of Economic Theory*. New York: Kelley, 1960.

Ingham, Geoffrey. "'Babylonian Madness': On the Historical and Sociological Origins of Money." Chapter 2 in *What is Money?* Edited by John Smithin. Abingdon, England: Routledge, 2000.

———. "The Emergence of Capitalist Credit Money." In *Credit and State Theories of Money—The Contribution of A. Mitchell Innes*. Chapter 7. Edited by L. Randall Wray. Cheltenham, UK: Edward Elgar, 2004.

———. *The Nature of Money*. Cambridge, UK: Polity Press, 2004.

International Monetary Fund. "The World Economic Outlook (WEO) Database 2000." Accessed March 25, 2015. www.imf.org/external/pubs/ft/weo/2000/02/data/index.htm.

Jones, William Thomas. A *History of Western Philosophy: Kant and the Nineteenth Century*. Volume IV. Second Edition, revised. Fort Worth: Harcourt Brace Jovanovich College Publishers, 1980.

Kant, Immanuel. *Fundamental Principles of the Metaphysic of Morals*. Translated by T. K. Abbott. London: Longmans Green and Co., 1927.

Karl, Terry Lynn. "Ensuring Fairness. The Case for a Transparent Fiscal Social Contract." In *Escaping the Resource Curse*. Edited by M. Humphreys, J. D. Sachs, and J. E. Stiglitz. New York: Columbia University Press, 2007, 257–285.

———. "Institutional Act Number 1, April 10th, 1964." In *All the Constitutions of Brazil*. São Paulo, Brazil: Editora Atlas S.A., 1979.

Kay, John. "Should We Have 'Narrow Banking'?" (blog). June 2, 2011. *Future of Finance, the LSE Report*. www.johnkay.com/2011/06/02/should-we-have-narrow-banking

Kaye, Joel. *Economy and Nature in the Fourteenth Century—Money, Market Exchange, and the Emergence of Scientific Thought*. Cambridge: Cambridge University Press, 2000.

Kennedy, Peter. "A Marxist Account of the Relationship between Commodity Money and Symbolic Money in the Context of Contemporary Capitalist Development." Chapter 10 in *What is Money?* Edited by John Smithin. Abingdon, England: Routledge, 2000.

Keynes, John Maynard. *A Treatise on Money, Volume I, The Pure Theory of Money*. New York: Harcourt, 1976.

———. *The General Theory of Employment, Interest, and Money*. New York: Prometheus Books, 1997.

Kindleberger, Charles. *The World in Depression 1929–1939*. Revised edition. Berkeley: University of California Press, 1986.

King, Peter (7th Baron King). *Thoughts on the Restriction of Payments in Specie at the Banks of England and Ireland*. London: Cadell and Davies, Strand; and J. Debrett, Piccadilly, 1803. Reprinted on demand in 2014 by Paige M. Gutenborg—The Harvard Book Store.

Klein, Peter G., and George Selgin. "Menger's Theory of Money: Some Experimental Evidence." Chapter 11 in *What is Money?* Edited by John Smithin. Abingdon, England: Routledge, 2000.

Knapp, G. F. *The State Theory of Money*. London: Macmillan & Co., 1924; San Diego: Simon Publications, Inc., 2003.

Koning, J. P. (2013) "Real or Unreal: Sorting Out the Various Real Bills Doctrines." (blog). *Moneyness*. Accessed on June 14, 2013. jpkoning.blogspot.com/2013/06/real-or-unreal-sorting-out-various-real.html.

Krueger, Anne O. "The Political Economy of the Rent-Seeking Society." *American Economic Review* 64, no. 3 (June, 1974): 291–303.

Lachmann, L. M. *The Legacy of Max Weber*. London: Heinemann Booksdon, 1970.

Lagos, Ricardo. "Asset Prices, Liquidity, and Monetary Policy in the Search Theory of Money." *The Federal Reserve Bank of St. Louis Review* (July/August, 2010).

Laidler, David E. W. *The Demand for Money , Theories, Evidence & Problems*. New York: HarperCollins College Publishers, 1993.

———. "Some Aspects of Monetarism Circa 1970: A View from 1994." In *Macroeconomics in Retrospect: The Selected Essays of David Laidler*. Northampton, MA: Edward Elgar Publishing, Inc., 2004.

Lassalle, Ferdinand (1862) *On the Essence of Constitutions*. Speech Delivered in Berlin, April 16, 1862. Available at: www.marxists.org/history/etol/newspape/fi/vol03/no01/lassalle.htm.

Lasser, Joseph R., Gail G. Greve, William E. Pittman, and John A. Caramia, Jr. *The Coins of Colonial America: World Trade Coins of the Seventeenth and Eighteenth Centuries*. Williamsburg, VA: The Colonial Williamsburg Foundation, 1997.

Laures, John S. J. *The Political Economy of Juan de Mariana*. Auburn, AL: Mises Institute, 2008.

Leeson, Peter T. "The Political Economy of Peter Boettke." *The Journal of Private Enterprise* XXVI, no. 1 (Fall, 2010): 47–56.

Lerner, Abba P. "Functional Finance and the Federal Debt." *Social Research* 10 (February, 1943): 38–51.

Levin, Michael. "A Hobbesian Minimal State." *Philosophy and Public Affairs* 11, no. 4 (Autumn, 1982): 338–353.

Liggio, Leonard P. "Jacksonian Movement and the Tea Party Movement." Working paper, February 2011.

———. "Murray Rothbard and Jacksonian Bank Policy." In *Durrell Conference Papers* (September, 1995). Winchester, VA: Durrell Foundation, Shenandoah University.

Listhaug, Ola. "Oil Wealth Dissatisfaction and Political Trust in Norway: A Resource Curse?" in *We st E u r o p ea n Po l i t i c s* 28, no. 4 (September, 2005): 834–851.

Locke, John. "Further Considerations concerning raising the Value of Money. Wherein Mr. Lowndes's Arguments for it, in his late Report concerning an Essay for the amendment of the Silver Coin, are particularly Examined." 1695. In *The Works of John Locke , in nine volumes*. Volume 4, twelfth edition. London: C. Baldwin. 1824.

———. "Some Considerations of the Consequences of lowering the Interest, and raising the Value of Money. In a Letter sent to a Member of Parliament, in the Year 1691." In *The Works of John Locke, in nine volumes*. Volume 4, twelfth edition. London: C. Baldwin. 1824.

Lopez, Juan Luis. "Historia Legal de la Bula Llamada." In *In Coena Domini*. 1768. Reprint, c, 2011.

Mack, Eric. "The Ethics of Taxation: Rights Versus Public Goods." *Taxation and the Deficit Economy*. Edited by Dwight Lee. Chapter 18. San Francisco: Pacific Research Institute, 1986: 487–515.

Madureira Prates, Marcelo. "Why Prudential Regulation Will Fail to Prevent Financial Crises. A Legal Approach," *Working Papers* 335, Banco Central do Brasil, ISSN 1518–3548, 2013.

Magliocca, Gerard N. "The Gold Clause Cases and Constitutional Necessity." *Social Science Research Network* (January 11, 2012). Electronic copy available at ssrn.com/abstract=1707175.

Mann, F. A. *The Legal Aspect of Money*. Oxford: Oxford University Press, 1982.

de Mariana, Juan. *De Monetae Mutatione*, in *Tractatus* VII. Cologne: 1609.

Martin, Felix. *Money the Unauthorized Biography*. New York: Alfred A. Knopf, 2014.

Martin, Thomas. "Why Did the Greek Polis Originally Need Coins?" In *Historia*, Band XLV/3. Stiz Stuttgart, Germany: Franz Steiner Verlang Wiesbaden GmbH, 1996.

Marx, Karl. *A Contribution to the Critique of Political Economy*, Part II, Money or Simple Calculation. Moscow: Progress Publishers, 2009, originally published in 1859. www.marxists.org/archive/marx/works/1859/critique-pol-economy/ch02_1.htm.

———. *Capital*, Volume 1. London: Penguin Books, Ltd, 1990.

———. *Capital*, Volume 3. London: Penguin Books, Ltd., 1991.

———. *Capital, A Critique of Political Economy, Volume 1, The Process of Capitalist Production*. Chicago: Charles H. Kerr and Co., 1906. Available electronically at www.econlib.org/library/YPDBooks/Marx/mrxCpContents.html.

———. *Grundrisse*. London: Penguin Books, Ltd., 1993.

———. *The Poverty of Philosophy*. New York: International Publishers, 1992.

Maurer, B. *Mutual Life, Limited: Islamic Banking, Alternative Currencies, Lateral Reason*. Princeton, NJ: Princeton University Press, 2005.

May, Larry. *Limiting Leviathan —Hobbes on Law and International Affairs*. Oxford: Oxford University Press, 2013.
McCloskey, D. "The Rhetoric of Economics," in *Journal of Economic Literature* vol. 21, no. 2 (June 1983): 481–517.
McKinnon, Ronald I. *Money & Capital in Economic Development*. Washington, DC: The Brookings Institute, 1973.
Meckling, William H. "Values and the Choice of the Model of the Individual in the Social Sciences," in *Schweizeriche Zeitschrift fur Volkswirtshaft und Statistki-Revue Suisse d'Economie Politique et de Statistique* (December 1976).
Meikle, Scott. "Aristotle on Money." Chapter 8 in *What is Money?* Edited by John Smithin. Abingdon, England: Routledge, 2000.
Meltzer, Allan H. *A History of the Federal Reserve —Volume 1: 1913–1951*. Chicago: University of Chicago Press, 2003.
Menger, Carl. On the Origin of Money. New York: Cosimo Classics, 2012. (First published in *Economic Journal* 2 (1892): 239–255).
———. *Principles of Economics*. Grove City, PA: Libertarian Press, Inc., 1871/1994.
———. *Problems of Economics and Sociology*. Chicago: University of Illinois Press, 1963.
Merquior, J. G. *A Natureza do Processo*. Rio de Janeiro: Editora Nova Fronteira, 1982.
Mill, John Stuart. *The Positive Philosophy of Auguste Comte*. Honolulu: University Press of the Pacific, 2002.
Miller, Robert C. B. "The Austrians and the Crisis." *Journal of the Institute of Economic Affairs* 29, no. 3 (2009): 27–34.
Minsky, Hyman P. "Securitization." In *The Levy Economics Institute of Bard College Policy Note* 2008/2 (June, 2008).
———. *Stabilizing an Unstable Economy*. New Haven: Yale University Press, 1986.
Mises, Ludwig von. *The Historical Setting of the Austrian School of Economics*. Online edition. Auburn, AL: Ludwig von Mises Institute, 2003.
———. *Human Action: A Treatise on Economics*. Indianapolis: Liberty Fund, Inc., 1949/2007.
———. *Nation, State, and Economy*. Indianapolis: Liberty Fund, Inc., 2006.
———. *Notes and Recollections*. Translated by Hans Sennholz. South Holland, IL: Libertarian Press, 1978.
———. *The Theory of Money and Credit* . Indianapolis: Liberty Fund, Inc., 1981.
———. *The Theory of Money and Credit*. Translated from the German by H. E. Batson. New York: Harcourt Brace & Co, 1935.
Moreno-Villalaz, Juan Luis. "The Cost of Using the Dollar as Currency." Ministry of Planning, Panama, 1998. Mimeographed.
Mueller, Antony. "The Ghost that Haunts Brazil." Published online in *Mises Daily*. Auburn, AL: Ludwig von Mises Institute, 2002.
Narveson, Jan. *The Libertarian Idea*. Peterborough, Ont.: Broadview Press Ltd., 2001.
Neary, J. Peter. "Real and Monetary Aspects of the 'Dutch disease.'" In the *UCD Centre for Economic Research Working Paper Series*, no. 5. Published by the University College Dublin, School of Economics, 1982. hdl.handle.net/10197/1398.
Nelson, Anitra. *Marx' s Concept of Money; The God of Commodities*. Abington, UK: Routledge, 2005.
North, Douglass C., and Barry Weingast. "Constitutions and Commitment: The Evolution of Institutions Governing Public Choice in Seventeenth-Century England." *Journal of Economic History* 43, no. 4 (1989): 803–832.
———. *Institutions, Institutional Change, and Economic Performance*. Cambridge: Cambridge University Press, 2005, 27.
Nozick, Robert. *Anarchy, State and Utopia*. New York: Basic Books, 1974.
Oakeshott, Michael. *On History and Other Essays*. Indianapolis: Liberty Fund, Inc., 1999.
O'Driscoll Jr., Gerald P. "A Free Market Money: Comment on Yeager." *Cato Journal* 3, no. 1 (Spring, 1983).

Oresme, Nicolas. *The De Moneta of Nicolas Oresme and English Mint Documents*. Edited by Charles Johnson. London: Thomas Nelson and Sons Ltd., 1956.

Pacheco-Rodriguez, Emilio J. *Utility and Rights: The Science of Morals in Britain in the First Half of the Nineteenth Century*. Doctoral dissertation, St. Antony's College, Oxford University, Trinity, 1986.

Paganelli, Maria Pia. "David Hume on Banking and Hoarding.," *Southern Economic Journal* 80, no. 4 (April 2014): 968–980.

Parguez, Alain, and Mario Seccareccia. "The Credit Theory of Money: The Monetary Circuit Approach." Chapter 5 in *What is Money?* Edited by John Smithin. Abingdon, England: Routledge, 2000.

Paterson, Dennis. *A Companion to the Philosophy of Law and Legal Theory*. Hoboken, NJ: Wiley-Blackwell, 2000.

Peacock, Mark. *Introducing Money*. Abingdon, UK: Routledge, 2013.

Plato. *The Republic*, Book I. 2nd edition (revised). London: Penguin Books, 1974.

Postali, Fernando Antonio Slaibe. "Petroleum Royalties and Regional Development in Brazil: The Economic Growth of Recipient Towns." *R e so u r c e s P o l i c y* 34 (2009): 205–213.

Priddat, Birger P. "Theory of Subjective Value in German National Economics." *International Journal of Social Economics* 25, no. 10 (1998): 1509–1519.

Pulak, Cemal. "Discovering a Royal Ship from the Age of King Tut: Uluburun, Turkey." *Beneath the Seven Seas—Adventures with the Institute of Nautical Archeology*. Edited by George F. Bass. London: Thames & Hudson Ltd., 2005.

———. "The Uluburun Shipwreck:; An Overview." *The International Journal of Nautical Archeology* 27, Issue 3 (August, 1998): 188–224.

Quiggin, Hingston A. *A Survey of Primitive Money —The Beginnings of Currency*. London: Methuen & Co. Ltd., 1949.

Quint, Thomas, and Martin Schubik. *Barley, Gold, or Fiat—Toward a Pure Theory of Money*. New Haven, CO: Yale University Press, 2014.

Rand, Ayn. "The Ethics of Emergencies." In *The Virtue of Selfishness*. Signet Centennial Edition. New York: New American Library, 1963.

———. "What is Capitalism?" In *Capitalism: The Unknown Ideal.* Signet Centennial Edition. New York: New American Library, 1965. Originally published in *The Objectivist Newsletter* (November and December, 1965).

Rappleye, Charles. *Robert Morris: Financier of the American Revolution*. New York: Simon & Schuster, 2010.

Rasmussen, Douglas. "Perfectionism and the Alleged Naturalistic Fallacy.," Parts one and two. Working Paper, n.d.

Reden, Sitta von. *Exchange in Ancient Greece*. London: Gerald Duckworth & Co. Ltd., 2003.

Reisman, George. *Capitalism: A Treatise on Economics*. TJS Books, 1996.

Reti, Steven P. *Silver and Gold—The Political Economy of International Monetary Conferences, 1867–1892*. Westport, CO: Greenwood Press, 1998.

Ricardo, David. *The Principles of Political Economy and Taxation*. 3rd Edition, London: J. M. Dent, 1821, reprinted in 1965.

Riegel, E. C. *Private Enterprise Money—A Non-Political Money System*. Public domain, 1944.

Rist, Charles. *History of Monetary and Credit Theory, From John Law to the Present Day*. New York: Augusts M. Kelley Publishers, 1966.

Rogers, Collin, and T. K. Rymes. "The Disappearance of Keynes's Nascent Theory of Banking between the *Treatise* and the *General Theory*." Chapter 13 in *What is Money?* Edited by John Smithin. Abingdon, England: Routledge, 2000.

Rogoff, Kenneth S. "Costs and Benefits to Phasing Out Paper Currency." *NBER Working Papers*, No. 20126. Issued in May 2014.

Ross, Michael L. "Does Oil Hinder Democracy?" *World Politics* 53 (April, 2001): 325–361.

———. "The Political Economy of the Resource Curse." *World Politics* 51, no. 2 (January, 1999): 297–322.

Rostovtzeff, M. *The Social & Economic History of the Roman Empire*. London: Clarendon Press, 1926.

Rothbard, Murray. *A History of Money and Banking in the United States: The Colonial Era to World War II*. Auburn, AL: Ludwig von Mises Institute, 2005.

———. *America's Great Depression* . Auburn, AL: Ludwig von Mises Institute, 2008.

———. *An Austrian Perspective on the History of Economic Thought*. Auburn, AL: Ludwig von Mises Institute, 2006.

———. *Man, Economy, and State with Power and Market*. Scholar's 2nd edition. Auburn, AL: Ludwig von Mises Institute, 2009.

———. *What Has Government Done to Our Money?* Auburn, AL: Ludwig von Mises Institute, 1990.

Rudd, David. "An Empirical Analysis of Dutch Disease: Developing and Developed Countries." *Research Honors* (Spring), at http://digitalcommons.iwu.edu/cgi/viewcontent.cgi?.

Salerno, Joseph T. "The Place of Human Action in the Development of Modern Economic Thought." *The Quarterly Journal of Austrian Economics* 2, no. 1 (1999): 35–66.

———. "The 'True' Money Supply: A Measure of the Supply of the Medium of Exchange in the U.S. Economy." *Austrian Economics Newsletter* (Spring, 1987): 1–6.

Sargent, Thomas J., and François R. Velde. *The Big Problem of Small Change*. Princeton: Princeton University Press, 2002.

Sarjanovic, Ivo. "Procesos de Mercado: precios en desequilibrio + moneda en desequilibrio." In *La crítica como método—Ensayos en honor de Rogelio T. Pontón*. Edited by Rafael E. Beltramino and Pablo F. Marchetti. Rosario, Argentina: Fundación Libertad, 2007.

Scherman, Harry. *The Promises Men Live By—A New Approach to Economics*. New York: Random House, 1938.

Scheussinger, Jr., Arthur M. *The Age of Jackson*. New York: Little, Brown, and Co., 1945.

Schuler, K. "Should Developing Countries Have Central Banks? Currency Quality and Monetary Systems in 155 Countries." *Research Monograph* 52. London: IEA, 1996.

Schumpeter, Joseph A. *History of Economic Analysis*. London: Routledge, 1997.

———. *The Economics and Sociology of Capitalism*. Princeton, NJ: Princeton University Press, 1991.

———. "Money and Currency." *Social Research* 58, no. 3 (Fall, 1991): 499–543. Published by: The New School. Article Stable URL: www.jstor.org/stable/40970658.

Selgin, George. *Good Money—Birmingham Button Makers, The Royal Mint, And the Beginnings of Modern Coinage, 1775–1821*. Ann Arbor: Michigan University Press and The Independent Institute, 2008.

———. *Less Than Zero—The Case for a Falling Price Level in a Growing Economy*. London: Institute of Economic Affairs, 1997.

———. "Synthetic Commodity Money." *Social Science Research Network* (April 10, 2013). Accessed at ssrn.com/abstract=2000118.

Selgin, George, and Lawrence H. White. "A Fiscal Theory of Government's Role in Money." *Economic Inquiry* (January 1999).

———. "In Defense of Fiduciary Media—or, We are Not Devo(lutionists), We are Misesians!" *The Review of Austrian Economics* 9, no. 2 (1996): 83–107.

Science Daily—University Of Cambridge. "New Research Confirms 'Out Of Africa' Theory of Human Evolution." ScienceDaily (May 10, 2007). Retrieved January 3, 2008, from www.sciencedaily.com/releases/2007/05/070509161829.htm.

Seltman, Charles. *Greek Coins*. London: Methuen & Co., Ltd., 1933.

Senna, José Júlio. *A M ã o Visivel: Problemas e Controvérsias da Política Econômica Brasileira*. Rio de Janeiro: IBMEC, 1983.

Shaxson, Nicholas. "Oil, Corruption and the Resource Curse." *International Affairs* 83, no. 6 (2007): 1123–1140.

Shostak, Frank. "The Mystery of the Money Supply." *The Quarterly Journal of Austrian Economics* 3, no. 4 (Winter, 2000): 69–76.

Simmel, Georg. "The Metropolis and the Mental Life." In *On Individuality and Social Forms*. Edited by Donald N. Levine. Chicago: The University of Chicago Press, 1971.

———. *Philosophie des Geldes*. 2nd edition. Leipzig: Duncker und Humblot, 1907.

———. *The Philosophy of Money*. Second enlarged edition. Edited by David Frisby, translated by Tom Bottomore and David Frisby. London: Routledge, 2001.

Simon, Julian. *The Ultimate Resource*. Princeton, NJ: Princeton University Press, 1983.

Simpson, Brian P. *Money, Banking, and the Business Cycle . Volume I: Integrating Theory and Practice*. Hampshire, UK: Palgrave MacMillan, 2014a.

———. *Money, Banking, and the Business Cycle . Volume II: Remedies and Alternative Theories*. Hampshire, UK: Palgrave MacMillan, 2014b.

Smith, Adam. *An Inquiry into the Nature and Causes of the Wealth of Nations*. Indianapolis: Liberty Fund, Inc., 1981.

Smith, Barry. "Aristotle, Menger, and Mises: An Essay on the Metaphysics of Economics." In *Carl Menger and His Legacy in Economics*. Edited by Bruce J. Caldwell. Annual supplement to volume 22, History of Political Economy. Durham, NC: Duke University Press, 1990.

———. *Austrian Philosophy: The Legacy of Franz Brentano*. Peru, IL: Open Court Publishing Co., 1996.

Smith, Vera C. *The Rationale of Central Banking and the Free Banking Alternative*. Indianapolis: Liberty Fund Press, 1990.

Smithin, John. *Essays in the Fundamental Theory of Monetary Economics and Macroeconomics*. Singapore: World Scientific Publishing, 2013a.

———. "Requirements of a Philosophy of Money and Finance." Chapter 1 in *Financial Crises and the Nature of Capitalist Money—Mutual Developments from the Work of Geoffrey Ingham*. Edited by Jocelyn Pixley and G. C. Harcourt. Hampshire, UK: Palgrave MacMillan, 2013b.

———. "What is Money? Introduction." Chapter 1 in *What is Money?* Edited by John Smithin. Abingdon, England: Routledge, 2000.

Steiner, Hillel. "Invisible Hand Processes and the Theory of Money." In *Rationality, Markets and Morals—Studies at the Intersection of Philosophy and Economics*. An open access journal published by Frankfurt School Verlag (RMM), volume 4, special topic: Can the Social Contract Be Signed by an Invisible Hand? (2013): 44–52. Available at: www.rmm.journal.de/.

Strange, Susan. "The Westfailure System." *Review of International Studies* 25, issue 03 (July, 1999): 345–354.

Subercaseaux, Guillermo. *El Papel Moneda*. Santiago, Chile: Imprenta de Cervantes, 1912. Reprinted from the collections of the University of California Libraries. Lexington, KY: 2014.

Sylla, Richard, Richard Tilly, and Gabriel Tortella, eds. *The State, the Financial System, and Economic Modernization*. Cambridge: Cambridge University Press, 2007.

Tavares de Araujo Jr., José. "Conversibilidade do Real e Inserção Internacional da Economia brasileira." *Fundação Alexandre de Gusmão*—FUNAG, Rio de Janeiro, Brazil (July 23, 2009): 1–18.

Taylor, John B. "Discretion Versus Policy Rules in Practice." *Carnegie-Rochester Conference Series on Public Policy* 39 (1993): 195–214.

Timberlake, Richard H. "Gold Standards and the Real Bills Doctrine in the U.S. Monetary Policy." *Econ Journal Watch* 2, no. 2 (August 2005): 196–233. econjournalwatch.org.

Tovar, Camilo. "DSGE Models and Central Banks." in *Working Papers*, no. 258 (September 2009). Bank for International Settlements.

Tullock, Gordon. *The Selected Works of Gordon Tullock, Volume I: Virginia Political Economy*. Indianapolis: Liberty Fund, Inc., 2004.

Turner, John D. *Banking in Crisis—The Rise and Fall of British Banking Stability, 1800 to the Present*. Cambridge, UK: Cambridge University Press, 2014.

US Bureau of Labor Statistics. "International Index of Consumer Prices: 18 Countries and Areas, 1999–2013." Accessed March 25, 2015. www.bls.gov/fls/intl_consumer_prices.pdf.
Velde, François R. "Bitcoin: A Primer. Essays on Issues," *Working Papers*, Number 317, December 2013, The Federal Reserve Bank of Chicago.
Vélez Rodríguez, Ricardo. *Patrimonialismo e a Realidade Latino-americana*. Rio de Janeiro: Documenta Histórica Editora Ltda., 2006.
Viera, Edwin Jr. "The Forgotten Role of the Constitution in Monetary Law." *Texas Review of Law & Politics* 2, no. 1 (Fall, 1997): 77–124.
Walras, Leon. *Elements of Pure Economics*. New York: Routledge. Reprint 2010.
Weatherford, J. *The History of Money*. New York: Three Rivers Press, 1997.
Weber, Max. *Economy and Society*. Volume 1. London: University of California Press, Ltd., 1978.
White, Lawrence H. *Competition and Currency—Essays on Free Banking and Money*. New York: New York University Press, 1989.
———. "Did Hayek and Robbins Deepen the Great Depression?" *Journal of Money, Credit and Banking* 40, issue 4 (2008): 751–768.
———. *Free Banking in Britain, Theory, Experience, and Debate, 1800–1845*. London: Institute of Economic Affairs, 1995.
———. *The Theory of Monetary Institutions*. Malden, MA: Blackwell Publishers, Inc., 1999.
Williams, J. *Money: A History*. London: The British Museum Press, 1997.
Winder, G. *A Short History of Money*. London: Newman Neame and IEA, 1959.
Withers, Hartley. *The Meaning of Money*. London: Smith, Elder & Co., 1909. Reprinted on demand by Kessinger Publishing, LLC, USA, 2014.
World Gold Council Website, at www.gold.org.
Wray, L. Randall. *Credit and State Theories of Money, The Contributions of A. Mitchell Innes*. London: Edward Elgar Publishing Limited, 2004.
———. "Modern Money." Chapter 3 in *What is Money?* Edited by John Smithin. Abingdon, England: Routledge, 2000.
Yeager, Leland B. *The Fluttering Veil, Essays in Monetary Disequilibrium*. Indianapolis: Liberty Fund, Inc., 1997.
———. "The Significance of Monetary Disequilibrium." *Cato Journal* 6 (Fall, 1986): 369–399.
———. "Stable Money and Free-Market Currencies." *Cato Journal* 3, no. 1 (Spring 1983): 305–333.
Younkins, Edward W. *Flourishing and Happiness in A Free Society—Toward a Synthesis of Aristotelianism, Austrian Economics, and Ayn Rand 's Objectivism*. University Press of America, 2011.
———. "Murray Rothbard's Randian Austrianism." 2004. In *Solopassion—Sense of Life Objectivists* website: (rebirthofreason.com/Articles/Younkins/Murray_Rothbards_Randian_Austrianism.shtml).
———. "Social Cooperation, Flourishing and Happiness." 2005. In *Solopassion—Sense of Life Objectivists* website: solohq.solopassion.com/Articles/Younkins/Social_Cooperation,_Flourishing,_and_Happiness.shtml.
Zanotti, Gabriel J. "A Proposal to Overcome the Current Deadlock of Austrian School of Economics' Epistemology." Lecture to the International Conference "The Austrian School of Economics in the 21st Century." Universidad Católica Argentina, Campus Rosario, Argentina, August 5–7, 2010.
Zarlenga, Stephen. "Comprehensive Explanation of Monetary Reform." Posted on the website of the American Monetary Institute, 2011. Accessed at monetary.org/wp-content/uploads/2011/09/32-page-brochure.pdf.
Zelmanovitz, Leonidas. "In Face of Changes in the Demand for Money, What is the Proper Response by the Central Bank?" in *Criterio Libre* vol. 8, no. 13 (July–December 2010): 69–94.

Index

About the Author

Leonidas Zelmanovitz has been a Liberty Fund fellow in Indianapolis, Indiana, since January 2006; before that he was a businessman in Brazil.

Dr. Zelmanovitz has a law degree from the Federal University in Porto Alegre, Brazil, a master's degree in Austrian economics from the Universidad Rey Juan Carlos in Madrid, Spain, and a PhD in applied economics from the same university.

He was born in Brazil in 1961; he is married and has a son and a daughter.

Lightning Source UK Ltd.
Milton Keynes UK
UKHW011353121119
353366UK00009B/10/P

9 780739 195130